JUDAISM IN THE FIRST CENTURIES OF THE CHRISTIAN ERA THE AGE OF THE TANNAIM

VOLUME II

JUDAISM

IN THE FIRST CENTURIES OF THE CHRISTIAN ERA
THE AGE OF THE TANNAIM

GEORGE FOOT MOORE

VOLUME II

SCHOCKEN BOOKS · NEW YORK

First SCHOCKEN PAPERBACK edition 1971

Library of Congress Catalog Card No. 72-146791
Published by arrangement with Harvard University Press
Manufactured in the United States of America

Second Printing, 1975

IN MEMORIAM

M. H. M.

OBIIT MDCCCCXXIV

CONTENTS

PART IV

OBSERVANCES

PART V

MORALS

PART VI

PIETY

PART VII

THE HEREAFTER

PART IV

OBSERVANCES

CHAPTER I

RELIGIOUS PRINCIPLES. CULTUS

IN THE practice of any religion on a stage of advancement comparable to Judaism we may, from our point of view, distinguish three elements. There are, in the first place, certain rites, public, domestic, or personal, by which the favor of the deity is cultivated, and to which for this reason the general designation 'cultus'[1] is given. The gods are believed to approve conformity to ancestral custom in all spheres, and the sanction of religion thus attaches to a multitude of acts of daily life and to conventional ways of doing things which to extraneous apprehension have no religious significance. On the negative side many acts are interdicted by religion as obnoxious to the gods, and the doing of them is believed to expose the transgressor to the vindictive displeasure of the gods,[2] for the prohibition of which — whatever explanation we may give of them — we discern no rational or moral ground. This whole sphere of practical religion, positive and negative, may be comprehended under the name 'observances.'

Among the things which the religious law or the *mos maiorum* with religious sanction prescribes or forbids are many that fall within our conception of morality, and it will be convenient to treat them separately under the head of 'morals.'

Finally, there is the subjective side of religion, the attitude of the community or the individual toward God in thought and feeling and will, which we may call 'piety.'

As has already been intimated, this division of the subject is made from our point of view, not from that of the religions themselves, in which morals are not assigned a sphere of their own

[1] Colere deos.

[2] It is to such interdictions that the word *religio* in the old Roman religion primitively applied, from a time when gods had not yet assumed the vindication of them.

separate from what we have called 'observances,' much less set over against them. Primitive morality consisted in habitual conformity to all the obligatory customs (*mores*) of the community, however we may classify them. What we call ceremonial observances are in this sense of moral obligation, and conversely the morals of the community in our sense are to its apprehension religious observances. Again, piety expresses itself in scrupulous conformity to the observances of religion as well as to what we call its moral injunctions and prohibitions. Nor is this interlacing of observance, morals, and piety by any means confined to an elementary stage of development; it persists through the entire history of religion.

In this complex the element we have called observances has throughout been an essential part of practical religion. The organization and institutions of religion, its ministry, rites of worship, domestic ceremonies, forms of personal devotion, regulation of behavior in daily life, things to be done and ways of doing them, and things to be shunned, are the most salient and distinctive features of particular religions. The worship in which the community participates and the observances recognized by all its members as obligatory are the bond that holds it together and unites it with other local communities in a national religion or in an international church. Augustine justly says: "In no kind of religion, true or false, can men be held together, unless they are united in some sort of fellowship in visible symbols, or sacraments," and he defines sacrament in the most general sense as such a *sacrum signum* in whatever religion.[1] Agreement in beliefs or doctrines, or the acceptance of a theory of religion, may be the constitutive factor of a sect or school, but the lasting cohesion of such a body is only possible when its ideas are embodied in certain forms.

[1] This is true also of society as a whole and of social classes. Men are bound together not only by common interests or agreement in opinions, but even more strongly by common observances, and the penalty of disregard or defiance, which in primitive society is outlawry, is here its civilized counterpart, social outlawry.

Religious observances are often called the externals of religion, and reformers, reacting against the inclination of the common mind to attend to the form more than the substance, or repelled by the character of the inherited forms, have sometimes endeavored to abolish them altogether, thinking thus to make religion purely spiritual; but, as is most instructively illustrated in the Society of Friends, the rejection of all historical forms itself became a formalism of a most rigid type, which as such furnished the cohesive factor to a body that was in its beginnings and its persistent theory an enthusiastic mysticism of a radically individualistic type. Similarly in pietistic circles within various Protestant churches, the depreciation of all externals was accompanied by a formalizing of the modalities of religious experience and the inner life which gave them the bond that held them together, notwithstanding the centrifugal tendencies of pietistic individualism.

In Judaism the whole range of religious observances, the morality prescribed or commended by it, and the specific type of its piety, are all integral and inseparable parts of a revealed religion, and correlated to the revelation of God's nature and character and his relation to his people collectively and individually, of the nature of man, his religious and moral obligations under divine law, of the consequences and remedies of default, the means of expiation, and the salutary efficacy of repentance — topics which have been discussed in the preceding parts of this work. The norms of belief and practice were given in the two-fold law, "the Torah in writing" and "the Torah orally transmitted," which together constitute the unitary revelation, in all parts and in every particular of divine origin and authority, and as such of equal and identical obligation. To impress this on men, God attached the same sanction — prosperity and long life — to what intrinsically might be called "the lightest of the light commandments," the prohibition of taking the mother bird from the nest with the nestlings or the eggs (Deut. 22, 6f.), and the "weightiest of the weighty," the injunction to honor one's parents (Deut. 5, 16; Exod. 20, 12).[1] The direst of all dooms, to be cut off from his people (by God)[2] is denounced not only upon abominable crimes such as incest, or upon neglect of a fundamental observance like circumcision, but on eating suet from the kinds of animals admissible as sacrificial victims (Lev. 7, 25), or flesh of any kind in which blood remains (Lev. 17, 14), or leavened bread at the Passover season (Exod. 12, 19).[3]

On the other hand man honors God with his substance (Prov. 3, 9), by setting aside the overlooked sheaf and the corner of the field, and the priest's portion (*terumah*), and the various tithes, and the bit of dough; by keeping Tabernacles with the palm branches, by the horn-blowing, by wearing the prayer boxes (*tefillin*) and the fringes (*ṣiṣit*), by feeding the hungry and giving drink to the thirsty, etc.[4]

It is obvious from these examples that the Scripture gives no warrant whatever for dividing the law into ceremonial and moral, and attributing to the latter perpetuity and superior obligation, while regarding the former as of less moment in the eyes of God, and negligence in the observance of it as a venial offence on the part of men. Jewish teachers were quite aware of the intrinsic difference between laws which the common intelligence and conscience of mankind recognize apart from revelation, things which "if they were not written in the law would on grounds of reason have to be written" — idolatry, incest, homicide, robbery, blasphemy — and such laws as the prohibition of eating pork, or wearing garments of linsey-woolsey (Deut. 22, 11; Lev. 19, 19), loosing the shoe in the refusal of levirate marriage (Deut. 25, 7–10), the ritual of purification of the leper (Lev. 14), and the

[1] Jer. Ḳiddushin 61b, below; cf. Ḳiddushin 39b. Tanḥuma ed. Buber, Teṣè §2 (f. 17b).

[2] A catalogue of the offenses which expose the perpetrator to this fate is drawn up at the beginning of M. Keritot.

[3] These interdictions are repeated in many places with great emphasis, and there are numerous others of a similar kind.

[4] Jer. Ḳiddushin 61b, below.

scapegoat (Lev. 16), which men might be tempted to call futile performances. For this reason the Scripture adds: 'I am the Lord.' I, the Lord, have ordained it, and you have no right to have notions of your own about it.[1]

They might even go further, as Johanan ben Zakkai did in regard to the purification by the ashes of the red heifer in water (Num. 19) of a house in which a death had occurred and persons who had been in actual or constructive contact with the dead: "Death does not make unclean, nor the water make clean." It is a decree of the Sovereign King of kings. God says, I have prescribed a statute for you; I have issued a decree to you. You have no right to transgress my decree, for it is written (Num. 19, 2), 'This is the statute of the law.'[2]

That is the logical attitude of a revealed religion. Its observances — the ceremonial law in the widest extension of the term — are statutory. It is not for man to cavil about its prescriptions or interdictions, or to exempt himself from any of them because he can discover no rational or moral ground for them. It should be observed also that what we call the moral law is delivered in statutory form,[3] and that its obligation in such a religion rests not on the consensus of men, however unanimous, that certain acts are intrinsically right and others wrong, but on the fact that they are commanded or forbidden by divine law.[4] Obedience to God's law in its entirety is the supreme *moral* obligation of man, irrespective of the subject matter of the particular article. The modern distinction of duties to God as *religious* obligations, and those to our fellow men or in our personal conduct as *moral* obligations, is, from the point of view of revealed religion, a false

[1] Sifra, Aḥarê Pereḳ 13 (ed. Weiss f. 86a); Yoma 67b.

[2] Tanḥuma ed. Buber, Ḥuḳḳat § 26, and parallels.

[3] Laws that we distinguish as ceremonial or moral are not only given in the same form, but indiscriminately in the same contexts, as for example in Lev. 19.

[4] That the will of God, whether impressed on the common conscience of mankind (*lex naturae*) or more explicitly revealed in Scripture (*lex divina*) makes the difference between right and wrong is a doctrine that has been held by many Christian theologians.

division of an indivisible unity. Even ignorant or inadvertent deviations from the law are offenses which demand expiation, while knowingly and purposely to violate it is to "throw off the yoke" of the sovereign whose will it is — to rebel against God.[1]

A modern scholar who construes the history of the religion of Israel on the basis of an analytic criticism and chronological ordering of the sources, and interprets it in the light of the comparative study of other religions, sees in a large part of the observances of Judaism survivals of a remote past and of stages of development long since outgrown. Much which is elaborated in what from the critical point of view are the latest strata of the legislation is substantially of prehistoric antiquity, common to diverse races on similar levels of culture or specifically to Semitic peoples, the motive and meaning of which have been completely forgotten. Perpetuated in custom by the obstinate conservatism of religion, always stronger in matters of form than in ideas, it was eventually formulated, fixed in writing, and incorporated in the collection of divinely revealed laws supposed to have been delivered by Moses to the Israelites.

Evolutionary criticism of this kind may distinguish between observances which embody and symbolically express the great principles of Judaism and antiquated survivals of lower stages of religion which have no relation to its ideas and principles, or are even at variance with them, and may draw the practical consequence that the latter are obsolete and no longer obligatory. It is obvious, however, that this critical attitude, no less than a rationalistic discrimination between observances which commend themselves to the reason and conscience and those which have no such intrinisic validation, is an abandonment of the very conception of revealed religion as entertained by the teachers of Judaism on the basis of revelation itself. The case was somewhat the same with those Hellenistic Jews who, having by allegory discovered the religious and moral significance of the observances,

[1] See Vol. I, p. 465.

deemed their obligation fulfilled by accepting the truths and practising the moral principles which were the reason and meaning of the injunction or prohibition, and held themselves exempt from literal compliance with the commandment, reasoning doubtless that, as they had extracted the kernel, why should they preserve the empty and now worthless shell? Philo, than whom none was more proficent in such use of allegory, rightly condemns this inference and the conduct which justified itself thereby.[1]

> There are some who, understanding the letter of the laws to be a symbol of intellectual things, are very particular about the latter but readily neglect the former. I, for my part, should blame such for unscrupulousness; for it is necessary to attend to both, the exact investigation of the things not manifest, and the uninterrupted preservation of the manifest. But now, as though living in a desert alone by themselves, or as having become bodiless souls, and knowing neither city nor village nor family, no association of men of any kind, looking contemptuously upon the opinions of the many, they explore the naked truth itself by itself. The sacred word teaches that such men have conceived an excellent idea;[2] but at the same time not to relax aught of what is found in the customs which inspired men, better than those of our time, have ordained.

The attitude of Jesus and his immediate followers toward the so-called ceremonial law was, as has already been observed, entirely orthodox.[3] Not only does he declare in the most sweeping terms the perpetuity of the whole Law,[4] but he enjoins obedience to it in ritual details such as the cleansing of a leper,[5] and even approves of rabbinical extensions like the tithing of garden herbs.[6] That justice and compassion and fidelity are "weightier matters," does not mean that neglect of mint, anise, and cumin is commendable. The disciples in Jerusalem had so little notion

[1] De migratione Abrahami c. 16, especially §§ 89f. (ed. Mangey I, 450).

[2] Namely, that the letter of the law is a symbol of intellectual things.

[3] See Vol. I, pp. 269 f. [4] Matt. 5, 18.

[5] Matt. 8, 4; Luke 5, 14; cf. 17, 14.

[6] Matt. 23, 23. See M. Ma'aserot 4, 5; M. Demai 1, 1; 2, 1, etc. The general principle, Matt. 23, 2 f.

of exempting themselves from the ceremonial law that they were slow to admit that Gentile believers could be saved without assuming by circumcision the obligation to keep every article of it.

For Paul the dispensation of law had come to an end — the moral law as statutory law no less completely than the ceremonial. The fundamentals of the moral law are implanted in the intelligence and the conscience of all mankind (Rom. 1, 19–32; 2, 14–16). Gentiles who ignored the law of nature and Jews who transgressed the revealed law were all under the same condemnation. Neither the one law nor the other has succeeded in making men righteous. Morality cannot be achieved by outward regulation, but only by the spontaneity of a new divine life, the indwelling of Christ, or the spirit of Christ. The peculiarity of Paul's antinomianism is the substitution of enthusiasm, in the literal sense, for the law of nature reflected in the individual and the common conscience, as well as for the law in Scripture and tradition; and it was precisely in the moral field that this theory had the most radical consequences.

A large part of what is commonly called the ceremonial law has to do with the sacrificial cultus — the temple, its plan, furniture; the ministry, their vestments and services; the varieties and modalities of offering (*sacra publica*, *sacra privata*), propitiatory and expiatory offerings, votive and thank offerings; the celebration of festivals. All this was in the hands or under the authority of the priesthood, who carried out the provisions of the written law in accordance with their own traditional practice. The legislation on these matters in the Pentateuch was also the subject of assiduous exegetical and comparative study in the schools of the Law, whose interpretations are preserved in the legal Midrash and concisely formulated in the codified rules to which the name Mishnah was given. Of especial interest to us are the parts of these collections which describe the cultus of the temple in the generation preceding its destruction.[1]

[1] E.g. Tamid, Kippurim (Yoma).

An account in detail of the cultus and what goes with it lies outside the purpose and plan of the present work, and will properly be sought in treatises on the religious antiquities of the Jews, or, for particular features, in the relevant articles in encyclopaedias and the monographic literature there cited.[1]

In its general character and in many particulars the cultus is very similar to that of contemporary religions, especially, as we should expect, to those of the neighboring lands. Certain peculiarities, impressed upon it by the history and principles of the religion are to be briefly noted here.

First and foremost, it is the worship of *one* God, the only being in the universe to whom in its proper sense that name can be given or divine homage paid. No subordinate power of nature, not the highest ranks of his angelic ministry, no prophet, and no saint, has a place beside Him or beneath Him in His temple and in the cultus of this uncompromising monotheism. As a corollary to the soleness of God it had long been established that the temple in Jerusalem was the only seat of this cultus; there alone sacrifices could be offered to Him and expiation made by a legitimate priesthood in conformity to a ritual of His own ordaining.[2] Neither in the temple nor elsewhere was any image of God, public or private, tolerated — a feature of Judaism which observers and reporters found most singular.

But though Jerusalem was its sole seat, the sacrificial worship of God was not a local cult; its *sacra publica* were maintained by the annual didrachm tax collected from Jews in all the countries to which they had spread, for the benefit of the whole nation. The wide dispersion of the Jews had long since made obsolete the ancient laws which required appearance of all males at the sanctuary with an offering three times in the year. Even for dwellers in the remoter parts of Palestine this must have been impossible. But at these festivals multitudes from near and far streamed to

[1] A summary description of the cultus (by the present author) may be found in the Encyclopaedia Biblica, col. 4201–4226.

[2] The temple of Onias in Egypt was founded at a time when the temple in Jerusalem was in the hands of the hellenizers or the heathen.

Jerusalem. The figures given by Josephus for the attendance at the Passover in 66 A.D., though professedly computed upon an enumeration by the priests of paschal victims,[1] are quite beyond the bounds of credibility, but the concourse, especially at the Passover, was unquestionably enormous. Many residents of remoter regions probably made the long journey but once in their lives, many others not at all; but in the pilgrims from all lands the whole Jewish nation was ideally gathered at the feast, while those who remained at home, through the festival services of the synagogue, participated in spirit in the celebration.

For the vast majority of Jews, not alone in the dispersion but in Palestine itself, the synagogue had become, long before the destruction of the temple, the real seat of religious worship, though so long as the temple stood they may not have used of it the word 'worship' historically appropriated to the sacrificial cultus. Significant evidence of this is the existence within the temple precincts of a synagogue for the priests, and the interpolation, so to speak, of features akin to the synagogue service in the ritual of the daily morning sacrifice, where, after preparation had been made for the offering, the priests left the parts of the victim and the other materials of sacrifice lying on the ramp of the altar, and assembled in an adjacent hall to recite their Shema' and a series of Benedictions,[2] after which the sacrificial ritual was resumed. R. Joshua ben Hananiah gives from his own experience an interesting account of the continuous alternation of sacrificial rites and synagogue services through the entire day and night at the festival of Water-Drawing at the season of Tabernacles which left the priests no time for sleep.[3]

Another link between the temple worship and the synagogue was the so-called *ma'amad*.[4] To make sure of the presence at the

[1] Josephus, Bell. Jud. vi. 9, 3 § 424; 255600 lambs, on which he estimates a total presence of 2700000. In ii. 14, 3 § 280 he makes them a round 3000000.

[2] M. Tamid 5, 1.

[3] Tos. Sukkah 4, 5; Sukkah 53a. A somewhat different version in Jer. Sukkah 55b.

[4] M. Ta'anit 4, 1–4; Tos. Ta'anit 4 (3), 1–4. Elbogen, Der jüdische Gottesdienst, pp. 237 ff.

sacra publica (and private sacrifices in the absence of the offerer) of a representation of the laity as well as priests and levites, there was constituted for each of the twenty-four 'courses'[1] of the priests and levites a corresponding 'attendance' composed of all three classes, whose duty it was to be present in the temple during the week in which a given course of priests was in service, roughly, therefore, once in six months. The priests and levites were presumably supplied by that part of the weekly 'course' which was not actually on duty on that day. How the lay deputation was made up is not known. Many of them were probably residents of Jerusalem or the vicinity; but inhabitants of remoter parts of the land were among the "men of attendance."[2]

Those who went up to the temple not only stood by at the sacrifices, but four times a day held a service of their own, consisting of prayers and the reading or memoriter recitation of Scripture.[3] Those who were unable to go up to Jerusalem abstained from work throughout the whole week, and assembled in the synagogues of their own towns, where they kept the same hours of prayer and read the same portions of Scripture.[4] Both in Jerusalem and at their homes the members of the 'attendance' fasted from Monday to Thursday.[5]

The cessation of the sacrificial cultus, which in any other ancient religion would have been in a short while the end of it, was in Judaism not even a serious crisis, so completely had the worship of the synagogue come to satisfy its religious needs. The only noteworthy consequence of the destruction of the temple was that the synagogue was henceforth for all Jews, not only practically — as it had long been for most of them — but in thought and feeling the place where God was worshipped and

[1] משמרות.

[2] M. Bikkurim 3, 2. A leader (ממונה) conducted them, at least when the first fruits were brought up.

[3] M. Ta'anit 4, 3. The Mishnah prescribes the reading seriatim from Gen. 1, 1–2, 3. Cf. Megillah 31b.

[4] Tos. Ta'anit 4 (3), 3. Cf. M. Ta'anit 4, 2.

[5] So the common text (M. Ta'anit 4, 3); but the clause is lacking in some important witnesses.

religion cultivated. It was natural that such features of the temple liturgy as could be detached from the sacrificial cultus, the blowing of the ram's horn at New Years, the palm branches and willows at Tabernacles, and the like, were transferred, with the necessary adaptations, to the synagogue, as, indeed, some of them had already been; but in the character of its services there was no essential change.

Much more important than all this is the fact that, as has been shown above, the religious leaders of Judaism had fully assimilated the teaching of the prophets and other scriptures concerning the cultus. Its efficacy as a means of propitiating God or expiating sin lay not in itself *ex opere operato*, but was dependent upon the moral character and religious spirit of those in whose behalf the sacrifices were offered. In making repentance and good works the *conditio sine qua non* of the divine forgiveness, they put it in a position to become the sole condition when the performance of the rite itself was rendered impossible.

It is not to be imagined that teachings which thus reduced the cultus to a secondary place in religion found general acceptance or even understanding. The great mass of the people doubtless regarded the divinely instituted and prescribed rites as an effective means of securing the favor of God or expiating offences against his laws. So inseparable was the connection between sacrifices and the forgiveness of sins in the Law itself that in the context from which we have quoted above Rab Asi says:[1] "Were it not for the *ma'amadot* (attendance on the sacrifices), heaven and earth would not endure." The proof is taken from Abraham's question in Gen. 15, 8 ('How shall I know that I shall inherit it?') and God's answer bidding him offer a sacrifice. To Abraham's further question, But how will it be when the temple no longer exists? God replies, When they read before me the laws about sacrifices, I will impute it to them as if they offered

[1] Ta'anit 27b. In Megillah 31b attributed to his contemporary, R. Ammi (3d cent.). Jer. 33, 25 is cited (cf. Nedarim 32a, where the same is said of circumcision and of the Torah).

the sacrifices before me, and will have mercy upon them for all their misdeeds.[1] According to R. Abahu the prayers which are offered before God ('the bullocks of our lips,' Hos. 14, 3), are an equivalent for the sacrifices.[2] Much older than these passages is Sifrè Deut. § 41 (ed. Friedmann f. 80 a, top) where both study of the law and prayer are shown to be called in Scripture 'service' (specifically of sacrificial worship), and the words of Deut. 11, 13 ('and serve him') interpreted accordingly.[3]

[1] Ta'anit and Megillah ll. cc. Cf. Pesiḳta ed. Buber f. 60b.

[2] Pesiḳta ed. Buber f. 165b, with Buber's notes (nos. 180, 181) there. See Elbogen, Der jüdische Gottesdienst, p. 251, who contrasts with this the attitude of Rabban Johanan ben Zakkai (Vol. I, p. 503).

[3] See below, Part vi, Piety.

CHAPTER II

CIRCUMCISION. SABBATH

THE two fundamental observances of Judaism are circumcision and the sabbath. In Exod. 19, 5: 'If ye hearken diligently to my voice and observe my covenant, then ye shall be a people peculiarly my own from among all peoples,' etc. R. Eliezer (ben Hyrcanus) understood by the 'covenant' the covenant of the sabbath, R. Akiba the covenant of circumcision.[1] The two are elsewhere coupled by R. Eliezer as the fundamental commandments. Finding in the "seven" and "eight" of Eccles. 11, 2 the sabbath and circumcision respectively,[2] he puts into the mouth of Elijah in his prayer on Carmel the words: "Lord of the world, if there remained to Israel these two commandments only, the merits of keeping them should suffice that rain descend on them."[3] That the precedence belongs to circumcision appears, as the rabbis observe, from the fact that the sabbath law is suspended in order that circumcision be performed at the normal time on the eighth day of the boy's life, although other reasons for postponement are admitted.

Circumcision, using the term in a broad sense for an operation of one kind or another upon the prepuce, is customary among peoples of unrelated races in widely remote quarters of the globe, from Polynesia and Australia to the American continent; it is practised in all parts of Africa, but not by all races or tribes. In

[1] Mekilta, Baḥodesh 2 (ed. Friedmann f. 62b; Weiss f. 70b). The Mekilta de-R. Simeon ben Yoḥai inverts the attributions. There are some other uncertainties in the text of the Mekilta, which do not here further concern us. See the editors' notes.

[2] The interpretation of this verse as a command to observe the sabbath and circumcision was known to Jerome (Commentary on Eccles. 11, 2). Bacher, Agada der Tannaiten I, 156.

[3] Pesiḳta ed. Buber f. 192a; cf. Eccles. R. on Eccles. 11, 2. The connection with Elijah's prayer is made through 1 Kings 18, 43 f. (seven times, and then once more, the servant of the prophet goes to look for signs of rain).

Asia it is confined to Semites, except for peoples that have embraced Mohammedanism; and in Europe to Jews and Moslems. The Indo-Germanic peoples and the Mongols (exception being made for the influence of Islam), so far as our evidence goes, have never had such a custom. According to Herodotus (ii. 104), it was practised by the Egyptians, the Ethiopians (Nubians), the Phoenicians, and the "Syrians of Palestine," and further by certain tribes in Asia Minor, and by the Colchians (whom he regards as of Egyptian race), all of whom he believes to have got the custom from Egypt.

In the Bible 'uncircumcised' is an opprobrious epithet bestowed distinctively on the Philistines, from which it is to be inferred that the inland Canaanites like those on the sea-board whom Herodotus calls Phoenicians were circumcised. Jeremiah (9, 24 f.) names as circumcised peoples[1] whom the Lord will visit with judgment, Egypt, Judah, Edom, the Ammonites, Moab, the bedouin Arabs. When he continues, 'For all the heathen are uncircumcised, and all the house of Israel are uncircumcised in heart,' his meaning is that the circumcision in the flesh will not save them in the day of visitation — it is not the true circumcision. The circumcision of the Arabs is the presumption of the narrative of the circumcision of Ishmael in Genesis 17, 23–26, where there is probably also a further reflection of the fact that circumcision among the Arabs was customarily performed at a later age than by the Jews, originally, there is reason to think, at the age of puberty as a preliminary to marriage, as is the case frequently among the peoples that practise it.[2] In Mohammed's time it was so universal among the Arabs that he did not think it necessary to enjoin it in the Koran.

Into the various theories of the origin of the wide-spread custom it is unnecessary to enter here. To the Jews it was a divine institution, given by God to Abraham for himself and his pos-

[1] כל מול בערלה.

[2] See Louis H. Gray, Encyclopaedia of Religion and Ethics, III, 662 f.

terity, and so inseparably connected with the covenant promises that it is not only the sign of the covenant (Gen. 17, 11), but is itself called the covenant: 'My covenant shall be in your flesh for an everlasting covenant' (Gen. 17, 13; cf. vss. 10 f.). Circumcision is therefore called 'the covenant of Abraham.' The neglect of this ordinance has the direst consequence: 'The uncircumcised male who is not circumcised in the flesh of his foreskin, that person shall be cut off from his people; he has nullified my covenant' (Gen. 17, 14).

In view of the eminent place thus given to circumcision it was a natural question why it was not commanded in the Decalogue. In one version of the story the question is addressed to R. Eliezer by Aquila the proselyte;[1] in another by King Agrippa.[2] In both the answer is that it had already been given, and is presumed in Exod. 19, 5, or in the repeated mention of 'the *ger* (circumcised proselyte) who is in thy towns.'

It is the duty of the father to circumcise his son, or have him circumcised on the eighth day,[3] and the master has the same obligation for a slave, whether born in his household or the child of a foreign slave woman acquired by purchase.[4] If the father or master neglected this obligation, rabbinical law made it the duty of the court to have the circumcision performed.[5] An adult gentile slave should be circumcised on the day on which he became the property of a Jewish owner.[6] If he did not consent, he might be kept, so to speak on probation, for twelve months, at the expiration of which period, if he still refused, he must be sold to a gentile.[7] If, however, such a slave while in the possession of

[1] Pesiḳta Rabbati ed. Friedmann f. 116b–117a.

[2] Tanḥuma, Lek leka, near the end; Agadat Bereshit c. 17 (ed. Buber, p. 36). See the editor's notes, and Bacher, Agada der Tannaiten, I, 117. The same question by a Gentile lady to R. Jose bar Ḥalafta, Pesiḳta Rabbati f. 117a.

[3] For certain exceptions see below, p. 19.

[4] The various cases that may arise under the latter head need not be detailed here. See Maimonides, Hilkot Milah 1, 3–5.

[5] Ḳiddushin 29a.

[6] Female slaves in similar case were baptized.

[7] Yebamot 48b.

his former gentile owner, made a condition that he should not be circumcised, it was permissible for the Jewish purchaser to keep him, provided he agreed to observe the seven commandments given to the descendants of Noah, his status being then comparable to that of the resident alien (*ger toshab*).[1] The female slave might make a similar condition with regard to baptism. The circumcised foreign slave was admitted to eat the Passover (Exod. 12, 43–45), and the slave of a priest might eat consecrated food, which was prohibited to any lay Israelite (Lev. 22, 10 f.).

In a system of domestic slavery such as that of the Israelites, the incorporation of slaves into the family as a religious group was natural — the *sacra* of the master are the *sacra* of his household — and from a practical point of view almost necessary. If a manumitted slave voluntarily adhered to the Jewish religion, he became a *ger ṣedeḳ* and, since circumcision could not be repeated, received a second baptism.

The circumcision of converts has been considered in a previous chapter.[2]

As has been already noted, the rule that the circumcision of a child should be performed on the eighth day takes precedence of the law of the sabbath. Other circumstances may, however, cause the postponement of the operation to the ninth, tenth, eleventh, or even the twelfth day. If the newborn infant was ill, it was postponed until after his recovery.[3] If a mother has lost two sons by the fever following circumcision, the operation on a third should be deferred till he is grown and strong.[4] The principle is one frequently affirmed and illustrated by the rabbis: The laws were given that men should live by them, not that they should die by them.[5]

Among the measures which Antiochus Epiphanes adopted to annihilate the Jewish religion none struck so directly at its very

[1] Ibid. On the Ger Toshab, see Vol. I, pp. 339 f.

[2] Vol. I, pp. 330 ff.

[3] See Shabbat 134a, end.

[4] Yebamot 64b (second century authorities). Such a man, though not circumcised, is regarded as an unexceptionable Israelite. Ḥullin 4b and 5a.

[5] Lev. 18, 5. 'Abodah Zarah 27b and often.

existence as the prohibition of circumcision.[1] Hadrian's rescript making it a capital crime equally with castration, to which it was assimilated, was one of the provoking causes of the revolt of the year 132 A.D.[2] and the desperation of the ensuing war. Antoninus Pius exempted the Jews — and them alone — from this statute so far as to permit them to circumcise their sons; it is to be inferred that the circumcision of slaves or proselytes remained subject to the penalty of the law of Hadrian. The frequent repetition by later emperors, pagan [3] and Christian, of laws expressly to this effect is evidence that legislation in large measure failed to accomplish its end.[4]

To circumcise their sons is a commandment which the Israelites received with joy and rejoice in keeping; while such as they received with reluctance, like the law of prohibited degrees, they keep with reluctance. It, like the prohibition of idolatry, is one of the commandments for which Israelites deliver themselves to death rather than obey a conflicting edict of the government, and is therefore tenaciously held by them, while such commandments as the wearing of phylacteries (*tefillin*) are held laxly.[5] Every period of persecution proved the tenacity with which the Jews clung to the token of the Abrahamic covenant in their flesh (Gen. 17, 11, 13 f.)[6] as an assurance that God on his part would fulfil the covenant promises. All the more bitter was the feeling toward the apostates who, in effacing the physical evidence of their Judaism, renounced the religion itself and openly united themselves to the gentiles. Ἐποίησαν ἑαυτοῖς ἀκροβυστίαν, καὶ ἀπέστησαν ἀπὸ διαθήκης ἁγίας, καὶ ἐζευγίσθησαν τοῖς ἔθνεσιν (1 Macc. 1,15).[7]

1 1 Macc. 1, 41–50.

2 Historia Augusta, Hadrian, 14, 2.

3 Septimius Severus (ibid. 17, 4), "Judaeos fieri sub gravi poena vetuit."

4 On the history of the legislation see Juster, Les Juifs dans l'empire romain, I, 263ff.

5 Shabbat 130a; Sifrè Deut. § 76.

6 1 Macc. 1, 60f. (cf. 2 Macc. 6, 10; 4 Macc. 4, 25). Under the edict of Hadrian, Mekilta, Baḥodesh 6 (ed. Friedmann f. 68b; ed. Weiss f. 75b). See below, pp. 105 f.

7 Vol. I, p. 49.

The animosity to Paul was not alone because he maintained that Gentile believers in Christ should be admitted to the church without circumcision, a point which concerned the church only, but — what was of vital interest to all Jews — because he was reported to foment apostasy from Moses by teaching all the Jews in the dispersion not to circumcise their children nor observe the customs of their religion (Acts 21, 21).

The second of the fundamental observances of Judaism was the sabbath, the keeping of every seventh day as a 'holy' day by religious abstention from every kind of labor. It is called 'an eternal covenant,' 'an eternal sign' (cf. Ezek. 20, 12) between God and Israel (Exod. 31, 16, 17; cf. ibid. vs. 13).[1] Like circumcision (Gen. 17, 14), the sanction is extirpation: 'Every one who does work on it, that person shall be cut off out of the midst of his people' (Exod. 31, 14).[2] Here, as in the case of circumcision and for the same reason, an exploration of the antecedents of the Jewish sabbath and of analogous customs or institutions among other races is irrelevant. Days or seasons in which certain ordinarily licit acts and enterprises, or all ordinary occupations, are interdicted are common upon all planes of culture and acquire a fixed place in the calendar of many peoples.[3] The origin and motives of such interdictions are obviously diverse. To huddle them all together under the title ancient "taboo-days" is to deceive one's self with the imagination that when one has put a label — preferably a jargon label — on a phenomenon he has explained it, or dispensed himself from the necessity of understanding it. The jargon of anthropologists (and anthropological theologians) is getting to be as portentous as that of the mediaeval alchemists, with this difference, that the alchemists' jargon was for the mystification of outsiders,

[1] Compare the expressions about circumcision in Gen. 17, 7, 13.

[2] It is also punishable by the hands of men: Whoever profanes the holy day shall be put to death (ibid. vss. 14 and 15).

[3] The old Roman religion is a peculiarly instructive example. See G. Wissowa, Religion und Kultus der Römer, 2 ed., pp. 432 ff., 443.

while the anthropologists mystify not only the unlearned but themselves unawares with their Totem, Mana, Taboo, and the rest. The sabbath as a "taboo-day" means nothing but that it was a day on which certain doings were interdicted under a supernatural sanction, which is the very definition of the sabbath, as everybody knew before.

To the Jews the sabbath was an institution peculiar to their religion; it belongs to their God (Jehovah),[1] and is sacred unto him;[2] he calls them 'My sabbaths.'[3] It is 'an eternal covenant' between Him and Israel, an 'eternal sign.'[4] Greeks and Romans recognized it as an observance distinctive of Judaism, and as such, rulers who aimed to suppress the religion put the sabbath among the first of their prohibitions along with circumcision.

The hebdomadal sabbath was in fact exclusively Jewish; nothing corresponding to it existed in the Greek and Roman world, nor, so far as is known, elsewhere in antiquity.

In old Israel the new moon — the day after the crescent was first sighted in the sky — was celebrated by sacrifice and feasting (1 Sam. 20, 18–34), and, as may be inferred from 2 Kings 4, 23, by the suspension of every-day occupations. The prophets couple it with the sabbath, regularly naming it in the first place ('new moon and sabbath').[5] Amos 8, 5 shows that trading was prohibited on both. In Hos. 1, 13 (E.V. 1, 11) and Isa. 1, 13 f. it stands at the head of the list, preceding the seasonal festivals, and was, like the sabbath and those festivals, the occasion of a 'convocation'[6] (A.V. 'solemn assembly'), a proclamation calling the people to observe the day. The offerings appointed for the new moon (Num. 28, 11–15; cf. Ezek. 46, 4–7)[7] exceed those

[1] Exod. 16, 25.
[2] Exod. 16, 23.
[3] Ezek. 20, 12, 16, 20, and repeatedly; Isa. 56, 4.
[4] Exod. 31, 13, 16f.
[5] Note also Colossians 2, 16.
[6] Isa. 1, 14.
[7] It is not mentioned in Deut., nor elsewhere in the legislation, a fact about which various conjectures have been made.

on the sabbath, and in post-exilic sources (Chron., Ezra, Neh.) it maintains its precedence in the order of enumeration. No express prohibition of labor on the new moon is found in the Law (Num. 28, 11–15 has to do solely with the offerings for the day) nor is a 'holy convocation' appointed for it, but this is true in the passage cited of the sabbath also.[1] In later times at least labor was not suspended on the new moon.[2] The new moon retained its prime importance for the fixing of the calendar with the dates of all the annual festivals, but the religious observance of the day outside the ritual of the temple seems to have early declined.[3]

The sabbath is frequently joined with the annual festivals, and is, like the high days of those festivals, New Years, and the Day of Atonement, a day of 'holy convocation.' The three great annual festivals, the Passover with the Feast of Unleavened Bread at the vernal full moon, the Harvest Feast, or Feast of Weeks, in midsummer, and the Feast of Ingathering, or of Booths, at the time of the vintage, marked in ancient Palestine the three great seasons of the agricultural year, and in the age in which they were celebrated at the local holy places or at some more famous pilgrim shrine must have somewhat overshadowed the weekly sabbath with its predominantly negative features. Even after the suppression of the 'high places' and translation of the high festivals to the capital of the little kingdom of Judah, this doubtless continued in a measure to be the case, but from the fact that the sabbath was the one local observance left, it would gain relatively in importance. Before a generation had passed, however, the reforms of Josiah went down in the catastrophe of the kingdom.

For the Jews colonized in Babylonia or scattered in other lands, the sabbath alone of all the sacred calendar remained, and

[1] Contrast Num. 28, 18, 25; 29, 1, etc.

[2] Ḥagigah 18a (second century).

[3] After the adoption of an astronomically fixed calendar, about the middle of the fourth century, the coming New Moon was announced in the synagogue on the preceding Sabbath after the reading of the lessons.

its importance was thus greatly enhanced. It was the one observance historically associated with the cultus that could still be maintained wherever there were Jews,[1] and the observance of it was the most conspicuous sign of allegiance to the national God and the institutions of their fathers. This conception of it appears with striking emphasis in the great historical indictment of Israel for rebellion against the laws of God, not only in the present but in every period of its past, drawn by Ezekiel. In the specifications, which gather force by the very monotony of iteration, the profanation of the sabbaths regularly forms the climax — they walked not in my statutes and rejected my ordinances and profaned my sabbaths.[2]

Conversely in Isa. 56, 2, 4, 6; 58, 13, for the Jews and for the aliens who join themselves to them,[3] the observance of the sabbath is the symbol of adhesion to the covenant religion and the condition of participation in the coming restoration with all its blessings. In Augustine's sense it may properly be called a sacrament, a sacred sign by which a religious community is bound together, and through the long centuries and in all the lands of their ever widening dispersion it was such to the Jews.

It was in this respect even more significant than circumcision. The latter sign of the covenant was imposed on an infant by his parents without his understanding or will, solely by virtue of his descent; whereas the keeping of the sabbath in the face of persecution or the permanent and more insidious temptations of worldly interest was a standing evidence of the intelligent and self-determined fidelity of the man to the religion in which he was brought up from a child.

Of particular features of sabbath observance the Bible gives but few and incidental glimpses. Agricultural labor is expressly

[1] The abstention from labor on the appointed days was the only part of the festival laws that could be everywhere observed.

[2] Ezek. 20, 13, 16, 21; cf. 20, 12, 20. See also 44, 24. Probably 'sabbaths' here include not only the weekly sabbath but the other sabbatical days and the seventh year fallow as parts of one system.

[3] Proselytes.

forbidden, even in plowing time and harvest (Exod. 34, 21; cf. Neh. 13, 15); and from the social and economic conditions of the times it may be inferred that the general interdiction primarily contemplated every-day agricultural and domestic occupations. From Amos we know that trading on that day was prohibited (8, 5); from Isa. 58, 13 (end), pursuing one's own business or talking about it. Jeremiah lays particular stress upon the bearing of burdens and bringing them in by the gates of Jerusalem, and carrying burdens out of houses (17, 19–27);[1] and from the way Jeremiah speaks of them it would seem that corresponding prohibitions were familiar in an ancient law. The story of the man who was stoned to death for gathering sticks for firewood on the sabbath (Num. 15, 32–36) is familiar, and the kindling of fire in any habitation is expressly forbidden (Exod. 35, 3).

These are plainly only casual instances of a much more comprehensive customary law, which was probably extended in course of time to meet changing conditions.

The penalty of violating the law of the sabbath, whether death inflicted by the courts or extirpation by God, fell upon the guilty person. Ezekiel, in making the profanation of the sabbaths by the people as a whole from the beginning a national sin, which over and over again had provoked God to the point of meditating the destruction that after many postponements finally befel the nation,[2] gave the observance a collective sanction, so to speak the extirpation (*karet*) of the guilty nation, with all the evils in which it involved the individual members of the people. In the same sense Isa. 58, 13 f. attaches to the observance of the sabbath in the true spirit of it the crowning promises of the age of restoration.[3] In the conviction that God's great deliverance waited for the conformity of all the people to the revealed will of God, the sabbath is sometimes taken as the critical instance:

[1] Cf. Neh. 13, 15–22, where it appears that the Sabbath had been made a market day. [2] Ezek. 20.

[3] For the individualizing interpretation of these promises, see below, pp. 291 f.

"If Israel should keep two sabbaths strictly according to rule, they would be delivered forthwith."[1]

When Antiochus Epiphanes undertook by force of arms to compel the Jews to obey his edict of conformity, the recalcitrants at first not only would not bear arms on the sabbath, but did not even move a hand in their own defense, and let themselves be massacred with their wives and children rather than profane the sabbath (1 Macc. 2, 29–41).[2] It may be conjectured that it was not solely a case of personal fidelity at any cost, but that with this was joined the belief that such fidelity was the condition of the deliverance of their people by divine intervention. However this may be, it is certain that in that sifting time, when many sought to emancipate themselves from the restrictions of the law, partly because they found them unreasonable as well as onerous, partly because they wanted to break down partitions and fraternize with the gentiles,[3] while others yielded to the stress of persecution, the strict observance of the sabbath became in Judaea the touchstone of allegiance, distinguishing the true Jew from the cosmopolite or the apostate, as in the dispersion it distinguished Jew from heathen, or from the slough of Jewry which was presently engulfed in the surrounding mass of heathenism.

The crisis passed, and the attempt to modernize Judaism from within after foreign patterns was not renewed,[4] but the effects remained in a heightened consciousness of separateness, and greater tenacity in maintaining and emphasizing the distinctive observances of Judaism.

Such glimpses of sabbatical prohibitions as we get from the

[1] R. Simeon ben Yoḥai (Shabbat 118b). The exegetical derivation is from Isa. 56, 7, combined with vs. 4. Cf. Levi in Jer. Ta'anit 64a: If they should keep one sabbath as prescribed, the Son of David would come forthwith. Parallels with variations in the homiletic Midrash.

[2] See also 2 Macc. 5, 25 f.; 6, 11; 8, 26; 12, 38; esp. 15, 1 ff.

[3] Cf. 1 Macc. 1, 11.

[4] The conflicts of Pharisees and Sadducees were of an entirely different character.

period shortly preceding the Christian era [1] exhibit numerous details of which our scanty previous sources make no mention. The spirit is one of strict observance, and the particulars for the most part correspond to those which we find in the authoritative Halakah — a fact of all the greater significance because the Damascene sect was pronouncedly schismatic, and Jubilees, besides other idiosyncrasies, is contentious on points — especially the calendar — which contradict and condemn the teaching of the schools. Where the sabbath observance in these writings differs substantially from the Tannaite Halakah, it is generally in the direction of greater strictness; this tendency however was not peculiarly sectarian, it was the character of the older Halakah in general,[2] resulting chiefly from greater literalness in interpreting and applying the written law.

It can hardly be doubted that the more methodical labors of the schools upon the Law and the discussion of actual or hypothetical cases led to new definitions or more exact formulations of the rules, and to a multiplication of rabbinical regulations hedging the Torah with precautions. The codification of the rules of sabbath observance in the Mishnah represents the conclusion of a long process, to be immediately recommenced in another form in the Talmud. It includes the agricultural and industrial occupations of the Mishnaic period.

The enumeration of thirty-nine principal species of prohibited acts is an attempt to bring them under one head with a biblical warrant for the whole. This was found in Exodus 35, where in immediate sequence upon the prohibition of 'work' on the sabbath, the same word (*mal'akah*), is repeatedly used in the directions for the construction and furnishing of the tabernacle, the vestments of the priests, etc.[3] By cataloguing the various occu-

[1] Jubilees 2, 26–33; 50, 6–13; Damascene Sect (Schechter's text) 10, 14–11, 21. See Vol. I, pp. 198 f., 201.

[2] The differences in other fields are much wider than in the sabbath laws.

[3] Cf. Exod. 36, 1–7; and see also 31, 1–11, immediately followed by the sabbath law (31, 12–17).

pations specified or implied in the making of the tabernacle, the acts forbidden under the indefinite name 'work' in the sabbath law could be defined.[1]

The number thirty-nine is, however, not the sum of an actual count, a method by which, from the nature of the operation, independent agreement in the result would have been impossible. The "forty less one" was taken from Deut. 25, 2 f., and the count in Exodus made to come out to that figure, just as the number 613 for the commandments and prohibitions in the Law [2] was the starting point, not the conclusion, of the enumeration.

Of these thirty-nine principal species (*abot*) there are many derivative varieties (*toledot*). R. Johanan and R. Simeon ben Laḳish are said, as the outcome of three years and a half of study, to have discovered thirty-nine such in each of the species named in the Mishnah, making a total of 1521;[3] a compliment is paid to their persistent diligence and the subtlety of their analysis.

The striking disproportion between the multitudinous rules of sabbath observance and their biblical authority was early remarked: "The (provisions for) release from vows float in the air, there is nothing to support them; the regulations (*halakot*) about the sabbath, and offerings at the festivals (*ḥagigot*), and the misappropriation of sacred things (*me'ilot*) are like mountains hanging by a hair, for they are very little Bible and a great many rules." [4] This is contrasted with the state of the case in various other titles of the law which have abundant support in Scripture.

The thirty-nine principal species of infraction of the sabbath catalogued in the Mishnah are defined to cover cognate operations. 'Plowing,' for example, includes spading the ground and

[1] M. Shabbat 7, 2; Mekilta, Wayyaḳhel 1; Shabbat 49b; Baba Ḳamma 2a. These and other passages are translated in Strack–Billerbeck, Kommentar zum Neuen Testament aus Talmud und Midrasch, on Matt. 12, 2.

[2] See below, p. 83. [3] Jer. Shabbat 9 b–c.

[4] M. Ḥagigah 1, 8, שהן מקרא מועט והלכות מרובות; cf. Tos. Ḥagigah 1, 9; Tos. 'Erubin 11 (8) 23 f. (ed. Zuckermandel p. 154 line 14 ff.).

digging a trench; 'sowing' covers planting trees, layering and pruning; reaping comprehends not only harvesting grain and legumes, but picking grapes, cutting clusters of dates, stripping off olives from the tree, and plucking figs.[1] These operations are in each case brought under one head by the end common to them — preparing the soil, getting something to grow and bear fruit, gathering the increase.

The derivative restrictions (*toledot*) are laid upon actions that, though not to the same end, are in some way analogous to one of the principal species; for example, if a man takes a bar of metal and rubs it in order to use the powder as goldsmiths do, the operation resembles 'grinding,' and constructively falls under that head as a secondary prohibition. When the disciples of Jesus, walking on a path through a grain field on a sabbath, plucked ears of wheat and ate them (Mark 2, 23 and parallels), which was lawful on week-days (Deut. 23, 26), they were transgressing such a secondary prohibition of 'reaping.'[2]

Besides these classes of prohibitions there were others which rested solely on rabbinical authority. A list of such, which applied to the sabbatical days of the festivals as well as to the sabbath, is found in the Mishnah.[3] Some of them are expressly noted as in themselves permissible, others are things prescribed by the law itself, but forbidden by the learned to be done on those days. Those that were prohibited 'for the sake of sabbatical observance' were climbing a tree, riding on a beast, swimming, clapping hands, smiting on the thigh, dancing. There follow: holding court, betrothing a wife, performing the ceremony of loosing the shoe (Deut. 25, 8–10), or entering into levirate marriage; in another category are consecrating anything, valuing (in commutation of vows, Lev. 27, 1 ff.), dedicating by a ban.[4]

[1] Shabbat 73b; Maimonides, Hilkot Shabbat 7, 2–4.

[2] Since they must have rubbed out the grains in their hands — though only Luke thinks it necessary to mention this — they were also constructively threshing.

[3] M. Beṣah 5, 2.

[4] These because they are assimilated to transactions involving the passage of money or the like.

The sabbath was thus hedged about by a multitude of restrictions. They are, however, only specifications of a general rule which might be formulated thus: All ordinary agricultural, industrial, and domestic work is forbidden, unless it is, by its nature or in the circumstances of the case, necessary, i.e. such that it could not have been done the day before or be put off to the following day without serious consequences. What is new in the rabbinical laws of the sabbath is not the interdiction of every kind of work — that is emphatically biblical — but the direct or round-about provision for the necessary exceptions, which in their turn demanded definition. For example, it is a general principle that when a human life is in danger the sabbath laws are set aside by the higher obligation. It may safely be assumed that this was ancient commonsense custom. The Maccabees acted on it, when, enlightened by the fate of the rigid sabbatarians of their day, they decided to take up arms in defence of their lives and those of their wives and children if attacked by their enemies on the sabbath; and in the persecution under Hadrian a council of rabbis at Lydda decided that to save his life a Jew might yield on any point but three (idolatry, incest, murder),[1] for which concession R. Ishmael found a warrant in Lev. 18, 5 — the laws were given 'that a man should *live* by them,' not *die* by them. The same principle is expressly applied by R. Ishmael to the sabbath, with an argument a *fortiori* from Exod. 22, 1.[2] We have already noted that the circumcision of an ailing child is postponed if the operation would be dangerous, and there are many other cases[3] in which danger to life (even possible though uncertain danger) supersedes[4] all the sabbath laws. Even in such a case as that of a child who has accidentally got

[1] Sanhedrin 74a, and elsewhere.

[2] Mekilta Ki tissa 1 (ed. Friedmann f. 103b; ed. Weiss f. 109 a–b); Yoma 85a; cf. Tos. Shabbat 15 (16), 17, attributed to Akiba. See Bacher, Agada der Tannaiten, I, 260 and note (correcting the reference to Yoma as above).

[3] A comprehensive enumeration in Maimonides, Mishneh Torah, Shabbat 2, 1 ff.

[4] The technical term is דחה, 'push out' (and take its place).

locked up in a room, the door may be broken down to let it out.[1] The general principle is: The sabbath was committed to you, not you to the sabbath (Mekilta on Exod. 31, 13; cf. Mark 2, 27).

An attentive survey of the most attenuated casuistry on the sabbath will show that the motive for most of it is to make the law practicable. One or two illustrations may be adduced here. Jeremiah 17, 22 forbids carrying a burden [2] out of a house on the sabbath day. The Mishnah (M. Shabbat 1, 1), and upon it the Talmuds, show how two persons between them can pass something into the house or out of it without either of them transgressing the law. There is no prohibition of carrying things from one room to another in the same house, even if it should be occupied by more than one family. If there were several separate houses surrounding a court, this court could be converted into the central court of one tenement by what we should call a legal fiction. If the families living in private houses around this court prepare, before the beginning of the sabbath, a meal to which each contributes something and to which all have access, they constitute themselves for the occasion one family, and the court with the houses about it for the time being a single private domain in joint occupation.[3] In the case of a larger complex, the street entrance may be converted into a constructive doorway by erecting jambs on the sides and (or) a beam overhead for a lintel.[4] In some cases an even wider extension may be given to the principle.[5]

1 See Tos. Shabbat 15 (16), 11 f.; Yoma 84 a–b. See Rashi on Yoma 84b. The child might be badly frightened and die of fright, Maimonides 2, 17. The objection to Jesus' treatment of the sick on the Sabbath was that the sufferers were in no danger. A man with a withered arm (Mark 3, 1–6) or other malady of years standing could just as well have waited till Sunday.

2 Carrying into a house is on a parity with carrying out.

3 It seems not unlikely that this device was introduced in the first instance to facilitate social meals on the sabbath.

4 It was not necessary that this doorway should be a solid structure; what might be described as scenery sufficed.

5 The differences between the schools of Shammai and Hillel over the details of these arrangements show that the permissibility of such combinations had long been established beyond question.

At the first mention of the sabbath (Exod. 16, 29), in connection with the giving of the manna, the injunction is added, 'Remain every man where he is; let no man go out from his place on the seventh day.'[1] This was taken as a prohibition of locomotion and extended from the particular occasion to the sabbath in general. From Josephus (B. J. ii. 8, 9 § 147) it seems that the Essenes took this with extreme literalness. The Samaritans are said to recognize nothing corresponding to the Jewish 'sabbath day's journey.' The latter is a distance of 2000 cubits reckoned from the outer boundary of the city or town[2] from which a man starts out. This regulation is found, in complete accord with the authentic Halakah, in the laws of the Damascene schismatics,[3] and must therefore have been established at least as early as the second century before the Christian era. Within the sabbath limits of his city or town a man might move about freely. For the purpose of fulfilling a religious act (*miṣwah*), such as to go to a house of mourning or a wedding party, or to meet his master (rabbi) or his colleague returning from a journey, the permissible distance might be doubled by a 'combination of limits.' A man who has such a reason for going to a more distant place (within 4000 cubits of the town bounds) on the sabbath may establish a constructive domicile at any point within the limit of sabbath locomotion by depositing there on Friday provisions for at least two meals,[4] from which point he may go on up to 2000 cubits more.

In the Decalogue in Exodus (20, 8–11) the institution of the sabbath is connected with the rest of God on the seventh day, after the completion of his six days creative work, 'wherefore the Lord blessed the sabbath day and made it holy.' In Deut-

[1] On the distinction of the two terms תחתיו (the four cubits), and מקומו (the 2000 cubits, Num. 35, 5), see Mekilta, Beshallaḥ 5 (ed. Friedmann, f. 51a; ed. Weiss f. 59a); 'Erubin 51a.

[2] The way in which this figure was arrived at does not here concern us, nor the minute prescriptions concerning the delimitations.

[3] See L. Ginzberg, Eine unbekannte jüdische Sekte, p. 155.

[4] M. 'Erubin 8, 1 f. The texts are collected in Strack-Billerbeck on Acts 1, 12.

eronomy (5, 12–15) to the identical prohibition ('Thou shalt not do any work, thou nor thy son nor thy daughter nor thy slave nor thy maid servant,[1] nor thine ox nor thine ass nor any of thy cattle, nor the alien sojourner [2] in thy gates, in order that thy slave and thy maid servant may rest like thyself'), Israel is reminded that it was in servitude in Egypt and was delivered by its God with a strong hand and an outstretched arm, 'therefore the Lord, thy God, enjoins thee to keep the sabbath day' (5, 15). It is a day of respite from toil for man and beast, master and slave, Israelite and alien. The humane motive is here urged, as so often in Deuteronomy; the periodical abstention from labor is not only a divine ordinance, but a refreshing pause in the round of daily toil.

There are many restrictions on sabbath occupations which have no resemblance to work, such as talking about business, looking over plantations to see what they need, hiring workmen, casting up accounts, and the like.[3] The biblical authority is found in Isa. 58, 13: 'If thou turn away thy foot from the sabbath, from pursuing thy business on my holy day . . . and honor it by not doing thy wonted ways, nor pursuing thy business nor talking of it,' etc. Everyday occupations are to be demitted on the sabbath in honor of the day. That these are not late refinements is proved by their place in the law of sabbath observance contained in the text of the schismatic Damascene sect: "On the Sabbath day a man shall not engage in foolish and vain talk; he shall not claim anything back from his fellow; he shall not have an argument with him about money matters; he shall not talk about work and labor to be done next morning."

[1] Minors for whom the father is responsible; uncircumcised and unbaptized slaves (התושבים), who are not under personal obligation to keep the Sabbath. Mekilta de-R. Simeon ben Yoḥai on Exod. 20, 10 (p. 108); Midrash Tannaim on Deut. 5, 14.

[2] Some understood this of proselytes; others of the *ger toshab*. See Vol. I, p. 339.

[3] Shabbat 150a; Maimonides, Hilkot Shabbat, c. 24; Shulḥan 'Aruk, Oraḥ Ḥayyim §§ 306 f.

There is another side of Jewish sabbath observance to which due attention is not always paid, namely its festal character. The spirit of such a celebration is well expressed in Neh. 8, 9–12. On New Years Day (the first day of the seventh month), which was a high sabbath[1] on which all labor was forbidden (Lev. 23, 24f.), the people broke out into weeping as Ezra read the Law to them. Nehemiah and Ezra stopped this ill-timed demonstration of penitence: 'This day is holy to the Lord your God; do not mourn nor weep. . . . Go, eat of the richest viands and drink of the most delicious wine, and send portions to those who have nothing provided, for this day is holy unto our Lord; do not be mournful. . . . So all the people went their way to eat and drink, and to send portions, and to make a great festivity.'

Parallel with the laws for the religious festivals in Leviticus and Numbers where the sabbatical character of the celebration, or of certain days of the feast, is noted and labor on them forbidden, are the laws in Deuteronomy in which the joyousness of the festivals, and of all the occasions that bring men to the sanctuary, is uniformly emphasized. To eat and drink and be joyful before the Lord is in fact the salient characteristic of the sabbatical seasons.[2]

Modern critics have laid much stress on the contrast between this temper and that of the laws regulating the cultus in other books of the Pentateuch. Deuteronomy and the Law-Book of the Priests represent, it is said, widely separated stages in the history of the religion. Deuteronomy preserves, notwithstanding the transplantation to Jerusalem, the natural festive character of the old Israelite religion in Canaan; while in the Law-Book of the Priests everything natural, spontaneous — in a word, human — has been supplanted by a meticulous formalism in every sphere, and the joyousness of the ancient cultus by sin offerings and trespass offerings and multiplied piacula, culminating in the Day of Atonement, when it was a man's most sacred obligation to fast and afflict his soul for his sins.

[1] שבתון.

[2] See Deut. 12, 6 f., 12, 18; 14, 23–26; 16, 10f., 13 f.

Whatever may be thought otherwise about this method, one thing is sure — the Jews were wholly innocent of it. For them the laws were not conflicting but complementary; to be joyful at the feasts, with the natural concomitants of good cheer, was as truly a divine commandment as to abstain from laborious occupations.

The Book of Jubilees is in some notable particulars more stringent about abstention from such ordinary occupations than the Mishnah; but it names in one breath eating and drinking and resting from all labor and praising God for the gift of this holy day as the duty of the sabbath, and continues: "For great is the honor that God has shown Israel, that they should on this day eat and drink to satiety, and rest on it from all labor." This distinction belongs to Israel alone,[1] "He hallowed no people or peoples to keep sabbath on this day, except Israel only; to it alone he granted to eat and drink and keep sabbath on it."[2]

From Isa. 58, 13 it was deduced that the sabbath observance approved and requited by God included not only showing peculiar honor to the day, but the indulgence in some unusual luxury[3] on it, especially in the way of food and drink. It was laudable for a man to be as lavish with his table as his means permitted, and even the poorest should have some unusual dish, however small it might be, for even some little thing done in honor of the sabbath is 'a luxury.' In order to have a better appetite for the sabbath meal (on Friday evening), men ate sparingly on Friday, even if they were at a wedding feast.[4] Consequently the sabbath was a favorite day for entertaining guests at dinner. Luke 14, 1–24 is a scene in the house of one of the leading Pharisees, whose guest at such a meal Jesus was. Provision was made for three meals, one on Friday evening, one on Saturday morning, and a light meal following the time of afternoon prayer (*minḥah*).

[1] Jubilees 50, 9 f. Cf. Mekilta, Ki tissa 1 (ed. Friedmann f. 104b; ed. Weiss f. 109b); Beṣah 16a.

[2] Jubilees 2, 31.

[3] ענג. Shabbat 118 a–b; Maimonides, Hilkot Shabbat 30, 7 ff.

[4] Tos. Berakot 5, 1; Jer. Pesaḥim 37b; Pesaḥim 99b.

All preparations were made on Friday, and, inasmuch as cold victuals were not a luxury then any more than now, devices were introduced to keep them hot (with due precautions against cooking going on) until the meals might be served.[1]

It was an ancient custom, for which minute regulations are given in the Mishnah,[2] on Friday afternoon before dark to light a lamp which was to be left burning through the evening of the holy day. In the Talmud this is declared to be obligatory.[3] The master of the house was responsible for seeing that all preparations were according to rule, but the lighting of the lamp fell to the housewife, and negligence on her part was a very serious dereliction.[4]

The advent of the Sabbath was marked by a 'sanctification' (*ḳiddush*) which set the day apart from the week-day that preceded. The head of the house, at the table surrounded by his family and guests, took a cup full of wine, pronounced over it the usual blessing (Blessed art thou, O Lord our God, King of the World, who createst the fruit of the vine) [5] and the Blessing of the Day.[6] Then he, and after him those seated with him at the table, drank from the "cup of blessing." [7] The blessing on the bread (Who bringeth forth bread from the earth), two loaves of which were before the head of the house, symbolizing the double portion of manna on the Sabbath,[8] followed, and the meal proceeded.

1 M. Shabbat 3 and 4, with the Talmud.

2 M. Shabbat 2.

3 Shabbat 25b (with Tosafot in loc.); cf. Maimonides, Hilkot Shabbat 5, 1. The blessing in the liturgy speaks of it as a divine command (וצונו להדליק נר של שבת). Baer, 'Abodat Israel, p. 173; Singer, Prayer Book, p. 108.

4 M. Shabbat, 2, 6. One of the causes of death in childbirth, Tos. Shabbat 2, 10; Jer. Shabbat 5b.

5 M. Berakot 6, 1.

6 The core of it is thanks to God for the gift of the sabbath to the Jews as a heritage.

7 כוס הברכה; cf. 1 Cor. 10, 16.

8 On the two loaves and the ceremonial breaking of the bread see Shabbat 117b, below; Berakot 39b.

A counterpart of these ceremonies, the 'separation'[1] (*habdalah*), in which spices were used as well as wine, signified that the Sabbath was over.[2]

The domestic character of the rites will be noted. In later times this feature was further developed, and it became customary for parents to give their blessing to their children, and for the husband to recite the beautiful eulogy of the model housewife from Proverbs 31, 10–31.

Everything that might damp the joyous spirit of the day was shut out. The period of strict mourning was interrupted by the sabbath or other sabbatical day. Fasting, accompanied by demonstrations of grief or distress and prayer for relief or compassion, was forbidden, except in the case of certain imminent perils.[3] The spirit and practice of days of mourning and fasting and those of the sabbath were mutually exclusive. So far is this carried that we read that certain second century authorities prescribed that if one visited the sick on the sabbath — which was a pious act — he should say: "It is the sabbath, one must not complain; you will soon be cured," the motive being to encourage the sick, so that they may not grieve on the day. There follow various forms of expression employed on such occasions by exemplary teachers of the time. R. Ḥanina (third century) significantly adds: "Only with difficulty was permission granted to console mourners or visit the sick on the sabbath."[4]

Here, as in many other points, the Jews may seem to have overdone the logic of a situation, but nothing could be more conclusive testimony to the dominant idea of the sabbath — a day of sheer gladness, uncontaminated even by natural sympathy with suffering.

As the Scribes learned from Isa. 58, 13 that God meant the sabbath to be set apart from other days not only by the things

[1] I.e. of the holy day from the following week.
[2] See the article 'Habdalah,' Jewish Encyclopedia, VI, 118–121.
[3] Specified in M. Ta'anit 3, 7.
[4] Shabbat 12 a–b.

that were not done on it, but by what was done, that it was a day for men to enjoy themselves on, and in accordance with the notions of feast days in the Scriptures, gave a front place in this enjoyment to more sumptuous eating and drinking than on other days ('luxury'), so they found there also that it was His will that the sabbath should be honored, and defined what belonged to the honor of the day. A man should bathe his face and hands and feet in warm water on Friday, and wash his clothes clean; he should dress differently on the sabbath from week-days, and so on.

The rise of the synagogue and its growing importance in the religious life of Judaism gave to the sabbath another character. The fact that the sabbath was a day of leisure made it the natural day for such assemblies, and in the course of time a larger and larger part of it was occupied by them. It is true that attendance on the synagogue formed no part of the obligatory sabbath observance prescribed in the Scriptures or interpreted and applied in the regulations of the Scribes, but it came by custom to belong to the proper way of spending the day. Thus from being only a day of recreation and good cheer, the sabbath became a day for religious instruction and edification. The exercises of the synagogue, consisting of prayer, the reading and interpretation of Scripture, and expository homilies thereupon, were a rational worship, which even while the temple stood was of far greater actual moment in the religious life of the Jews than the sacrificial cultus, and after the cessation of that cultus the only form of worship. The further development of the 'study-house,' [1] to which many devoted the afternoon hours, completed the transformation by which the sabbath was filled by exercises directed to instruction in religion and the cultivation of a religious spirit.

If the legal observance of the sabbath was, in the sense previously defined, a sacramental bond holding together all ad-

[1] Bet ha-Midrash.

herents of the Jewish religion, the use of the sabbath for the worship of God in the study of the revelation of his character and his will for men gave it a positive religious value in comparison with which its negative aspect becomes wholly subsidiary. In any representation of the Jewish sabbath as it was in the centuries with which we are here primarily concerned — and as it has been ever since — it is a stupendous error to concentrate attention on the micrologic casuistry of external restrictions or relaxations, ignoring the real significance of the day for religion itself. Enough has been said about this in a former chapter and it is unnecessary to summarize it here.[1]

[1] It is pertinent to add that many popular representations of the so-called Puritan sabbath err in exactly the same way.

CHAPTER III

ANNUAL FESTIVALS

It has been remarked above that after the destruction of Jerusalem if not earlier, various features of the temple service which could be detached from the sacrificial cultus were, with the necessary adaptation, transferred to the synagogue. In two of the great festivals, Passover and Tabernacles, there was an original connection with the home which was maintained by the side of the pilgrim celebration in Jerusalem. The laws which forbade the eating of leavened bread during the Passover season and even the presence of leaven in the house,[1] applied to every Jewish family. The searching of the house for leaven or bread was probably early ceremonialized as such things naturally are; and it would also be natural that the domestic meal on the eve of the fifteenth of Nisan,[2] at which the unleavened cakes (*maṣṣot*) were first eaten, should be given by this fact a note distinguishing it from the weekly sabbath or another festival day,[3] and be associated with the deliverance from Egypt as was done in the synagogue lessons. So long, however, as the Passover was celebrated in Jerusalem, where the pilgrims made up temporary groups to provide for the Paschal meal and partake of it, in place of the natural family observance in the home,[4] these features were doubtless subordinate. But when the temple worship ceased, the Passover most naturally fell into place in the home, to which, in the narrative of the institution and by its whole character, it belonged before Jerusalem became the sole legitimate seat of sacrificial worship.[5]

1 Exod. 12, 15, 19; 13, 7.

2 Evening of the 14th in our way of counting.

3 Yom Tob.

4 Only men were required to attend, though women and girls might be present.

5 Deut. 16, 1–8.

In the domestic celebration the sacrificial features necessarily disappeared when the lamb or kid could no longer be slaughtered in the temple and its blood conveyed to the altar by the priests. The Paschal meal itself, eaten as it was in private houses, with its unleavened cakes and bitter herbs, the successive cups of wine, the blessings, and the psalms, could be closely reproduced without profanation.

In some places it was customary to eat a roast on the Passover night; in others not. The Mishnah authorizes the following of the local custom.[1] We are told in this connection that a certain Theodorus [2] introduced in Rome the custom of roasting a kid for this occasion, trussed in the peculiar manner prescribed for the Paschal sacrifice, which was highly disapproved because it made those who partook of it eat consecrated food outside of Jerusalem, or, more correctly, have the appearance of it.[3] If an animal is dressed and roasted in this general manner, it must be made in some way to differ from the Paschal victim, as for instance if one limb be cut off.

The rite, in all its essential features, as it is observed to this day, is described in the Mishnah (Pesaḥim 10).[4] The head of the family resumes his primitive function and conducts the service as the priest of his own household. The children are present, and the question of one of them,[5]—"Why is this night different from all other nights?" gives occasion to explain the ritual and its significance as a memorial of the deliverance of Israel from the oppression in Egypt, followed by an exposition of Deut. 26, 5–9.[6] "In every age a man is bound to regard himself as if *he* went forth out of Egypt, as it is written, 'And thou shalt tell thy son in that day, saying, It is because of what the Lord did for *me* when I came out of Egypt'" (Exod. 13, 8).[7] The

[1] M. Pesaḥim 4, 4. [2] תודוס.

[3] Pesaḥim 53 a–b; Beṣah 23a; Jer. Pesaḥim 34a; Jer. Beṣah 61c, below. See also Berakot 19a.

[4] Cf. Tos. Pesaḥim 10. [5] Exod. 13, 8; cf. 12, 26 f.; 13, 14.

[6] 'A wandering Syrian was my father,' etc.

[7] Pressing the first person singular. Cf. Pesiḳta ed. Buber f. 105a; Tanḥuma ed. Buber, Yitro § 7 (ביום הזה, Exod. 19, 1).

catch-words of these obligatory topics at the Passover, according to Rabban Gamaliel, are "Passover," because God passed over the houses of our fathers in Egypt (sparing the first-born); "Unleavened Cake," because our fathers were delivered from Egypt;[1] "Bitter Herbs," because the Egyptians made bitter the lives of our fathers in Egypt. For this deliverance their descendants are bound to give thanks, and to laud and praise and honor and exalt "Him who wrought for us and for our fathers all these miracles. He brought us out from slavery to freedom, from sadness to joy, from mourning to festivity, from darkness to great light, from oppression to deliverance."[2] With this introduction the recital of the Hallel began (Psalms 113–114), 'In exitu Israel' being peculiarly appropriate. The recitation concluded with the 'Ge'ullah,' a liturgical close magnifying God for saving his people from Egypt. The retrospect invites the prospect of the future deliverance. The Mishnah records a prayer of R. Akiba for the time when the celebration of the festivals may be renewed in Jerusalem, and sacrifices and Passovers may be eaten there, happy in the rebuilding of God's city and rejoicing in his worship.[3]

In later times a place was set for Elijah, the forerunner of the Messiah. In the intimate circle in which it was repeated and the happy spirit of the festivity, the Passover Story (*Haggadah shel-Pesaḥ*) was free from constraint, and developed in popular forms fitted to interest the young and the unlettered, and was accommodating enough to pick up elements of quite unbiblical character, some of them of modern origin, like the Ḥad Gadya, a rhyme whose nearest English analogue is "The House that Jack Built." A healthy religious sense found no incongruity between the serious and the playful in the celebration. The primitive sacrificial meal thus became completely symbolical, enshrining the most precious memories and the most exalting hopes of the Jew-

[1] With the unraised dough in their kneading troughs, Exod. 12, 34.
[2] M. Pesaḥim 10, 5.
[3] M. Pesaḥim 10, 6.

ish people in a rite not only of sacramental significance, but of singular and moving beauty.

In the centuries preceding the Christian era the Feast of Tabernacles had become the culminating festival of the year, as it doubtless had been in the agricultural calendar of Palestine from immemorial antiquity, the Harvest Home in the time of the vintage and the oil-pressing. The sacrifices during the seven days of the feast, with the closing rites on the eighth (*shemini 'aṣeret*),[1] were more lavish than at any other, requiring, besides other species, seventy bullocks as holocausts,[2] and all the courses of priests were on duty.

A characteristic feature of the celebration in the temple was the carrying of the Lulab and the Etrog by the worshippers in conformity with Lev. 23, 40 as interpreted by the Jewish authorities.[3] Josephus describes the former as an *εἰρεσιώνη* of myrtle and willow with a spray of palm leaf; in another place he calls them compendiously *θύρσοι* of palms and citrons, the latter being the Etrog.[4] At certain points in the recitation of the Hallel (Psalms 113–118) the branches were waved in concert. The Mishnah names particularly the beginning of Psalm 118 ('O give thanks unto the Lord, for he is good') and vs. 25 ('We beseech thee, O Lord, save us now'), registering some minor diversities.[5] After the supplemental sacrifices of the day (*musaf*) had been

[1] Eventually a ninth day; cf. 2 Chron. 7, 8–10 with 1 Kings 8, 66.

[2] On the first day, 13; the second, 12, and so on decreasing to 7 on the seventh day. These burnt offerings were made, according to an often repeated explanation, in behalf of the seventy heathen nations; the *one* on the eighth day for the unique people, Israel. When the heathen destroyed the temple, they destroyed the atonement that was made for them. Sukkah 55b; cf. Pesiḳta ed. Buber f. 193b–194a.

[3] Samaritans, and later the Karaites, interpreted Lev. 23, 40 of materials for the construction of the booths. Cf. Neh. 8, 15.

[4] Jos. Antt. iii. 10, 4 § 245; xiii. 13, 5 § 372. In the former passage the Etrog is *μῆλον τῆς περσέας*. The word is the Persian name of *Citrus medica a cedra* Hayne [Ascherson, in Löw]. See also Jubilees 16, 20–31; 2 Macc. 10, 6 f.

[5] M. Sukkah 3, 9. Some commentators understand the words תחלה וסוף in the Mishnah to refer to the first and the last verses of Psalms 118 (vss. 1 and 29), others to the first and last parts of vs. 1.

offered, the people marched in procession around the altar, carrying their branches and citrons and intoning the Hosanna (Psalm 118, 25); on the seventh day they made seven such circuits.[1]

A unique character was given to the festival by the libation of water made together with the usual wine at the morning service in the temple on each of the seven days, and the ceremonies attending it, and by the illumination of the temple courts on the night of the first day. Both of these are enrichments of the liturgy introduced possibly in the Hellenistic period. According to the Mishnah, a golden flask[2] holding about three pints was filled with water from the fountain of Siloam, carried up to the Water Gate,[3] where the procession was greeted by three calls on the ram's horn (*shofar*)[4] by the priestly musicians. The officiating priest ascended the ramp on the south side of the great altar, and turned to the left (west), where there were two silver basins of peculiar form, one for the ritual libation of wine, into the other the water was poured. Through orifices in the bottom of these basins the wine and the water emptied out simultaneously.[5] At the moment when the priest was about to pour the water into the basin, the people shouted to him, Raise your hand! because once a certain priest spilled it on his feet.[6] It is not improbably to this incident that Josephus refers when he says that once at the Feast of Tabernacles, when Alexander Jannaeus, the high priest, stood on the altar about to offer, they pelted him with the citrons they carried in their hands.[7] Why he — if it was he — chose to manifest contempt for the rite by spilling the water is not told; one might surmise

[1] M. Sukkah 4, 5.

[2] צלוחית.

[3] On the south side of the temple area. M. Sheḳalim 6, 3 (cf. Neh. 8, 1). So called from this ceremony, Tos. Sukkah 3,3. (The whole passage should be read.)

[4] Teḳi'ah, Teru'ah, Teḳi'ah. See 'Shofar,' Jewish Encyclopedia, XI, 301–306.

[5] M. Sukkah 4, 9.

[6] M. Sukkah, ibid. The Talmud calls this high priest a Sadducee. The rite was not biblical, and for the Sadducees tradition had no authority.

[7] Jos. Antt. xiii. 13, 5 § 372.

that it was because the Pharisees, with whom he was on bad terms, showed an especial interest in it. The endeavor to find a biblical warrant for the rite led to various far-fetched solutions.[1] The ingenuity of a Babylonian scholar of the late third century, Rab 'Ena, discovered at least a felicitous text: 'Therefore with joy shall ye draw from fountains of salvation' (Isa. 12, 3).

Pouring out water is an ancient and common way of making rain, and, as the Feast of Tabernacles falls at the time when the first autumnal rains are due, it is a plausible conjecture that the rite is a survival of an old rain ceremony, which in the context of a higher religion became a symbol of rain. It is to be noted that in Zech. 14, 16–19, where it is predicted that, in the coming golden age, all that are left of the nations which once came up against Jerusalem shall come up from year to year to worship and keep the Feast of Tabernacles, the punishment of those who neglect this pilgrimage is that upon them no rain shall fall, or in Egypt the inundation shall fail. The rite is associated with rain, as if the connection was universally recognized. R. Akiba in giving reasons for various prescriptions of the festival ritual (the '*omer* sheaf at Pentecost, etc.) thus explains it: "Why does the Law say, Make a libation of water at the Feast? The Holy One, blessed is He, says, Make a libation of water before me at the Feast in order that the rains of the year may be blessed to you."[2] At this season judgment is passed by God concerning the rains of the coming year.[3] A symbolical interpretation was given by Joshua ben Levi. "Why was it called *bet sho'ebah* (lit. 'place of drawing')?[4] Because from it they draw the holy spirit (prophetic inspiration), according to Isa. 12, 3, 'Ye shall

[1] According to Neḥunya of Bet Ḥoron it was a traditional rule "of Moses from Sinai," i.e., without support in the Scriptures.

[2] R. Judah (ben Ila'i) in the name of Akiba, Rosh ha-Shanah 16a. Cf. Tos. Sukkah 3, 18 (Akiba quotes Zech. 14, 17); Tos. Rosh ha-Shanah 1, 12.

[3] M. Rosh ha-Shanah 1, 2 and the places cited in the preceding note. The prayer for rain began to be recited in the Tefillah at this time (גבורות גשמים, M. Berakot 5, 2.); M. Ta'anit 1, 1.

[4] Applied especially to the night ceremony.

draw with joy from fountains of salvation,' "[1] The origin of this interpretation is to be sought in the association of a sacred joy (joy in the fulfilment of a commandment) with inspiration: the Presence (Shekinah), or the holy spirit, does not rest on a sad heart but only on a glad one.[2]

On the night of the first day of the feast there was a great illumination in the temple.[3] Tall pillars were set up in the court of the women, like gigantic candelabras, each bearing four basins holding fifteen gallons apiece as saucer-lamps; for wicks cast off breeches and girdles of the priests were used. Youths of the priesthood mounted ladders and poured their jars of oil into the basins. The light was so bright that it illumined every courtyard in Jerusalem. Two galleries were erected around three sides of the court for the spectators; in the upper one the women sat, in the lower the men.[4] Men of conspicuous piety and good works danced before them, with flaming torches in their hands, uttering words of song and praise. Rabban Simeon ben Gamaliel is reported to have been so expert that, with eight torches going, not one of them touched the ground when he prostrated himself, touched his fingers to the pavement, bent down, kissed it, and at once sprang up.[5]

The levitical orchestra with harps and lutes and cymbals and trumpets — innumerable instruments — stood on the fifteen steps that led down from the court of Israel to the court of the women,[6] corresponding to the fifteen "Songs of the Steps" in the Psalter (Psalms 120–134), while in the gate behind them were two priests with trumpets. An interesting feature of the ceremony was the march through the court of the women, beginning at a signal on the trumpets of the two priests, and moving with

[1] Jer. Sukkah 55a; Pesiḳta Rabbati 1 (ed. Friedmann f. 1b) on Isa. 66, 23.

[2] Jer. Sukkah 55a; Shabbat 30b. Cf. Tosafot on Sukkah 50b, top.

[3] M. Sukkah 5, 2 ff.

[4] The separation of the sexes was a precaution against the kind of 'levity' to which the enthusiasm of the hour incited.

[5] Tos. Sukkah 4, 4. A somewhat different description, Sukkah 53a.

[6] Tos. Sukkah 4, 7–9.

continuous trumpeting to the gate opening to the east. There they turned about, facing west, and said: "Our fathers who were in this place 'stood with their backs to the temple and their faces eastward, and worshipped the sun toward the east' (Ezek. 8, 16); but our eyes are unto the Lord," or as more fully reported, they repeated twice, "But we (worship, or confess) the Lord, and upon the Lord our eyes (wait)."[1] The jubilation at this ceremony exceeded anything to be seen elsewhere or at another time: "A man who has never seen the rejoicing of the water-drawing has never seen rejoicing in his life."[2]

The Feast of Tabernacles (more exactly of Booths) has its name from the booths in which all native Israelites[3] were required to dwell at this season for seven days (Lev. 23, 42). It is a probable surmise that the booths were originally the temporary shelters in which men lodged in the vineyards at the vintage season,[4] as is still the custom in other wine-growing countries. As the population became more largely urban the custom would naturally fall into desuetude. In the account in Neh. 8 of the celebration in conformity to the directions which they found written in the law of Moses as Ezra read it to them, it is said that the Israelities had not done so — i.e. erected booths on the roofs of houses, in the courts of the temple, and the open squares of the city — since the days of Joshua. The law in Leviticus (23, 42 f.) gives a memorial significance to the festival, 'That your generations may know that I made the Israelites dwell in booths when I brought them out of the land of Egypt.' Thus detached from other agricultural associations than the season at which it was held, and given, like the Passover and Feast of Unleavened Bread,[5] a historical origin and meaning, it was adapted to become a permanent institution.

With the destruction of the temple most of this ritual came to an end. The custom of carrying the palm branches and citrons

1 M. Sukkah 5, 4; Sukkah 53b, end.
2 M. Sukkah 5, 1.
3 Understood of men and boys only.
4 See Isa. 1, 8.
5 Exod. 12, 39; 13, 3–7.

(Lulab and Etrog) was maintained, however, a procession around the reading desk in the synagogue [1] taking the place of that around the altar, in which, especially on the seventh day (which got its name Hosh'ana Rabbah therefrom), the repetition of the refrain, Hosh'ana, 'Deliver now' (Psalm 118, 25), was a characteristic feature.

The command to dwell in booths for seven days was independent of the temple observance, and was incumbent on all (male) Israelites, wherever they were, whether in Palestine or outside of the land. In cities and towns the booth was often necessarily a very slight shelter representing a booth, rather than a habitable structure, and the rabbinical rules and discussions on the question what was enough of a 'booth' to satisfy the requirements of the law are extended and refined. What is of importance for us is that the observance of the festival was thus perpetuated in every Jewish house as well as in the synagogue, and that the jubilant note runs through the whole celebration; it is eminently 'the season of our rejoicing.'

The transformation of the agricultural festivals into historical commemorations was complete when the old Harvest festival (*ḳaṣir*, Exod. 23, 16) at the end of the wheat harvest, or Feast of (seven) Weeks (Exod. 34, 22),[2] was taken to be the time when the Law was given at Sinai.[3] Starting from Exod. 19, 1, taking *ḥodesh* as the *first day* of the month, and counting the days enumerated in the following verses, it was found that the giving of the Law (more exactly the Ten Commandments) occurred on the sixth day of the month Sivan, or, as others counted, the seventh.[4] How old this arithmetic may be is unknown.

[1] But not (as had been the practice in the temple) on the sabbath, even when that was the first day.

[2] Tobit 2, 1, ἁγία ἑπτὰ ἑβδομάδων. In the Mishnah עצרת.

[3] There is no intimation of this in Scripture, nor in Philo or Josephus. In Pesaḥim 68b it is assumed as generally accepted opinion.

[4] Mekilta, Yitro, 3 (on Exod. 19, 10; ed. Friedmann f. 63b; ed. Weiss f. 71b); Yoma 4b; Ta'anit 28b; Shabbat 86b; see also 88a, top; cf. Mekilta de-R. Simeon ben Yoḥai on Exod. 19, 10. The Palestinian Targum on the verse is acquainted with the computation.

This one-day festival cannot have drawn many pilgrims from a distance to the temple, and we possess no information about any special ceremonies on that occasion other than those prescribed in the laws (especially Num. 28, 26–31). When in later times the 'Joy of the Law' (*Simḥat Torah*) found a place in the calendar, it was not on this day, but on the eighth day which closed the celebration of the Feast of Tabernacles, and was associated with the reading of the Law in Neh. 8, rather than with the giving of the Law, marking the completion of the reading of the Pentateuch in course in the annual cycle.

The most conspicuous features of the ceremonies in the temple at the Feast of Tabernacles were, as we have seen, supplementary to the ritual prescribed in the Pentateuch. In a similar way whole festivals were introduced of which the Law knows nothing. One of these, beginning on the 25th of Kisleu, was instituted in the year 165 by Judas Maccabaeus and his brothers 'and the whole assembly of Israel' as an annual eight-day celebration of the reëstablishment of worship in the temple after three years' interruption, to be observed with joy and gladness (1 Macc. 4, 59). The corresponding account in 2 Maccabees (10, 6–8) adds that the festival was patterned after the Feast of Tabernacles,[1] the season of which only a little while before they had passed living among the mountains and in caves like wild beasts. They carried thyrsi and fair branches, as well as palm leaves, and sang praises to him who had helped them to purge his temple. The festival is called in the Gospel of John (10, 22) 'Ἐγκαίνια,[2] corresponding to its Hebrew name Ḥanukkah, we might say 'Rededication.' Josephus tells us that in his time it was called 'Lights' (φῶτα), a name doubtless given to it from the illumination of houses which was a characteristic feature of the celebration.

The rules for this illumination date from an early time; a difference between the schools of Shammai and Hillel about a particularly fine illumination with a redundant number of lamps is

[1] Cf. 2 Macc. 1, 18–36. [2] Cf. 1 Macc. 4, 54, 56.

recorded.[1] Every house should burn at least one such lamp on every one of the eight evenings; those who made a finer show of it lighted one for each inmate of the house. The lamps were placed in the doorway, so as to cast their light out into the court or street; if a house had doors on two sides, a lamp must be set at each; tenants of upper stories set theirs in a window opening on a public place. So much importance is attached to the observance that if a man has not money enough for both he should buy oil for the Ḥanukkah lamp rather than the wine to 'sanctify' the advent of a holy day.[2] Even a temporary guest in a house is bound to light a lamp for himself at the festival. The illumination was originally solely domestic; later, lamps were lighted in the synagogues also. As at the Feast of Tabernacles, the Hallel (Psalms 113–118) was recited complete on each of the eight days.[3] During this period mourning and fasting are forbidden. Josephus, who does not mention the illumination itself, surmises that the name 'Lights' was given to the festival because, contrary to expectation, the power to restore the temple worship had been manifested to the Jews. The Talmud gives a legendary explanation of the rite: When the Asmonaeans got possession of the temple after the heathen occupation, all the oil was unclean, and they found only one small jar of oil bearing the seal of the high priest, containing enough for but one day. With this they lighted the lamps, and by miracle it lasted eight days. The next year they made these days a festival with praise and thanksgiving (Hallel and Hoda'ah).[4] It is this miracle that is commemorated by the Ḥanukkah lamps.

In the comparison of the celebration to the Feast of Tabernacles, one important difference must not be ignored: during the eight days of the Dedication festival there was no total or partial

[1] Shabbat 21b. The former would begin with eight lamps and light one less each day; the latter began with one and added one each day.

[2] Shabbat 23b (Raba).

[3] Tos. Sukkah 3, 2; Shabbat 21b.

[4] Shabbat 21b. A different story in Pesiḳta Rabbati 2 (ed. Friedmann f 5a). Cf. 2 Macc. 1, 18 ff.

abstention from ordinary occupations, nor were the beginning and end marked by a 'holy convocation.'

A popular festival that had a still greater place among Jewish observances was Purim,[1] commemorating the deliverance of the Jews from the wholesale destruction Haman had planned for them. The appointment and inauguration of the celebration are set forth in Esther 9, 16 ff. It was kept on the fourteenth or the fifteenth day of the month Adar — on the former by the people of the villages and unwalled towns (9, 19), on the fifteenth by the inhabitants of fortified cities (9, 18). 'The Jews ordained and took upon them, and upon their posterity, and upon all such as attached themselves to them (proselytes), so that it should not fail, that they would keep these two days as prescribed at the appointed time every year,' etc. (9, 27 f.). 'The days in which the Jews had rest from their enemies, and the month which was turned for them from sorrow to gladness and from mourning to festivity,' were to be made 'days of feasting and gladness and of sending portions one to another, and gifts to the poor' (Esther 9, 22 f.).[2] In accordance with the pronouncedly secular character of the Book of Esther, there is no mention of any religious observance,[3] nor even of gratitude to God for their deliverance; and the secular character remained the signature of the celebration through all its history, notwithstanding its adoption into the religious calendar.

When the festival, which was probably of Oriental origin,[4] was introduced in Palestine is not to be determined with any exactness. A note at the end of Greek manuscripts tells that the

[1] Esther 9, 26, cf. 24.

[2] Cf. Neh. 8, 10–12. Jos. Antt. xi. 6, 13 § 292: All the Jews in the world keep a festival on those days, sending portions to one another.

[3] A sacrificial celebration in Persia was not imaginable.

[4] Samuel bar Judah had at least an inkling of the history. Purim was originally appointed for Susa, and later for all the world. Esther sent to the learned (in Palestine) saying, Appoint me (i.e., the celebration of what I did) for all time; they replied, You stir up resentment against us among the heathen, etc. Megillah 7a.

translation of the "Purim Epistle," the work of Lysimachus son of Ptolemaeus of Jerusalem, was introduced (into Egypt) in the fourth year of Ptolemy and Cleopatra. Which of the various Ptolemies who had Cleopatras for partners of the throne is meant is a mere guess. Older scholars pitched on Philometor (181–145 B.C.) ; more recent ones favor Soter II (Lathyrus) and reckon the year to be 114 B.C.[1] The worth of the somewhat strangely worded note is dubious. "Mordecai Day" appears as a calendar date in 2 Macc. 15, 36: The Jews of Palestine enacted that the anniversary of the defeat and death of Nicanor should be celebrated on the thirteenth of the twelfth month, Adar, the day before Mordecai Day.[2]

We have already seen that in Palestine objection was raised to the new festival.[3] On the other hand the elaborated regulation of the days on which the Roll of Esther should (or may) be read is attributed in the Talmud to the Men of the Great Assembly, i.e. is regarded as of immemorial antiquity.[4]

The distinctive observance of the season is the reading of the Book of Esther, which by rabbinical authority was made incumbent on all, women as well as men[5] (for women also shared in the wonderful deliverance), proselytes, and freedmen.[6] Children were prepared for the reading as they approached the age at which it would become obligatory for them. The obligation might be fulfilled by reading the book privately or in the synagogue, or by hearing it read by another. In the second century some commenced the reading, not at the beginning of the book but at a later point (2, 5; 3, 1; 6, 1). The eventual decision was that the whole should be read.[7] As was the custom with the

[1] See B. Jacob, Das Buch Esther, u. s. w., Zeitschrift für alttest. Wissenschaft, X (1890), 278.

[2] Many scholars think that Purim is meant by the nameless feast of the Jews in John 5, 1, falling between the winter (4, 35, four months till harvest) and Passover (6, 4), to which Jesus went up to Jerusalem, though Purim was not a temple festival.

[3] Vol. I, p. 245.

[4] Megillah 2a.

[5] 'Arakin 2b–3a; Megillah 4a.

[6] Tos. Megillah 2, 7.

[7] M. Megillah 2, 3 (R. Meir); Jer. Megillah 73b; Megillah 19a.

lessons from the Pentateuch in the synagogue, certain benedictions were naturally attached to the reading of Esther, but the attestation of particular formulas is comparatively late. The Hallel psalms were not recited. Numerous rules are found in the Mishnah which need not detain us here.[1] It is worthy of note, however, that Esther was read from a separate roll, containing that book only.

During the two days, fourteenth and fifteenth of Adar, mourning and fasting was prohibited to all Jews everywhere, whether they kept the one day or the other.[2] Labor on the day kept in any place was not forbidden, though in some places it was suspended by public opinion.[3]

The command to celebrate the day by rejoicing and feasting (Esther 9, 19, 22) was taken with somewhat exaggerated literalness. A Babylonian authority of the fourth century, Raba, took it that a man should drink till he cannot distinguish between Cursed be Haman! and Blessed be Mordecai![4] It is narrated in the context that in such confusion of persons a famous Babylonian teacher of the time killed another with whom he was feasting. Fortunately, he was able to bring him to life again next day; but the resuscitated rabbi declined an invitation to dine in such dangerous company the following year, quoting, 'Miracles do not happen every time!' (Cf. Pesaḥim 50b.)[5]

In accordance with Esther 9, 22 it was customary, and indeed obligatory, for families to send choice viands from their feast to one another and make presents to the poor either in food or money.

1 The Mishnah prescribes as the Purim lesson Exod. 17, 8–16 (Amalek). M. Megillah 3, 6. The association is Haman the Agagite — Agag king of the Amalekites (1 Sam. 15).

2 In an intercalary year Purim was kept in the Second Adar, but if the intercalation was announced after Purim had been kept in Adar I, the reading of Esther was repeated in Adar II. M. Megillah 1, 4.

3 Megillah 5b; Babylonian instance.

4 Megillah 7b. The two phrases have numerically the same value, 502. Others add, till he cannot distinguish between Cursed be Zeresh! and Blessed be Esther! Cursed be all the wicked, and Blessed be all the Jews. Tosafot, Megillah 7b, דלא.

5 Megillah 7b.

The whole celebration resembles the modern observance of the Christmas season in Western Europe and America and the pagan festivals that have survived in it, and the resemblance extends to the large license allowed the merrymakers.[1]

A popular festival in the days of the second temple was kept on the fifteenth of Ab, on which, as on the Day of Atonement, the girls of Jerusalem danced in the vineyards and challenged the young men to choose partners in marriage. On this day the general offering of wood for the temple also was brought, but the two features of the day are doubtless of independent origin.

In the Megillat Ta'anit, an ancient calendar, many glorious deeds or joyous events in the external or internal history of the Jews in the Hellenistic and Roman periods are enumerated, but with such laconic brevity that the identification of the occasion is frequently a matter of uncertain conjecture, and the scholia compiled at the end of the Talmudic age have no historical authority.[2]

These days were kept as semi-holidays; public fasts were not appointed on them, and on a considerable number of them mourning was prohibited. In the course of time most of them ceased to be observed, and the memory of the events they commemorated faded out. Our interest in the "Fasting Roll"—*lucus a non*—is the evidence it gives that Purim and the Dedication (Ḥanukkah) were not the only examples of commemorative festivals instituted from time to time by the religious authorities of their own motion. Of the mode of the celebration, which, it may safely be assumed, embraced features of distinctive appropriateness, tradition was early lost with the desuetude of the observance.

[1] See 'Purim,' Jewish Encyclopedia, X, 274–280; I. Abrahams, Jewish Life in the Middle Ages (Index *s.v.* Purim).

[2] See Vol. I, p. 160.

CHAPTER IV

PUBLIC FASTS

WHILE festive joy is the note of the holy seasons hitherto described, the Day of Atonement on the tenth of Tishri is a time for men to 'afflict their souls,'[1] and as feasting goes with rejoicing, fasting belongs so inseparably with affliction that 'afflicting oneself' is synonymous with fasting.[2]

The Day of Atonement is signalized as one of the great festivals of the year by supplementary burnt offerings with corresponding oblations as a sweet savor[3] to the Lord, and a he goat for the accompanying sin offering, exactly as prescribed for New Years. The distinctive rites of the day, however, are piacular. These are of two types. The first, in their nature and original intent, are a disinfection of the sanctuary from the pollution that may have been contracted during the preceding year from the presence of men who were defiled by any of the varieties of uncleanness detailed in the laws.[4] To this end the high priest, after incensing the adytum of the temple, which none but he might ever enter and he only this one day of the year, brought into it, first, the blood of a bullock offered as a sin offering for himself and all the priesthood, which he sprinkled within the curtain, and then repeated the rite with the blood of the goat, a sin offering for the people. With the blood of the bullock he aspersed the curtain from without, and did the same with the blood of the goat; he next applied the blood of both, mingled, to the four corners of the altar of incense which stood in the front room of the temple, and to the surface of the great altar in the court.[5]

[1] Lev. 16, 31; 23,27, 29, 32; Num. 29, 7. Cf. Isa. 58, 3–7.
[2] ענה נפש = צום. [3] ריח ניחח.
[4] Lev. 16, 16, 19; Ezek. 45, 18–20.
[5] For the ritual see Lev. 16, 2–19, with Sifra on the passage; M. Yoma 5. For a commentary taking due account of tradition, see D. Hoffmann, Das Buch Leviticus, I, 432–464.

Of a different kind is the second part of the ritual. After the ceremonies described above, 'When he has finished expiating the sanctuary and the meeting-tent and the altar' (Lev. 16, 20),[1] the high priest took a second goat, which in the first stage of the ritual had been drawn by lot 'for Azazel,' and pressing both his hands on the animal's head, confessed over it 'all the iniquities of the Israelites and all their transgressions, even all their sins,' and lading them on the head of the goat sent it, 'bearing upon it all their iniquities,' under conduct of a man previously appointed, to an isolated region, where it was let go into the wilderness.[2]

Similar rites of riddance, commonly called 'scapegoat'[3] ceremonies from the present instance — though the carrier may be man[4] or beast or an inanimate vehicle such as a boat, and what is thus got rid of may be a contagious disease such as smallpox — are found among many races.

A peculiar feature of the ritual, plainly symbolic, is to be noted. The high priest on this one day, and for this part of its rites only, is vested, not in his gorgeous pontificals of crimson and gold, but in pure white linen from head to foot. These are in an eminent sense 'the holy vestments'; before putting them on he must bathe himself in water, and this is repeated when, after the dismissal of the goat, he lays them aside. For the subsequent sacrifices of the day he resumes his pontificals.

The ancient directions of Lev. 16, which have been summarized in the foregoing paragraphs, must be supplemented by the traditional interpretation and liturgical practice preserved in the Midrash Torat Kohanim (Sifra) on Leviticus, and in the Mishnah

[1] Cf. Ezek. 45, 18, Thou shalt *un-sin* the sanctuary; ibid. 20, Ye shall expiate the house.

[2] According to the Palestinian Targum the goat was hurled down a precipice to its death by a gust of wind sent by God; in M. Yoma 6, 6 it is pushed backward over a cliff by the man who led it into the wilderness.

[3] Lev. 16, 8, 10 in the English version, following the Septuagint and Vulgate (*caper emissarius*).

[4] As, e.g., in the Attic Thargelia. See, in general, J. G. Frazer, Golden Bough, Vol. IX, The Scapegoat.

and Tosefta on the Day of Atonement, if the rites are to be represented as they were performed in the Herodian temple. A description of the ceremonies in detail does not belong to our present task; but certain significant changes in the apprehension of the meaning and effect of the piacula, some of which are impressed on the ritual itself, are not to be overlooked.

The first of these is the introduction of a general confession of sin, twice pronounced, into the ritual of the sin offering brought for himself and the priesthood:[1] "O Lord (pronouncing the Name), I have done wickedly, transgressed, sinned, before thee, I and my house; O Lord (as before) forgive the wickednesses and transgressions and sins that I have committed and transgressed and sinned before Thee, I and my house, as it is written in the law of Moses thy servant, 'For on this day shall atonement be made,'" etc. (Lev. 16, 30); with the response of the priests behind him: "Blessed be His glorious Name whose kingdom is forever and ever."

The confession of the sins of the people said over the head of the goat that is to be sent away is of the same tenor:[2] "O Lord (the Name), Thy people, the house of Israel, have done wickedly, transgressed, sinned before Thee. O Lord (as before) forgive now the wickednesses and transgressions and sins that Thy people the house of Israel have committed and transgressed and sinned before Thee, as it is written in the law of Moses thy servant, 'For on this day shall atonement be made to purify you; from all your sins before the Lord shall ye be purified'" (Lev. 16, 30). When he uttered the ineffable Name, the priests and the people who were standing in the court knelt and worshipped and fell on their faces, and made the same response as the priests in the former case.

These confessions show, whatever may have been the origin of the rites, that the atonement was not a disinfection of the sanctuary with blood or a physical riddance of guilt conveyed away by the scapegoat, but an act of divine forgiveness; in other

[1] M. Yoma 3, 8; 4, 2.

[2] M. Yoma 6, 2.

words, the cardinal doctrine of Judaism that the forgiveness of God is bestowed upon the sinner who seeks it of him in penitence with confession has here given its own meaning to the rites, which thus, consciously or unconsciously, become symbolical of it.

In Sifra on Lev. 16, 16[1] an interpretation of the 'uncleannesses of the Israelites' is proposed which would take the words of the three cardinal sins, heathenism (*'abodah zarah*), incest and kindred crimes (*gilluy 'araiyot*), and homicide (*shefikat damim*), to each of which the epithet 'unclean' is applied in the Scriptures (Lev. 20, 3; Lev. 18, 3; Num. 35, 34).[2] On exegetical grounds the soundness of which cannot be denied, this theory is rejected, but the inclination to moralize the conception of defilement is not devoid of interest.

The Day of Atonement was not, like the three great festivals, in idea a concourse of all Israel, and though from its proximity to Tabernacles some pilgrims from a distance may have timed their arrival in Jerusalem so as to witness what they could of its solemnities, it is probable that the attendance of the laity was chiefly from the city and its vicinity. Long before the destruction of the temple the domestic observances of the day and the services of the synagogue had become of far greater moment in the religious life of the Jews in all lands than the expiation made for them by the high priest in Jerusalem.

The Day of Atonement was a sabbath of eminent sanctity.[3] The prohibitions of every kind of labor on it are emphatically iterated (Lev. 23, 28, 30, 31; 16, 29); they apply to native and alien in the land alike. While the violation of an ordinary sabbath was punishable by death, God threatened himself to destroy whoever does any work on the Day of Atonement (Lev. 23, 30).

In other respects it was most unlike the weekly sabbath. On the latter feasting and rejoicing were not only permissible but belonged to the duty of the day; on the Day of Atonement, from

[1] Ed. Weiss f. 81c; quoted in Shebu'ot 7b.

[2] These are the sins that cause the withdrawal of the divine Presence (Shekinah).

[3] *Shabbat shabbaton*, Lev. 23, 32.

evening to evening, strict fasting is enjoined under penalty of extirpation (Lev. 23, 29). The Mishnah defines:[1] "On the Day of Atonement it is forbidden to eat[2] or drink,[3] or bathe or anoint oneself or wear sandals, or to indulge in conjugal intercourse."[4] Young children were not made to fast, but were accustomed to a measure of privation a year or two before the fast became obligatory for them. Mitigations were allowed in the case of pregnant women, people who were ill, and various others; particularly where there was thought to be danger to life.[5]

The services in the synagogue, which began in the evening, and were resumed in the morning and continued throughout the day, were of penitential character; confession of sin and prayer for forgiveness are the substance of them for the congregation and for the individual. The confessions of the high priest for himself and for the people which have been quoted above were carried over into the synagogue in the part of the liturgy which brings before the congregation the course of the temple ritual, the Seder 'Abodah. Independent of this is the confession which forms a part of the synagogue liturgy, being pronounced by the Leader in Prayer[6] in the Tefillah at each of the hours of prayer (including the Ne'ilah, which is peculiar to the day),[7] and recited by individuals before the public prayer on each occasion. The first words of several such confessions are given in the Talmud in the name of teachers of the third century,[8] showing that the forms were not yet stereotyped. Some of these confessions have been perpetuated in the later prayer books, doubtless in greatly expanded forms according to the whole tendency of the liturgy. One of these, cited in the name of Rab,[9] runs in the modern prayer book: "Thou knowest the secrets of eternity and the

[1] M. Yoma 8, 1 (cf. 2).
[2] A quantity as large as a big date.
[3] As much as a mouthful altogether.
[4] The last was prohibited on the sabbath also by some of the older sects. Jubilees 50, 8. The rabbinical law is to the contrary.
[5] M. Yoma 8, 4–7.
[6] שליח צבור.
[7] Yoma 87b.
[8] Yoma 87b; cf. also Jer. Yoma 45c.
[9] Abba Areka, d. 247.

most hidden mysteries of all living. Thou searchest the innermost recesses, and triest the reins and the heart. Naught is concealed from thee, or hidden from thine eyes. May it then be thy will, O Lord our God and God of our fathers, to forgive us for all our sins, to pardon us for all our iniquities, and to grant us remission for all our transgressions." [1] The following long specification of sins ('Al Ḥeṭ) belongs to a later stage in the development of the liturgy, and has been much amplified since its first appearance. Another of the forms of confession in the same passage of the Talmud, in the name of Mar Samuel, stands now in an inconspicuous place in the preface to the alphabetical Ashamnu.

In the name of Hamnuna (fourth century) is quoted entire a prayer which still stands in the prayer books at the end of the Tefillah of the day: "O my God, before I was formed I was nothing worth, and now that I have been formed I am but as though I had not been formed. Dust am I in my life; how much more so after my death. Behold I am before thee like a vessel filled with shame and confusion. O may it be thy will, O Lord my God and God of my fathers, that I may sin no more, and as to the sins I have committed, purge them away in thine abounding compassion, though not by means of affliction and sore diseases." [2]

The ritual of atonement in the temple was performed by the priest for the whole people, who had no other part in it than to utter their doxology in response at a certain point in the service. In the synagogue the day was one long act of penitence on the part of the congregation, and pre-eminently of its members individually. The confession of sins, which in the temple was an incident of the rite, was here the substance of it, and all the circumstance was of a kind to deepen the sense of sin in the apprehension of judgment, to give poignancy of sorrow for sin, to fortify the resolve of amendment, and to add urgency to the prayer

[1] Singer's translation, page 259: cf. Abrahams, p. cci.
[2] Yoma 87b; Singer, Prayer Book, p. 263; Abrahams, p. cci.

for forgiveness — in a word, to cultivate the spirit of genuine and sincere repentance. From ceremonies of expiation and riddance, which at the most might be made symbolical of purification of heart and annulment of guilt, the service became a spiritual exercise.

It has already been noted that the Day of Atonement was not only a fast but a high festival. R. Simeon ben Gamaliel declared that the Israelites had no more joyous festivals than the fifteenth of Ab (the day of the Wood Offering), and the Day of Atonement,[1] for it was a day of pardon and propitiation.[2] The women of Jerusalem used to go out dressed in newly washed white garments, all borrowed for the occasion in order that those that owned no festal attire might not be put to shame; the maidens danced in the vineyards, and playfully challenged the young men to make their choice, whether for beauty, or family, or merit.[3] The vineyard dance is an old popular custom (Judges 21, 19 ff.); the religious motive given in the Mishnah, which takes allegorically Cant. 3, 11 ('Go forth ye daughters of Zion and gaze upon King Solomon, on the crown with which his mother crowned him on his wedding-day, and on the day of the gladness of his heart') — the wedding day being the giving of the Law (the restoration of the Decalogue, Exod. 34, 27 ff.), the day of gladness, the building of the temple (M. Ta'anit l.c.), is a pious afterthought.[4] If it is deemed necessary to correlate the dances with the ritual of the day, it may be supposed that they took place after the completion of the piacula, when the High Priest resumed his gorgeous vestments and proceeded to the festival sacrifices.

In the observance of the day in the synagogue there was no place for such secular performances, even with the reference to

[1] M. Ta'anit 4, 8. [2] Ta'anit 30b.

[3] M. Ta'anit 4, 8; Ta'anit 31a. The handsome girls said, Set your eyes on beauty, for a woman is only for beauty; the well-born said, Set your eyes on the family, for a woman is only for children; the ill-favored said, Take your choice for piety's sake (לשום שמים, i.e., not for any worldly reason), only crown us with gold coins (bridal ornaments). Cf. ibid. 26b.

[4] It is not unlikely that the verse itself was used in the festivities.

the speedy rebuilding of the temple with which the Mishnah concludes (4, 8).

To the seriousness of the day it doubtless contributed not a little that it had become the culmination of a penitential period which began ten days before with New Years. It had come to be believed that New Years (the first of Tishri) was an annual day of judgment on mankind. "On New Years Day all who come into the world pass before Him like sheep,[1] as it is said, 'He who fashions the hearts of all, who scrutinizes all their doings'" (Psalm 33, 15; see also 13–14). In the Tosefta additional texts are quoted (Psalm 81, 4 and 5).[2] The judgment is passed on New Years, and the decree is sealed on the Day of Atonement (R. Meir). These are the earliest mentions of the notion, and it will be observed that it is associated with three other judgment days in the course of the year — at Passover for the crops, at Pentecost for the fruits, at Tabernacles for the rains.[3]

According to R. Johanan, there are three tablets, on which are inscribed respectively the names of the entirely righteous, the entirely wicked, and the betwixt-and-between. The first two are sentenced on New Years Day to life or death; for the third class sentence is suspended, and they are given ten days for repentance between New Years and the Day of Atonement; if they repent they are inscribed in the list of the righteous, if not, in that of the wicked. Biblical support for the notion is sought in Psalm 69, 29:[4] 'Let them be blotted out of the book of the living

[1] So the obscure words כבני מרון (M. Rosh ha-Shanah 1, 2) are understood by the commentators. See Rosh ha-Shanah 18a below (כבני אימרנא, and other guesses there); R. Ḥananel *ad loc.* and Rashi. In Tos. Rosh ha-Shanah 1, 11, the Erfurt manuscript reads מרון; the Vienna manuscript, נומרין, i.e. a troop of soldiers (*numerus*); probably rightly. A similar interpretation is given by R. Judah (b. Ezekiel) in the name of Samuel, Rosh ha-Shanah 18a.

[2] Tos. Rosh ha-Shanah 1, 11

[3] See also R. Judah (ben Ila'i) in the name of Akiba, Rosh ha-Shanah 16a.

[4] Jer. Rosh ha-Shanah 57a, below; Rosh ha-Shanah 16b; cf. also Pesiḳta ed. Buber f. 157b–158a, where eternal life or reproach and eternal abhorrence (Dan. 12, 2) are the alternative issues. Cf. Gen. R. 24, 3 (Bar Ḳappara). It is perhaps not superfluous to repeat that this is homiletic, not dogmatic.

and not be written with the righteous.' [1] Pious Jews accordingly fast most of the ten penitential days from New Years (beginning the day before) to the Day of Atonement, but not on the day immediately preceding it, on which, indeed, fasting is forbidden.[2]

The beginning of the agricultural year in the fall, coinciding roughly with the autumnal equinox, was fixed in the calendar, as we know it, on the first of Tishri, independently of the cycle of festivals beginning in the spring with the Passover and closing with Tabernacles (Tishri 15–22, 23). The day was doubtless celebrated from ancient times in the same way as other New Moons, to which special observances were added marking it as the beginning of the year.[3] In Lev. 23, 24 f. it is a high sabbath, on which no servile work is to be done, a sacred convocation, with sacrifices to the Lord. Besides these features, which it has in common with other holy days, it is peculiarly noted as 'a commemoration signalized by a blast of horns.' [4]

The same reasons which led to the introduction of the second day of all festivals except the Day of Atonement applied with peculiar force to New Years, and the observance of the second day of this festival is said to have been ordained by the ancient prophets.[5] At what point in the ritual the horn-blowing was performed in the temple is not recorded; one would suppose at an early stage in the morning service. In the synagogue it seems originally to have had a corresponding position, from which, we are told, it was transposed to a later hour, in the Musaf prayers, because on one occasion their enemies took the blasts for a call to arms and acted accordingly.[6] It retained this place in the

1 Cf. Rev. 3, 5; 13, 8; 17, 8, etc.; Phil. 4, 3. — Exod. 32, 32 f.

2 Yoma 81b.

3 The critical questions which beset the history of the Jewish calendar did not occur to the Jews in our age.

4 זכרון תרועה. See also Num. 29, 1–6, where the sacrifices of the day are specified. It is there also a יום תרועה, vs. 1. On the Zikronot in the liturgy see below, p. 64.

5 Jer. 'Erubin 21c.

6 Jer. Rosh ha-Shanah 59c.

liturgy, but what might be called an anticipatory horn-blowing was introduced, when the congregation was seated after the close of the morning prayer and the reading of the law.

The characteristic features of the New Years liturgy are the three proper benedictions introduced into the Tefillah, known respectively by the names Malkuyot, Zikronot, Shofarot. Each is made up of verses, three from the Pentateuch, three from the Hagiographa, three from the Prophets, concluding with another from the Pentateuch.[1] The theme of the first is God as king, concluding with the future universality of his kingdom (Zech. 14 ,9) and the confession of the divine unity (Deut. 6, 4). The theme of the second is God as judge, who is mindful of all men's deeds and judges them as they deserve, mindful also of his covenant and his promises to his people. The third brings together verses in which the horn (*shofar*) is named, from the revelation at Sinai to the blast that shall be the signal for the gathering of the dispersion to worship the Lord in Jerusalem.

The introductions which now precede each of these pieces, whatever their age, are appropriate to the theme, and the first of the series, the 'Alenu, is very fine. Each of the three is followed by a prayer ending in a benediction, of which the same may be said. In the Zikronot the thought of the judgment day is developed: "This day, on which was the beginning of thy work, is a memorial of the first day,[2] for it is a statute for Israel, a decree of the God of Jacob. Thereon also sentence is pronounced upon countries — which of them is destined to the sword and which to peace, which to famine and which to plenty; and each separate creature is visited thereon, and recorded for life or for death. Who is not visited on this day? For the remembrance of every creature cometh before Thee, each man's deeds and destiny, his works and ways, his thoughts and schemes, his imaginings and achievements. Happy is the man that forgetteth Thee not,"[3] etc. The dominance of the idea of judgment gave the day a peculiarly

[1] This disposition is prescribed in the Mishnah, Rosh ha-Shanah 4, 6.
[2] The creation according to one opinion began on the first of Tishri.
[3] Singer's translation, Daily Prayer Book, p. 250.

serious character, comparable to that of the Day of Atonement, even in the very protracted services, but it was not, like it, a fast day.

There are interesting analogies to this development in the history of the Christian liturgy. In the so-called Advent season preceding the festival of the Nativity, the thought of the church was centred, not on the approaching commemoration of the birth of the Saviour, but on his coming as the judge to the last assize with all its terrors. It was a season of mourning: the Gloria in Excelsis was omitted in the Mass; the organ was silent; the pictures in the churches were covered; the altar cloths and the stoles of the priests were violet, the color of mourning. Fasting was prescribed; marriages were not solemnized. Another similarity may be noted: in the Latin Church Advent became the beginning of the ecclesiastical year. The parallel is the more noteworthy because the history of the Christian Advent makes it evident that the two are entirely independent. The case may well be a warning against the fallacy of that abuse of the "comparative method" which jumps at derivation wherever it finds analogies.

Of regular fast days, aside from those already described, the Jewish calendar had very few. During the seventy years of the exile four such days were kept annually in the fourth, fifth, seventh, and tenth months (Tammuz, Ab, Tishri, Ṭebet) respectively,[1] in memory of disastrous events in the final conflict with Babylonia [2] from the investment of Jerusalem by Nebuchadnezzar (Ezek. 24, 1 f.) to the murder of Gedaliah (2 Kings 25, 25).[3] With the rebuilding of the temple the reason for these fasts ceased, and by an oracle to Zechariah they were discontinued. After the destruction of the second temple by Titus, the fast of the ninth of Ab commemorated both that event and the like catastrophe under Nebuchadnezzar, and with it the other three

1 Zech. 8, 19; cf. 7, 5 f.
2 Rosh ha-Shanah 18b.
3 Sifrè Deut. §31 (ed. Friedmann f. 72b, top).

old historical fasts were revived. After the war under Hadrian Bether also was added to the sorrows of the ninth of Ab.[1]

The accumulation of the direst calamities on this day gave it an importance that outdid its old companions and the numerous fast days that were at one time or another inserted in the calendar. The fast was now prolonged, including the night as well as the day time. In view of the nature of the events commemorated it was natural that the observance of the day should take the character of mourning. "All the laws that are observed in mourning are observed also in keeping the Ninth of Ab:[2] it is forbidden to eat or drink, to bathe or anoint oneself or to put on sandals, or indulge in conjugal intercourse; forbidden also to read the Law, Prophets, or Hagiographa, or study any branch of the unwritten law." One might, however, study unfamiliar and difficult parts of the Law, written or unwritten — which was no recreation — or read Job, Lamentations, and the ominous prophecies in Jeremiah. R. Judah (ben Ila'i) would permit only the latter.[3] School children had a holiday because the commandments of the Lord rejoice the heart (Psalm 19, 9) — a mood unsuitable to the sadness of the day.[4]

R. Judah carried the resemblance to mourning still farther; he would have the bed upset, but the majority did not agree with him.[5] It is reported, however, that he himself passed the day exactly like one in mourning for one near of kin whose dead body lay before him.[6]

The teachers of the second century are very emphatic about the strict fast; eating and drinking on the Ninth of Ab is as bad as on the Day of Atonement.[7] Work was not everywhere suspended, and it was licit to follow local custom;[8] but labor on the day was strongly disapproved. Akiba declared that a man who worked on the Ninth of Ab would never see a sign of blessing,

1 M. Ta'anit 4, 6, where two more misfortunes are added; see the Talmud *in loc.* f. 29a.

2 Ta'anit 30a. 3 Ibid. 4 Ibid.

5 M. Ta'anit 4, 7. 6 Ta'anit 30a–b.

7 R. Simeon ben Gamaliel, Ta'anit 30b. 8 Ibid.

and the majority of the learned said that no one who worked on that day and did not mourn over Jerusalem should behold her rejoicing (Isa. 66, 10).[1]

Occasional public fasts appointed by authority were in Palestine most frequently observed when the autumn rains, which were expected soon after the Feast of Tabernacles, were so long deferred as to arouse apprehension of a failure of the crops. The Book of Joel gives a vivid description, doubtless on some dire occasion, of the devastation wrought by prolonged drought and the plague of locusts which frequently concurred with it, and summons the people to a solemn mourning fast, bewailing their calamitous state, repenting of their sins, and pleading with God for compassion and relief. His gracious response followed (Joel 2, 18 ff.). The great fast of the repentant Ninevites (Jonah 3, 5–10) and the revoking of the doom pronounced upon them also gave a biblical picture of such an observance, and its lesson is the boundless mercy of God towards repentant sinners — even heathen.

One of the primitive motives for fasting, private or public, is to excite the pity of a god by the spectacle of distress, and obviously there is such an appeal to God's compassion in the biblical instances just adduced. Noteworthy disasters were generally attributed to the wrath of the gods whom men had in some way offended, and lamentations for the offense, known or unknown, were ordinary on such occasions. Under the teaching of the prophets, Judaism had come to conceptions of sin and repentance far beyond these beginnings, but the old modes of expression were perpetuated.[2] If by the seventeenth of Marḥeshvan the

[1] Ta'anit 30b. According to Giṭṭin 57a, Kefar Sekanya in Galilee, which has elsewhere Nazarene associations, notwithstanding the virtues of its inhabitants, was destroyed because they did not mourn over Jerusalem. For Kefar Sekanya של מצרים (Egypt!) read של נוצרים, Nazarenes.

[2] See Eleazar (ben Pedat): Three things annul a dire decree (of God), namely, prayer, and charity, and repentance, and all of them are found in one verse (2 Chron. 7, 14). Jer. Ta'anit 65b, top. Cf. Bacher, Paläst. Amoräer II, 13 (n. 2–4).

autumn rains had not begun, the religious heads of the community began to fast in a mitigated fashion. If this did not avail they appointed a general fast on three days (Monday, Thursday, Monday), then a severer fast on three days (Thursday, Monday, Thursday); finally seven public fast days, on which the shops were closed and the Shofar blown. The chest in which the rolls of the Law were kept was carried out into a public square and ashes were strewn upon it.[1] The dignitaries and all the people put ashes on their heads; the eldest among them spoke affecting words: "Brethren, it is not said of the men of Nineveh, God saw their sackcloth and their fasting, but God saw their works, that they turned from their evil ways (Jonah 3, 10); and in the Prophets He says, Rend your hearts and not your garments" (Joel 2, 13).[2] The modifications of the daily prayer (Tefillah), the Psalms to be read,[3] and the special prayer to be said, are minutely prescribed. The Mishnah affectingly depicts the scene and the service on such an occasion.[4]

Public fasts were appointed by the authorities in other perils or calamities,[5] or when for any reason the Jews believed themselves to be under divine displeasure, after such biblical examples as Judges 20, 26; 1 Sam. 7, 6; 2 Chron. 12, 5–8; Neh. 9, 1, etc.; and this custom has continued to modern times.

An appendix to the commentary on Megillat Ta'anit enumerates various commemorative fasts, among which are several dedicated to the martyrs of the time of Hadrian on the days of their martyrdom, and the fast on the tenth of Ṭebet, the day on which the Law was written in Greek in the time of King Ptolemy, when there was darkness over the world for three days.[6]

[1] M. Ta'anit 2, 1. For the reason for these ceremonies see Ta'anit 16a; Jer. Ta'anit 65a.

[2] M. Ta'anit 2, 1. [3] Psalms 120, 121, 130, 102. [4] M. Ta'anit 2.

[5] M. Ta'anit 3 (Ta'anit 19a). Cf. 1 Macc. 3, 47; 2 Macc. 13, 12, etc.

[6] Cf. Soferim 1, 7. The Greek translation put the Law into the hands of the Gentiles, and particularly of the Christians, who claimed it as their Scripture and interpreted it to support their doctrine. This experience made the Jews more careful to guard the traditional law by prohibiting putting it into writing. Tanḥuma ed. Buber, Ki tissa § 17; cf. ibid. Wayyera § 6.

The higher teaching of Judaism about the fast that is acceptable to God, in contrast to the external form, has its classical expression in Isa. 58, 3 ff.,[1] which is appointed (Isa. 57, 14–58, 14) for the prophetic lesson at the morning service on the Day of Atonement.[2] The self-imposed fasting of individuals will be considered in a later connection.[3]

[1] See Tos. Ta'anit 1, 8; Jer. Ta'anit 65b near the top (Eleazar ben Pedat). See, in general, Jer. Ta'anit on M. Ta'anit 2, 1.

[2] Megillah 31a.

[3] See below, pp. 257 ff.

CHAPTER V

TAXATION. INTERDICTIONS

ANOTHER class of observances which was of large importance in the economic and domestic life of the Jews had to do with the support of the ministers of religion. The maintenance of the public cultus in the temple was provided for by the annual half-shekel poll-tax collected not only in Palestine but throughout the whole diaspora. The priests officiating in private sacrifices, whether obligatory or voluntary, had a share for their services according to a legal tariff.[1] But the very numerous clergy of different ranks were maintained by a system of religious taxation, which also embraced what we call poor-relief.

The basis of this system, as defined in the fundamental law,[2] were the annual tithes of agricultural produce to be paid to the levites, who in their turn tithed to the priests.[3] This law contains no provision for the collection of the tithe, everything being apparently left to the conscience of the tax-payer, which all experience proves to be a slender reliance. Even in the very narrow limits of Judaea under Persian rule the voluntary method evidently did not work, and the compact in Neh. 10, 33 ff. provides for the collection of the tithes in the agricultural communities by levites accompanied by a priest (Neh. 7, 38 f.); even this plan was not successful, for in Neh. 13, 10, we read that the tithes were not paid, and the levites deserted the temple to get a living by tilling their own fields.[4] In the first century of our era the tithes were collected by the priests for themselves; [5] and in the evil days before the rebellion of the year 66, avaricious high priests

[1] With the destruction of the temple in 70 A.D. these revenues ceased.

[2] Num. 18

[3] *Terumat ma'aser.* See in general the article "Tithes" in the Encyclopaedia Biblica, IV, cols. 5102–5105.

[4] See also Mal. 3, 8 f.

[5] Josephus, Vita cc. 12 and 15.

sent bands of bravos who seized the tithes on the threshing floors and beat the priests who tried to keep what they had a right to.[1] So far as the collection of the tithes by the priests instead of the levites is concerned, the Talmud recognizes the departure from the law as of long standing, and legitimizes it: Ezra took away the tithes from the levites because so few of them were willing to return.[2]

Another of the priestly revenues prescribed in the laws were the first fruits of crops of grains and fruits,[3] the amount of which is fixed in the Mishnah as a fortieth, fiftieth, or sixtieth of the crop by estimation of value, according to the liberality of the owner.[4] Mention must also be made of the Ḥallah, a portion of every batch of dough to be given to a priest in a proportion also defined in the Mishnah.[5] Into the details of these requirements as they were interpreted in our period it is needless to go further here.[6]

All of these applied in the letter of the law only to the land of Israel, however at any time its boundaries might be defined. From the discussion in M. Yadaim 4, 3, participated in by leading authorities of the second century, it appears that it had so long been customary in Babylonia to set apart the tithes that it was regarded as an institution of the prophets; in Egypt it had been established by the elders, i.e. it was less ancient; and so also in Ammon and Moab.[7] Elsewhere we learn that Syria was in this respect treated substantially like the land of Israel.[8]

The system is adapted to very primitive economic conditions;

1 Jos. Antt. xx. 8, 8 § 181; 9, 2 §§ 206f.

2 Ḥullin 131b; Ketubot 26a; Yebamot 86a–b.

3 *Terumah gedolah.* Num. 18, 11–13.

4 M. Terumot 4, 3; 1, 7.

5 Num. 15, 17–21. M. Ḥallah 2, 7.

6 The biblical law applied only to the Land of Israel; the extension to other countries is rabbinical. On the disposition of the Ḥallah (a bit of the dough cast into the fire) reference must be made to the codes.

7 M. Yadaim 4, 3. According to R. Eliezer (ben Hyrcanus), on the contrary, it was a Mosaic tradition. Cf. Tos. Yadaim 2, 16.

8 M. Demai 6, 11; Tos. Kelim i. 1, 5. "Syria" stands for regions conquered by David.

it supposes a population occupying a small territory within easy reach of the temple, and chiefly engaged in small agriculture, on which the whole burden of the religious taxation falls. Moreover, the system, with its numerous and various payments in kind, was complicated, while the method of collection, so far as there was such a thing, had the semblance — and doubtless often the substance — of extortion by the beneficiary.

It is small wonder that the peasant earned the reputation of being very "untrustworthy" in acquitting himself of his religious obligations in this sphere. Even the most scrupulous of the class doubtless followed in this as in other matters the prescriptive usage of their fathers, heedless of the stricter interpretation of these laws in the schools and of the refinements of the oral law. Investigation showed, we are told, that the only law that was generally observed was the separation of the Terumah Gedolah, which could be eaten only by priests and their families in a state of ritual cleanness; some set apart the several tithes, others did not.[1] This negligence gave great concern to the religious leaders, but evidently their efforts to secure conformity to their standard had small success. Nor was the laxity of the common man in such matters his private affair which he might have to settle for himself with God. Such robbery of God was a national crime which was visited on the whole people; the favor of God and his blessing could be recovered only by complete amendment (Mal. 3, 8–12).[2]

It was also the individual concern of every truly pious man. What should such a one do who bought grain, fruit, vegetables, wine or oil, which were subject to tithing, from the country people who brought them to market, or bread from a baker or dealer? There was not only the uncertainty whether the tithe had been properly separated and disposed of, but further

[1] The investigation and subsequent regulation are attributed to Johanan the High Priest (John Hyrcanus). See Soṭah 48a; [M.] Soṭah 9, 10; Tos. Soṭah 13, 10.

[2] Midrash Tehillim on Psalm 57, 3 (ed. Buber f. 148b, f.). The neglect of tithing was one of the causes of the exile.

doubt whether the seller was telling the truth when he averred — as he would be sure to do — that it was all right. The question was a serious one, for it was taught that the failure to separate the tithe of the (levites') tithe which should go to the priest was a mortal sin equally with the Terumah Gedolah. Things to which this doubt attached were called Demai, "Dubious," and the various cases and what is to be done about them are dealt with under that title in a treatise in the Mishnah and Tosefta, and in the Palestinian Talmud.[1] The general rule is that the buyer of "dubious" produce should separate from his purchase a hundredth part (tenth of a tenth), the *terumat ma'aser* spoken of above.[2]

The religious leaders no doubt endeavored, through instruction and exhortation, to impress upon the people the magnitude of their offending in thus defrauding God in the person of his ministry, but they certainly did not succeed in bringing about a great reformation. Societies were also formed whose members pledged themselves to one another to be "trustworthy"[3] in these matters, and scrupulous in keeping other laws about which there was much laxity, especially in matters of uncleanness and purification. These were not made up of the educated class solely; on the contrary they sought to draw in the common people, who were received on the same conditions, to instruct them in the exact requirements of the laws, and to get them to give their solemn word to be henceforth "trustworthy" in fulfilling them. The members of these societies called themselves *Ḥaberim*, 'associates'; it seems likely that to them the name Pharisees was originally applied, being subsequently extended to all who exhibited a similar scrupulousness. The *Ḥaberim* are contrasted in this respect with the *'Amme ha-'areṣ*, 'the (ignorant) people of the land,' who could not be trusted in such matters.[4]

[1] There is no Babylonian Talmud upon these parts of the Mishnah.
[2] Mishneh Torah, Hilkot Ma'aser 9, 2.
[3] *ne'eman* (M. Demai 2, 2).
[4] See Jackson and Lake, The Beginnings of Christianity, Part I, Vol. 1, Appendix E (pp. 439–445).

On other Jewish observances we can be more summary. A large class fall under the head of avoidance of things stigmatized in the laws as 'unclean.'[1] It was, for example, a peculiarity often noted by pagan writers that the Jews regarded swine's flesh with abhorrence.[2] Numerous other species were similarly prohibited in the Law, but, inasmuch as most of them were creatures that no civilized man would eat anyhow, these restrictions on diet belonged to learning rather than to life.[3]

Of fundamental importance, on the other hand, was the often repeated injunction not to eat any flesh with blood in it, a monstrous offence, the penalty of which is extirpation from the people by God.[4] The prohibition in the Scripture is as indefinite as it is emphatic,[5] and it was left to the oral law, based, no doubt, on immemorial practice but elaborated in detail by the labors of the schools, to prescribe a mode of slaughter by which the danger that there should be a remainder of blood might be eliminated. The laws also forbade eating the flesh of an animal that died from natural causes (*nebelah*) or was torn (by beasts or birds of prey — *ṭerefah*).[6] In the regulations for the correct slaughtering of animals for food, precautions were accordingly taken that the beast should not die of anything but the effusion of blood, especially not of suffocation, which would make it *nebelah*.[7] The prohibition of *ṭerefah* was extended to include injuries and organic diseases, for instance of the lungs, which would eventually cause death. The latter could only be determined by inspection of the

1 'Clean' and 'unclean' in religious definition. Both 'unclean' and 'holy' have their root in ancient interdictions.

2 Théodore Reinach, Textes d'auteurs grecs et romains rélatifs au Judaisme, *passim*. The abhorrence was intensified when the beast was a sacrificial victim. Isa. 65, 4; 66, 3, 17; 1 Macc. 1, 47; 2, 23; 2 Macc. 6, 18–31.

3 A comparison of the so-called 'dietary laws' of other religions, e.g. in India, is instructive.

4 The *karet*. See above, p. 6.

5 Gen. 9, 4; Lev. 3, 17; 7, 25f.; 17, 10f.; 19, 26; Deut. 12, 16, 23; 15, 23.

6 Lev. 17, 15; 22, 8.

7 Acts 15, 19 f., 28 f.; 21, 25. The inclusion of "things strangled" in these places is, however, secondary. See J. H. Ropes, The Text of Acts (1926), pp. 265–269.

inwards after the animal had been killed. The flesh of animals which had not been killed in the prescribed way or which were not found on inspection to be sound was forbidden food to every Jew.

These regulations made it difficult for a Jew who strictly observed the laws to eat meat at the table of a Gentile, who lay under the presumption of observing none of them, though he might invite a Gentile to his table.[1] The first serious conflict in the new Christian community arose over this point, and the danger of a schism was narrowly averted. It should be added that there was another and even more cogent motive deterring the Jew from accepting the hospitality of Gentiles, namely the possibility that he might partake of the flesh of an animal that had been offered to a heathen God or of wine from which a libation had been made,[2] and thus be constructively guilty of joining in a sacrificial meal, an act of 'heathenism.'[3]

Closely associated with the prohibition of blood is that of the abdominal fat (*ḥeleb*)[4] of neat cattle, sheep, and goats. The original motive of the prohibition seems to have been that this fat was exclusively reserved to be burnt on the altar, as the blood was an atonement upon the altar (Lev. 17, 11), but the cessation of sacrifice did not abrogate the law.

Another observance which even more profoundly than these has affected the Jewish kitchen and diet is developed from the ancient law, 'Thou shalt not seethe a kid in its mother's milk,'[5] which grew into a segregation so complete that the bringing of any kind of flesh and any kind of milk or any dish prepared with milk into any kind of juxtaposition in the kitchen or on the table at the same meal is regarded as a violation of the law.[6]

[1] Legend tells of banquets which the Patriarch Judah gave to "Antoninus," both on the Sabbath and on week days. Gen. R. 11, 2.

[2] יין נסך

[3] '*Abodah zarah*. See 1 Cor. 8.

[4] Lev. 3, 17 (cf. vs. 14f.); 7, 23–25, etc. The more precise definition of what is *ḥeleb* need not be gone into here.

[5] Exod. 23, 19; 34, 26; Deut. 14, 21. Targum Onkelos in all three places, "You shall not eat flesh with milk." See Mekilta, Mishpaṭim c. 20 (ed. Friedmann f. 102a–b; ed. Weiss f. 108a–b).

[6] For the refinements of these rules see Maimonides, Hilkot Ma'akalot Asurot 9, 1 ff.; Shulḥan 'Aruk, Yoreh De'ah §§ 87–97.

There is a multitude of things that are in the religious definition 'unclean' and may communicate uncleanness by contact and sometimes through an intermediary, demanding therefore, 'purification'—a species of contagion requiring religious disinfection. Death is the most redoubtable of these, and next to it sexual functions, normal or pathological; a very high degree of uncleanness attaches to the various skin diseases comprehended under the general name 'leprosy.' The contamination is in many cases transmissible. There are also many animal kinds, especially vermin, which contaminate by contact. All these topics and others like them have an extensive and minute development which fills a large space in the Mishnah and cognate works.

By very many of these laws the common man was little troubled. The rabbinical interpretation was that he need not be particular about them unless he was going to visit the temple, or where it was a question of consecrated food, the priest's portion, and the second tithe. Otherwise he might eat ordinary food (*ḥullin*) regardless of questions of levitically clean or unclean.[1] Those forms of uncleanness which demanded an ablution could be removed in that way. Outside the land of Israel most laws prescribing ritual purifications were not in force, and with the destruction of the temple they ceased in Palestine also. The supererogatory piety of the "associates" undertook in such matters to maintain a supersacerdotal standard, by eating their unconsecrated food in a state of purity and keeping themselves at all times from every kind of uncleanness.[2]

Notions and customs of the same general character, and often strikingly similar in particulars, are found all over the earth and through all known ages, and in scrupulousness about them the so-called 'primitive' peoples are unsurpassable. They come out of a prehistoric past and persist through all stages of culture. Many

[1] Maimonides, Hilkot Ṭum'at Okelin 16, 8–11. See Sifra, Shemini Pereḳ 4 (ed. Weiss f. 49a); Rosh ha-Shanah 16b.

[2] Maimonides l.c. § 12: From this these *ḥasidim rishonim* were called *perushim* (Pharisees), etc. M. Ḥagigah 2, 7; cf. 'Abodah Zarah 20b; Jer. Sheḳalim 47c, below (Phineas ben Jair).

modern scholars have been much interested in the beginnings of these things — how 'primitive' men ever came to think and do thus and so — and often seem to assume that in the answer would be found an explanation of the phenomena as they survive in religions far removed from primitiveness. It is demonstrable, however, that customs often outlive the ideas that engendered them so long that those who practice them know as little about their origin or significance as we, and when curiosity raises the question, a myth is invented to answer it or a rationalistic explanation is excogitated.[1]

When religious custom comes not only to be put under divine sanction, but is believed to have been ordained and made known to men by God, and when finally such ordinances become part of a body of divine legislation, the all-sufficient answer to the question why this or that is done or left undone is that God has so commanded — "it is a statute of the King of kings." Nothing can be learned about what the observances of religion meant in Judaism by an investigation of their primitive analogies or prehistoric origins. Eating pork may be labelled an ancient 'food-taboo' — though the outlandish word does not suggest the smallest idea *why* their ancestors excluded swine's flesh from their diet — but the Jews themselves could give no other reason for abstinence than that God had prohibited it. For some laws God had given a reason, for others not; but whether he had or not, and whether in the latter case men could divine a reason or not, they were bound to obey his command. To repeat what has been emphasized more than once before in this volume, this is the logic of a revealed religion. Upon its premises, any other attitude is *ipso facto* a rejection of the religion and of God who is its author.

There is no reason to imagine that the observances of which we have spoken were new in the so-called post-exilic period, and still less that they were introduced or revived by Ezra and other

[1] An example of the former kind in the Bible is the 'sinew that shrank', Gen. 32, 33.

reformers to keep the Jews a separate people by increasing the difficulty of mixing with their neighbors. If they came to be casuistically developed and more scrupulously attended to in the last centuries before the Christian era and in those that followed, at least in the circles of the pious and the associations of the Pharisees, it was a consequence of a clearer and more consistent notion of what is involved in the possession of a revealed religion, and a deeper conviction that the fulfilment of all the great promises of the Scriptures was dependent on the fulfilment of their conditions in the conformity of the people, collectively and individually, to the will of God made known to them in the two-fold law.

If this is what is meant by the "legalism" of the Scribes and Pharisees, the name cannot be denied them, though another derivative of *lex*, 'loyalty,'[1] would express their conscious attitude better. It is pertinent to add that from this point of view observances are not the 'externals' of religion, the outgrown vestments of ideas; conformity to the revealed will of God is the essence of religion.

The effect of this conception of religion in theory and practice on Jewish piety will be discussed in a later chapter. Meanwhile it must suffice to repeat that this conception, being given in revelation itself, was the only one possible in Judaism with the Bible in its hands.

[1] English 'lealty' (legality), fealty (fidelity) to the sovereign and his law — On another use of 'legalism' see below.

PART V

MORALS

CHAPTER I

GENERAL CONSIDERATIONS

In a previous chapter it has been remarked that the splitting of the law into ceremonial and moral has no warrant in the religion itself, which claims for its sphere the whole of life, and not only of the outward life but of the inward life which we call piety.[1] The Jews, as we have seen, did not fail to distinguish between commandments and prohibitions which were, we may say, of natural obligation, recognized by the reason and conscience of all right thinking men and by the legislation of all nations, and statutory laws given to Israel alone, which are known only through divine revelation; but they made no attempt to carry this distinction through, and had no reason to do so. Right and wrong were for them not defined by the reason and conscience of men, naïve or reflective, nor by national custom or the *consensus gentium*, but by the revealed will of God; and constituted a distinctive Jewish morality which as a whole was different from that of other peoples, as the observances of Judaism, whatever their resemblance to the rites and ceremonies of other religions, constituted a distinctive Jewish cultus and observance.[2]

Morals had thus a legal character, whether in form they were mandatory like the categorical injunctions and prohibitions in the laws, or hortatory, as in large part they are not only in the Prophets but in the Law itself, or the examples of good and bad men in the narratives, or counsels of wisdom commended by experience in Proverbs, or the outcome of piety as in the Psalms — in substance all belonged to the God-given rule of life. It was as such that they were apprehended, interpreted, developed, and inculcated in the school and the synagogue. It was through

[1] See above, Part iv.

[2] See M. Lazarus, Die Ethik des Judenthums, I, chap. v. (Versittlichung ist Gesetzlichkeit).

the influence of the Scribes (biblical scholars) and their successors, from the days of the Men of the Great Assembly down, that a normative Jewish ethic was established as well as a normative observance.

In the present chapter we shall have to do chiefly with the moral teaching of these recognized authorities.

Writings such as the Testaments of the Twelve Patriarchs are instructive as showing how substantially the same teachings — for the most part lying on the surface of the Bible — were popularized in a characteristic literary form. In another way Sirach is of the greatest value for the evidence he gives of the unbroken continuity, in this as in other things, of the teaching from the days of the early Scribes to the Talmud.

The main source here as in other parts of our undertaking is the consecutive exposition of the Pentateuch (Exodus to Deuteronomy) in the schools of the second century,[1] and the quotations of similar origin and character in the Talmud (Baraita). It is not exclusively from the interpretation and application of the moral precepts of the Law that the teachings of the rabbis are to be gathered. The more strictly juristic parts of the same works, and the systematic formulation of the law (Halakah) in the Mishnah of the Patriarch Judah and kindred works, both in criminal and civil law and in procedure, as well as in connection with observances, exemplify the same principles in various ways. Many illustrations of this will appear in the course of our subsequent inquiry.[2]

Of the extent to which the conduct of the Jews at large was shaped by these standards there is no means of judging. The teachers had in the synagogue a unique institution for the education of all classes in religion and morals and made the most of it; but the experience of similar endeavors in more modern times shows that multitudes of men evade their opportunities of educa-

[1] Mekilta, Sifra, Sifrè.

[2] M. Lazarus notes especially laws relating to business transactions, Baba Meṣi'a 44a–60b. Ethik des Judenthums, I, 293 ff.

tion, and that being well instructed in duty and consistently doing it are different things. The Jews unquestionably felt that in morality they were superior to the nations among whom they lived, and in some things they doubtless were so; but as flatteringly fallacious modern examples again show, the comparison may be between moral ideals on the one side and immoral reality on the other. Strictures or satires in Greek and Latin literature, on the other hand, generalize from the morals and manners of the proletariat of great cities, with an unconcealed dislike and contempt for the whole race which should warn the historian against taking their prejudiced utterances as objective testimony. Fortunately these are questions into which we are not called to enter here; our concern is with the moral teaching of Judaism and the conduct of those who most faithfully translated principles and rules from doctrine into practice.

Before we address ourselves to this task certain preliminary observations remain to be made. The first is that the Jews did not develop ethics as a branch of philosophy, a science of conduct and character, such as we have in mind when we speak of the ethics of the Greeks. Hellenistic Jews like the author of the so-called Fourth Book of Maccabees and especially Philo appropriated the definitions and terminology of Greek ethics, and endeavored to show that the morality taught and exemplified in the Scriptures was in complete accord with what the philosophers taught in more abstract form on the authority of right reason, which was itself another mode of divine revelation. In the Middle Ages a succession of Jewish thinkers, among whom Maimonides is the most famous name, undertook the same demonstration from their own philosophical point of view. The motive of these enterprises was, however, not to construct a Jewish system of ethics but to prove to educated Jews and others the rational and moral excellence of Jewish ethics, and while of very great interest, they must be regarded as a chapter of apologetics rather than as a constructive essay in ethical theory. With such partial exceptions, what are called Jewish ethics are in substance and form more exactly described as preceptive morals; they are the morals of a religion, and their obligation lies not in the reason and conscience of men but in the authority of the sovereign Lawgiver.

Furthermore, no attempt is made to systematize these precepts for paedagogic ends by classifying them under general topics of any kind, as was done in the Mishnah for civil and criminal laws, for the cultus, and for the whole range of observances, public and private. The fact is of itself most significant. Things that are susceptible of exact definition and quantitative determination, such as the taxes for the support of the ministry and of the poor, or the keeping of the sabbath and other holy days, or forbidden kinds of food and the whole field of clean and unclean, are treated in that way, and carried by juristic casuistry to the utmost refinements; while such virtues as filial piety, philanthropy, charity, have no measure or norm,[1] but are left to the conscience and right feeling of the individual.

These and many other things are in the rabbinical phrase *masūr la-lēb*, 'committed to the heart.'[2] Generalizing from Lev. 19, 14 and 32; 25, 36 and 43, they say, Wherever something is thus left to conscience, the Scripture says of it, 'And thou shalt revere the Lord thy God.'[3] Judaism never developed a systematic ethical casuistry such as we find in the Stoics[4] or in the Christian church, not only in Roman Catholic treatises on Moral Theology but among Protestants,[5] though particular problems are occasionally treated in that way. A very interesting example from the end of the first century of our era is the discussion of the question what should be done if, of two wayfarers in the desert, one had a little water while the other had none. If one of them should drink all the water, he would be able to get out; if

[1] For the phrase see M. Peah 1, 1; cf. Tos. Peah 1, 1.

[2] Baba Meṣi'a 58b; Ḳiddushin 32b near the end. M. Lazarus, Ethik des Judenthums, I, 95, 400–402.

[3] Sifra on Lev. 25, 36, ed. Weiss f. 109d. Perles, Boussets Religion des Judentums, p. 76. See further below, p. 92.

[4] For example in Cicero, De officiis (after Panaetius).

[5] See R. M. Wenley, 'Casuistry,' Encyclopaedia of Religion and Ethics, III, 239 ff.

they should divide it, both would die. Ben Paṭuri said they should both drink, and die, for it is written, 'And thy brother shall live *with* thee' (Lev. 25, 36); R. Akiba replied, 'Thy brother shall live with *thee*' — thy life takes precedence of his life.[1]

Though the Jewish teachers made no attempt to classify the virtues,[2] they sought in the Scripture passages or verses in which the essence of morality was compendiously expressed. By an ingenious conceit to which reference has been made above, it was reckoned that Moses gave to the Israelites as many positive commandments as there are members and organs in the human body (248), and as many negative commandments (prohibitions) as there are days in the solar year (365), in all six hundred and thirteen.[3] R. Simlai, in a homily, starting from these six hundred and thirteen commandments, continues: "David came and comprehended them in eleven (Psalm 15, quoted entire).[4] Isaiah came and comprehended them in six: 'He that walketh righteously, and speaketh uprightly, he that despiseth the gain acquired by oppression, that shaketh out his hands from holding of bribes, that stoppeth his ears from hearing of blood, and shutteth his eyes from looking upon evil; he shall dwell on high,' etc. (Isa. 33, 15). Micah came and comprehended them in three: 'He has told thee, O man, what is good and what the Lord requireth of thee. Only to do justice and to love mercy and to walk humbly with thy God' (Micah 6, 8). Isaiah further compre-

[1] You must be alive, if he is to live with *you*. Sifra on Lev. 25, 36 (ed. Weiss f. 109c); Baba Meṣi'a 62a. Bacher, Tannaiten, I, 60, cites the problem of the two shipwrecked men in Cicero, De officiis iii. 23, 90.

[2] In Hellenistic writers we find the common quadripartite scheme. Thus, 4 Macc. 1, 2–4 (*φρόνησις, σωφροσύνη, δικαιοσύνη, ἀνδρεία*), cf. 1, 18; 5, 23; Wisdom of Solomon 8, 7; Philo, Legum allegoriarum i. 19 § 63 (the four rivers flowing out of Eden, *φρόνησις, σωφροσύνη, ἀνδρεία, δικαιοσύνη*, proceeding from one source, the generic virtue, *ἀγαθότης*), etc. See Grimm on 4 Macc. l. c.

[3] Another way of arriving at the number 613 is by adding to the numerical value of תורה (611) the two commandments uttered by God himself, Exod. 20, 2 and 3. Makkot 23b–24a.

[4] Typical examples of these virtues are adduced in the Talmud from the Bible and famous rabbis, in this and the following cases. See Bacher, Pal. Amoräer, I, 558 and notes.

hended them in two: 'Observe justice and do righteousness' (Isa. 56, 1). Amos came and comprehended them in one: 'Seek me and live' (Amos 5, 4)." Another finds the one comprehensive word in Habakkuk: 'The righteous man shall live by his faithfulness' (Hab. 2, 4; cf. Rom. 1, 17; Gal. 3, 11: 'The just shall live by faith').[1]

The commandments in the Pentateuch, however they may be counted, are largely concerned with ritual and observance; the 'law in a nutshell' in these summaries is solely moral. The selection also demands a word of note. One would seek far in the Scripture to find a finer ideal of the virtuous man than Psalm 15, and the essence of religion has never been so pregnantly expressed as in Micah 6, 8. R. Simlai's often quoted sermon is not solitary. Bar Ḳappara asks, What short passage is there upon which all the essentials of the Law depend? 'In all thy ways know (acknowledge) Him, and He will make thy paths straight' (Prov. 3, 6).[2] Of Leviticus 19 it is said that it was delivered in the assembly of all Israel because most of the essentials of the Law depend upon it.[3]

The motto of Simeon the Righteous was: "The world is sustained by three things, by the Law, by Worship, and by Charity."[4] By the Law is meant not alone the objective revelation, without which the world could not endure,[5] but the knowledge of the Law acquired and cultivated by learned and pious study. Worship was in his day the cultus in the temple, including not only the sacrificial ritual but the praises and prayers by which it was accompanied; after the cessation of the cultus the word was natur-

[1] Makkot 24a. Without the illustrative examples, Tanḥuma ed. Buber, Shofeṭim § 10. Numerous other parallels, יפה עינים on Makkot l. c.

[2] Berakot 63a.

[3] Sifra on Lev. 19, 1 f. (ed. Weiss f. 86c). The 'essentials of the Law' (גופי תורה) may, according to the connection, be in the sphere of observance or of morals. For instance, see Abot 3, 18; Tos. Shabbat 2, 10; M. Ḥagigah 1, 8 (Bacher, Terminologie, I, 11 f.); Ḥullin 60b, etc.

[4] Abot 1, 2.

[5] Cf. Nedarim 32a (R. Eliezer): If it were not for the Torah, heaven and earth could not endure (Jer. 33, 20).

ally transferred to the worship of the synagogue and of the home — prayer, in the customary form (Tefillah), is worship of God in the heart.[1] Charity is personal service and helpfulness to fellow men, the active expression of the love enjoined in Lev. 19, 18.[2] The great exemplar is God himself. The Talmud finds one verse of Scripture which implicitly contains them all (Isa. 51, 16).[3] R. Simeon ben Gamaliel also names three things by which the world is sustained — fundamental conditions of social stability — Justice, Truth, and Peace; as in Zech. 8, 16.[4]

When R. Akiba declared 'Thou shalt love thy neighbor as thyself' (Lev. 19, 18) to be the most comprehensive rule in the Law,[5] he was thinking of a rule of moral conduct, as Paul did when, two generations earlier, he said, 'The whole law is fully expressed in one sentence, Thou shalt love thy neighbor as thyself.'[6] Ben 'Azzai found, as we have seen above, a broader principle still in Gen. 5, 1: 'These are the generations of man; (in the day that God created man, in the likeness of God created He him').[7] Reverence for the divine image in man is of wider scope than love to our fellow-man. The question of the lawyer (Matt. 22, 36), 'What is the greatest commandment in the law,' was therefore one which was mooted in the Jewish schools. In his answer Jesus quotes Deut. 6, 5, 'Thou shalt love the Lord thy God with all thy heart and with all thy soul and with all thy means,' and Lev. 19, 18, 'Thou shalt love thy neighbor as thyself' — the essence of religion on its Godward and its manward sides respectively. The preëminence of the first was recognized in the place it occupies in the Shema', and was impressed on the

1 Sifrè Deut. § 41 (ed. Friedmann f. 80a, top), on Deut. 11, 13.

2 On this virtue (*gemīlūt ḥasadīm*), which is far higher than mere almsgiving (*ṣedaḳah*), see below, pp. 171 ff.

3 Jer. Ta'anit 68a, near the end.

4 Abot 1, 18, cf. Jer. Ta'anit, l. c.

5 Sifra ad loc., Ḳedoshim Pereḳ 4 (ed. Weiss f. 89b); Jer. Nedarim 41c, middle; Gen. R. 24, end (see Theodor's note).

6 Gal. 5, 14; cf. Rom. 13, 8–10; James 2, 8.

7 See the references in note 5, above. Akiba on the prerogative of man, created in the image of God, and the love of God shown in creating him thus and revealing the fact to him, Abot 3, 14. See Vol. I, pp. 397 f., 446 f.

Jew every time he recited his confession of Unity; in the second, as we have just seen, Akiba found the most comprehensive formulation of man's duty to his fellow. 'On these two commandments the whole Law depends[1] and the Prophets.'

'Thou shalt love thy neighbor as thyself' assumes that self-love is not only natural but good. A sound morality must take account of our own interests equally with those of others. Hillel expresses himself in the spirit of the principle when he says: "If I am not for myself, who is for me? And when I am for myself only, what am I? And if not now, when?"[2]

The two precepts are brought into juxtaposition in more than one place in the Testaments of the Twelve Patriarchs, thus: "Love the Lord and your neighbor, and have compassion on the poor and feeble" (Issachar 5, 2); "Love the Lord with all your life, and one another with sincere heart" (Dan 5, 3). Issachar says of himself, "I loved the Lord with all my strength; likewise I loved every man with all my heart" (7, 6). The association is in fact a natural one, and it is a gratuitous suspicion that the Testaments have in this particular been improved by a Christian hand.[3]

In substance, though not in form, the two are brought together in Sifrè on Deuteronomy 32, 29: "What did it (the Law) say to them? Take upon you the yoke of the kingdom of Heaven,[4] and excel one another in the fear of Heaven,[5] and conduct yourselves one toward another in charity."[6] Hillel's answer to a foreigner who asked to be taught the whole Law while he stood on one foot was: "Do not do to your fellow what you hate to have done

[1] For the expression, see above, p. 84 (cf. p. 28).

[2] Abot 1, 14.

[3] An interpolator is not likely to have been so subtle as to disguise in every case his reminiscence of the Gospel.

[4] The fundamental obligations of religion, as a Jew does in reciting the Shema' (Hear, O Israel, the Lord our God, the Lord is One; and thou shalt love the Lord thy God, etc.).

[5] Reverence for God — the nearest equivalent in the Scriptures for 'religion.' See below, p. 96.

[6] גמילות חסדים, the works of love; see below, pp. 171 ff.

to you.[1] This is the whole Law, entire; the rest is explanation. Go, learn!" [2] This often quoted summary of the Law was not original with Hillel upon the occasion; it seems rather to have been proverbial. Parallels from Jewish sources and in various other literatures have frequently been collected, and the catalogue need not be repeated here.[3] We may see in it a negative formulation of Lev. 19, 18 for practical application, precisely as is done by Paul in Rom. 13, 8–10, where, after recalling the commandments, Thou shalt not murder, steal, commit adultery, he finds them all summed up in Lev. 19, 18, and concludes, 'Love works no harm to the neighbor; the whole content of the law, therefore, is love." [4]

In the Gospels this so-called Golden Rule is phrased affirmatively, 'All that you would wish that men should do to you, so do ye also to them. This is the Law and the Prophets.' (Matt. 7, 12; cf. Luke 6, 31).[5] It is often said that the substitution of the positive form of the rule for the negative makes a very different thing of it. That is a point about which it is not worth while to argue. Jewish teaching about the treatment of others, countrymen or aliens, friends or enemies, was not deduced from an aphorism, but based upon the positive general rule in Lev. 19, 18 (cf. vss. 33–35) and the many specific injunctions and exhortations, both positive and negative, in which the Scriptures abound in all parts; and these virtues are exemplified by instances in the

[1] דעלך סני לחברך לא תעביד.

[2] Shabbat 31a. Compare the story of Akiba and the donkey driver, Abot de-R. Nathan, ed. Schechter, p. 26 (second recension).

[3] A recent list of such collections, may be found in the Harvard Theological Review, XIV (1921), 193 f. (W. H. P. Hatch).

[4] Cf. the Epistle of Aristeas: Our law commands to do harm to no man either in word or deed (ed. Wendland § 168).

[5] So also by Maimonides, Hilkot Ebel 14, 1: "Thou shalt love thy neighbor as thyself. All the things that you wish that others should do to you, do you to your brother." On the other hand the Teaching of the Twelve Apostles (1, 2) gives the negative form: "The Way of Life is this: First, thou shalt love the God who made thee, secondly, thy neighbor as thyself; and whatsoever thou wouldst not have done to thyself, do not thou to another." In the negative form it is found in the so-called "Western" text of Acts 15, 20 and 29, and in the Apostolic Constitutions vii. 2. [Tobit 4, 16.]

familiar narratives of the Bible and by the character and conduct of eminent rabbis. No one who knows this topic in the ethics of the school and the synagogue, or in the Halakah itself, would attribute to it a distinctively negative type, any more than he would discover a distinctively positive type in the New Testament or the legislation of the church.

This leads to a more general observation. Such condensations of the essentials of the moral law into a dozen great precepts or into one comprehensive rule are of interest to us as exhibiting a sound estimate of religious and moral values, and for the intrinsic unity of fundamental principle. They were never meant to be taken for sufficient regulatives of conduct, for which, indeed, they are wholly inadequate, and the broader and more elevated they are, the less they are adapted to any such end. At the most they may serve the ethical philosopher as a criterion, like Kant's, "Act so that the maxims of thy will at all times may likewise be valid as the principle of a universal legislation." For the actual conduct of life, and above all for the practical morals of a community or a people in any age, explicit rules, defining cases and prescribing what is to be done in concrete instances, are indispensable. Such rules may be conventional, the custom of a given society, or they may be embodied in legislation, civil, or religious, or both at once. The Jews possessed such a legislation in the form and with the authority of divine revelation, and on it the ethics of Judaism were founded, not on deductions from general principles, which were themselves at best only inductions from its particular regulations.[1]

[1] It is needless to enlarge on the fact that the Christian church from the beginning did the same thing.

CHAPTER II

MOTIVES OF MORAL CONDUCT

THE motives of moral conduct have as wide a range as in the Scriptures from which they are derived. We shall find an advance, however, in the discriminative estimation of the relative ethical value of motives, and correspondingly of the acts which are prompted by them, and, secondly, in the emphasis laid on certain religious motives of the highest rank in this estimation which are developed from implications and suggestions of Scripture, but have there no corresponding prominence.

What we should call the natural and social consequences of evil courses are fully recognized, but they occupy a minor place in comparison with books like Proverbs and Sirach which endeavor, by exhibiting these consequences, to make men see that vice is disastrous folly, and virtue practical wisdom. In Judaism, as we should expect, the religious view prevails. Conformity to the law of God is righteousness, disobedience is sin — both primarily religious conceptions.[1] God punishes sin and rewards obedience. This is the constant teaching of Scripture. From the simple notion that God was well-pleased with those who did his will and showed them favor in return, while he was angry with those who ignored or defied his commands and made them feel his displeasure, there had grown, under the influence of the prophetic teaching, a doctrine of retribution in which God's justice was committed to requite men strictly according to their deeds.[2]

Reward and punishment are the motives to which the mass of mankind is most amenable, and the Jewish teachers, though well aware that they are not the highest, do not scruple on that

[1] It is to be noted that the definition of sin in the New Testament is identical. Synonyms of *ἁμαρτία* are *ἀδικία* and *ἀνομία*. So in Paul, Rom. 7, 13; 5, 13; etc. 1 John 3, 4 *ἡ ἁμαρτία ἐστὶν ἡ ἀνομία*.

[2] God's reward as wages (שׂכר), Gen. 15, 1; Prov. 11, 18 (עקב); Psalm 19, 12; Prov. 22, 4. See also Isa. 49, 4.

account to appeal to them.[1] It was better to lead a man to obey the law of God from an inferior motive than that he should not obey it; and, as is frequently observed, if he is diligent in keeping the law from a lower motive he may come to do it from a higher.

From the point of view of retribution, they believed that wrong-doing deserved the punishment God threatened, and no less that good deeds deserved the favor of God and the reward he promised. Subjectively, if a reproving conscience voices the consciousness of ill-desert, an approving conscience is the consciousness of good desert.

The reflection may be made that man's good deeds do not of themselves lay God under an obligation; God does not *owe* him a recompense for doing his duty. But God has put himself under obligation by his promise of reward, and in this sense man, in doing what God requires of him, deserves the recompense. Judaism has no hesitation about recognizing the merit of good works, or in exhorting men to acquire it and to accumulate a store of merit laid up for the hereafter.[2]

The most familiar examples are the words of Jesus in the Gospels. To the rich young man who wanted to be set on doing some good thing to possess eternal life, and who thought an every-day keeping of the Ten Commandments too small a task for so great a reward, Jesus said: If you wish to be perfect, go, sell your property and give it to the poor, and you shall have treasure in heaven; and come, follow me.[3] In the Sermon on the Mount he exhorts his hearers: 'Do not lay up for yourselves treasures on the earth where moth and rust consume, and where thieves break through and steal; but lay up treasures for yourselves in heaven,[4] where neither moth nor rust consumes, and

[1] They are as freely employed by Jesus in the Gospels.

[2] See Marmorstein, The Doctrine of Merits in Old Rabbinical Literature, 1920.

[3] Matt. 19, 21; Mark 10, 21; Luke 18, 22. On God's reward in general cf. Matt. 6, 1, 6, 18; 10, 41, 42; Luke 6, 35, etc.

[4] I.e. with God.

where thieves do not break through nor steal. For where thy treasure is, there will thy heart be."[1]

Of these treasures of good works there is repeated mention in the apocalypses from the end of the first century, Fourth Esdras and the Syriac Baruch. Thus Esdras is assured by the angel: "Thou hast a treasure of works laid up with the Most High, but it will not be shown to thee except in the last days."[2] The voice from heaven tells Baruch: "Lo, the days are coming when the book will be opened in which are written the sins of all that have sinned, and likewise the treasuries in which the righteousness of those who have conducted themselves righteously in the creation is collected."[3]

Most instructive for the Jewish conception of the treasury of merit are the words put into the mouth of Monobazus, king of Adiabene in the middle of the first century of our era.[4] The story goes that in years of famine he distributed all his treasures to the poor. His kinsmen remonstrated against such squandering of the family wealth: "Your fathers laid up treasures and added to the treasures of their fathers, and you have come and squandered your own wealth and that of your fathers!" He replied: "My fathers laid up treasures for below (this earth), but I have laid up treasures for above (Psalm 85, 12); they laid up treasures in a place over which force may prevail; I in a place over which no force can prevail (Psalm 89, 15). My fathers laid up treasures which bear no fruit (interest); I have laid up treasures that bear fruit (Isa. 3, 10). My fathers laid up treasures of mammon; I have laid up treasures of souls (Prov. 11, 30). My fathers laid up treasures for others; I, for myself (Deut. 24, 13). My fathers

1 Matt. 6, 19; cf. Luke 12, 33 f. See also 1 Tim. 6, 17–19.

2 4 Esdras 7, 77.

3 Syr. Baruch 24, 1. See also 14, 12; 4 Esdras, 7, 77; 8, 33, 36. Cf. further Tobit 4, 8 f. (longer recension); Test. of Twelve Patriarchs, Levi, 13, 5; Psalms of Solomon, 9, 9, etc. See Dalman, Worte Jesu, 169 f.; Strack-Billerbeck on Matt. 6, 19 f.

4 Monobazus like his brother Izates and his mother Helena had embraced Judaism; see Vol. I, p. 349.

laid up treasures in this world; I, for the World to Come (Isa. 58, 8)."[1]

The beginning of M. Peah enumerates works the fruits (interest) of which man enjoys in this world, while the principal is secured for him in the World to Come, viz., honoring one's parents, and deeds of lovingkindness, and making peace between a man and his fellow, and the study of the Torah, which is equal to all the others.[2] It will be noted that all the items of this 'capital in heaven' are things that cannot be defined or measured by law — things that by their nature are 'committed to the heart' of the individual. Elsewhere it is said that there is no least commandment which is not rewarded in this world, while its reward in the world to come is incalculable.[3]

God not only, in general terms, threatened punishment for wrong-doing and promised reward for doing his will, but he had attached particular penalties to particular offenses and particular blessings to obedience to certain commandments. It was natural to suppose that this was the case with all of them, and that the keeping of each prohibition or injunction had its own reward appropriate in kind and measure.[4] A certain R. Hananiah ben 'Aḳashya says: "The Holy One, blessed is He, was pleased to justify Israel, therefore he multiplied for them Law (to study) and commandments (to do), as it is written, 'The Lord was pleased, for the sake of his (Israel's) righteousness,[5] to make the Law great and glorious'" (Isa. 42, 21).[6] The multiplied com-

[1] Tos. Peah 4, 18; Jer. Peah 15b, below; Baba Batra 11a.

[2] See also Ḳiddushin 39b; especially 40a, with proof texts and exposition of the ideas of the principal and the interest of merit (זכות); Shabbat 127a, end, a list of six in the name of Johanan; taking in wayfarers, visiting the sick, devoutness in prayer, being early in the school house (Bet ha-Midrash), bringing up sons in the study of the Torah, and judging one's fellow on the good side.

[3] Menaḥot 44a, top.

[4] M. Makkot 3, 15 (R. Simeon, son of the Patriarch Judah). See also Tanḥuma ed. Buber, Teṣè § 2 (f. 17b).

[5] Probably pronouncing *ṣaddĕḳo* instead of *ṣidḳo*, 'for the sake of justifying him.' Bacher, Tannaiten, II, 376.

[6] M. Makkot 3, 16.

mandments are to give Israel ampler opportunity to acquire merit by obedience and by avoiding transgression.[1] As there is no end to the words of the Law (Job 11, 9), so there is no end to the giving of its reward (Psalm 31, 20, 'How abundant is thy goodness, which Thou has laid up for them that fear Thee').[2]

The kind and measure of the reward of most of the commandments are not annexed to them in the Scriptures, lest men should pick out those that promised most and neglect the others, but should keep them all in faithfulness, or of their own accord (disinterestedly).[3] A man should be as careful about a light commandment as about a grave one, since he does not know how they are to be rewarded, nor which has in it for him the issues of life.[4]

Upon R. Ḥanina's word, "Everything is in the power of Heaven except the fear of Heaven" (God can do everything except make a man religious) [5] the question is raised, Is then the fear of Heaven a small thing! and Ḥanina quotes R. Simeon ben Yoḥai, "God has in his treasure house no treasure but the fear of Heaven, as it is written, 'The fear of the Lord is his treasure'" (Isa. 33, 6).[6] It is perhaps not pressing the words too hard if we put on them the meaning, What God prizes in men's good works is not the acts themselves but the religious motive from which they spring.

The prejudice of many writers on Judaism against the very idea of good works and their reward, and of merit acquired with God through them, is a Protestant inheritance from Luther's controversy with Catholic doctrine, and further back from Paul's contention that there is no salvation in Judaism, for 'by the

[1] See Maimonides and Rashi *in loc.*

[2] Pesiḳta ed. Buber, f. 107a; cf. f. 73b.

[3] Tanḥuma ed. Buber, 'Eḳeb § 3; Teṣê § 2, end. See Jer. Peah 15d, near the top.

[4] Judah the Patriarch, Abot 2, 1; cf. Menaḥot 44a, top, and the following story, ending with the same phrase.

[5] Berakot 33b. Above, Vol. I, p. 456.

[6] A slightly different version, Johanan in the name of R. Eleazar ben Simeon, Yalḳuṭ on Deut. 10, 12, § 855: God has nothing in his world save only the fear of Heaven (Deut. 10, 12; Job 28, 28).

works of the law shall no flesh be justified in His sight.' Paul's assertion is the corollary of his first proposition, that the one universal and indispensable condition of salvation is faith in the Lord Jesus Christ.[1] Luther is bent on proving that salvation is wholly and solely the work of God's free grace, which takes no account of man's works. Both involve the question in the doctrine of salvation.

Judaism did not come at it from the theoretical side at all; it got its ideas from the Scriptures and developed them by the same methods it employed on the other teachings of Scripture. It was concerned not solely with the individual but with the nation, not with the hereafter alone but with the present life. All the good things God promised in this world or the world to come were conditioned upon conformity to his righteous will as revealed in the Law. He did not expect an impossible perfection of creatures in whom he himself implanted the 'evil impulse,'[2] and therefore, in foresight of their failure, provided repentance as the remedy for their shortcomings. Not only does he freely forgive, but he gives them merit that they have not earned. When he showed Moses all the treasuries of merit prepared for the righteous, one for those who give alms, one for those who provide for orphans, and so on, Moses saw one large treasury and asked whose it was. God replied: To the man who has (merit), I give of his own; and on him who has none I bestow gratis, as it is written, 'And I will show favor to whom I will show favor' (Exod. 33, 19).[3]

It should be remarked, further, that "a lot in the World to Come,"[4] which is the nearest approximation in rabbinical Judaism to the Pauline and Christian idea of salvation, or eternal life,

[1] His implicit assumption is that God cannot forgive the penitent sinner without expiation.

[2] See Vol. I, pp. 480 f.

[3] Tanḥuma ed. Buber, Ki tissa § 16. Contrast Paul's use of this text in support of the arbitrariness of election (Rom. 9, 15, 18). On the imputation of merit see Vol. I, pp. 536 ff.

[4] After the resurrection, in an endless life on a transformed earth. See pp. 378 f.

is ultimately assured to every Israelite[1] on the ground of the original election of the people by the free grace of God, prompted not by its merits, collective or individual, but solely by God's love,[2] a love that began with the Fathers.[3] For this national election Paul and the church substituted an individual election to eternal life, without regard to race or station.

These facts are ignored when Judaism is set in antithesis to Christianity, a "Lohnordnung" over against a "Gnadenordnung." "A lot in the World to Come" is not wages earned by works, but is bestowed by God in pure goodness upon the members of his chosen people, as "eternal life" in Christianity is bestowed on the individuals whom he has chosen, or on the members of the church. If the one is grace, so is the other.

A word may be said in this connection about the corresponding conception of sin as debt, for example in the petition, 'Forgive us our debts as we forgive our debtors' (Matt. 6, 12). The expression, which is very common in Jewish literature, was evidently so strange to Greek readers that Luke substitutes 'sins' for Matthew's 'debts,' and in the immediate sequel in Matthew παραπτώματα is introduced as if in explanation.[4] Man *owes* God obedience, and every sin, whether of commission or of omission, is a defaulted obligation, a debt.[5] A guilty man, who is liable to punishment, is said to be 'owing the penalty.'[6]

However legitimate the motive of reward may be, there is a higher obedience than that which is rendered from this motive. The otherwise unknown Antigonus of Socho, the next in the succession of teachers after Simeon the Righteous, was made forever memorable by one saying: "Be not like slaves who serve

[1] M. Sanhedrin 10, 1; Sanhedrin (11, 1) 90a ff.; Jer. Sanhedrin 27b ff. The specific exclusions emphasize the universality. For a widely different outlook see 4 Esdras.

[2] Deut. 7, 6–11. See Vol. I, pp. 536 ff.

[3] Deut. 10, 15.

[4] English version, 'trespasses.'

[5] It may be remembered that Anselm's argument in his "Cur deus homo?" starts with the same postulate.

[6] Reatus poenae.

their master in the expectation of receiving a gratuity;[1] but be like slaves who serve their master in no expectation of receiving a gratuity; and let the fear of Heaven be upon you."[2] R. Eliezer comments on Psalm 112, 1 ('Blessed is the man who fears the Lord, and in his commandments delights greatly'): "In His commandments, and not in the reward of His commandments," and cites as authority the Mishnah Abot just quoted.[3]

The concluding words are also to be noted, "And let the fear of Heaven be upon you," in our terms, reverence for God.[4] Instead of expectation of recompense let your motive be purely religious. For religion is in the Hebrew of the schools, as in the Bible, 'the fear of the Lord,' and the usual way of saying 'a religious man' is 'one who fears the Lord.' 'Reverence' would often be a better word, for though reverence in fact as well as in etymology preserves the element of fear, it is a fear that is not inconsistent with love, though it may be contrasted with it, as it is sometimes by the Jewish teachers.[5]

It is worthy of note that this disparagement of an obedience into the motive of which the thought of recompense even as a gratuity enters comes from the man who stands at the head of what may not improperly be called the Pharisaic tradition, the connecting link between the Men of the Great Assembly and the Pairs. There is a certain irony in the fact that the first recorded word of a Pharisee should be a repudiation of the supposed "Pharisaic" wage-theory of righteousness.[6]

That the law of God and every commandment in it should be kept 'for its own sake,'[7] not for any advantage to be gained by it among men or with God, is frequently emphasized. Thus, if a man occupy himself with the Law for its own sake, his study of the Law is made for him a life-giving elixir (Prov. 3, 8, 18;

1 פרס.

2 Abot 1, 3.

3 'Abodah Zarah 19a.

4 Cf. Baba Meṣi'a 58b., etc. Above, p. 82.

5 See below, pp. 99 f.

6 See L. Ginzberg, in Jewish Encyclopedia, I, 629. On the varieties of Pharisees whose conduct and motives are condemned, see below, p. 193.

7 לשמה, i.e. because it *is* the law.

8, 35); but to him who occupies himself with it not for its own sake, it is made for him a deadly poison [1] (Deut. 32, 2; 21, 4). In the parallel in Sifrè [2] the contrast is between *doing* the words of the Law for their own sake and doing them not for their own sake; in the former case they are life, in the latter they kill (Prov. 4, 22; Deut. 21, 4; Prov. 7, 26).[3] From Psalm 111, 10 ('The first principle of wisdom is the fear of the Lord (religion); all those who do them [4] have good understanding') Raba deduces: "It is not said, 'who learn them,' but 'who do them'; and who do them for their own sake, not those who do them not for their own sake. Whoever does a commandment not for its own sake (from other than a religious motive), it were better for him that he had never been created!" [5]

R. Eleazar ben Zadok says: Do the words of the Law for the doing's sake, and discuss them for their own sake.[6] He goes on to declare the sin of the man who uses for his own ends the instrument with which this world and that to come were created [7] greater than Belshazzar's use of the vessels of the temple for which (though they were already profaned, Ezek. 7, 22),[8] the king was rooted out of this world and the world to come. The same fate is doubly deserved by him who so profanes the Law. The maxim of his father Zadok was: "Do not make it (the Law) a crown to magnify thyself by, nor a hoe to dig with." So Hillel was wont to say, "He who uses the crown for his own ends, passes away.[9] Lo, thou hast learned, Every one who makes a profit of the words of the Law does his life away from the world." [10] There are many warnings in the same spirit against turning the Law to worldly advantage; it is needless to multiply instances.

[1] סם חיים, סם מות. Ta'anit 7a. See Bacher, Tannaiten, II, 540 and n. 3.

[2] Sifrè Deut. § 306, ed. Friedmann f. 131b, end.

[3] See also Abot 6, 1.

[4] The injunctions of God, verse 7.

[5] Berakot 17a, below.

[6] Sifrè Deut. § 48, end (on Deut. 11, 22); cf. Nedarim 62a. On the difference of reading see Bacher, Tannaiten, I, 48 f.

[7] The Law, see Vol. I, pp. 397 f.

[8] See Bekorot 50a, below.

[9] (Abot 1, 13).

[10] Abot 4, 5. Parallels, see Kobryn, Catena, p. 91a–b.

There is sound insight into human nature in the saying ascribed to Rab: Let a man always occupy himself diligently with the study of the Law and the doing of the commandments, even if not for their own sake; for out of doing it not for its own sake comes doing it for its own sake.[1]

Another common expression for the religious motive is 'for the sake of Heaven' (God)[2] Those who labor with the community should do so for God's sake (*le-shem Shamaim*), i.e., from an unmixed religious motive (Abot 2, 2). "Let thy neighbor's property be as dear to thee as thine own; and address thyself to acquire knowledge of the Law, for it does not come to thee by inheritance; and let all thy deeds be done for God's sake" (ibid. 2, 12). "Every assembling of yourselves together which is for God's sake will in the end stand; one that is not for God's sake, will not stand in the end" (ibid. 4, 11). The same thing is said of controversies for God's sake, like those of the schools of Shammai and Hillel, in contrast to that of Korah and his company with Moses (ibid. 5, 17). The motive in the former was religious, aiming at an exact understanding and application of the Law; the other was prompted by personal ambition.

In the Old Testament the religious attitude toward God which translates itself into a motive for doing his will is the fear of God or the love of God. In Deuteronomy, in particular, the two occur in exactly similar contexts, without any apparent consciousness of a difference between them, much less that they were conflicting.[3] In a notable passage the sum of God's demands is put thus: 'And now, O Israel, what doth the Lord thy God require of thee, but to fear the Lord thy God, to walk in all his ways, and to love him, and to serve the Lord thy God with all thy heart and with all thy soul; to keep for thy good the com-

[1] Pesaḥim 50b; Sanhedrin 105b; Nazir 23b, etc. Compare the prayer of R. Safra, Berakot 16b–17a: May it be Thy good pleasure that all who labor in the Law for other motives may come to labor in it for its own sake.

[2] לשם שמים, e.g. Abot 2, 2; 4, 11.

[3] Compare Deut. 5, 26; 6, 2, 13 (Fear the Lord and keep his commandments, serve him, etc.), with 11, 1, 13, 22; 19, 9; 30, 6, 16, etc.

mandments of the Lord,' etc. (Deut. 10, 12). In the Psalms godly men are those who fear the Lord, or love Him, with no discoverable distinction of two kinds of religiousness. If the phrase be pulled to pieces, however, a distinction may be made between an obedience the motive of which is fear and one whose motive is love, and some of the rabbis, having done this, estimated obedience out of love superior to obedience from fear — love is the higher motive.[1] Rabbi Simeon ben Eleazar said, "Greater is he who acts from love than he who acts from fear."[2] In Sifrè on Deut. 6, 5,[3] it is said: "The Scripture makes a difference between the man who acts from love and him who acts from fear, and the reward of the former is far greater than of the latter, according to his word, 'The Lord thy God thou shalt fear, and him thou shalt serve, (and to him thou shalt cleave.' Deut. 10, 20). It sometimes happens that a man is afraid of his fellow, and when the latter is troublesome to him, leaves him and makes off. But do thou act from love, for where love is there is no fear, and where fear is there is no love, except in relation to (במדת) God only."

It was a moot point whether Job served God from love or from fear. A certain R. Joshua ben Hyrcanus maintained that Job served God purely out of love, proving it by Job 13, 15 and 27, 5, to the great indignation of R. Joshua (ben Hananiah), who broke out: "Who will clear away the dust from thine eyes, Rabban Johanan ben Zakkai, who didst teach all thy days that Job served God only out of fear (Job 1,1), and here is Joshua (ben Hyrcanus), the pupil of thy pupil, teaching that he acted out of love!"[4] R. Meir shows that the two expressions are not exclu-

[1] On this point see the exposition of Maimonides, Hilkot Teshubah 10, 1 ff. Under service from fear he puts everything that has a selfish end in this life or another. It is the religious motive of the ignorant masses, of women and children, who have not yet got far enough to serve God from love.

[2] Soṭah 31a. See Bacher, Tannaiten, II, 425. Cf. Philo, Quod Deus sit immutabilis c. 14 § 69 (ed. Mangey I, 283).

[3] Sifrè Deut. § 32, ed. Friedmann f. 73a; cf. Midrash Tannaim, p. 25.

[4] M. Soṭah 5, 5. Cf. Tos. Soṭah 6, 1, where this view of Job's motive is ascribed, with a different proof-text, to Ben Paṭuri. Bacher, Tannaiten, I, 61.

sive: 'God-fearing' is said of Abraham (Gen. 22, 12), as well as of Job (Job 1, 1). As God-fearing in Abraham's case sprang from love, so also did Job's. For Abraham himself this is proved by Isa. 41, 8, 'The seed of Abraham who loved me.'[1] As evidence that Job's piety was inspired by love R. Nathan quotes Job 13, 16.[2]

Love to God should be the sole motive. So Sifrè on Deut. 11, 13:[3] " 'To love the Lord your God.' Should you say, I will learn Torah that I may become rich, or that I may be called Rabbi, or that I may acquire a reward, the Scripture says, 'To love the Lord your God' — whatever you do, do not do it except from love." The same more at large in a Baraita, quoting Deut. 30, 26: "That a man say not, I will study the Scriptures that men may call me a learned man (חכם), I will study tradition that I may become an elder and sit in the session house;[4] but learn out of love, and honor will come in the end" (Prov. 7, 3; 3, 17; 3, 18).[5]

If it be asked, How shall men love God with all their heart? (Deut. 6, 5), the Scripture answers, 'And let these words which I command thee this day be upon thy heart' (Deut. 6, 6). "Put them upon thy heart (keep them ever in mind), for thence thou shalt recognize God and cleave to his ways."[6]

This is sufficient to exemplify Jewish teaching about the love of God as a motive of virtuous conduct. As an element of Jewish piety we shall recur to the subject in a later chapter.[7]

Thus far we have had to do with motives that are explicit and emphatic in the Scriptures and could not fail to be recognized and applied by the teachers of the Law. The one we have next

See further the discussion in Jer. Soṭah 20c; Jer. Berakot 14b. Note in the latter the place assigned to both motives in accordance with the two commands to love God and to fear Him.

[1] Soṭah 31a.

[2] Tos. Soṭah 6, 1; Jer. Soṭah 20c.

[3] Sifrè Deut. § 41, ed. Friedmann f. 79b–80a.

[4] ישיבה, academy.

[5] Nedarim 62a. With the honor that comes unsought at the end compare Matt. 6, 33.

[6] Sifrè Deut. § 33, ed. Friedmann f. 74a, top.

[7] See Part vii.

to consider is indeed derived from Scripture,[1] but is developed into what may fairly be regarded as the most characteristic feature of Jewish ethics both as principle and as motive, "the hallowing of the Name,"[2] with its opposite, "the profaning of the Name."[3]

The hallowing of the Name is familiar in the beginning of the Lord's Prayer (Matt. 6, 9; Luke 11, 2), and in the same position in the Jewish prayer, Ḳaddish.[4] In both it is followed by the establishment of God's kingdom. But besides prayer that God would cause his name — that is, Himself — to be universally revered as holy, and besides the proclamation of his holiness as in the Trisagion of the liturgy, 'Holy, Holy, Holy, is the Lord of Hosts' (Isa. 6, 3),[5] the Name of God is hallowed by the actions of men. For ancient apprehension, and for primitive apprehension everywhere, the name is not a *flatus vocis*, the accidental appellation by which we designate a person or thing; rather it is the distinctive essence of the thing, so that the name is often equivalent to the thing itself. So it is in biblical language. When God causes his name to dwell in a place (e.g. Deut. 12, 11),[6] it is a way of saying that he himself dwells there, as in 1 Kings 6, 13 (of the place meant in Deuteronomy), 'I will dwell there among the children of Israel.' When God does something 'for his name's sake' it is usually quite the same as for his own sake. Thus in Isa. 48, 9, 'For my name's sake will I defer my anger,' and in verse 11, 'For my own sake, for my own sake will I do it.'[7]

At a certain stage in the religion of Israel, the Holy One was a favorite word for God, and his holiness an equivalent for his

1 See Lev. 22, 32: Ye shall not profane My holy name, and I will be hallowed in the midst of the Israelites; I am the Lord, who hallow you. Cf. Ezek. 22, 26; 36, 20–23; Mal. 1, 11 f.

2 קידוש השם. 3 חילול השם.

4 Authorised Daily Prayers (ed. Singer), pp. 37, 75, 77, 86. I. Abrahams, Companion to the Authorized Daily Prayer Book. Revised edition (1922), pp. xxxix ff. See further, below, pp. 212 f.

5 Ḳedushah. Daily Prayers, l.c. p. 45 (cf. 39).

6 Men of a later age said, 'causes his Shekinah (Presence) to dwell there.'

7 Observe the interchangeableness of the two modes of expression in the Psalms.

deity; and however strong the connotation of moral perfection came to be, this never became, as it is for us, the denotation of the words.[1]

God hallows his own name (himself) by demonstrating his supreme godhead and compelling the nations to acknowledge it. His restoration of exiled Israel is such a demonstration: 'I do not do this for your sake, O house of Israel, but for my holy name,[2] which ye have profaned among the nations whither ye came And I will hallow my great name . . . and the nations shall know that I am the Lord, saith the Lord JHVH, when I shall be hallowed in you before their eyes.'[3] He is hallowed in the destruction of Gog, 'that the nations may know me.'[4]

In the same way God's hallowing of his name was understood by the rabbis. On Deut. 32, 3[5] ('I will proclaim the name of the Lord, give ye greatness to our God') we read in the Sifrè: Our fathers went down to Egypt only in order that the Holy One, blessed is He, might work miracles and do mighty works for the purpose of hallowing his holy name in the world. He inflicted the ten plagues on Pharaoh and on Egypt only because they did not hallow his great name in the world; for at the beginning of the passage he (Pharaoh) says, Who is the Lord (JHVH) that I should hearken to his voice? (Exod. 5, 2), and at the last he says, The Lord (JHVH) is the one who is in the right, and I and my people are the wicked (Exod. 9, 27). The text goes on to assert the same thing of the miracles and mighty deeds God wrought for the fathers at the Red Sea and the Jordan and the valleys of the Arnon — they were all for the purpose of hallowing his name, and accomplished this end by inspiring terror in the kings and people of Palestine (Josh. 5, 1; 2, 10 f.).[6] So also Daniel was cast

[1] Historically, the epithet was not applied to God because he was conceived to be morally perfect, but the meaning of moral perfection attached to the word because such perfection belonged to the character of the Holy One (i.e. of God).

[2] Literally, for my name of Holy One.

[3] Ezek. 36, 22–33. Cf. 20, 41 f.; 28, 25; 39, 27.

[4] Ezek. 38, 16.

[5] Sifrè Deut. § 306 (ed. Friedmann f. 132b.).

[6] Cf. Mekilta, Beshallaḥ 3, near the end.

into the lion's den to hallow God's name, and his safety there leads the king to issue a decree acknowledging Daniel's God (Dan. 6, 26–28). So it was, too, with the three youths in the fiery furnace, whose miraculous deliverance drew from Nebuchadnezzar the decree in Dan. 3, 31.

God 'hallows his name' (makes it holy), therefore, by doing things that lead or constrain men to acknowledge him as God. And as it is God's supreme end that all mankind shall ultimately own and serve him as the true God, so it is the chief end of Israel, to whom he has in a unique manner revealed himself, to hallow his name by living so that men shall see and say that the God of Israel is the true God.[1] This is the meaning of the Ḳiddush ha-Shem, the hallowing of the Name, as the supreme principle and motive of moral conduct in Judaism.[2]

God's holiness is his nature; how then can men 'hallow' Him (make him holy)? This reflection and the solution are the subject of a notable passage in the Sifra on Lev. 19, 2:[3] "'Ye shall be holy.' Be ye separate (*perushim*).[4] 'Ye shall be holy, for I the Lord your God am holy.' As much as to say, If ye make yourselves holy, I impute it to you as though ye hallowed me; and if ye do not make yourselves holy, I impute it to you as though ye did not hallow me. Can the meaning be, If ye make me holy, then I am made holy, and if not, I am not made holy? The Scripture shows, 'For I am holy'—I abide in my holiness, whether ye hallow me or not."[5]

In this sense are to be understood the words of R. Simeon ben Yoḥai: "'Ye are my witnesses, saith the Lord, and I am God' (Isa. 43, 10). When ye are my witnesses, I am God, and when

[1] Cf. Matt. 5, 14–16: Ye are the light of the world. . . . Let your light so shine before men that they may see your good works and glorify your Father which is in heaven.

[2] It is the duty of Israelites only, not of other nations. Jer. Shebi'it 35a, end ('in the midst of the *Israelites*').

[3] A section delivered to the whole congregation, 'because on it depend most of the essentials of the Law.' Above, p. 84.

[4] See on the etymology of the name Pharisees, Vol. I, p. 61.

[5] Sifra, Ḳedoshim, *init.* (ed. Weiss f. 86c).

ye are not my witnesses, I am not God."[1] In the context are found other utterances of similar purport.[2] "When Israel is of one counsel on earth, God's great name is praised in heaven, as it is said, 'And He was king in Jeshurun' (Deut. 33, 5). When? When 'the heads of the people are gathered, the tribes of Israel as one.' When they are made one band (אגודה), not when they are made several bands; and so it says: 'He who built in the heavens his upper stories, and has founded his band (אגודה)[3] on earth'" (Amos 9, 6). R. Simeon ben Yoḥai illustrates this by the figure of a palace built on two boats lashed together, and the consequence if the boats are separated. Similarly, he continues: "'This is my God, and I will make him lovely' (Exod. 15, 2).[4] When I praise him, he is lovely, and when I do not praise him, he is, so to speak, lovely in himself. . . . Again, 'Unto Thee do I lift up my eyes, O Thou that sittest in the heavens' (Psalm 123, 1). Otherwise, I should not be sitting in the heavens."[4]

A less characteristic expression which is a substantially synonymous antithesis to profaning God's name, is to make his name great (magnify his name).[5] Thus, on Exod. 15, 2 ('My father's God, and I will exalt him'), R. Simeon ben Eleazar says: "When the Israelites do the will of God, then his name is made great in the world, as it is said, 'When the kings of the Amorites heard, etc.' (Josh. 5, 1); and so Rahab said to the messengers of Joshua, 'We have heard how the Lord dried up the waters of the Red Sea before you, . . . And as soon as we heard it, our hearts melted, neither did any more spirit remain in any man because of you; for the Lord your God, he is God in heaven above and

[1] Sifrè Deut. § 346; cf. Pesiḳta ed. Buber f. 102b.

[2] A number of striking sayings to the same effect will be found in Midrash Tannaim ed. Hoffmann, p. 72.

[3] English version 'troop.' Targum, 'congregation' (synagogue). Modern interpreters, from the context, 'vault.' See Bacher, Tannaiten, II, 140.

[4] See Mekilta, Shirah 3 (ed. Friedmann f. 37a; ed. Weiss f. 44a). More at length, Shabbat 133b; cf. Nazir 2b.

[5] In the beginning of the Ḳaddish the two words are coupled, יתגדל ויתקדש שמה.

on earth beneath' (Josh. 2, 10 f).[1] And when they do not do his will, his name is, so to speak, profaned in the world, as it is said, 'And when they came unto the nations whither they came, they profaned my holy name' (in that men said of them, These are the people of the Lord, and are gone forth out of the land." Ezek. 36, 20).[2]

The name of God is hallowed by an extraordinary act of charity. A Midrash tells how, when the heathen said that the infant Isaac was not the child of Sarah, but of Hagar, God dried up the breasts of their wives. The ladies came and kissed the dust at Sarah's feet, begging that she would do a good deed and nurse their children. Abraham said to her, Sarah, this is no time for modesty; hallow the name of the Holy One, blessed is He, and sit in the market place and nurse their sons.[3]

It is said that it was the practice of R. Ishmael, when a case came before him for adjudication one of the parties in which was an Israelite and the other a heathen, to give judgment according to whichever law (Jewish or foreign) was the more favorable to the Israelite.[4] This chicanery was condemned by R. Akiba, "because of hallowing the name," i.e., because it reflects dishonor on the religion.[5] A just judgment by R. Jonathan drew from a Roman the exclamation, Blessed is the God of the Jews![6]

But while the Name is hallowed by everything in the conduct of his people that exhibits the superiority of their religion and makes others honor their God, it is supremely hallowed by the devotion which makes men ready to lay down their lives rather than abandon their religion or violate the law of God. R. Johanan (reported by R. Levi) found in Abraham the first example

[1] The same passages cited in the Sifrè, above, p. 104, on the hallowing of the name.

[2] Mekilta, Shirah 3, near the end (ed. Friedmann f. 37b; ed. Weiss f. 44b); Mekilta de-R. Simeon ben Yoḥai on Exod. 15, 2.

[3] Pesiḳta ed. Buber f. 146b. Cf. Gen. R. 53, 9, where the beginning of the story is missing.

[4] Sifrè Deut. § 16, citing Deut. 1, 16b. R. Simeon ben Gamaliel declared this discrimination inadmissible.

[5] Baba Ḳamma 113a, near the end.

[6] Jer. Baba Batra 13c.

of such devotion. When he was cast into the fiery furnace by Nimrod,[1] he hallowed the name of the Holy One and proved steadfast in his trial.[2]

Abraham, according to the legend, was cast into the fire because of his attacks on idolatry and his refusal to worship other gods at the command of Nimrod. It was for the same refusal that the three Jewish youths were cast into Nebuchadnezzar's superheated furnace; for this that Daniel was thrown into the cage of lions. The resistance of the Maccabaean martyrs to eating swine's flesh was to what was understood on all hands to be an overt act of apostasy, as Christians refused to burn incense to the gods or to the images of the emperor. After the rebellion under Hadrian, not only were the observances of the Jewish religion, and especially the teaching of the Law, prohibited in Palestine, but it appears that Jews were in some cases required to prove their loyalty by the performance of some rite of idolatrous worship. The generation of the persecution gave their lives for the hallowing of the Name.[3]

The number of those who got into the clutches of the law by one violation of the edict or another became so great that a council at Lydda decided that, under duress, to save his life, a Jew might transgress any article of the law except idolatry, incest and other sexual sins, and homicide.[4] R. Ishmael, on this point at variance with his colleagues, held that even an idolatrous act might, under such circumstances, be done, provided it was

[1] For the story see Gen. R. 38, near the end (§ 13). See L. Ginzberg, The Legends of the Jews, I, 198 ff.

[2] Tanḥuma ed. Buber, Lek leka § 2; (Abraham says) I will give my life for the hallowing of the Name. Num. R. 1, 12.

[3] Pesiḳta ed. Buber f. 87a. As in the persecution by Antiochus IV, there seems to be no certain evidence that the edicts were enforced upon Jews in other countries, say in Rome or in Egypt. They were a retaliation for the revolt of Palestine.

[4] Sanhedrin 74a, middle; Jer. Sanhedrin 21b, above; Jer. Shebi'it 35a, below. Some rabbis, however, notably Akiba and Ḥanina ben Teradion, held themselves bound by what we might call professional ethics to defy the prohibition of teaching and take the consequences. See 'Martyrdom, Restriction of,' Jewish Encyclopedia, VIII, 853 f.

in private,[1] on the principle, so often cited, that the Law was given that a man should live by it (Lev. 18, 5), not die by it. If, however, the act was done openly, all were agreed that a Jew should resign himself to death rather than yield to such a demand: 'Ye shall not profane my holy name, and I will be hallowed among the Israelites, I am the Lord that hallow you' (Lev. 22, 32).[2] The Sifra adds: "'And I will be hallowed.' If ye hallow my name, I will hallow my name through your instrumentality. As Hananiah, Mishael, and Azariah did, when all the heathen were prostrate before the idol, but they were standing straight as palm trees. . . . I said . . . This day I will be exalted in them in the eyes of the heathen who deny the Law; this day will I punish their enemies for their sake."[3]

In their case God hallowed his own name by a miracle; but when in Trajan's time, the brothers Lullianus and Pappus were tauntingly asked why, if they were of the people of Hananiah, Mishael, and Azariah, their God did not come and deliver them as he delivered the three youths from Nebuchadnezzar, they replied that Hananiah and his comrades were perfectly righteous and worthy that a miracle should be wrought for them, while they themselves deserved of God death.[4] It is the way of the martyrs of all faiths to justify God's justice in dealing thus with them; we shall find other Jewish examples further on.[5]

In Lev. 22, 32 ('Ye shall not profane my holy name; and I will be hallowed among the children of Israel; I am the Lord who hallow you'), the words, 'I will be hallowed,' etc., could be taken to mean, 'Give thyself up (to the persecutors)and hallow my name.' This interpretation is set aside, and a decision is cited: "If a man gives himself up in the expectation of a miracle's being wrought for him, no miracle is wrought for him; and if with no

[1] Sifra, Aḥarè Pereḳ 13 (ed. Weiss f. 86b).
[2] Sanhedrin, 74a; 'Abodah Zarah 27b; Sifra, l. c.
[3] Cf. Tanḥuma ed. Buber, Noah § 15.
[4] Ta'anit 18b. On these martyrs see S. Krauss in Jewish Encyclopedia, IX, 512.
[5] See Sifrè Deut. § 307 (Ḥanina ben Teradion and his wife).

such expectation, a miracle is wrought for him," as in the case of Hananiah, Mishael, and Azariah (Dan. 3, 24,30).[1]

The opposite of the hallowing of the Name is the profanation of the Name (*ḥillūl ha-Shem*).[2] It includes every act or word of a Jew which disgraces his religion and so reflects dishonor upon God. The world judges religions by the lives of those who profess them — the tree by its fruits. It was thus that the Jews judged other religions; the vices of the heathen prove the nullity of the religions which tolerated such behavior, and even encouraged it by the examples of their gods. A favorite topic of Jewish apologetic was the superiority of Jewish morals, not merely in precept but in practice, and they argued from it the superiority of their religion, thus inviting a retaliation which the heathen world let them experience in full measure. Individuals, sects, religions, which profess to be better than others must always expect to have their conduct observed with peculiar scrutiny and censured with peculiar severity.

The Jews had therefore especial reason for precaution against giving an only too welcome occasion for such strictures. This is the significance of the warnings against the profanation of the Name. The climax in an enumeration of the five kinds of sinners for whom there is no forgiveness is, "every one who has resting on him the guilt of profaning the Name."[3] R. Ishmael taught that while all other classes of sins are atoned for, according to their heinousness, by repentance, the Day of Atonement, chastisements cumulatively, not all together suffice to atone for the man through whom the Name is profaned; such guilt is only wiped out by the day of death.[4] God forgives every thing else;

[1] Sifra, Emor Pereḳ 9 (ed. Weiss f. 99d, top).

[2] An example of the antithesis, Jer. Sanhedrin 23d, middle, where it is also said that in a conflict of obligation the positive commandment to hallow the Name takes precedence of the prohibition of profaning it.

[3] Abot de-R. Nathan c. 39 (beginning). Bacher, Tannaiten, I, 270 f., finds grounds for attributing the list to Akiba.

[4] Tos. Yom ha-Kippurim 5, 6–8; Yoma, 86a. See Vol. I, p. 546, and Bacher, Tannaiten, I, 250.

the profaning of the Name He punishes at once.[1] "If a man profanes the Name of Heaven in secret, he will be requited openly. In the profanation of the Name, there is no distinction of inadvertent and presumptuous." [2]

It is unnecessary to specify applications of the criterion of conduct given in the principle of profaning the Name, but an illustration or two from different spheres may be in place. The name of God may be profaned through erroneous teaching. A master of the days of the last Asmonaeans warned his hearers: "Scholars, be cautious in your words, lest ye incur the penalty of exile, and ye be exiled to a place where the waters are bad, and your disciples who follow you drink of them and die, and it come to pass that the name of Heaven is profaned." [3] R. Yannai somewhat hyperbolically sees a profanation of the Name when one scholar attains such repute that his colleagues are put to shame.[4] To rob (defraud) a Gentile is worse than to rob an Israelite 'on account of the profanation of the Name' [5] — the Israelite lays the wrong to the individual, the Gentile blames the religion. Similarly in the case of lost property of a 'Canaanite' (heathen inhabitant of Palestine), which under a strict construction of the law in Deut. 22, 3 ('thy brother's') an Israelite was not required to return to the owner, Phineas ben Jair held that if this would give occasion to the profanation of the Name, the finder was forbidden to keep it.[6]

The injunction, 'Ye shall be holy; for I, the Lord your God, am holy' (Lev. 19, 2) suggests a likeness between the holiness of God by nature and the holiness of character which men are to strive after.[7] This holiness may be conceived as separateness, as

[1] Sifrè Deut. § 328. This is the meaning also of Ḳiddushin 40a, below: In the profanation of the Name, whether inadvertent or presumptuous, the account is not allowed to run up.

[2] Abot 4, 4. Johanan ben Beroḳah.

[3] Abṭalion. Abot 1, 11.

[4] Yoma 86a. To put a fellow to shame is a great sin; see below, pp. 147 f.

[5] Tos. Baba Ḳamma 10, 15.

[6] Baba Ḳamma 113b.

[7] On the Imitation of God, see I. Abrahams, Pharisaism and the Gospels, Second Series, pp. 138–182. For Philo, see the references in James Drummond, Philo Judaeus, II, 286 f.

in the Sifra on Lev. 19, 2 quoted above:[1] "'Ye shall be holy.' Be ye separate (*perūshīm*)." On Lev. 11, 44 ('For I am the Lord your God; hallow yourselves, therefore, and be ye holy; for I am holy') the same Midrash has: "As I am holy, so are ye holy; as I am separate, so be ye separate (*perūshīm*)."[2] Here the likeness of God is in purity. More frequently, however, in rabbinical literature, it is God in his gracious character that is commended to men's imitation. The vexed word אנוהו in Exod. 15, 2,[3] was interpreted by Abba Saul: "I will imitate Him. As He is merciful and gracious, be thou also merciful and gracious."[4] To the same effect, on Lev. 19, 2, he said: "What is the duty of a king's train? To imitate the king (do as the king does)." [5] The character of God proclaimed in Exod. 34, 6, the first words of which are quoted by Abba Saul in the former of these two sayings, is set before men for their imitation in several places. Thus on Deut. 10, 12, the sum of what God requires: "'To walk in all His ways.' These are the ways of the Holy One, as it is said: 'The Lord, the Lord, a God merciful and gracious, slow to anger, and abundant in goodness and truth; keeping lovingkindness to thousands (of generations), forgiving iniquity and transgression and sin, and clearing' (Exod. 34, 6).[6] And it says, 'Every one who is called [7] by the name of the Lord shall be delivered' (Joel 3, 5). How is it possible for a man to be called by the name of the Holy One? Nay, as God is called merciful and gracious, so

[1] Page 103.

[2] Sifra, Shemini Pereḳ 12 (ed. Weiss f. 57b). In the context, 'apart from uncleanness.' See also Lev. 20, 26, and Sifra, Kedoshim Pereḳ 11 end (f. 93d).

[3] זה אלהי ואנוהו. See above, p. 104.

[4] Mekilta, Shirah 3 (ed. Friedmann f. 37a; ed. Weiss f. 44a); Mekilta de-R .Simeon ben Yoḥai ed. Hoffmann p. 60 "הִדַּמֵּה"; Jer. Peah 15b (אדמה); Shabbat 133b. Rashi on Shabbat l.c. supposes Abba Saul to have resolved the word into אני והוא, "I and He," by the method called Notarikon on which see Bacher, Terminologie, I, 125 f. See Abrahams, *op. cit.*, pp. 174–176.

[5] Sifra, Ḳedoshim, *init.* (ed. Weiss 86c, below).

[6] The quotation breaks off short, stopping before the ominous words 'he will not clear the guilty.'

[7] Our versions, with the Massoretic text, 'Whoever shall call on the name,' etc. The Midrash would pronounce the verb as a passive.

do thou also be merciful and gracious and give gifts freely to all; as the Holy One is called righteous — as it is said, 'Righteous is the Lord in all his ways and kindly (*ḥasid*) in all his works' (Psalm 145, 17) — so be thou also righteous; as the Holy One is called kindly in all his works, so be thou also kindly. Therefore it is said, 'Every one who is called by the name of the Lord shall be delivered.' And it says, 'Every one that is called by my name, for my glory I have created him, formed him, yea made him' (Isa. 43, 7). And it says, 'The Lord made every thing for his own sake'" (Prov. 16, 4).[1]

R. Ḥama ben Ḥanina said: "What does the Scripture mean which says, 'After the Lord your God ye shall walk.' Is it possible for a man to walk after the Presence (Shekinah)? Is it not said, 'For the Lord thy God is a devouring fire'? Nay, but to walk after the attributes of the Holy One (imitate his character). As he clothes the naked (Gen. 3, 21), so do thou clothe the naked. He visits the sick (Gen. 18, 1); do thou also visit the sick. He comforts mourners (Gen. 25, 11); do thou also comfort mourners. He buries the dead (Deut. 34, 6); do thou also bury the dead."[2]

[1] Sifrè Deut. § 49.
[2] Soṭah 14a. Cf. Vol. I, p. 441.

CHAPTER III

DUTIES TO RULERS

In Plato and Aristotle ethics stand in the closest connection with politics. The individual with whom they are concerned is thought of as a citizen of a Greek city, actual or ideal. His rights and duties are related not only to individuals of his own status or another, or to a social aggregation of such individuals, but to the state as an organic whole. In Judaism the conditions of such an association did not exist. The Jews had for centuries been under foreign rule — Babylonian, Persian, Ptolemaic, Seleucid, and finally Roman. From the beginning of the sixth century, through deportation, colonization, and emigration, they were in ever increasing numbers widely dispersed in other countries, East and West. The home land, a shrunken Judaea whose limits in all directions were visible from the heights about Jerusalem, was a petty subdivision of an outlying province.

The general policy of the empires which succeeded one another in dominion left to the Jews a large measure of autonomy in their own affairs, much as the Turkish empire since the fifteenth century did with the subject Christian populations in its territory. If the tribute assessed on Judaea was punctually paid into the treasury, the empire concerned itself little about how the Jews managed the rest. The high priest and the council of elders had, therefore, large authority, and were upheld in it by the central government, which, on the other hand, held them responsible for the collection and rendering of the tribute, and the maintenance of order.[1]

It is evident that under such conditions there was no place for the political virtues in fact or in theory; submission is the one virtue of the subject of an absolute power.

[1] Our testimony comes from the Greek period, but it is probable that a similar policy was pursued by the Persians. The Roman system was different.

The outcome of the conflict which Antiochus Epiphanes provoked by the desecration of the temple and the interdiction of the Jewish religion was the creation of an autonomous Judaean state under the Asmonaean dynasty, whose priestly rulers eventually assumed the title King, and by conquest brought under their dominion for a time a territory as wide as the ancient Davidic kingdom. This period of independence lasted eighty years and was ended by Pompey in the year 63 B.C. The liberation of Judaea from the yoke of foreign rule it had borne so long, and the subsequent expansion over the old Land of Israel, was naturally accompanied by an exaltation of the national spirit; but, on the other hand, the political aims and worldly policies of the Asmonaean princes alienated from them the religious leaders and their following among the people.

When Pompey gave a hearing at Damascus to the rival claims of Aristobulus and Hyrcanus II, representatives of the people appeared against them both, seeking the abolition of kingly rule, and the restoration of their ancient constitution under which they were governed by the priests.[1] The feeling of the Pharisees toward the Asmonaean princes is well illustrated by the second of the Psalms of Solomon, which denounces them as usurpers and accuses them of every kind of evil. It was for their crimes that God permitted his sanctuary to be desecrated by the entrance of Pompey. Herod, king of Judaea by the grace of the Romans, was in the eyes of the Jews a foreign ruler. The heads of the Pharisees, Sameas and Pollio, used their influence to bring the people to submit to him, and were honored by him; but when he demanded of the Jews an oath of allegiance, they and most of their disciples refused, and the king was wise enough to let it pass.[2]

Fidelity to their religion and the authority of the interpreters of the Law had completely displaced political loyalty and the sense of civic duty. The principle which Paul lays down in Rom.

[1] Josephus, Antt. xiv. 3, 2 § 41.
[2] Josephus, Antt. xv. 10, 3 § 370; see also xvii. 2, 4 § 42.

13, 1 ff. expresses the general attitude of the Jewish teachers: 'Let every one be in subjection to the authorities that are set over him; for no authority exists unless by God's will, and those that actually exist have been appointed by him, so that one who arrays himself against the authority puts himself in opposition to the ordinance of God, and those who oppose this will bring on themselves (God's) judgment.' But to this broad principle they made one exception: If rulers command their subjects to do what is forbidden by their religion or forbid them to do what it requires, they are not to be obeyed — God is to be obeyed rather than men — and may be resisted.

The kings of this earth rule by the appointment of Heaven.[1] In the time of persecution under Hadrian, R. Jose ben Ḳisma asserted this particularly of the Romans in a warning addressed to Ḥanina ben Teradion:[2] "You know, my brother, that this people (the Romans) has been given the kingdom by Heaven, for it has ruined his house, and burnt his temple, and slain his pious ones and destroyed his good men, and still it stands."[3] This was but the application to the present of the consistent teaching of the prophets, most conspicuously of Jeremiah about Nebuchadnezzar.[4]

It was probably while the rebellion that broke out in the year 66 was brewing that R. Ḥanina, the prefect[5] of the priesthood, uttered his warning, "Pray for the welfare of the government, for if it were not for the fear of it, men would swallow one another up alive" — words that are an ominous prevision of what actually happened in the war and the siege of Jerusalem by the Romans. A later rabbi quotes this saying in connection with Hab. 1, 14 ('And thou makest man like the fishes of the sea'): "As it is with the fishes in the sea, the one that is bigger than

[1] See Berakot 58a.

[2] Ḥanina disregarded the warning and the edict against teaching, and became one of the martyrs. Sifrè Deut. § 307; 'Abodah Zarah 17b–18a.

[3] 'Abodah Zarah 18a.

[4] E.g. Jer. cc. 34–39. Cf. Syriac Baruch 1, 1–4; cc. 6–8; Pesiḳta Rabbati, ed. Friedmann f. 131a.

[5] *Sagan.*

another swallows the other up,[1] so with human kind; were it not for fear of the government everyone that is greater than his fellow would swallow him up. This is what Ḥanina, the prefect of the priesthood said, Pray for the welfare of the government, for were it not for the fear of the government, a man would swallow up his neighbor alive." [2]

Here again Jeremiah had shown the way: 'Seek the welfare of the city whither I have caused you to be carried away captive, and pray unto the Lord for it; for in its welfare shall ye have welfare' (Jer. 29, 7).[3]

As a matter of fact, sacrifices for foreign rulers were an immemorial custom,[4] and were doubtless accompanied by prayers for their welfare.[5] The stopping of the offering for the emperor in 66 A.D. was, as Josephus observes, equivalent to a declaration of war.[6]

Even after the war under Hadrian, R. Simeon ben Laḳish found in the repeated, 'And behold it was very good' in Gen. 1, an intimation of the mission of Rome. " 'And behold it was very good.' This is the kingdom of Heaven (the divine government of the world). 'And behold it was very good.' This is the earthly kingdom. Is then the earthly kingdom very good? Yes, for it exacts justice of mankind. As it is said, 'I made the earth, and created man upon it' " (Isa. 45, 12).[7]

These utterances are to be understood in the light of the circumstances which gave occasion for them. Both the heads of the priesthood in Jerusalem and the leading Pharisees were opposed to the rebellion of the year 66. Ḥanina, the prefect of the

[1] Cf. Hab. 1, 13.
[2] 'Abodah Zarah 4a.
[3] Cf. Baruch 1, 11f.; 1 Tim. 2, 1 f.
[4] See I Macc. 7, 33; Philo, Legatio ad Gaium c. 23 § 152 f.; c. 45 §§ 355–357.
[5] Yoma 69a, below. Josephus Bell. Jud. ii. 10, 4 § 197.
[6] Bell. Jud. ii. 17, 2; cf. Giṭṭin 56a, top. See Schürer, Geschichte des jüdischen Volkes, II, 302–304.
[7] Gen. R. 9, near the end. Instead of *adam*, 'man,' the author pronounced *edom* (Edom–Rome), 'I created Rome over it.' See Theodor's note.

priesthood, doubtless expressed the well-grounded apprehensions of both classes. Johanan ben Zakkai is said to have predicted the calamitous outcome of the war, and during the siege of Jerusalem, like Jeremiah in a similar situation in the days of Nebuchadnezzar, counseled peace with the Romans as the only salvation. When the strife of factions in the doomed city destroyed all hope, he made his escape to the camp of the besiegers, and got permission from Vespasian to establish himself at Jamnia,[1] where even before the fall of the city he was laying the ground for the restoration of Judaism.

The situation under Hadrian was different. Whether the rebellion was provoked by the prohibition of circumcision or by the emperor's purpose to erect a heathen temple on the site of the ruined temple of the Lord, it was in defence of their religion that the Jews rose, and some of the most prominent rabbis of the time were zealous for the war, Akiba even acclaiming Simeon bar Kozibah as the Star out of Jacob [2] of Num. 24, 17–19, who should triumph over Edom (Rome). The event proved to Jose ben Ḳisma that the empire had been given to the Romans by God, and that defiance of their edicts was inviting doom, and Simeon ben Laḳish could find its administration of justice intimated in the 'very good' of Gen. 1.

The duty and the limits of obedience are defined in the Tanḥuma on Gen. 8, 16, after Eccles. 8, 2 ('I [counsel thee], keep the king's commands, and that on account of the oath of God'): God said to Israel, I adjure you that if the government imposes on you harsh decrees, you do not rebel against it, whatever it decrees. But if it decrees that you shall nullify the Law and the commandments, do not listen to it, but say to it, I will keep the king's command in everything necessary to you, but 'on account of the

[1] There is a story that at this interview he foretold to Vespasian that he should become emperor. Abot de-R. Nathan 4, 5. Josephus attributes to himself a similar prediction. Bell. Jud. iii. 8, 9; cf. Suetonius, Vespasian 5.

[2] Hence the name Bar Cocheba in Christian writers. The point lies in vs. 18, Edom (Rome) shall be conquered, etc.

oath of God,' . . . 'do not stand in an evil thing' (Eccles. 8, 3); for they are not stopping you from the commandments, but making you deny God; therefore, 'on account of the oath of God.' This is what Hananiah, Mishael, and Azariah did when Nebuchadnezzar set up the image, etc. (Dan. 3, 13–18). They said to him, whatever you impose upon us, levy of produce (*annona*), duties and tolls, or poll-tax, we will obey thee; but to deny the Lord, we will not obey thee, 'on account of the oath of God.'[1]

The most striking historical illustration of this attitude is the protest of the Jews against the statue of Caligula which the emperor had ordered Petronius, the governor of the province of Syria, to install in the temple in Jerusalem, by force if necessary. The Jews appealed to their law, which forbade an image of God, much more of a man, not only in the temple but anywhere in the land. They offered sacrifices for the emperor twice every day; but if he insisted on setting up images, he would first have to sacrifice the whole Jewish nation; they were ready to offer themselves for the slaughter with their wives and children.[2]

The arbitrary and extortionate exactions of the collectors of octroi tolls (מוכסים), who were not inaptly classed with highwaymen, early gave rise to casuistical discussion of the permissibility of deceiving them by representing the goods as the portion set apart for the priests (Terumah) or as belonging to the government; and even of fortifying the declaration by an oath, a point on which the schools of Shammai and Hillel were divided in the first century of our era.[3] In the Talmud this is held not to apply to officers appointed by the government to collect a fixed tariff on the goods, on the general principle later formulated by Mar Samuel,[4] "The law of the state is law."[5] This

[1] Tanḥuma ed. Buber, Noah § 10; cf. § 15.

[2] Josephus, Bell. Jud. ii. 10, 4.

[3] M. Nedarim 3, 4.

[4] Head of the school at Nehardea in Babylonia in the first half of the third century.

[5] Nedarim 28a; cf. Baba Ḳamma 113a. See Maimonides, Hilkot Gezelah 5, 11 ff.

laconic dictum, in its manifold application, has governed the relation of the Jews to the laws of the countries in which they have lived. In the same sense Jesus answered the question whether it was lawful to pay taxes to the Romans: 'Render unto Caesar what belongs to Caesar, and to God what belongs to God.'[1] But Samuel's pronouncement was of wider scope, and carried authority.

[1] Matt. 22, 21. See I. Abrahams, Pharisaism and the Gospels, I, 62.

CHAPTER IV

THE FAMILY

MARRIAGE was regarded not only as the normal state, but as a divine ordinance. It was a generally accepted opinion that the world was created for the multiplication of the species (Gen. 1, 26), alleging Isa. 45, 18, 'He created it not a waste; to be inhabited He formed it.'[1] On Gen. 2, 18 ('It is not good that man should be alone; I will make him a helper corresponding to him') the Midrash collects sayings of various rabbis about the things that the unmarried man lacks. R. Jacob says: "One who has no wife remains without good, and without a helper, and without joy, and without a blessing, and without atonement," and adduces scripture for all these deficiencies. Others add without peace (welfare) and without life. Another[2] says, He is not a whole man,[3] for it is said, And He blessed *them*, and He called *their* name, 'man' (Gen. 5, 1). The two of them together were called 'man.' Others still say that the unmarried man diminishes the likeness (of God), 'In the image of God He made the man, and thereafter, 'And do ye (plural) increase and multiply.'[4]

Celibacy was, in fact, not common, and was disapproved by the rabbis, who taught that a man should marry at eighteen, and that if he passed the age of twenty without taking a wife he transgressed a divine command and incurred God's displeasure.[5] Postponement of marriage was permitted students of the Law that they might concentrate their attention on their studies, free

[1] M. Eduyot 1, 13.

[2] R. Ḥiyya ben Gamda.

[3] Similarly R. Eleazar (ben Pedat): He is not a man, as it is said, Male and female created He them, and called *their* name 'man.' Yebamot 63a.

[4] Gen. R. 17, 2; cf. Yebamot 62b, below, and 63a, b. The last inference was drawn by several teachers of the second century. Tos. Yebamot 8, end; Yebamot 63b, end; Gen. R. 34, 8 f. Bacher, Tannaiten, I, 408.

[5] R. Ishmael, Ḳiddushin 29b, end.

from the cares of supporting a wife.[1] Cases like that of Simeon ben 'Azzai, who never married, were evidently infrequent. He had himself said that a man who did not marry was like one who shed blood,[2] and diminished the likeness of God. One of his colleagues threw up to him that he was better at preaching than at practicing, to which he replied, What shall I do? My soul is enamored of the Law; the population of the world can be kept up by others.[3] Whether the commandment to marry applied to women was disputed;[4] the decision was in the negative.

It is not to be imagined that pronouncements about the duty of marrying and the age at which people should marry actually regulated practice. A man must be able to support a wife before he takes one, and no fixed age could be set for the fulfilment of that condition. Early marriages were, however, favored for sound moral and social reasons. The institution of marriage had for its object children, and this was, as we have seen, the motive expressed in the Law.[5] For girls there were no independent careers to compete with motherhood; and to remain unmarried or to have no offspring was a bitter misfortune.

Stress is laid upon parity of rank in a society which set great store by family and station;[6] but it is not wise to take a wife of superior rank — rather go down a step in the scale in choosing a wife.[7] There is a good deal of similar worldly wisdom about the whole subject of marriage, as there is in Proverbs and Sirach, which has no bearing on our present theme. The catalogue of prohibited degrees of kinship, based on Lev. 18, 6–18

[1] In general a man should pursue his studies and then marry; but if he cannot get along without a wife, he may marry, and study afterwards. Tos. Bekorot 6, 10; Yoma 72b; Menaḥot 110a; Ḳiddushin 29b. In the last two passages a Babylonian ruling is recorded, that a man should marry first, and study afterwards.

[2] He took the life of his potential offspring. Yebamot 63b, end.

[3] Yebamot l.c.; Tos. Yebamot 8, end.

[4] M. Yebamot 6, 6; Yebamot 65b.

[5] Another reason for marrying, corresponding to Paul's counsel, 1 Cor. 7, 2 (cf. 9), Maimonides, Ishshut 15, 3.

[6] Ḳiddushin 49a.

[7] Yebamot 63a, below.

(cf. 20, 11–21), was extended by the rabbinical authorities by the inclusion of 'secondary relations,' on the principle "make a precautionary regulation in addition to my regulation" (Lev. 18,30),[1] and R. Ḥiyya introduced 'tertiaries.' Most of these are, however, so many steps up or down in the generations that they have no practical importance.[2] It may be mentioned that marriage of cousins-german was not barred, and that the marriage of a man to his niece (especially his sister's daughter) is approved.[3] There were other restrictions in the Law, and special rules for priests which need not be recounted here.

Marriages were usually arranged by the parents of the parties. It was one of the duties of a father to give his son a wife, and to get a husband for his daughter as soon as she was old enough to be wedded.[4] Betrothal [5] was a formal act by which the woman became legally the man's wife; unfaithfulness on her part was adultery and punishable as such; if the relation was dissolved a bill of divorce was required. Some time elapsed after the bridegroom claimed the fulfilment of the agreement [6] before the bride was taken to her husband's house [7] and the marriage consummated; [8] preparations had to be made on both sides. The term

[1] Yebamot 21a; 22a.

[2] See Jewish Encyclopedia, 'Incest,' VI, 572–574, with a table of prohibited degrees.

[3] Yebamot 62b–63a; Tos. Ḳiddushin 1, 4. The Damascene sect regarded this connection as incestuous, as did the Samaritans and the Karaites. See L. Ginzberg, Eine unbekannte jüdische Sekte, pp. 31 f. — It may be added that marriage with a deceased wife's sister was unobjectionable. R. Tarfon contracted such a marriage on the funeral day. Jer. Yebamot 6b.

[4] M. Ḳiddushin 2, 1. A proverb ran: When a daughter is adult, free your slave and give him to her (rather than let her remain longer unmarried). Pesaḥim 113a. Cf. Ecclus. 7, 24 f. — On the forms and ceremonies of marriage see Jewish Encyclopedia, s.v.; S. Krauss, Talmudische Archäologie, II, 24 ff.

[5] ארוסין.

[6] A girl might be betrothed by her father while still a minor (*ḳeṭannah*) (under twelve years and a day), and if the contract was dissolved a bill of divorce was necessary. On the circumstances under which the betrothal (or marriage) could be annulled by the girl, see Jewish Encyclopedia s.v. 'Miun', VIII, 623 f., and references there.

[7] נשואין.

[8] According to M. Ketubot 5, 2, twelve months was the normal interval in the case of a maiden, thirty days in the case of a widow.

employed for betrothal, *ḳiddushin*, has religious associations; it is an act by which the woman is, so to speak, consecrated to her husband, set apart for him exclusively.[1]

Polygamy was legitimate under the Mosaic law, not only with women of the husband's status but with bondwomen, and the rabbinical law corresponds.[2] In our epoch it was evidently not common among Palestinian Jews. Our information is largest about the learned class, and among them convincing instances of polygamous marriages are at least very rare.[3] The Gospels and the whole Tannaite literature evidently suppose a practically monogamous society. The great mass of the people, indeed, lived in circumstances which precluded polygamy. The rabbinical institution of the marriage contract and settlement [4] operated not only as a check upon the freedom of divorce but upon plural marriages.

The law of divorce in Deut. 24, 1 contained a restriction of the natural right of the man to put out of his house a wife who did not please him: he must give her a written certificate that he had no further rights in her, and that consequently she was free to marry another.[5] The formalities of the rabbinical law regarding the drafting, attesting, and service of this instrument [6] involved a measure of delay which may sometimes have given time for the husband to get over a fit of temper and change his mind. Even after the bill of divorce (*gēṭ*) had been delivered, there was no hindrance to a reunion by consent, unless suspicion of unfaithfulness was the ground or the woman in the meantime had been married to another. A more effective restraint was the

[1] קידש אשה.

[2] The Damascene sect condemns the religious authorities in Judaea for permitting a man to take a second wife while the first was living, see Vol. I, p. 202.

[3] The case of R. Tarfon (Tos. Ketubot 5, 1) is not in point. Bacher, Tannaiten, I, 343.

[4] Ketubah.

[5] The requirement of a bill of divorce is presumed by this law, not created by it.

[6] See Maimonides, Hilkot Gerushin 1, 1 ff.

fact that the sum he settled on his wife at marriage had to be paid to her if he divorced her. It was a lien on his whole estate, and collectible by legal process.[1] From this obligation, or any part of it, a wife could not release her husband,[2] but she could forfeit her right to the fulfilment of the contract by certain kinds of misconduct.[3] Malachi 2, 16 was taken by R. Johanan to mean, Hateful (to God) is the man who puts away his wife (cf. vs. 14);[6] but the same words are interpreted by R. Judah, If you hate her, put her away.[4] R. Ḥanina (ben Papa) deduced from the same passage ('the God of Israel,' vs. 16) that only in Israel has divorce a religious sanction.[5] R. Eleazar, from vss. 14 and 16, that the very altar drops tears on every one who divorces his first wife ('the wife of his youth,' vs. 14).[6]

But however the rabbis might disapprove of divorce and seek to impose restraints upon it, the law in Deut. 24, 1 recognized the man's right to dismiss his wife: 'If a man takes a wife and has intercourse with her, and she does not please him[7] because he finds in her some unseemly thing, and he writes for her a bill of divorcement and delivers into her hand, and sends her out of his house,' etc.[8]

In the first century the schools of Shammai and of Hillel differed about what constituted under this law a legitimate ground of divorce.[9] The former admitted only the discovery of unchas-

[1] The liability for the payment of the Ketubah is said to have been introduced by Simeon ben Shaṭaḥ, in the first century before our era. Tos. Ketubot 12, 1; Ketubot 82b. For an illustration of the way this worked in preventing divorce see the story of R. Jose the Galilean, Gen. R. 17, 3. He was unable to pay his insolent wife the sum for which he was obligated, until a colleague gave him the money. [2] M. Ketubot 5, 1.

[3] M. Ketubot 7, 6; Ketubot 72a–b; cf. Giṭṭin 90a–b.

[4] Bacher surmises that this was Judah son of Ḥiyya. Pal. Amoräer, I, 49, n. 3.

[5] See Bacher, Pal. Amoräer, II, 524, n. 2, for other references and the variants. Strack–Billerbeck on Matt. 5, 31 (I, 312).

[6] Giṭṭin 90b. Eleazar ben Pedat.

[7] Cf. vs. 3, If her later husband hates her.

[8] On this whole subject see Strack-Billerbeck, Kommentar zum Neuen Testament aus Talmud und Midrasch, on Matt. 5, 32.

[9] M. Giṭṭin 9, 10; Sifrè Deut. § 269.

tity; the latter not that alone but less serious faults, even down to scorching her husband's food.[1] The controversy turned on the interpretation of the phrase rendered above 'unseemly thing.' The school of Hillel interpreted 'unchastity *or* something (else)'; the school of Shammai as if the words were transposed, 'matter of unchastity.'[2] Akiba, from the words, 'if she does not please him' (lit. 'find favor in his eyes') inferred that a man might divorce his wife if he found another fairer than she.

Whatever may be thought of the exegetical argument of the school of Hillel in this particular, the conclusion is unquestionably in accordance with the older interpretation of the verse,[3] and eventually the Halakah of the school of Hillel, in this as in other controverted matters, became the rabbinical law.

These deliverances of the schools of Shammai and Hillel are often compared with the answer of Jesus to the question of certain Pharisees whether it was a man's right to divorce his wife for whatever cause — Hillel's position.[4] Jesus bases his reply, not on an interpretation of Deut. 24, 1, but on Gen. 1, 27[5] together with 2, 24, and brands as adultery the union of either the

[1] Bad cooking is a more serious ground for divorce than some modern ones. It is possible, however, that the expression is proverbial in some other meaning.

[2] The arguments are set out in the Baraita, Giṭṭin 90a (translated in Strack-Billerbeck, I, 313 f.); cf. Sifrè Deut. § 219–269. Cf. Jer. Soṭah 16b. The phrase ערות דבר occurs besides only in Deut. 23, 15, in a context in which 'unchastity' is out of the question: excrement lying about uncovered in the camp is 'an indecency of a thing' (appositional genitive), that is an indecent thing.

[3] Cf. Josephus Antt. iv. 8, 23 § 253; *καθ' ἁσδηποτοῦν αἰτίας, πολλαὶ δ' ἂν τοῖς ἀνθρώποις τοιαῦται γίνοιντο, κ.τ.λ.* Philo, De spec. legg., iii. 5 § 30, *καθ' ἣν ἂν τύχῃ πρόφασιν.* The Septuagint renders *ὅτι εὗρεν ἐν αὐτῇ ἄσχημον πρᾶγμα*, and there is no record of a different interpretation in the subsequent Jewish versions. Vulgate, *propter aliquam foeditatem.* Cf. Deut. 23, 15, *ἀσχημοσύνη πράγματος* (vs. 14, *καλύψεις τὴν ἀσχημοσύνην σου* — צאתך).

[4] Matt. 19, 3 ff.; Mark 10, 2 ff. Cf. Matt. 5, 31 f.; Luke 16, 18. — In Matt. 5, 32, *παρεκτὸς λόγου πορνείας* is verbatim Shammai's formulation (דבר ערוה, by transposition of the ערות דבר of Deut. 24, 1), as noted above.

[5] The Damascene sect quoted these words, together with Gen. 7, 15, and Deut. 17, 17, in support of their condemnation of polygamy. Schechter, Documents of Jewish Sectaries, I. Hebrew text p. 4, ll. 20 ff. That they did not exclude divorce, see L. Ginzberg, Eine unbekannte jüdische Sekte, p. 26.

husband who has divorced his wife or the divorced woman with a second partner.[1] His own disciples were so impressed by the unhappy case a man might find himself in if marriage was to be an indissoluble bond that they felt it would be safer not to marry at all. In setting these utterances by the side of those of Hillel and Shammai, it should be remembered that they were jurisconsults called upon to pronounce authoritatively what the law was; while Jesus, having no such authority or responsibility, undertook to say what, on ideal principles, the law ought to be, Moses to the contrary notwithstanding.

Divorce was not only a right, but in some cases a duty. After the death penalty for adultery had ceased to be enforced and the ordeal of jealousy was done away by Rabban Johanan ben Zakkai, it was the duty of a husband to divorce a wife whom he suspected of unchastity, but in such a divorce she retained her right to the marriage settlement and dowry. In this case the husband could not remarry her. In a case of proved adultery the husband was required by the court to divorce her even if he was willing to condone the offense. Barrenness was a ground for divorce, and if after ten years of married life a wife bore no child, it was the duty of the husband, in compliance with the commandment, Be fruitful and multiply, to take another wife.[2] A woman divorced under these circumstances received the marriage settlement and was free to marry again. In Jewish law a woman could not divorce her husband, but she could sue for divorce in the courts, which would for certain causes require him to give her a bill of divorce. Such causes were impotence, denial of conjugal rights, unreasonable restriction of her freedom of movement, such as keeping her from going to funerals or wedding parties, loathsome ailments, or nasty occupations such as tanning.[3]

How frequent divorces were there is no way of knowing — whether, for instance, the ratio of divorces to marriages was

[1] In Matt. 5, 32, the man who marries a divorced woman is guilty of the same offense. All this is quite foreign to Jewish law.

[2] M. Yebamot 6, 6; Yebamot 64a, etc.

[3] M. Nedarim 11, 12; M. Ketubot 5, 5; 7, 2–5; 7, 9 f.

higher or lower than in the statistics of consecutive polygamy in some modern Christian countries. Several anecdotes have for their subject the vexations great scholars had to endure from their wives; but of divorce on this ground R. Jose is the one prominent example, and in his case the motive of the story is his generous treatment of the divorced wife and her second husband in their fallen fortunes, installing them in a house he owned and providing for them as long as they lived.[1] R. Ḥiyya also had a shrewish wife. Once when he was making her a present wrapped up in a cloth, his nephew and disciple, Rab, exclaimed, And this when she plagues you so! Ḥiyya replied, All we can expect of them is that they bring up our children and keep us from sin.[2] But though he endured the affliction, he wished Rab better fortune: May God keep you from what is worse than death (Eccl. 7, 26, 'I find more bitter than death the woman whose heart is snares and nets and her hands as bands,' etc.).[3] The good wish was not effectual, for Rab himself had a contrary spouse — if he told her to cook him a mess of lentils she was sure to set before him peas, and vice versa, so that his son learned, when he took a message about dinner from his father to his mother, to ask for the opposite of what his father wanted.[4] Yet though these women belonged to the class of 'bad wives' and gave abundant cause, there is no intimation that their husbands divorced them.

The legal status of woman under Jewish law compares to its advantage with that of contemporary civilizations, and represents a development of the biblical legislation consistently favorable to woman.[5] Her place was in the home of her father till she

[1] Gen. R. 17, 3; Lev. R. 34, 14; more briefly, Jer. Ketubot 34b, below.

[2] Yebamot 63a, end. [3] Ibid. [4] Ibid.

[5] Minor or unmarried daughters had a right to maintenance from the estate of their deceased father, even though it left nothing for the sons to inherit and they had to beg from door to door. M. Ketubot 13, 3 (a decision rendered shortly after the death of Jesus). A clause to this effect is introduced in the Ketubah. M. Ketubot 4, 10 f. Daughters who were minors at their father's death had also a claim on the estate for a dowry equal to that which their elder sisters received. M. Ketubot, 6, 6.

was married, then in that of her husband as wife, mother, and housekeeper. For emancipated women there was in the ancient world only one calling.

The husband was bound by the marriage contract to work for his wife, support, and provide for her food, clothing, etc.;[1] the wife's household duties were to grind meal, bake, wash clothes, cook, nurse her child, make the bed, and work in wool (carding, spinning, weaving). If she brought with her female slaves, she was relieved of these occupations in proportion to their number—if they were as many as four, "she may sit in her chair" like a lady.[2] Complete idleness, however, was disapproved as perilous to her morals.[3] Peasant women no doubt had to help in the field and garden, but this is not included in the normal occupations of the housewife.

The father was expected to support his children during their early years, and had a right to their services or earnings during their minority.[4] His obligations to a son are defined: he must circumcise him, redeem him,[5] teach him Torah, teach him a trade, and get him a wife — some say also, teach him to swim.[6] The duty of educating a son in the Law and commandments is inculcated in many places.[7] Emphasis was laid on teaching him a handicraft by which he could make a living. R. Judah (ben Ila'i) said, A man who does not teach his son a trade, teaches him robbery.[8] Secular pursuits were commended, however, not

[1] For the formula of the marriage contract in which these obligations are assumed see Jewish Encyclopedia, s. v. 'Ketubah' (VII, 472).

[2] This does not exempt her from certain personal attentions to her husband, such as washing his face and hands, etc.

[3] M. Ketubot 5, 5. R. Simeon ben Gamaliel held that if a husband restrained his wife from doing any work, he should divorce her and pay the Ketubah, for idleness is a cause of insanity. See also Yebamot 63a (woman a helper to man).

[4] I.e. to the age of twelve years and six months. M. Ketubot 4, 4.

[5] Redemption of a first born son, Exod. 13, 15; cf. Num. 18, 16.

[6] Tos Ḳiddushin 1, 11; Jer. Ḳiddushin 61a (with proof texts); Ḳiddushin 29a–b, 30a; Tanḥuma ed. Buber, Shelaḥ § 26 with note 108, etc.

[7] On the educational ideal see Vol. I, pp. 316 ff.

[8] Tos. Ḳiddushin l. c. See there the benefits of knowing a handicraft. The trades of many rabbis are known from the Talmud; see the Jewish Encyclo-

alone because they gave an assured livelihood, but because unremitting application to studies was not favorable even to study itself. Rabban Gamaliel (III), son of the Patriarch Judah, said: "Study combined with a secular occupation is a fine thing, for the double labor makes sin to be forgotten. All study of the Law with which no work goes will in the end come to naught and bring sin in its train." [1]

Girls were brought up in domestic occupations and thus prepared to assume the like duties and responsibilities in homes of their own. Some of them may have been taught by their fathers or their husbands at home to read in the Bible,[2] but since this involved the learning of the ancient Hebrew language, it is probable that such cases were rare. Yet it is said that in the household of Rabbi (the Patriarch Judah) the maid servants spoke biblical Hebrew, and were able to enlighten professional scholars on some rare words in the Scripture.[3] Instruction of women in the unwritten law was naturally still more rare.[4] The one famous instance is Beruriah, daughter of R. Ḥanina ben Teradion and wife of R. Meir, who in an anecdote about R. Simlai and R.

pedia, X, 294 f. On the choice of a respectable trade, M. Ḳiddushin 4, 14 and the Talmuds thereon. Bacher, Tannaiten, II, 14.

[1] Abot 2, 2. Cf. M. Ḳiddushin 1, 10.

[2] There was no commandment in the Bible to instruct daughters in the Law. Ḳiddushin 29b, 30a. Women are exempt from the commandment to study the Law. Ḳiddushin 34a. The fact that a woman might read a portion of the Sabbath lesson in the synagogue assumes, however, that there were women competent to do so. See below, p. 131.

[3] Rosh ha-Shanah 26b; Megillah 18a, below; Nazir 3a. The Patriarch himself had been taught Greek in his father's house, and gave the preference to that language over Aramaic in Palestine. Soṭah 49b.

[4] There were rabbis who strongly disapproved it. To a learned woman who asked him a question about the sin of the golden calf and its consequences R. Eliezer ben Hyrcanus replied: A woman has no learning except about the spindle (Yoma 66b; Jer. Soṭah 19a, top). Let the words of the Law burn up but let them not be transmitted to a woman. Jer. Soṭah l.c. One who teaches his daughter Torah is as if he taught her frivolity (M. Soṭah 3, 4). Ben 'Azzai, on the contrary, taught that a man is bound to teach his daughter Torah. See also R. Joshua, *ibid.* In the following sentence, R. Joshua: "A pious fool, and a shrewd rascal, and a she Pharisee, and the plague of Pharisees, use up the world." See Soṭah 21b, 22a; Jer. Soṭah 19a. See below, p. 194.

Johanan is said to have studied three hundred talmudic topics in a day, and to have spent three years on the Book of Genealogies.[1] She even gave opinions on points of law, and on one such, a question of clean or unclean, Rabbi approved her decision, though it went counter to the prevailing opinion of the learned.[2] Several anecdotes illustrate her familiarity with the Scriptures and skill in rabbinical methods of interpretation and application, and her ability to quote the rabbinical law with effect.[3]

Women were exempt from certain religious obligations incumbent on men,[4] namely, the recitation of the Shema', and the wearing of phylacteries on the head and left arm (Tefillin), but were required to recite the prayers (Tefillah, the Eighteen Prayers) and the table blessings, and to maintain the Mezuzah on the doors of houses.[5] A more general rule is that women are exempt from all positive commandments ('thou shalt') for the performance of which a fixed time is set.[6] Such are the booth, the palm branches, and the ram's horn (at Tabernacles), the fringes, the phylacteries.[7] All other positive commandments are binding on women as well as men,[8] and all prohibitions except the few which by their nature apply only to men and the prescriptions concerning the ritual of sacrificial worship.[9] There are also laws which apply exclusively to women.[10] Others in the domestic economy, naturally fall to women to carry out, such as the separation of the Ḥallah (the portion of dough from every baking which is the priest's due) and the lighting of the sabbath lamp with the proper benediction.[11] A peculiar responsibility rests on

[1] Pesaḥim 62b. The three hundred is not to be taken numerically.

[2] Tos. Kelim ii. 1, 6. Examples of a similar kind have been not uncommon in Islam; some women are famous as traditionists.

[3] Berakot 10a; 'Erubin 53b–54a.

[4] As are also slaves and children.

[5] M. Berakot 3, 3.

[6] M. Ḳiddushin 1, 7; Tos. Soṭah 2, 8; Berakot 20b.

[7] Ḳiddushin 33b–34a.

[8] Like other general rules, these are not without exceptions. Ḳiddushin 34a.

[9] M. Ḳiddushin 1, 7–8.

[10] Especially observance of the rules about menstruation (Niddah).

[11] M. Shabbat 2, 6 (three things for the neglect of which women die in childbirth); cf. Gen. R. 17, 8, end.

the wife for the scrupulous fulfilment of these laws, though the obligation was really on the householder, i.e., in most cases the husband.

Women were not required to attend the three annual festivals (Exod. 3, 17). In conformity with Deut. 14, 22–27 the so-called second tithe, in kind or in the proceeds of redemption, was to be consumed in a family feast in Jerusalem two years out of three, or rather since the seventh year was fallow, in four years of each sabbatical period.[1] Firstlings and voluntary sacrifices were also to be brought to the temple. Nothing prevented combining this with a festival season, and presumably this was often done. In the temple, women had access to a fore-court, called for that reason the Woman's Court, within the sacred precincts, but separated from the inner enclosure surrounding the Holy House and the great altar where the sacrificial worship was performed. In the Woman's Court such popular festivities as those at the Feast of Tabernacles took place, and seats were especially provided for women in a raised gallery.[2]

Sacrifices of purification (sin offerings) were required of women after childbirth (Lev. 12, 6–8), and in other cases.[3] They could also bring offerings in fulfilment of vows,[4] or as a free-will offering or a thank-offering, any of which might be either a burnt offering or a peace offering. The question was early raised whether the imposition of hands (Lev. 1, 4; 3, 2, etc.) was necessary in the case of a woman's sacrifice.[5] The decision was that it was required of men but not of women. Some authorities held that though it was not obligatory, it was permissible if she chose, and a case is reported in which the victim was taken out into the woman's court for this purpose, "not because it was necessary, but to gratify the women."[6]

[1] In the third and sixth years the tithe was set apart for the poor of the owner's neighborhood.

[2] Above, p. 46.

[3] E.g. Lev. 14, 1–32; 15, 25–30, etc.

[4] Subject to the right of the father or husband to nullify the vow of a woman not *sui juris*, Num. 30.

[5] She could not come into the inner court to perform this part of the rite.

[6] Ḥagigah 16b, below. Cf. Sifra, Wayyiḳra Pereḳ 2 (ed. Weiss f. 4b).

Women could not be counted to make up a quorum (*minyan*) for public worship in the synagogue, for which ten free adult males were required. A woman might, however, take part as one of the seven in the reading of the Sabbath lessons, though this was disapproved on grounds of propriety and no instance is reported.[1] Many women frequented the synagogue services, not only on Sabbaths and festivals but on week days.[2] Of the presence of women in the synagogues of the dispersion the Acts and the letters of Paul give evidence.

No apology is necessary for this digression into the social and religious position of woman in Judaism, which is itself a moral achievement, and fundamental in the morals of the Jewish family.[3]

Among all the commandments the 'weightiest of the weighty' is filial piety:[4] 'Honor thy father and thy mother, that thy days may be long upon the land which the Lord thy God giveth thee' (Exod. 20, 12).[5] In Exod. 20, 12 the father is named first; in Lev. 19, 3 the mother, showing that both parents are equally to be honored and revered.[6] Dear to God is the honoring of father and mother, for the Scripture employs the same expressions about honoring, revering, cursing parents, as about honoring, revering, or cursing Himself, thus, according to a hermeneutic rule, equating the things themselves.[7] The rewards attached to

[1] Tos. Megillah 4 (3), 11; Megillah 23a, below.

[2] 'Abodah Zarah 38a–b. Bacher, in Hastings Bible Dictionary, IV, 640a.

[3] That it was no recent achievement in our period is shown by the eulogy of the good wife and mother in Prov. 31, 10–31.

[4] On this subject see Philo, De decalogo c. 22–24 (ed. Mangey, II, 198 ff.); De spec. legg. ii. (De parentibus colendis, ed. Cohn u. Wendland, V, 141 ff.).

[5] Deut. 6, 15; Lev. 19, 3, etc. It may be remarked that an anonymous opinion in the Mekilta de-R. Simeon ben Yoḥai on Exod. 20, 12 and Ketubot 103a extends the commandment to a step-mother and a step-father during the lifetime of the son's own father or mother, and to the oldest brother.

[6] Mekilta, Baḥodesh 8 (ed. Friedmann f. 70a; ed. Weiss f. 77b; Sifra Ḳedoshim, *init.* (ed. Weiss f. 87a, top); Gen. R. 1, 15, end.

[7] Mekilta on Exod. 20, 12 (ed. Friedmann f. 70a; ed. Weiss f. 77b); attributed to the Patriarch Judah; cf. Mekilta de-R. Simeon ben Yoḥai, Exod. 20, 12; Sifra on Lev. 19, 3 (Ḳedoshim, *init.* ed. Weiss f. 86d); Jer. Peah 15c, below; Ḳiddushin 30b.

them are equivalent. It is logical that father, mother, and God should be thus joined, for they are so to speak partners in bringing the child into life.[1]

Simeon ben Yoḥai said: "Great is the honoring of father and mother, for God makes more of it than of honoring Himself. It is said, 'Honor thy father and thy mother,' and it is said, 'Honor the Lord with thy substance.' Honor Him, that is, with what He has graciously bestowed on you — setting apart the forgotten sheaf, and the corner of the field; setting apart the priest's dues, first and second tithes and the poor-tithes, and the portion of dough; making the booth, and the palm-branches, and the horn, and phylacteries and fringes, and feeding the poor and hungry — if you have substance, you are obligated to all these, and if you have not, you are not obligated to any of them. But when it comes to honoring father and mother, whether you have substance or not, 'Honor thy father and thy mother,' even if you have to beg your living from door to door."[2] When a man honors his father and his mother, God says, I impute it to you as if I were dwelling among them and they honored me.[3] When a man does despite to his father and his mother, God says, I have done well not to dwell among them, for if I dwelt among them they would do despite to me.[4] If a case should arise, however, in which the parents bade their son[5] transgress any one of the commandments delivered in the Law, for instance, in the matter of sabbath observance, he should not listen to them; the duty to honor God, which rests on the parents as well as the son, takes precedence.[6]

Reverence requires that a son should not sit in the place where his father usually sits, not talk in a place where he is accustomed

[1] Mekilta de-R. Simeon ben Yoḥai l.c.; Ḳiddushin l.c., cf. Niddah 31a. Cf. Philo, De decalogo c. 22 § 107 (ed. Mangey, I, 198–199); De spec. legg. ii. §§ 224 f.

[2] Jer. Peah 15d, top.

[3] Ḳiddushin 30b, end.

[4] Ibid. 31a.

[5] Or daughter.

[6] Sifra l.s.c.; Yebamot 5b–6a. A particular application of this rule, M Baba Meṣi'a 2, 10, and the Gemara f. 32a.

to talk, not contradict him.[1] A variant of the tradition has, not to stand in his place, nor sit in his place, nor contradict his words, nor decide against his opinion.[2] Honor includes providing the father with food and drink, clothing and covering and shoes, conducting him in and out.[3] The honor a man owes to his father he owes him living or dead.[4] A bastard (*mamzer*) is bound to honor and reverence his father. Nor is a son dispensed from the obligation by the fact that his father is a bad man and a transgressor of the law.[5] If a son see his father breaking a commandment, respect should keep him from saying, Father, you have transgressed words of the Law; he should say, Father, thus it is written in the Law, or rather, In the Law the following verse is written.[6] Similar deferential forms of speech are to be employed in discussing a difference of opinion.[7] The Talmud has a collection of anecdotes illustrating the lengths — or the extravagances — to which filial piety could go. Some of them are told of eminent scholars, such as the stories of R. Tarfon and his mother;[8] but the model son who best showed how far a man could go in honoring father and mother was Dama ben Netina, a heathen of high rank in Ashkelon.[9]

Trivial questions are raised about the precedence of obligations where a conflict exists; for example, if father and mother ask their son for a drink at the same moment,[10] or if the father ask

[1] Sifra, Ḳedoshim, *init.* (ed. Weiss f. 87a); cf. Jer. Peah 15c, end.

[2] Ḳiddushin 31b, end. The case in mind is of a father and son both of whom are scholars; see Rashi on the passage. In general, Maimonides, Hilkot Mamrin 6, 1 ff.

[3] See the places cited in the two preceding notes. The case contemplated is that of a father who is dependent on the son for such services and personal attentions.

[4] Ḳiddushin 31b, end.

[5] Maimonides, Hilkot Mamrin 6, 11. Others make the father's repentance a condition. See the commentators on the passage.

[6] Ḳiddushin 32a.

[7] Ibid. 31b, below.

[8] Jer. Ḳiddushin 61b; Jer Peah 15c. A Babylonian version of the story in Ḳiddushin 31b.

[9] References in the preceding note, and 'Abodah Zarah 23b–24a.

[10] Ḳiddushin 31a.

for a drink at a time when the son has an opportunity to do an act of charity (which is a religious duty, *miṣwah*) to another.[1]

A man's master, who instructed him in the revelation God had made in his two-fold law and the religious doctrines and duties therein contained, stood to him in this capacity *in loco parentis*, and as his spiritual father — to use a modern phrase — was entitled to the honor and reverence due to the literal father.[2] This is a topic on which the rabbinical literature is expansive; there is a code of etiquette for the relation of pupil and teacher, about which they were very punctilious. In the Babylonian schools the question was even raised whether, if a master of his own accord waived the honor due him, he could release others from the obligation, as a father could, and as God did.[3]

The Mosaic law prescribes the death penalty for a son who strikes his father or mother (Exod. 21, 15; Lev. 20, 9), or curses them (Exod. 21, 17).[4] A stubborn and rebellious son may be accused by his parents before the elders of the town, and put to death by stoning (Deut. 21, 18 f.). The severity of these laws was mitigated in various ways by the rabbinical law. Thus, he was guilty of cursing his parents (living or dead) only if he uttered one of the special names of God;[5] if he used an epithet or metonymy[6] he is not held to be guilty. The process in case of the unruly son as defined in the Mishnah,[7] like much else in this treatise, reads more like juristic theory than actual practice. But the mitigating tendency is evident. The offence cannot be committed by a minor child; both parents must unite in the

[1] Ibid. 32a, below. One rabbi gave the unconditional preference to the latter; the rule, however, follows the opinion of Isi ben Judah, that if the *miṣwah* can be performed by another, the duty to the father takes precedence.

[2] Sifrè on Deut. 6, 7 (§ 34, ed. Friedmann f. 74, below): Biblical proof that students are called sons, and the master (*rab*) called father.

[3] Ḳiddushin 32a–b.

[4] See also Prov. 20, 20; 30, 11; 30, 17.

[5] I.e. one of the seven names that may not be erased, viz., El, Elohim, Jhvh, Adonai, Jah, Shaddai, Ṣebaot (Shebu'ot 35a, end).

[6] Such as Great, Mighty, Terrible, etc., or Gracious, Merciful, etc., Shebu'ot 35a. M. Sanhedrin 7, 8.

[7] M. Sanhedrin 8, 1–5.

action; for a first offence the son is formally warned and flogged by the local court of three; if he continues stubborn he is tried before the court of twenty-three; but he can only be executed when the first judges are present, etc. One who strikes his father or mother is guilty only if he has wounded them.[1] The requirement of at least two eye-witnesses and of a warning, in this as in the former case, made conviction difficult. The penalty was probably obsolete long before these circumstantial procedures were defined in the second century; but the law remained to impress God's abhorrence of the abuse of parents.

Slavery [2] under the Mosaic law was of two kinds according as the slave was an Israelite or of alien race. In the former case the master acquired the right to the services of the slave for a term of six years,[3] or till the Year of Jubilee with its general release came around. The master is reminded that he is a brother and exhorted to treat him as such. He is, in fact, not to be treated like a slave at all, but like a hired servant, and must not be sold as slaves are sold. They are God's slaves, by virtue of the deliverance from Egypt.[4] Nor must the master assert his authority over them harshly. These commandments were interpreted and regulated in the rabbinical law, and invariably in a sense favorable to the servant.

Slaves of other than Israelite race were in an entirely different case.[5] They were really slaves in the ordinary meaning of the word in its ancient and modern use. The legal and social status of slaves was substantially the same as in contemporary pagan

[1] Ibid. 11, 1. See the Talmud on the Mishnahs cited. Other texts in Strack-Billerbeck on Matt. 15, 4 (I, 709–711).

[2] See Maimonides, Hilkot 'Abadim; L. N. Dembitz, art. 'Slaves and Slavery,' Jewish Encyclopedia, XI, 403–407; S. Krauss, Talmudische Archäologie, II, 83 ff.

[3] Exod. 21, 2–11; Deut. 15, 12–18; Lev. 25, 39–43. On the ways in which such servitude might arise it is unnecessary to dwell here.

[4] See e.g., Sifra on Lev. 25, 39–43 (ed. Weiss f. 109 c–d); cf. Mekilta, Mishpaṭim 1 (ed. Friedmann f. 75b; ed. Weiss f. 82a).

[5] The term Canaanite slave in the Mishnah includes aliens of all sorts, in contrast to the Hebrew slave.

countries.[1] Unlike the tendency of the rabbinical law concerning Hebrew slaves, its development was not to the advantage of the foreign slave, a fact probably due in part to the altered conditions of the institution itself, in part to environment.

One peculiar feature of Jewish slavery has been referred to in another connection. A Jew who bought a heathen slave was required by the Mosaic law to have him circumcised. If after a year's time the slave refused to submit to the operation, the rabbinical law prescribed that he must be sold to a heathen master, and the same rule applied to the baptism of a female slave. In the case of slaves these rites, though bringing them "under the wings of the Shekinah," did not carry with them the obligation to observe the whole law, as they did for proselytes; nor did they, as in the latter case, put them on an equality with the native born in point of legal rights. In respect of obligations they were on the same footing as Jewish women and minor sons. A slave could eat the Passover with his master's family; but he might not be counted to make up the quorum of ten for public prayer in the synagogue, and an anecdote is told of a rabbi, who, finding the congregation one short, manumitted on the spot the slave who accompanied him to complete the required number.[2]

The number of slaves owned by Jews in Palestine probably varied widely at different times within our period with the prosperity of the country and other circumstances. It is to be borne in mind that under the economic conditions slavery was chiefly domestic. There were no industries in which slave labor could be profitably employed in mass, nor was the nature of the land and its products adapted to agriculture on a great scale. The wars of the Asmonaeans must have brought in at times many

[1] It may be remarked that the slave was not a "chattel," as in a famous American decision, but is assimilated to real, rather than personal, property.

[2] R. Eliezer. Giṭṭin 38b, above. A form of virtual emancipation was for the master to put Tefillin on his slave, or to bid him read three verses from a roll of the Law in the presence of the congregation. The owner was thereupon required to give him the usual written instrument (*geṭ*). Giṭṭin 40a.

captives, and we may well suppose that the houses and estates of the aristocracy of Jerusalem were amply supplied with them.[1] We may safely assume that this was true also under Herod, and after him down to the revolt of 66–72. The war and its consequences greatly impoverished the land, and multitudes of Jews were themselves carried off into slavery. Even more disastrous was the war under Hadrian. When in the following generations we hear of hundreds or even thousands of slaves belonging to a single master we are justified in taking the numbers homiletically rather than arithmetically; but there is no reason to doubt that, in fertile and populous Galilee especially, there were many heathen slaves, and even considerable slave houscholds.

The reputation of slaves was no better among the Jews than in the rest of the world. An aphorism attributed to Hillel runs: "The more property the more anxiety; the more wives the more witchcraft;[2] the more slave girls the more licentiousness; the more slaves the more robbery."[3] Five things Canaan taught his descendants:[4] "Love one another (stick together), and love robbery, and love licentiousness, and hate your masters, and do not speak the truth."[5] Sirach's advice about the way to deal with slaves (Ecclus. 30, 33 ff.) is: "Hay and a stick and burdens for the ass; bread and discipline and labor for the menial slave. Make the boy work and you will have no trouble with him; if you take your hand off him, he will be seeking freedom. A yoke and a strap bow the neck,[6] and for a rascally slave there are the rack and torture. Plunge him into work that he may not be idle, for idleness teaches much badness. Set him to work as

[1] Since the rule was *partus sequitur ventrem*, and the child of a slave mother was a slave whether the father was slave or free, many were bred in slavery.

[2] The most estimable of woman kind is addicted to witchcraft. Jer. Ḳiddushin 66c (Simeon ben Yoḥai); Jer. Sanhedrin 25d, above; 'Erubin 64b; Bacher, Tannaiten, II, 86 f.

[3] Abot 2, 7.

[4] The foreign slave was a "Canaanite slave"; see above.

[5] Pesaḥim 113b, below. For other utterances of similar purport see S. Krauss, Talmudische Archäologie, II, 92 f.

[6] Of a plow-beast.

befits him, and if he does not obey lade him with heavy fetters. But do not go beyond bounds with any man, and do nothing you have not a right to do." The significance of this is not diminished by the bit of prudence that follows: "If you have a menial slave, treat him like yourself, for he is as necessary to you as your life. If you maltreat him, and he up and runs away, in what quarter will you look for him?"

There is no reason to think that the author of this drastic counsel was a peculiarly hard-hearted master, or that the lot of slaves was greatly ameliorated in later times. Flogging was a common punishment, and the rods, whips, and scourges with which it was administered in progressive degrees of severity are often named.[1] Of good slaves and good masters we naturally hear less, but it may well be believed that relations such as existed between the Patriarch Gamaliel II and his slave Ṭabi [2] were not uncommon.

Hired servants were doubtless much more common in Palestine than slaves, both in the household and in husbandry,[3] replacing the native term-servitude, which had almost passed out of use. In agriculture the need of more hands at certain seasons of the year made it necessary to employ such laborers, who were recruited for the time either from the class of small peasant proprietors, who supplemented the living they got off their own land by hiring themselves out to the holders of larger estates, or from the landless population of the towns. In the house, also, the well-to-do had to have many servants in consequence of the subdivision of employment — men could not be set at women's work, not women at men's, and where any special skill was required, the servant did that one thing, and did not expect to be generally useful. Artisans of all kinds — masons, carpenters, smiths, and the like — were hired for the occasion, as for example

[1] See Krauss, l.s.c. 95 ff.

[2] See Jewish Encyclopedia, s. v.

[3] Evidence of this is found in the parables of Jesus, the Laborers in the Vineyard, Matt. 20, 1–16; the Prodigal Son, Luke 15, 11 ff.; cf. also Zebedee's fishermen, Mark 1, 20.

in the building or repair of a house. Another important class of laborers were the porters who carried burdens on their shoulders.

The biblical law prescribed that the wages of a hired laborer (probably presumed to be in kind) should be given him at the end of each day. 'Thou shalt not defraud thy neighbor and thou shalt not rob. The wages of a hired servant shall not remain with thee over night until morning' (Lev. 19, 13; cf. Deut. 24, 14 f.). The law applies also to the *ger*, that is in rabbinical interpretation a proselyte or a resident alien. The gravity of the offence is duly emphasized in the rabbinical law.[1] The Mishnah affirms the servant's right to such payment if he asks it, but does not make it obligatory unless he does — he may prefer to let his wages accumulate. It accommodates itself to a more complex society by allowing payment to be made by an order on a shop-keeper or on a money-changer.[2] There are various regulations on agreements to work for wages, and on the duties and rights of both parties. Such engagements might be made for a day, or a week, a month, a year, or a longer period.[3] The interests of the wage earner are protected; for example, the employer may not insist on a longer day's work than is customary in the place, even though he pays higher wages than usual. If a man was hired by the day to do one kind of work and finished it before night, he could not be put at another kind, unless it was lighter than that for which he was engaged.[4] A craftsman employed as such could not be required to do other work. Where it was the local custom for the employer to furnish food, that would be understood to be covered by his contract.

In general, in defining the law as well as in the judicial application of it, the rabbis observe the principle laid down for judges and witnesses in Lev. 19, 15,[5] 'Thou shalt not show partiality to

[1] See Sifra in loc. (ed. Weiss f. 88 c–d); Sifrè Deut. §§ 208 f; Midrash Tannaim ed. Hoffmann, pp. 158 f.

[2] M. Baba Meṣi'a 9 12.

[3] In these cases he could claim his wages only at the expiry of the term M. Baba Meṣi'a 9, 11.

[4] On the whole subject see S. Krauss, Talmudische Archäologie, II, 101 ff.

[5] Cf. Exod. 23, 3.

a poor man, nor pay respect to the person of a great (rich) man; with righteousness shalt thou judge thy countrymen.' A peculiar character is given to the rabbinical laws, however, by the fact that the interpretation of the civil and criminal legislation in the Pentateuch, with its elaboration and amplification in the unwritten law, is not purely juristic, but is consciously guided and controlled by the moral and social principles which are equally a part of the divinely revealed Torah. In technical phrase, Jewish ethics are impressed upon the Halakah, as well as expressed in the Haggadah. What is to be learned from the former has hitherto received little attention in comparison with the popular moral teaching of the Haggadah. The investigation and exposition of this subject is a task to which Jewish scholars, learned in that field, might profitably address themselves.

CHAPTER V

UNLAWFUL GAIN. WRONGS IN WORDS

The influence on Jewish jurisprudence of the broad principles to which reference has been made is manifest in the mitigation by the rabbinical law of much of the severity of the Mosaic legislation. It was not, we may safely say, a sentimental humanitarianism, nor the mere advance of civilization, that animated the Pharisees, in contrast to the Sadducees, in the substitution of damages for the ancient talio, for example, or in the development of rules of evidence and of procedure which made the proof of capital crimes such as adultery or blasphemy close to an impossibility. The important distinction is also drawn between legal and moral responsibility. Thus, in a question of liability for damages, the rabbis ruled: "He is not liable in a human court, but he is liable in God's court."[1] Numerous cases of this kind are noted in the laws of bargain and sale. Thus, if the consideration has passed but the thing purchased has not been formally taken in possession by the purchaser, either party may legally retract; but "He who exacted retribution of the generation of the Flood and the generation of the Dispersion (at the Tower of Babel) will exact it of the man who does not stand by his word."[2]

While we are upon this topic it may not be amiss to cite one or two other examples from the same tractate of the Mishnah. As a man may wrong another in business transactions, so he may also wrong him by words. One should not say, How much will you sell me this for? when he has no intention of buying.[3] To

[1] Baba Meṣi'a 82b, and elsewhere.

[2] M. Baba Meṣi'a 4, 2; Baba Meṣi'a 49a, top; 74b; Tos. Baba Meṣi'a 3, 14, adding, A bargain made by words only is not binding, but the learned say, The learned are not content with a man who nullifies his words.

[3] Arousing false expectations, a kind of cheating.

a man who has repented, one should not say, Remember your former deeds; nor to a proselyte, Remember the deeds of your fathers (Exod. 22, 20).[1] There is an interesting paragraph on unfair competition. R. Judah (ben Ila'i) held that a shop-keeper should not give children sweetmeats (parched grain and nuts) to attract them to buy things at his shop when they were sent on errands; and that a shop-keeper should not cut prices to draw custom away from other dealers. The majority were not of his mind. Of the merchant who sells under the market price they say, he should be gratefully remembered, for the community gets the advantage of the reduction others also will have to make.[2]

In a similar way the subject of adulteration of food is dealt with. If, for example, water accidentally gets into a wine jar, the owner may not sell the wine at retail without apprising the buyer of the dilution, and he may not sell it to a merchant at all, even with such notice, it being assumed that he would buy it (at a reduced price) only with a fraudulent purpose. The tricking up of articles for sale to make them look better than they are is prohibited.

Rabbi Jose, a disciple of Rabban Johanan ben Zakkai,[3] said: "Let thy neighbor's property be as dear to thee as thine own; and set thyself diligently to learn Torah, for the knowledge of it is not inherited; and let all that thou doest be for God's sake." [4] The first of these maxims may be illustrated by the treatment of the subject of usury in the rabbinical law.[5] In the Pentateuch it is forbidden to lend anything to a fellow Israelite upon interest,

[1] M. Baba Meṣi'a 4, 10; cf. the Talmud on this Mishnah (f. 58b–59a). There will be occasion to recur to this subject later.

[2] M. Baba Meṣi'a 4, 12. A convenient introduction to this part of the law is H. E. Goldin, Mishnah, a Digest of the Basic Principles of Early Jewish Jurisprudence. Baba Meziah. New York. Putnam's. 1913.

[3] See Bacher, Tannaiten, I, 72.

[4] Abot 2, 12; cf. Abot de-R. Nathan c. 17, 1 ff.

[5] It is worth observing that the code of the widest authority among modern Jews, the Shulḥan 'Aruk (1555) of Joseph Caro, treats the whole subject, not in the juridical part of the work but in the Yoreh De'ah among moral and religious duties.

that is on condition of receiving back more than was lent.[1] The supposition of the early laws is that the borrower is in need, and that it would be oppressive for his more fortunate brother Israelite to take advantage of his necessity for his own profit.[2] In the more complex society of a later time the rabbis extended the principle of this legislation to transactions of various kinds in which one party would gain and the other suffer a corresponding loss, and even to some cases where the borrower suffered no detriment and the lender received no advantage, to exclude a possible misconstruction by outsiders ignorant of the facts.

The prohibition of the Mosaic law, in rabbinical interpretation, is simple:[3] "If a man lends a *sela* (a silver coin of the value of four *denars*) on condition of receiving five *denars* at the expiration of the term, or two *seahs* of wheat to receive three, this is usury (*neshek*)."[4] 'Increase' (*tarbit*, *marbit*,[5] Lev. 25, 36, 37) is illustrated by a more complicated example.[6] A man (A) buys of another (B) a quantity of wheat at the market price of twenty-five *denars* a *kor*, and pays cash for it, but leaves the grain warehoused with the seller (B). The market price goes up to thirty, and A claims delivery of the wheat, proposing to sell it and with the proceeds buy wine. The original seller (B) offers to buy back the wheat at the current price of thirty denars,[7] and to give

[1] Exod. 22, 24; Lev. 25, 35–38; Deut. 23, 20 f. Cf. Ezek. 18, 8, 13, 17; Psalm 15, 5. To take interest from an alien is expressly allowed in Deut. 23, 21.

[2] R. Ishmael taught that when one was asked for such a loan it was not optional with him to grant or refuse it. Mekilta, Mishpaṭim 19 (ed. Friedmann f. 96a; ed. Weiss f. 102a). So Matt. 5, 42, 'do not turn away one who wants to borrow of you.'

[3] On the whole subject see Mekilta on Exod. 22, 24 (ed. Friedmann f. 96a–b; ed. Weiss f. 102a–b); Sifra on Lev. 25, 35–38 (ed. Weiss f. 109b–c); Sifrè Deut. § 162. These and other texts in translation, Strack–Billerbeck, Kommentar zum Neuen Testament, u. s. w. on Matt. 5, 42 (I, 346 ff.). Tos. Baba Meṣi'a 4–6.

[4] M. Baba Meṣi'a 5, 1.

[5] Under this term (in later Hebrew *ribbit*) rabbinical usury, in distinction from biblical, is here defined.

[6] M. Baba Meṣi'a 5, 1, with the Talmud (60b, ff.). See Goldin, op. cit., pp. 98 ff.; Jewish Encyclopedia, XII, 388 (L. N. Dembitz).

[7] This is legitimate.

to A wine of equivalent value at the then ruling market price, having at the time of the negotiation no wine in his possession.[1] This is constructively usurious, because in the interval before delivery the price of wine may advance, and A may thus receive more than his due.[2]

The effect of this and similar regulations was to prohibit dealings in futures which have so large a place in modern speculation. The evasion of the law by what we should call a premium or a bonus,[3] that is a gift made by a prospective borrower in anticipation of a loan, or a gift to the lender when the loan is repaid, is defined as usury, advanced or postponed, as the case may be.[4] Many other transactions are forbidden as usurious, as, for example, if a man who has a piece of land for sale offers it to a buyer for 1000 *zuzim* cash or 1200 after the harvest;[5] for here the higher price is evidently charged by the owner for waiting for his money, which is plain usury. Another example of the rabbinical legislation to guard against an unfair advantage on the part of a capitalist is found in a subsequent paragraph.[6] A man may not give a shop-keeper produce to sell with an agreement to share equally the profits made in disposing of it at retail, nor give him money to buy at wholesale and sell at retail on the same conditions, unless he pays him wages, because, if the venture proves unprofitable, the shop-keeper will be out of his time and labor, besides the risk of loss by fire or larceny, or by depreciation.[7]

[1] An agreement of this kind is not enforceable in law, but it was assumed that B would stand by it as morally binding.

[2] It is interesting to note that legislation of like intent, compelling merchants by law to deliver everything they sell and to acquire possession of it before selling, has been frequently proposed in recent times, not so much, however, in the interest of individuals as to prevent manipulation of the market.

[3] A very common way of evading modern laws making illegal a rate of interest above a fixed per cent ('usury' in the modern definition).

[4] Rabban Gamaliel, Sifrê Deut. § 263; M. Baba Meṣi'a 5, 10.

[5] M. Baba Meṣi'a 5, 2.

[6] M. Baba Meṣi'a 5, 4.

[7] The supposition is that for one half the grain, fruits, or what not, the shopkeeper is a borrower and for the other half a bailee. See Goldin, op. cit. p. 107 f.; Jewish Encyclopedia, XII, 389.

All persons involved in any way in usurious transactions, whether in the biblical or the rabbinical definition, are guilty of violating the prohibition — the lender, the borrower, the surety, the witnesses, and the scrivener who draws up the contract.[1] Interest actually paid may be recovered at law [2] during the lifetime of the lender (but not from his estate). What may be called usurious profits cannot be recovered.[3] The lender may sue for the principal alone, but not for interest.[4]

These illustrations taken from a single title of the Mishnah may suffice to show how the rabbis endeavored to apply broad moral principles to the regulation of every day matters of business. Many of the rules they laid down must seem to the reader who considers them in the light of modern conditions, not merely unpractical but impracticable; and so, in fact, they often proved under their own conditions,[5] as appears plainly in the Talmud, where the jurists find legal ways of getting around the law. It is, however, precisely in the impracticable provisions of their laws that the ideals of legislators are most evident, and in the present instance it is with the moral ideals that we are concerned, not with the adaptation of the laws to concrete conditions.

The idealistic character of much in rabbinical jurisprudence is an inheritance from the Law and the Prophets. Particularly in Deuteronomy what nowdays is called idealism is palpably utopian. Striking examples are in the law of war (Deut. 20) and the septennial wiping out of all debts (Deut. 15, 1–11),[6] but the same spirit runs through the book and appears in many other places in the Pentateuch. Intelligent and religious men could not have spent their lives in the study of the Scriptures without

1 M. Baba Meṣi'a 5, 11; Mekilta, Mishpaṭim 19, on Exod. 22, 24 (ed. Friedmann f. 96b; ed. Weiss f. 102b).

2 Some opinions were averse even to this.

3 Baba Meṣi'a 61b, 62a.

4 Ibid. 72a.

5 A usurer is represented by R. Simeon ben Yoḥai as saying: Our master Moses was wise and his Law is true; but if he had known what profit there was in the business, he would not have written this law. Baba Meṣi'a 75b.

6 Cf. also the law of the monarchy, Deut. 17, 14.

recognizing and appropriating this spirit, and interpreting the law in it. The Law was not for the Jewish Doctors of the Law merely a Corpus Juris, a volume of statutes on all kinds of subjects, ritual and ceremonial, criminal and civil; it was — to give it modern expression — a revelation of God's ideal for men's conduct and character. Their task was, therefore, not solely to give a juristic definition of the statutes, with application to the various cases that were expressly or by implication covered by them, but to widen the scope of the law in accordance with its spirit and principle, as in the examples above where the biblical law against taking interest on a loan is stretched into a rabbinical prohibition of a variety of business transactions which were assimilated to usury by the possibility that one of the parties might profit at the expense of the other.[1]

Modern writers on the application of moral principles to business have frequently laid down the doctrine that in an equitable exchange of whatever kind both parties should profit by the transaction, each getting what he wanted on fair terms. An anticipation of this conception may be seen in the rabbinical legislation we have had under consideration.

Another example of the broad extension of a biblical precept and its many applications may appropriately be given here.[2] The law of jubilees[3] in the context of which (Lev. 25, 37–38) occurs the prohibition of lending on interest cited above, allows no sale of agricultural lands in fee simple; they are entailed to the heirs of those to whom they were originally allotted in the division of the land, and revert to them at the end of every half-century. All that could be sold was the leasehold of such lands till this term, and the price was to be based on the number of crops in

[1] There are things which have a value in the estimation of one person which they have not for another, such as a copy of the Pentateuch or a pearl. Here the owner may set a price without doing a wrong to the buyer, no matter how much profit he makes. M. Baba Meṣi'a 4, 9 (R. Judah); Baba Meṣi'a 58b.

[2] M. Lazarus has used this to illustrate the rabbinical development of the Law. Die Ethik des Judenthums, I, 293 ff.

[3] Lev. 25, 8 ff.

the intervening years (Lev. 25, 8–17). In this transaction neither party is to overreach the other (vs. 17).[1] The significant repetition of this injunction leads the Sifra [2] to distinguish between a wrong affecting material interests, as in the case of certain kinds of property (*hona'at mammon*) [3] and an injury inflicted by words (*hona'at debarim*).

Examples of the latter have been cited above; [4] numerous others might be collected. If affliction or illness come upon a man, or he has buried his sons, do not say, as Job's friends said to him, 'Is not thy fear (of God — religion) thy confidence, and thy hope the integrity of thy ways? Remember, pray, who ever perished, being innocent, (or where were the upright cut off?' Job 4, 6 f.).[5] R. Johanan quotes a saying of R. Simeon ben Yoḥai that injurious words are a greater wrong than a monetary injury, for to the former the solemn words are annexed, 'and thou shalt fear thy God' (Lev. 25, 17).[6] The one affects a man personally, the other only in his property.[7] The one can be made good, the other not.[8] Whoever makes his neighbor's face blanch (from shame) before others, is as if he shed blood; [9] quite true, for the red disappears and the white comes. To put one's fellow to an open shame is counted one of the gravest sins. R. Eleazar of Modiim puts the man who is guilty of it alongside of him who nullifies the covenant of Abraham (the apostate who obliterates his circumcision) in his list of those who, no matter how much learning and good works they possess, have no share in

[1] ולא תונו איש את עמיתו ויראת מאלהיך. In more general terms: 'If thou sell anything unto thy countryman, or buy from thy countryman, ye shall not wrong one another' (Lev. 25, 14). 'Ye shall not wrong one another, but thou shalt fear thy God' (Lev. 25, 17).

[2] Sifra on Lev. 25, 17 (ed. Weiss f. 107d); cf. Baba Meṣi'a 58b.

[3] For cases which do not fall under the legal definition of *honayah* (*hona'ah ona'ah*), see M. Baba Meṣi'a 4, 9 (with the discussion in the Talmud *ibid.*, f. 56b); Sifra on Lev. 25, 14 (ed. Weiss f. 107c).

[4] Vol. I, p. 394; above, pp. 141 f.

[5] Baba Meṣi'a 58b; with other examples.

[6] Ibid.

[7] Ibid. R. Eleazar (ben Pedat).

[8] Ibid. R. Samuel ben Naḥman.

[9] Ibid. More to the same purport in the sequel.

the World to Come.[1] R. Ḥanina puts him among the three kinds of sinners who go down to hell and never come up again, viz., the adulterer, the man who puts his fellow to open shame, and he who calls him by an opprobrious name.[2] The rabbis are somewhat liberal in such denunciations of future punishment, particularly in cases which are not reached by human justice. It is precisely to things which for this reason are left to the conscience of the individual [3] that the ominous words are appended, 'Thou shalt fear thy God.' It is in the same spirit that Jesus says: He who says, 'Thou fool! is liable to the penalty of hell fire' (Matt. 5, 22).[4] The law, 'Ye shall not wrong one another' extends to the resident alien (*ger*); [5] in our period *ger* had become the name for a proselyte, and as in the case of a fellow Jew, the prohibition was taken to include injurious words as well as material wrongs.

Beyond most other literature of the kind, the Jewish Scriptures abound in condemnation of speaking ill of others,[6] whether it be a malicious slander or a hearsay retailed out of that love of scandal which seems to be an inveterate trait of human nature.[7] The Jewish moralists are no less emphatic upon this topic. The law in Lev. 19, 16, was understood as in the English version, 'Thou shalt not go up and down as a talebearer among thy people,'[8] to

[1] Abot 3, 11.

[2] Even if he is used to it. Baba Meṣi'a 58b, end.

[3] מסור לֵלב; see above, p. 82.

[4] 'Fool' in the Bible has a moral implication. — See Strack-Billerbeck on Matt. 5, 22 (I, 279 f.).

[5] Exod. 22, 20; Lev. 19, 33. Cf. Deut. 23, 17, a runaway slave who has taken refuge in Jewish territory.

[6] False testimony in a civil or criminal case (Deut. 19, 16–21; cf. Exod. 23, 1 f.) need not here be considered. On the '*ed zomem* see M. Makkot 1 with the Talmud. The false witnesses, it should be noted, are often the accusers. Nor need we expand on the particular case of false accusation in Deut. 22, 13–19.

[7] See Exod. 23, 1; Lev. 19, 16; Jer. 6, 28; 9, 3; Ezek. 22, 9; Psalm 15, 3; 101, 5; 50, 19 f.; Prov. 10, 18; 11, 13; 20, 19; 30, 10; and at length Ecclus. 28, 12–26, etc. Many other verses of Scripture are cited by the rabbis.

[8] Going from house to house like a peddler (*rokel*). Jer. Peah 16a, above; one interpretation in Sifra (ed. Weiss f. 89a); cf. the Palestinian Targum.

forbid the peddling of gossip, a mischievous business, even if the report was true and told without malice.[1] The offense was much greater if it was circulated with malicious intent to injure a man's reputation or to expose him to contempt or derision; and gravest of all if it was invented for this purpose. The name for the last two cases was 'the evil tongue,'[2] 'slander, calumny.' That a true statement may do as much harm as a falsehood is illustrated by the report Doeg the Edomite made to Saul of the aid and comfort Ahimelech, the priest of Nob, gave to David in his flight from Saul, with its consequences (1 Sam. 22, 9–19).[3]

Except in the case mentioned above[4] the biblical law provides no judicial remedy for slander; the Psalmist prays that God may cut off the offender.[5] For this reason, probably, the 'evil tongue' was all the more vehemently inveighed against by the rabbis. It is punished by God in this world, but the complete retribution is reserved for the world to come, as in the case of the cardinal sins, idolatry, incest, and murder — "and calumny is equal to all of them."[6] Four classes of men will not be received in the divine presence: scoffers, liars, hypocrites, and retailers of slander.[7] The case of Miriam, who was smitten with leprosy because she spoke evil of Moses (Num. 12) leads to the reckoning of calumny as one of the seven sins on account of which leprosy comes upon men.[8] A man does not utter a calumny until he has

[1] Maimonides, De'ot 7, 1 f.

[2] לשון הרע. One who puts out a false accusation is מוציא לשון הרע; one who circulates a report, however true, with malicious intent is מספר לשון הרע. Note the denominative מלשין, Psalm 101, 5.

[3] Jer. Peah 16a. The worst of all evil-tongued men were the delators.

[4] Pages 148 n., 186.

[5] Psalm 12, 4; cf. 101, 5, cited in Jer. Peah 15d, end; cf. 'Arakin 16a. The principle of the rabbinical law was that there was no injurious *act*. Verbal *insults* are discussed in Baba Ḳamma 91a, and there also the authorities hold that there was no redress by fine or damages.

[6] Tos. Peah 1, 2; Jer. Peah 15d, below. Cf. Midrash Tehillim on Psalm 12, 4 (ed. Buber f. 53a).

[7] Sanhedrin 103a, below; Soṭah 42a.

[8] 'Arakin 15b; 16a, cf. b. A severe and dangerous kind of sore throat is also a visitation on this sin. Shabbat 33a–b.

denied God;[1] for such men say, 'We will give rein to our tongue; our lips are in our own control. Who is lord over us?'[2] In all other transgressions a man sins on earth, but these sin in heaven and on earth (Psalm 73, 9).[3] Another says: "Of him who circulates a calumny God says, I and he cannot both abide in the world.[4] In Palestine the Aramaic name for the *lashōn ha-ra'* was *lishan telita'e*,[5] 'third tongue.' In explanation of this singular phrase it was said that slander kills three, the man who told it, and the one who accepted it, and the one it was told about.[6]

There is a less serious form of this fault which is called 'dust of evil speech' (tongue),[7] which we might perhaps call unchari table comment on our neighbors, a thing that even good men find it very hard to avoid. Even laudation is to be shunned, lest it call out detraction from some hearer who dislikes him who is praised (Prov. 27, 14).[8] Many more utterances of similar purport ranging through several centuries might be quoted.[9] The moral principle is succinctly formulated by R. Eliezer, "Let the honor of thy fellow be as dear to thee as thine own."[10] "This teaches that as a man has regard for his own honor, so he should have regard for the honor of his fellow; and as he does not wish any slander to come upon his own honor, so he should wish not to bring any slander upon the honor of his fellow."[11] The disciples

1 כופר בעיקר; see Vol. I, p. 467.

2 Psalm 12, 5. Jer. Peah 16a; cf. 'Arakin 15b.

3 Ibid. Cf. 'Arakin 15b (Resh Laḳish); from the same verse in the Psalm: He who circulates a calumny accumulates guilt even to heaven.

4 Psalm 101, 5, pronouncing *'itto* instead of *'oto*, 'I cannot abide with him' instead of 'I cannot abide him.'

5 So in the Palestinian Targum in Lev. 19, 16, for the Hebrew *rakil*, and in Gen. 1, 16, in the story of how the moon was diminished in brightness for speaking evil of the sun (cf. Ḥullin 60b).

6 Jer. Peah 16a; 'Arakin 15b, below. Cf. Ecclus. 28, 14. The 'third tongue' is a go-between (Rashi).

7 אבק לשון הרע. Baba Batra 164b–165a. Named with sinful (especially unchaste) thoughts and distraction in prayer.

8 'Arakin 16a; Baba Batra 164b, below.

9 See especially Jer. Peah 16a; 'Arakin 15b–16a.

10 Abot 2, 10. Cf. Gen. R. 1, 5: R. Jose bar Ḥanina said, He who honors himself by the disgrace of his fellow has no share in the world to come.

11 Abot de-R. Nathan 15, 1.

of R. Eliezer, gathered about his sick bed, asked him: "Master, teach us the ways of life, that by them we may attain the life of the World to Come (eternal life). He answered, "Be careful about the honor of your fellow, and restrain your sons from (mere) reading,[1] and set them between the knees of scholars, and when you pray, know before whom you stand; and thus you will attain to the life of the World to Come."[2]

The two maxims, 'Let the property of another be as dear to you as your own,' and, 'Let the honor of another be as dear to you as your own,' are particular cases of the general law, 'Thou shalt love thy neighbor as thyself.' Both are developed to an ethical ideal that makes no concessions to what we call human nature and the way of the world. A world in which men do not speak evil of their fellows or enjoy hearing them evil spoken of is a remoter Utopia than one in which they do not take advantage of one another in business; but this is said to the credit of these moralists, for all ethics worth the name propose an unrealizable ideal, a perfect man in a perfect society. Unlike the philosophers, however, the Jewish moralists conceive this end as the divine ideal, revealed not alone as a law for human life but as a constituent factor of religion.

There is a similar utopian strain in the teaching of Jesus as it is reported in the Gospels. The principle of non-resistance, for example, in Matt. 5, 39–41, is carried to extravagance: If a man cuffs you on the right cheek, turn to him the other also;[3] if he wants to sue you at law and take your shirt, let him have your cloak too; if he impresses you to go a mile, go with him two. Much else in the Sermon on the Mount is so impracticable that many modern scholars think it necessary to save Jesus' reputation for common sense by taking such utterances, not as universal

1 Without the traditional explanation, explaining for themselves.

2 Berakot 28b.

3 The rabbinical law allows the injured party in such a case exemplary damages. M. Baba Ḳamma 8, 6. In Tos. Baba Ḳamma 9, 31, it is expressly said that in a trifling assault the damages are not for the pain the blow gave, but for the insult of it.

rules of conduct, but as counsels of perfection for the little group of his disciples in anticipation of the imminent crisis that should usher in the reign of God — it was what is called an "interim ethic."

This theory ignores a striking feature of the biblical legislation itself. By the side of laws which represent ancient custom and the amendments made necessary by experience or changing conditions, there are laws that leave the ground of reality altogether and set forth in statutory form ideals which in the world of reality are manifestly impossible — take for a single example the law of war in Deuteronomy 20. It is more serious that those who entertain this theory take no account whatever of what I have called the utopian element, not alone in the ethical maxims of the rabbis and in commendations of ideal standards of conduct such as we expect from moralists, but in the prosaic pages of the laws about bargain and sale, usury, and the like, of which examples have been given above. It would be easy to multiply indefinitely illustrations from other fields of this tendency to interpret and apply the biblical law in the spirit of equity and charity. That this often carries them beyond the strict letter of the law they were well aware. "Here is the line of legal right," but on higher grounds men are urged, and sometimes constrained,[1] not to confine themselves to it in dealings with their fellows, but to act "within the line of legal right." [2]

A sensitive regard for the honor and for the feelings of others is impressed also upon the difficult duty of admonishing one who has done a wrong, or warning one who is on the verge of doing so. The law runs: 'Thou shalt not hate thy brother in thy heart. Thou shalt not fail to reprove thy fellow and not bear sin because of him. Thou shalt not take revenge, nor nurse a grudge against the members of thy people; but shalt love thy neighbor as thyself' (Lev. 19, 17 f.).[3] The fulfilment of this precept was felt to be extremely difficult, especially when it was the aggrieved party who had to undertake it. Several teachers of the beginning

[1] M. Giṭṭin 4, 4. [2] Mekilta on Exod. 18, 20. [3] Cf. Amos 5, 10.

of the second century give strong expression to this difficulty, one declaring that in that generation there was no one able thus to reprove his fellow, another that there was no one who was able to accept the reproof, and a third that there was no one who knew how to administer reproof.[1] An example of the spirit of love under rebuke is given by Johanan ben Nuri in the same context: "I call heaven and earth to witness that more than four or five times Akiba was censured on my account before Rabban Gamaliel because I complained to him of him,[2] and, for all that, I know that he loved me the more." [3] A man is bound to persist in his admonitions until the offender violently repulses him and positively refuses to hear him; but it must be in all kindness, and above all not in a way to put him to shame.[4]

A similar injunction of Jesus to his disciples is recorded in Luke 17, 3 f.: 'If thy brother sin, reprove him, and if he repent forgive him. And if seven times in the day he sin against thee, and seven times turn to thee saying, I repent, thou shalt forgive him.' [5] In the corresponding passage in Matthew (18, 15–17), a procedure is prescribed, beginning with a private interview, a repetition, if necessary, in the presence of one or two others, and eventually a complaint to the assembly (church). 'If he refuse to listen to the assembly, let him be to thee like a heathen or a toll-man.' [6] What in Jewish law is obligatory on all, is in Luke a precept addressed to the circle of disciples, and in Matthew is developed into a process of church discipline.[7]

[1] Contrast the generation to whom the words of Moses (Deut. 1) were addressed, Sifrè Deut. § 1 (ed. Friedmann f. 64a, below). Sifra on Lev. 19, 17 (ed. Weiss f. 89b); 'Arakin 16b (Yalkut I § 789).

[2] See Bacher, Tannaiten, I, 366 and note 3.

[3] Sifra l.c. In the parallel in 'Arakin 16b, Prov. 9, 8 is quoted: 'Reprove not a scorner, lest he hate thee; reprove a wise man and he will love thee.' See Bacher, l.c.

[4] He is bound to desist short of this point (see above, p. 147), for the law says, 'And not take upon thyself sin on his account.'

[5] Cf. Matt. 18, 21 f.

[6] With whom you have no dealings.

[7] It has been embodied as such in the ecclesiastical law of some Protestant churches.

On the other hand, it is the bounden duty of one who has wronged another by deed or word to make full reparation and seek the forgiveness of the injured party, and of the latter to accept the amends and forgive the suppliant. "Sins that are between a man and God the Day of Atonement expiates; sins that are between a man and his fellow the Day of Atonement does not expiate until he has conciliated his fellow."[1]

A procedure is laid down by Samuel:[2] One who has sinned against his fellow ought to say to him, I have done very wrong to you. If he accepts it, well and good. If not, he should take men with him and set them in a row,[3] and appease him in their presence, confessing his sin ('I have sinned, and perverted what was right, and was not requited.' Job 33, 27); if he does so, the Scripture says of him, 'He redeemeth his soul from going into the pit, and his life will see the light' (Job 33, 28).[4] In the case of man as well as God the condition of forgiveness is repentance and confession.[5] When the wrong-doer makes this amends, it is the duty of the injured party to forgive him: "When thou hast mercy upon thy fellow, thou hast One to have mercy on thee; but if thou hast not mercy upon thy fellow, thou hast none to have mercy on thee."[6]

With this may be compared the development of the same ideas in Sirach: "Vindictiveness and anger — these also are abominable, and a sinful man will make them his own. He who avenges himself will experience vengeance from the Lord, and He will surely lay up his sins for him. Forgive the wrong done by thy neighbor, and then when thou dost ask it thy sins will be remitted. Will a man cherish anger against a man and seek healing

[1] M. Yoma 8, 9; cf. Sifra, Aharè Pereḳ 8 (ed. Weiss f. 83a); Yoma 87a. See also the parable of Jose ha-Kohen, Rosh ha-Shanah 17b.

[2] Died 254 A.D.

[3] With a peculiar twist of the words ישר על אנשים.

[4] Jer. Yoma 45c; cf. Tanḥuma ed. Buber Wayyera § 30 (Pesiḳta Rabbati, ed. Friedmann, f. 165a).

[5] In that of man, reparation also.

[6] Tanḥuma, l.c. Matt. 6, 14 f., cf. vs. 12. Luke 17, 3; Matt. 18, 21 f. See Vol. I, p. 512.

from the Lord! On a man like himself he has no mercy, and he begs pardon for his own sins! Being flesh himself, he nurses a grudge. Who will make propitiation for his sins?"[1]

In the Testaments of the Twelve Patriarchs, Gad warns his children at length and with much earnestness against hatred, envy, and cognate sins. Particularly notable is chapter 6: "Put away hatred from your heart, and love one another in deed and word and thought. . . . Love one another from the heart; and if a man sin against thee, speak peaceably to him, and do not hold guile in thy soul; and if he repent and confess, forgive him. But if he deny, do not wrangle with him, lest, if he swear, thou sin doubly. . . . If he deny it, and be shamed by the reproof, desist. . . . But if he is shameless and persists in his badness, even so, forgive him from the heart, and leave the retribution to God."[2]

The passage is of critical importance for the evidence it gives that when the Hebrew original of the Testaments was written,[3] the Jewish law defining the way in which a man who has been wronged by another should treat the wrong-doer had been developed in all its particulars as has been set forth in our preceding pages, so that moralists embodied it in their teaching and exhortations.

Later teachers discuss the question whether a more excellent way is not to abstain from reproof altogether[4] out of humility, that is, lest, in admonishing another, a man seem to be arrogating to himself superior rectitude. For humility is the greatest of all virtues.[5]

[1] Ecclus. 27, 30–28, 5.
[2] Gad 6, 1, 3–4, 6a.
[3] Probably in the latter half of the second century B.C.
[4] Even 'for its own sake,' i.e. as a religious duty.
[5] 'Arakin 16b. The question is raised by R. Judah son of R. Simeon (Simeon ben Pazzi; see Bacher, Pal. Amoräer, III, 160 f.). On the pre-eminence of humility, see 'Abodah Zarah 20b, and below, pp. 273 ff.

CHAPTER VI

RELATIONS OF SOCIAL CLASSES

THE ideal of the religion of Israel was a society in which all the relations of men to their fellows were governed by the principle, 'Thou shalt love thy neighbor as thyself.' Social and economic conditions had changed in many ways, but there is no reason to think that reality came nearer to this sublime ideal in the days of the Asmonaeans or of Herod than in those of Uzziah and Jeroboam II, when the prophets thundered against the wrongs that the rich and powerful inflicted upon their less fortunate countrymen. In many of the Psalms which may be probably assigned to the Persian or Greek periods there is a strident note of class conflict. 'Rich' becomes a frequent synonym for 'wicked.' The rich oppress the poor and rob them by force or fraud; they pervert justice, so that there is no remedy. The distinctive thing in this outcry is that the social strife deepens into a religious cleavage. The poor and humble are in their own consciousness the pious;[1] they denounce their adversaries as ungodly.[2] The ill-treatment they suffer is conceived as persecution for righteousness' sake.[3] The Psalms of Solomon testify eloquently to the feeling of the pious[4] toward the later Asmonaean princes and the aristocracy, lay and clerical, that surrounded them. Still more vehement is Enoch 94–104, a half century or more earlier, where the same charges and worse are made by the Pharisaean party apparently against John Hyrcanus[5] or Alexander Jannaeus.

What remained of the Asmonaean nobility was superseded under Herod by his own creatures, and under the procurators a

[1] *Ḥasidim.*

[2] *Resha'im*, 'wicked,' in the religious sense.

[3] See also Wisdom of Solomon, 2, 10 ff., and elsewhere.

[4] Ὅσιοι (*ḥasidim*).

[5] After his breach with the Pharisees.

Judaean aristocracy played no part, though some of the great families may have been very wealthy. In the war of 66–72 many of the well-to-do perished; others were sold into slavery. The revenues which had flowed to Jerusalem from the diaspora through the poll-tax for the maintainance of the *sacra publica* or been expended there by the multitudes of pilgrims, ceased. The demand for sacrificial victims, the rearing of which must have been of considerable economic importance, was at an end.[1] In Judaea all classes were impoverished; Galilee probably soon recovered a measure of prosperity, through its fertility and its trade with the Phoenician coast. Then came the wars under Trajan, which were disastrous for the Jews in Mesopotamia and a great part of Greek-speaking Jewry, and the war under Hadrian which again devastated Judaea. Of the old social cleavage between the rich and powerful and the poor and oppressed much less is heard.[2] Poor and pious are no longer synonyms opposed to rich and wicked.

The new division is between the class who are instructed in their religion and scrupulous in the performance of its obligations, and the ignorant and negligent masses. The Scribes and Pharisees are the older representatives of the former class; the learned and their students[3] succeed them. They called the masses, "the people of the land,"[4] a name which in Ezra and Nehemiah is applied to the half-heathenish native population of Judaea, and carried over this derogatory connotation into the rabbinical use.[5]

This division appears in the utterances of teachers of the first century as something universally understood,[6] but its consequences were more fully developed in the schools of the second

[1] For a somewhat similar case see Pliny, Letter to Trajan, x. 96, near the end.

[2] Some echoes of it are heard in Luke, e.g. 6, 20 ff.

[3] *Ḥakamim*, *Talmidè ḥakamim*.

[4] *'Ammè ha-areṣ*.

[5] See Strack und Billerbeck, Kommentar zum Neuen Testament aus Talmud und Midrasch, II (1924), 494–519; G. F. Moore, in Jackson and Lake, The Beginnings of Christianity, I (1920), Appendix E (pp. 439–445).

[6] See Hillel's words. Abot 2, 5: No boor (*bor*) fears to sin, and no *'am ha-areṣ* is pious.

century in Galilee, where the scholars who migrated thither after the war under Hadrian probably found both in town and country a population which knew less about the traditional law than the corresponding class in Judaea, and was more negligent in the observance of the law they knew.[1]

Apart from the conviction that the neglect of His laws by the mass of the people perpetuated the disfavor of God under which the whole nation manifestly lay, those who undertook for themselves personally to conform strictly to the laws, written and unwritten, were constantly in danger of being defeated in their endeavor by the ignorance and negligence of others. If such a man was a guest at the table of a common man (*'am ha-areṣ*) or bought country produce of him in the market, what assurance had he that the priest's portion and the tithes had been set apart and delivered to their proper destination, or the laws about the fruits of the fallow year complied with?[2] If they had not, he himself violated the law in eating such food, and his ignorance of the fact was no apology.

Then there was the large category of uncleanness. The food set before him, or what he purchased, might have been rendered unclean, and therefore religiously prohibited, in any one of many ways. The clothing, seat, or couch of the common man might be unclean, and communicate their contagious defilement to any one who even accidentally or unwittingly touched them, with secondary consequences that might be most serious.[3]

In these circumstances self-protection dictated the general presumption that the common man was not exact in matters of agricultural taxation, and that he and his belongings were unclean. In the former case the scrupulous buyer could for himself remedy

[1] The Jews in Galilee seem previously to have run more to a militant patriotism than to punctiliousness in their religious obligations. In Babylonia the *'am ha-areṣ* question does not appear ever to have had anything like the same importance.

[2] These laws continued in force "in the Land," notwithstanding the destruction of the temple.

[3] These interdictions, it should be observed, are biblical; they are not rabbinical extensions.

the seller's neglect by setting apart the proper proportion of the suspected purchase;[1] but the presumption of uncleanness was a serious bar to social intercourse, and indeed to friendly relations of any kind.

The religious leaders tried to instruct the peasantry in the somewhat complicated laws of tithing and the like, and to induce them to fulfil the requirements. From a man who was recognized as "a tither"[2] the scrupulous could buy without being under the necessity of tithing over again for themselves, and it would be only natural that they should do their marketing with him. Later, one who has undertaken to observe the regulations about these matters was certified as "trustworthy" (*ne'eman*).

The punctilious Jews, on their side, formed a voluntary association, the members of which pledged themselves in the presence of three associates[3] to observe strictly the laws regarding uncleanness and the precautions by which they were surrounded, as well as those noted in the preceding paragraphs. The specific obligations assumed are thus enumerated: The Associate shall not give Terumah or tithes to (a priest or levite who is) an *'am ha-areṣ;* perform his purifications in the presence of a man of this class; be the guest of one, or entertain one in his house unless he leave his outer garment outside; he shall not sell him of the products of the soil either "dry" (grain and the like) or "moist" (garden vegetables or fruits), or buy from him any but "dry" things (which are not liable to contract uncleanness by contact), etc.[4] He should not travel in company with one of the class, visit him, study the Law in his presence, and much more to the like effect. The "people of the land" were not to be summoned as witnesses, nor their testimony admitted; no secret was to be entrusted to them; one of them might not be appointed guardian of an orphan, or custodian of the poor rates, etc.[5] Mar-

[1] The oldest law on this subject (Demai) is attributed to the high priest Johanan (John Hyrcanus). Soṭah 48a. See Strack-Billerbeck, Kommentar zum Neuen Testament, u. s. w., II, 500. [2] מעשר.

[3] M. Demai 3, 2 f.; cf. Tos. Demai 2, 2. Strack-Billerbeck, II, 501.

[4] Bekorot 30b. [5] Pesaḥim 49b.

riage between the two classes was condemned in terms of abhorrence. Admission to the association was open to men of the common people on the same conditions as to the educated class, with provision for the instruction of the former in the obligations he assumed in a probationary period. It was, in fact, one of the means by which conscientious Jews tried to secure a more general knowledge of the law and regard for it. It may be suspected that the animosity which many of the teachers of the second century express in most emphatic language toward the "people of the land" was provoked by the fact that few of them responded to this uplifting enterprise; the majority remained wilfully in their ignorance and negligence.

The splitting of society on such lines involves graver evils than the reciprocal antipathy of classes, however ugly the feeling and the expression of it may be, and the worst effect of it is upon those of whom better things are justly expected. The educated had the common pride of learning in double measure because it was religious learning. It was impossible to obey the divine laws without knowledge of the Law, written and traditional. Hillel had put it in a word, "No ignorant man (*'am ha-areṣ*) is religious."[1] They were no less proud of the pains they took to keep the laws in all their refinements, and particularly, as we have seen above, those about which common men were most careless. They were led in this way to lay especial stress on articles in the laws which from our point of view seem of the smallest religious significance — the taxation of agricultural produce for the support of a hereditary clergy that after the destruction of the temple no longer had any sacerdotal functions, and the various kinds of uncleanness which, detached from their relation to participation in the cultus, were extended to social intercourse.

The large development of these sides of the law long antedates the Christian era, and pre-occupation with such things is the only notion many have of Pharisaism. So far as that is concerned, the

[1] Abot 2, 5 אין בור ירא חטא ולא עם הארץ חסיד; Tos. Berakot 7, 18, illustrated by a parable. Cf. John 7, 49.

Pharisee or the Schoolman would have replied: God gave these laws for reasons sufficient to himself; it is not for men to set them aside as antiquated or unimportant. In the application of them many cases arise which require a definite ruling and a practice in conformity to it. You may think them small commandments by the side of those whose obligation the reason and conscience of all men recognize; but fidelity to the revealed will of God is not a small matter, and the crucial test of it is precisely solicitude about keeping the commandments whose obligation is solely positive — God has commanded thus and so. It is, as has been repeatedly remarked, the unimpeachable logic of revealed religion.

The effect of such a situation as we have been considering goes farther than this putting of all obligations in principle on the same plane. In all sects, and in every *ecclesiola in ecclesia*, it is the peculiarities in doctrine, observance, or piety, that are uppermost in the minds of the members; what they have in common with the great body is no doubt taken for granted, but, so to speak, lies in the sectarian subconsciousness.

Worse than this displacement of values by emphasis on the differential peculiarities is the self-complacency of the members of such a party or association and the self-righteousness that comes of believing that their peculiarities of doctrine or practice make them singularly well-pleasing to God. With this goes censoriousness towards outsiders, which often presumes to voice the disapprobation of God. The Pharisees and the Associates, who seem to have numbered among them in the second century most of the learned and their disciples, conspicuously illustrate these faults. It is not without detriment to himself that a man cherishes the consciousness of being superior to his fellows, and the injury to his character is not least when he has the best reason for his opinion. To this point we shall have occasion to recur when we come to the subject of piety.

CHAPTER VII

PRIVATE AND PUBLIC CHARITY

Solicitude for the poor is broadly impressed on the biblical legislation. The laws for their benefit contemplate a population living in simple conditions, chiefly on the land. When a piece of grain is harvested the corners are to be left uncut; a sheaf that has been overlooked in the field is not to be reclaimed; nor is the field to be gone over to gather up the loose heads that have fallen. Similarly not all the grapes on the vines are to be gathered; the olive trees are not to be gone over a second time. The gleaning of the grain fields and of the orchards and vineyards are for the poor.[1] In the seventh year, when the fields lay fallow and the vineyards were not pruned, what grew of itself was free to the whole community as well as to the proprietor.[2]

The biblical laws on these subjects are frequently indefinite and sometimes apparently at variance with one another. A real conflict between divine commandments was, however, inconceivable,[3] and it was the task of the learned not only to harmonize them by interpretation but to combine them for practical observance. The mere repetition of laws between which there seems to be no difference made it necessary to find something in the one that was not explicit in the other.[4]

These agricultural laws apply to the land of Israel; but of the territory to which that name might have been given in the days of the kingdoms, or included within its ideal boundaries, the Jews in the period with which we are concerned formed a com-

[1] Lev. 19, 9 f.; Deut. 24, 20 f.

[2] Exod. 23, 10 f.; Lev. 25, 2–7.

[3] The modern critical explanation of these diversities, namely that they come from different sources and represent different periods in the history of the legislation, contradicts the very idea of revealed religion which was the foundation of Judaism. See Vol. I, pp. 112, 235 f, 247 ff.

[4] This is an accepted hermeneutic principle.

pact population only in a much reduced Judaea, and a predominant element in Galilee. The question where these laws were to be treated as in force called urgently for decision. Again, the taxes and contributions for the support of the ministry after the cessation of the worship in the temple required regulation. The first of the six grand divisions of the Mishnah is devoted to these subjects, dealing with the details of observance and the rights of the poor as well as of priests and levites under the various laws. It is evident from our sources that the provisions for the poor contemplated by the laws, even with a liberal interpretation, was inadequate under the actual conditions, and that other measures were necessary.[1]

In the laws about loans it is presumed that a man borrows only in case of need, and the lender is forbidden to profit by his neighbor's necessity by getting back more than he lent ('usury'). At the end of the seventh year all debts were to be cancelled.[2] If an Israelite was so reduced that he had to sell his services to another, he served six years, being meanwhile supported by his master, and at the end of the term was released, the master being enjoined to furnish him out liberally from the flock, the threshing floor, and the wine press, so that he may be started on the way to self-support.[3]

The poor had a prescriptive right to share in the family or communal feasts at the holy places, and under the Deuteronomic law at Jerusalem. The same law provides that the tithes of every third year are to be laid up in the village or town where the tither lives, for the support of the local poor.[4] Certain classes

[1] See below, pp. 174 ff.

[2] Deut. 15, 2.

[3] Exod. 21, 2–4; Deut. 15, 12–15. The term-service contemplated in these laws is a benevolent provision for enabling a man who has fallen into debt to work off his obligation and start afresh.

[4] Deut. 14, 28 f. Jewish law distinguished (1) the tithe of agricultural products paid for the support of the ministry; (2) the "second tithe," to be consumed by the proprietor with his family, dependents, and guests, in a feast in Jerusalem; (3) the "poor tithe" which took the place of (2) in the third and sixth years of each septennial period. See Encyclopaedia Biblica, IV, cols. 5102–5105.

are frequently specified in Deuteronomy as objects of charity: the levite, the alien living in an Israelite community (*ger*), the orphan, and the widow.[1] The two first named own no land from which to get a living; the orphan and the widow have lost their natural providers. They are all under the peculiar patronage of God.[2]

Such provisions as are outlined above were not adapted to a large urban population, but in Jerusalem, so long as the temple stood, the festivals and the many family feasts, at which generosity was law and custom, doubtless in some measure supplied the deficiency, but much must have been left to public and private almsgiving. The injunction of liberality is finely put in Deut. 15, 11: 'The needy will never disappear from the land; therefore I command thee, Open thy hand to thy poor and needy brother in thy land.'[3] How a good man fulfilled his duty to those who needed his help is ideally described in Job 29, 12–16: 'I delivered the poor that cried, the fatherless also that had none to help him. The blessing of him that was ready to perish came upon me; and I caused the widow's heart to sing for joy. I put on righteousness, and it clothed itself with me; my justice was a robe and a diadem. I was eyes to the blind, and feet was I to the lame. I was a father to the needy, and the cause of him that I knew not I searched out.'

Or again (31, 16–22, 29–32): 'If I have withheld aught that the poor desired, or have caused the eyes of the widow to fail; or have eaten my morsel myself alone, and the fatherless hath not eaten thereof — Nay, from my youth he grew up with me as with a father, and I have been her guide from my mother's womb. If I have seen any wanderer in want of clothing, or that the needy had no covering; if his loins have not blessed me, and if he were not warmed with the fleece of my sheep; if I have lifted up my hand against the fatherless, because I saw my help in the gate;

1 Deut. 16, 11, 14; 24, 19, 20, 21; 26, 12, 13.

2 Deut. 10, 18; 24, 17; 27, 19; Jer. 7, 6; 23, 3; Zech. 7, 10; Psalm 10, 14, 18.

3 Cf. Lev. 25, 35–37.

then let my shoulder fall from the shoulder-blade, and mine arm be broken from the bone.'

'If I rejoiced at the destruction of him that hated me, or exulted when evil found him — Yea, I suffered not my mouth to sin by asking his life with a curse. If the men of my tent said not, Who can find one that hath not been satisfied with his meat? The stranger did not lodge in the street; my doors I opened to the roadside.'

It is needless to multiply quotations here from the many places in all parts of the Scripture commanding or commending beneficence to the poor.[1] The same theme runs through the uncanonical literature. It is frequent in Sirach.[2] Tobit begins with a recital of his charities to the living and the dead.[3] The exhortations of Jesus in the Gospels are in the same vein,[4] as are also the Apostolic writings.[5]

The jurists of our period interpreted the Mosaic legislation on the subject of charity in its spirit, sometimes, to our notions of exegesis, straining the letter in doing so, and in their application adapted it to the conditions of their own time.[6] An instructive example is the oldest juristic commentary on Deut. 15, 7–11.[7] In the context the passage is a warning against refusing to lend to a necessitous countryman, especially in the immediate prospect of the septennial cancellation of debts. The Midrash extends it to gifts,[8] and only incidentally touches on loans secured by a pledge (vs. 8).

1 Familiar examples are, Isa. 58, 7, 10; Ezek. 18, 17 f.; Psalm 37, 21; 41, 2; Prov. 14, 20 f., 31; 19, 17; 21, 26; 28, 27; 3, 27 f., etc.

2 Ecclus. 4, 1–6; 29, 1–13, cf. 21–28; 18, 15–18, etc. See also 10, 22 f.

3 See also Tobit 4, 7–11; 12, 8 f.

4 Matt. 5, 42; Luke 6, 30–38.

5 James 1, 27 (cf. 5, 1–6; 2, 6); Hebrews 13, 16; 1 John 3, 17.

6 On these regulations see S. Krauss, Talmudische Archäologie, III, 70–74, and notes pp. 271–273.

7 Sifrè Deut. §§ 116–118 (ed. Friedmann f. 98a–b). For a translation of the whole passage see Strack-Billerbeck on Matt. 5, 42 (Kommentar zum N. T. aus Talmud und Midrasch, I, 346 f.). With Sifrè, this part of which comes from the school of Akiba (Simeon ben Yoḥai), should be compared Midrash Tannaim ed. D. Hoffmann, pp. 81–85.

8 Deut. 15, 10.

The Scripture (vs. 7) forbids a man to harden his heart toward his needy brother or close his hand — there are men who are perplexed [1] whether to give or not to give, and men who stretch out their hand and afterwards contract it. From vs. 9, 'Beware lest there be in thy heart a wicked thought, and thou be evil-eyed toward thy needy brother and thou give him naught,' the lesson is drawn: "Be careful not to refuse charity, for every one who refuses charity is put (by the text) in the same category with idolaters, and he breaks off from him the yoke of Heaven (God), as it is said, *wicked*, that is *without yoke*." [2] The hard-hearted and close-fisted man who will not give to his poor brother will one day be reduced to receiving alms from him.

A man's hand is to be open wide for the relief of need (vs. 8, cf. 11), and not once but a hundred times.[3] The gift is to be sufficient for the need — men are not required to enrich the recipient.[4] If he needs a loaf of bread, that is to be given him, or dough, or money; if the food has to be put into his mouth, he is to be fed in that way. On the other hand, 'whatever he lacks' (vs. 8, end) is taken to mean not merely what is necessary for a living, but whatever he lacks that belongs to his social station and former habit of life, even a horse to ride and a slave to run before him, as is illustrated by an anecdote about Hillel, who once did exactly this for an impoverished son of a good family,[5] and by a story about a town in Upper Galilee where the people provided a man who in his better days had been accustomed to luxury with a pound daily of the flesh of birds. By a more subtle com-

[1] So Yalkuṭ, Rashi, and Midrash Tannaim (from Midrash ha-Gadol); cf. vs. 10. The printed text of Sifrè has "who cause pain."

[2] Both these sins are found in the word conventionally translated 'wicked,' in Hebrew *beliya'al* (familiar in the phrase, 'sons of Belial'). The idolatry comes by way of Deut. 13, 14; 'breaking off the yoke,' by taking *beliya'al* as a compound, equivalent to *bĕli* (without) *'ol* (yoke). Cf. Sanhedrin 111b, end. It is the most radical of sins, the rejection of the authority of God. See Vol. 1, pp. 465 f.

[3] Deduced on Akiba's principles from the repetition, פתח תפתח.

[4] To make him better off than he was before.

[5] Once when there was no slave at hand, Hillel himself ran before him three miles. Ketubot 67b; cf. Sifrè on Deut. 15, 8.

bination it was made out that if a man was too poor to marry, the last words of vs. 8 required that he should be enabled to support a wife.[1]

Again, from the phrase, 'Thou shalt give *to him*' (vs. 10), it is deduced that a gift to the poor must be made privately, with no one else present; and as an illustration reference is made to a chamber in the temple in Jerusalem where peculiarly scrupulous persons[2] deposited their charitable donations in secrecy, while with equal privacy the impoverished members of good families drew from this fund their sustenance.[3]

The intent of the legislator in vs. 8 is plain: A loan sufficient for the need of the borrower is to be made on the security of a pledge.[4] The rabbis, who interpreted the whole passage of charitable *gifts*, explained the mention of security in harmony with this assumption in various ways. From the repetition,[5] according to the hermeneutics of the school, it was inferred that more than one case was contemplated.[6] If a man has property but is unwilling to consume it on his living, they provide what he needs nominally as a gift, and collect from his estate after his death. If a man has nothing and is not willing to be supported by charity, they spare his feelings by letting him take it in the name of a loan, and afterward let him have it as a gift (they do not try to collect it).[7] The innocent fiction in the latter case shows a noteworthy delicacy. An illustration may be added from another source. On the words in Deut. 15, 8, 10, 'Thou shalt open thy hand' (פתח תפתח), R. Ishmael said, "If it is a man of good

[1] אשר יחסר לו and Gen. 2, 18, אעשה לו עזר כנגדו.

[2] Literally, "the sin-fearing." Midrash Tannaim (p. 83, end) reads, "the righteous."

[3] On this chamber, לשכת חשאים, see M. Sheḳalim 5, 6; Tos. Sheḳalim 2, 16. According to the latter, there was a similar institution in every city. The name means "chamber of the silent." With the Essenes it has nothing to do beyond a fortuitous resemblance of sound to Ἐσσαῖοι.

[4] Cf. the same expression in vs. 6.

[5] תעבט תעביטנו.

[6] The different opinions are more fully reported in Ketubot 67b.

[7] Ketubot 67b; cf. Sifrè Deut. § 116. The authorities cited by name (R. Meir, R. Judah, R. Simeon) flourished in the middle of the second century.

family and he is ashamed (to ask alms), 'open' to him with words, My son, perhaps you need a loan. Hence the authorities say, Alms is given like a loan."[1]

The promise of God's blessing on the benevolent (vs. 10) includes not only the man who gives for the relief of the poor but one who solicits others to give; and if, unable to give anything else, he expresses his sympathy in words, that too has its reward.[2] On the other hand, warning is given that the poor man refused an alms may cry to the Lord against him who refused him, 'and it will be sin in thee.' Sin it is in any case, but God will be quicker to punish when the unfortunate cries to him.

It will no doubt have occurred to the reader that most of this fine doctrine about charity is interpreted into the text, not out of it. And that is precisely the thing to be observed about it. The fundamentals of Jewish teaching on the subject from a far earlier time are here ingeniously worked into a single passage only a few verses long.

Parallels to them all can be adduced in multitude.[3] When Jesus said: 'Give to him who begs of thee, and do not turn away him who wants to borrow from thee' (Matt. 5, 42), it is not, like the preceding injunctions of non-resistance, what the Jews called conduct that keeps "inside the line,"[4] but an exact summary of what they laid down as prescribed by divine law.

To lend to a would-be borrower is not optional but obligatory,[5] and no less obligatory to give to the poor according to the measure of his need and to the ability of the giver.[6] One should not withhold the needed relief out of apprehension that if he distributes all his property to others he may himself be reduced to

[1] Midrash Tannaim ed. Hoffmann, p. 82. See also the story in Lev. R. 34, 1.

[2] בגלל הדבר הזה.

[3] A comprehensive methodical exhibition of these teachings is to be found in Maimonides, Mishneh Torah, Hilkot Mattenot 'Aniyim.

[4] See above, p. 152.

[5] Mekilta on Exod. 22, 24 (Mishpaṭim 19, ed. Friedmann f. 96a; ed. Weiss f. 102a); Mekilta de-R. Simeon ben Yoḥai on Exod. 22, 24.

[6] See above, pp. 166 f.

want and come to be a charge on the community; he should trust the promise of Deut. 15, 10b — if he does his part, God will do His. He has the best of security, for 'he who befriends the poor lends to the Lord, and He will repay him for his good deed' (Prov. 19, 17).[1] The donor, who owes God all he has,[2] becomes a creditor of God — if it was not so written in Scripture, no one would venture to say such a thing![3] God says to Israel: "My sons, whenever you give food to the poor, I impute it to you as though you gave me food, as it is said, 'my offering, even my food for my fire sacrifice' (Num. 28, 2). Does God eat and drink! Nay, but whenever you give food to the poor I impute it to you as though you gave me food."[4]

On the other side, to one who has means but withholds relief from the needy, God says: Keep in mind that it is I that made him poor and thee rich; I can send reverses on thee and make *thee* poor.[5] In the same connection another takes occasion from the expression בגלל[6] in Deut. 15, 10 to compare the ups and downs of men's fortunes to the turning of a wheel (גלגל). God says: I made him poor and thee rich. Do not cause me to turn the wheel over, and make thee poor.[7] The general principle applied to the particular case is: "To every one who shows mercy

[1] Midrash Tannaim on Deut. 15, 10 (ed. Hoffmann, pp. 83–84). See the discussion of Rabban Gamaliel (II) with a "philosopher" (cf. 'Abodah Zarah 54b), *ibid.*, p. 84.

[2] Exod. R. 31, 15.

[3] Baba Batra 10a, below; Lev. R. 34, 2 (on Lev. 25, 25). Bacher, Pal. Amoräer, I, 407.

[4] Midrash Tannaim on Deut. 15, 9 (ed. Hoffmann, p. 83, below). Cf. Matt. 25, 40: The King will say, In so far as you did it to one of these humblest brothers of mine you did it to me.

[5] Tanḥuma ed. Buber, Mishpaṭim § 8.

[6] Instead of the more common למען. Similarly R. Ishmael, Shabbat 151b.

[7] For the figure of the wheel see Exod. R. 31, 14 (on Exod. 14, 25), 'God is judge; one he brings down and one he lifts up' (Psalm 75, 8). The author has in mind a wheel such as is used in irrigation; the buckets at the bottom come up full; those at the top go down empty. Not every one who is rich today will be rich tomorrow, and not every one that is poor today will be poor tomorrow. The world is a wheel. Other references, יפה עינים on Shabbat 151b. See also Lev. R. 34, 3.

to other men, mercy is shown from Heaven; but to him who shows no mercy to other men, no mercy is shown from Heaven."[1]

In the great distress that followed the war under Hadrian, some of those who still had means seem to have been moved to part with all their possessions to relieve their perishing countrymen. Wiser heads recognized that, however commendable the spirit of such uncalculating generosity might be in itself, the voluntary impoverishment of this class would but increase the evils it was meant to alleviate. The rule was accordingly laid down that no one should in this way dissipate more than one fifth of his property.[2] In the corresponding passage in the Jerusalem Talmud this is explained as one fifth (of the capital) to begin with and a fifth (of the income) each succeeding year.[3]

A man's first obligation is to support the dependent members of his own family,[4] then to relieve the necessities of his kinsfolk and his townsmen.[5] He is not bound to give to the beggar who goes around from door to door; of such cases it is the business of the organized charity of the community to take care.[6] The Gentile and the foreigner have a place in Jewish charity, but the fellow Israelite has a prior claim.[7]

If one has nothing to give to a needy man, he should express his deep regret that he is unable to relieve his necessity, thus fulfilling Isa. 58, 10 ('If thou draw out thy soul to the hungry').

It is very significant that the usual word for alms in this

[1] Shabbat 151b; cf. Midrash Tannaim on Deut. 15, 11. Matt. 5, 7, and Strack-Billerbeck ad loc.

[2] This ordinance was adopted at Usha, where the leaders assembled under the presidency of R. Simeon ben Gamaliel, and is reported by a contemporary, R. Ila'i. Ketubot 50a; 'Arakin 28a; Jer. Peah 15b. The obligation of a man to support his minor children was laid down at the same gathering. Jer. Ketubot 28d, middle.

[3] Jer. Ketubot 28d, near the end; Jer Peah 15b.

[4] Cf. Ketubot 50a (Psalm 106, 3).

[5] On the precedence among charitable claims see Mekilta, Mishpaṭim 19 (ed. Friedmann f. 96b; ed. Weiss f. 102a–b); Baba Meṣi'a 71a, top; Tanḥuma ed. Buber, Mishpaṭim § 8.

[6] Tos. Peah 4, 8. See below, pp. 176 f.

[7] Mekilta l. c.

period [1] is *ṣedaḳah*, which in the English version of the Bible is all but uniformly rendered 'righteousness,' whether used of God or of man. Like every such conventional equivalent, this one not infrequently misleads the reader, all the more because 'righteousness' is frequently coupled with 'justice' (*mishpaṭ*), and because the Christian reader brings to the word Pauline associations. The 'righteousness' of God is frequently shown, however, in his vindication [2] of his people by delivering them from their enemies or from other evils, so that the word becomes parallel to the words for deliverance, salvation,[3] blessing,[4] kindness,[5] and, as a result, even to property, wealth.[6] The Greek translators sometimes render it not by *δικαιοσύνη* but by *ἐλεημοσύνη*, as better expressing the implications of the context as they understood it.[7] In Dan. 4, 24 (English version 4, 27) the corresponding Aramaic *ṣidḳah* is 'alms-giving': 'Redeem thy sins by alms-giving[8] and thine iniquities by showing mercy to the poor.'

Another word for charity is *miṣwah*, literally, 'a commandment,' meaning not a specific commandment, but any particular opportunity to fulfil the comprehensive duty of men to their fellows; and the development of this sense also throws light on the mental attitude of the Jews toward the whole subject.

There is a higher form of this virtue which not merely relieves bodily needs by private almsgiving or through contributions to the organized charities of the community,[9] but gives personal attention, sympathy, and service. For this there is a special name, *gemīlūt ḥasadīm*.[10] "Almsgiving and deeds of lovingkindness are equal to all the commandments of the Law. Almsgiving is exer-

[1] This use is much older; it occurs in the Elephantine papyri (fifth century) as well as in the Hebrew Sirach.

[2] The verb הצדיק is not only *justificare* but *vindicare;* cf. שפט, 'judge, deliver.'

[3] Frequently in Isa. 40 ff.

[4] Psalm 24, 5.

[5] חסד, Psalm 36, 11; 103, 17.

[6] Prov. 8, 18.

[7] Deut. 6, 25; 24, 13; Isa. 1, 27; 28, 17; 59, 16; Psalm 24, 5.

[8] So correctly both Greek versions, Latin, Syriac. Protestant translators shy at the doctrine and woodenly render, 'righteousness.'

[9] See below, pp. 174 ff.

[10] Literally, doing deeds of lovingkindness.

cised toward the living, deeds of lovingkindness toward the living and the dead; almsgiving to the poor, deeds of lovingkindness to the poor and to the rich; almsgiving is done with a man's money, deeds of lovingkindness either with his money or personally."[1] In all these the superiority of deeds of lovingkindness is affirmed.[2] Almsgiving itself is requited (by God) only in proportion to the love (*ḥesed*) that there is in it.[3] Alms given in this spirit are more than all the sacrifices (Prov. 21, 3),[4] and deeds of lovingkindness more than almsgiving (Hos. 10, 12). In the words of Simeon the Righteous, the world is upheld in being by three things, the Law (knowledge of divine revelation), the cultus (in the temple), and lovingkindness to men.[5] For the last in the Abot de-R. Nathan Hos. 6, 6 is adduced, and it is told how Johanan ben Zakkai consoled a disciple who was lamenting over the destruction of the temple, the place where atonement was made for the sins of Israel: "My son, do not be grieved; we have one atonement that is equal to it. What is that? Deeds of lovingkindness, as it is said, 'I desire lovingkindness (*ḥesed*) and not sacrifice'" (Hos. 6, 6).[6]

Of this virtue God is the great exemplar. The world itself was created solely in lovingkindness.[7] R. Simlai observes that the Pentateuch begins with an act of lovingkindness — God made garments of skins to clothe the man and his wife — and ends with another — He buried Moses in the valley.[8] It is in such gracious deeds that man can and should imitate God, who clothes the naked, visits the sick, comforts mourners, buries the dead.[9] No one, however dignified his station, should think himself too good for the humblest offices of human help and sympathy. In the words of Micah 6, 8, 'to walk humbly with thy God,' is

1 בגופו, Jer. Peah 15b–c; Tos. Peah 4, 19; Sukkah 49b.

2 Sukkah l.c.

3 R. Eleazar (ben Pedat), ibid.

4 Ibid. Cf. Matt. 9, 13; 12, 7 (Hos. 6, 6). — Prov. 21, 3 is a favorite text for this preference. Hos. 6, 6; Abot de-R. Nathan c. 4.

5 Abot 1, 2. After the destruction of the temple prayer takes the place of sacrificial worship. See below, pp. 217 f.

6 Abot de-R. Nathan 4, 5.

7 Psalm 89, 3 (*'olam*, 'world').

8 Soṭah 14a.

9 Ibid. See above, pp. 110 f.

found the duty of joining the funeral procession or the company conducting the bride to the wedding.[1] For to rejoice with those who rejoice is no less an act of kindness than to mourn with mourners.

The high estimate put on deeds of lovingkindness might be illustrated by many quotations.[2] More significant than any such accumulation of eulogiums, however, is a passage in Sifrè in which it sums up the whole of the manward side of religion. On the words, 'If they were wise, they would consider this' (Deut. 32, 29), the comment runs: "If Israel would consider the words of the Law that was given to them, no nation or kingdom would have dominion over them (see vs. 30). And what does it (the Law) say to them? Take upon you the yoke of the kingdom of Heaven, and try to excel one another in the fear of Heaven; and conduct yourselves one to another with lovingkindness."

The first two clauses comprehend that part of religion which has to do with man's relation to God. "The yoke of the kingdom of Heaven" is the acknowledgement of God's sole sovereignty and of the obligation to love him with mind and soul and substance, which man makes when he recites the Shema' (Deut. 6, 4) — the daily renewed profession of his religion. The second clause carries this religion into practice as it is summarized in Deut. 10, 12 f.: 'And now, Israel, what doth the Lord thy God require of thee, but to revere the Lord thy God, to walk in all his ways, and to love him, and to serve the Lord thy God with all thy heart and with all thy soul; to keep for thy good the commandments of the Lord and his statutes which I command thee this day.' Try to excel one another in an obedience to God's revealed will, inspired by reverence and love.

Finally the Midrash condenses into one clause what religion requires of men in their relations to one another. This part of

[1] Sukkah 49b. When such a procession passed his school, R. Judah used to dismiss his disciples, saying, Doing takes precedence of studying. Jer. Ḥagigah 76c. A majority vote in the contrary sense is reported, *ibid.* See S. Krauss, Talmudische Archäologie, II, 38 f., 66, and 458, n. 317.

[2] See Kobryn, Catena, on Abot 1, 2 (f. 6a–7b

Sifrè is from the school of R. Akiba, who found in Lev. 19, 18, 'Thou shalt love thy neighbor as thyself,' the most comprehensive principle of the Law.[1] We have seen how this principle was applied to the protection of the property, the reputation, and the feelings of others.[2] As in Paul, however, this application is primarily negative, 'Love worketh no ill to his neighbor; therefore love is the fulfilling of the law' (Rom. 13, 10). The Sifrè goes far beyond the safeguarding of others' *rights* when it makes *gemīlūt ḥasadīm* in all the wealth of meaning that was put into that phrase the principle of all human intercourse. It requires an active charity, and makes the measure of the duty, not the rights but the needs of others.[3]

In various connections it has already appeared that the relief of the poor was not left wholly to the benevolence of individuals; the community assumed its obligation to care for those permanently or temporarily in need. The regulation of particulars in the Tosefta Peah c. 4 shows that the system was well-established and familiar at the end of the second century, and other evidence makes it probable that it was organized or reorganized under Simeon ben Gamaliel and the scholars who gathered around him in Galilee after the war under Hadrian. For the preceding period our sources give but scanty intimations.[4] For the second century they are ample.

In each municipality two collectors [5] were appointed, men of unimpeachable probity whose character warranted leaving the whole business in their hands without any accounting.[6] They made their rounds together every Friday to the market and the

[1] Sifra, Ḳedoshim Pereḳ 4 (ed. Weiss f. 89b). See above, p. 85.
[2] Above, pp. 142 ff., 147 ff.
[3] Compare the parable of the good Samaritan, Luke 10, 25–37.
[4] Ḥanina ben Teradion, who taught at Siknin in Galilee and was one of the victims of the persecution of teachers under Hadrian, had a proverbial reputation as an administrator of the community alms-chest (Baba Batra 10b; 'Abodah Zarah 17b). Akiba also figures as collector (charity tithe assigned to him, M. Ma'aser Sheni 5, 9; Ḳiddushin 27a).
[5] גבאי צדקה. M. Peah 8, 7; Baba Batra 8b.
[6] Baba Batra 9a (2 Kings 12, 16). Various regulations were made to protect them from suspicion.

shops and to private houses, taking up the weekly collection for charity in money or in kind.[1] If a man was not prepared to pay on the spot, they could require him to give a pledge;[2] they must, however, not be oppressive either in the matter or the manner of their demands, lest they incur the sentence of Jer. 30, 20.

Their duties were responsible and difficult. It is a harder thing to make others give than to give oneself, and the desert and reward are correspondingly great.[3] Still more difficult than the collection was the distribution, which was made also on Fridays by a commission of three members,[4] since they had to investigate the various needs and sometimes competing claims of the recipients. In case of necessity they might have to make up the deficiency themselves[5] or borrow to meet it. The difficulty and responsibility of the apportionment were so great that R. Jose ben Ḥalafta prayed that his lot might be among the collectors rather than the distributors.[6]

To the poor of the town there was given every Friday enough to provide for the coming week (fourteen meals); clothing also was furnished as it was needed. A temporary resident from another city who was out of money also received aid from this fund.

Upon the community fell also the support of orphan children, and the seeing of them married and launched in life for themselves by renting and furnishing a house for a man,[7] fitting out a girl with clothing, and giving her a dowry, for which a minimum sum is fixed.[8] If the funds in the community chest were low, the orphan girl was universally given priority over the boy.[9] For the

1 Baba Batra 8b.
2 Ibid.
3 Baba Batra 8b, applying Dan. 12, 3, "those who make the many give alms" (shall shine as the stars forever and ever).
4 M. Peah 8, 7; Baba Batra 8b.
5 Baba Batra 11a, top.
6 Shabbat 118b.
7 Tos. Ketubot 6, 8.
8 M. Ketubot 6, 5 (fifty *zuz*); Tos. Ketubot 6, 7.
9 Tos. Ketubot 6, 8.

burial of the poor provision was made from the public funds, and also for the ransom of captives, an obligation to which every other was postponed.[1] For these extraordinary expenses special collections were made.

An interesting feature of this institution was that in providing for the impoverished regard was had, so far as funds were available, to the social position of the beneficiary and his former manner of life — the kind of food and dress to which he was accustomed,[2] and so also in the garments furnished the orphan bride.[3]

Besides the collection for this community chest,[4] there was a daily collection of victuals from house to house called *tamḥui*.[5] This was received and distributed by a committee of three to such as were in pressing need of food for the coming day.[6] No one who had two meals in the house could claim relief from this source, as no one who had provision for a week could claim it from the *ḳuppah*.[7] While the latter was for residents, the *tamḥui* was for strangers also. For the vagrant[8] a minimum ration of bread was prescribed; if he stayed over night, he was given lodging, oil, and pulse; over sabbath, food for three meals, oil, pulse, fish, and fresh vegetables;[9] if he is known to them, they may give him clothing also. Public provision for the relief of such cases being made, begging from door to door was disfavored; charitable housewives often gave food to such mendicants, but the

1 Baba Batra 8a–b. Here also, the woman first, M. Horayot 3, 7.

2 Even to a horse to ride and a slave to run before him — fortified by an anecdote of Hillel. Sifrè on Deut. 15, 8 (see above, p. 166); Tos Peah 4, 10; Ketubot 67b.

3 M. Ketubot 6, 5.

4 קופה (*ḳuppah*, literally 'basket'). Also כיס, 'purse' and ארנקי, 'bag.'

5 תמחוי (*tamḥui*), the name of a tray or shallow dish with compartments for different kinds of food. Cooked food, presumably remnants, was thus collected.

6 Baba Batra 8b.

7 M. Peah 8, 7.

8 עני עובר ממקום למקום, 'the poor man passing from place to place.'

9 The more generous fare which belonged to sabbath observance, to make it a delight. Tos. Peah 4, 8.

latter then forfeited their right to assistance from the overseers of the poor.[1]

Public as well as private charity has always had its chapter of impostors, and the Jews were no exception. Their rule was that if a man pleaded hunger he should be fed without further question, but if an unknown beggar asked for clothing the case should be investigated. There were mendicants who made themselves out to be blind, or gave themselves wounds on their legs, or simulated a dropsical swelling of the belly; and they are warned that before they die they will suffer in reality from the infirmities they now pretend.[2] Similarly, one who takes alms which he does not need will come to genuine poverty before he ends.[3]

Men should make every effort not to become a public charge. Rather make your sabbath a week day (by foregoing the sabbatical luxury) than become a burden to your fellow men.[4] A pointed application of this principle is made by Rab: "Skin the carcass of a dead beast in the market place for hire, and do not say, I am a great man, it is beneath my dignity."[5] Earn your own living even by the most repugnant employment.

Many of the most eminent scholars, as is well known, supported themselves and their families by manual labor, some of them by unskilled labor.[6] Every father was enjoined to teach his son a trade, not only because it secured him a livelihood but because of the moral influence of labor.[7] Shemaiah's motto was, "Love labor, shun office, and do not cultivate intimacy with the authorities."[8] The dignity and the blessings of labor are a frequent theme in the literature of all periods.

[1] Tos. Peah 4, 8; Jer. Peah 21a. One dried fig *pro forma* discharged all their obligations to him.

[2] Tos. Peah 4, 14; Ketubot 68a.

[3] Ketubot 68a.

[4] Shabbat 118a; Pesaḥim 112a, 113a.

[5] Baba Batra 110a; Pesaḥim 113a (I am a priest; I am a great man).

[6] Maimonides, Hilkot Mattenot ʿAniyim 10, 18.

[7] See above, pp. 127 f.

[8] Abot 1, 10. Under Herod. On the last clause cf. ʿAbodah Zarah 17a, above (Prov. 5, 8b).

To the collections for public charities all were required to contribute in the measure of their ability and of the current or occasional need. Men who moved into the town were liable to the daily collection of victuals (*tamḥui*) after thirty days residence; after three months to the weekly collection for the poor of the place (*ḳuppah*); after six to the collection for clothing; after nine to the burial fund; and at the end of the year for the defences of the city.[1] Minor orphans, even though they inherited property, were not assessed for charity,[2] nor even for the ransom of captives; nor were, naturally, the women and children of a household. From women the collectors were allowed to receive only small voluntary contributions.[3] The poor, even those themselves dependent on charity, were permitted to make a small contribution to the *ḳuppah*, but not urged to do so.[4] Where there was a suspicion that the contributor was not really the owner, it was forbidden to accept what he offered.[5,6]

In the concluding chapter of the treatise on charity[7] Maimonides enumerates eight degrees in a descending scale. The highest of all is what we might call preventive charity, which lays hold of a man who is failing, and keeps him from falling and becoming a public charge by a gift or a loan or a partnership, or by finding him work. The principle is clearly enounced in Sifra on Lev. 25, 35.[8] Such a man is like a load resting on the top of a wall; so long as it is in place one man can take hold of it and keep it there; once it is fallen to the ground, five cannot raise it up again. Next to this comes remedial charity so managed that neither

1 Baba Batra 8a, below. Cf. Tos. Peah 4, 9 (inferior text).
2 Baba Batra 8a, end.
3 Tos. Baba Ḳamma 11, 6.
4 Giṭṭin 7b, top.
5 M. Baba Ḳamma 10, 9; Tos. Baba Ḳamma 11, 9 ff.; Baba Ḳamma 119a.
6 On the almsgiving of heathen and contributions by influential Gentiles to Jewish charity funds, see Baba Batra 10b.
7 Mattenot 'Aniyim c. 10.
8 Sifra, Behar Parashah 5 *init.* (ed. Weiss f. 109b). See Rashi on Lev. 25, 35. With Maimonides' examples cf. Shabbat 63a, bottom (Bacher, Pal. Amoräer, I, 358).

donor nor the beneficiary knows who the other is.[1] This was one of the things which was accomplished by contributions to the public chest, officially collected and distributed. At the bottom of the scale comes the man who gives with a sullen mien; for the spirit and manner in which the thing is done is of the essence of the deed.[2] There are many other features in this system which it would be interesting to pursue farther did space permit, but for our present task, the place of charity in Jewish moral teaching and practice, what has been said must suffice.

[1] Baba Batra 10b, top; see above, p. 167.
[2] Maimonides l.s.c. 10, 14, cf. § 4.

CHAPTER VIII

JUSTICE, TRUTH, PEACE

In no sphere is the influence of the highest conceptions of Judaism more manifestly determinative than in that to which we give the general name of justice, including under it, *first*, fair dealing between man and man, the distributive justice which gives to each his due; *second*, public justice, the function of the community in defining and enforcing the duties and rights of individuals and classes; and, *third*, rectitude, or integrity of personal character.[1] In all parts of the Bible justice in the broad sense is the fundamental virtue on which human society is based. It is no less fundamental in the idea of God, and in the definition of what God requires of men.

We have already seen how distributive justice is summarized in the maxim that the property and the honor of another should be as dear to a man as his own, and what care is enjoined to avoid any act or word that might hurt his feelings. Some of the applications of this principle in business relations and in the censure of slander and gossip have been set forth in a former chapter.[2] It is unnecessary to enlarge further upon this aspect of the subject here. Attention may, however, be called again to the fact that the ordinary, and one may say technical, name for almsgiving in Judaism is *ṣedaḳah*, a right, or just, act, and that it is taught not only that it is the duty of those who have means thus to relieve the need of others, but that the poor have a right to such relief — a right of which God declares himself the vindicator [3]— and that in the organized charities which have been

[1] The English word 'righteousness' most frequently used in our versions for the Hebrew *ṣedeḳ* fastens the attention too exclusively on the religious quality of rightness in relation to God or in his judgment.

[2] See above, chapter 5.

[3] Deut. 15, 9.

described above the community itself enforces this right against those who neglect their individual duties.

In what we may properly call the legislation of the Tannaite period the task of the jurists was to interpret the Mosaic laws in the light of the prophetic teaching and of the examples which biography and history supplied, to adapt them to existing conditions, and to formulate them in authoritative regulations; and here also the influence of the highest religious and moral conceptions is constantly evident. In this way many of the injunctions and admonitions in the Pentateuch are drawn out into rules of conduct by a development of implications which, with our different notions of the end and method of exegesis, we should never think of. A study of the Tannaite Midrash from this point of view would be most instructive. A single illustration is all that can be given here. Leviticus 19, 16 reads: 'Thou shalt not go about as a talebearer among thy people; thou shalt not stand against the blood of thy fellow.'[1] The last clause is generally translated in this way (*against*), and understood in the sense of Exod. 23, 1–3, 7, as directed against bearing false witness on the strength of which a man might be condemned to death.[2] The phrase can, however, by itself with equal propriety be interpreted, 'Thou shalt not stand (idly) *by* the blood of thy fellow,'[3] that is, when his life is in danger. From this it is deduced in the Sifra, among other things, that if a man knows of any evidence in favor of the defendant he is not at liberty to keep silent about it, since he might thus become responsible for his death.[4] Further, that if a man sees another in peril of his life by falling into a river, or attacked by robbers, or some evil come upon him, he is bound not to stand idly by but to come to his rescue. Again, if he sees a man pursuing another to kill him, or to ravish a man or boy or a betrothed girl, he is bound to prevent the commission

[1] לא תעמוד על דם רעך.

[2] Οὐκ ἐπιστήσῃ (ἐπισυστήσῃ) ἐφ' αἷμα τοῦ πλησίον σου. Non stabis contra sanguinem proximi tui. So most modern commentators.

[3] So it is rendered in the version of the Jewish Publication Society (1917).

[4] Sifra, Ḳedoshim Pereḳ 4 (ed. Weiss f. 89a). Lev. 5, 1. M. Sanhedrin 4, 5.

of the capital crime even by taking the life of the offender.[1] Similar examples might be accumulated without number.

The administration of public justice must be without respect of persons. In a cause in which one of the parties is a poor man and the other rich, the judges must not favor the poor man because he is poor, nor show regard to the other because he is rich, but decide between them with impartial justice (Lev. 19, 15; cf. Exod. 23, 3).[2] He must not say to himself: "This man is poor; and inasmuch as this rich man is under obligation (by the general duty of charity) to support him, I will give judgment in his favor, and he will be able to make an honest living."[3] In the converse case, regard to the rich man, the judge must not reflect: "This man is rich, this one well-connected. Can I see him shamed? How much less put him to shame myself"[4] (by making him lose his case). Not only in the decision but in the whole procedure the parties are to be treated without partiality. One is not to be allowed to state his case at length and the other bidden to cut it short; one must not be allowed to be seated in court and the other kept standing, and the like.[5]

Judges who pervert justice to the disadvantage of the poor are familiar figures in the denunciations of the prophets and the prohibitions of the laws; but the ideal of even-handed justice is that which is as little swerved from the line of right by sympathy for the small man as by the fear or favor of the great.

Nowhere is the endeavor to develop the highest principles of the Law in ordinances and regulations more conspicuous than in the sphere of judicial procedure. From the Scriptures themselves little is to be learned about the constitution of courts and their jurisdiction, and still less about their procedure; and of the

[1] See also M. Sanhedrin 8, 7, and the Talmud in loc.

[2] See also Deut. 1, 17; 16, 19, etc.

[3] Sifra on Lev. 19, 15 according to the reading in Yalḳuṭ; the editions of Sifra have, "Inasmuch as *I and* this rich man are under obligation to provide for him," etc. The reflection, either way, is somewhat subtle.

[4] So the Yalḳuṭ.

[5] Sifra, l.c., Ḳedoshim Pereḳ 4 (ed. Weiss, f. 89a). Cf. Tos. Sanhedrin, 6, 2: Shebuot 30a, below.

actual administration of justice under the Asmonaeans or under Herod our sources give us hardly any information. Under the procurators the Jews were left to administer their own laws in their own way in civil cases in which only Jews were involved, and in criminal cases at least so far as the death penalty was not invoked. But so long as the Sanhedrin in Jerusalem under the presidency of the high priest remained the constitutional supreme court, with original jurisdiction in certain cases and appellate jurisdiction in others, it is probable that it followed its own precedents both in substantive law and in procedure, without much attention to the theories of the law schools.

With the fall of Jerusalem in 70 the old Sanhedrin went out of existence, and in the reorganization at Jamnia a high court was established whose members were all learned in the Law. This self-constituted body had only a moral authority,[1] but for the religious-minded Jews in Palestine under the influence of the Pharisees the authority of a council of the Doctors of Law was supreme. They had free hand to define the law and determine the mode of administering it, in accordance with Scripture, as they interpreted it, and tradition, of which they were the depositaries.

So long as the local judges settled the cases that came before them after a customary law and with a rude kind of equity, they had no need for much learning; but the growth of a scholastic law with its exact definitions and manifold refinements made it necessary that from the lowest courts to the highest the judges should be learned in the Law. That this was recognized by those who constituted the high court at Jamnia can hardly be doubted. The times favored the putting into practice what under other circumstances might have been a difficult innovation, for the war and the devastation of Judaea must have left many communities without even a rudimentary organization. A similar state of things existed after the war under Hadrian, and from this time

[1] They had, however, a formidable weapon in excommunication, and the patriarch was soon invested by the Romans with extensive powers.

on even the courts of three judges are required to be made up of legally trained men, at least in all cases which involve penalties or damages.[1] In what we might call the superior courts twenty-three judges sat, and in the supreme court, seventy-one.[2] The former had original jurisdiction in capital crimes.[3]

In the trial of such cases as described in the Mishnah every precaution is taken to exclude the possibility that by condemning an innocent man the witnesses and the judges should themselves incur the guilt of judicial murder. The biblical law which requires at least two eye-witnesses [4] to the commission of the crime prevented many cases from being brought to trial at all, since such crimes are seldom committed with so much publicity.

Circumstantial evidence of the most conclusive kind was not admitted. Simeon ben Shaṭaḥ gives an instance as of his own experience: "I saw a man chasing another into a ruin; I ran after him and saw a sword in his hand dripping with the other's blood and the murdered man in his death agony. I said to him, You villain! Who killed this man? Either I or you. But what can I do? Your life is not delivered into my hand, for the law says, At the mouth of two witnesses shall he that is to die be put to death.[5] But He who knows the thought, will requite that man who killed his fellow." [6]

Certain classes and occupations are incompetent on the pre-

[1] For actions on contract this was not necessary. Judges in such cases were a kind of arbitrators. See Dembitz, 'Jurisdiction,' Jewish Encyclopedia, VII, 394 f.

[2] On the cases that fell under the jurisdiction of these courts severally, see M. Sanhedrin 1.

[3] With an academic reservation to the supreme court of certain cases which in this period could not occur. M. Sanhedrin 1, 5.

[4] Deut. 19, 15; cf. 17, 6; Num. 35, 30. This rule was extended to less serious crimes and to civil actions also. Sifrè Deut. on 19, 15 (§ 188). It was inferred that a single witness might testify in favor of the accused. Sifrè Num. on 35, 30 (§ 161); cf. Tos. Sanhedrin 9, 4. The ultimately prevailing opinion did not admit this. Jer. Sanhedrin 22b; Sanhedrin 33b–34a.

[5] Deut. 17, 6.

[6] Sanhedrin 37b. Even Simeon ben Shaṭaḥ himself was not a witness to the act; he only drew the kind of inference against which witnesses are warned. See Tos. Sanhedrin 8, 3.

sumption that they are habitually untruthful or dishonest,[1] and individuals who fall in the wide category of "wicked" (רשע, Exod. 23, 1). The testimony of near relatives by blood or marriage is not admissible.[2] Nor is that of women or slaves.[3]

At the opening of the court a solemn charge was given to the witnesses, cautioning them against testifying to anything that is their own inference, or that they know only at second hand, however trustworthy they believe the informant to be. They are bidden remember that where only property is at stake errors can be redressed, but that when a man's life is involved his blood and that of his (potential) posterity sticks to the author of his death to the last human generation; but are urged not to be deterred by this reflection from giving testimony.

The witnesses are interrogated separately about the exact time and place of the crime, and their recognition of the parties. Any material discrepancy in their testimony leads to immediate acquittal. Another question is whether they had warned the accused that he was about to commit a crime the penalty of which is death.[4] That such a warning had been given, and that in spite of it the man had rejected it and gone right on to the perpetration of the criminal act, was proof that he had done it with full knowledge of the crime and its consequences, and therefore with complete moral responsibility.[5]

The cross-examination by members of the court took a wide range. The presumption of innocence was given to the accused, and the questioning was directed to bringing out grounds for acquittal.

[1] Gamblers, usurers, pigeon-fliers, dealers in the produce of the fallow year. M. Sanhedrin 3, 3.

[2] M. Sanhedrin 3, 4. The degrees are there specified.

[3] Sifrè Deut. on 19, 17 (§ 190); M. Shebu'ot 4, 1; M. Rosh ha-Shanah 1, 8. Josephus, Antt. iv. 8, 15 § 219.

[4] M. Sanhedrin 5, 1; Tos. Sanhedrin 11, 1–5; Sanhedrin 40b, 41a; and especially Jer. Sanhedrin 22a–b.

[5] The biblical precedent for warning one who is seen to be committing (or about to commit) a crime is found in Num. 15, 32. Sifrè Num. § 113; Sifrè Zuṭa, ibid.; Sanhedrin 41a. Other verses from which the requirement is deduced are Lev. 20, 17; Exod. 21, 14; Deut. 22, 24.

The possibility that two witnesses whose testimony agreed had conspired to fasten the guilt on the accused was provided for. Besides general prohibitions of false witness and impressive warning of the guilt thereby incurred,[1] the law in Deut. 19, 16–21, prescribes the penalty for giving false testimony. If the judges on investigation find that a witness, with malicious intent, has testified falsely, he shall be liable to the same penalty which the accused would suffer if convicted on his testimony — a species of *talio*, the injury which he planned in this way to do to another recoiling upon himself.

In the interpretation of this law the Sadducees held that in case of a capital crime the false witnesses become liable to the death penalty only when the accused had actually been executed; the Pharisees, that they were liable from the moment that the sentence had been pronounced, though the subsequent detection of their falsity might have prevented the execution and led to acquittal.[2] But even in the case of such a conspiracy the utmost care was taken that there should be no mistake.

In the deliberations of the judges considerations tending to acquittal were given precedence. The decision was by a majority; a majority of one acquitted, but for conviction there must be a majority of at least two. Even when the condemned man was on the way to the place of execution, if he or any one else had anything to offer in defence, he was recalled and the new evidence taken. Once acquitted, however, he could not a second time be put in jeopardy, whatever new evidence against him might come to light.[3]

It is clear that with such a procedure conviction in capital cases was next to impossible, and that this was the intention of the framers of the rules is equally plain. The Mishnah itself

[1] Exod. 20, 13 (16); Deut. 5, 17. Exod. 23, 1–3, 7; Lev. 19, 16.

[2] Sifrè Deut. § 190; M. Makkot 1, 6. The difference of interpretation was old; see Ḥagigah 16b (Judah ben Ṭabai and Simeon ben Shaṭaḥ). On the way in which witnesses may be convicted of plotting against the accused, see M. Makkot 1; Maimonides, Hilkot 'Edut 18–19; Jewish Encyclopedia s. v. 'Alibi' (L. N. Dembitz).

[3] Sanhedrin 33b.

brands a court which executes one man in seven years as ruinous.[1] R. Eleazar ben Azariah said "one in seventy years." R. Tarfon and R. Akiba said, "If we had been in the Sanhedrin, no man would ever have been put to death," on which R. Simeon ben Gamaliel makes the obvious reflection, "They would multiply murderers in Israel."[2] It should be observed, however, that when the court was convinced of the guilt of the accused, though the evidence did not warrant his conviction and execution, they might imprison him on bread and water.[3]

These rules of procedure impress us as purely academic. They purport to be based on biblical laws or precedents, from which they are frequently derived by subtilities of scholastic exegesis which would have amazed the law-givers as much as Akiba's perplexed Moses when, sitting in the last row, he heard that great authority discover in his laws what he had never thought of.[4] In the realities of a wicked world they have as little place as the laws of war in Deut. 20. It cannot be imagined that any government charged with the maintenance of public order and security ever devised and put into practice a code of procedure the effect and intent of which was to make the conviction of criminals impossible.[5] Such rules can have been conceived even in the schools only at a time when the administration of justice in such cases was in foreign hands.[6]

The unreal character of the procedure should not, however, lead us to ignore the idea which inspired it. Exodus 23, 7, enjoins on judges, 'Keep thee far from a false matter, and the

[1] חובלנית, 'destructive.'

[2] M. Makkot 1, 10. Tarfon and Akiba probably mean that by acute cross-examination they would have made the witnesses contradict each other or themselves. They are evidently referring to the old Sanhedrin in Jerusalem as an institution that had ceased to exist.

[3] M. Sanhedrin 9, 5.

[4] Menaḥot 29b.

[5] The inquiry whether the trial of Jesus was "legal," i.e. whether it conformed to the rules in the Mishnah, is futile because it assumes that those rules represent the judicial procedure of the old Sanhedrin.

[6] Not less palpably academic are the modes of execution.

innocent and the righteous [1] slay thou not; for I will not justify a wicked man.' God will not acquit those who, through accepting false testimony, or through an unjust or even erroneous judgment, make themselves guilty of judicial murder. The whole procedure in capital cases is devised to make it impossible for the judges to expose themselves to this condemnation. That these precautions would enable the guilty to escape the penalty of the law and thus encourage crime [2] was in the eyes of those who prescribed them the less of two evils.

The obligation to speak the truth is naturally most emphasized in the warning against false witness and against starting or retailing slander, that is in cases where a falsehood obviously injures another man in his material interests or his good name. But the Scriptures also commend truthfulness and condemn falsehood and deceit by themselves.[3] The later moralists reiterate these utterances.[4]

The rabbinical literature of all periods abounds in similar sayings. R. Simeon ben Gamaliel's motto was, "The world stands fast on three things, on justice, on truth, and on peace." [5] A few of the most familiar sayings about truth and falsehood are quoted here. "There are three that God hates: The man who says one thing with the mouth and another in the mind; [6] the one who could give testimony in another's case and does not give it; and the one who sees some scandalous sin in another and testifies to

[1] The man who is in the right of it. The juristic Midrash interprets differently.

[2] See the words of R. Simeon ben Gamaliel, above, p. 187.

[3] See e.g. Lev. 19, 11; Mic. 6, 12; Jer. 9, 3; Isa. 59, 4; Zech. 8, 16; Psalm 12, 3 f.; 15, 2; 89, 34 f.; 101, 7; Prov. 12, 19; 13, 5; 17, 7; etc. ,

[4] See Ecclus. 7, 12 f.; 20, 24–26; 28, 13; Testaments of the Twelve Patriarchs, Reuben 6, 12; Dan 1, 3; 2, 1, 4; 5, 1; 6, 8; Asher 6, 1 f.; Issachar 7, 4 f.; 3 Esdras 4, 38–40, etc.

[5] Abot 1, 18. Cf. the triad of Simeon the Righteous, ibid. 1, 2 (above, p. 84). A large collection of such sayings is to be found in the Talmudic catena on Abot by R. Noah Kobryn, with commentaries (Warsaw, 1868), f. 25b–27a.

[6] Cf. Midrash Tehillim on Psalm 12, 3, בלב ולב ידברו. Iliad ix, 312 f.

ἐχθρὸς γάρ μοι κεῖνος ὁμῶς 'Αΐδαο πύλησιν
ὅς χ' ἕτερον μὲν κεύθῃ ἐνὶ φρεσίν, ἄλλο δὲ εἴπῃ.

it singly."[1] "Four classes are excluded from the presence of the Shekinah (God), scoffers (Hos. 7, 5), hypocrites (Job 13, 16), liars (Psalm 101, 7), and retailers of slander (Psalm 5, 5)."[2] One who has given his word and changes it is as bad as an idolator.[3] R. Jose ben Judah (ben Ila'i) bases on Lev. 19, 36 the precept, "Let your *Yes* be righteous and your *No* be righteous."[4] "Teach thy tongue to say, I do not know, lest thou make up something and be taken."[5] Do not promise a child something and not give it to him, for by so doing you will teach him falsehood (Jer. 9, 4).[6] The school of Shammai condemned "the conventional lies of civilized society" when at a wedding procession the bride was eulogized as pretty and charming, though she might in fact be lame or blind — "Avoid a false word!" (Exod. 23, 7). The school of Hillel did not take so seriously compliments which deceived no one, and the second century authorities thought that to make oneself agreeable under such circumstances was the proper thing.[7]

To deceive another is a kind of theft, and this "stealing a man's thought" is the first of seven kinds of theft, and is as bad as all the rest together.[8] It is forbidden thus to cozen any one, Israelite or foreigner.[9] Flattery or blandishment, one of the common ways of accomplishing such deceit, is correspondingly repro-

[1] Pesaḥim 113b. — Inasmuch as the testimony of a single witness is legally none, the making public of the fault, lacking the motive of public justice, is an injury to the man's reputation which falls under the condemnation of the "tale-bearer" (רכיל).

[2] Soṭah 42a; Sanhedrin 103a, below.

[3] Sanhedrin 92a. R. Eleazar (ben Pedat), who is very strong against liars and hypocrites, deduces this equality by analogy of expressions from Gen. 27, 12 and Jer. 10, 15.

[4] The law requires honest measures. For *hin ṣedeḳ*, an honest *hin*, R. Jose pronounces *hen* (affirmative particle, Yes)! *ṣedeḳ*. Sifra in loc. (ed. Weiss f. 91b); Baba Meṣi'a 49a. Cf. Matt. 5, 37, ἔστω δὲ ὁ λόγος ὑμῶν ναὶ ναί, οὒ οὔ.

[5] Berakot 4a.

[6] Sukkah 46b.

[7] Ketubot 17a, top. Among themselves the crowd sometimes exchanged uite different comments. Midrash Tehillim on Psalm 24, 1.

[8] Tos. Baba Kamma 7, 8. גונב דעת חבירו; cf. κλέπτειν νόον, φρένα.

[9] Ḥullin 94a; Maimonides, Hilkot De'ot 2, 6.

bated in Scripture, and there are on the other hand many warnings against being taken in by such cajolements.[1]

In the eyes of the rabbis flattery is a form of hypocrisy, and in some contexts the word *ḥanufah* is properly so translated, but in most instances it stands for any kind of hypocrisy in word or act. A Baraita in the name of R. Nathan says: "The Israelites made themselves liable to extermination when they flattered Agrippa,"[2] by crying out to him, Thou art our brother![3] thus recognizing this descendant of the Idumaean Herod as an Israelite and a legitimate king, contrary to Deut. 17, 15, which excluded all proselytes and their posterity. That it is permissible to flatter the wicked in this world is argued by two rabbis of the third century from Isa. 32, 5, and Gen. 33, 10, respectively;[4] but the behavior of Jacob to Esau is justified by R. Levi on the ground that Jacob thought himself in danger of his life, which suspends all such laws.

Very strong language is used about hypocrisy and the fate of hypocrites. They are one of the classes that cannot come into the presence of God. R. Eleazar (ben Pedat) is emphatic: Every man in whom there is hypocrisy brings (God's) wrath upon the world (Job 36, 13); not only that, but his prayer is not heard (ibid.); he is cursed (by all mankind) even by unborn infants in their mother's womb (Prov. 24, 24); he goes down to hell (Isa. 5, 20, 24), etc. A community in which hypocrisy exists is as disgusting as a menstruous rag (Job 15, 34); such a community will finally go into exile (Job 15, 34, and Isa. 49, 21).[5] The moral in-

[1] See Psalm 12, 3 f.; 5, 9; Prov. 2, 16; 6, 24; 7, 21; 26, 28; 28, 23; 29, 5. Cf. Isa. 30, 10.

[2] Tos. Soṭah 7, 16; Soṭah 41b. Cf. Midrash Tannaim on Deut. 17, 15: From that hour sentence of exile was passed on our fathers, because they flattered him.

[3] See the story in M. Soṭah 7, 8; Sifrè Deut. §157; Midrash Tannaim l. c.

[4] Soṭah 41b. Simeon ben Pazzi and R. Simeon ben Laḳish. The 'wicked' of the latter, at least, are probably the Roman officials. Bacher, Pal. Amoräer, I, 371; cf. II, 442. To decide a point out of deference to the opinion of a great scholar is a kind of flattery which is censured. Ketubot 63b, end; 84b, below.

[5] Soṭah 41b–42a.

dignation is here the significant thing; the ingenuity by which far-fetched proof-texts are discovered for it or twisted to serve it is secondary.

Truth belongs to the integrity (*ṣedeḳ*) of a godly man — truth not only in speech or in fidelity to a word given but in his whole character and deportment. Hypocrisy is a living lie.

The ideal of integrity is the man of whom it can be said תוכו כברו,[1] he is inwardly just what he is outwardly. The pithy phrase sounds like a popular proverb rather than a product of the schools, and the way it comes into the contexts in which it occurs seems to confirm this conjecture. Whatever its origin, it became proverbial. Rabban Gamaliel II caused it to be proclaimed at Jamnia, "Let no student who is not inwardly what he is outwardly enter the lecture hall."[2] In another place such insincerity is sharply condemned. The ark was to be plated with pure gold within and without (Exod. 25, 11). Raba said: A student[3] who is not inwardly what he is outwardly is no student. Another adds, He is called 'abominable,' as it is said, 'Abominable and impure, a man who drinks iniquity like water' (Job 15, 16). R. Jonathan applies Prov. 17, 16 ('Wherefore is there a price in the hand of a fool to buy learning, when he has no intelligence?'), "Woe to the students who labor at the Law with no fear of Heaven in them"[4] — an irreligious study of religion.

It may be the pretense of a learning that a man does not possess. A late homilist applies Eccles. 4, 1, to these "hypocrites of learning" (Torah). Everybody supposes that such a man is a biblical scholar, and he is nothing of the kind; that he is versed in tradition (Mishnah), and he is not. He wraps his cloak about him and has his phylacteries on his head (like a pious man), 'And behold the tears of the oppressed, and they have no com-

[1] Literally, "his inside is as his outside."

[2] Berakot 28a. There may have been special reasons at the time for this exclusion. See Weiss, Dor. II, 80.

[3] Talmid ḥakam.

[4] Yoma 72b. See also in the sequel, by way of contrast, the kind of study of the Law that has a blessing in it. See above, pp. 96 ff., also pp. 244 f.

forter.' God says, It is for me to punish them, for it is written, 'Cursed is he who does the work of the Lord deceitfully' (Jer. 48, 10).[1]

This pretender to learning cultivated the confidence of the multitude by the aspect of piety, wrapped in his prayer shawl with his Tefillin on his head.[2] The word hypocrite is more commonly associated with an ostentatious pretense of superior religiousness or virtue. That the harmless Greek name for a stage-player has acquired this sinister meaning[3] is a consequence of the invectives against the "scribes and Pharisees, hypocrites!" in the Gospel of Matthew.[4] And, conversely, 'pharisaism' has got its place in English dictionaries as a synonym for hypocrisy in the sense defined above. Not less vehement is the denunciation of hypocrites in the Psalms of Solomon 4;[5] but the poet voices the judgments and sentiments of the Pharisaean party — his hypocrites are Sadducees.[6]

Men who make a show of more piety or virtue than they possess are not peculiar to any creed or age, and the higher the value set on religiousness the more they have flourished. The Pharisees had endeavored by teaching and example to establish a higher standard of religion in Judaism, and had gained the reputation of being more religious than their Sadducean opponents or the ignorant and negligent mass of the people. That many men cared more for the reputation than for the reality, is only

[1] R. Benjamin, Eccles. R. in loc. Benjamin applies Eccles. 5, 5, in a similar sense to the pretenders to learning, חניפי תורה. Cf. Midrash Tehillim on Psalm 52, 1.

[2] For an example of a use of the Tefillin as a pious act, see Jer. Berakot 4c, top.

[3] The Hebrew חנף is translated ὑποκριτής in Job 34, 30; 36, 13; Vulg. *hypocrita, simulator*. See also Ecclus, 1, 29; 32 (35), 15; 33 (36), 2; 2 Macc. 5, 25; 6, 21; 6, 24, 25 ('dissimulate,' 'play a part.'). The actor assumes a rôle, or character, not his own.

[4] See especially the cumulative indictment in Matt. 23.

[5] *ἐξάραι ὁ θεὸς τοὺς ἐν ὑποκρίσει ζῶντας μετὰ ὁσίων*, vs. 7.

[6] These party names do not occur in the Psalms of Solomon. The authors assail the later Asmonaean rulers and the upper classes in Jerusalem among whom the Sadducees were chiefly found.

what human nature would lead us to expect; and that many sincere Pharisees thought better of themselves in comparison with other men than it is good for any man to think, and that their superior airs were often very disagreeable, may be taken for granted. But that the Pharisees as a whole were conscious and calculating hypocrites whose ostentatious piety was a cloak for deliberate secret villainy is unimaginable in view of the subsequent history of Judaism.[1] For it was men of the Pharisaean party who tided Judaism over the two great crises of the destruction of Jerusalem and the war under Hadrian, and in the three quarters of a century following consolidated the labors of their predecessors and added their own to create the type of Judaism which it is the aim of this volume to record and interpret. Judaism is the monument of the Pharisees.

That many who bore the name Pharisee were a disgrace we have on rabbinical testimony. Both Talmuds have a list of seven varieties of Pharisee, of which only one— or none at all — gets a word of approval. The first four are designated by what were perhaps old nicknames at the enigmatic significance of which those who recorded them in the Talmuds could only guess, and did not guess alike. In the Palestinian Talmud they are the "shoulder Pharisee," who packs his good works on his shoulder (to be seen of men); the "wait-a-bit" Pharisee, who (when some one has business with him) says, Wait a little; I must do a good work; the "reckoning" Pharisee, who when he commits a fault and does a good work crosses off one with the other; the "economizing" Pharisee, who asks, What economy can I practice to spare a little to do a good work? the "show me my fault" Pharisee, who says, show me what sin I have committed, and I will do an equivalent good work (implying that he had no fault); the Pharisee of fear, like Job; the Pharisee of love, like Abraham. The last is the only kind that is dear (to God).[2]

[1] Hypocrisy cannot be more severely condemned than it was by R. Eleazar. See above, p. 190.

[2] Jer. Berakot 14b; Jer. Soṭah 20c, middle; Soṭah 22b.

The motive of love and the motive of fear exemplified by Abraham and Job belong to the schools;[1] the others show us the Pharisees as the people saw them. There is no malice in these characterizations nor in the enlargements in the Talmud; those who drew them evidently found the subjects ridiculous rather than obnoxious[2] in the vanity of the "good works," done to be seen of men (Matt. 23, 5). Earlier and more earnest is R. Joshua (ben Hananiah) in his list of those who bring ruin on the world; "a fool saint, a subtle knave, a woman pharisee, and the plagues[3] of Pharisees."[4] The "plagues of Pharisees," according to the Babylonian Talmud, are the kinds enumerated above; the Palestinian finds "the plague of Pharisees" in scholars (lawyers) who give counsel by which, apparently in strict form of law, the law may be circumvented.[5] Nowhere is there any connivance at the pretenses of such sham Pharisees, who brought an historically honorable name into disrepute. Nor were the religious teachers blind to the evils of exaggerated self-esteem, or self-righteousness, to which the most sincere were exposed, as will be shown in another place.[6]

In conclusion one or two passages may be cited in which truth is made the very character of God.[7] Truth (*emet*) is the seal of

[1] See above, pp. 99 f.

[2] The humor is broader in the Babylonian Talmud, where one of them in his mock humility trails his feet on the ground and stubs his toes, another goes with his eyes half shut for fear he should see a woman and bloodies his head by running into a wall, etc.

[3] Jer. Soṭah, sing., "the plague."

[4] M. Soṭah 3, 4. Here also the two Talmuds give different explanations or illustrations of the words. See Bacher, Tannaiten, I, 163.

[5] The examples are the same which in the Babylonian Talmud (Soṭah 21b) are adduced to illustrate the "subtle knave." In Jer. Soṭah 19a the "subtle knave" is one who interprets the law, when applied to himself, in a way to lighten its requirements, but in a more burdensome way for others — an iniquity frequently condemned. See Matt. 23, 4. Strack-Billerbeck, Kommentar, u. s. w. I, 913 f.

[6] See below, pp. 245 f., 273 f.

[7] The truth of God (his constancy in goodness, his fidelity to his promises which is an aspect of his righteousness, etc.) is found in so many and so familiar passages of Scripture that it would be superfluous to adduce the testimony here.

God.[1] Since a seal usually bore the name of its owner, invention was exercised to find a name of God in this inscription. One took the letters as shorthand, the initials of three words, Elohim Melek Tamid, and interpreted, "Living God and eternal king." [2] R. Simeon ben Lakish had a more ingenious explanation: *Alef* is the first letter of the alphabet, *Mem* is the middle letter, and *Tau* the last, as much as to say, 'I the Lord am first,' for I did not take over the rule from another; 'and beside me there is no god,' for I have no partner; 'and with the last I am He,' [3] for I shall not hand it over to another [4]—perhaps aimed at the Christians.

At the close of the daily Common Prayer (Tefillah), every Jew recites the personal petition: "O my God! guard my tongue from evil and my lips from speaking guile," turning the divine injunction of Psalm 34, 13 (keep *thy* tongue) into a prayer that God may keep him from this sin.[5]

The third pillar of the social world in R. Simeon ben Gamaliel's motto is peace—justice, truth, peace.[6] The Hebrew *shalōm* [7] has a wider meaning than the English 'peace.' For the individual it is welfare of every kind, sound health, prosperity, security, contentment, and the like. In the relations of men to their fellows it is that harmony without which the welfare of the individual or the community is impossible; aggression, enmity, strife, are destructive of welfare, as external and internal peace, in our sense, is its fundamental condition.

On the priests' benediction, 'The Lord lift up his countenance upon thee[8] and give thee peace' (Num. 6, 26), the Sifrè has col-

[1] Shabbat 55a (R. Ḥanina); Sanhedrin 64a; Yoma 69b. The origin of the notion that אמת was inscribed on the seal of God is Dan. 10, 21.

[2] Jer. 10, 10: The Lord God is Truth (אמת); He is a living God and eternal King.

[3] See Isa. 44, 6; 41, 4.

[4] Jer. Sanhedrin 18a, near the end; cf. Gen. R. 81, 2; Deut. R. 1, 9; Cant. R. on 1, 9. (Abahu). Bacher, Pal. Amoräer, II, 118; cf. p. 8.

[5] Berakot 17a (private prayer of Mar son of Rabina); Singer, Authorised Daily Prayer Book, p. 54; Baer, 'Abodat Israel, p. 104.

[6] Above, p. 188.

[7] Etymologically, wholeness (cf. 'health'), soundness.

[8] Show thee favor.

lected encomiums on peace by a long series of teachers each beginning, Great is peace! and citing Scripture to prove how highly it is esteemed by God and how excellent a gift of His to men.[1] The importance of the subject in the eyes of later generations is shown by the fact that the passage is substantially repeated in several of the Midrashim.[2]

It is peace in the relation of men to one another, however, that R. Simeon ben Gamaliel has in mind. To make peace by reconciling those who are at strife is a duty that is strongly emphasized and illustrated by many examples. One of the four things the profit of which a man enjoys in this world while the capital is laid up for him in the other world is making peace between men.[3] Hillel made Aaron the great exemplar of this virtue: "Be disciples of Aaron, loving peace and pursuing peace,[4] loving mankind and drawing them to the Law (religion)."[5] Moses, it is said, was for uncompromising justice — let justice pierce the mountain![6] (*fiat justitia ruat caelum*), but Aaron loved peace and pursued it, and made peace between a man and his fellow, as it is written, 'He walked with Me in peace and uprightness, and turned many away from iniquity' (Mal. 2, 6).[7] Among the rabbis of the second century, R. Meir is noted for his attention to this duty. The story is told that on one occasion, to make peace between a man and his wife, he allowed the woman to spit in his face in the presence of his disciples, and when they remonstrated at his submission to such an indignity not alone to him-

[1] Sifrè Num. § 42 (ed. Friedmann, f. 12b–13a); cf. Sifrè Zuṭa, ed. Horovitz, p. 248–250. See also the catena on Abot 1, 18 (f. 27 f.).

[2] Lev. R. 9, 9; Num. R. 11, 7; Deut. R. 5, 15.

[3] M. Peah 1, 1: Honoring father and mother; deeds of lovingkindness (*gemīlūt ḥasadīm*); making peace between a man and his fellow; and the study of the Law, which is equal to them all. See also Ḳiddushin 40a. Cf. Matt. 5, 9, *μακάριοι οἱ εἰρηνοποιοί*.

[4] These phrases are favorite names for Jewish synagogues, Ohabè Shalom, Rodefè Shalom. Cf. 1 Peter 3, 11.

[5] Abot 1, 12.

[6] Cf. Yebamot 92a.

[7] Sanhedrin 6b, top. Legends of Aaron as a peacemaker are narrated in Abot de-R. Nathan, c. 12.

self personally but to the Law of which he was a teacher, replied, Is it not enough that Meir's honor should be as that of his Creator? If, to make peace between a man and his wife, the Holy Name, which is written in holiness may be washed off into water,[1] should not this apply all the more to the honor of Meir?[2] Another example was his reconciliation of two men against whom Satan was wrought up, who quarrelled violently every evening (or every Sabbath eve). R. Meir went to the house and spent three evenings with them until he had made peace between them. Then he heard one (Satan) saying, Ow! R. Meir has driven this person (me, Satan) out of his house![3]

Such stories at least illustrate the notions of the duty and the merit of peace making, which Judaism cultivated.

Other aspects of morals more intimately related to the inner life of the individual will be taken up in subsequent chapters on Piety.

[1] In the ordeal of jealousy, Num. 5, 23.

[2] Jer. Soṭah 16d, with parallels in the Midrashim. Cf. Sukkah 53b, above. For a very different use of the argument from Num. 5, 23 (destruction of heretical books, names of God and all — R. Ishmael) see Tos. Shabbat 13 (14) 5.

[3] Giṭṭin 52a.

PART VI

PIETY

CHAPTER I

THE FATHER IN HEAVEN

IT HAS already been pointed out in more than one connection [1] that in Judaism the religious man is one who loves the Lord and walks in all His ways as He has made them known through revelation. Love to God is not merely an affection or a pious sentiment, but the motive of obedience in all things that God requires.[2] The pious, or godly, man [3] must therefore be scrupulous in the observances prescribed in the Law in the modes defined by those who are expert in interpretation and application of the Law and give their decisions with authority conferred on them in the Law. The same thing is true of the moral law — in which civil and criminal law is included — with all the extensions and refinements of the exegetes and jurists.

But while godliness, or piety, in Judaism thus includes both observances and morals, there is an aspect of religion to which we often apply the name piety in a more limited sense, the attitude of the individual to God in thought, feeling, and will, and the manifestations of this inwardness of religion in word and deed. It is in this narrower sense, for which the phrase personal religion is sometimes employed, that piety is used in the title of this part of our subject and in the following chapters.

The premises and principles of Jewish piety are the beliefs and conceptions about God's nature and character, his relation to men and particularly to Israel; the complete and final revelation of religion — what man is to believe concerning God and what duty He requires of men — in Scripture and Tradition; the nature and consequences of sin; the remedy for sin, repentance;

[1] See above, pp. 6 ff., 79.

[2] Deut. 8, 6; 10, 12; 11, 22; 26, 17; 1 Kings 8, 58. Individualized, e.g., Ezek. 18, 9; Psalm 119, 3; 128, 1.

[3] חסיד.

the ends of God in history; his purpose for his people and the world; the judgment after death and the lot of the righteous and the wicked — topics which are treated at length in other parts of these volumes.[1]

A characteristic of the piety of this age is the increasing frequency with which God is addressed in prayer as father, or "father in heaven" used as a surrogate for "God." In the Scriptures God is the father of the nation and Israel is his son, his firstborn;[2] or he is the father of the Israelites, and they are the sons of God, collectively or severally.[3] To cite but one salient verse: 'For Thou art our father; for Abraham ignores us and Israel does not acknowledge us. Thou, O Lord, art our father; our Redeemer from Everlasting is thy name' (Isa. 63, 16).

Similarly in Jubilees 1, 24f. After the repentance of the Israelites and the transformation God works in them,[4] "Their soul will follow me . . . and will do according to my commandment, and I will be their father and they will be my sons, and they shall all be called sons of the Living God, and all angels and spirits shall know and recognize that they are my sons, and I their Father in fidelity and righteousness, and that I love them."[5] Sirach prays: "O Lord, father and master (δεσπότης) of my life," (23, 1); and "O Lord, father and god of my life" (23, 4).[6] The prayer of Eleazar in 3 Maccabees begins, "O sovereign King, Most High, Almighty God," etc. and introduces the next petition, "O father!"[7] and a little below, "Thou didst show Jonah again, unharmed, to all his kinsfolk, O father!"[8] In the Wisdom of

[1] See especially Parts ii, iii, and vii.

[2] Exod. 4, 22; Deut. 32, 6, 18; Hos. 11, 1; Jer. 31, 9.

[3] Deut. 14, 1; Isa. 1, 2; Jer. 3, 19; Isa. 45, 11; 63, 16; 64, 8; Mal. 1, 6; 2, 10.

[4] After Deut. 30, 6; Ezek. 36, 26 f.; 11, 19, etc.

[5] See also 1, 28, "Father of all the sons of Jacob and King on Mt. Zion forever." — Other examples, Jub. 19, 29; Tobit 13, 4; Wisdom 2, 16; 3 Macc. 5, 7; 7, 6.

[6] See also 51, 10 (Hebrew); cf. the Syriac, and the Aldine Greek.

[7] 3 Macc. 6, 2–4. It is proper to remember that 3 Maccabees is written in florid Greek, and that πάτερ can be Greek rhetoric as well as Jewish piety.

[8] Ibid. 6, 8.

Solomon the unbelieving enemies of the upright man find it a grievance that "he praises the end of the righteous, and boasts that God is his father." [1]

In the rabbinical literature the paternal-filial relation between God and man is a common theme. R. Akiba's words have already been quoted: "Beloved (of God) are the Israelites, in that they are called sons of God; still more beloved in that it is made known to them that they are called sons of God" (Deut. 14, 1).[2] R. Judah (ben Ila'i) thought that the name sons was given them only when they behaved themselves like sons; [3] but R. Meir refuted him by quoting passages in which they were called foolish sons (Jer. 4, 22), untrustworthy sons (Deut. 32, 20), breed of evil-doers, vicious sons (Isa. 1, 4) — but sons notwithstanding. Instead of its being said to them, Ye are not my people, they shall be called sons of the Living God (Hos. 2, 1, E. V. 1, 10). The relation is not annulled by sin.[4]

The fatherly care of God for Israel is a familiar idea in Scripture.[5] R. Judah ben Ila'i says on Exod. 14, 19 ('The angel of God who went before the camp of Israel removed and went behind them'): "A rich verse the idea of which is found in many places." "It is like a man who was walking on the way and letting his son go on before him; came robbers in front to take the boy captive, the father put him behind him; came a wolf from behind, he put him in front; came robbers in front and wolves

[1] Wisdom 2, 16; cf. 5, 5.

[2] Abot 3, 14.

[3] Cf. the story of Tineius Rufus and Akiba, Baba Batra 10a, where Akiba quotes Deut. 14, 1, and the Roman replies, When you do the will of God you are called sons, and when you do not you are called slaves. See also Pesiḳta Rabbati c. 27 (ed. Friedmann f. 132b), on Jer. 2, 4: Hearken to thy Father who is in heaven, who begat thee (Prov. 23, 22), and deals with thee like an only son; otherwise he deals with thee like slaves (Deut. 32, 6). If thou doest the will of thy father, thou art his son, and if not . . . thou art his slave (Jer. 2, 14).

[4] Ḳiddushin 36a. See Sifrè Deut. on 14, 1, § 96; § 308 (ed. Friedmann f. 133 a–b); § 320 (f. 137a). Cf. Midrash Tannaim ed. Hoffmann, p. 71. Similarly, Philo, Frag. (ed. Mangey II, 635, 10 ff.).

[5] See Deut. 1, 31; Isa. 63, 8 f.; cf. 46, 3 f. — Wisdom 11, 10.

behind, he took him up in his arms; did he begin to be troubled by the heat of the sun, his father stretched his own garment over him; was he hungry, he gave him food, thirsty, he gave him to drink. Just so God did, as it is written," etc. He led Israel, his son, and took it in his arms (Hos. 11, 1–3); spread over it a cloud to shelter it from the heat (Psalm 105, 39); fed it with bread from heaven (the manna, Exod. 16, 4); brought streams out of the rock for it to drink (Psalm 78, 16).[1] 'God has compassion as a father on his sons (Psalm 103, 13), and comforts like a mother (Isa. 66, 13.)'[2]

New in this period is the phrase "Father in heaven" for God. It is to be observed at the outset that it is never "*the* Father in heaven," which might express God's relation to the universe,[3] but always with the note of personal relation, "*Our* Father who is in heaven" or "my (thy, his, your) Father who is in heaven." The metonymy is very frequent, and occurs in commonplace contexts as well as in connections where it has an especial appropriateness.[4] Its significance, however, is not lost, and it does not become a mere proxy for the name of God or the word "God," like Heaven, or The Place, or the Holy One, blessed is He, or He who spoke and the world was.[5] It is worth noting also that the phrase Father in heaven is peculiar to the rabbinical sources, which represent normative Judaism, in distinction from the sects or circles that produced the apocalyptic literature (in which, indeed, the thought of God as father has very little place), and from Hellenistic Judaism, so far at least as this may be legitimately inferred from Philo. In the New Testament it is found only in

[1] Mekilta, Beshallaḥ 4 (ed. Friedmann f. 30a; ed. Weiss f. 36a–b). Cf. also Tanḥuma ed. Buber, Niṣṣabim § 8: God keeps Israel as a father keeps his son — Lo! He that keeps Israel slumbers not nor sleeps (Psalm 121, 4).

[2] Pesiḳta ed. Buber f. 139a (R. Samuel ben Naḥman); cf. Yalḳuṭ on the verses.

[3] As often in Philo, e.g., De Abrahamo c. 12 § 58 (ed. Mangey, I, 10). Cf. Wisdom 14, 3; Sibyll. iii, 604 (ἀθάνατον γενέτην πάντων ἀνθρώπων).

[4] It is very common in the (mediaeval) Seder Eliahu Rabbah, where it sometimes occurs several times on a page.

[5] See Vol. I, pp. 429 ff.

the Gospel of Matthew, in which the Palestinian impress is much stronger on both thought and expression than in the others.[1]

The words "who is in heaven" have in them no suggestion of the remoteness of God, exalted above the world in his celestial habitation; they remove the ambiguity of the bare word "father"[2] by thus distinguishing between God and an earthly father.

From its biblical associations the phrase is often used of doing the will of the Father in heaven. If a man keeps the law and does the will of his Father in heaven, he is like the celestial creatures (angels; Psalm 82, 6); if he does not keep the law and do the will of his Father in heaven, he is like the creatures here below (*ibid.* vs. 7).[3] That it is the will of his Father in heaven is the all-sufficient reason and motive for abstaining from what He forbids. On Lev. 20, 26, R. Eleazar ben Azariah says: "A man should not say, I have no desire to wear a garment of mixed stuff, I have no desire to eat swine's flesh, I have no desire for forbidden sexual connections. He should say, I have the desire, but what shall I do, since my Father in heaven has laid a prohibition on me. This we learn from the words, 'I have separated you from the nations to be Mine.'" Keeping aloof from transgression and accepting the rule of Heaven go together.[4] A certain R. Judah ben Tema said: "Be strong as a leopard and swift as an eagle and fleet as a gazelle and brave as a lion to do the will of thy Father who is in heaven."[5]

Biblical associations are recognizable also when deliverances are ascribed to the Father in heaven. In the battle with Amalek

[1] Mark 11, 25 (cf. Matt. 6, 14) is the one exception. Verse 26 is rightly athetized by modern critical editors; Luke 11, 2 (in the Lord's Prayer) is conformed to Matthew; 11, 13, read ὁ πατὴρ ἐξ οὐρανοῦ δώσει πνεῦμα ἅγιον.

[2] E.g., Prov. 23, 15. Sifrè Deut. § 48 (ed. Friedmann f. 84b, middle): Man's learning in the Law rejoices the heart not only of his father who is on earth but also of his Father who is in heaven. R. Simeon ben Yoḥai.

[3] With reference to the dual nature of man. See Vol. I, pp. 451 f. Sifrè Deut. on 32, 2 (ed. Friedmann f. 132a below). Cf. Matt. 7, 21.

[4] *Malkut Shamaim.* Sifra, Ḳedoshim, end (ed. Weiss f. 93d).

[5] Abot 5, 20; Pesaḥim 112a.

(Exod. 17, 8–13) it was not Moses' uplifted arms that miraculously made Israel prevail. The Scripture teaches that when the Israelites looked upward and subjected their mind and will (לבם) to their Father in heaven, they prevailed, and when they did not they fell down slain. It was not the brazen serpent that healed, by looking at it, those that were bitten by the serpents in the desert (Num. 21, 4–9); but when the Israelites looked upward, and subjected their mind and will to their Father in heaven they were healed, and if not they perished.[1]

The deterioration that followed the destruction of the temple is painted in dark colors by R. Eliezer the elder (ben Hyrcanus): From the day when the temple was destroyed the learned began to be like schoolmasters, the schoolmasters like sextons, the sextons like the ignorant masses, and the masses go their way to ruin and no one inquires about it. And who is there for us to lean upon? Upon our Father who is in heaven.[2] To the pious Phineas ben Jair, a century later, is attributed a similar lament: Since the destruction of the temple, the Associates[3] and the men of the better classes are ashamed and cover their faces, the workers[4] have become weak, the violent and the insolent have multiplied. There is none that investigates or inquires or asks. And whom have we to lean upon? On our Father who is in heaven.[5]

On Exod. 20, 6 R. Nathan said: "'And keep My command-

[1] M. Rosh ha-Shanah 3, 8. In another, in some respects more original version, the *faith* of the Israelites in God who gave this command to Moses leads Him to work miracles for them. A third example is the blood on the houses of the Israelites in Egypt (Exod. 12, 7, 13). In this version the Holy One takes the place of the Father in heaven. See Mekilta, Amalek 1 (ed. Friedmann f. 54a; ed. Weiss f. 62a); cf. Mekilta de-Simeon ben Yoḥai on Exod. 17, 11 (ed. Hoffmann, p. 82 f.), where it is ascribed to R. Eliezer. The desire to eliminate the magical semblance of the narratives is to be noted.

[2] [M.] Soṭah 9, 15.

[3] Ḥaberim; see above, p. 73.

[4] Men of (good) works? or Workers of miracles? See Büchler, Types of Jewish Palestinian Piety, pp. 81 ff.

[5] M. Soṭah 9, 15. The close of M. Soṭah (9, 11 ff.) is an appendix, describing the decadence of the times and leading over to the still worse things that portend the imminent coming of the Messiah.

ments.' These are the Israelites who remain in the land of Israel and give their lives for the commandments.[1] Why art thou going forth to be put to death? Because I circumcised my son. Why art thou going forth to be burned? Because I read in the Law. Why art thou going forth to be crucified? Because I ate unleavened bread.[2] Why art thou beaten with a scourge? Because I carried the palm branches.[3] 'The wounds I received in the house of those who made me to be beloved' (Zech. 13, 6). These wounds cause me to be beloved by my Father who is in heaven."[4]

When Jeremiah at God's command bade the Israelites repent, they replied, How can we repent? With what countenance can we come before Him? Have we not provoked Him, have we not insulted Him? These mountains and hills on which we worshipped other gods, are they not still there? (cf. Hos. 4, 13). 'Let us lie down in our shame and let our confusion cover us' (Jer. 3, 25). When Jeremiah repeated their speech to God, he was bidden return and say to them: If ye come near to me, is it not to your Father in heaven that ye come near? as it is written, 'For I became a father to Israel, and Ephraim is my first born' (Jer. 31, 9).[5]

Of the general pardon on the Day of Atonement R. Akiba said: Blessed are ye, O Israelites! Before whom do ye purify yourselves, and who purifies you? Your Father who is in heaven. As it is said, 'I will dash upon you pure water and ye shall be pure' (Ezek. 36, 25). And it says: 'Font of Israel (the Lord).'[6] As a font purifies the unclean, so the Holy One purifies Israel.[7]

These examples are quoted in full to illustrate not only the

[1] In the persecution after the revolt under Hadrian.

[2] Observing the feasts was prohibited.

[3] At the time of Tabernacles.

[4] Mekilta, Baḥodesh 6, end (ed. Friedmann f. 68b; ed. Weiss f. 75b). In Zech. 13, 6, the Midrash takes מאהבי causatively. Cf. Midrash Tehillim on Psalm 12, 19, and Lev. R. 32, 1.

[5] Pesiḳta ed. Buber f. 165a. R. Isaac (third century).

[6] Jer. 17, 13; 14, 8. Akiba plays on the ambiguity of the word *miḳweh*, 'hope' (e.g. Jer. 50, 7), and 'cistern, tank' (Lev. 11, 36), in rabbinical use especially for the ablutions prescribed in the laws of purification.

[7] M. Yoma 8, end.

lexical use of the phrase [1] but the variety of what I may call the emotional context.

In prayer, where the address to God leaves no room for misunderstanding, the specification, "who art in heaven" is unnecessary.[2] In the Ḳaddish of the liturgy the petition in behalf of Israel, and particularly for teachers and scholars everywhere and all who apply themselves to the study of the Law, is that they may have abundant peace, favor, lovingkindness, mercy, long life, ample sustenance, and salvation "from their Father who is in heaven," [3] which corresponds to the indirect form of the prayer. Elsewhere in the common prayer we find the simple, "Our Father" (Abinu) as, e.g. in the fifth and sixth petitions, "Make us return, O our Father, to thy Law," etc.; "Forgive us, O our Father, for we have sinned," etc.[4] The Palestinian recension has in the fourth petition, "Grant us, O our Father, knowledge from thee," etc.[5]

In the common prayer, even when it is said by a man by himself, he associates others with him in the petitions, and a Babylonian teacher of the fourth century would have this the rule even for the private prayer of a solitary wayfarer for God's protection; he should not say, May it be Thy good pleasure, O Lord our God, to lead *me* in safety, but to lead *us*.[6] In earlier sources we hear of no such rule or practice. We shall find in the private prayers of the rabbis many strictly individual petitions; [7] and it is told of R. Gamaliel II, that once when he with some of his disciples was

[1] Instances of this use can easily be multiplied; e.g., Berakot 3a, 30a; 'Abodah Zarah 16b, end; Mekilta, Pisḥa 1 (ed. Friedmann f. 3a); Tos. Shabbat 13 (14), 5.

[2] Prayers beginning, Our Father who art in heaven, are found in Seder Eliahu R. c. 7 (ed. Friedmann, p. 33, top); c. 19 (p. 110); c. 28 (p. 149). On the other hand, in the prayer which Jesus taught his disciples, Luke (11, 2) has in the oldest manuscripts simply πάτερ (Vulg. *pater;* Syr. Sin. אבא).

[3] Ḳaddish de-Rabbanan, Singer, Daily Prayer Book, p. 86; Baer, 'Abodat Israel, p. 153. See below, pp. 212 f.

[4] Singer, p. 46; Baer, p. 90.

[5] Dalman, Worte Jesu, p. 297.

[6] Abaye (died 339), Berakot 29b–30a.

[7] See below, pp. 215, 216.

at sea in a storm and they asked him to pray for them, he prayed, O our God, have mercy on us! and then, at their instance, *My* God, have mercy on us.[1] Naturally, however, even when the petition is personal, the form of address to God is 'our God,' 'our Father,' though there is no hesitation in speaking about *my* Father in heaven.

With the address to God, Our Father, is frequently joined, Our King. In the fifth petition of the Tefillah in the common version these stand in adjacent clauses: "Cause us to return, O our Father, unto thy Law; draw us near, O our King, unto thy service," and the sixth, "Forgive us, O our Father, for we have sinned; pardon us, O our King, for we have transgressed." More often they stand side by side, "Our Father, our King." Thus in the ancient prayer, Ahabah Rabbah (or Ahabat 'Olam),[2] "With abounding (or, eternal) love, thou hast loved us, O Lord our God," etc.; we read, "Our Father, our King, for our fathers' sake who trusted in thee, and whom thou didst teach the statutes of life, be thou gracious to us likewise and teach us." It is related that in a great drouth, when the twenty-four prayers pronounced by R. Eliezer were not answered, R. Akiba prayed: "Our Father, our King! [Thou art our Father, and] we have no king but Thee. Our Father, our King for thine own sake have compassion upon us!" whereupon the rain descended.[3]

The names are coupled in the same way in a prayer in the additional (Musaf) service for certain festivals: "Our Father, our King! Make manifest upon us the glory of thy kingdom."[4]

[1] Midrash Tannaim on Deut. 26, 3, ed. Hoffmann, p. 172. The story is told in illustration of the opinion that it is permissible to appropriate the name of God to an individual, e.g., "his God" (as of Moses, Exod. 32, 11).

[2] Berakot 11b. Singer, Daily Prayer Book, p. 39 f. and p. 96. I. Abrahams, Companion to the Daily Prayer Book, xlviii. ff.; Baer, 'Abodat Israel, p. 80, p. 164 f.

[3] Ta'anit 25b. The words in brackets are supplied from the commentary of R. Ḥananel and the 'En Jacob. The latter has also the confession, [We have sinned before thee], have compassion upon us.

[4] Singer, p. 234; Baer, p. 352, 396.

In the long litany recited on the ten Penitential Days, every petition begins with the words, Our Father, our King, whence it has its name, Abinu Malkenu;[1] clauses of Akiba's prayer introduced and concluded the whole, which, like other litanies, has grown inordinately in the procession of the centuries and the rites.

The invocation of God as King has good biblical warrant, for example, 'For the Lord is our judge (ruler), He is our lawgiver, He is our king; He will save us.'[2] He is the King of the universe, but in a peculiar sense the King of Israel.[3] In the additional service for New Years Day, in the so-called "Kingdom Verses" (Malkuyot), passages from all three parts of the Bible are brought together to magnify God as king, from "He was king in Jeshurun" (Deut. 33, 5), through his sovereignty in history and nature, to the climactic, "The Lord shall be King over all the earth: in that day shall the Lord be One and his name One" (Zech. 14, 9). "And in thy Law it is written saying, Hear, O Israel, the Lord our God, the Lord is One."[4]

The frequency of the collocation, Our Father, our King, is conclusive proof that the latter title did not connote to the Jews "the arbitrariness of the tyrant and the unapproachableness of the despot."[5] What thoughts and feelings they did associate with it is to be learned from the content and spirit of the prayers addressed to God in this name,[6] not from preconceived notions about what the word king means to Orientals.

[1] Singer, pp. 55–57; Baer, pp. 108–111; 392 f.

[2] Isa. 33, 22; cf. 44, 6, the king of Israel and his redeemer. See above, p. 195.

[3] He is our God; there is no other. Of a truth He is our King, there is none besides him. 'Alenu, Singer, p. 247; Baer, p. 398 (quoting Deut. 4, 39).

[4] Singer, p. 248; Baer, p. 398 f. M. Rosh ha-Shanah 4, 5; Sifrê Num. § 77 (on Num. 10, 10); Rosh ha-Shanah 32a; also 16a, below, and 34b.

[5] Bousset, Religion des Judentums, 2 ed. pp. 431 f. See Vol. I, pp. 431 ff. — It might have occurred to this author that a prayer for the Kingdom of God, whether in the Ḳaddish or in the Lord's Prayer, did not really express a desire for the establishment of a universal arbitrary despotism.

[6] A common, and perhaps the original, association is with prayers for deliverance (in a comprehensive sense), and it may pertinently be remarked

That God is so often called our Father who is in heaven,[1] or invoked in prayer, O our Father! does not indicate that the age had a new conception of God, or put a new emphasis on one element of the conception. What these phrases express is not an idea of God, but a characteristic attitude of piety, and therein lies their significance. This is the type of piety in which Jesus and his immediate disciples were brought up, and the Gospel of Matthew is a most instructive illustration of it.[2]

Experience shows that the language of piety when it becomes usual tends to become conventional and to be repeated with little of the meaning or feeling that it originally expressed; and doubtless by many Jews, as by many Christians through the centuries, 'Our Father who is in heaven,' was repeated as a consecrated formula without further thought. For others it not only symbolized more adequately than any other phrase the relation of the soul to God, but expressed their deepest religious experience. Each put into it what he brought to it.

that the two titles are thus associated in the Scriptures, where God is the deliverer both as father and as king. Compare Isa. 63, 16, Thou art our father, our Deliverer from Everlasting is thy name, with 33, 22, The Lord is . . . our king, He will deliver us; 44, 6; The king of Israel and his deliverer. See the close of the Ne'ilah prayer on the Day of Atonement. Singer, p. 268; Baer, p. 438.

[1] Or with other personal pronouns, my, his, your, their, father who is in heaven.

[2] See Detached Note.

CHAPTER II

PRAYER. FAITH

THE true nature of a religion is most clearly revealed by what men seek from God in it. The public and private prayers of the Jews thus show not only what they esteemed the best and most satisfying goods, but their beliefs about the character of God and his relation to them, and their responsive feelings toward him.

The order of Daily Prayer as it was fixed about the end of the first century of our era (Shemoneh 'Esreh, Tefillah), which was recited in the synagogue and by individuals privately, has been described in another place.[1] After ascriptions to "our God and our fathers' God," the mighty God, the Holy God, the first petitions are that he, the giver of knowledge, would graciously bestow on his suppliants knowledge, discernment, and understanding; that he would bring them back to his Law and draw them near unto his worship,[2] and turn them to him in perfect repentance; that he would look upon their affliction, and redeem them speedily for his name's sake; restore the sick to health; bless the year with abundant crops, etc. The condensed prayer [3] which may be said in place of the twelve petitions of the Eighteen in stress of circumstances, begins: Grant us, O Lord our God, to have knowledge of thy ways; circumcise our hearts to revere thee; [4] and forgive us, that we may be redeemed, etc.[5]

Another ancient prayer is the Ḳaddish, the opening sentence of which is: "Magnified and hallowed be his great name in the world

[1] Vol. I, pp. 291 ff.

[2] In prayer, "the worship of God in the heart."

[3] Habinenu. Singer, Daily Prayer Book, p. 55; Baer, 'Abodat Israel, p. 108.

[4] Deut. 10, 16 f.; cf. 30, 6.

[5] See M. Berakot 4, 3 f. The form in the Prayer Books is given in the Babylonian Talmud, Berakot 29a, on the authority of Samuel (early third century). See also the summary, Jer. Berakot 8a: "Grant us [intelligence], accept our repentance, forgive us, O our Redeemer, heal our diseases, bless our years."

which he created according to his will; and may he make his kingship sovereign in your life time and in your days."[1] It will be observed that the prayer Jesus taught his disciples begins in the same way, "Hallowed be thy name; thy kingdom come, thy will be done," etc.

The beautiful prayer, Ahabah Rabbah, "With abounding love thou hast loved us, O Lord, our God; with great and exceeding pity thou has pitied us,"[2] which precedes the recitation of the Shema' with its 'Thou shalt love the Lord thy God,' goes on: "O our Father, the merciful Father who showest mercy, have mercy upon us, and put it in our hearts to discern and to understand, to hear, to learn, to teach, to keep, to do, to fulfil all that is learned by the study of the Law, in love."

The first petitions in the Eighteen Prayers, as we have seen, are individual in their nature — knowledge[3] of God's law, repentance, forgiveness, health — though all men need them and ask them for their fellows with themselves. The second half is national in character, containing prayers for independence, and the gathering again of the dispersion to their own land, for the restoration of a national government as in the good old times, and that God alone should be king over them; that Jewish apostates may perish, and righteous converts be rewarded;[4] that Jerusalem may soon be rebuilt to be God's lasting abode, and the throne of David be set up; and that the Scion of David may speedily appear.

In other parts of the liturgy, ancient and modern, prayers for the great restoration, the fulfilment of so many prophecies, fill a large room. When the Jews asked why this restoration, so long

[1] וימליך מלכותה בחייכון וגו׳. The prayer was originally said (in Aramaic) by the preacher at the end of his discourse, which explains the *your*.

[2] See above, p. 209. This prayer, with the alternative introductory phrase, With everlasting love (Ahabat 'Olam), is familiar to authorities of the second century. Berakot 11b.

[3] Cf. James 1, 5 f.

[4] A similar juxtaposition in contrast of proselytes and apostates in Philo, De monarchia, c. 7 §§ 53 f. (ed. Mangey II, 219 f.); De poenitentia, c. 2 §§ 181 f. (Mangey II, 406).

and ardently prayed for, was still withheld, they read in the prophets that their sins stood between them and the fulfilment, and that only repentance could remove this barrier. The expansion of the liturgy century by century was consequently greatest in the direction of the confession of sins, sometimes developed in lengthy litanies of enumeration,[1] and in prayers for forgiveness, frequently in poetical form (Seliḥot). The Middle Ages were prolific in compositions of this kind. The persecutions and outrages to which the Jews in Christian countries were subjected for centuries account for the exorbitance of this side of religion and give pathos to the mere volume of production and to the monotony of its content.

In the period with which we are concerned, in spite of all the calamities of the age, religion was more healthy-minded; nevertheless, in no ancient religion is normal piety so pervaded by the consciousness of sin, the need of repentance, and the conviction that man's sole hope is the forgiving grace of God. The appeal is to his promise, to his mercy, to his knowledge of man's frailty, as, for example, "Our Father, our King, be gracious unto us, and answer us, for we have no good works; bestow on us charity[2] and lovingkindness, and save us."[3] The general tenor of these supplications is well represented by the fine prayer for the service with which the Day of Atonement terminates, from which a few words may be quoted here: "What are we? What is our life? What is our piety? What is our righteousness? What help is there in us? What strength? What valor? What can we say before Thee, O Lord, our God and our fathers' God?"[4]

More intimate glimpses of Jewish piety are opened to us by the prayers of individual rabbis, of which a considerable number are preserved in the Talmud. Place was given, after the con-

[1] E.g., the Ashamnu, and especially the 'Al Ḥeṭ in the liturgy of the Day of Atonement; Singer, p. 258; 259–262; Baer, p. 415; 417–420.
[2] צדקה. What God does for men is as it were an alms.
[3] Singer, p. 65; Baer, p. 118.
[4] Ne'ilah. Singer, p. 267 f.; Baer, p. 436 f., 438.

clusion of the appointed daily prayers, for private petitions silently offered.[1] These doubtless often became habitual and the master's practice was noted by his disciples. They range over three or four centuries, and include Babylonian as well as Palestinian teachers, but this is hardly perceptible in the prayers themselves, in which personality makes more difference than time or place. There are also prayers composed by the rabbis for private use of themselves and others; and many ejaculatory "benedictions" (exclamations of thanks to God).

A short prayer by R. Eliezer ben Hyrcanus, to be said in a moment of danger is: "Do Thy good pleasure in heaven above, and give composure of spirit to those who revere Thee here below, and what is good in Thy sight, do. Blessed art Thou, O Lord, the hearer of prayer!"[2] An anonymous prayer in the same group runs: "The needs of Thy people Israel are many, and their wit is scant. May it be Thy good pleasure, O Lord our God, to give to each one all his needs, to each several person the supply of his lack. Blessed is the Hearer of prayer."[3]

A prayer to be said on waking in the morning which has found a place in all the prayer books as a form of private devotion is: "My God, the soul Thou didst put within me is pure; Thou didst form it in me; Thou didst breathe it into me; and Thou dost preserve it within me. And Thou wilt take it from me and wilt return it to me in the hereafter. So long as the soul is within me, I will give thanks to Thee, O Lord my God and my fathers' God, lord of all the ages, lord of all souls. Blessed art Thou, O Lord, who dost return souls to dead bodies."[4]

[1] In the Tefillah itself the individual introduced his personal needs either into the sixteenth prayer, "Hearer of prayer," or into the appropriate petitions; e.g., in case of illness in his family, into the common petition for the sick, "Heal us, O Lord"; if he lacked food, into the petition for God's blessing on the year, etc. 'Abodah Zarah 8a, top.

[2] Berakot 29b; Tos. Berakot 3, 7.

[3] Tosefta, l. c. Maimonides (Hilkot Tefillah 4, 19) has in conclusion, "And what is good in Thy sight, do!"

[4] Berakot 60b. Singer, Daily Prayer Book, p. 5; Baer, 'Abodat Israel, 39 f. Cf. the corresponding prayer on going to bed at night, Berakot, ibid.; Singer, p. 293; Baer, p. 573.

Raba, a famous Babylonian master of the fourth century, when he had finished the appointed prayers used to say: "My God, so long as I was not created, I had no claim (to be created); and now that I have been created I am as if I had not been created. Dust am I while alive, how much more when I am dead. I am before Thee as a vessel full of shame and ignominy. May it be Thy good pleasure, O Lord my God, that I sin no more, and the sins I have committed, wipe out by Thy great mercy, but not by means of chastisements and sore illnesses." [1]

R. Alexander's prayer was: "Lord of the worlds, Thou knowest perfectly that our will is to do Thy will. And what hinders? The leaven in the dough [2] and the tyranny of the (heathen) empires. May it be Thy good pleasure to deliver us from their power, and that we return to fulfil the dictates of Thy will with a perfect heart." [3]

Quotations such as these could be multiplied page after page. I will add but one more. R. Eleazar (ben Pedat, contemporary of Johanan) prayed: "May it be thy good pleasure, O Lord our God to cause to dwell in our allotted place love and brotherliness and peace and fellowship; and enlarge our bounds with disciples; and bring us to a good latter end and all we hope; and appoint our portion in Paradise. Stablish us by good associates and a good impulse in this Thy world, that when we arise we may daily find our heart waiting to revere Thy name, and let the satisfaction of our soul's desire be graciously granted by Thee." [4]

The sense of dependence on God for all man's needs and of gratitude for his constant goodness are renewed by giving thanks to him at the table for the food he provides. Formulas of this kind are given in the Mishnah, for example: For the products of the soil, Blessed is the Creator of the fruits of the soil; over

[1] Berakot 17a.

[2] The evil impulse which God himself implanted in man's nature. See Vol. I, p. 480.

[3] Berakot, ibid.

[4] Berakot 16b; cf. Jer. Berakot 7d (attributed to R. Johanan). Many other prayers are brought together in Berakot 16–17; Jer. Berakot iv. 2 (7d).

bread, Blessed is He who brings forth bread from the earth (Psalm 104, 14); over fruits, Blessed is the Creator of the fruits of the trees; over wine, Blessed is the Creator of the fruit of the vine, etc.[1]

At the end of the meal a longer grace is said, of which the four essential constituent prayers and their order are prescribed in a Tannaite tradition,[2] but which has been greatly expanded in the prayer books, and varied for different days, seasons, and circumstances.[3] It includes thanksgiving for sustenance; for the goodly heritage of the land of Israel, and for the Law; a prayer for God's mercy in the restoration of Jerusalem and the temple;[4] and a (later) more general prayer of praise and petition.

Ten synonyms for prayer in the Scriptures are enumerated in Sifrè on Deut. 3, 23, with examples.[5] Of them all it is the supplication for God's free grace (תחנה) that is the "nearest," as it is written, 'Let these my words wherewith I have made supplication before the Lord be near unto the Lord our God day and night' (1 Kings 8, 59).[6]

The most characteristic thing that is said about prayer in this age is that it is the worship of God in the heart. On Deut. 11, 13 ('to love the Lord your God, and to serve (worship) him with all your heart and with all your soul') we read in Sifrè: 'To worship Thee.'—This is prayer. May it not mean literally sacrificial worship? . . . Is there such a thing as worship in the heart? The text says, 'to worship him in all your hearts.' So David says: 'Let my prayer be set forth as incense before Thee, the

[1] M. Berakot 6, 1.

[2] Berakot 48b. The variation for the Sabbath is also prescribed there. See the whole passage.

[3] Singer, pp. 278–285 (cf. I. Abrahams, Companion to the Daily Prayer Book, pp. ccvii–ccx); Baer, pp. 554–561. A shorter form will be found in Singer, p. 286; Baer, p. 562.

[4] Said to have been framed after the slaughter at Bether.

[5] Sifrè Deut. § 26 (ed. Friedmann f. 70b.).

[6] Midrash Tannaim, p. 14. The name תחנונין was given to the personal supplications which individuals silently addressed to God at the close of the appointed prayers, and eventually to the forms for such prayers which were provided in the prayer books.

lifting up of my hands as the evening sacrifice' (Psalm 141, 2). So also Daniel's prayer in Babylonia, where there was no Jewish cultus, is called worship. "Just as the worship of the altar is called worship, so prayer is called worship."[1] The point lies in the word for service or worship, '*abodah*, which was used specifically of the sacrificial cultus in the temple. Prayer is such worship in the inner man.[2]

That prayer takes the place of sacrifice was deduced from Hosea 14, 3: 'Say unto Him, Altogether forgive iniquity and accept what is good; so will we render (instead of) bullocks (the words) of our lips.' R. Abahu said: What shall replace the bullocks we formerly offered to thee? 'Our lips,' in the prayer we pray to Thee.[3] So long as the temple stood we used to offer a sacrifice and thus atonement was made; but now we have nothing to bring but prayer.[4] The offerings and pure oblations that are brought to God throughout all the world (Mal. 1, 11) are not literal sacrifices and incense (which can only be offered in the land of Israel), but prayer.[5] Moses foresaw that a time would come when the temple would be destroyed and the bringing of first fruits (Deut. 26, 1 ff.) would cease, so he ordained that Israelites should pray thrice each day, "for prayer is dearer to God than all good works and than all sacrifices."[6] That an hour

[1] Sifrè Deut. § 41, f. 80a. Study also is worship, as we shall see.

[2] This conception is expressed in various other places. Jer. Berakot 7a, middle; Yalḳuṭ I § 863; Midrash Samuel 2, 10; Pirḳè de-R. Eliezer c. 16, where '*abodah* in the words of Simeon the Righteous — the three foundations of the world (Abot 1, 2), Torah, 'Abodah, Gemilut Ḥasadim — is understood of prayer. With this identification of prayer with worship in the heart Maimonides begins his treatise on Prayer (Hilkot Tefillah 1, 1).

[3] Pesiḳta Shubah, end (ed Buber p. 165b). See also R. Abahu and R. Isaac, ibid.

[4] Tanḥuma Korah § 12, near the end. Cf. Pesikṭa ed. Buber f. 181a (the generations that have no king, no prophet, no priest, no oracle — only prayer); Midrash Tehillim on Psalm 102, 18 ('He regarded the prayer of the destitute, and hath not despised their prayer'), ed. Buber, f. 215b–216a.

[5] Mal. 1, 11. Tanḥuma Aharè § 14, ed. Buber f. 34b–35a, (quoting again Psalm 141, 2).

[6] Tanḥuma Ki tabo, beginning; ed. Buber § 1, with a slightly different text (more than a hundred good works). Prayer greater than sacrifices, Berakot 32b (Isa. 1, 11). R. Eleazar ben Pedat.

of prayer avails more with God than good works is argued by R. Eliezer ben Jacob from the example of Moses. His life time of good works did not win for him permission to view the promised land which he might not enter, but when he prayed, the answer came, 'Go up unto the top of Pisgah' (Deut. 3, 23–27).[1] The ranking of the relative importance of this and that is to be taken as it was meant — these are homiletical improvements for ends of edification; but they are not for that reason without significance.

From the prayer of Moses in Deut. 33, supported by the examples of David (Psalm 149) and Solomon (1 Kings 8, 23 ff., 2 Chron. 6, 14 ff.), the principle is derived that prayer should begin with ascriptions of praise to God, go on to present petitions for men's needs, and close as it began, with praise; on this scheme the Eighteen Prayers are arranged.[2] Opinion was divided whether one should put up petitions for his personal needs before or after the recitation of the common prayer, and biblical warrant was alleged on both sides. R. Eliezer ben Hyrcanus took the former view; Joshua ben Hananiah the latter.[3] One evidently gives the precedence to what is for the individual the more urgent; the other to what is in itself the worthier, the needs of the community.

It has already been noted that the prayers for the common needs are phrased in the plural; when a man prays by himself he does not ask these things for himself alone but for his fellows as well.[4] If it is in his power to beseech God's compassion on another individual, it is a sin not to do it, as Samuel says, 'Far be it from me that I should sin against the Lord by ceasing to pray for you.'[5]

Private prayer was offered by Daniel, according to his custom, three times a day (Dan. 6, 10). David prayed, evening, morning,

1 Sifrè Deut. § 29; cf. Berakot 32b, top, Eleazar (ben Pedat).

2 Sifrè on Deut. 33, 2 (§ 343), and R. Simlai, 'Abodah Zarah 7b, end, arguing from Deut. 3, 24 ff. Cf. Jer. Berakot 4d, below; Maimonides, Hilkot Tefillah 1, 2. Vol. I, pp. 291, 293 f.

3 'Abodah Zarah 7b. See Bacher, Tannaiten, I, 109 f.

4 Above, p. 208.

5 1 Sam. 12, 23. Berakot 12b; cf. Jer. Berakot 7a.

and in the middle of the day (Psalm 55, 18). This ordinance was attributed to Moses.[1] The usage went back, it is said, to the patriarchs. Abraham instituted the morning prayer, Isaac the afternoon prayer (*minḥah*), and Jacob the evening prayer.[2] By the side of this midrash stands the better grounded opinion of the learned that the hours of prayer in the morning and afternoon corresponded to the times of the regular daily sacrifices (*tamidin*).[3] For the customary evening prayer there was no such obvious correspondence with the cultus in the temple.[4] The obligation of this prayer was one of the points in the controversy between Rabban Gamaliel II and some of his colleagues, and his tyrannical treatment of R. Joshua ben Hananiah, who maintained that it was optional, so exasperated the rest that they deposed Gamaliel from the principalship of the academy and elected R. Eleazar ben Azariah to the office.[5]

The real issue was, however, a deeper one. R. Gamaliel had given to the daily common prayer a fixed content and order, and prescribed that in this form it should be used by every Israelite three times a day. This regulation of devotion was not universally approved. Some seem to have objected on principle to the trammels thus imposed on the freedom of the individual in his use of a traditional directory of worship.[6] R. Joshua held that it was sufficient to repeat the substance of the Eighteen; R. Akiba, that if a man can say his prayers fluently, he should recite the Eighteen; if not, say the substance of them. R. Eliezer goes farther: If a man makes his prayer a fixed task, his prayer is not, as it should be, a plea for God's grace.[7]

[1] See above, p. 218.

[2] Berakot 26b; Jer. Berakot 7a; Tanḥuma ed. Buber, Miḳeṣ § 11.

[3] Jer. Berakot 7b. Of the supplementary prayers, corresponding to the *musaf* sacrifice it is unnecessary to speak here.

[4] A somewhat far-fetched association was eventually discovered.

[5] Berakot 27b–28a; Jer. Berakot 7c–d. See also Berakot 4b.

[6] Against this inference, Bacher, Tannaiten, I, 108, n. 1.

[7] M. Berakot 4, 3–4. The same sentiment is ascribed to another disciple of R. Johanan ben Zakkai, R. Simeon ben Nathaniel: Do not make your prayer a fixed task, but a plea to God for grace and mercy. Abot 2, 13.

The word here rendered "fixed task" (קבע) is explained in the Talmud in various ways: one thinks that it is addressed to the man to whom his prayer is like a burden — an obligation he has to work off; others refer it to one who is confined to the words of the text and unable to frame his own supplications or to extemporize in prayer, and uses the same words day after day.[1] R. Eliezer is said to have followed his own advice by saying a new prayer every day, and R. Abahu a new benediction.[2] Whatever temporary controversial point such utterances may have had, the outcome was that the Jewish common prayer is a noteworthy endeavor to achieve order without sacrificing freedom.

If prayer is of such importance, should not a man pray continually, all day long?[3] This is one of the questions said to have been addressed by "Antoninus" to the Patriarch Judah: What about praying at every hour? Forbidden! was the answer. Why? Lest a man get into the way of calling on the Almighty thoughtlessly. Antoninus did not see the force of the answer until Rabbi tried it on him by presenting himself once an hour, beginning in the early morning, and greeting him with nonchalant familiarity, Good morning, Sir; O Emperor; Your good health, O King. The emperor indignantly exclaimed, What do you mean by treating royalty with such disrespect! If you, a mere mortal king, resent being saluted thus every hour, the rabbi replied, how much more the sovereign King of Kings.[4]

When the disciples of R. Eliezer ben Hyrcanus asked their dying master to teach them the ways of life by following which they might attain to the life of the World to Come, he gave them as his last word: "When you pray, realize before whom you stand."[5] A wholesome reverence keeps the note of intimacy in

[1] Berakot 29b, and Rashi there; cf. Jer. Berakot 8a, below. What in no case is to be done is to say it as if one was reading a document (word for word).

[2] Jer. Berakot, l. c.

[3] See Tos. Berakot 3, 6; Jer. Berakot 8a–b; Berakot 21a, below (R. Johanan).

[4] Tanḥuma ed. Buber, Miḳeṣ § 11.

[5] Berakot 28b. Cf. Tanḥuma Wayyera § 1: Be careful in your prayer, for there is no better quality than this, and it is greater than all sacrifices (Isa. 1, 11).

Jewish piety from degenerating into vulgar familiarity. Reverence characterizes not only the phraseology of prayer, but all its circumstances. Ḥoni ha-Me'aggel, famous for the miraculous efficacy of his prayers in making it rain while he stood in the ring he had drawn on the ground, so to speak challenging God, would have been excommunicated by Simeon ben Shaṭaḥ for his irreverent importunacy, if he had not been so visibly a spoilt child of God.[1]

Prayer at the appointed times may be said in any clean and proper place; but preferably in the synagogue,[2] and if elsewhere, 'the acceptable time' (Psalm 69, 14) is the hour when the congregation is gathered in the synagogue.[3] The worshippers turn toward the earthly abode of God.[4] Abroad, they turn their faces toward the land of Israel; in the land, toward Jerusalem; in Jerusalem toward the temple; in the temple they direct their thoughts to the holy of holies. Thus all Israelites, wherever they are, pray toward one place and in spirit *in* one place. A blind man, or one who can not fix the points of the compass, shall direct his thought to his Father who is in heaven.[5]

Ablutions — washing the hands — are an obligatory preparation for prayer, as for other religious acts. The prayers were regularly said standing, in a reverent attitude. In the opinion of some, the eyes should look down; others would have them raised up; another says, eyes down, mind up![6] Genuflexions and prostrations occur at certain points in the recitation.[7] Decorum was to be observed in dress, posture, and in the undertone in

[1] Ta'anit 23a.

[2] God is found in the synagogue; when ten men are praying together, the Shekinah is in the midst of them. Berakot 6a.

[3] Berakot 8a, top.

[4] Dan. 6, 11; 3 (1) Esdras 4, 58.

[5] Sifrè Deut. §29 (ed. Friedmann f. 71b–72a); Tos. Berakot 3, 16 f.; Berakot 30a.

[6] Yebamot 105b, above. To the end of the second century there was evidently no fixed rule.

[7] Berakot 34b, above. Bowing and kneeling are also mentioned. See L. Ginzberg, 'Adoration,' Jewish Encyclopedia, I, 210 f.; S. Krauss, Synagogale Altertümer, pp. 400 ff.

which the prayers were pronounced. These things were the natural expression of reverence; attention to them also tended to impress on the worshipper the sacredness of the act in which he was engaged.

The essential thing in prayer, to which these outward acts were auxiliary, is the direction of the thoughts and desires. For this there is a technical term, Kawwanah, which includes attention and intention; perhaps "concentration" comes as near as any word to expressing this conception of the spirit of devotion. It is, in fact, the element of intention that gives meaning to any action, and makes a reality of a religious form. The Scripture requires a worship of God with all your heart and with all your soul (thought and emotion), and R. Eliezer ben Jacob takes this as a warning to the priests not to let their minds wander (or be distracted) in their sacrificial service.[1] The principle has many applications, for example to the priest's benediction (which was taken over into the synagogue service). The priests are warned not to recite this blessing (Num. 6, 24–26) as though they were forced into service[2] and in a hurry to get through with it, but to bless the people with an intent mind in order that the blessing may be effective.[3] The principle is concisely formulated, "Commandments demand intention."

The mere doing of a thing that is commanded in the law is not the fulfilment of the commandment; to make it such it is necessary that in the act a man should have in mind that it is a commandment and mean to fulfil it for that reason.[4] This is a generalization of the particular case contemplated in the Mishnah: When a man is reading in the Pentateuch and comes to Deut.

[1] Sifrè Deut. § 41 (on Deut. 11, 13; ed. Friedmann f. 80a). The sacrifice (e.g., of the Passover victim) may be invalidated by such defect of intention. M. Pesaḥim 5, 2.

[2] The Greek word ἀγγαρεία is used.

[3] Tanḥuma ed. Buber, Naso § 18, end.

[4] Whether every commandment required such conscious intention was a point on which opposite opinions are reported: Berakot 13a; 'Erubin 95b–96a; Pesaḥim 114b, top; Rosh ha-Shanah 28b, top (Raba).

6, 4 (Hear O Israel) just at the time for saying the Shema', if he reads the passage intending it to be his Shema', he fulfils his obligation, otherwise not.[1] The explicit rule is, one who recites the Shema' must fix his mind upon it.[2] Whether this applied to the whole (R. Akiba), or to the first part only (R. Eliezer), the confession of God's unity and the obligation to love him wholly, was decided in the former sense.[3]

The term means more, however, than the intention to perform in the prescribed way a religious duty. A good definition, with especial application to prayer is given by Maimonides: It means that a man should clear out his mind of all thoughts of his own, and regard himself as if he were standing before the Shekinah (in the manifest presence of God).[4] Without this a prayer is no prayer.[5] "He who prays must direct his mind intently to Heaven." (Cf. Psalm 10, 17b.) Prayer should always be offered in a serious frame of mind. Men should not go straight to prayer from states or surroundings that make it impossible to collect themselves — from grief or indolent vacuity or laughter or light talk or frivolity or idle pastimes; they should bring to it the joy of the commandment.[6] A drunken man's prayer is an abomination, and even a man who has imbibed more moderately is in no frame of mind to pray.[7]

The learned, on their part, should not go directly to their prayers from trying a case in court or from the discussion of legal norms (Halakah), which would run on in their mind while they were praying.[8] Even the excitement of returning from a journey

[1] M. Berakot 2, 1. So in the case of other religious acts. M. Rosh ha-Shanah, 3, 7; Tos. Rosh ha-Shanah 3 (2), 5 f. (Everything depends on the intention; Psalm 10, 17).

[2] Tos Berakot 2, 2.

[3] Berakot 13a–b.

[4] Maimonides, Hilkot Tefillah 4, 16.

[5] Ibid., 4, 15.

[6] M. Berakot 5, 1; Berakot 30b–31a; Tos. Berakot 3, 21; Jer. Berakot 8d; Tanḥuma ed. Buber, Wayyera § 9.

[7] 'Erubin 64a; Berakot 31a.

[8] Halakah already decided and about which there can be no controversy is no such obstacle. Berakot 31a.

may so occupy a man that it will be two or three days before he can concentrate his mind on prayer, and it is better that he should not pray at all than go through the empty form.[1] Another Babylonian authority of the fourth century lays it down as a general principle, Let no man say his prayers whose mind is not composed.[2]

It is difficult to command such detachment when the appointed time finds a man engaged in his necessary occupations. Hence the pious men of old times[3] used to sit quiet for an hour before their prayer in order to fix their mind on their Father in heaven; and did not allow even a salutation from a king, or a snake coiled at their feet, to interrupt their meditation.[4]

There was no attempt, however, to make such saints of common people. Men said their prayers, when the time came, where they were, in the house, the field, or on the road, with necessary accommodations of customary form to unusual circumstances. Laborers who were picking olives or figs might even say them without coming down from the tree,[5] it being assumed that they felt perfectly secure there and were not distracted by apprehension of falling.

The Jewish ideal of prayer as it is disclosed to us in Tannaite sources comprises under the word Kawwanah (*kawwanat ha-leb*) attention, intention, concentration of mind, devoutness of spirit. The same conception runs through the Talmudic period as some of the examples cited above show. The most systematic writings of mediaeval authors from Saadia on lay great stress on the necessity of inwardness in religion. Baḥya ibn Paḳuda, in his "Duties of the Inner Man," makes the spiritual element, devotion in the largest sense (Kawwanah), the essence of religion,

[1] 'Erubin 65a, below.

[2] Ibid., middle. This does not refer to personal appeals to God's mercy.

[3] חסידים הראשונים.

[4] M. Berakot 5, 1. According to the Talmud they waited an hour after prayer also. Jer. Berakot 8d; Berakot 32b.

[5] Berakot 16a. The employer, however, must come down, because, being not accustomed to the situation, he cannot help being distracted by it. Cf. Rashi.

apart from which all outward observances are worthless, because meaningless.[1] Judah ha-Levi agrees that outward acts done without devotion have no value; but that equally valueless is the contemplation and emotion which ends in itself and is not translated into action. The attitude of Maimonides has already been indicated.[2]

The teaching of the Tannaim and their successors on this point is evidence of the degree to which the Psalms not only furnished types and phrases to the public and private prayers, but inspired their piety.

By the side of this went discussions of the proper form, time, and circumstance of prayer in the interest of liturgical — and sometimes of doctrinal — correctness and of uniformity.[3] It lies in the nature of the juristic sources that these things occupy a large space in them and are treated as matters for legal definition. But in this literature itself, as previous citations have shown, strong protests are made against the excess of regulation and obligation, and emphatic assertions of the essential necessity of the spirit of devotion. It can hardly be doubted that in providing a simple form of prayer which united praise and gratitude to God with petitions expressing common needs and desires, and in fixing certain times for concerted prayer in the synagogue or the private prayer of individuals, the leaders of Judaism made an inestimable contribution to the religion of their times. In these prayers the common man participated in the worship of God on a complete equality with the educated class, and without the mediation of priest or rabbi. They furnished him with simple and appropriate language to express what in his simplicity he would have found no words for. The reverent attitude was adapted reflexively to promote the spirit of reverence. That all

1 Similarly many Moslem mystics.

2 See on the whole subject H. G. Enelow, "The Struggle for Inwardness in Judaism," in Studies in Jewish Literature. . . in honor of Professor Kaufmann Kohler (Berlin, 1913), pp. 82–107.

3 Contentious differences of usage might give rise to serious dissensions, as is abundantly exemplified in Christian history.

this must have done much for the spread and cultivation of an intelligent piety among the masses is evident.

It corresponds to all experience, however, that the practice of devotions at particular times, places, and circumstances, and in regular forms tends to become a matter of routine, and to be performed by force of habit with but slight attention to the meaning of the act.[1] It is another common observation that those who are more punctilious than the rest in the performance of such observances are prone to feel themselves on that account peculiarly religious and to pride themselves upon it. Against this tendency to formalism the teaching about the spirit of devotion which has been set forth above is directed. Such high doctrine, however explicit and emphatic, makes little impression on most men's minds. If they understand it at all, they dismiss it as a counsel of perfection for saints. All higher religions have had the same experience.

The Jewish order of prayer in the age with which we are here concerned was a directory rather than a formulary. It was not only licit but commendable for the individual to vary the phraseology and to extemporize upon its themes.[2] When such improvisations or private petitions were inserted (in an undertone) in the common prayer of the congregation, they were properly brief, in order not to get out of step, so to speak, with the other worshippers.[3] Even in private prayers, brevity is commended. So, for example, R. Meir: "Let a man's words before God always be few, as it is said, 'Be not rash with thy mouth, and let not thy heart be hasty to utter a word before God; for God is in heaven and thou on earth, therefore let thy words be few.'"[4] An example

[1] I. Abrahams (Pharisaism and the Gospels, 'Some Rabbinic Ideas on Prayer,' 2d. Series, p. 84) remarks: "The fixation of times and seasons and formulae for prayer does tend to reduce the prayer to a mere habit." But, he pertinently adds, "What can be done at any time and in any manner is apt to be done at no time and in no manner."

[2] See above, p. 221.

[3] Such, it is said, was the practice of R. Akiba — he abridged more than all of them. Tos. Berakot 3, 5.

[4] Eccles. 5, 1. Berakot 61a, top.

of a very brief prayer is that said by a student after he has lain down in bed: Into Thy hands I commit my spirit. Thou hast redeemed me, O Lord, faithful God (Psalm 31, 6).[1]

There were, however, biblical examples of protracted prayer, and Meir elsewhere cites the case of Hannah (1 Sam. 1, 12), who prayed long before the Lord, and drew from it the lesson that whoever remains long in prayer is answered.[2]

There are times when prolonged prayer is inopportune. God interrupted Moses on the brink of the Red Sea: "Moses, my children are in straits; the sea shuts off their way and the enemy pursues, and you stand there and make a long prayer! 'Why criest thou unto me?' There is a time to prolong prayer, and a time to make it short." As an example of a brief prayer, Moses' prayer for Miriam is cited, O God, pray heal her! (Num. 12, 13), and his forty days intercession for the people after the sin of the golden calf (Deut. 9, 18, 25) as an instance of long continued prayer.[3] The same examples of the shortest and the longest prayers recorded in Scripture are used by R. Eliezer with particular application to the abridgment or expansion of the benedictions in the prayers.[4] The private prayers which various rabbis were accustomed to say after the conclusion of the Tefillah, of which some specimens were quoted above,[5] are none of them longer than would take a minute or two to repeat. But it is told of the same Akiba, who abridged more than all the rest in the common prayer, that when he prayed by himself, one might leave him praying on one side of the synagogue and on returning later find him on another side, so many were the genuflexions and prostrations he made.[6] And doubtless many long prayers were made that were not "for a pretense."

[1] Berakot 5a, top.

[2] Jer. Berakot 7c, top.

[3] R. Eliezer ben Hyrcanus. Mekilta, Beshallaḥ 3 (ed. Friedmann f. 29a; ed. Weiss f. 35a). Cf. the exposition of the same verse (Exod. 14, 15) by R. Joshua (ibid.) — Moses, the Israelites have only to march forward! Cf. Soṭah 37a.

[4] Mekilta on Exod. 15, 25, Wayyassa' 1 (ed. Friedmann f. 45b; ed. Weiss f. 53a); cf. Berakot 34a; Mekilta de-R. Simeon ben Yoḥai, in loc. As an answer to questions of his disciples, Sifrè Num. § 105 (on Num. 12, 13).

[5] Pages 215 f.

[6] Tos. Berakot 3, 5.

Multiplication of eulogistic titles for God was censured by R. Ḥanina. In his presence a man once began: O God, the Great, the Mighty, the Awful, the Noble, the Powerful, the Terrible, the Strong and Puissant, the Indubitable, the Glorious! Ḥanina waited till he had finished, and said, "Have you finished all these praises of your Lord? What are all these for! We have three that we use (Strong, Mighty, Awful), and we should not venture to use these had not Moses uttered them in the Law (Deut. 10, 17) and the Men of the Great Synagogue appointed them in the Prayer. And you run on with all these!" [1] Excess in recounting the praises of God is explicitly prohibited; [2] the liturgy is sufficient. R. Johanan finds in Job 37, 20 a proof text for the dictum, He who recites the praises of God inordinately will be extirpated from the world.[3] No doubt, if the rabbis could have imagined such blasphemy, they would have pronounced the same doom on the fondling of God in certain types of modern non-liturgical prayer!

In a classical manual of Christian devotion the counsel is given, "Let everything you see represent to your spirit the presence, the excellency, and the power of God." [4] The same thought was in the mind of the rabbis when they gave forms of ejaculatory "benedictions" to be said on various occasions to which the whole of the ninth chapter of the Mishnah on Prayers (Berakot) and the corresponding Talmud is devoted.[5] For example, at the occurrence of comets, earth-quakes, lightning, thunder, and winds, one should say, "Blessed is He whose almighty power fills the world." No less, for the everyday sights of nature, mountains, hills, lakes, rivers, deserts, "Blessed is the Author of creation"; at the sight of the Mediterranean, "Blessed is He who made the Great Sea." On seeing crowds of men, "Blessed is He

[1] Berakot 33b, below.

[2] Megillah 18a, middle, quoting Psalm 106, 2, 'Who can utter the mighty acts of the Lord, or proclaim all his praise?'

[3] Megillah *ibid.*

[4] Jeremy Taylor, Holy Living, i. 3 ("The Practice of the Presence of God").

[5] See also (at still greater length) Tos. Berakot 7 (6).

who is wise in secrets," for not two of them are alike in features nor in thoughts.[1] On seeing men of striking physical peculiarities, "Blessed is He who makes his creatures various." For rains, and for good news, "Blessed is the Good and the Beneficent"; on the receipt of evil tidings, "Blessed is the faithful Judge." For it is man's duty to bless God for the untoward events of life just as he blesses him for the good; as it is written, 'Thou shalt love the Lord thy God with all thy heart, and with all thy soul and with all thy might.' With all thy heart — with the good and evil impulse[2] — and with all thy soul (life) — even though he take it from thee — and with all thy might — that is, means (material possessions).

Whatever difference there may be about the length of prayers in general, there is no question about perseverance in prayer. Moses was not prevented from pleading for the mercy of God even when God himself said to him, 'Enough for thee! Speak no more to me of this matter' (Deut. 3, 26). How much less should other men desist when their prayer is not answered![3] Moses' intercession for Israel after the sin of the golden calf was granted only after forty days.[4] Hezekiah, in his mortal illness, did not give up even when Isaiah announced to him in the name of the Lord that he should die and not live. We have a family tradition, he said in dismissing the prophet, that even if a sharp sword is resting on a man's throat he should not refrain from craving mercy. Thereupon he prayed, and was granted fifteen more years of life (Isa. 38, 1–5).[5] It is a commonplace that prayer, repentance, and almsgiving (*ṣedaḳah*), are the three things that cause a dire decree (of God) to be rescinded.[6]

[1] Tos. Berakot 7, 2.
[2] See Vol. I, p. 491.
[3] Sifrè Deut. § 29. In the sequel the words of R. Eliezer ben Jacob about the superiority of an hour of prayer to good works, above, p. 219.
[4] Above, p. 228.
[5] Berakot 10a. R. Johanan and R. Eleazar quote in this connection 'Though He slay me, yet will I trust in Him.' (Job 13, 15). See the sequel, 10b. Prov. 14, 32b.
[6] Jer. Ta'anit 65b, top; Jer. Sanhedrin 28c, near top; Gen. R. 44, 12; Pesiḳta ed. Buber f. 191a; Tanḥuma ed. Buber, Noah § 13, etc.

That God hears and answers prayer is taught and exemplified in a thousand ways in the Scripture. In the Psalms this fundamental truth of religion becomes a fact of experience, the faith by which men live. The Jewish conception and belief cannot be more adequately summarized than in the words of the Psalmist: 'The Lord is nigh unto all them that call upon him, to all that call upon him in truth. He will fulfil the desire of them that fear him; he also will hear their cry, and will save them.'[1] Yet, notwithstanding so many promises and prophecies, the prayer for the great deliverance which had been on the lips of Israel for centuries had not been answered. For this two explanations were found in the Scriptures. One was that the deliverance and the golden age which it should inaugurate were, as the prophets insistently taught, conditional upon the repentance of the people as a whole. They would come only when all classes did their best to think and feel and act as God required in his Law. The other was that the history of the world was a great plan of God, in which things came to pass at epochs fixed by him from the beginning, and that the predestined time for the great crisis in the fortunes of Israel had not yet arrived (Hab. 2, 2 f.).[2] Some presumptuous arithmeticians undertook, by combinations of assumed data in Scripture, to calculate the exact time — always in their immediate future — and gave out their results as revelations made to ancient seers, and saw signs of the approaching end in the conditions and events of their days; but the soberer sense of the rabbis regarded the time of the end as a secret which God kept to himself.

It was a matter of experience also that the concerted prayers of the community, for example for the seasonable rain on which their wellbeing depended and for fruitful years, were not always answered, and epidemics came from time to time notwithstanding the prayers for health. Even the most urgent specific petitions of individuals brought no response. Jewish piety met this

[1] Psalm 145, 18 f. Cf. Deut. 4, 7.
[2] On these two theories see more fully below, p. 351.

experience in the same spirit as other religions which share its faith in God's goodness and its assurance that he hears and answers prayer, and it made similar reflections.

In what has been said above about perseverance in prayer it has been seen that prayers are not always answered immediately. In the Scriptures, to wait on, or for, the Lord [1] connotes confidence, and the connotation often predominates, so that the word becomes a synonym for to trust in Him. The exhortation of Sirach, "Do not be discouraged (or despairing) in prayer," implies "let not your faith fail." [2] Long delay in answering prayer may then be a trial of man's abiding trust in God, by which such are distinguished from those lacking in faith.[3] When a wicked man prays and is not answered, he says: As I prayed before an idol and got nothing at all, so I have prayed before God and got nothing at all.[4]

It may be, also, that God knows that the thing which a man most desires is not for his real good. In the same context from which the preceding extract is taken in the Midrash, the prayer of the righteous is submitted to the judgment of God: If it be suitable in Thy sight, grant it; if not, not. At the dedication of the temple Solomon prayed: [5] "Lord of the World, when an Israelite comes and prays and asks for sons or something else, if it be suitable give it to him, and if not do not give it to him, as it is written, 'And give unto every man according to all his ways

[1] For a selection of passages and the lesson derived from them see Midrash Tehillim on Psalm 40, 1 (ed. Buber f. 129a). Most readers of the familiar English version are hardly aware that 'wait' in these phrases (e.g., Psalm 40, 1) means *wait* (cf. Isa. 25, 9). The Prayer Book version of Psalm 27, 16, "O tarry thou the Lord's leisure," makes the meaning plainer. Cf. (with other words) Psalm 37, 7.

[2] Ecclus. 7, 10. The Hebrew text has אל תתקצר בתפלה, which has been rendered "be not impatient," and comes to much the same thing, if impatient be not made equivalent to petulant.

[3] מחוסרי אמנה. On this phrase, and the synonymous קטני א׳, see Strack-Billerbeck, Kommentar zum N. T., u.s.w. on Matt. 6, 30 (I, 438 f.).

[4] Tanḥuma ed. Buber, Toledot § 14. The immediate application is to Esau. Cf. the story of Manasseh, Vol. I, p. 524.

[5] 1 Kings 8, 12.

as Thou knowest his heart' (1 Kings 8, 39);[1] but if a foreigner comes and prays in the temple, give him whatever he asks, as it is written, 'And also to the foreigner, . . . when he shall come out of a far country for Thy name's sake . . . hear Thou in heaven, and do according to all that the foreigner calleth to Thee for'" (1 Kings 8, 41–43).[2] The stranger's whole faith in the God in whose temple he worships depends on his getting what he asks, and if he succeeds he will become a worshipper of the true God (1 Kings 8, 43); the Israelite's faith rests on a securer basis, and it is part of his faith that God will give or withhold the thing he asks as in his wisdom he knows to be for the best good of his worshipper, which is what every man really wishes, though in his ignorance of his own good he may ask something else. Again, the denial even of good things may be part of that chastening discipline to which God submits those whom he peculiarly loves.[3]

Other explanations are offered. How does it come, asks R. Meir, that two men may take to bed, one as ill as the other, or two may go to court to be tried for exactly the same offense, and one get up from his illness, the other not, one be acquitted and the other not? One prays and is answered, the other prays and is not answered. Why is this discrimination? His response is that the prayer of the former was perfect, that is in the true spirit of prayer;[4] the other lacked this vital element. The latter was not answered because it was not really a prayer at all. Others referred the difference to the decree of God. When His unalterable decree had been issued, and the predestined hour of death had come, no prayer was effectual.[5]

Many prayers in lesser matters are futile because they ask

[1] If God knows, e.g., that the sons will provoke God to anger, or that the possessions he asks will lead the petitioner to 'kick' (like Jeshurun when he waxed fat, Deut. 32, 15), let him not give them. Tanḥuma, Terumah 9.

[2] Tanḥuma ed. Buber, Toledot § 14; cf. ibid. Bemidbar § 3, and Terumah § 8.

[3] See below, pp. 254 f.

[4] *Kawwanah* (see above, pp. 223 ff.). So Rashi on Rosh ha-Shanah 18a.

[5] Rosh ha-Shanah 18a (see also the preceding discussion, 17b).

God to make undone what has already been done, for example, if a man whose wife is with child prays that she may bear a son.[1] Marriages also are predestined — "every day a heavenly voice (*bat ḳol*) goes forth, saying, So and so's daughter is for so and so"[2] — and no other can by prayer get ahead of the designated spouse. A Babylonian authority, Raba, once heard a man praying that a certain girl might be his mate. The rabbi disapproved the petition: If she is the right one for you, she will not be parted from you (prayer is superfluous); if not, your unanswered prayer may lead you to lose faith in God.[3]

The commonest introduction to a petition is, "May it be Thy good pleasure to grant (or to do) thus and so," in which the suppliant expressly makes his request dependent upon the will of God, as is done in the prayer in imminent danger quoted above, What is good in thine eyes, do![4] It is in thus leaving the answer to the wisdom and good pleasure of God, and in accepting the giving or withholding of the thing asked in equal faith, that prayer essentially differs from an incantation or a magical formula, which is imagined to be efficacious in and of itself to attain the desired end.[5]

The experience of all religions which have attained to the higher conception of prayer with which we have been dealing proves how difficult it is for the mass of men to expel from their minds the delusion that prayer is an efficacious means of moving God to do what the petitioner wants, rather than the submission of his desires to the wiser goodness of God; and Judaism would have got far beyond Christianity, ancient or modern, if it had

[1] תפלת שוא. M. Berakot 9, 3; Berakot 60a. According to an author in the Babylonian Talmud, such a prayer is proper down to the fortieth day after conception, at which time the sex of the embryo is determined.

[2] Sanhedrin 22a, bottom; Soṭah 2a. The decision is made before the birth of every boy. See Vol. I, pp. 439 f.

[3] Mo'ed Ḳaṭon 18b. (Rashi.)

[4] Page 215.

[5] Magical means frequently fail; but the explanation then given and accepted is that there was some defect in the performance, or that they were thwarted by more potent charms opposed to them.

succeeded in overcoming human nature to this extent. There are, said Rab, three sins from which no man escapes for a single day: letting his imagination play with sin, and calculating on prayer,[1] and injurious speech.[2] The sin consists in man's presumption that God will grant his request as a compensation due for his praying.[3] It is no wonder that the disappointment of such false confidence should make men "sore at heart." [4]

Judaism also had its heroes of prayer, whose supplications were answered where others failed. One such case has already been mentioned, Akiba's prayer for rain.[5] R. Eliezer had recited twenty-four "benedictions" without result; Akiba said only, Our Father, our King . . . for Thine own sake have compassion upon us," and was at once answered.[6] Among these virtuosi in prayer with whom legend made itself busy was Ḥanina ben Dosa, at whose intercession a son of R. Johanan ben Zakkai was restored to health from a grave illness, and later a son of Gamaliel II.[7] Another was Ḥoni called ha-Me'aggel, who was famous for the efficacy of his prayers in bringing rain. On one occasion when he was sent for on this business, and the rain did not at once follow on his prayer,[8] he drew a ring on the ground and taking his stand within it, after the example of the prophet Habakkuk (Hab. 2, 1), addressed God in the following familiar fashion: "Lord of the World, thy children are looking to me, and I am like a household servant of thine. I swear by thy great name that I will not budge from this place till thou hast compassion on thy children." First it did not rain hard enough, and he said,

[1] עיון תפלה.
[2] Baba Batra 164b, bottom.
[3] See Rashi in loc. (other explanations in Tosafot). See on this point, I. Abrahams, Pharisaism and the Gospels, Second Series, p. 78 f.
[4] Berakot 32b; 55a, top, quoting Prov. 13, 12, with a midrashic twist.
[5] Above, p. 209.
[6] Ta'anit 25b. Cf. Jer. Ta'anit 66c–d, the parable by which Akiba interpreted the incident to the honor of his teacher R. Eliezer.
[7] See Vol. I, pp. 377 f.; Jewish Encyclopedia, VI, 214–216.
[8] A later Amora explains, Because he did not come in humility. Jer. Ta'anit 66d.

That is not the kind of rain I asked for; then it poured, and he made the same complaint; finally it rained steadily but so long that the people of the city had to take refuge on the temple mount and begged him to pray that the rain should be gone.[1]

For such prayers and the answers to them there were abundant precedents in the Scripture, and for that reason the stories of such miraculous results have little bearing on the general rabbinical teaching about prayer. It is further to be observed that Ḥoni the rain-maker belongs to another age, the times of Queen Alexandra, and that Simeon ben Shaṭaḥ is said to have declared that he deserved to be excommunicated for his irreverence — a report which we may take as a reflection of the impression the story made on the rabbis of the second century.

It is said that when Ḥanina ben Dosa prayed for persons seriously ill he had a premonition that one would live, another die, and when he was asked how he knew replied, If my prayer comes easily, I know that it is accepted; if not, I know that it is rejected.[2] When the son of Rabban Gamaliel II fell ill, the father despatched two scholars to R. Ḥanina [3] asking him to intercede for his son. He went up to a chamber on the roof and prayed for him. When he came down he said, Go back, the fever has left him. They said, Are you a prophet? He replied, Neither a prophet nor the son of a prophet (Amos 7, 14); but I have it by tradition that if my prayer comes easily I know that it is accepted, if not I know that it is rejected. They seated themselves and wrote down and noted the time exactly. When they came to R. Gamaliel, he said, By the divine service![4] you put it neither sooner nor later; at that very hour the fever left him and he asked us for a drink of water.[5]

[1] Ta'anit 23a. Compare the story of the flood raised by an anonymous saint (*ḥasid*) in Tos. Ta'anit 3, 1. For many other examples see A. Büchler, Types of Jewish-Palestinian Piety from 70 B.C.E. to 70 C. E., chap. iv.

[2] M. Berakot 5, 5.

[3] The parallel in Jer. Berakot notes that his residence was in another town.

[4] I.e. the sacrifice on the altar; a frequent form of oath.

[5] Berakot 34b; cf. Jer. Berakot 9d. Cf. John 4, 46–53.

Faith, in Judaism, is confidence in God. It was in this confidence that the forefathers, in the decisive moment of the nation's history, at his command marched straight toward the sea which barred their way, and their faith was justified by the cleaving of its waters before them.[1] When we read in the Epistle to the Hebrews (11, 29), 'By faith they crossed the Red Sea as on dry ground,' we may recall the words of the Midrash: (God said to Moses) "The faith they have shown (in obeying the command to march forward) is sufficient reason that I should divide the sea for them." [2] "Great is the faith with which Israel confided in Him who spake and the world came into being, for in requital for Israel's confiding in the Lord, the holy spirit rested upon them and (inspired by it) they uttered the Song (Exod. 15), as it is said, They had faith in God and in Moses his servant" (Exod. 14, 31).[3] The Israelites were delivered from Egypt only as a reward for faith, as it is written, And the people believed, etc. (Exod. 4, 31).[4] These miracles in the past are a ground for faith in the future.[5]

Abraham is the great exemplar of faith; by virtue of faith he became heir of both this world and the world to come — He put faith in the Lord and it was accounted unto him for righteousness (Gen. 15, 6).[6] The whole passage from which the last two extracts are taken is a laudation of faith, supported by numerous quotations of texts of Scripture in which the word *amunah* or *amanah* occurs. Both, like πίστις, *fides*, and the English 'faith' itself, cover fidelity as well as confidence, and as in the famous case of Hab. 2, 4, 'The righteous man shall live by his faith,' [7] the in-

[1] Note the place given to this miracle in the Psalms.

[2] Mekilta, Beshallaḥ 3, on Exod. 14, 15 (ed. Friedman f. 29b; ed. Weiss f. 35b), attributed to Rabbi. An anonymous version, agreeing on the point of faith, in Mekilta de-R. Simeon ben Yoḥai in loc.

[3] Mekilta, Beshallaḥ 6, on Exod. 14, 31. (Friedman f. 33b; Weiss f. 40b, end.) [4] Mekilta, l. c. [5] Sifrè Deut. § 25 (on 1, 29).

[6] Mekilta, l. c.; cf. Rom. 4, 3, 9, 20–21; Gal. 3, 6; James 2, 23 f.

[7] Gal. 3, 11; Romans 1, 17; Hebrews 10, 38. According to one opinion the single verse in which the substance of revelation is summed up. Makkot 24a, below. See above, p. 84.

terpreter may be at a loss whether to say 'faith' or 'faithfulness.' The compiler in the Midrash (and very likely the authors) did not feel what to us seems an ambiguity. Be that as it may, fidelity to God was in Jewish thought inseparable from confidence in God.

Confidence in God is manifested in the assurance that what he promises he will fulfil, as in the classic example of Abraham (Gen. 15, 1–6). In the period with which we are occupied these promises were extended beyond the golden age of the national hope to the life beyond the tomb and the World to Come. Fidelity was exercised in the endeavor to know and do the whole will of God. In relation to the dispensations of Providence in this life, confidence in God has its complete expression in the words of R. Akiba, A man should habitually say, All that the Merciful [1] does is for the best.[2]

In conclusion it may not be superfluous to remark that the words for faith in the literature and the thought of this age are not used in the concrete sense of creed, beliefs entertained — or to be entertained — about God.

[1] A common Jewish-Aramaic name for God, which was taken over by Mohammed, *el-Raḥmān*.

[2] Berakot 60b, below, with a story about Akiba illustrating the way in which what seem to be most unfortunate accidents may prove the truth of the saying.

CHAPTER III

STUDY

In a former chapter it has been shown that the school was one of the fundamental institutions of Judaism,[1] and was so regarded. It must now be added that the study of the divine revelation in the Scriptures, and of the interpretation and application of revelation was an integral part of Jewish piety.[2]

It is a religious duty the fulfilment of which is requited in this world, but whose full reward is reserved for man in the World to Come, like that of honoring father and mother, doing deeds of lovingkindness, and making peace between a man and his fellow, "and the study of divine revelation (Talmud Torah) is equal to them all." [3] This is not a boastful claim of the superiority of learning to the fulfilment of the highest human obligations in the Law itself; it is a way of saying that the study of the Law is a religious duty of the first rank.[4] The revelation itself is God's most precious gift.[5] The whole world is not equal in worth to one word of the Law; all the commandments of the Law are not equal to one word of the Law.[6] It should receive attention adequate to its unique worth. To give all one's time and thought to it would be the ideal life. Such was God's charge to Joshua: 'Thou shalt meditate therein day and night, that thou mayest observe to do according to all that is written therein' (Josh. 1, 8); and on him whose delight is in the law of his God,

[1] Part i, Chapter 6.

[2] For a collection of passages expressing a similar estimate of study, see Friedmann, Introduction to Seder Eliahu Rabbah, p. 109.

[3] M. Peah 1, 1.

[4] On the priority of study or deed see below, pp. 246 f.

[5] The incomparable worth of wisdom (e.g., Prov. 8, 11) is applied to the Torah (see Vol. I, pp. 263 ff.); Jer. Peah 15d, etc.

[6] Ibid. There is no greater proof of God's love to Israel than the multitude of commandments he has given it. Sifrè Deut. § 36, end; Menaḥot 43b, etc.; cf. the evening prayer, Ahabat 'Olam, Singer, Daily Prayer Book, p. 96.

and who meditates therein day and night His blessing rests (Psalm 1, 2 f.).[1]

The study of revelation, as we have seen, did not end with the study of Scripture; it included all the branches of learning which dealt with the interpretation of the Scriptures and the application of their teachings to life — exegesis, legal rules and religious and moral lessons.[2]

Study, as well as prayer, is worship, like it called by the name of the service of the altar (*'abodah*).[3] Like every other religious act, study is made such by the "intention" (Kawwanah) with which it is performed, the directing of the mind intently to Heaven. R. Johanan went to visit R. Eleazar, who was lying ill, and finding him weeping asked, "Why are you weeping? Is it because you have not mastered the Law? We have the authority of tradition, It matters not whether much or little, if only a man directs his mind to Heaven." [4] The rabbis of Jamnia, in their antidote to the self-conceit which is the besetting sin of scholars in all ages,[5] comparing their work with that of peasants in the fields, conclude: "If a scholar should say, I do much and the peasant does little (my work is of great value and his of small), we have learned, Whether much or little, if only a man directs his mind to Heaven." [6]

[1] See, e.g., Tanḥuma ed. Buber, Re'eh § 1 init. That the command to Joshua is not to be understood to exclude secular occupations is observed by R. Ishmael, Sifrè § 42 (on Deut. 11, 14); cf. Berakot 35b. According to Johanan, Josh. 1, 8, is not a commandment (מצוה) nor an obligation (חובה) but a blessing (ברכה). Menaḥot 99b, bottom.

[2] Midrash, Halakot, Haggadot. Sifrè Deut. § 48 (ed. Friedmann f. 84b). One who loves the Torah (here the study of Scripture) will not be satisfied with Torah, but go on to Mishnah, and finally, for the same reason, to Talmud. Lev. R. 22, 1.

[3] Sifrè Deut. on Deut. 11, 13 (§ 41; ed. Friedmann f. 80a, top). On prayer as worship, see above, pp. 217 f.

[4] Berakot 5b. The Tannaite authority is found in M. Menaḥot 13, 11, where it is deduced from the laws about burnt-offerings, which range from a bullock to a bird.

[5] See below, p. 245.

[6] Berakot 17a. The saying is quoted in various other applications; see Yoma 42a, top; Shebu'ot 15a; Shabbat 96a.

Instances are cited in which study was regarded as a superior obligation to the appointed prayers, and the interruption of the learned labors of the school when the hour of prayer came around disapproved.[1] The rabbis to whom this opinion or practice is attributed are, however, not a sufficient support for an inference that a similar attitude was taken in the period with which we are concerned.[2] That scholars recited their prayers, when the time came, in the lecture room (Bet ha-Midrash) [3] instead of the synagogue may very well have been an older custom, though there seems to be no early evidence of it.

Like every other religious duty, the study of revelation should be pursued "for its own sake," [4] that is with no admixture of self-regarding motive. The one true motive is love of God. Suppose you say, I am learning Torah that I may get rich, or that I may be called Rabbi, or that I may gain reward (from God), the teaching of Scripture is, 'To love the Lord thy God' (Deut. 11, 13); whatever ye do, do it only out of love.[5] To the same intent on Deut. 11, 22: Suppose you say, I will learn Torah in order to be called learned, in order to have a seat in the academy, in order to have endless life in the World to Come, the teaching is, 'To love the Lord thy God.' Honor and blessing follow the study that is not done for their sake.[6]

The good consequences of such study are frequently mentioned.[7] But here, as in the field of morals, it is taught that doing

[1] See J. D. Eisenstein in Jewish Encyclopedia, X, 166; I. Abrahams, Pharisaism and the Gospels, Second Series, p. 84 n. 1.

[2] The R. Judah who is said to have recited the prayers only once a month (Rosh ha-Shanah 35a) is not, as a reader of the articles cited above might imagine, Rabbi Judah (ben Ila'i), the disciple of Akiba, and one of the great authorities of the second century, but Rab Judah (ben Ezekiel), a Babylonian Amora (disciple of Rab), who died ca. 300 A.D. R. Zeira (Shabbat 10a) was a disciple of Judah who migrated to Tiberias; Raba, who commented unfavorably on R. Hamnuna's long praying when he was studying (Shabbat 10a), died in 352. All these examples come from one line of Babylonian scholars.

[3] Berakot 8a. The special prayers they said on entering the place of study (M. Berakot 4, 2; Jer. Berakot 7d; Berakot 28b) are another matter.

[4] See above, pp. 96 ff.

[5] Sifrè Deut. § 41.

[6] Sifrè Deut. § 48; Nedarim 62a.

[7] E.g., Sanhedrin 99b, R. Alexander; Tanḥuma ed. Buber, Berakah § 4.

right from an imperfect motive should be encouraged in the hope that it may end in doing it from a higher one. A Babylonian rabbi of the latter half of the fourth century used to pray at the close of the appointed prayer: "May it be thy good pleasure, O Lord our God, to make peace in the household above [1] and the household below, and among the students who occupy themselves with thy Law, whether they do so for its own sake or not; and may those who do not occupy themselves with it for its own sake come to do so." [2] To Rab is attributed the exhortation: "Let a man always labor in the study of the Law and doing the commandments, even though it be not for its own sake, for from this he will come to doing it for its own sake." [3]

The benefit of the study is enjoyed only by those who study the Law for its own sake. To one who does so his learning is made for him (by God) a life-giving elixir (according to Prov. 3, 8, 18; 8, 35); to him who studies it not for its own sake it is made a deadly poison (quoting Deut. 32, 2).[4]

The Law is not to be regarded as an antiquated edict (διάταγμα) to which nobody pays any attention, but as a new one which every one runs to read.[5] Every day when a man busies himself with the study of the Law, he should say to himself, It is as if this day I received it from Sinai.[6] The Law is called 'a fire of a law' (אש דת): Every one who comes to occupy himself with the Law should regard himself as if he were standing in fire.[7] In

[1] *Familia*. The angel princes who are over the heathen nations (cf. Dan. 10, 13, 20), for their strife brings the nations into conflict on earth.

[2] Berakot 16b–17a.

[3] Pesaḥim 50b; Sanhedrin 105b; 'Arakin 16b; and several other places. A quite similar saying of Rab Huna, Pesiḳta ed. Buber f. 121a.

[4] Ta'anit 7a. The poison is got out of Deut. 32, 2, by somewhat violent exegesis. Cf. Sifrè on this verse (§ 306), and see Bacher, Tannaiten, II, 540 n. 3. The author, R. Bena'ah, was a Palestinian rabbi of the end of the second century.

[5] Sifrè Deut. § 33 (on Deut. 6, 6), reading סופנה with Midrash Tannaim. Similarly, Pesiḳta ed. Buber f. 102a (R. Eleazar); 107a; cf. 105a (Ben 'Azzai).

[6] Tanḥuma ed. Buber, Yitro § 7 (Ben Zoma). The midrash in Pesiḳta as well as Tanḥuma plays on the words "*this* day" in Exod. 19, 1, where "*that day*" would be expected.

[7] Pesiḳta ed. Buber, f. 200a (Johanan).

what seem to us fanciful forms, the rabbis sought to impress on themselves and others that the student is himself receiving the Law from the Lawgiver as really as if he stood at the foot of Sinai amid the awe-inspiring scenery depicted in Exod. 19, and Deut. 4, 10 ff. A solemn responsibility rests on the scholar whose calling it is to teach and interpret this revelation. It is narrated that Neḥunya ben ha-Ḳanah, a contemporary of Johanan ben Zakkai, was accustomed, on entering the school, to pray that no occasion of sin or error might occur by his fault, and on leaving it briefly gave thanks that God had appointed his lot in life among those who frequent the synagogue and the school, not the theatre and the circus, nor those that loaf on the street corners.[1]

To carry the devotional spirit into the learned study of Scripture has been a Christian ideal also. We are told of men who studied the Bible on their knees; but it may be doubted whether they understood it any better for the posture of body or mind, whatever edification they may have derived from it. Jewish scholars knew that understanding is an intellectual function, which is not promoted but perturbed by the intrusion of any mystical or emotional element. They prayed for intelligence, and to be kept from error, but they looked for the answer in the working of their own minds, and did not expect any supernatural illumination.

In the school of R. Ishmael it was taught, from Josh. 1, 8 ('This book of the Law shall not depart from thy mouth'), that the obligation to study the Law is not like a debt, which a man can discharge by paying a fixed amount and be done with it; it is an abiding duty from which no one has authority to release himself.[2] Shammai's maxim was, "Make thy study a regular thing; say little and do much; and meet every man with a

[1] M. Berakot 4, 2. The prayers themselves are reported in the Talmud in loc. (Jer. Berakot 7d; Berakot 28b). Cf. his prayer after the Tefillah, Jer. Berakot 7d (Bacher, Pal. Amoräer, II, 12 n. 6).

[2] Menaḥot 99b, end. In the preceding context different opinions are recorded on a minimum fulfilment of this duty. Cf. Mekilta on Exod. 16, 4 (ed. Friedmann f. 47b; ed. Weiss f. 55b).

friendly mien."[1] A commentary on the first of these recommendations is the saying come down from Judah ben Ila'i: Former generations made their study the regular thing and their secular occupation incidental, and both prospered in their hands; recent generations make their secular occupation the regular thing and their study incidental, and neither prospers in their hands.[2] A later homilist will have it that a man who makes his study of the Law a matter of convenient seasons breaks the covenant (Psalm 119, 126).[3] Many scholars, however, had to earn their own living, and there are not lacking opinions that secular occupation within limits was a good thing for learning too.[4]

R. Meir advises: "Be not much engaged in business, and busy yourself with the Law, and be lowly in spirit before every man.[5] If you give yourself a vacation from study, you will find many reasons for wasting your time; but if you study industriously, He has a great reward to give you."[6]

The benefits of such study are the subject of an eloquent passage in the appendix to Abot (c. 6), called from this passage at the beginning of it Ḳinyan Torah or Pirḳè R. Meir: "Whosoever labors in the Torah for its own sake merits many things, and not only so, but the whole world is indebted to him: he is called friend, beloved, a lover of the All-Present, a lover of mankind: it clothes him in meekness and reverence; it fits him to become just, pious, upright and faithful; it keeps him far from sin, and brings him near to virtue; through him the world enjoys counsel and sound knowledge, understanding and strength, as it is said, 'Counsel is mine, and sound knowledge; I am understanding; I have strength' (Prov. 8, 14); and it gives him sovereignty and

[1] Abot 1, 15.

[2] Berakot 35b. Cf. the similar saying of the same rabbi in Abot de-R. Nathan 28, 10.

[3] R. Simon. Jer. Berakot 14d, top.

[4] R. Gamaliel, son of the Patriarch Judah, Eccles. R. on Eccles. 7, 11. Above, pp. 127 f.

[5] Willing to learn from those less proficient than yourself.

[6] Abot 4, 10.

dominion and discerning judgment; to him the secrets of the Torah are revealed; he is made like a never-failing fountain,[1] and like a river that flows on with ever-sustained vigour; he becomes modest, long-suffering, and forgiving of insults; and it magnifies and exalts him above all things." (Singer's translation.)

Study of the divine revelation is here eulogized as — in Christian phrase — a means of grace, and it must be admitted that it would not be easy to exhibit the fruits of such study more comprehensively.

The learned as well as the pious have always been tempted to think of themselves more highly than they ought to think in comparison with others. Paul has to warn his Christians against it, and to remind them that the measure of faith is a gift unequally distributed by God.[2] Johanan ben Zakkai, who lived in memory as the unrivalled master of all branches of Jewish learning,[3] gave a like warning: "If you have learned a great deal of Torah, do not claim credit for yourself, for that is what you were made for." [4]

Humility is the condition of true learning. "As wine does not keep in vessels of gold or silver, but in the meanest of vessels, earthenware, so the words of the Law (the results of study) keep only in one who humbles himself." [5] It was a current saying of the rabbis of Jamnia: "I am a creature (a human being) and my fellow is a creature; my work is in town and his work is in the field; I rise early to my work, and he to his. As he does not esteem his occupation superior to mine, so I do not esteem mine

[1] Not like a cistern, which only retains what is put into it. Cf. Sifrè Deut. § 48 (ed. Friedmann 84a, above); Abot, 2, 8, where R. Johanan ben Zakkai compares Eliezer ben Hyrcanus to a cemented cistern from which not a drop escapes, and Eleazar ben 'Arak to a welling spring.

[2] Romans 12, 3.

[3] Bacher, Tannaiten, I, 27 f. On his reputation as a religious man as well as a scholar and teacher see Sukkah, 28a.

[4] Abot 2, 8. Cf. Sanhedrin 99b, top (Eleazar ben Pedat).

[5] Sifrè Deut. § 48 (on 11, 22; ed. Friedmann f. 84a). The parallel in Midrash Tannaim (p. 42), reads: "The words of the Law do not keep in one who is in his own esteem like a vessel of silver or of gold, but in one who is in his own esteem like the lowliest of vessels, an earthenware jar."

superior to his. Perhaps you may say, I accomplish much and he little, but we are taught, It matters not whether much or little, if only a man directs his mind to Heaven." [1] The scholar and the peasant respect each other's calling, and the scholar recognizes that in God's sight it is not the nature of a man's work nor its intrinsic importance that counts, but the whole-heartedness of the thought of God with which it is done.[2]

Advanced studies in the Law, with all the benefits that accrue from them, are not the privilege of any class — sons of elders or great men or prophets — the Scripture teaches that all men are on an equality in this field.[3] Learning is a pure democracy, in which the private person is on an equality with a king.[4] Among the great scholars and teachers all social classes were represented — the contemporary heads of two great schools, Ishmael and Akiba, may be taken as examples of the extremes.

Another thing that the Scripture makes too plain to be ever forgotten is that though knowledge of divine revelation is properly an end in itself, it can — even for its own sake — never be divorced from the doing of God's revealed will. A single quotation may suffice for the attitude of Judaism on this point. On Deut. 11, 22 ('If ye pay good attention to all this commandment,' etc.) the exegetical question is raised, Is it to be inferred that if a man pay attention (in study) to words of the Law, he may sit still and not do them? It is to exclude this inference that the words are added, 'which I command you to *do* — you shall turn (from study) to do them.[5]

Every scholar is familiar with the conflict of obligations which frequently arises between the jealous claims of his calling as a scholar and the opportunities — or importunities — of "practical usefulness," in rabbinical phrase, between learning and good

[1] Berakot 17a.

[2] These utterances, it may be remarked, come from the earliest and most authoritative Pharisaic sources.

[3] Deut. 11, 22; cf. 33, 4; 29, 9. Sifrè Deut. § 48 (ed. Friedmann f. 84b, top). Read ישנו (Midrash Tannaim, p. 43). Cf. ibid. § 41 (f. 79b, middle).

[4] Sifrè Deut. § 161, on 17, 19 f. (105b, below).

[5] Sifrè Deut. § 48 (f. 84b, below).

works. The question of the priority of obligation in such cases was propounded to a conference of rabbis at Lydda: Is studying the greater thing, or doing? R. Tarfon gave his voice for doing, but R. Akiba for study; and the decision was unanimous in his favor, on the ground that "study leads to doing," [1] or as it is expressed elsewhere, "doing is dependent on learning, not learning on doing." [2]

It is obvious that in the complexity of life no such simple rule will always meet the case; but those who framed it at least understood that, in the logic of it, right doing depends on knowing what to do and how to do it.

It would be interesting, if space and the immediate purpose of these pages permitted, to quote the many sound maxims about the method of learning, for example, the fundamental paedagogic principle, *repetitio est mater studiorum*, the abandonment of which in the vagaries of "educational psychology" is one of the chief causes of the inferiority of our "new education." The Jewish ideal of religious learning may be read in the following extract from a Christian aid to piety: In hearing the word of God, "be sure you be of a ready heart and mind, free from worldly cares and thoughts, diligent to hear, careful to mark, studious to remember, and desirous to practice all that is commanded, and to live according to it." [3]

The Law of God perpetually in man's mind (Deut. 6, 6 f.) guides him on his way, guards him in his sleep and converses with him when he wakes — guides him through this world, guards him in the hour of death, will be with him when he awakes in the days of the Messiah, and converses with him in the World to Come.[4]

[1] Ḳiddushin 40b. The decision is cited in several other places: Megillah 27a; Baba Ḳamma 17a; Jer. Pesaḥim 30b; Jer. Ḥagigah 76c (Bacher, Tannaiten, I, 303).

[2] Sifrè Deut. § 41, on 11, 13 (ed. Friedmann f. 79a, below). The heaviest penalty is denounced upon the neglect of study — 'they have spurned the law of the Lord of Hosts' (Isa. 5, 24); 'there is no knowledge of God in the land' (Hos. 4, 1). Ibid. 79a–b.

[3] Jeremy Taylor, Holy Living, iv. 4.

[4] Sifrè Deut. § 34 (ed. Friedmann f. 74b, top), after Prov. 6, 22.

CHAPTER IV

CHASTISEMENT

A NOTABLE feature of the piety of this age is its attitude toward the afflictive dispensations of Providence in the development of the idea of chastisement. With the Scriptures in their hands the rabbis could not but recognize that many of the inflictions which befall the people or the individual are retributive, the penalty of transgression or neglect of the holy will of God. This was the moral of the history of the nation as it was drawn by the prophets, looking backward and forward over it. The comminations in Lev. 26, 14–39 and Deut. 28, 15–68, as appalling as were ever penned, denounce every conceivable kind of evil on the people that will not hearken unto God and will not do all his commandments.[1] These threats, which like those of the prophets were originally collective, in the personalizing of the whole doctrine of retribution, were applied, so far as their nature permitted, to individuals also.

In the study of such lessons in the Law and the Prophets an association was discovered between specific offenses and corresponding penalties,[2] and it was inferred that such correspondence was a principle of divine retribution. Accordingly we find certain diseases, for example, said to come for certain sins of the individual, or as epidemics for prevalent sins in the community. Leprosy, which had always been in a peculiar way the stroke of God, was inflicted on account of peculiarly grave sins. Johanan enumerated seven: slander, homicide, false swearing, licentiousness, haughtiness, robbery, and stinginess.[3] Women die in childbirth for neglect of the three obligations which rest exclusively on

[1] Lev. 26, 14 f., 27; Deut. 28, 14, 58.

[2] In this proceeding large use was made of Lev. 26. See a list of eight by Eleazar ben Judah of Bartota, Shabbat 32b–33a. Bacher, Tannaiten I, 443–444, and notes.

[3] 'Arakin 16a. Tanḥuma ed. Buber, Meṣora' § 10 and parallels raise the count to eleven.

them.[1] Children die for the sins of their parents, several of which are specified by rabbis of the second century.[2]

Some ingenuity is displayed in matching diseases with sins, as when R. Eleazar ben Jose makes out that a disease [3] that cut off the breath and was accounted the worst of nine hundred and three kinds of death [4] comes in consequence of slander, in support of which a later rabbi finds a text in Psalm 63, 12, 'The mouth of them that speak lies shall be stopped.' [5] An epidemic of this dreaded disease was attributed to neglect of the study of the Law, which was a cause of the death of children by other ailments.[6]

It is unnecessary to expand further on this topic; [7] most of the opinions recorded are mere midrash, which is not to be taken more seriously than it was meant. So far as they have any other motive, it is not to serve as an inventory of crimes and penalties,[8] but to be a warning against transgression or negligence, as in the Mishnah (Shabbat 2, 6) cited above.[9] That men, like Job's comforters, inferred their neighbor's sin from his suffering, and great sin from great suffering, is a logical consequence of an unqualifiedly moral conception of Providence, and had abundant biblical warrant.[10]

To whatever uncharitable judgments this led when it was applied to others, it had its merits when a man was led by affliction

[1] M. Shabbat 2, 6. The Talmud on this Mishnah (32a–33b) is the principal locus for this whole subject.

[2] Shabbat 32b.

[3] אסכרא. Probably diphtheria.

[4] Berakot 8a. The 903 deaths have the numerical value of the word תוצאות in Psalm 68, 21 ('the issues of death.').

[5] יסכרו פי דוברי שקר, etymologizing אסכרא. Shabbat 33b. Cf. Eccles. R. on 9, 2; the spies who brought back an evil report of the land died thus.

[6] Shabbat 33b and 32b.

[7] A sufficient collection will be found by the curious in Strack-Billerbeck, Kommentar zum Neuen Testament aus Talmud und Midrasch, II, 193–197 (on Luke 13, 2).

[8] Strack-Billerbeck, l. c. p. 193: So gewann man ein förmliches Strafverzeichnis für die einzelnen Sünden. (See the sequel.)

[9] See also Tos. Shabbat 2, 10 (Jose ben Ḥalafta).

[10] The principle of 'measure for measure' is often enounced, e.g., Sifrè Deut. § 308 (on 32, 5; ed. Friedmann f. 133b), quoting 2 Sam. 22, 27; Sanhedrin 90a, end (all God's dealings with men are 'measure for measure'). Striking examples from law and history, M. Soṭah 1, 7–9.

to examine himself, with a view to repentance and amendment.[1] A Midrash thus applies Isa. 26, 20 ('Come, my people, enter thou into thy chambers, and shut thy doors behind thee,' etc.): "Search in the inner chambers of thy heart, and see whether it be not on account of thy sins that I have brought upon thee afflictions — thy chambers are the chambers of the reins (Prov. 20, 27) — and if afflictions have come upon thee, do not complain of God's justice, but 'close thy doors behind thee; hide thyself a little moment, till the indignation passes.' Afflictions do not come to last forever; they are passing, as the text says."[2] If a man see that afflictions are coming upon him, let him examine his conduct, as it is said, 'Let us search and try our ways, and turn to the Lord' (repent).[3]

Examples of self-examination and of the help intimates may give in the inquiry are not infrequent. A story is told about R. Eliezer ben Hyrcanus, that he was once arrested on a charge of being a Christian.[4] He was discharged; but returned home much chagrined that he should have fallen under this suspicion, and unable to explain why such a visitation should have befallen him, until Akiba suggested that it might be that he had listened too complacently to some heretical utterance, whereupon he remembered that he had once heard from one of the disciples of Jesus of Nazareth, Jacob of Kefar Sekanya, a response of Jesus to a halakic question, which pleased him well, thus transgressing the injunction of Scripture, 'Remove thy way far from her,[5] and come not near the door of her abode; for she has laid low many slain' (Prov. 5, 8, combined with 7, 26).[6]

[1] Suffering and the consciousness of sin, see Psalm 31, 11 ff.; 38, 4 ff.; 39, 9–12; 40, 13; 41, 4 f., etc.

[2] Tanḥuma ed. Buber, Wayyeṣè § 5, end.

[3] Lam. 3, 40. Berakot 5a. — On the self-examination of the righteous see also Psalms of Solomon, 3, 5–10.

[4] The sequel shows that the 'heresy' (*minut*) for which he was taken up by the Roman authorities was so understood by the narrator.

[5] The 'strange woman' of the Proverbs is heresy. Cf. the similar interpretation of Eccles. 7, 26 in Eccles. R.

[6] Tos. Ḥullin 2, 24; 'Abodah Zarah 16b–17a (in uncensored texts).

A more trivial case is that of Rab Huna, who had four hundred large jars of wine go sour on his hands. His colleagues, hearing of his loss, bade him review his conduct. Do you suspect me? he asked. Is God to be suspected of injustice? they replied. — If any one has heard anything about me, let him say so. — Why does not the master give cuttings to the vine-dresser?[1] — Is there any of it left for me when he is through? He steals them all! — People say, Steal from a thief, and you get the same flavor.[2] — He thereupon pledged himself to give him the cuttings; and some say that the vinegar turned to wine again, and some that the price of vinegar went up so that it sold at the price of wine.[3]

In his self-examination a man was guided by the belief that in divine retribution there was a principle of *talio*, evil deeds were requited in kind.[4] "Where the sin began, there the retribution sets in." It is so of a member of the human body, as in the effect of the ordeal of the bitter water on the adulteress — her belly will swell and her thigh fall away (Num. 5, 27).[5] The principle is illustrated by numerous examples of other kinds.[6]

The notion is familiar. In the Testaments of the Twelve Patriarchs, Reuben, for incest with Bilhah, his father's concubine, was smitten with a grievous ailment in his loins, and and was sick unto death for seven months.[7] Gad hated Joseph for his tale-bearing and for his dreams, and as his liver was merciless toward Joseph, whom he would have liked to consume out of the land of the living as an ox licks up the grass of the field, God sent upon him a liver complaint of which he suffered mercilessly

[1] To which the farmer on shares (metayer) had a right (Baba Meṣi'a 103b).

[2] It is theft.

[3] Berakot 5b.

[4] This principle is enounced in Mekilta, Beshallaḥ 6, on Exod. 14, 27 (ed. Friedman f. 32b; ed. Weiss f. 39a), with an array of examples and proof-texts, beginning with the Egyptians who meant to drive the Israelites into the sea to drown.

[5] Cf. M. Soṭah 1, 7. So it came that Samson's eyes were put out; that Absalom was hanged by the hair he was so proud of; he was pierced by ten darts because of the ten concubines of his father whom he lay with (ibid. 1, 8).

[6] Sifrè Num. § 18 (on 5, 27).

[7] Reuben 1, 6 ff.

for as many months as he had cherished his hatred of his brother; "for whereby a man transgressed, thereby he is punished." [1]

Retribution, even thus conceived as in this sense retaliatory in kind and measure, was not vindictive, or was so only in the case of the irreclaimably bad who persisted in provoking their doom. God's end in punishment was not to make the sinner suffer what he deserved, but through suffering to bring him to penitence and amendment. So the prophets had taught both for the nation and the individual, and so Judaism understood. For afflictions sent to this intent and received in this spirit, chastisement is in our language an apter name than punishment, and Judaism makes the same distinction between afflictive dispensations conceived as of the nature of fatherly discipline, and the exaction of a penalty.[2]

To Deut. 6, 5 ('Thou shalt love the Lord thy God . . . with all thy soul and with all thy means') the Midrash significantly attaches an anthology of sayings about the worth of chastisements from seven or eight of the leading Tannaim, chiefly of the third generation.[3] If one remembers that several of these were men who had witnessed the catastrophe of their people in the war under Hadrian or lived in the misery of the generation following, he will feel a deeper pathos in their eulogies of suffering, and gratitude to God in it and for it.[4] To appreciate the passage, it should be read as a whole; here only a summary can be given.

Akiba, the teacher of four of those who contribute to this collection, himself one of the victims of Hadrian's edict against teaching, once in company with three colleagues visited R.

[1] *Δι' ὧν γὰρ ὁ ἄνθρωπος παρανομεῖ δι' ἐκείνων κολάζεται.* Gad 5, 10. In almost the same words, במה שחטאו בו נפרע מהם, Tanḥuma ed. Buber, Bereshit § 33, near the end. See also Wayyera § 28 (Abimelech, Judges 9, 53); Jubilees 4, 31 (Cain); 2 Macc. 5, 10; 9, 5 f; 13, 8; Wisdom 11, 16, etc.

[2] The former are *yissurin* (chastisements); the latter, *pur'anut* (retribution, punishment). Since both are sufferings, both words can be used more loosely.

[3] Sifrè Deut. § 32 (f. 73a–b); also Mekilta, Baḥodesh 10 (ed. Friedmann f. 72b–73a; ed. Weiss f. 79b).

[4] Out of the same situation comes the saying of R. Simeon ben Gamaliel (II) in Shabbat 13b, "We also cherish afflictions, but they are so many that time would fail to record them."

Eliezer (ben Hyrcanus) who lay ill. The others paid the great scholar extravagant compliments — he was worth more to Israel than the sun, than rain, than parents — when it came Akiba's turn he said, "Precious [1] are chastisements," and supported his estimate by the example of King Manasseh, for whom chastisement did what all his father's instruction did not do, made him know that the Lord was God (2 Chron. 33, 10–13).

To Akiba [2] is also properly attributed the application of Deut. 6, 6 ('Thou shalt love the Lord thy God . . . with all thy means'): "In whichever measure He metes out to thee,[3] whether the measure of good or the measure of punishment." For the former Psalm 116, 13, and Job 1, 21b, are quoted; for the latter, Job 2, 9 f. That men should give thanks to God for ill fortune as well as for good is a reiterated teaching. "A man is bound to give thanks for the evil just as he gives thanks for the good (Deut. 6, 6). . . . 'With all thy means.' With whatever measure He metes out to thee, be very thankful to Him." [4]

Akiba goes further than this: A man should rejoice in chastisements [5] more than in good fortune; for if a man lives in good fortune all his days his sin is not remitted. How is it remitted? Through chastisements.[6] That sufferings, borne as chastisements,

[1] Dear, חביבים.

[2] So Yalkuṭ I § 837, in an extract from Sifrè Deut. § 32. Our texts of Sifrè have R. Jacob. See Bacher, Tannaiten, I, 321.

[3] In *me'od* (E. V. 'might'), he finds *middah*, 'measure.' By a similar procedure R. Meir found in Gen. 1, 31, טוב מאד ('very good,') the lesson, טוב מות, '*death* is good.' Gen. R. 9, 5.

[4] The play on words cannot be imitated in translation. *Bekol middah umiddah shehu moded leka hewi modeh lo bim'eod me'od.* M. Berakot 9, 5. The obligation to give thanks for evil as for good, Berakot 33b; 48b; 54a, etc.

[5] Cf. Romans 5, 3, We rejoice in tribulations. See Shabbat 88b: Those who being reviled revile not again (cf. 1 Pet. 2, 23; 1 Cor. 4, 12), hearing disgraceful things said of them make no answer, act habitually out of love, and rejoice in afflictions (chastisements), of such the Scripture says: And those who love Him are as the sun when it goeth forth in its heroic strength (Judges 5, 31); also Giṭṭin 36b, end; Yoma 23a.

[6] Sifrè l. c. (f. 73b). An illustration of the belief that a man who has always fared well has "had his world" here, Sanhedrin 101a. Akiba by the sick bed of R. Eliezer: So long as everything went well with him, "I said, Is it possible — God forbid — that my master has received his world (here, and

are an atonement for sins is the common belief.[1] R. Nehemiah said: Precious are sufferings (*yissurin*), for as sacrifices atone so do sufferings atone (Lev. 1, 4; Lev. 26, 43); they are a better atonement than sacrifice, for sacrifices are of a man's property, sufferings in his person, and 'all that a man hath will he give for his life' (Job 2, 4).[2]

On the other hand, chastisements are an evidence of God's love, and through them man becomes dearer to God. So R. Eliezer ben Jacob: "'Whom the Lord loveth he correcteth, even as a father the son in whom he takes pleasure' (Prov. 3, 12) [3]— What makes a son pleasing to his father? You must say, chastisements." Meir: "'Thou shalt know in [4] thy heart that as a man chastises his son, so the Lord thy God chastises thee' (Deut. 8, 5). — Thou and thy heart (conscience) know the deeds thou hast done and the chastisements I have inflicted upon thee, that I have not inflicted on thee anything like what thy deeds deserved." [5] R. Jose ben Judah: Precious to God are chastisements, for the Glory of God lights on those on whom chastisements come, as it is said, 'The Lord thy God (in person) chastises thee.' [6]

Three great gifts which the peoples of the world vainly desire were given to Israel only through sufferings, viz., the Law, and the Land of Israel,[7] and the World to Come. Proof of the last is Prov. 6, 23, 'For the commandment is a lamp, and the Torah is light, and the way of life is disciplinary correction.' What is the

has no prospect beyond). Now that I see my master in tribulation I rejoice." Cf. Luke 16, 25.

[1] Chastisements wipe out all a man's sins. Berakot 5a, below. For the teaching of R. Ishmael on this point (in some cases a *partial* expiation), see Mekilta, Baḥodesh 7 (ed. Friedmann f. 68b; ed. Weiss f. 76a), and the numerous parallels cited in Encyclopaedia Biblica, IV, col. 4224. Cf. Psalms of Solomon, 13, 9 f.

[2] Mekilta, Baḥodesh 10 (ed. Friedmann f. 73a; ed. Weiss f. 79b, end); Sifrè Deut. § 32 (ed. Friedmann f. 73b, middle), etc.

[3] Hebrews 12, 5 f.; Revelation of John 3, 19.

[4] עם, 'with.'

[5] Cf. Syr. Apocalypse of Baruch 79, 2.

[6] For this and the preceding utterances see Sifrè l. c. (f. 73b).

[7] Proof-texts for the first two, Prov. 1, 2; Psalm 94, 12; Deut. 8, 5, 7.

way that brings a man to the World to Come? "You must say, chastisements." [1]

The biblical sources of these beliefs about chastisements and the spirit in which it should be received are in part apparent from the quotations. Others that might have been brought in are Lam. 3, 27–33 and Job 5, 17. The same teachings appear, as we should expect, in Sirach: "A man's compassion is for his neighbor; the compassion of the Lord on all flesh, correcting, and disciplining and instructing,[2] and turning back, as a shepherd his flock. On those who accept his discipline he has compassion, and those who hasten to keep his laws." [3] "He who hates correction walks in the track of the sinner, and he who fears the Lord will turn (repent) in his heart." [4] The theme is frequent in the Psalms of Solomon: "Blessed is the man whom the Lord remembers with correction and turns him from an evil way with the rod, that he may be purified from sin and not make it more." [5] God "warns the upright like a dear son, and his discipline is like that of an only son" (13, 8 f.).[6] It is the same in the literature of the Greek-speaking Jews. "Being chastised a little they will receive great good; for God tried them and found them worthy of himself. As gold in the crucible he proved them, and accepts them as a whole burnt offering." [7]

Parallels to the extracts given above from the Sifrè and variations on the theme could be cited in numbers,[8] but those adduced exhibit in sufficient completeness the attitude of the great masters of the second century.

[1] Sifrè Deut. § 32 (f. 73b, middle). See above, p. 253, n. Pesiḳta ed. Buber f. 152b, The way of life are chastisements (Prov. 6, 23). Acts 14, 22, Through many tribulations must we enter into the Kingdom of God.

[2] ἐλέγχων παιδεύων διδάσκων.

[3] Ecclus. 18, 13 f.; cf. 35, 14 f.

[4] Ibid. 21, 6; cf. 35, 17 (32, 21).

[5] Psalms of Solomon 10, 1–3, 6, 11–15; see also 3, 4 f.; and incidentally in numerous other places.

[6] The whole passage, 13, 5–10. See also the Syriac Apocalypse of Baruch 78, 3; 79, 2 (in the Letter of Baruch).

[7] Wisdom of Solomon 3, 5 f. (note the context); see 12, 2, 20 ff.; etc. 2 Macc. 6, 13–16; 7, 32 f.; 10, 4.

[8] See e.g. Berakot 5a.

There are afflictions for which self-examination discovers no explanation either in the way of transgression or of negligence.[1] For such a special category was made, "chastisements of love." 'Whom the Lord loveth he correcteth' (Prov. 3, 12). Every one "in whom the Holy God takes pleasure, he crushes with sufferings, as it is said, 'The Lord took pleasure (in him); he crushed him, made him ill'" (Isa. 53, 10).[2] Such evidences of God's peculiar love must be accepted in corresponding love: 'If thou makest his life a sacrifice of restitution (אשם).'—As a restitution-sacrifice is made with consciousness (of the reason), so chastisements (are to be received) with consciousness (of the reason, *sc.* God's love). Then only do they have the consequences promised in the second half of the verse, 'He shall see his posterity and prolong his days; and the purpose of the Lord shall succeed through his instrumentality' (Isa. 53, 10b).[3]

In the Babylonian schools the question was further discussed by what external signs such chastisements might be recognized. Some thought that only such afflictions as did not interrupt study or interfere with prayers were to be so regarded. Leprosy and the loss of children could not be chastisements of love.[4] Upon these refinements it is unnecessary to dwell; in any case they belong to a later period.

[1] For example, insufficient diligence in study, an extensive possibility. Raba (or R. Ḥisda), Berakot 5a.

[2] The translation is accommodated to the preceding midrash.

[3] Berakot 5a. Raba, through an intermediary, from Rab Huna, head of the academy at Sura, d. 296/7 A.D.

[4] Berakot 5b. This sentence is fittingly attributed to R. Johanan, who had lost ten sons.

CHAPTER V

FASTING

In an earlier chapter some account has been given of the calendar fasts and of the occasional fasts appointed by public authority when calamity threatened the community.[1] We have here to do with fasting as a phase of personal piety.[2] It is to be observed, however, that as the act of penitence on the Day of Atonement and in the preceding days from New Years on[3] was individual, though universal, so the obligatory strict fast on the Day of Atonement and the voluntary abstinences imposed on themselves by pious Jews on some of the intermediate days are individual in their character.

The regulations for mourning do not prescribe fasting,[4] of which it was an ancient concomitant, though in the interval between the death and the burial (unless on a Sabbath) the mourners must abstain from flesh and wine.[5] The story of Judith, who through all her widowhood fasted every day except Friday and Saturday of each week and the festivals with the day before, is told as an exceptional instance of wifely devotion.

Examples of self-imposed abstinence as a penance for mortal sin are given in the Testaments of the Twelve Patriarchs. For seven years Reuben drank no wine or other liquor, no flesh passed his lips, and he ate no appetizing food, but continued mourning over his sin, for it was great.[6] In the fear of the Lord, Simeon afflicted his soul with fasting for two years for his hatred

[1] Above, pp. 55 ff.

[2] On this subject see I. Abrahams, Pharisaism and the Gospels. First Series, pp. 121–128.

[3] Above, pp. 62 f.

[4] Maimonides, Mishneh Torah, Hilkot Ebel 4, 6–9; 5, 1 ff. — Biblical examples of fasting in mourning for an eminent man are 1 Sam. 31, 13; 2 Sam. 1, 12; 3, 35.

[5] Mo'ed Ḳaṭon 23b.

[6] Test. Reuben 1, 10.

of Joseph.[1] Judah, in repentance for his sin with Tamar, to his old age took neither wine nor flesh, and saw no pleasure.[2] By the side of these instances we may put an utterance of R. Meir about the penance of Adam; for a hundred and thirty years (Gen. 5, 3), he lived apart from Eve, and all that time wore a girdle of fig-leaves next his skin.[3]

In all these legendary cases it is probable that there lurks a vague notion of satisfaction which justifies us in using of them the word penance. The authors assumed that the transgression had been repented of, confessed, and pardon besought and bestowed. That fasting has an expiatory value is distinctly expressed in the Psalms of Solomon (3, 8 f.): The righteous man continually investigates his household to remove the guilt incurred by transgression. He makes atonement for inadvertent sins by fasting, and afflicts his soul.

A Babylonian rabbi of the third century[4] would have his fasting received in commutation of sacrifice. When he was fasting he used to pray at the close of the Tefillah: "Lord of the Worlds, thou knowest that while the temple stood if a man sinned he brought a sacrifice, and they offered only the fat and the blood of it and atonement was made for him. And now I have sat fasting, and my fat and blood have been diminished; may it be thy good pleasure that this diminution of my fat and blood be as though I had offered a sacrifice upon thine altar, and be thou gracious to me." It is perhaps in this aspect especially that it is associated with almsgiving.[5]

The prevailing notion, however, is that fasting is an act of humiliation before God. This conception, expressed by the

[1] Test. Simeon 3, 4.

[2] Test. Judah 15, 4. It should not be forgotten, however, that beside these examples of penance, the Testaments have a very high conception of the effect of true repentance. See especially the fine passage in the Testament of Gad (5, 6–8) on its effect on the penitent himself.

[3] 'Erubin 18b. Cf. the Latin Vita Adae et Evae §§ 4 ff.

[4] R. Sheshet. Berakot 17a.

[5] Tobit 12, 8. The merit in fasting is the almsgiving, Berakot, 6b. What a man thus spared he gave to the needy, e.g. Testament of Joseph 3, 5.

phrase 'afflict one's soul,' so predominates that it has almost completely superseded the old word for 'fast' (*ṣūm*), which conveys only the physical fact of abstinence from food. The association of the phrase in the meaning 'fast' is with the law of the Day of Atonement, which connects it indissolubly with the act of penitence. And, like every rite of propitiation, its virtue lies, not in the outward circumstance, but in the sincerity of the repentance which is the substance of it. The words of Psalm 25, 3, 'They shall be put to shame that behave deceptively without cause,' are once explained: "These are the men who (on occasion of a public fast) fast without repentance."[1] Long before, Sirach wrote: "A man who performs his ablution to purify himself from contact with a dead body, and then touches it again — of what avail was his ablution? So is a man who fasts to get rid of his sins and goes again and does the same thing — who will listen to his prayer, and what profit is there in his humbling himself."[2] Of such vain fasting the Testament of Asher says: "Another commits adultery and fornication, and abstains from food; and (even) while fasting does evil to others."[3]

In the case of an individual as in that of the community, fasting in one aspect is connected with mourning customs, a gesture of sorrow for wrong-doing; in another it is an appeal to the mercy of God through the spectacle of his client's distress. Fasting is always a potent auxiliary of prayer, not only for forgiveness, but for the other needs and desires of the suppliant.[4] "If a man prays and is not answered, he should fast — 'The Lord will answer thee in the day of distress'" (Psalm 20, 1; cf. 51, 15).[5] In the common text of Matt. 17, 21, Jesus explains to his disciples, who asked why they failed in an exorcism, that the species of demon

[1] Midrash Tehillim on Psalm 25, 3 (ed. Buber, f. 106a).

[2] Ecclus. 31 (34), 30 f. See Vol. I, pp. 508 f.

[3] Testaments of the Twelve Patriarchs, Asher 2, 8 f.

[4] See e.g. Psalm 35, 13 f.; Ezra 8, 21 ff.; Dan. 9, 3. The classical example is David, 2 Sam. 12, 15–23.

[5] Jer. Berakot 8a, top; Jer. Ta'anit 65c, top. "Distress" (צרה) taken for fasting.

they were dealing with [1] can be expelled only through prayer and fasting. The verse is omitted by recent editors as an amplified intrusion from Mark,[2] but it very early found its way into the manuscript tradition both in the East and the West, and expresses a belief entertained by Christians and Jews alike that fasting gives more force to prayer.[3]

Mention may also be made of fasting as a preparation for revelation, as in the example of Moses (Exod. 24, 15 f.; [4] Daniel 9, 3, 20–22; 10, 2 ff.).[5]

Besides the fasts which individuals observed for specific reasons, fasting was also practiced as a religious exercise by such as aspired to a superior piety. We read that the disciples of John the Baptist did not understand why the disciples of Jesus did not fast as they and the Pharisees did, apparently at set times.[6] Among the Pharisees Monday and Thursday were the customary days thus observed.[7] The teaching of the Twelve Apostles enjoins: "Let not your fasts coincide with those of the hypocrites. For they fast on Mondays and Thursdays; but do you fast on Tuesdays and Fridays." [8] The only reason given for the choice of the second and fifth days of the week is a piece of far-fetched midrash: [9] after the sin of the golden calf Moses went up to the mountain on Thursday and came down again (at the end of forty days) on a Monday. Therefore the learned ordained that men should fast on those days.

[1] See the fuller description in Mark 9, 17–27.

[2] Mark 9, 29, by prayer. The Shema' and the recitation of certain Psalms, particularly Psalm 3 and 91, were believed to be peculiarly efficacious.

[3] For an example in a case of general supplication, see 2 Macc. 13, 10–12.

[4] Yoma 4b (R. Jonathan). Bacher, Tannaiten, I, 388 n. Cf. Exod. 34, 28.

[5] In the later apocalypses this becomes a regular procedure; see 4 Esdras 5, 20; 6, 35; 9, 26 f.; 12, 51. Syr. Baruch 5, 7; 9, 2; 20, 5 f.

[6] Mark 2, 18; Matt. 9, 14; Luke 5, 33. The disciples of John had prayers of their own, as those of the rabbis had. Luke 11, 1.

[7] In the Pharisee's prayer, Luke 18, 12, he says, "I fast twice a week and tithe everything that I get."

[8] Didachè c. 8. They are (like the Jews) to say their prayers three times a day; but to use the Lord's Prayer instead of the Tefillah.

[9] Tanḥuma ed. Buber, Wayyera § 16.

We have already seen that these days were appointed for the public rain fasts.[1] Considerations of a practical character probably determined the choice; it interposed one day on each side of the Sabbath between that season of religious joy and a fast day, and it left the longest possible interval between the two fasting days. The same reasons applied to the voluntary fasts of individuals.[2] A man might impose upon himself by a vow the obligation to fast every Monday and Thursday throughout the year;[3] it was understood, however, that if one of these was a festal day on which fasting was not permissible, his private vow gave way to the general rule.[4] The fast, like all Jewish fasts except the Day of Atonement and the Ninth of Ab, which were from evening to evening, lasted from dawn to the first appearance of the stars after sunset. There was no objection to hearty meals before and after these limits.

The motives that might lead men to resolve to keep such fasts are various. When it became the custom of pious people, doubtless many adopted it because it was the custom of such people. Others may have vowed it in mourning for some public calamity or private affliction, or in penance for some sin. But it seems likely that a motive of less personal character had a large part in it. Like the scholars who devoted their lives to the knowledge of the Law, like the Pharisees with their scrupulousness in the utmost refinements of the religious and charitable taxes or the rules of ceremonial purity, or like the martyrs who were faithful to their religion unto death, those who made semi-weekly fasting a rule of life for themselves felt that in so doing they represented their people before God as it was in the ideal. Theirs was in this

[1] See above, pp. 67 f.

[2] Monday and Thursday were also the week days on which a service with the reading of lessons from the Scriptures was held in the synagogues, which was believed to be an ordinance of Ezra. Jer. Megillah 75a; Baba Ḳamma 82a. See Vol. I, p. 296.

[3] Ta'anit 12a.

[4] In Ta'anit l. c. the case is contemplated of the proclamation of a new day of this kind after the vow was made. In that case his private vow takes precedence of the general festal day.

sense a vicarious piety which might incline God to overlook the deficiency of others and be gracious to the whole nation. In some vague way, at least, we may believe that this representative relation was in the the minds of seriously religious men among them. An analogy existed in the public fasts for rain, in which, if the rains did not begin at the seasonable time the religious heads of the community first fasted alone, and only if this did not suffice proclaimed a general fast.[1]

The destruction of Jerusalem with its temple by Titus in the year 70, the disastrous issue of the wide-spread rising under Trajan, and the final catastrophe in the war under Hadrian, revived the temper in which the four memorial fasts in Zechariah had been kept.[2] These fasts, which apparently were discontinued after the rebuilding of the temple in 516 B.C., were renewed. The Ninth of Ab now commemorated the destruction of the second temple as well as the first, and to these was added the fall of Bether.[3] It could hardly be but that under these evidences of divine displeasure the penitential aspect of fasting should have become predominant; and that private fasting should have become more frequent, and that some should have prescribed for themselves modes of continual penance.

After the destruction of the temple some altogether gave up eating meat and drinking wine, because the daily sacrifice and libation had ceased; but the leading rabbis disapproved their abstinence. R. Joshua (ben Hananiah) pointed out to such that their logic would carry them much farther; they could not eat figs and grapes because the first fruits had not been brought, nor bread because there were no more "two loaves" and shew bread, nor drink water because there was no water libation at Tabernacles.[4]

After the war under Hadrian R. Ishmael ben Elisha said: From the day when the temple was destroyed we should by rights make a decree binding upon ourselves not to eat flesh nor drink

[1] Above, pp. 67 f.
[2] Zech. 7, 3–5; 8, 19.
[3] M. Ta'anit 4, 6.
[4] Tos. Soṭah 15, 11 f.; cf. Baba Batra 60b.

wine, but it is a principle not to impose on the community a decree that the majority of the community cannot live up to.[1] And from the triumph of the heathen empire which imposes upon us dire and cruel edicts and stops the study of the Law and fulfilment of the commandments, and does not let us circumcise our sons, we should by rights make a decree for ourselves not to take a wife or beget sons, so that the race of Abraham might come to its end in this way.[2] Such a decree, however, would not be observed; and the deliberate violation of it would be worse than marrying without seeing anything wrong in it.[3]

In these manifestations of Jewish piety there is no ascetic strain, in the historical and usual sense of the term. The characteristic of asceticism is not the pains and privations to which a man subjects himself, but the end which he proposes thus to achieve. One wide-spread and primitive motive is the attainment of supernormal psychico-physical powers, whether exercised immediately or through control over spirits. A higher end is the liberation of the rational soul from the trammels of sense and from bondage to the appetites and passions that have their seat in the flesh. To a crasser dualism matter was inherently and irremediably evil, and the human body with all its functions was part and parcel of a material world whose evil was not only physical but moral. The soul was essentially divine, and when once it realized its own nature there was war without truce between it and the body. The freedom of a man's soul could be won only by the subjugation of the flesh; and only when it had thus conquered its liberty could it attain salvation, or, in mystical form, achieve its destiny in union with God, or, more metaphysically, in identity with Absolute Reality. Jewish theology, as it has been

1 Horaiyot 3b; 'Abodah Zarah 36a.

2 Baba Batra 60b, below. The same utterance is reported in the name of R. Simeon ben Gamaliel, and the latter ascription is the more probable. Tos. Soṭah 15, 10.

3 A principle repeated elsewhere; Shabbat 148b; Beṣah 30a. Bacher, Tannaiten, II, 330 n. 1.

exhibited in a former chapter, is in contradiction with this philosophy at every point. The premises of an asceticism such as was in vogue in certain pagan circles and early took root in the Christian church, were altogether lacking.

This is confirmed by another observation, which is in itself of wider scope. The goal of the true ascetic, whether in India or in the West, is purely individualistic; the most logical type is the solitary hermit, whose sole all-absorbing concern is his own soul. Now it can hardly fail to impress every one familiar with the sources that such desperate concern of the individual about his own precious soul is conspicuously absent in Judaism; and that for reasons that lie deep in its religious thinking.

It would be saying a great deal more than we know, and indeed much more than is probable, to affirm that the dualism so widely current in those centuries had had no influence upon Jews who came in contact with foreign thought. The problem of the Essenes and the Therapeutae at once suggests itself. Nor is it impossible that solitaries like that Bannus with whom Josephus consorted[1] had picked up notions that did not circulate in the schools and the synagogues under Pharisaic teaching, though it is quite as likely that he took his models from the Old Testament. But what can be said with much confidence is that these ideas enjoyed no countenance from the leaders of religious opinion and practice, and left no permanent mark on orthodox Judaism. When we read, therefore, of extravagances of piety, of which there were no doubt many more than got into the record, we do not need to set them down as illustrations of an ascetic tendency in the proper sense of the word.

There is no such significance, for example, in the story of Joseph's fasting as a prophylactic against the allurements of Potiphar's wife;[2] nor of the comely young shepherd who took the Nazarite's vow because his beauty, as he saw himself with his flowing locks reflected in water, awakened in him emotions like

[1] Vita c. 2 § 11.

[2] Test. of Joseph 3, 4 f.; 10, 1 f.

those of Narcissus.[1] It was natural that those who had witnessed the fatal consequences of drink in others, should take an oath never again to touch wine,[2] or for a man who found habit growing strong upon him to vow total abstinence for a year.

Many rabbis disapproved such self-imposed abstinences. A vow of abstinence is an iron collar (such as is worn by prisoners) about a man's neck; and one who imposes on himself a vow is like one who should find such a collar lying loose and stick his own head into it. Or, a man who takes a vow is like one who builds an illegitimate altar (*bamah*), and if he fulfils it, like one who sacrifices on such an altar.[3] R. Isaac (reported by R. Dimi) said: "Are not the things prohibited you in the Law enough for you, that you want to prohibit yourself other things."[4] An ingenious interpretation of Num. 6, 11, discovers that the Nazarite had to make atonement by sacrifice for having sinned against his own soul by making himself miserable by leaving off wine. Such a man is called (in the text) a sinner, and *a fortiori* if one who has denied himself the enjoyment of nothing more than wine is called a sinner, how much more one who denies himself the enjoyment of everything.[5] In this spirit is the often quoted saying of Rab: "A man will have to give account on the judgment day of every good thing which he might have enjoyed and did not."[6]

Such sentiments, however frequent they may have been, must not be taken as the voice of an anti-ascetic "spirit of Judaism."

[1] Jer. Nedarim 36d; Nedarim 9b; Nazir 4b. The tale purports to be told by Simeon the Righteous. The familiar Narcissus story, Ovid, Metamorphoses, iii, 402 ff.

[2] Num. R. 10, 4; with reference to the ordeal of jealousy.

[3] Jer. Nedarim 41b. The former simile is ascribed to R. Simeon ben Laḳish; the latter to R. Jonathan. Other expressions of similar tenor are to be found in the same context.

[4] Ibid. Maimonides quotes this as the most noteworthy principle he knows on the subject. Eight Chapters, c. 4 (ed. Gorfinkle, p. 27; transl. p. 66).

[5] Nazir 22a, R. Eleazar ha-Ḳappar. The interpretation was so much liked that it is repeated in several other places. Also quoted by Maimonides, l. c., p. 25 (63).

[6] Literally, "which his eyes saw and he did not eat." Jer. Ḳiddushin, 66d, end.

They are expressions of personal temperament, circumstance and surrounding, and not to be broadly generalized. From an early time, also, antipathy to Christian monasticism was an influence not to be left out of account. The treatment of the subject by Maimonides has in view both Christian asceticism and similar tendencies in pietistic and mystical circles among Jews.

CHAPTER VI

CHASTITY. MODESTY. HUMILITY

THE three deadly sins in Judaism were, *'abodah zarah*, 'alien cultus,' which covered heathenism with all its ways and works; *shefikat damim*, 'shedding of (human) blood,' murder; and *gilluy 'araiyot*, strictly 'incest,' which was extended to comprehend all illegitimate intercourse between men and women and the various abuses or perversions of sexual instincts. The biblical laws on these subjects go much beyond what is common in the legislation of other ancient peoples, and in some important particulars beyond the moral ideals of the most enlightened, to say nothing of common custom.[1] The jurists carried still further the principles and precedents they found in the Scriptures, and where specific penalties were out of the question, pronounced the severest condemnation on acts or practices at which the world in general took no serious offense. We may dismiss this phase of the subject here, with the remark that in the most important points Christian moral teaching follows Jewish.

It is more relevant to our present purpose to remark that the Jewish teachers recognized that the imagination of sin is not only a temptation, but if dallied with instead of resolutely expelled, is itself a sin. The eminent association of 'evil impulse' with 'lust'[2] — also a specialized association — lent force to this conception. When Jesus said: "You have heard that it was said, 'Thou shalt not commit adultery'; but I say unto you that whoever gazes at a woman with desire has already debauched her in his mind," he was not only uttering a Jewish commonplace, but with

[1] It is no paradox that the greater stringency of the Hebrew law results in considerable measure from its more primitive character.

[2] *Yeṣer ha-ra'*. (See Vol. I, pp. 479 ff.) Compare the common modern specialization of "immoral" and "virtuous."

a familiar figure, "adultery of the eyes." Job says, 'I made a covenant with my eyes; how then should I look upon a virgin?'

On this topic there are many dicta. "Thou shalt not commit adultery. Neither with hand nor foot nor eye nor mind. . . . Whence do we learn that the eyes and the mind commit fornication? From the text, 'Do not go about after your mind and your eyes, after which ye commit fornication.'" For the adultery of the feet Prov. 19, 2 is cited; for the hand, Isa. 1, 10, with an application *ad hoc*.[1] R. Simeon ben Laḳish says: "You are not to say (merely) that he who commits the physical act is called an adulterer; one who commits adultery with his eyes is called adulterer, as it is said 'The eye of the adulterer'" (Job 24, 15; cf. Prov. 7, 9), etc.[2] A closer verbal parallel to the words of Jesus is found in the extra-talmudic Tract, Kallah (c. 1): Whoever gazes on a woman intently is as though he lay with her.[3]

That the coincidence of the Gospel with the rabbinical teaching is not fortuitous is demonstrated by the next following verses in Matthew: 'If thy right eye is an occasion of sin to thee, tear it out and cast it from thee. . . . If thy right hand is an occasion of sin, cut it off and cast it from thee.' The hand is not named here because of its value to man, but because it may be a minister to the same sin with the eye, as in the first extract quoted above.[4] To this offense the Talmud applies the laconic words of the Mishnah Niddah 2, 1, "The hand . . . shall be cut off." R. Tarfon (about 100) would literally cut it off, and *in situ*,[5] which, as was objected to him, would make a gash in the belly. Better, he replied, that his belly be split than that he should go down to the

[1] Mekilta de-R. Simeon ben Yoḥai on Exod. 20, 14 (ed. Hoffman, p. 111).

[2] Lev. R. 23, 12; cf. Pesiḳta Rabbati, ed. Friedmann f. 124b.

[3] Other references: Sifrè Num. § 115 (ed. Friedmann f. 35a); Jer. Berakot 3 c (the mind and the eyes two go-betweens of sin); cf. Tanḥuma ed. Buber, Shelaḥ § 31; Niddah 13b. Yalkut I § 750, on Num. 15, 39, citing Sifrè Zuṭa, counts up fourteen prohibitions which the adulterer transgresses.

[4] Niddah 13b. Cf. Latin *masturbari*, according to the popular etymology, *manu stuprare*. The sin deserved death. כל המוציא שכבת זרע לבטלה חייב מיתה (Gen. 38, 9 f.). Niddah 13a. Compare the application of Isa. 1, 10 above.

[5] Niddah 13b. יד לאמה תקציץ ידו על טבורו.

pit of perdition.[1] 'It is better for thee that one of thy members should perish and not thy whole body go off to hell.' [2]

Sirach's warnings about behavior with women (9, 1–9) emphasize the consequences of imprudence. The rabbis, in their endeavor to "keep man a long way off from sin," took manifold precautions against the excitement of lustful thoughts through the senses, and administer their warnings with liberal threats of damnation, as is a common way with moralists when they want to be impressive. Thus, under no circumstances should a man walk behind a woman, not even his own wife. One who walks behind a woman crossing a stream has no share in the World to Come. One who pays money out of his hand into a woman's so as to get a look at her, though he have as much learning and good works as our master Moses, will not get off from condemnation to hell, as it is said, 'Hand to hand! the wicked man will not get off' (Prov. 11, 21) — from condemnation to hell.[3] With less extravagance of language the advice is derived from Deut. 23, 10 ('Thou shalt keep thyself from every evil thing'), teaching that a man should not gaze on a handsome woman, even an unmarried one; not on a married woman even if she is ugly; and not on a woman's high-colored attire [4] — the fine clothes she wears to enhance her charms. Whoever looks at a woman will in the end fall into transgression.[5]

More dangerous still was protracted conversation with a woman. To R. Jose ben Johanan [6] is attributed the counsel that a man should not talk long with any woman. Some one who thought that this needed elucidation added: "One who prolongs conversation with a woman does himself harm, and wastes the

[1] Psalm 55, 24.

[2] Matt. 5, 30.

[3] Berakot 61a (cf. Erubin 18b). See also Berakot 24a. Many similar utterances may be found in Strack-Billerbeck, Kommentar zum Neuen Testament aus Talmud und Midrasch, I, 299–301.

[4] 'Abodah Zarah 20 a–b; Midrash Tannaim, ed. Hoffmann, p. 147. On the effect of the colored garments, cf. M. Zabim 2, 2. See also Mekilta de-R. Simeon ben Yoḥai, p. 111, expanding on woman's allurements in Isa. 3, 16 ff.

[5] Nedarim 20a.

[6] Second century B.C.

time he should be putting on the study of the Law, and in the end will occupy a place in hell."[1] Such counsels are addressed especially to students, who, having the reputation of their calling to sustain, are urged to avoid not only the occasion of sin but everything that might give rise to the slightest suspicion. The surprise of the disciples of Jesus, as narrated in John 4, 27, at finding their master talking with a woman was quite in accord with rabbinical ideas of propriety; so also was the respect which restrained them from asking, What are you after? Why are you talking with her?

It may be questioned, whether the exponents of Jewish piety, like Christian saints, did not think more about the snares of women and the lusts of the flesh than was good for them; but the fundamental difference between the two must not be overlooked. For the Christian ascetic the instinct itself was evil, and the aim of those who aspired to higher religiousness was to extirpate it, root and branch. To the Jew its aberrations were deadly sin, but marriage and the begetting of children was not only good and lawful, but voluntary celibacy ran counter to the very oldest commandment of God, Increase and multiply![2] Continence was a moral ideal on which due weight was laid;[3] abstinence was not a superior virtue, confounded with chastity, but was in conflict with the purpose of creation.

The Jewish teachers, as we have seen, counted "adultery of the mind" (thoughts) among the varieties of the sin of unchastity. The stimulus may come from sights in the natural world from which man should turn his eyes away;[4] sometimes from listening to obscene or licentious talk. Sometimes the "evil impulse," which is in his own nature and yet somehow his bosom enemy, seems to set upon him without occasion, bent on his

[1] Abot 1, 5. Many sayings in the same vein are collected in Kobryn, Catena, on Abot 1, 5 (f. 12a–b) and 3, 13 (ff. 67a–68a).
[2] See Vol. I, p. 119 f.
[3] See Maimonides, Hilkot De'ot 5, 4.
[4] 'Abodah Zarah 20b, top.

undoing. If he lets this impulse occupy his mind and his imagination play with the gratification of it,[1] he is guilty of this sin. To escape falling into it everything is to be avoided which in any way, physically or mentally, tends to excite this state.[2] If it occurs, in spite of these precautions, the rabbis understood human nature well enough to know that the remedy is not to struggle against it, which only keeps it in the centre of attention, but to divert the mind from it altogether by an engrossing occupation with something else. Their way was to concentrate all the faculties on the study of the Law in the school.[3]

The epithet 'holy' (*ḳadosh*) is given to the man who keeps aloof from all unchastity. The juxtaposition of the section 'Araiyot (Lev. 18) with Ḳedoshim (Lev. 19) is to teach that wherever you find restraint upon sexual relations, there you will find holiness, as is proved by many texts (Lev. 21, 7, 8; ib. 14, 15).[4] It is quite likely that in fact the connection in Lev. 18–20 of the idea of holiness with avoidance of the whole catalogue of venereal transgressions [5] led to the special application of the adjective 'holy' — we might say 'saintly' — to men distinguished by scrupulousness in the observance of these laws in the wide extension given them by the scribes.[6] A similar appropriation is familiar to us in our popular use of 'virtuous.' The Jewish idea of holiness was, however, not confined to the avoidance of the illicit; its ideal included the hallowing of the licit. The man who keeps aloof from unchastity is one who follows the maxim to hallow himself in what is lawful for him.[7] Various instances of conjugal chastity

[1] הרהור עבירה. Berakot 12b; Niddah 13b; Baba Batra 164b, end. Yoma 29a, top: The imagination indulged is worse than the act.

[2] See Akiba's words, Abot 3, 13: Sport and frivolity familiarize a man with lewdness (ערוה).

[3] See Vol. I, pp. 489 ff.

[4] Joshua ben Levi, Lev. R. 24, 6; Judah ben Pazzi, *ibid.;* also Jer. Yebamot 3d.

[5] See e.g. Lev. 20, 10–26, with the conclusion, 'Ye shall be holy unto me,' etc.

[6] "Secondary prohibitions by the words of the Scribes," M. Yebamot 2, 4.

[7] Yebamot 20a. Niddah 70b; Shebu'ot 18b. Cf. Sifrè Deut. § 104 (f. 95a, below) on Deut. 14, 21.

and modesty are reported of eminent rabbis of the second century.[1]

Modesty[2] is not only closely associated with chastity, but is itself a virtue highly esteemed in men and women. Some extraordinary, not to say extravagant, examples are recited, like that of the mother of seven sons who functioned as high priests, the rafters of whose house had never seen her hair uncovered nor the hem of her shift.[3] The patriarch Judah is said to have acquired the epithet "the holy" by singular modesty maintained through his whole life.[4]

Phineas ben Jair, a contemporary of the Patriarch Judah, is the author of a kind of Saint's Progress[5] which is preserved with slight variations in several places: "Heedfulness leads to cleanness; cleanness to purity; purity to holiness; holiness to humility; humility to the fear of sin; the fear of sin to saintliness; saintliness to the (possession of the) holy spirit; the holy spirit to the restoration of the dead; the restoration to life brings him to Elijah of blessed memory (the precursor of the new age. Mal. 3, 23)."[6] Jellinek was so impressed by this ladder of piety that he pronounced it a precious remnant of an Essene Baraita, and of great importance also for the primitive history of Christianity,[7] and the opinion has been confidently affirmed by others.[8] There

[1] A. Büchler, Types of Jewish-Palestinian Piety, pp. 43 f.

[2] *Ṣenī'ūt.* One of the etymologies proposed for the name of the Essenes is *ṣenī'īm*, 'the (preëminently) modest,' which at least corresponds to a conspicuous characteristic of the sect.

[3] Jer. Yoma 38d, above; Jer. Horaiyot 47d; Yoma 47a, below; Pesiḳta ed. Buber f. 174a, etc.

[4] Jer. Megillah 74a.

[5] In a late reproduction (Jellinek, Bet ha-Midrasch, VI, 117) they are called ten steps or stages in the ascent of the righteous.

[6] Jer. Sheḳalim 47c, below; Jer. Shabbat 3c, above; Midrash Tannaim ed. Hoffmann p. 148 (on Deut. 23, 15); Cant. R. on 1, 1. [M.] Soṭah 9, 9; 'Abodah Zarah 20b. Proof texts are annexed in the Palestinian sources.

[7] Bet ha-Midrasch, VI (1877), xxix n. 1 (text, p. 117).

[8] Bacher, Tannaiten, II, 497. (Not improperly called an Essene Baraita, though the author is not on that account to be regarded as an Essene.) K. Kohler, 'Essenes,' Jewish Encyclopedia, V, 31. (Phineas ben Jair, the last Essene of note.)

is nothing in other reported sayings of Phineas ben Jair or the stories told about him that suggests a sectarian affiliation; nor is there anything specifically Essene, so far as our information about the Essenes goes, either in the enumeration or procession of moral qualities in the passage quoted above.[1] The sense in which these stages were understood is indicated by the texts of Scripture adduced for them in the Palestinian sources, elucidated by the abundant particular parallels in the Tannaite literature, which show that the terms have no esoteric meaning. We may take it therefore as an expression of a rabbinical ideal.

Of one of the virtues in this sequence, humility, something has been said above in relation to the character and demeanor of scholars. The appreciation of this quality, however, has a wider scope. In the Babylonian Talmud, R. Phineas ben Jair is represented as closing his catalogue with the words, "and saintliness (*ḥasīdūt*) is the greatest of them all,[2] as it is said, 'Then Thou spakest in vision to Thy saints'" (Psalm 89, 20). R. Joshua ben Levi disagreed: Humility is the greatest of them all, for it is said, 'The spirit of the Lord God is upon me, to bring good tidings to the humble' (Isa. 61, 1). It is not said 'to the saints,' but 'to the humble,' whence you learn that humility is the greatest of them all.[3]

That the lowly enjoy the especial regard of God and that he resents the arrogance of the proud is a frequent theme in the Psalms. 'A man's pride will bring him low, but a man of lowly spirit will attain to honor' (Prov. 29, 23).[4] The biblical history from Adam down yielded abundant examples. Moses was marked in the Scripture itself as the great exemplar of humility

[1] See Büchler, op. cit. p. 42–67. It is to be observed that the *perīshūt*, of which a good deal is made by those who discover Essene principles in the saying, is not found in any Palestinian source, and that *ṣenī'ūt*, supposed to be especially conspicuous in Essene notions and practice, is not mentioned at all.

[2] חסידות (ὁσιότης) is the distinguishing quality of the pious, the saints.

[3] 'Abodah Zarah 20b; quoted as a general maxim, 'Arakin 16b.

[4] Cf. Prov. 15, 33; 18, 12.

(Num. 2, 3). Hillel was conspicuous for this virtue, and is proposed for imitation.[1] When he died the elegy over him was: Alas! the humble man, the pious man, the disciple of Ezra![2] A sentence of his own is: "My abasement is my exaltation, and my exaltation is my abasement."[3] The general principle here individualized is: Every one who humbles himself, God exalts; and every one who exalts himself, God humbles; one who runs around for greatness, greatness flees from, and one who flees from greatness, him greatness runs after.[4] With Prov. 29, 23, for a text and Saul for an elaborated example, we read: One who flees from office-holding, office pursues.[5] The Gospel advice to take a low seat at a dinner in order to be honored by an invitation to a better place has a parallel in advice, with the same motive, to take a place in the lecture room two or three rows back of that to which the order of precedence would entitle a man.[6]

Beyond these prudential motives there is a higher doctrine. It was Moses' humility (Num. 12, 3) that fitted him to be the medium of revelation. "The Scripture teaches that every one who is humble in the end causes the Presence of God (*Shekinah*) to dwell with mankind on the earth, as it is said, 'The High and Lofty One, inhabiting eternity — and Holy is his name — I dwell in the high and holy place; and with one who is contrite and humble of spirit' (Isa. 57, 15 f.); and again, 'The spirit of the Lord is upon me to bring good tidings to the humble' (Isa. 61, 1); and again, 'All these things My hand made, . . . and on this man will I look, on him that is humble and of contrite spirit (Isa. 66, 2); and again, 'The sacrifices of God are a broken spirit; a broken and a contrite heart, O God, thou wilt not spurn' (Psalm

[1] Shabbat 30b. Many anecdotes illustrate this quality.

[2] Jer. Soṭah 24b; Tos. Soṭah 13, 3; Soṭah 48b.

[3] Lev. R. 1, 5. Psalm 113, 5b–6a, is cited in support.

[4] 'Erubin 13b, below. Matt. 23, 12. (The passives are idiomatic: God will bring him down.)

[5] Tanḥuma ed. Buber, Wayyiḳra § 4. The other recension (§ 3) gives also the converse — office runs away from the office-hunter.

[6] Lev. R. 1, 5 (Prov. 25, 6 f); Tanḥuma ed. Buber, Wayyiḳra § 2; Abot de-R. Nathan c. 25 near end.

51, 19). But a man proud of heart causes the land to be defiled and the Presence of God to withdraw from it, as it is said, 'One who is haughty of eye and proud of heart, I cannot abide with him' (Psalm 101, 5).[1] Those who are lifted up with pride are called 'abomination,' as it is said, 'Every one that is proud of heart is an abomination to the Lord' (Prov. 16, 5); heathenism also is called 'abomination' (Deut. 7, 26). As heathenism defiles the land and causes the Presence of God to withdraw from it, so pride causes the same things."[2]

A Palestinian saying is: Who is a son of the World to Come? One who is humble and of lowly demeanor, bows low as he enters and leaves; who studies the Law continually and claims no credit for it.[3]

God cannot live in the same world with the proud and arrogant man.[4] Let man always learn from the mind of his Creator, who let alone all the high mountains and peaks and caused his Presence to rest on Mt. Sinai, which is no great ascent. His character is not like men's; among men one of exalted station regards one of the same rank, not one far beneath him; but God is exalted, yet regards the lowly — 'God is high yet regards the lowly' (Psalm 138, 6).[5] The passages in which, as it is said, God puts himself on a level with the hearts of the contrite have been noted in another connection.[6]

There is nothing novel in the condemnation of pride or the commendation of humility, it is emphatically taught in many places in the Scripture. But it is also made a constituent element of the Jewish conception of piety. Pride is hard to subdue, and none so hard as the joint pride of piety and learning, and when men have made a painful effort to eradicate their pride they may become inordinately proud of their humility.

[1] Pronouncing *itto* as in 'Arakin 15b; see below, Soṭah 5a.
[2] Mekilta (on Exod. 20, 21), Yitro 9 (ed. Friedmann f. 72a; ed. Weiss f. 79a).
[3] Sanhedrin 88b. See above, p. 245.
[4] Soṭah 5a. Many bad things about arrogance (גסות רוח, etc.) and its consequences are said on this page.
[5] Soṭah l.c. [6] See Vol. I, pp. 440 f. Tanḥuma ed-Buber, Wayyera § 3.

PART VII

THE HEREAFTER

INTRODUCTORY

In an exposition of Jewish notions about the hereafter of the individual, the nation, and the world, it is necessary to take account of a peculiar class of writings which profess to be revelations of these things. From the Greek title of a Christian work of this kind, the Revelation of John,[1] the name Apocalypse is extended to the others, and collectively they are spoken of as an apocalyptic literature. The revelation is generally made in a vision interpreted to the seer by an angel commissioned for this service; in others the seer makes a tour through the heavens or unknown regions of earth under conduct of an angelic guide who explains to him the sights and their significance.[2] It usually purports to have been made to some man of note in the sacred history, from the antediluvians down, and the motive in the selection is frequently obvious. The visionary form has biblical antecedents, among which Ezekiel is of especial importance; but the fiction of the ancient seer makes its appearance in the literature known to us only in the second century B.C.

Many of these revelations have to do with a great crisis in the history of Israel and the world, which the authors believed to be imminent. The imaginary seer in the remote past is shown in symbolic visions the successive epochs of history from his own day to the situation of the author on the eve of the crisis, to the crisis itself and what comes after it. We can follow the panorama stage by stage as long as the seer's pretended foreknowledge is really the author's knowledge of past and present. When this correspondence ceases, we know that the author had passed from

[1] The title in the manuscripts is itself taken from the first words of the book: The revelation of Jesus Christ, which God gave to him to show to his servants, what is to come to pass speedily; and he signified it by sending through his angel to his servant John, etc.

[2] This fiction was peculiarly apt to Enoch, who was translated to heaven (Gen. 5, 24).

relating to predicting, and guessed wrong. When he is definite enough, and we know the events with sufficient particularity, it is possible to fix the date of the writing within narrow limits. Sometimes, however, the failure of fulfilment led to a recasting of the prediction to adapt it to a later situation; occasionally the original may be discerned under the repainting, so that two dates, or at least limits, can be made out.

Much in the revelation, however, is transacted in another sphere and beyond the end of history. In such matter the indications of age are much more obscure, and the best the historian can do is to give dates relatively, loosely, and with inferior confidence. The difficulty is made greater by the fact that this material and the way of handling it soon became an apocalyptic tradition, with conventional figures, scenes, and stage properties.

The apocalypses may for our purposes be divided into two groups, those before the fall of Jerusalem in 70 A.D. and those after that event. The principal representatives of the former class come from the second and first centuries before the Christian era; the latter from the last generation of the first century of that era. In the first group are Daniel and the various writings collected under the name of Enoch; in the second Fourth Esdras, the Apocalypse of Baruch, and the Revelation of John in the New Testament.

With the exception of the last, all these apocalypses were written in Hebrew or in Aramaic,[1] though they have been transmitted to us only in translations from an intermediate Greek version and in Christian hands. There is no recognizable sectarian peculiarity in them, except again in the New Testament Apocalypse, where it is manifestly superimposed. The opinion entertained by some scholars that the apocalyptic literature originated with the Essenes lacks evidence.[2] If it were true, it

[1] This is true also of the Jewish sources of the Revelation of John.

[2] From Josephus (Bell. Jud. ii. 8, 7 § 142) we learn that a postulant for admission to the order swore to keep secret the books of the sect and the names of the angels, but that these esoteric books were of the apocalyptic variety is not suggested by anything in the passage.

would contribute nothing to our understanding of the books themselves.

These pseudonymous revelations, which in their time were very popular, are ignored by the rabbis; it is not unlikely that they are included in the "outside books" reading out of which, according to Akiba, costs a man his portion in the World to Come. At a much later time Enoch and what he saw in the heavens appear in Hebrew writings whose resemblance to features of our Book of Enoch suggests subterranean channels of communication, if not literary acquaintance.[1]

The visions of Daniel in the book that bears his name found a place in the third part of the Jewish canon, the miscellaneous "Writings," and consequently in the Christian Bible, where it is put among the Prophets. The author describes in his way the desecration of the temple by Antiochus Epiphanes (168 B.C.), but not the recovery and re-dedication by Judas Maccabaeus in 165; and the angel's prediction of the sudden end of Antiochus in his camp between the Great Sea and the beauteous holy mountain (Jerusalem), in another Egyptian campaign, did not come true—he died on an expedition in the East at Gabai in Persis in 164/163.[2]

The Book of Enoch is a collection of writings of different character, authorship, and age, and incorporates, besides revelations in the name of Enoch, pieces of a similar kind taken from a book (or books) of Noah. The obvious divisions of the book are: (I) chapters 1–36; (II) cc. 37–71; (III) cc. 72–82; (IV) cc. 83–90; (V) cc. 91–105. Some of these parts are themselves manifestly composite and the analysis uncertain. Dislocations and interpolations complicate the problems of the critic. The authors themselves, in conformity to the conventions of apocalyptic, convey their allusions to historical persons and events in riddles which invite divination rather than submit to interpretation.

[1] Several such are to be found scattered through the five volumes of Jellinek, Bet ha-Midrasch.

[2] E. Meyer, Ursprung und Anfänge des Christentums, II, 220.

For our purpose it is unnecessary to entangle ourselves in these intricate and controversial questions. It is now generally agreed that the so-called Parables (cc. 37–71), for which at first many scholars assumed a Christian origin, are Jewish, and probably come from the earlier decades of the first century before our era. The other parts of the book with which we are concerned represent less advanced conceptions, and, so far as this constitutes a presumption of age, are older. The oldest which seems to offer a more definite indication of time is what is commonly called the apocalypse of the Seventy Shepherds (cc. 83–90); but opinions are divided between a date before the death of Judas Maccabaeus (161 B.C.), making it but a few years later than the visions in Daniel (before the end of 165), and the reign of John Hyrcanus (135–104 B.C.) — probably not in his last years.[1]

Of the other parts of the book it is sufficient to say that from their general affinities they may be assigned to the century which lies between the Maccabaean rising and the appearance of the Romans upon the scene.

The Book of Enoch as a whole is preserved only in Ethiopic. Of a Greek version intermediate between the Hebrew (or Aramaic) original and the Ethiopic there are extracts in Georgius Syncellus, and part of a manuscript covering chapters 1–32, about one fifth of the book, were found in a tomb at Akhmin in Egypt in 1886–87.

English Translation: R. H. Charles, The Book of Enoch . . . with Introduction, Notes, etc. Oxford, 1912; and in his Apocrypha and Pseudepigrapha. — German: G. Beer, Das Buch Henoch (in Kautzsch, Apokryphen und Pseudepigraphen des A. T., Vol. II); Joh. Flemming und L. Radermacher, Das Buch Henoch, 1901.

For editions of the text and other literature reference may be made to Charles's Introduction, or to Schürer, Geschichte des jüdischen Volkes, u. s. w., Vol. III.

Three apocalypses fall in the generation between the destruction of Jerusalem in 70 A.D. and the close of the century, Fourth

[1] The difference turns on the identification of the 'big horn' in 90, 9 seq. with the one or the other of these heroes.

Esdras, the (Syriac) Apocalypse of Baruch, and the Christian Apocalypse of John.

Fourth Esdras (in the English Bible, Second Esdras), contains revelations purporting to be made to Ezra in Babylon in the thirtieth year after the fall of Jerusalem and its devastation by the armies of Nebuchadnezzar.[1] The theme of the first half of the book (3, 1–9, 25) is the problem of theodicy — how the existence of sin in the world from Adam down, with all its dire consequences here and more dreadful hereafter, can be reconciled with the character of God. Ezra urges the question; he finds the replies of the angel unconvincing, and returns to the argument a second and a third time (3, 1–5, 19; 5, 20–6, 34; 6, 35–9, 25). The problem has its national aspect — grant that Israel has deserved its doom, is heathen Babylon better? — as well as its concern with the fate of individuals, Jews and Gentiles, at death and beyond. There is in Jewish literature no such searching analysis of the problem as it presented itself to the twofold eschatology of the author's age.

The second part of the book is a series of three visions: The Mourning Mother (9, 26–10, 60); The Eagle and the Lion (11, 1–12, 51); The Son of Man (13, 1–58). Finally, Ezra's account of the restoration of the sacred books (14, 1–50).

In the use that is made of 4 Esdras in the following pages the substantial unity of the book is presumed. The fall of Jerusalem in 70 A.D. is never long out of the author's thought and still less out of his feeling. For a closer date departure is generally taken from the vision of the eagle with twelve wings (besides eight winglets) and three heads, both wings and heads representing Roman emperors, the heads unmistakably the three Flavians (11, 1–12, 51). The date of the vision thus falls in the reign of Domitian (81–96), and this is the probable time of composition; the two winglets of ch. 12, 2 f., which carry us into the beginning of the reign of Trajan (98–117), are then an addition — whether by the

[1] Some guess that by this "thirtieth year" the author meant cryptically to indicate that he wrote in the year 100 A.D.

same author or not — made when the expected crisis, the appearance of the Messiah, did not arrive. The book need not have been issued all in one piece, but we shall not go far astray if we put at least the main part under Domitian.

Fourth Esdras enjoyed great popularity among Christians. Written in Hebrew, it was early translated into Greek, and thence, directly or mediately, into various languages — Latin, Syriac, Armenian, Georgian, Arabic, Ethiopic. The Greek version itself as well as the original has perished.

A synoptic edition of these versions (except the Georgian) by Bruno Violet in 1910. German translation, with notes based on this apparatus, by the same author: Die Apokalypsen des Esra und des Baruch. 1924. An earlier German translation of 4 Esdras with commentary, by Hermann Gunkel, in Kautzsch, Apokryphen und Pseudepigraphen des A. T. — English Translation: G. H. Box, The Ezra-Apocalypse, . . . with critical Introductions, Notes, and Explanations, etc. 1912; also in Charles's Apocrypha and Pseudepigrapha. For the literature see his Introduction. — The Georgian version is published by R. P. Blake in the Harvard Theological Review, XIX (1926), 299–375.

The Apocalypse of Baruch falls in the same generation with 4 Esdras, and in many ways has so great an affinity to it, not only in subject and treatment but in close parallels of idea and phrase, that a literary relation is commonly assumed. Some think that 4 Esdras preceded and influenced Baruch; others *vice versa*. Whichever way it was, there is no question that the author of Fourth Esdras was by far the more original man.

The fiction of the book is that the revelations contained in it were given to Baruch, whom we know in the Old Testament as the amanuensis of Jeremiah. They begin before the fall of Jerusalem, which is announced to him by the word of the Lord as imminent; in c. 11 the ruin is already accomplished. The imaginary date is therefore thirty years before that of 4 Esdras, but no inference is to be drawn from this to the relative age of the two books. The same problems are raised as in 4 Esdras, but the individual aspect is less prominent than the national, and there is a marked difference in the temperament of the authors. The visions of the messianic age and the eschatology exhibit the same scheme, and, in its separation of the national golden age from the age beyond the resurrection and last judgment, it is the same which through the Tannaim became the standard conception of Judaism.

Nor is this the only thing in which these apocalypses are closely related to what we call the rabbinical sources. The authors had the learning of the schools. Baruch has a wealth of Haggadah which in almost every point is verifiable in the Midrash.[1] The questions with which both wrestle had been mooted in the schools in preceding generations, but became more harassing with the fall of Jerusalem.[2] The dogmatic pronouncement of the authorities of the next generation, "All Israelites have a portion in the World to Come," sounds like a deliverance to close a controversy in the schools in which it was held on the other part, as it is in 4 Esdras, that only a very few would be saved — an opinion which crops up again later in more than one place. The attempt has even been made to connect the authors with the teachings of particular schools,[3] and if the evidence is insufficient for this, it does establish their relation to the tendencies of the schools.

The attempt to decompose 4 Esdras, reconstruct its sources, and define the part of the compiler ("Redactor"), was soon followed by a similar decomposition of the Apocalypse of Baruch by the same critic. The chief recent exponent of the theory is R. H. Charles, whose analysis is carried into great complexity.

[1] The parallels to the Antiquitates Biblicae which passes under the name of Philo, to which attention has recently been directed, are chiefly midrashic commonplaces.

[2] The schools of Shammai and Hillel are said to have argued for two years and a half over the question whether it would have been better for man never to have been created, which the former maintained, the latter disputed. The majority eventually decided that it would have been better for man if he had never been created; but inasmuch as he has been created, he must closely scrutinize his doings. 'Erubin 13b, below.

[3] F. Rosenthal, Vier apokryphische Bücher aus der Zeit und Schule R. Akibas. 1885.

Parts of the book, in his opinion, were written before the fall of Jerusalem, and others in the first generation of the second century.

The fortunes of the book were strikingly dissimilar to those of 4 Esdras. The popularity of the latter is evinced by the number and wide distribution of the versions. Baruch is preserved in Syriac only, and (except for the letter to the nine-and-a-half-tribes, at the end) in but a single known manuscript; though there are other apocalypses of Baruch, or remnants of such, in various languages.

The Syriac text was published from a manuscript of the 6th century by Ceriani in 1871, and in the facsimile of the great Milan Peshitto. More accessible and convenient is the edition by M. Kmosko in Graffin's Patrologia Syriaca, Vol. II (1907), 1056 ff., with a parallel Latin translation and a concordantial Index Verborum. — English Translation: R. H. Charles, Apocalypse of Baruch, 1896; also in his Apocrypha and Pseudepigrapha; German: V. Ryssel, in Kautzsch, Apokryphen und Pseudepigraphen, Vol. II; B. Violet, Die Apokalypsen des Esra und des Baruch, 1924.

The Greek Apocalypse of Baruch is an entirely different work, with which we are not here concerned.

The Christian Revelation of John not only adopts the conventional forms of Jewish apocalyptic, but appropriates and adapts a large part of its substance from Jewish sources. It is only with these, and as such, that in these chapters we have to do. The book as we have it probably comes from the reign of Domitian, though it incorporates pieces from the time preceding the destruction of the temple, and even earlier.

The language throughout is a strongly hebraized Greek. It must be assumed that the ultimate sources of the elements taken over from Jewish apocalyptic were in Hebrew like the rest of that literature. Of the versions the most important is the Latin. The Syriac church did not admit the book to its canon, consequently there is no early Syriac translation of it.

CHAPTER I

RETRIBUTION AFTER DEATH

In old Israel the common notions about what becomes of a man at death were like those which are found among various peoples on comparable planes of civilization. Death is the departure from the body of the life, or, as we say, soul, concretely imagined as the vital breath (Gen. 2, 7) or as the blood, or *in* the blood (Lev. 17, 14).[1] The body was buried in a natural cave, a rock-cut tomb, or a shaft grave; structural tombs are probably a later development.[2] Such elaborate burial was naturally the privilege of the great; neither literature nor extant remains have anything to say about the graves of the multitude.[3] To lie unburied, without the customary funerary rites, or to be cast out of the tomb, was an aggravation of death;[4] to bury those who were thus neglected or cast out was a deed of charity and of piety.[5] The tomb was the abode of the dead. There the body reposed, and it was doubtless believed that the ghost also inhabited the tomb, an attenuated material double of the body,[6] ordinarily invisible, but sometimes seen in dreams or as an apparition in waking states; the conscious wraith of the man that had been.

[1] Cf. Lev. 17, 11. Gen. 9, 4. It is on this ground that eating blood (or flesh with blood in it) is so strictly forbidden.

[2] Burning was not usual in any period. The case of Saul and his sons (1 Sam. 31, 12 f.) is explained by the circumstances. Whether in the burnings for kings (Jer. 34, 5; cf. 2 Chron. 16, 14; 21, 19) the body itself was consumed, may here be left undecided. Cf. 'Abodah Zarah 11a.

[3] A solitary mention in 2 Kings 23, 6 suggests a common grave, perhaps for the very poor; what in Greek is called πολυάνδριον (LXX, Jer. 2, 23; 19, 2, 6; Ezek. 39, 11, 12, 15, 16; 2 Macc. 9, 4, 14).

[4] Jer. 16, 4, 6–8; 22, 18 f.; 25, 33; 8, 2.

[5] Tobit 1, 17; 2, 3–10. The מת מצוה; see Vol. I, p. 71.

[6] Immateriality, or in ancient phrase "incorporeality," is an abstraction remote from natural thought.

Among many peoples similar beliefs are associated with rites of tendance; the tomb is furnished with articles of use and ornament; food and drink are left by the side of the body at the burial, and periodically brought to the tomb thereafter. In Egypt this tendance of the dead grew to vast proportions, and in China what is called ancestor worship has been from the earliest times a most prominent branch of religion.

It is antecedently probable that, at least in rudimentary forms, the tendance of the dead was customary among the ancestors of the Israelites, as it certainly was among the Canaanites; but of the persistence of such customs in historical times there is scanty indication. In the formal profession which is required of the Israelite concerning the tithe set aside in the third and sixth years of every seven,[1] he has to declare: 'I have not eaten any of it when I was in mourning, and I have not separated any part of it when I was unclean; nor have I given any of it to the dead.' The point of this part of the declaration is that no uncleanness adheres to the things thus dedicated to charity. The last clause is frequently thought to refer to a funereal offering, but it may equally well be a contribution to a funeral feast such as is supposed in Jer. 16, 7.[2] That the prophets found no occasion to denounce anything even remotely resembling a cult of the dead is evidence as strong as silence can be that such customs were not prevalent in their times.[3]

The tombs of men famous in history or legend have all over the world been venerated not merely as monuments, but because there men felt themselves in a peculiar way in the presence of the mighty dead. This presence was not, as for us, a sentiment,

[1] Deut. 26, 12–15.

[2] Vulgate: nec expendi ex his quidquam in re funebri, — which was probably the interpretation of Jerome's Jewish teachers. In Sifrè Deut. § 303 R. Eliezer explains: I have not purchased out of this fund a coffin and grave-clothes for a dead man. M. Ma'aser Sheni 5, 12 adds, "and I have not given it to other mourners."

[3] Isa. 65, 3–5 is not to the contrary. It describes some strange cult or mystery; but does not specify offerings to the dead. Cf. Psalm 106, 28 (Baal Peor). Ecclus. 30, 18 is an allusion to a foreign practice.

but a reality, and at the tombs offerings were brought and petitions made to the superhuman power lodged in them. The hero shrines of the Greeks are a familiar instance.[1] Palestine and the neighboring lands today are dotted over with reputed tombs of holy men — saints, prophets, weli's — frequented by people of all the varieties of religion represented in the country. The tomb at Hebron, where the patriarchs are believed to repose in the Cave of Machpelah which Abraham bought as a burial place for Sarah (Gen. 23), is venerated by Jews, Moslems, and Christians alike.

Besides the patriarchs, the burial place of many of the great men of Israel, especially in the story of the exodus and the conquest and in the days of the judges, is noted in the narrative,[2] but of resort to their tombs to do them homage or to seek their aid there is no reminiscence in the historical books or the prophets.

Another notion of the whereabouts of the dead was that they went to a common abode of all the dead in the depths of the earth. The proper name of this nether world was Sheol.[3] It was a dark cavern, a kind of universal tomb such as Hades is imagined in Homer.[4] Its inmates are the dead, limp shades,[5] the semblance of their former selves bereft of all strength, as in Homer. They are shut in by gates and bars;[6] from Sheol there is no exit.[7] Or it is imaged as a monster with gaping jaws that greedily swallows men down and is never sated.[8] The association with the tomb lends to Sheol the imagery that belongs to the dissolution of the body — worms and decay (Job 17, 13–16; 24, 19 f.). Sometimes, indeed, Sheol seems to be only a metaphori-

[1] See Pauly-Wissowa, Real-Encyclopaedie der classischen Altertumswissenschaft, VIII, 1111–1145; Rohde, Psyche, 2 ed. I, 146 ff., II, 348 ff.

[2] See e. g. Josh. 24, 29–33. Samuel, 1 Sam. 25, 1; Saul, 1 Sam. 31, 13, etc.

[3] Poetical synonyms are Abaddon ('perdition'), Mawet ('death'), Bor, Shaḥat ('pit'), Ṣalmut ('darkness'), etc.

[4] Especially Odyssey xi. Cf. also Vergil, Aeneid vi.

[5] Refa'im, 'impotent.'

[6] Isa. 38, 10; Job 38, 17; Psalm 9, 14; 107, 18.

[7] Compare the Babylonian Aralu, the Land Without Return.

[8] Isa. 5, 14; Hab. 2, 5; Prov. 27, 20; 30, 15 f.

cal equivalent for the grave. Between the presence of the dead in their several tombs and the assembly of the dead in Sheol no contradiction was felt, and no attempt was made to reconcile the two notions.[1]

Necromancers professed to summon ghosts to answer the questions of the living,[2] or to have at their bidding familiar spirits which gave responses with twittering voices;[3] but this, like other heathenish forms of divination, was forbidden on pain of death.[4]

More picturesque glimpses of Sheol are given in Isa. 14, 3–21, and Ezek. 32, 17–32 (cf. 31, 15–18), where the descent of the king of Babylon and of the Egyptian Pharaoh respectively are described, and the reception they meet from those who were before them there. In Ezekiel the several nations that had earlier ruled and fallen occupy quarters of their own in the vast netherworld,[5] and it was doubtless believed that the Israelite dead had a place by themselves, and were not indiscriminately mingled with the heathen.[6]

To this gloomy realm all must one day go, great and small, good and bad. Those who have had bitter experience of the misery of the life on earth may covet the release, where 'the wicked cease from troubling and the weary are at rest';[7] to those who have rounded out their years it is the appointed end; but to be cut off out of the land of the living and sent down to Sheol in God's anger before one's time is the direst doom of the wicked.[8]

These ideas prevail in the later writings of the Bible as well as in the earlier. The Book of Job has already been cited. The

[1] Here again the Greeks are a corresponding example, in contrast to the Egyptians.

[2] 1 Sam. 28. [3] Isa. 8, 19; cf. 29, 4. [4] Lev. 20, 27.

[5] Similarly Menippus sees the population of the Acherusian plain living κατὰ ἔθνη καὶ κατὰ φῦλα. Lucian, Menippus c. 15.

[6] This is the probable meaning of such phrases as "Abraham . . . died . . . and was gathered to his people" (אל עמו, Gen. 25, 8, and elsewhere).

[7] Job 3, 11–19; cf. 17, 13–16.

[8] Psalm 73, 18–20.

Psalms throughout represent Sheol in the same way.[1] Sirach makes no advance beyond the biblical conceptions.[2]

Of a revivification of the dead there is no hope. On this point Job is peculiarly emphatic: A tree that is felled may spring up again from the root if there is moisture in the ground; but when a man dies he lies down never to rise; 'till the heavens be no more they will not awake nor be roused out of their sleep.'[3] Nor is there in Sheol itself any compensation for the unmerited sufferings of the upright in this life. The difficult passage in Job 19, 25–27 expresses Job's conviction that when he is dead God will vindicate him and he will know it.[4] The expectation of a resurrection of the flesh in the common English version, and more uncompromisingly in the Latin Bible,[5] is read *into* the text, not *in* it.

At first sight it may appear strange that the Jews, with their strong faith in the righteousness of God, should have been so tardy in extending the sphere of retribution over the existence beyond death, as other religions with which they were in contact — Egyptians, Persians, Greeks — had long since done. The religious development of Judaism was, however, radically different from that of those nations. The prophets of Israel had delivered their message to the nation, and their teaching about retribution, repentance, and restoration, because it was national, was of this world, not of another sphere of existence. In Judaism the old vague belief that God shows favor to those who please him by conformity to the established rule of right — civil, moral,

[1] Psalm 6, 6; 30, 10; 88, 11–13; 115, 17, etc.

[2] Ecclus. 14, 16; 41, 4; 17, 27 (cf. Psalm 6, 6). See also Baruch 2, 17; 3, 19; Test. XII Patriarchs, Reuben 4, 6; Psalms of Solomon 4, 15 (cf. Isa. 5, 14) — reminiscences of the O. T.

[3] Job 14, 7–15; cf. 20, 7.

[4] This at most implies no more than that the shades in Sheol may be aware of things that go on in the world they have left, as was naturally imagined; see Isa. 14.

[5] Scio enim, quod redemptor meus vivit, et in novissimo die de terra surrecturus sum, et rursum circumdabor pelle mea, et in carne mea videbo Deum meum, quem visurus sum ego ipse, et oculi mei conspecturi sunt, et non alius; reposita est haec spes mea in sinu meo.

religious — and brings evil upon those who violate or neglect it, was made definite by the individualizing of the prophetic doctrine, by the statutory conception of divine law, and by the dominating idea of the justice of God. God's favor and displeasure thus became in the proper sense retributive — reward and punishment in the kind and measure of desert.

On this principle, in a particular situation, Ezekiel laid down a rigorous doctrine of individual retribution (Ezek. 18). Generalized, as it is by Job's friends, this doctrine in application makes inevitable their conclusion that extraordinary inflictions argue extraordinary guilt, and their zeal to defend God's justice threatens to undermine Job's faith in it altogether. In the end he acquiesces in the inscrutable mystery of God's ways; but he will not belie his good conscience, nor admit that his calamities are explicable on premises of justice. The author has no theodicy of his own to substitute; it is enough for him to refute a complaisant orthodoxy.

Ecclesiastes puts man completely on a level with the beasts. The end of both is the same; what happens to the one happens to the other; as the one dies, so dies the other. All are of dust and to dust all return. The vital breath (spirit) in them is the same, so that man has no preëminence over the beast. 'Who knows whether the spirit of man goes upward and the spirit of the beast goes down to the earth?' (Eccles. 3, 18–22). The last sentence suggests that the author had heard some such discrimination of human and animal souls as was current in Greek circles, and flings at it his skeptical, Who knows?[1]

In the Hellenistic world current notions of what is after death, popularizing earlier Greek thinking, postulated the dual nature of man. His true self is an imperishable soul,[2] which during

[1] Cf. Eccles. 9, 4–6; Job 14, 19–22. The "impious" in the Wisdom of Solomon (1, 16–2, 9) are outspoken in their disbelief of a hereafter, and in the consequences they draw for the present.

[2] The *immateriality* of the soul (Platonic doctrine) is not necessarily assumed, and being unimaginable probably never got beyond those who had

what we call life is the inmate of a mortal body. At death it leaves this tenement, which presently dissolves into its material elements and perishes, while the soul flits away to the realm of spiritual or noumenal existence to which by its essential nature it belongs. Inasmuch as the soul is the thinking and willing subject which moves the body and uses it as an instrument, and is potentially the ruler of the natural appetites and passions, the responsibility for man's character and conduct rests upon the soul alone, and the destiny of the disembodied souls is made for themselves by the deeds done in the body. The good are happy and the bad are miserable. Poetical imagination had early busied itself with these blessed and wretched states;[1] but everyone was free to picture them to please himself. Good and bad were such as were judged so by the social and civil standards of their fellows, or by the ethical principles of philosophers; there was in Greek religion no definition of righteous and wicked such as the Jews had in the Law, nor was the idea of retributive justice grounded in the character of God fundamental, as it was in Judaism. In Greek thought the separation of good and bad belonged to the natural fitness of things rather than was established by divine ordinance.

The ideas of immortal souls and of the happy lot to which the souls of the good go at death seemed to some Jews to fit in so well with their own religious conceptions as to belong to them. The author of the Wisdom of Solomon appropriates them in an eloquent passage: 'The souls of the righteous are in the hands of God,[2] and no torment can touch them. In the eyes of the senseless they seemed to be dead, and their departure was regarded as an evil fate, and their going from us as destruction, but they are in peace. For though in the sight of men they be punished, yet

minds for metaphysics. The Stoic universe had no room for immaterial reality, and the popular notion of soul as spirit implied its material nature.

[1] E.g. Pindar, Olymp. 2, 55 ff.; Frag. nos. 129–130, 131, 133. Plato, Phaedrus, 246 ff.; Republic, x. 614 ff. Cf. the parody in Lucian, True History, ii.

[2] Cf. 5, 5, "His lot is with the holy (angels)."

are they filled with the hope of immortality.[1] Having endured a little chastisement they will receive great blessings, for God put them to proof and found them worthy of himself; He tested them as gold is tested in the crucible, and accepted them as a whole burnt offering.'[2]

Before the wicked the prospect of manifold and great evils in this life, their just desert, is held up and there is no good for them beyond. 'If they turn out long-lived, they will be naught accounted of, and dishonor will be their reward in the end; and if they die early, they have no hope,[3] and no consolation in the day of inquest.'[4] 'They will see the death of the wise man, and will not understand what He planned for him nor why the Lord brought him into security. They will see, and make light of it; but the Lord will deride them. After that they will become a dishonored corpse and an object of scorn among the dead for ever.[5] For he will hurl them down speechless, headlong, and will shake them from their bases. And to the end they will be desolate and will be in anguish, and the memory of them will perish.'[6]

It will be observed that in what the author has to say about the fate of the wicked he keeps closely to biblical representations, of which there are reminiscences in every line.[7] In particular the "visitation of souls," "the day of inquest" (or discrimination), and the judgment scene depicted in the sequel,[8] with belated confession of the sinners (4, 20–5, 14); the final fate of the righteous and discomfiture of the wicked (5, 15 ff.), are specifically Jewish not only in imagery but in conception. It is a consequence of these antecedents that the representation

[1] Cf. 5, 15 (16), "The righteous will live forever (εἰς τὸν αἰῶνα ζῶσι), and their reward is in the Lord, and care for them with the Most High."

[2] Wisdom 3, 1–6. The passage contemplates particularly such as had suffered for righteousness' sake; see the preceding. — See also chaps. 4 and 5.

[3] In contrast to the hope of immortality, 3, 4.

[4] ἐν ἡμέρᾳ διαγνώσεως, cf. ἐν ἐπισκοπῇ ψυχῶν, vs. 13.

[5] Cf. Isa. 66, 23 f.

[6] Wisdom 4, 17–19.

[7] This will be still plainer if the whole context is read.

[8] Note the participation of the righteous in this judgment, 4, 16. See also 3, 7 f.

oscillates between the destiny of the individual after death and the triumph of the Lord in the day when he arms himself for war with his adversaries (5, 17–23).[1]

In Philo the immortality of the soul is entertained in philosophical form,[2] and in the hereafter this only is considered. These writings are frequently taken as representatives of a Hellenistic Judaism which is supposed to have been prevalent among Greek-speaking Jews. What currency such conceptions had outside the numbers of those whose education had gone as far as philosophy, or who had picked up some looser acquaintance with them from their intellectual environment in a centre like Alexandria, is unknown.

Whether Greek ideas of the immortality of the soul and retribution after death — popular or philosophical — were widely entertained, or not, in a centre of Hellenic culture like Alexandria in the first century before the Christian era, it is certain that the development of conceptions of the hereafter in authentic Judaism went its own way unaffected by the alien influence. The premises were totally different; on the one side the dualism of soul and body, on the other the unity of man, soul and body. To the one the final liberation of the soul from the body, its prison-house or sepulchre, was the very meaning and worth of immortality; to the other the reunion of soul and body to live again in the completeness of man's nature. What to Philo would have seemed the greatest imaginable evil was to the Pharisees the highest conceivable good. The resurrection of the body, or, in their own phrase, the revivification of the dead, thus became a cardinal doctrine of Judaism.

How this came about we have now to inquire.

In the canonical Scriptures a restoration of the dead to life is found in Isa. 26, 17–19: 'As a woman with child that draws near her delivery is in pain and cries out in her pangs, so have

[1] The fate of the Egyptians at the Red Sea furnishes striking figures.
[2] Cf. also 4 Maccabees.

we been before thee, O Lord. We have been with child, we have been in pain; it was as though we brought forth wind.[1] Deliverances we have not wrought in the earth, nor are inhabitants of the world brought forth.[2] Thy dead shall live, my dead bodies shall stand up. Wake, and sing, ye that dwell in the dust! For Thy dew is a dew of lights,[3] and the earth shall yield up the shades.'

The passage is difficult in itself, and the difficulty of interpretation is increased by our ignorance of its age and occasion. In the surrounding chapters (24–27) the chief theme is a great crisis not only in history but in nature, one might say the *dies irae* of the world and its inhabitants, of the kings of the earth and the celestial powers that are allied with them.[4] Upon this follows the vindication of God's people before the eyes of the nations (ch. 25–26). The travail is long, and seems fruitless; the deliverance so ardently yearned for is not achieved. But it will come. And not only those who survive the catastrophe, but the dead in their dusty abodes will awake and break into a jubilant song; the earth will yield up the shades.

The author's interest is in the renascence of the people, multiplied by the revival of generations dead and gone, rather than in the return to life of individuals. It may be surmised that the suggestion came from Ezek. 37, 12–14; cf. Isa. 66, 7–9. But the concluding verse (26, 19) furnished a frequent proof-text from the Prophets for the Pharisaic doctrine of resurrection.[5]

The visions in the Book of Daniel, starting with the Babylonian or the Medo-Persian empire, recapitulate the course of history

[1] Contrast Isa. 66, 7–9.

[2] The last clause may be otherwise understood: nor do the inhabitants of the world (cf. 26, 13 f.) fall.

[3] Perhaps "a (reviving) dew on plants." — The dew is a sign of the revivification of the dead. Tanḥuma ed. Buber, Toledot § 19, adducing Micah 5, 6, and applying Isa. 26, 19 to the martyrs of the Hadrianic persecution. In Ḥagigah 12b (below) the dew by which God will revive the dead is stored up in the heaven *'arabot*, where are also the souls of the righteous.

[4] For this aspect of the judgment see especially 24, 16–23.

[5] See below, p. 382.

through the conquest of Alexander and the division of his empire, sometimes, as in chapter 11, in great detail, down to Antiochus Epiphanes; dwell upon his desecration of the temple and his attempt to suppress the Jewish religion,[1] and foresee his doom.[2] At the pitch of his power and his pride, he is suddenly cut off by no human hand; his kingdom falls with him — the last of the great kingdoms of this world — and in its place is established the world-wide kingdom of the holy people of the Most High, which shall have no end, and to which all the kingdoms under the whole heaven will be subject.[3] The final catastrophe of the world-empires, the inauguration of the eternal dominion of the Most High and his people, is at hand. The calculation of the end proves that the "seventy weeks" [4] are all but fulfilled — only half of the last week (three and a half years) remains.

Then Michael, the angelic champion of the Jews, will arise in their defence. The conflict will be a time of such distress as history has never known, but in it the Jews will be delivered, 'every one that is found written in the book.' [5] 'And many of those that sleep in the dusty ground will wake, these to eternal life, and those to ignominy and eternal abhorrence.' [6] In the context it lies nearest to suppose that in the former class are such as had given their lives for religion's sake in the persecution or had fallen in battle in defence of it, brought to life again to share in the triumph and the glorious age to follow,[7] while the latter are the Hellenizers and apostates. A resurrection of all Israelites, righteous and wicked, is not to be pressed on the word "many," much less of the heathen, and there is no suggestion of a judgment scene like that in chapter 7.

The fate of the second class reminds us of Isa. 66, 24, where all mankind, who in the future will come to worship the Lord at

[1] Dan. 7, 24 f.; 8, 11–14, 25; 9, 26 f.; 11, 36–39.

[2] Dan. 7, 9–11, 26; 8, 25; 11, 45.

[3] Dan. 2, 44; 7, 13 f., 18, 22, 26 f.

[4] Weeks of years (490 years). Dan. 9, 24–27.

[5] The register of the faithful.

[6] Dan. 12, 1 f. — "To eternal life" is here "to live forever," (cf. Wisdom of Solomon 5, 15), and "forever" may be hyperbolic.

[7] As in the Revelation of John 20, 4.

Jerusalem, go out from month to month and week to week and see the corpses of those who rebelled against Him, 'for their worm will not die and their fire will not go out, and they will be an abhorrence [1] to all mankind.'

Some find in Dan. 12, 2 a resurrection of the righteous only. Ibn Ezra quotes the Gaon (Sa'adia): "Those who wake will be unto eternal life, and those who do not wake will be unto ignominy and eternal abhorrence." The "many" are the minority, as in instances cited. The sense, as he takes it, is that the righteous who died in the exile will live when the redeemer [2] comes, for concerning them it is written, 'As the days of a tree so are the days of my people' (Isa. 65, 22); and then they will enjoy Leviathan and Ziz and Behemoth.[3] "They will die another time, and will live in the revival of the dead (the general resurrection), when they are in the World to Come, where men do not eat and drink, but enjoy the effulgence of the Shekinah." [4] In the mediaeval commentary on Daniel which is printed in the Rabbinical Bibles under the name of Sa'adia [5] a similar interpretation is given: "'Many who sleep in the dusty earth will wake.' This is the resurrection of the dead of Israel whose lot is unto eternal life; and those that do not wake are those who abandoned the Lord, who will go down to the lowest level of Gehenna and be an abhorrence to all mankind." (Isa. 66, 24).

In the sequel in Daniel special mention is made of the students and teachers of the Law: 'Those who cultivate intelligence will shine as the splendor of the firmament, and those who make the many righteous, as the stars for ever and aye.' [6]

[1] The word thus rendered, דראון, is found only in these two places, which it thus links together.

[2] גואל, the Messiah.

[3] Whose flesh is the pièce de résistance of the messianic banquet. See below, pp. 363 ff.

[4] Only the first part of this interpretation is strictly apposite to our question, but the rest, which represents a systematized eschatology, has its own interest.

[5] Not by the Gaon.

[6] See the comments on this verse in Sifrè Deut. § 10 and § 47; Midrash Tannaim on Deut. 11, 21. R. Simeon ben Menasya takes the words 'who

Second Maccabees, and presumably Jason of Cyrene from whom it is abridged, is in accord with these Palestinian conceptions rather than with exponents of what is called Hellenistic Judaism like the Wisdom of Solomon. This is the more noteworthy because the author had evidently been through a Greek school of language and literature, and attained a proficiency in the art of rhetoric of which, to judge from his display, he was not a little vain.

The martyr brethren, in the extremity of their torture, about to depart from life, declare their faith that God will raise them up to an endless life. The severed and mutilated members of which the tormentors have deprived them, they expect to receive back from God.[1] For the tyrant, on the contrary, there will be no rising up to life.[2] The situation assumed in these martyr stories is the persecution by Antiochus Epiphanes, and, as in Daniel, the crisis of deliverance is at hand. With that crisis the restoration to life of those who laid down their lives for their religion is immediately connected. It had, in its origin, nothing to do with a dramatic world-assize at the end of the age, as in the ultimate development of Jewish eschatology.

The author's belief in a revivification of those who fell in the struggle is illustrated by the story of the expiation Judas caused to be made in Jerusalem for the slain who had invited their doom by wearing heathen amulets[3] under their shirts when they went into battle. He did this reflecting upon their rising again, "For if he had not expected that the fallen would rise again, it would have been idle and silly to pray for dead men; and further having regard to the rich and gracious boon that is laid up for those that sleep in godliness" (2 Macc. 12, 42–45).

make the many righteous' as equivalent to 'who make them love God.' Those who love God are like the sun when it comes out in its power (Judges 5, 31); greater far are those who make others love him.

[1] The King of the world will raise us, who die for his laws, to an eternal renewal of life (εἰς αἰώνιον ἀναβίωσιν ζωῆς ἡμᾶς ἀναστήσει), 2 Macc. 7, 9 (cf. 11); 7, 14, 36; cf. 7, 29. Cf. the prayer of Razi, 2 Macc. 14, 46.

[2] σοὶ μὲν γὰρ ἀνάστασις εἰς ζωὴν οὐκ ἔσται (7, 14; see also vs. 36).

[3] ἱερώματα τῶν ἀπὸ Ἰαμνίας εἰδώλων.

In Enoch 85–90 the panorama of history is unrolled before the seer in a dream, from Adam and Eve to the Asmonaean times, in the midst of which the author stands. The situation seems to be a stage further on than the visions of Daniel, and like Daniel the author sees on the near horizon the great crisis looming. The throne of judgment is set up in Palestine, the books are opened,[1] the fallen angels of Gen. 6, 1–4, the seventy angelic shepherds who had abused their power over Israel, and the "blinded sheep"[2] (the apostate Jews), are cast into abysses of fire. Thereupon God brings a New Jerusalem in place of the old which is removed.[3] "And all that had perished and were scattered, and all the beasts of the field and all the birds of heaven (the converted Gentiles, vs. 30) came together in that house, and the Lord of the sheep rejoiced greatly, for they were all good, and had returned to his house." The Jews were to be cured of their heathenizing blindness. "And all the sheep were called to the temple, but it did not contain them. And the eyes of them all were opened, so that they saw clearly; there was none among them that could not see."

Then comes the birth of the white bull with great horns (the Messiah), and the metamorphosis of all the sheep into white bulls, with the further transformation of the leader.[4]

From vs. 33 it is commonly inferred that when the author sees gathered to the temple "those that had perished," they must have been brought to life again in a resurrection comparable to that in Daniel. There is, however, nothing else in these chapters to suggest resurrection, and it may well be doubted whether a single word in a translation at the second remove from the original is sufficient reason for attributing the belief to the author.[5]

[1] Enoch 90, 20. Cf. Dan. 7, 9–11. [2] Enoch 89, 74.

[3] Enoch 90, 28 f. Cf. Rev. of John 21, 2 ff.

[4] It is unnecessary here to go farther into the symbolism of this part of the vision.

[5] It is possible that the Hebrew had אבד, in the sense of 'be lost,' which would go better with the parallel. (Cf. the controversy about the return of the Ten Tribes turning on this word in Lev. 26, 38, below, p. 369.) In that case a reference to resurrection would not be implied.

In the composite Book of Enoch different conceptions find place. In the opening chapters (1–5) the judgment of God[1] is depicted in biblical imagery with no mention of a resurrection. The ungodly are destroyed, leaving their names to perpetual execration.[2] On the righteous, the elect, is bestowed remission of sins, and they are endued with wisdom so that they never sin again either through inadvertence or presumption, nor incur punishment, but live the full, long measure of their days in gladness and peace.

In another part of the book Enoch is conducted by angels through outlying quarters of the world beyond the bounds of human exploration (cc. 21–27). He sees the seven stars of heaven which trangressed the command of God, bound and burning for ten thousand years, the time of their sins;[3] the fiery abyss, the prison of the angels[4] where they are confined forever; the high mountain in the midst of a group, whose summit is like a throne, the seat of God, on which he sits when he comes down to visit the earth in goodness; and near it the Tree of Life, whose fruit after the great judgment will be made free for food to the righteous and holy, those who are chosen unto life. He is shown also the accursed ravine which is to be the place of eternal punishment for those who have blasphemed God (c. 27).

The judgment does not, as in Daniel and in Enoch 85–90, lie in the proximate future, and unlike them is not expressly connected with the deliverance of Israel from the dominion of the heathen;[5] it is a forensic act, which will come at its appointed time (22, 4).

This naturally leads to the question of the whereabouts of souls between death and the ultimate determination of their

[1] Not in forensic form, but as a crisis in nature and history.

[2] Dan. 12, 2.

[3] Cf. 18, 12–16. They did not at the beginning come forth at God's command. Contrast Isa. 40, 26.

[4] Cf. c. 19. The angels whose miscegenation with women is narrated in Gen. 6, 1–4. See Enoch 6–10; 12–16 (parallels).

[5] Note the absence of all militant features. It is to be observed also that in Enoch 1–36 there is no allusion to a messianic figure of any kind.

fate in the great judgment. At an early stage in his travels Enoch is shown a great mountain in the West in which are deep hollows with very smooth walls.[1] One of them was light and had a fountain of water in it, while the other three were dark.[2] The angel Raphael, who presides over the spirits of men (20, 3), tells him that these hollow places were created that in them should be collected all the souls of men until the time appointed for the great judgment. The one that is light and has the fountain in it is for the spirits of the righteous; the others for different classes of the wicked. One is for the sinners who die and are buried without judgment's having befallen them in their life time. "Here their spirits are separated for that great torment, until the great day of judgment, of the scourging and torments of the accursed, to the end that there may be a retribution of the spirits. There He will bind them forever" (22, 10 f.). Another was set apart for those who make complaint (to God), declaring how they were destroyed when they were slain in the days of the sinners (22, 12).[3] A third was created for "the spirits of the men who shall not be righteous, but godless sinners, and associates of the lawless (heathen). Their spirits will not be visited[4] in the day of judgment, nor will they be raised up from hence" (22, 13).[5]

The whole passage has in view Jews only; of the fate of the heathen there is no mention. The resurrection of the righteous Jews is assumed, not expressly asserted. That one class of sinners is reserved for torments after the judgment and will be bound in this fate forever, and that another will not be visited

[1] Probably to make it impossible to climb out. With these receptacles cf. 4 Esdras 7, 32 (*promptuaria*); Syr. Baruch 21, 23.

[2] And, it is to be inferred, waterless. Compare the parable of the thirsty Dives in torment.

[3] Cf. 22, 5–7. Abel is the typical instance.

[4] Punished, τιμωρηθήσονται. Cf. Psalms of Solomon 3, 14.

[5] The distribution is obscure, and the attempts to improve it by emendation are not convincing. The important point is that a separation not only of righteous and sinners but of different classes from one another is intended (22, 8).

and will not be raised up, implies the restoration to life on earth of others. The angel Remiel is set over those that rise.[1]

Enoch's journeyings are continued to the far East, where grow all sorts of balsamiferous and spice-bearing trees (cc. 28–32, 1), and farther east, beyond the Erythraean sea,[2] to the Garden of Righteousness (32, 3), the earthly paradise, among whose grand trees stands the Tree of Wisdom, of whose sacred fruit those who eat acquire great wisdom.[3] To his inquiry Raphael replies: This is the tree of wisdom, of which thy ancestors (Adam and Eve) ate,[4] and got wisdom, and knew that they were naked, and were driven out of the garden (32, 6).

The future is imagined as a restoration of paradisiacal conditions. The Tree of Life will, after the judgment, be transplanted to the Holy Place [5] beside the temple of God, the King of the World. The righteous and holy, those chosen unto life, who eat its fruit, "will rejoice and be glad, and will enter into the Holy Place. Its fragrance will be in their bones, and they will live on earth the longer life which the forefathers lived.[6] All their days no sorrow nor pain, no suffering nor affliction, shall touch them" (25, 6).[7] It may be surmised that the ban on the tree of knowledge (32, 3, 6) will be removed, and it be made lawful for men to enjoy it.

The second of what are commonly though inappropriately entitled the "Parables" of Enoch (cc. 45–57) enlarges on the theme of Daniel 7, 9–14, adapting it to a different situation and with

[1] ὃν ἔταξεν ὁ θεὸς ἐπὶ τῶν ἀνισταμένων (20, 8).

[2] The Persian Gulf and Indian Ocean (32, 2).

[3] ἐπίστανται φρόνησιν μεγάλην — wisdom for the conduct of life.

[4] Here the Greek text breaks off.

[5] As it had previously been removed from the earthly paradise to the mountain of God, where no mortal is able to touch it until the great judgment in which vengeance is taken on all the wicked and the final and endless consummation achieved (25, 4 f.).

[6] The centuries of the antediluvians in Genesis. Jubilees 23, 26–29; cf. verses 11 f., 15. There is no mention in Jubilees of a resurrection.

[7] Isa. 65, 19 f. Cf. Enoch 10, 17–11, 2, where the righteous who are delivered in the judgment live till they have begotten myriads of children, and all the days of their youth and old age will be lived in peace (prosperity).

a different conception of the 'one that looked like a man' (46, 1; Dan. 7, 13)[1] who appears in the judgment act.[2] After the great vindication in which the mighty of the earth who godlessly abuse their power are delivered into the hand of God's Chosen One, and are consumed as straw in fire, sink down like lead in water (Exod. 15, 7, 10; Obad. 18, etc.), leaving no trace behind (Enoch 48, 9 f.), and after space has been given for others, witnessing their fate, to repent before the final remediless decision (50, 1–5),[3] "the earth will restore what has been committed to it, and Sheol what it has received, and hell will give up what it owes. He[4] will pick out the righteous and holy among them, for the day when they shall be delivered is at hand. The Chosen One shall in those days sit upon My throne,[5] and all the secrets of wisdom will stream from the counsels of his mouth,[6] for the Lord of Spirits has given it to him, and glorified him. In those days will the mountains leap like rams, and the hills skip like lambs that have had plenty of milk;[7] and all will become angels in heaven.[8] And their countenance will shine with joy, because in those days the Chosen One has arisen; and the earth will rejoice, and the righteous will dwell upon it, and the chosen ones go to and fro in it" (51, 1–5).

The restoration is to a life on earth,[9] and, notwithstanding the universal expressions of 51, 1, a resurrection of Gentiles is not thought of.[10]

In subsequent chapters of this Parable, Enoch is shown, in

[1] On this point see below, pp. 334 ff.

[2] Various incongruities naturally result from this coupling of new ideas with phraseological reminiscences.

[3] Cf. 90, 30 and 35.

[4] God.

[5] Many manuscripts (chiefly later ones) read '*his* throne.' Cf. 61, 8; 45, 3.

[6] Isa. 11, 2.

[7] Psalm 114, 4, 6.

[8] Cf. Matt, 22, 30; Luke 20, 36. Enoch 104, 6; Syr. Baruch 51, 10; see also Enoch 69, 11. Charles (ed. 2) transposes, emends, construes, and translates: "And the faces of [all] the angels in heaven shall be lighted up with joy" — a somewhat insipid conclusion.

[9] See also 62, 13–16.

[10] Cf. 61, 4 f.

another part of the earth, a deep valley with burning fire, into which he sees the kings and the mighty cast,[1] and the enormously heavy chains that are being forged for the hosts of Azazel when they are hurled down into the abyss in the day of the last judgment (54, 1–6;[2] 55, 3–4; 56, 1–4). Then there is revealed to him the last outbreak of the heathen powers,[3] who are now the Parthians and the Medes, and their catastrophe (56, 5–8); and finally the return of the dispersion (c. 57).

In the other Parables (38–44; 58–69) the representations of the fortunes of the righteous and the wicked in the present and the future, of the issues of judgment, and of the final triumph of righteousness and wisdom, are similar, and need not be detailed here.

One other section of the book (cc. 91–105) demands brief remark. It includes (or incorporates) the apocalypse of the Ten Weeks, periods of the world's history from Enoch's own time to the great final judgment in which God exacts retribution from the angels. "And the first heaven will pass away and vanish, and a new heaven will appear,[4] and all the powers of heaven will shine with sevenfold brightness for ever.[5] And thereafter will be many weeks without number, forever, in goodness and righteousness, and thenceforth sin shall not be so much as named forever." This is the culmination of a series of judgments. In the second week was the great Flood; in the eighth week a sword is given to righteousness that just judgment may be executed on those who do violence, and the sinners will be delivered into the hands of the righteous (91, 12).[6] In the ninth "the righteous

[1] Isa. 24, 21 f.

[2] Rev. of John 20, 1 ff.

[3] Ezek. 38 f., Gog and Magog; cf. Rev. of John 20, 7 ff.

[4] Enoch 91, 16; Isa. 65, 17; 66, 22.

[5] Isa. 30, 26; cf. 60, 19 f.

[6] The seventh week (93, 9 f.) is that of the hellenizing apostasy; at its close "the chosen righteous of the eternal plant of righteousness" appear, and sevenfold instruction concerning God's whole creation is given them — the religious revival. Here is the standpoint of the author of the apocalypse

judgment will be manifested in the whole world, and all the works of the godless will disappear from the earth, and the world will be written down for destruction;[1] and all men will look toward the way of righteousness" (91, 14).

Apart from this little apocalypse and the introduction to it, 91, 1–10, the section is chiefly occupied with woes pronounced on the wicked, and exhortations to the righteous to maintain their faith in the assurance of a coming great reversal of the fortunes of the two parties. Even though they die before the crisis comes, they shall rise from the sleep of death to walk in the way of righteousness.[2] Their resurrection will justify their faith against the disbelief of the sinners who assert that there is no difference between the fate of righteous and wicked in death or after it (102, 6–11).[3] The author assures the righteous that all good, joy, honor, are prepared and written down (in the heavenly tablets and the holy books he has seen) for the spirits of those who have died in righteousness. Great is their recompense, and a better lot than that of the living. "The spirits of you who have died in righteousness will live, and will rejoice and be glad. Their spirits will not perish nor their memorial from before the Great One unto all the generations of the world" (103, 1–4). Wholly diverse is the fate of the wicked. Their souls will be sent down to the nether-world, and they will fare ill and be in great tribulation. "Into darkness, fetters, and flaming fire, will your spirit come, and the judgment will last for all the generations of the world. Woe to you; ye shall find no peace" (102, 7 f.; 103, 5 ff.).[4]

The several writings brought together in the Book of Enoch are distributed over almost a century, and come not only from different authors but out of widely different historical situations. That the revivification of the righteous dead occurs in so many

[1] This clause seems to intrude. The verse is probably to be understood of the conversion of the Gentiles who have witnessed the vindication.

[2] Enoch 92, 3–5; 91, 10.

[3] Eccles. 2, 14–16; 3, 19–21, etc. Cf. Wisdom of Solomon 2, 1–5.

[4] Isa. 48, 22; 57, 21.

parts of the book, with one conception or another, is evidence of the currency of the idea in that age.

Other writings, also, of the second or first centuries before our era attest the belief that at the expected turning-point in the history of the world the dead of former generations [1] would be brought to life again on earth; and exhibit the ways in which, by diverse combinations of Scripture, the crisis itself and the golden age to follow were imagined. In the Testaments of the Twelve Patriarchs the resurrection is extended to the dead of remote generations, back to the beginnings of the people. Judah says to his descendants: "And after these things,[2] Abraham and Isaac and Jacob will rise up to life, and I and my brothers will be chiefs of the tribes in Israel,[3] Levi first, I second, Joseph third, Benjamin fourth, Simeon fifth, Issachar sixth, and so all the rest in order. . . . And there shall be one people of the Lord, and one language; and Beliar's spirit of deceit shall be no more, for he will be cast into the fire forever. And those who died in grief will rise up in joy, and those in poverty for the Lord's sake will be enriched, and those in want will be fed full, and those in weakness will be made strong, and those who died for the Lord's sake will wake in life." [4]

In the Testament of Benjamin (c. 10) the original representation was similar: "Then ye will see Enoch, Noah and Shem, and Abraham, Isaac, and Jacob rising up on the right hand in exultation. Then shall we also rise, each over his own tribe, worshipping the King of heaven." There follows a resurrection of all, some unto glory and some unto dishonor,[5] and a judgment, first of Israel for their unrighteousness, and then of all the Gen-

[1] Generally the pious dead of Israel only.

[2] The restoration from the captivity and the rising of the star out of Jacob.

[3] See the word of Jesus to the Twelve: In the rebirth of the world, when the Son of Man shall sit on his glorious throne, ye also shall sit on twelve thrones judging the twelve tribes of Israel. Matt. 19, 28. Cf. the twenty-four elders in the Revelation of John.

[4] Test. Judah c. 25; see also Simeon c. 6; Zebulon c. 10.

[5] Dan. 12, 2.

tiles.[1] In the Greek text this passage has been heavily interpolated by Christian hands; both Jews and Gentiles are condemned for not believing in Christ.[2] The Armenian version is innocent of this palpable Christianization; but in what goes beyond the parallels cited from the other Testaments[3] is itself not exempt from suspicion of amplification by a second hand.

The resurrection, beginning with the patriarchs, is a restoration to a life on this earth, with the old tribal organization, in idealized conditions.[4]

The Psalms of Solomon represent the type of Judaism which we associate with the Pharisees. The references to the resurrection are in conformity with this origin. In Psalm 3, which contrasts the attitude of the righteous man and the sinner toward God and His dealings with them, and the outcome of their diverse character and behavior, we read: "If a sinner stumbles, he curses his life, the day of his birth and the pangs of his mother. He adds sins to sins as long as he lives; he falls — dire is his fall — and shall not rise up. The perdition of the sinner is forever, and when He visits the righteous, no mention will be made of him. This is the lot of the sinners forever. But they that fear the Lord will rise to eternal life, and their life in the light of the Lord will never again fail" (3, 11–16). Similarly in 13, 9-11: "The life of the righteous is eternal, but sinners will be carried off to perdition, and no memorial of them will be found."[5]

[1] Of the future of the righteous or the fate of the condemned nothing is said.

[2] The king of heaven "who appeared upon earth in the form of an humble man." The unrighteousness of the Jews was that "when God came to them in flesh as deliverer they did not believe" (10, 7–9).

[3] "Then shall we all be changed, some into glory and some into shame; for the Lord judges Israel first for the unrighteousness which they have committed, and then so (shall he judge) all the Gentiles. And He shall convict Israel through the chosen Gentiles," etc. (Charles's translation.)

[4] See especially Test. Levi c. 18; Dan 5, 9–13. Cf. Jubilees 23, 26–31, where, however, a bodily resurrection of the righteous of former generations is not contemplated: "Their bones will rest in the earth, and their spirit will have much joy, and they will know that it is God that holds judgment and shows favor to hundreds and thousands — to all who love him."

[5] Cf. 14, 6–10, etc.

It is to be noted that while the apocalypses bring the resurrection of the righteous into connection with the judgment act, in those psalms that extol the Messiah, son of David, and foretell his abolition of sinners, the destruction or subjugation of the heathen, and his righteous rule over the restored nation, the author says nothing of a resurrection.[1] It would be a mistake, however, to urge this silence; this part of the psalm is a tissue of biblical reminiscences, in which resurrection has no place.

The Gospels begin with a warning of a great crisis at hand, the immediate inauguration of the "reign of God."[2] It is assumed that this phrase and its meaning were familiar to all Jews; and whatever other ideas they may have connected with it, the summons to repentance, which is the burden of John the Baptist's prophesying presently taken up by Jesus, shows that it was thought of as a new order of things on earth suddenly instituted by God, in which only the righteous and the repentant sinners (whom Judaism classed with them) would survive. In the prayer Jesus taught his disciples, "May Thy reign come; may Thy will be done, as in heaven, also upon earth," the second clause gives the definition of the first in its religious and moral aspect.

In a second stage, this new era is associated with the appearance of the Messiah, son of David, in the person of Jesus of Nazareth.[3] Finally, after the messianic entry into Jerusalem[4] and the repudiation of these claims by the heads of the nation, the crisis is announced in eschatological form, the sign of Daniel's "abomination of desolation" standing in the holy place, the great tribulation, the Son of Man coming in the clouds of heaven, the gathering of the chosen from all quarters of the earth, the

[1] See especially Psalms of Solomon, 17.

[2] *Malkut Shamaim.* Kingdom of Heaven (Matt.), Kingdom of God (Luke). See p. 374.

[3] Mark 8, 27–30; Matt. 16, 13–20; Luke 9, 18–21. — Matt. 12, 22–30; Mark 10, 35–40; Matt. 20, 20–23. — Mark 10, 48 f. and parallels. Mark 12, 35–37.

[4] Mark 11, 1–10; Matt. 21, 1–9; Luke 19, 28–38. Cf. Zech. 9, 9; Isa. 62, 11 f.

final judgment of "all the nations," some going to eternal punishment, but the righteous to eternal life.[1]

The rôle of the Son of Man in this judgment act is similar to that in the Parables of Enoch.[2] It is noteworthy, however, that in Matt. 24–25 there is no express mention of a resurrection of the dead corresponding to Enoch 51, nor even of the restoration to life of the martyrs for their faith (Matt. 24, 9–14).[3]

The final separation of good and bad in the last judgment is the theme of two of the parables of the Kingdom of Heaven[4] in Matt. 13. The tares (the sons of evil) which the enemy (the devil) has sown in the wheat field are left to grow with the good grain until the harvest. At the completion of the age (world-period) 'the Son of Man will send out his angels, and they will gather up out of his kingdom all causes of offense, and those who do iniquity, and cast them into the furnace of fire. . . . Then shall the righteous shine as the sun in the kingdom of their Father' (Matt. 13, 40–43). Similarly, the kingdom is compared to a net that catches all manner of fish, which have to be sorted out when the draught is landed. 'So it will be in the completion of the age; the angels will go out and separate the wicked from among the righteous, and cast them into the furnace of fire' (Matt. 13, 49).[5]

The Gospels are also witnesses to the conflicting doctrines of the Pharisees and the Sadducees about the resurrection of the body and retribution after death,[6] on which point Jesus and his disciples were of the Pharisaic persuasion.[7] In an argument

[1] Mark 13, 4–37; Matt. 24, 4–25, 46. The specifically Christian adaptation of much of this is evident. Note particularly Matt. 25, 31–46.

[2] See Enoch 45–57, summarized above, pp. 303 ff., cf. 333 ff., and Enoch c. 52.

[3] According to Matt. 27, 53, as an accompaniment of the resurrection of Jesus, many bodies of saints that had fallen asleep were raised, and coming out of their tombs entered into Jerusalem and appeared to many; but these apparitions were understood by the author as signs, not as actual cases of resurrection.

[4] The Christian church has here become the kingdom of God.

[5] See also 16, 27 f.

[6] Mark 12, 18–27; Matt. 22, 23–33; cf. Acts. 4, 1 f.

[7] See also Acts 23, 6 ff.

with the Sadducees, Jesus adduces a proof of the resurrection from the Pentateuch (Exod. 3, 6) which might very well have been used by a rabbi.

The writings of which a cursory survey has been taken show how the belief in the better lot of the righteous after death arose among the Jews, and the various forms it took. Among the Greeks it started with anthropological notions of the constitution of man, an immortal soul in a mortal body. Their belief in immortality was promoted by a strong sense of the worth of personality, which demanded perpetuity as, so to speak, an inalienable right. There were mythical tales of the separation of good and bad [1] in the life beyond, which seemed so fitting that it was an article of popular belief; and imagination found occupation in inventing appalling tortures for the damned[2] and making the penalty fit the offense. The souls of the good went to the abode and company of gods and heroes, which poetical mythology furnished with all delights of refined sense, while philosophers made the delight purely intellectual. From beginning to end the conception was strictly individual; and the public religions of Greece had very little to do with the after life, which became the special field of the various mysteries and the salvationist sects, or was left to the speculations of philosophers.

Nothing was more deeply impressed on Judaism than the idea of national and religious solidarity. The individualizing of the principles of the prophets concerning sin and its consequences, repentance and divine forgiveness, was accomplished beside, not in place of, this solidarity. But there was one point at which the appropriation to the individual of the words of the prophets to the nation was not directly possible. They foretold, as the out-

[1] At first of the conspicuously good and the abominably bad.

[2] Lucretius sees in Epicurus the liberator of mankind from this fear of something after death, which kept men in bondage to fear and in subjection to superstitions cultivated by the priests for their own interest. See Book i, 62–126.

come of God's dealing with Israel and the nations, a final deliverance and an unending future of peace and prosperity, of universal righteousness and godliness. The nation clung to this faith even in its direst catastrophes, and when the worst that could happen seemed to have befallen it, believed the great revolution to be the next act in the world drama. But this could not, like the rest, be directly translated into individual terms. Happy, indeed, were the righteous who should be living when the great day came![1]

What the Jew craved for himself was to have a part in the future golden age of the nation as the prophets depicted it, the Days of the Messiah, or in the universal Reign of God, or in the Coming Age — always in the realization of God's purpose of good for his people. It was only so, not in some blissful lot for his individual self apart, that he could conceive of perfect happiness. The idea of salvation for the individual was indissolubly linked with the salvation of the people. This continued to be true in the subsequent development of eschatology, and gives its peculiar character to Jewish ideas of the hereafter.

The golden age to come, by whatever name it was called and however it was imagined, was a stage of human history on this earth. The deliverance of Israel from the yoke of the heathen with which it began, and the new era that followed, politically, socially, and economically, as well as in religion and morals, are what is called in the Scriptures in a preëminent sense "salvation,"[2] "the salvation of Israel" (Psalm 14, 7), "the salvation of our God" (Isa. 52, 10), and, in this sense,[3] only those who live in that age share in the great salvation. Most naturally it was felt that, of all men, the martyrs who had laid down their lives for their religion in the persecution, and the heroes who had fallen in the final conflict with heathenism, had earned a part in the salvation that was at hand; and it was easy to believe that

[1] Cf. Revelation of John 20, 6.

[2] ישועה; with especial frequency in Isa. 40 ff. and the Psalms.

[3] In distinction from the deliverance of the individual from his particular earthly distresses.

God, who must also recognize their desert, would bring them to life to enjoy it.

The promises of salvation in the prophets were made to Israel as a whole, and generations had lived in the hope of seeing it, and died, 'not having received the promises (the things promised), but having seen them and hailed them from afar.'[1] To them also the promise should be fulfilled. They too would be restored to life in the consummation. We have seen in the Testaments of the Twelve Patriarchs, how the antediluvians, Shem, Enoch, Noah, as well as Abraham, Isaac, and Jacob, will be seen rising up on the right hand, and the twelve patriarchs come, each at the head of his tribe.[2]

In general, in the sources we have hitherto examined, it is asserted or assumed that only the righteous dead are brought to life. That the wicked are left in the state of the dead is the simplest form of retribution for them. But their lot is not mere deprivation. A hell of torment is created not solely for the fallen angels, or for the godless tyrants who rule the earth, but for the apostates, or for all the wicked of Israel. In the crisis which ends the old order of things and ushers in the new era, the living sinners in Israel, for whom there is no room in it, perish.[3]

With the conception of a final assize, to appear bodily in which good and bad will be raised from the dead, we shall have to deal in another connection.[4]

I have dwelt on the genesis of these ideas somewhat at length in order to make it clear that, on the premises of Scripture, the only logical way in which the Jews could conceive the fulfilment of God's promises to the righteous was that they should live

[1] Hebrews 11, 13. [2] Above, p. 307.

[3] So in the Midrash. As in the three days of darkness in Egypt the wicked of Israel perished (Cant. R. on 2, 13; Pesiḳta Rabbati ed. Friedmann f.74a), so immediately before the days of the Messiah a great pestilence will come in which the wicked perish (Pesiḳta ed. Buber f. 51a; Pesiḳta Rabbati f. 75a; Cant. R. on 2, 12.) It is the conviction that at the advent of the "reign of God" the impenitent sinners will perish which gives point and effect to the summons of John and of Jesus to repent without delay.

[4] See below, pp. 362 f.

again upon earth in the golden age to come and share in the salvation of Israel. The resurrection seems, indeed, so necessarily the consequence of the whole teaching of Scripture concerning the salvation of the righteous and their great reward that it is not strange that the Pharisees found it explicit or by intimation in all parts of their Bible.[1]

The necessity may be looked at in another aspect. The overthrow of the last of the empires that had so long succeeded one another in oppressive dominion, the deliverance of Israel, and the establishment of the world-wide and eternal reign of God, was the vindication of God as true God, the ruler of the universe, as well as a vindication of Israel's faith in him and fidelity to him; and that the righteous dead were brought to life to share in the glories and the blessings of that time was their vindication before those who had scoffed at their fear of the Lord, averring that there is no divine providence in this life nor retribution beyond it.[2]

The emergence of this idea in the persecution of the religion by Antiochus Epiphanes and the insurrection of the faithful Jews in its defence, was at an opportune moment, and the situation, with the assurance that the hour of deliverance was at hand and the new era about to begin, gave both the motive and the limitation of the first conception of resurrection.

Those who were restored to life to share in the great salvation led their second existence on earth under the same conditions as the living who survived the great crisis. It was believed that the new era would be one of independence, peace, good government, justice, uprightness, prosperity, happiness — the consummation of all that is good in the actual world and the abolition of all that is evil in every sphere. The imagination of some of the apocalypses goes to the length of letting men attain the age of Methuselah, or beget myriads of children, and from youth to

[1] Below, pp. 382 f.

[2] See Enoch 102, 4–11; 103–104. Cf. Wisdom of Solomon 2, 1–5; 3, 2–4.

old age knowing no pain nor sorrow nor affliction.[1] But however superior to the present, it is a bodily and mundane existence. And this, as it was the original conception, doubtless continued to be the popular notion.[2] That only Jews were brought to life again to enjoy this happy state of things was the universal belief, a self-evident consequence of its origin; and that the ungodly Jews would perish in the crisis and not be heard of again was at least a common expectation, as it was the logical one.

In several connections the expectation appears that many living Gentiles, witnessing the vindication of God and his people, will be converted and join in the worship of the true God, thus escaping the final doom.[3] Certain other features of this apocalyptic literature and its congeners remain to be noted. One of the most striking is the elaboration of the myth of the fall of the angels, captivated by the charms of fair women, and the giant offspring of this miscegenation (Gen. 6, 1–4).[4] These angels taught men to work in metals and make for themselves armor and weapons of war, and for women jewelry and cosmetics; incantations and witches' brews, and the varieties of maleficent magic; astrology and divination by omens; and — not the least of their mischief — they taught men to write with pen and ink, "by which many sinned from age to age, unto this day," [5] and the all-potent adjuration by the secret name.[6]

The fallen angels are thus the authors of the corruption of mankind; [7] and consequently their imprisonment [8] till the last

[1] See above, p. 303.

[2] See Strack-Billerbeck, Kommentar zum Neuen Testament aus Talmud und Midrasch, I, 887–889.

[3] So in Enoch 90, 30; 91, 14; 50, 1–5. See Isa. 52, 13–53, 12.

[4] According to Jubilees 4, 15, they came down to teach men to practise justice and righteousness, but (5, 1) succumbed to the seductive beauty of their female pupils.

[5] Enoch 6–8; 69, 1–13 (the latter from a Noah apocalypse). Cf. 65, 6–10. The particular sin of pen and ink here specified is the introduction of contracts in writing.

[6] Ibid. 69, 13–21.

[7] See also Jubilees 5, 1, 10; 10, 5–11; 11, 4 f. (idolatry).

[8] Some of them, however, were left at large. Jubilees c. 10.

judgment and their final fate in the abyss of fire are standing elements in the apocalypses.[1]

Demons, by whatever name they are called,[2] maliciously tempt men, and seduce them into sin. In the future they will have no such power.[3] The new era will be free from sin, when once the sinners and the authors and solicitors of sin have been destroyed, and the survivors have been endued with wisdom.[4]

In Sirach, written only a few years before the crisis under Antiochus Epiphanes which is reflected in Daniel and in parts of the Book of Enoch, there is no suggestion of retribution after death. The author makes no difference among men in their end; death is the common lot of all, and from it there is no return. In 41, 1–4, where the author contrasts the feelings toward death of the prosperous, who see in it a calamity, and the unfortunate, to whom it is a release, he continues: "Be not afraid of the death that is decreed for thee; remember that the generations, former and later, are in the same case with thee. This is the lot of all flesh by the Lord's appointment, and why shouldst thou set thyself against the will[5] of the Most High? Whether it be a thousand years, or a hundred, or ten, in Sheol there is no complaint[6] about (the length of) life." In his advice to mourners not to indulge in excessive and protracted grief (38, 16 ff.) he says: "Do not forget that for him (the deceased) there is no hope.[7] Thou dost not help him, and thou harmest thyself. Remember that his fate is thine also,—'for me to-day and for thee to-morrow.' When a dead man is at rest, let the thought of him rest; and be comforted when once his spirit has departed."[8]

[1] Enoch 10; 12–16; 9; 21, 7–10; 67, 4–7; 0, 21, tc. Cf. Matt. 25 41; Rev. John 20, 1–3, 10. See also Testament of Judah 25, 3.

[2] Satan, the satans; Masṭema; Beliar, and the spirits of Beliar, etc.

[3] Testament of Judah 25.

[4] Enoch 5, 8 f.; 90, 32–36; 92, 5; 91, 17; 100, 5. No attempt is made here to discriminate among the various stages at which this consummation is attained.

[5] The Hebrew text has "the Law."

[6] Or, perhaps, 'reproach.'

[7] So the Hebrew. Greek ἐπάνοδος, coming up from the tomb.

[8] See also 10, 11; 40, 1, 11.

The outlook on what is beyond death here and elsewhere in Sirach is that of the Book of Job and of the Psalms which touch upon the point. This is only what would be expected of a biblical scholar in his day. There is no especial emphasis in his utterances, and certainly nothing controversial. If he was acquainted with the ideas current in the Hellenistic world about the immortality of the soul and the fortunes which awaited the souls of the good and the bad at death, his antagonism to the Hellenizing movement in his own people would not incline him to look more favorably upon them. For this conservatism he is sometimes labelled Sadducee, but there is no evidence that in his day parties were aligned on this issue, nor even that the question of retribution after death had come into the forum of discussion.

It is likely that the new ideas which emerged in the next generation made their way slowly among the Scribes, and not without opposition. All that we know for certain is that they became the distinguishing tenets of the Pharisees.[1]

That the resurrection of the dead was a party issue between the Pharisees and the Sadducees is familiar from the New Testament. In Josephus are two brief statements of the beliefs of the Pharisees on this point: "All souls are imperishable, but only the soul of the good passes into another body, while the souls of the bad are castigated with everlasting punishment."[2] To the same effect in the second passage, but somewhat more fully: "Their belief is that souls have a deathless vigor, and that beneath the earth there are rewards and punishments according as they have been devoted in life to virtue or to vice. For the latter everlasting imprisonment is prescribed; for the former capability of coming to life again."[3] By reason of these doctrines they have the greatest influence with the mass of the people, and in matters of religious observance, everything is done according to

[1] It may well be that this goes back to the very beginnings of the party.

[2] Bell. Jud. ii. 8, 14 § 163.

[3] Antt. xviii. 1, 3 § 14. — The Sadducees deny the survival of the soul — it perishes with the body — and the rewards and punishments in Hades (ll. cc.).

their interpretation. This description of the sects is written for Greek and Roman readers,[1] and the fact must be taken into account in interpreting the expressions; but the substantial accuracy of the report, so far as it goes, there is no occasion to doubt. It agrees with most of the sources we have discussed above in the return to bodily life of the souls of the good only, and the eternal punishment of the bad.

In the first century the Schools of Shammai and Hillel were agreed in defining the two classes in Dan. 12, 2 as the righteous, who are destined to eternal life, and the wicked, who are consigned to ignominy and eternal abhorrence. But they differed on a new question: What was to become of those who were neither totally righteous nor totally wicked, but betwixt and between?[2] — the great majority, in short. The School of Shammai held that those in whom good and evil were, so to speak, in equilibrium, will go down to hell, and dive and come up,[3] and arise thence and be healed (Zech. 13, 9; 1 Sam. 2, 6). For them the fires of Gehenna are purgatorial; they are refined like silver and assayed like gold. The School of Hillel maintained that God in his abounding mercy (Exod. 34, 6) would incline the balance to the side of mercy, and not send them down to Gehenna at all, arguing from Psalm 116.[4]

That the belief in retribution after death appeared in Judaism at so late a stage in its history gave it a distinct superiority over religions in which the notions of man's hereafter originated in

[1] There is reason to think that in both accounts Josephus is drawing directly or indirectly on a Greek source, presumably Nicolaus of Damascus. In that case the testimony is three quarters of a century older than Josephus.

[2] The בינונים. So among the Greeks, *οἱ δὲ τοῦ μέσου βίου, πολλοὶ ὄντες οὗτοι*. Lucian, On Mourning for the Dead, § 9. See Vol. I, pp. 495 f.; II, p. 62.

[3] מצפצפים. The rendering is dubious; see the commentators.

[4] Tos. Sanhedrin 13, 3; Rosh ha-Shanah 16b–17a. In the Baraita in Rosh ha-Shanah this is expressly said to take place at the day of judgment, meaning at the general resurrection in the last day. Daniel 12, 2 ('these are to ignominy and eternal abhorrence') is cited as a proof-text for the fate of the completely wicked who are consigned to hell.

ancient myths and were developed in mythical forms.[1] In Judaism all the great doctrines of the religion had long been fully established, and the extension of divine retribution beyond the tomb came as a necessary corollary to the idea of God's justice and the assurance of his faithfulness in fulfilling his promises to the righteous. Moreover, the conditions of God's favor, here or hereafter, had been completely moralized. Righteousness was conformity to his holy will as revealed in the twofold law he had given, which comprehended not only belief and observance but morals — man's conduct in all his relations to his fellows and in his personal character. Wickedness was deliberate defiance or habitual disregard of God's law, and the incorrigibly wicked are doomed to perdition. Sin was any transgression or neglect of its commandments or prohibitions. For sin thus defined there was but one remedy, the forgiving grace of God, and the *conditio sine qua non* of forgiveness was repentance, that is, contrition, confession, reparation of injuries to others, and a reformation of conduct undertaken and persisted in with sincere purpose and out of religious motives.

The ultimate salvation of the individual[2] is inseparably connected with the salvation of the people, and inasmuch as, in accordance with the prophetic teaching, this was made dependent on the righteousness or the repentance of the nation collectively, the conduct and character of the individual concerned not himself alone but the whole Jewish people. Those who by teaching and example made the multitude righteous merited especial honor, while the prevalence of wickedness, it was taught, deferred the fulfilment of God's promise of salvation to the nation.[3] The efforts of the religious teachers, the Scribes, and their following, the Pharisees, were not only to indoctrinate all their countrymen in the obligations of their religion, but to promote

[1] This is the element of truth in Warburton's famous paradox.

[2] חיי עולם, ζωὴ αἰώνιος. The opposite is חיי שעה 'the life of the (passing) hour,' e.g. Beṣah 15b; Jer. Mo'ed Ḳaṭon 82b, below.

[3] See below, pp. 350 ff.

among them by precept and example the fulfilment of these obligations in all spheres.

Besides all this there were the prophecies of the time to come when, after the destruction of the enemy nations, Judaism, the true religion, should be the religion of all mankind,[1] the universal "reign of God" should be made visible. Other passages make Israel the instrument in the enlightenment of the Gentiles, and the enlargement of God's salvation to the ends of the earth.[2] The expansion of Judaism by conversion in the centuries immediately preceding and following the Christian era is evidence of the zeal with which the Jews prosecuted this mission.[3]

A consequence of all this was that in Judaism the fate of the individual after death, however it might be emphasized as a motive for the fidelity of the Jew to every article of his religion, did not occupy the same place which it had in many contemporary religions in the Hellenistic world. The mysteries — which, in distinction from the public cults, we should call the personal religions of the age — were solely concerned with the salvation of the individual after death, each in its own particular way, of which they offered to their initiates the earnest and assurance. Whatever theology they had was a myth, upon which also their rituals as well as such scriptures as they possessed,[4] were based. They made no moral conditions of admission, but promised salvation indiscriminately to all their members. In general they constituted no organized communities,[5] and however wide their distribution, they were not united in a general organization. Men joined them for a guarantee of future blessedness; for the rest they continued to worship the gods of the public religions.

Judaism was the public as well as the personal religion of the Jewish people. A Jew did not embrace it nor adhere to it to

[1] Isa. 66, 18 ff.; 60, 6, 7; Zech. 14, 9, 16–21; Dan. 7, 13 f. Cf. Enoch 50, 2–5; 90, 30.

[2] Isa. 42, 1–7; 49, 6; 60, 3, etc.

[3] See Part I, chapter vii.

[4] E.g. the Orphica.

[5] The mysteries of Mithras are the conspicuous exception.

escape the perils of the soul beyond the tomb, much less the retributive justice of God. Religion, in the higher conception of Judaism, was not a means to that or any other end; it was the divinely appointed *end*. Whole-hearted and whole-souled love to God was its essence; its duties to God and man were truly done only when done for God's sake, or for their own sake, not from any self-regarding motive.

The question, What shall I do that I may inherit eternal life?[1] draws from Jesus the natural Jewish answer, Thou knowest the commandments (the Decalogue); if the questioner insists on some supererogatory good work, let him sell all his property and give the proceeds to the poor,[2] and he shall have treasure in heaven. When the disciples of R. Eliezer ask him the same question, he counsels them to be careful about the honor of their fellows, to watch wisely over the education of their children, and when they pray to consider in whose presence they stand.[3]

There is no indication that pious Jews were afflicted with an inordinate preoccupation about their individual hereafter. The anxiety of a few eminently godly men in the hour of death is recorded because exceptional;[4] it was never cultivated as a mark of superior piety.[5]

To the author of 4 Esdras it is self-evident that only a few will be saved, and he agonizes with the question how it comports with the character of God that the great mass, not only of mankind in general but of His chosen people, should be thus abandoned to perdition — for their own sin, no doubt, but why did not God prevent it? He might never have made Adam, or have

[1] Mark 10, 17; Matt. 19, 16; Luke 18, 18.

[2] The Nazarene Gospel expands on this point.

[3] Above, p. 151. The same rabbi contrasts the attendance on the instruction of the learned with secular occupations, חיי שעה . . . . חיי עולם.

[4] E.g. Johanan ben Zakkai, Berakot 28b. See below, p. 391. It is evidence in their case of a peculiarly sensitive conscience.

[5] Uncertainty of salvation is logical orthodoxy in those religions or theologies which make it depend on the inscrutable election of individuals, of which no man can be assured unless by immediate revelation from God.

kept him from transgression. The angel who is sent to enlighten Ezra confirms the fact,[1] but his explanations do not solve the difficulties nor satisfy the inquirer. Fourth Esdras stands by itself in Jewish literature in the pessimism of its premises — explicable enough in the circumstances of the time — as well as in the perception that the crux of the vital problem of theodicy lies here, and in the intellectual and moral earnestness with which it addresses itself to it.[2]

Retribution after death established itself in Judaism as a complement to the old belief in retribution in this life or in the article of death, not as a substitute for it. In a former connection it has been shown how the principle of retribution in kind, the infliction corresponding to the offence, was developed in detail.[3] Especially a signal calamity or misfortune invited an inference to the extraordinary guilt of the sufferer, for which the Scriptures gave ample warrant. The questions addressed to Jesus in the Gospels about the Galileans whose blood Pilate had mingled with their sacrifices and the eighteen persons on whom the tower in Siloam fell and killed them (Luke 13, 1–5),[4] or the man born blind (John 9, 1 f.), are illustrations of a natural inquiry, not in Jewry alone but in Christendom through all its centuries — wherever, in fact, it is believed that in all happenings the immediate volition and action of God is to be recognized. Jesus' answer to the former question is a warning of approaching doom: Unless you repent you will all likewise perish.[5]

[1] 4 Esdras 8, 1: The Most High made this world for the sake of many, but the future world for the sake of few. — 8, 3: Many have been created, but few will be saved. Cf. 7, 49–61. See Luke 13, 23 f.; Matt. 22, 14, etc.

[2] The Syriac Baruch, a work of about the same age, has much in common with 4 Esdras, but is far less poignant. Serious account is not to be taken of the homiletic conceits about the creation of this world and the world to come by ה or י respectively, and the significance of the latter (the smallest letter in the alphabet), viz. that the righteous who are in the world to come are few (Menaḥot 29b, below; cf. Jer. Hagigah 77c, below; v. Rashi on Gen. 2, 4).

[3] Part vi, Piety, pp. 248 ff. See also Strack-Billerbeck, Kommentar zum Neuen Testament aus Talmud und Midrasch, II, 192–197; 527–529.

[4] Evidently recent occurrences of which nothing else is known.

[5] See the preceding, Luke 12, 35–57.

CHAPTER II

MESSIANIC EXPECTATIONS

In the foregoing chapter we have seen how the belief in the ultimate retribution for the individual after death attached itself to the expectation of a great crisis in the history of the Jewish people or of the world, and in what diverse forms this crisis was imagined by the visionaries. It remains here to deal more particularly with these expectations.

By way of preamble it may be said that their religious significance lies not in attempts to make a picture out of the dissected puzzle of prophecy nor in the eschatological nightmares of the apocalypses, but consciously or unconsciously, in the idea that the history of the world is a plan of God, and in the faith that he will carry it out to the end. The value of the rest lay solely in that it helped men to give reality to their faith through an imaginative presentation. It must be observed further that, except on the single article of the revivification of the dead, there was no dogma and no canon of orthodoxy in this whole field, and that it was left for the Tannaim of the second century definitively to project the future in a perspective of receding planes.

For orderliness we may distinguish between the national form of the expectation, a coming golden age for the Jewish people, and what for want of a better word may be called the eschatological form, the final catastrophe of the world as it is and the coming in its place of a new world, which in so far as it lies beyond human experience of nature we may call supernatural. But it must be understood that in all the earlier part of our period the two are not sharply distinguished, but run into each other and blend like the overlapping edges of two clouds. In the older apocalypses the elements derived from the national expectation are drawn into the eschatology and suffer a transfiguration in their supernatural environment.[1]

The national, or as we might call it the political, expectation is an inheritance from prophecy. Its principal features are the recovery of independence and power, an era of peace and prosperity, of fidelity to God and his law, of justice and fair-dealing and brotherly love among men, and of personal rectitude and piety. The external condition of all this is liberation from the rule of foreign oppressors; the internal condition is the religious and moral reformation or regeneration of the Jewish people itself.[2]

This golden age to come presents itself to the imagination as a renascence of the golden age in the past, the good old times of the early monarchy, and, in this, the revival of the kingdom under a prince of the Davidic line. Thus in Amos 9, after the denunciation of relentless doom (vss. 1–4, 7–9) culminating in the sentence, 'All the sinners of my people shall die by the sword, that say, The evil shall not overtake nor confront us': 'In that day will I raise up the ruinous hut[3] of David, and wall up the breaches in it, and repair what of it has been demolished, and build it up as it was in bygone days.'[4]

For the prince in the restoration the figure of an offshoot is used in Jer. 23, 5: 'Days are coming, saith the Lord, that I will raise up to David a righteous scion,[5] and he will reign, a king, and prosper, and do justice and maintain righteousness in the land. In his days Judah will be delivered and Israel live in security; and this is the name by which he shall be called,

[1] The Parables of Enoch offer many illustrations of this.

[2] It need hardly be said that a scheme such as is here constructed for it does not occur in similar completeness and symmetry in prophecy itself.

[3] A 'hut,' a poor shelter, no longer a house, not to say a palace.

[4] That this sudden turn from destruction to restoration has displaced the original close of the prophecy, as many modern critics think, never occurred to the Jews. With the dates and circumstances of predictions they were not at all concerned; all were divine oracles, to which belongs as such the timelessness of revelation. Among them there was no progress, and above all no contrariety. See Vol. I, pp. 239, 358.

[5] צמח. Cf. the same figure (חטר, נצר) in Isa. 11, 1.

IHVH-Ṣidḳenu.'[1] Similarly in the twin passage, Jer. 33, 14–16, with the addition that the succession of Davidic kings and of Levitical priests shall never be cut off (vs. 17), and more expansively and emphatically in the following verses (Jer. 33, 19–22, cf. 23–33). In Zech. 3, 8, 'I am about to bring my servant, Scion,' it is used as a proper name or appropriated as a title,[2] and in 6, 12 is applied as such to Zerubbabel: 'Here is a man whose name is Scion; he will shoot up[3] from the spot where he is and build the temple of the Lord,[4] and will assume (royal) state,[5] and sit and rule upon his throne.'[6]

There was thus a moment when the Scion of David seemed in the way of becoming an established designation for the Davidic prince who should inaugurate the era of restoration, and even of passing into a name "Scion," much as the Lord's Anointed became in the use of later Jews and Christians "the Anointed" (Messiah).[7] A reminiscence of this is preserved or revived in the current form of the Eighteen Prayers, "Cause the Scion of David Thy servant speedily to sprout, and let his horn be exalted by Thy salvation."[8]

In other places the name David itself stands for the king in the restoration. Thus in Hos. 3, 5, after the people for their sins have long been deprived of king or prince, without sacrifice and oracle, 'Afterward the Israelites will return (repent) and

[1] There is no more propriety in translating this proper name than others, e.g. Jehoṣedeḳ or Ṣidḳiyahu, which have the like significance.

[2] Therefore without the article.

[3] *Yiṣmaḥ*, play on *Ṣemaḥ*, 'shoot.'

[4] Zech. 4, 7, 9. Cf. Haggai 2, 20–23.

[5] Lit. 'splendor.'

[6] See also Testament of Judah 24, 4–6 (*βλαστὸς θεοῦ ὑψίστου* vs. 4, as in Jer. 33 (40), 15 ed. Complut., Theodoret; cf. the Armenian version). The genuineness of the verse is suspected by Charles and others for reasons which are unconvincing.

[7] In Isa. 4, 2 צמח יהוה (E. V. 'the branch of the Lord'), is rendered by the Targum, 'the Anointed of the Lord' (Messiah); and in all the places cited above for the Scion, the Targum has the Messiah.

[8] No. 15 (14). Baer, 'Abodat Israel, p. 97; Singer, Prayer Book, p. 49. See Elbogen, Der jüdische Gottesdienst, p. 54. An older form has, "Have compassion on Israel thy people . . . and on the reign of the house of David thy righteous Messiah." Dalman, Worte Jesu, p. 300; cf. 303.

seek the Lord their God and David their king.' So also in Jer. 30, 9, when the yoke of foreign oppression that rested on the neck of the Jews is finally broken, 'They will serve the Lord their God and David their king, whom I will raise up unto them.'[1] David himself was God's Chosen, His Anointed,[2] and it is not strange that such passages as are adduced above should by some have been taken literally — David should be the instaurator of the golden age in the future as he was of the golden age of the nation in the past. Of such an expectation we have evidence in Jer. Berakot 5a, where the Rabbanan say on Hos. 3, 5 ('The Israelites will return and seek the Lord their God and David their king'): "This is the king Messiah. If he comes from among the living, David is his name, and if from those that sleep, David is his name," that is it will be David himself.[3] Of such a return in person of a great figure of former times, Elijah is the salient example (Mal. 3, 23 f.);[4] for another illustration of the belief see Mark 8, 27 f., where in answer to Jesus' question what men said about him, his disciples answer, Some say that thou art John the Baptist,[5] others Elijah. Jesus himself recognizes Elijah in John the Baptist,[6] and there is nothing to indicate that he said it in a metaphor.

To the interpretation which took the prophetic passages above of David in person, R. Tanḥuma opposes Psalm 18, 51: 'Making great the deliverances (wrought) for His king, and showing loving-kindness to His anointed' — it does not say, 'to David,' but 'to David and his posterity forever.'[7]

[1] See also Ezek. 34, 23 f.; 37, 24 f.; cf. Isa. 55, 3 f.; Psalm 78, 70–72.

[2] 1 Sam. 16, 1–13.

[3] Cf. Sanhedrin 98b, below, a different version attributed to Rab.

[4] See Ecclus. 48, 10 f.

[5] Matt. 16, 14 adds, 'Others, Jeremiah or one of the prophets.' Cf. Luke 9, 18 f., 'others, that one of the ancient prophets is risen from the dead.'

[6] Matt. 11, 10 (quoting Mal. 3, 1, and explicitly 11, 14. — On Elijah in Jewish expectation see Friedmann's Introduction to his edition of the Seder Eliahu Rabba (1902), esp. pp. 23 ff.; Ginzberg in Jewish Encyclopedia V, 122–127.

[7] Ekah Rabbati on Lam. 1, 16 (c. 51 end, Wilna). The reign of *the house of* David; Simeon ben Menasya, Midrash Samuel, 13, 4.

That the kingdom was secured in perpetuity to the house of David by the promise of God is said in express words in 2 Sam. 7, 16 (cf. 12–15) of which Psalm 89, 28–37 is an echo.[1] So it is for Sirach: the covenant promise to David is parallel to that to Aaron and his descendants (Ecclus. 45, 25); God "exalted his horn forever and gave him the statute[2] of the kingdom and established his throne over Israel" (47, 11).[3]

There are large tracts of prophecy in which there is no mention of the revival of the monarchy in the great restoration, and no place made for the king of the golden age — Isa. 40 ff. is the most conspicuous instance. The modern interpreter, from the premises of a critical dissection of the book, would describe such prophecies as exhibiting a theocratic form of the national hope, in distinction from the political type — an age in which the Lord alone is king.[4] The Jews, to whom there was only one Book of Isaiah — no Deutero- and Trito- — and to whom all prophecy was a unitary and consistent revelation of God, had no inkling of all this, and interpreted the latter part of the Book of Isaiah in accordance with the former.[5] Thus Isa. 42, 1, 'Behold my servant whom I uphold, my chosen one in whom my soul delighteth,' etc., is rendered in the Targum, "Behold my servant the Anointed (Messiah), I will draw him near, my Chosen in whom my word[6] delights; I will put my holy spirit upon him, and he shall reveal my judgment to the nations."[7]

There were times when the deliverance was of greater moment than the lineage of the deliverer. When the Asmonaeans conquered the independence of the Jews and extended their kingdom to the bounds of the ancient monarchy at its widest, it must have seemed to many that the prophecies of the restoration of the

[1] See also Psalms of Solomon 17, 4–6. [2] Or covenant.

[3] See also 47, 22 and 48, 15. 1 Macc. 2, 57, in the parting charge of Mattathias to his sons.

[4] For this the unhappy phrase "messianic age without a Messiah" has been invented.

[5] Christian interpreters all did the same thing until recent times.

[6] *Memri* here, as frequently, is equivalent to, "I myself."

[7] Cf. the Targum in 43, 10; 52, 13; 53, 10.

power and glory of the nation were being fulfilled in them. It is thought by many that Psalm 110 is a glorification, perhaps, by a court poet, of one of these militant rulers who, like Melchizedek, united in themselves the office and function of priests and kings.[1]

In everything except breaking the heads of the heathen (Psalm 110, 5 f.), the Asmonaean kings at the height of their power were at a remote extreme from the ideal of the ruler in the golden age as he is figured in such prophecies as Isa. 11, 1–5; 9, 6 f. It is very unlikely that the biblical scholars of the time as a class, and the party of the Pharisees, were inclined to bestow upon the priests who had mounted the throne the predictions of the restoration of the legitimate monarchy. If any indulged for a moment in this illusion it was completely dispelled by the conduct of Alexander Jannaeus and his sons, so that the representatives of the nation begged Pompey to abolish the royal form of government altogether.

The author of the seventeenth of the Psalms of Solomon recites God's choice of David to be king and God's oath concerning his descendants that his kingdom should never fail before Him (vs. 5). "Sinful men seized by force what they had no promise of;[2] they devastated the throne of David with arrogant exultation" (vs. 8). He prays that God raise up for his people their king, the son of David,[3] at the time acceptable to him, to reign over his servant Israel, and gird him with might that he may shatter tyrannical rulers[4] (vs. 23). The second of these Psalms descants on the vices of the people of Jerusalem in the days of the last of the Asmonaean rulers, vices which richly deserved the righteous judgment God inflicted on the city by the hand of Pompey.

[1] Psalm 45 is also sometimes referred to the marriage of one of these princes.

[2] These usurpers are the Asmonaeans, as is evident from the following context (Pompey).

[3] The earliest attested use of this phrase, so common in the Tannaite period, for the Messiah; cf. also vs. 36, "Their king will be the Lord's Anointed" (Messiah; emending, χριστὸς κυρίου).

[4] The Romans.

From the Gospels and the first part of Acts it appears that the expectation of the people attached itself to the Davidic promise, so that "the Son of David" [1] is equivalent to "the Messiah," which in the Gospels appears for the first time thus as a standing title.[2] In Mark 12, 35 (cf. Matt. 22, 41 f.) Jesus is said to have posed the question, "How do the scribes say that the Messiah is the son of David?" to lead up to a difficulty for this opinion in Psalm 110, 1. The genealogies in Matthew and Luke in different ways trace the lineage of Jesus himself through Joseph to David. In the Tannaite literature and thereafter "the Son of David" is a very common name for what we call the Messiah.[3]

Whether Davidic descent was claimed in his own time for Bar Cocheba, whom Akiba recognized as the Messiah of whom the conquest of Edom (Rome) was predicted (Num. 24, 17 f.), is unknown.[4] In fact his antecedents are wrapt in complete obscurity, and the assertion frequently made that he was not even of the tribe of Judah seem to have no other foundation than the silence of the sources.[5] The disillusion made the Jews glad to bury the whole episode. Even the name Bar Cocheba is preserved only in Christian writers; Jewish sources know only Bar Kozibah.

The Sibylline Oracles give evidence that similar expectations were entertained among the Hellenistic Jews, though the fiction of the heathen prophetess and the oracular mystification forbid

[1] Matt. 9, 27; 15, 22; 20, 30, 31, and parallels. The translators who thrust in the pronoun—'*Thou* son of David,' take the whole point out of the evangelist's intention.

[2] ὁ χριστός. In Enoch 48, 10; 52, 4, "His Anointed," as in the Old Testament, where it always has a defining genitive or pronoun.

[3] See e.g. Sanhedrin 97–98.

[4] Mediaeval statements (see Jewish Encyclopedia II, 507) that he was of the house of David, are probably inferred from the conviction that otherwise Akiba would not have proclaimed him the Messiah.

[5] Johanan ben Torta, who did not acknowledge him, is reported to have told Akiba that he would be long in his grave and still the *Son of David* would not come; but it would not be wise to lay much weight on the verbal exactness of the report.

an express identification of the coming ruler of the golden age. In Sibyll. iii, 46–50 we read: "When Rome shall rule also over Egypt, ... then the most mighty kingdom of the immortal King will appear to men. There will come a holy ruler, to wield the sceptre over the whole earth unto all the cycles of swift-rushing time.[1] Then will be inexorable wrath on Latin men, . . . Woe to thee, wretched city! When will that day come, and the judgment of the immortal God, the great King?" This oracle refers to a Roman triumvirate (vs. 52); opinions are divided between the first (60–53 B.C.) and the second (43–28 B.C.). Probability inclines to the latter; but in either case the date is not far from that of the Psalms of Solomon.[2]

The great deliverance was thus connected with the appearance of a descendant of David designated by God.[3] The deliverance itself was always the work of God.[4] There are prophecies in which the action moves on the stage of history. God gives the king victory over his enemies on all sides, subdues them under his dominion, creates durable peace; the ruler, endowed by God with wisdom and virtue, establishes order and enforces justice in his realm; and God bestows boundless prosperity on a righteous and God-fearing nation. The great days of the monarchy under David and Solomon, seen through the luminous haze which imagination throws over the good old times, the brighter by contrast with the dark clouds of the present, furnish the setting of the scene; prophetic teaching projects into the future its ideal of a golden age of righteousness and the fear of the Lord; poets depict it with the imagery of an earthly paradise; but, however magnified and glorified, it was not beyond the compass of imagination.

[1] Cf. Psalms of Solomon 17, 4 f.: "The kingdom of our God is forever over the heathen. Thou, O Lord, didst choose David as king over Israel," etc. (above, p. 326). — See also Orac. Sibyll. iii, 286 f.; 652–656; v, 108.

[2] Cf. psalm 17, 32–35; Enoch 48, 2–10.

[3] This is the significance of the phrases "the Lord's anointed," "the anointed son of David," "the anointed king."

[4] This is the consistent representation in the prophets (especially in Isa. 40 ff.) and the Psalms. So also in the Jewish prayers.

More frequently, however, in prophecies in which the figure of the king of the golden age appears at all, he is not the instrument of God in the conquest of independence and power; he appears on the scene only after the great deliverance has been wrought by God himself, as the ruler of a redeemed and regenerated Israel. This is naturally — one might say necessarily — the case when the act of deliverance is the liberation of the exiles and their restoration to their own land, as for example in Jer. 30–33.[1] It was the expectation of the prophets Haggai and Zechariah when they hailed Zerubbabel as the Scion.

In the following centuries, under the empires that succeeded one another in the dominion of their world, the Jews were made keenly aware of the impotence of little Judaea and its scattered sons over against the gigantic power of those vast empires. If for a short century in the decline and fall of the Seleucid kingdom they were able by arms and intrigue to establish and maintain a precarious independence, when once Rome reached out for the East, they found themselves in the grip of a power different from all its predecessors, mightier and more terrible than they.[2] Revolt they did, over and over again, on one occasion or another, but the outcome of each desperate attempt to throw off the yoke of bondage only riveted it upon them faster and heavier than before, and deepened the conviction that only by the immediate intervention of Almighty God could the might of the heathen kingdom be annihilated and the world made ready for the coming undivided and undisputed reign of God[3] or, in its national expression, the world-wide and eternal dominion of the holy people of the Most High.[4] And this all the more because, with a glimpse of the unitary conception of history, the empires that had dominated the world were seen to be but successive

[1] See Jer. 30, 8 f., 18–22; 33, 10–22, etc.

[2] Dan. 7. The fourth kingdom was now understood to be the Roman empire.

[3] Zech. 14, 9.

[4] Dan. 7, 27. So in the only occurrence of a messianic figure in Enoch (90, 37 f.) outside the Parables.

embodiments of *one* great ungodly and unrighteous power, the heathen world in its implacable enmity to the true God and his will for mankind. The overthrow of the empire that for any time-being represented this power was not enough; as a whole it must be reduced to subjection or destroyed.

A change came also in the representations of the divine judgment. From historical crises which determined the fate of nations, religiously interpreted as judgments in fact, it was transformed in imagination into a great assize at the end of the present epoch of history, with God sitting on his judgment throne pronouncing doom upon rulers and nations, as in Dan. 7, 9–14.

In Daniel this is not so much a new conception of the nature of judgment as the way in which, through the mechanism of vision, the ancient seer is supposed to see the decree of destiny upon Antiochus Epiphanes and his kingdom, which in the days when his book came to light, the time of the end (12, 4), was about to be executed. Elsewhere in the book the fate of the king overtakes him in the midst of his career, in a mysterious way, indeed, but on the stage of history.[1]

In Enoch 90, 20–27, however, the judgment is consistently forensic;[2] the stars, the fallen angels of Gen. 6, 1–4, and the seventy angelic shepherds, and the blinded sheep (apostate Jews), are brought before the throne of God set up in Palestine, tried, convicted, and cast into abysses of fire, before the beginning of the golden age, with its New Jerusalem and its transfigured head, in whom the traditional figure of the ruler of the golden age (Messiah) enjoys an otiose survival. The transition from visionary prophecy to eschatology is complete.[3]

Reminiscences of the prophecies of a conquering king are not infrequent in the literature of these centuries. Particular note is to be taken of Psalms of Solomon 17, 21–51 which moves completely in this circle of ideas, and in this as in other things

[1] Dan. 8, 25; cf. 2, 45.
[2] See above, p. 301. So also in Enoch 1, 4–9; 22–27 (see 22, 4; 27, 1–4).
[3] See below, p. 377.

proves its affinity to rabbinical conceptions. Other examples are to be found in the Sibyllines. Thus in iii, 652–659: Then [1] will God send from the sun [2] a king who will make the whole earth desist from dire warfare, slaying some and with some making firm treaties. Nor will he do all this by his own counsels, but in obedience to the good ordinances of the Great God.[3]

The apocalypses after the fall of Jerusalem assign to the Messiah [4] the rôle of denouncing the Roman empire or its last ruler for all their crimes, condemning, and making an end of them, but all, so to say, in a supernatural sphere. He will deliver the remnant of God's people and rule over them till the time of the last judgment or the end of the present age.[5] With this idea of a universal judgment *after* the Messianic Age we have reached another stage in eschatology to which we shall return further on.

In other parts of the apocalypses there is either nobody at all that corresponds to the Messiah,[6] or he has nothing to do in the deliverance of the Jews from their enemies and oppressors, but, as in the prophecies to which reference has been made, comes on the scene only when God has already done everything, and even then is often little more than a lay figure.[7]

It is different in the Parables of Enoch (cc. 37–71).[8] In them God's Chosen One — so he is usually called — has a very conspicuous place, and many things are ascribed to him which are

[1] After a time of commotion and savage warfare, 632 ff.

[2] Cf. v, 108 *θεόθεν*, 414, *οὐρανίων νώτων*. Others understand 'from the sunrising,' east, from the author's point of view.

[3] Contrast the destruction by the hand of God of the nations in their last onset on Jerusalem, ibid. 663–697, and see the idyllic picture of the golden age following, 702–731. The scheme, the Messiah, Gog and Magog, the New Era, is familiar in rabbinical sources also. See below, pp. 344 f. For the Messiah as deliverer and inaugurator of better times, see Orac. Sibyll. v, 108 f., 414–433.

[4] Expressly so named.

[5] 4 Esdras 12 (the Eagle Vision); Syr. Baruch 36–40 (Vision of the Cedar and the Vine); see also 72–74. The cedar forest is ultimately from Isa. 10, 33 f., immediately preceding the messianic oracle (11, 1 ff.); cf. the combination of cedar and vine in Ezek. 17. See below, pp. 338, 340 f.

[6] So in all parts of Enoch 1–36 and in 91–104.

[7] So in Enoch 90, 37 f.

[8] See above, pp. 303 f.

commonly associated with the so-called messianic prophecies. In two places the title "His (God's) Anointed" is appropriated to him; viz. 48, 10, where Psalm 2, 2 is in mind, and 52, 4, with a possible reminiscence of Psalm 72.

What is of more note is that the Chosen One is identified with the figure "like a human being" which Daniel sees in his vision (Dan. 7, 13 f.). At his first introduction (46, 1 f.), Enoch sees one with "an aged head, white as wool" (Dan. 7, 9), and with him another, "whose countenance was like the appearance of a man, and his face was full of graciousness like that of one of the holy angels." Thereafter he is called 'that (or this) son of man.'[1] What has happened here is plain. In Daniel the figure "like a human being" that comes in the clouds of heaven is explained by the angel as the kingdom of the holy people of the Most High (7, 27, cf. 13 f.), in contrast to the heathen kingdoms represented by the four monstrous beasts that came up out of the sea. In Enoch the four bestial empires have vanished from the scene, and the one in the likeness of a man has thus become an individual, naturally, then, the ruler to whom is given by God 'dominion and glory and a kingdom,' etc. (Dan. 7, 14), God's Chosen and Anointed One.

An individual, and then in the conventional sense "messianic," interpretation was in fact sure to be given[2] as soon as Dan. 7, 9–14 was taken by itself, without concern about the beginning of the chapter,[3] and is to be found both in the Midrash and in mediaeval Jewish commentators. R. Joshua ben Levi, one of the most highly esteemed masters of the Haggadah in the first half of the third century, harmonized Zech. 9, 9, 'Behold thy

[1] Enoch 46, 2; 48, 2, etc. The demonstrative pronoun is the only means in Ethiopic of giving an equivalent for the Greek article in ὁ υἱὸς τοῦ ἀνθρώπου, and this phrase itself is the rendering of Daniel's *bar 'enash*, a human being (*bar nasha*), or its Hebrew equivalent *ben adam* (indefinite).

[2] The more naturally since *bar 'enash* is a human being in contrast to God, as e.g. in the Targums on Num. 23, 19, and to angels, as the comparison in 46, 1 shows.

[3] Ancient interpreters concerned themselves little about total contexts.

king cometh unto thee . . . lowly, and riding upon an ass,'[1] with Dan. 7, 13, 'Behold, with the clouds of heaven came one like a human being,' thus: If they (Israel) are worthy, 'with the clouds of heaven'; if they are not worthy, 'lowly,[2] and riding upon an ass.'[3] The application of Dan. 7, 13 to the Messiah is presumed to be usual; Joshua ben Levi, of whom numerous such harmonistic solutions are reported,[4] only seeks to remove the difficulty in the two apparently opposite representations of the Messiah's coming.

That the messianic interpretation of the human figure who in Dan. 7, 13 comes with the clouds of heaven is much older is with great probability to be inferred from the Sibylline Oracles. In v, 414 we read: "There came from the wide heavenly spaces[5] a blessed man, holding in his hands a sceptre which God put in his grasp, and he brought all into subjection," etc.[6]

The use of the phrase "the son of man" in the Gospels is of extraordinary difficulty.[7] In eschatological contexts, however, with which alone we are here concerned, the Son of Man is plainly the figure of Daniel's vision, taken individually, and identified with the Messiah coming to judgment. Thus in Mark 14, 61 f. (cf. Matt. 26, 63 f.; Luke 22, 67 f.), to the high priest's question, Art thou the Messiah? Jesus replies, 'I am; and ye shall see the Son of Man sitting at the right hand of the Power,[8]

[1] See also Berakot 56b: If in a dream a man sees an ass, let him look for salvation, for it is written, 'Behold thy king cometh unto thee, righteous and saved is he, lowly, and riding on an ass.'

[2] The similarity of the words cannot be preserved in translation — *'im 'anane—'ani* (עם ענני — עני).

[3] Sanhedrin 98a, below; Jer. Ta'anit 63d, below.

[4] See Bacher, Pal. Amoräer, I, 151 f.

[5] ἦλθε γὰρ οὐρανίων νώτων ἀνὴρ μακαρίτης.

[6] Orac. Sibyll. v, 414; cf. iii, 652, "And then from the sun God will send a king"; see also iii, 46–50.

[7] It occurs in the Gospels only in the mouth of Jesus, and outside of them only in Acts 7, 56 in the dying words of Stephen, 'I see the heavens opened and the Son of Man standing on the right hand of God.' Not even, it should be observed, in the Revelation of John.

[8] Metonymy for God; in Hebrew *ha-Geburah.*

and coming with the clouds of heaven.'[1] The seat at the right hand of God is added to Daniel's picture from Psalm 110, 1, which was currently interpreted of the Messiah son of David (Mark 12, 35 f.).[2]

It was through this identification that the faith of the disciples of Jesus not only survived the shock of his death but found confirmation in his death. In Acts 1, 9, when they had witnessed his assumption — he was taken up, and a cloud received him out of their sight — an angel assures them that 'this Jesus who has been taken up from you into heaven will come in the same way that you have beheld him going into heaven,' i.e. in the clouds of heaven as in Daniel's vision.[3]

It is not likely that the discovery of the Messiah in Daniel's "son of man" was original with the followers of Jesus or with himself. Nor is it necessary to suppose, as is commonly done, that they got the idea from apocalyptic circles such as those from which we have the Parables of Enoch, any more than it is necessary to assume such a source for the interpretation to which Joshua ben Levi is a witness, or the midrash which finds in 'Anani ('cloud-man')[4] a name of the 'King-Messiah,' and his genealogy from David through Zerubbabel in 1 Chron. 3, 5–24.[5]

Much earlier evidence that a messianic interpretation of the vision could occur to a teacher of the Law is to be found in

[1] See also the passages where the Son of Man appears in a judgment scene: Matt. 16, 27 f.; 24, 15–31, 44; 25, 31 ff. (the king).

[2] Psalm 110 (and 1 Sam. 2, 10) are brought into this combination also in the messianic interpretation of Dan. 7, 13 in the mediaeval commentary printed under the name Sa'adia.

[3] The "Western" text seems originally to have read: *καὶ ταῦτα εἰπόντος αὐτοῦ νεφέλη ὑπέλαβεν αὐτὸν καὶ ἐπήρθη ἀπ' αὐτῶν.* J. H. Ropes, The Text of Acts, *in loc.* Cf. Apoc. Joan. 11, 12 (the two witnesses), *ἀνέβησαν εἰς τὸν οὐρανὸν ἐν τῇ νεφέλῃ.*

[4] In Sanhedrin 96b, end, the cloud-man is Bar-Naphli (*νεφέλη*), the Messiah. Quoted in Yalḳuṭ on Amos 9, 11 (§ 549).

[5] Tanḥuma ed. Buber, Toledot § 20. "Who is 'Anani? This is the King-Messiah, as it is said (Dan. 7, 3), 'I saw in night visions, and behold, with the clouds ('*anane*) of heaven,' etc. — This relatively late Midrash is not testimony that a similar interpretation was current in the first century; it is only an illustration of a *kind* that might have originated at any time.

Akiba's explanation of the 'thrones' (Dan. 7, 9), where the question, Why the plural? drew out various conjectures. Akiba's was, "One for Him and one for David" (the Messiah). His colleagues, who had no great opinion of the haggadic adventures of the famous jurist, induced him to adopt the opinion of R. Jose the Galilean, only to get another rebuff from R. Eleazar ben Azariah, who had one of his own;[1] but it remains that Akiba saw for himself no objection to assigning the second throne to the Messiah.

Some one who rejoiced in a divinatory faculty might even be tempted to guess that not only was Dan. 7, 9–14 taken messianically in the first century, but that the contrast between the Messiah coming with the clouds of heaven and the lowly Messiah coming riding on an ass had already attracted notice. Jesus' entry into Jerusalem in the latter character[2] stands over against the ominous advent of the Son of Man to judgment,[3] and Joshua ben Levi's formula might easily be inverted: If Israel is worthy, 'lowly and riding on an ass' (as a peaceful prince); if it is not worthy, 'with the clouds of heaven' (to judgment).

In 4 Esdras 13, 1 ff. the seer has a vision of something like a man[4] brought up by the wind from the depths of the sea, flying with the clouds of heaven, whose glance struck terror into all he looked at or who heard his voice. An innumerable multitude gather from everywhere to make war upon him,[5] but without weapons he burns them to ashes by the fiery breath of his mouth;[6] thereupon he calls to him a peaceful multitude.[7] In the interpretation this man is the one whom the Most High has for a long time kept, through whom to deliver his creation; he will make disposition of those that are left (alive).[8]

[1] Hagigah 14a; Sanhedrin 38b.

[2] Mark 11, 1–11; Matt. 21, 1–13.

[3] Mark 13, 24–37; Matt. 24, 27–51.

[4] Thereafter, as in Enoch, 'that man,' 'the man who arose from the sea.'

[5] The last assault of the heathen, Ezek. 38, 1 ff. (Gog and Magog).

[6] Isa. 11, 4 of the 'shoot out of the stock of Jesse,' the Davidic Messiah.

[7] The nine and a half (ten) tribes, 13, 40.

[8] About whom Esdras has inquired, vss. 13–20, and the angel replied, vss. 22–25. The meaning of "et ipse *disponet* qui derelicti sunt" is uncertain.

In the vision of the Eagle (4 Esdras 11, 1–12, 39) which represents the Roman Empire with its successive rulers, the Lion who comes roaring out of the forest, inveighs against the eagle upbraiding it with all its crimes, and predicts its fall, which presently comes to pass, is "the Messiah, whom the Most High has kept until the end of days, who will spring from the race of David,[1] and will come. . . . First he will set them (the rulers) alive before the bar of judgment, and when he has accused them, will annihilate them. But the remnant of my people he will mercifully deliver, those who were preserved in my land, and will make them joyful until the day of the final judgment of which I have spoken to thee before." [2]

A counterpart to this is the vision of the Cedar and the Vine, of the end of the Roman empire, and of the Messiah who will condemn and slay its last ruler, and protect the remnant of God's people. "His dominion will last forever until the perishable world comes to an end and the predicted times are fulfilled."[3]

In the visions of Esdras and Baruch the actual situation is evident; the destruction of the sacred city with its temple is fresh in memory; the end of the fourth empire of Daniel (Rome) is at hand. The Messiah has a more active part than in Enoch; he makes way with the last heathen ruler and liberates the remnant of the people. But the whole drama moves on a fantastic stage, like the last conflict with the hordes that gather to war upon him in 4 Esdras 13, and the Messiah is a symbol, not a hero.

An important feature of this revived apocalyptic is that the Messianic Age is not final; it endures only till the last judgment.[4] Most explicit is 4 Esdras 7, 26–44: "When the now invisible city becomes visible, and the land now concealed appears. . . . my

[1] The Davidic descent is found in all the Oriental versions, but not in the Latin.

[2] 4 Esdras 12, 31–34.

[3] Syr. Baruch 36, 1–11; 39, 1–40, 4. See also the apocalypse of the alternate turbid and clear waters, especially 70, 1–71, 3; 72, 1–74, 4.

[4] 4 Esdras 12, 34; Syr. Baruch 40, 4.

Messiah will manifest himself with those that are with him, and will bring joy to those who remain (alive) for four hundred years. After those years my servant the Messiah will die, together with all who have human breath, and the world will revert to primaeval silence seven days as at the beginning, so that no one is left alive. And after seven days the world will be awakened, which is not yet awake, and the corruptible will die. The earth will give back those that sleep in it, and the dust those that rest in it, the treasuries (*promptuaria*) will give up the souls committed to them. The Most High will be revealed upon his judgment throne. Mercy will cease, compassion withdraw, and long-suffering vanish; justice alone will remain, truth abide, faithfulness flourish. Requital will follow, reward will be shown; righteousness will awake, and unrighteousness not sleep. The pit of torment will appear, and opposite it the place of repose; the furnace of hell will be disclosed, and opposite it the garden of delight. Then will the Most High say to the peoples who have been brought to life: See and recognize whom ye denied, whom ye did not serve, and whose commands ye spurned. See before you, here joy and rest, there fire and torment. So will he speak to them on the judgment day."

This representation is noteworthy in more than one respect. In the Parables of Enoch the old expectation of a national golden age is translated into a confused eschatology; in 4 Esdras and the Apocalypse of Baruch the two are separated: the last judgment and its issues lie beyond the Messianic Age, which thus becomes not final and endless, but a limited period, and recovers something of its original character.

The Revelation of John is a Christian apocalypse closely contemporary with 4 Esdras and the Syriac Baruch. In it, as in them, the Roman empire is the last and worst of the kingdoms of which Daniel had visions.[1] It has now reached the culmination of wickedness and God-defying power. The count of its rulers is all but complete;[2] the hour of its total and final ruin is

[1] Rev. 13, 1 ff.; Dan. 7, 1–7. [2] Rev. 17, 10 f.; 4 Esdras 12, 10 f.

at hand. The agent of God in its destruction is the Messiah.[1] The entire eschatological scheme is similar to that in the Jewish apocalypses of the time; it is in fact an adaptation of current Jewish constructions to Christian uses.

A complete presentation of this scheme is found in Rev. 19, 11–21, 8, and to that we may for our present purpose confine ourselves. The seer has a vision of heaven opened, and of the coming conqueror mounted on a white horse at the head of the armies of heaven on white horses and clad in pure white linen; the leader's mantle alone is besplashed with blood.[2] On his head are many crowns, inscribed with a name known only to himself.[3] His eyes are a flash of fire; from his mouth issues a sharp sword with which to smite the heathen.[4]

An angel, standing in the sun, summons all the vultures under heaven to the great feast of God on the field of slaughter, to devour the flesh of kings and generals and mighty men, of horses and their riders, of freemen and slaves, of small and great.[5] The 'beast'[6] and the kings of the earth with their hosts assemble to make war with the mounted warrior and his army. The beast is seized together with his satellite the false prophet,[7] and the pair are cast alive into the lake of sulphurous fire; their followers are slain by the sword that issues from the mouth[8] of the leader of the armies of heaven, and the birds gorge on their carcasses.

In the next scene an angel descends from heaven with the key of the abyss, and a great chain in his hand. The devil is seized, fettered, and hurled into the abyss, which is locked and sealed after him that he may do no more mischief among men for a thousand years.

[1] Rev. 19, 11 ff.; 4 Esdras 12, 31–34.

[2] Or, dyed in blood. See vs. 15 (Isa. 63, 1–6).

[3] Cf. Pesiḳta ed. Buber f. 148a, the new name to be given in the future by God to the Messiah (Psalm 72, 17).

[4] Cf. vs. 21. Isa. 11, 4. He will rule them with a rod of iron, Psalm 2, 9.

[5] Ezek. 39, 17–20.

[6] Rev. 13, 1.

[7] Rev. 13, 11–18.

[8] Isa. 11, 4; 49, 2.

Then thrones [1] are set, and they [2] take their seats upon them, and judicial authority is given to them. The souls of the Christian martyrs [3] appear, and such as did not worship the beast nor his image, and did not bear his mark on their foreheads and hands.[4] These live and reign with the Messiah for a thousand years. Peculiarly fortunate is the lot of those who have part in this first resurrection. The rest of the dead do not come to life till the thousand years are finished.

When that time comes, Satan will be released from his prison, and will raise the heathen nations far and wide, an innumerable host, for the war of Gog and Magog. They invade Palestine and invest Jerusalem, but fire pours down from heaven and devours them. The final onslaught of the heathen powers thus ends in catastrophe. The devil who deceived them is cast into the lake of fire and brimstone where the beast and the false prophet are, and they will be tortured there forever and ever.

Thereupon ensues the grand assize. The seer beholds God himself sitting on his judgment throne, and all the dead, great and small, standing before it. The sea gives up the dead that are in it, and death and hades the dead that are in them. The books in which men's deeds are recorded are open, and another book, the book of life, in which are inscribed the names of those who from the foundation of the world (17, 8; 13, 8) were destined to eternal life. The dead are judged each according to his record. Death and Hades, the old enemies of mankind, are cast into the lake of fire which is the second death; and to it also is consigned every one who is not found inscribed in the book of life.

The judgment of this world thus ended, there appear a new heaven and a new earth — there is no more sea; the holy city,[5] a new Jerusalem, descends out of heaven from God. Hence-

[1] Dan. 7, 9.

[2] Observe the indefiniteness about the occupants of these thrones.

[3] Executed for bearing witness to Jesus and for the 'word of God' (1, 9).

[4] And, it is to be understood, had suffered death for refusing to worship the emperor.

[5] In 21, 10–22, 6 a closer vision of this city is granted to the seer.

forth, it is proclaimed, the habitation of God will be among men on earth. There will be no more death, no sorrow nor wailing nor distress — all that has passed away forever; there is God's word for it, 'I make all things new.'

The distinctively Christian traits in this delineation are scarce. The surest is that the 'first resurrection' brings to life at the beginning of the messianic millennium, to live and reign with the victor, none but the martyrs who were executed for the witness they bore to Jesus and for the word of God,[1] and those who did not worship the beast nor his image, and did not receive the mark on their forehead and their hand.[2] Christian is also the exhortation and warning appended to the vision in the name of God (21, 8). The name of the conquering hero, the 'Word of God' (19, 13), is evidently Christian,[3] but it may be doubted whether it is original.[4]

Otherwise the whole conception is Jewish. Jerusalem is to be the seat of the theocracy in the future as in the past. It is, indeed, a new Jerusalem which comes down from heaven in place of the old; [5] but it is Jerusalem on its old site that is henceforth to be the abode of God among men. The final stage in this eschatology is on earth, however transfigured — 'a new heaven and a new earth,' but earth still, and not somewhere above the sky. Life is human life, not what is called a spiritual existence; the very negations prove it — there is no more death, no sorrow nor wailing (of the bereaved) nor distress. Comparison with the other apocalypses abundantly confirms the internal evidence of the Jewish character of Rev. 19, 11–21, 8.

[1] The biblical proofs they alleged.

[2] Rev. 20, 4. They refused to do religious homage to the emperor, and suffered death for it. — Jews were by special privilege exempted from this demonstration of loyalty.

[3] John 1, 1.

[4] It stands in an awkward place, and only a few words before the author wrote that he has a name inscribed (presumably on the multiple crown) which no one knew but himself (see below, pp. 348 f). Vs. 16 is not parallel, for there the 'name' is only a title.

[5] See Enoch 90, 28 f.; Syriac Baruch 4, 2–7; 4 Esdras 7, 26; 8, 52; 10, 26 ff., 54; 13, 36. Cf. also Tobit 13, 16–18, with Rev. 21, 10 ff. The biblical antecedents may be found in Ezek. 40 ff.; Isa. 52, 1; 54, 11 f.; 60, 10–14, etc.

Imaginatively the vision of the conquering hero is superior to the corresponding visions in Esdras and Baruch with their grotesque allegorical Eagle and Lion [1] or Cedar and Vine, but the fundamental ideas are the same. In other parts of the book the Christian element is more prominent, and the visions are frequently unvisualizable.[2]

The apocalypses from the last decades of the first century show how after the catastrophe of the year 70 faith took refuge in visions of an imminent intervention to destroy the Roman empire and the city of Rome itself,[3] and usher in a new era in fulfilment of ancient prophecies. Occasionally there are veiled hints of real flesh-and-blood nations which might be the instruments of this overthrow, as in the Revelation of John the Parthian hordes [4] with the returning Nero,[5] but in general the visionaries keep on safer ground than contemporary history, even masked.

The premise of their fantasies is that historical events and personages are prefigured in a symbolic drama played on a celestial stage, as in Daniel the conflict with the Persian and Macedonian empires is symbolized by the single combat of the terrifying 'man' (angel) who appears to the prophet, supported by Michael the champion of the Jews, with the prince of Persia and the prince of Greece successively.[6] It is scenes of this mystifying drama that are exhibited to the seers and explained to them by angelic interpreters, who sometimes keep up the mystery.

The visionary form conditions the whole representation. The prophet predicted the Messiah in the nearer or more remote future; the visionary sees him on the celestial stage. The prophet may foretell the restoration of Jerusalem, greater and more glorious than ever; the visionary sees a new Jerusalem descending from heaven to take the place of the old. What else could

1 Symbols of Rome and Judah.
2 For example the rôle of the lamb.
3 As in Rev. 17, 1–19, 10.
4 Rev. 9, 13 ff. (Joel 2, 3); cf. 6, 2; 16, 12.
5 Rev. 17; cf. Ascension of Isaiah 4, 2 ff.
6 Dan. 10; cf. 12, 1.

he do?[1] Did he, therefore, imagine that the Messiah was really existent in heaven, waiting God's hour to be revealed, or his new Jerusalem as a real city built in heaven, one day to be let down to earth?[2] Or rather, was this the original conception; for after this manner of representation became an apocalyptic convention, writers may have taken thus realistically the imagery of their predecessors, and the common man was sure to do so.

It is the question of what with an ambiguous name is called "pre-existence," especially the "pre-existence of the Messiah," which has been given an exaggerated importance on account of its supposed relation to Christian beliefs. For Judaism it makes very little matter what the apocalyptic writers imagined about it. On that question it is pertinent to observe that Esdras and Baruch are contemporary with the great generation of Tannaim, the disciples of Johanan ben Zakkai and their successors; that the authors were evidently men of some respectable learning, which meant in those days a relation to the schools; and there is no sectarian eccentricity to be discovered in them. Under these circumstances there is a certain presumption that they were not consciously at variance with rabbinical teaching on this point. The Tannaim, as we shall see, counted "the name of the Messiah" among the things that preceded the world,[3] but not the person of the Messiah.

The eschatological scheme is in its general features the same in all these apocalypses. It was evidently the accepted construction, and is in conformity with what we find in the rabbinical sources. The Messianic Age comes to an end with a last great outbreak and onslaught of the heathen nations.[4] They invade

[1] When tours through the heavens came to be told of highly esteemed rabbis, as of Joshua ben Levi, for example, they also *see* the Messiah waiting for his hour; but it would be rash to impute to these Haggadists a belief in a "pre-existent Messiah."

[2] That there was in heaven a counterpart of the earthly city, or particularly of the temple, is an entirely different notion.

[3] Psalm 72, 17: 'His name is eternal, before the sun his name flourished.'

[4] Ezek. 38 f., Gog and Magog. Sometimes this act is put at the beginning of the messianic times, which was probably its original place.

the land of Israel only to be exterminated by God. The dead of all generations, righteous and wicked, rise from their graves to appear before God in the last judgment. The earth is transformed to be the unending abode of the righteous; the wicked are cast, soul and body, into a hell of fire.

This judgment with its issues is the definitive stage of individual retribution.

The calamitous outcome of the rebellion of the Jews in the reign of Nero, ending in the taking of the ruins of Jerusalem and the burning of the temple in 70 A.D., seemed to those who stayed their faith on prophecy to be the final chapter of God's judgments on the nation; the new leaf must be the beginning of the great deliverance which in the prophets follows so abruptly on the climax of catastrophe. And it was natural that the deliverance should present itself in political form; the appearance of the Messiah, the overthrow of the Roman empire, the establishment of the peaceful and prosperous national kingdom of the house of David. In the apocalypses from the last decades of the century we have seen that this expectation clothed itself in preternatural imagery. From the representative teachers of the last generation of the first century and the beginning of the second few well-attested utterances are reported. They had in the study and inculcation of the Law a task of greater moment than thinking about the when and how of deliverance — namely, to make their people capable of deliverance.

Then Hadrian's announced intention to rebuild Jerusalem as a heathen city, with a temple of Jupiter where once had stood that of the true God, raised the Jews of Palestine in desperate revolt again under the lead of Bar Kozibah, whom Akiba acclaimed as the Messiah, the Star out of Jacob who was to subdue Edom-Rome.[1] The hopelessly unequal conflict ended in bloody failure; the militant Messiah fell fighting with thousands of his followers. The disillusion was stunning. The attempt to desig-

[1] Num. 24, 17–19. See above, p. 116.

nate God's Messiah for him proved itself presumptuous; the deciphering of dates and unriddling of signs had been fatal mistakes.

This attitude and temper seem to express themselves in all that has come down to us from the rabbis for the remainder of the century. There is a noteworthy reticence, an evident disposition not to be wise beyond what is written, a sobriety in striking contrast to the enthusiastic constructions of the apocalypses. The following centuries are less reserved; the homilists especially use the freedom of their calling in messianic and eschatological interpretation, and bring out again much of this kind that had come down from earlier generations.

In this place we shall confine ourselves as closely as possible to the authentic utterances of the Tannaim. It must be premised that these utterances themselves are occasional, touching on particular points as they arise; they are not topics of a doctrine of the Messiah or of the Last Things. In exhibiting them here it is necessary to give them a semblance of system which they have not in the sources themselves. Further, with small exceptions — the resurrection is the most conspicuous — however generally accepted, they have no dogmatic authority.

Of fundamental importance in this whole sphere is the conviction that the end of God's ways in the history of the world, past, present, and to come, is the universal recognition of his own sovereignty, the time when the Lord shall be King (ruling) over all the earth; when the Lord shall be One and his name one (Zech. 14, 9).[1] This is the Malkut Shamaim, the sovereign reign of Heaven, the universality of the true religion.[2]

To this end the vindication in the eyes of the nations of Israel as the people of the Lord, and of the Lord himself as the God of Israel, is a necessary step, as is especially emphasized in Ezekiel and in Isaiah 40 ff. The low estate of the Jews in subjection to

[1] 'One,' as Israel confesses and proclaims in the Shema', and when all other names of gods shall disappear, and all men worship the one God under his name IHVH.

[2] See Vol. I, pp. 229 f.; 432 ff.

the heathen empires seemed to the Gentiles conclusive proof of the impotence of the god whom they called the only God in the whole world. The coming deliverance was, therefore, not only the fulfilment of the hope of the nation, it was the beginning of a new era for religion itself.

That this was all to come to pass the prophets had foretold with no uncertain voice; but to the question, How? many diverse answers could be found in them. To us this diversity reflects the changing historical situations, internal and external, in which the oracles were emitted; but to the Jews with their conception of unitary revelation this way of interpreting them was no way. At the most they could only refer them to different epochs in the unfolding of history yet to be.

What may be called the classic form of the expectation of a golden age for the nation pictured it as the reign of a wise and good king of the old royal line of Judah, who in this age was commonly called the Anointed King (Messiah).[1] The Davidic lineage of the ruler was found plainly and frequently in the Scriptures, and on this point there seems to have been complete agreement.[2] In place of the "Anointed One, son of David," "Son of David" by itself became a common designation of the Messiah. There were passages in the prophets where this figure is called simply "David," which opened the way to the surmise that the deliverer of the future and the king of the golden age would be no other than the deliverer from the oppression of the Philistines and founder of the kingdom himself.[3]

Others seem to have thought of Hezekiah in a similar rôle.[4]

[1] See above, p. 336.

[2] The opinion of a certain R. Hillel, not to be confounded with the great Hillel, "Israel has no Messiah (to come); they enjoyed (lit. consumed) him in the days of Hezekiah" (Sanhedrin 98b, 99a), is solitary, and was refuted by R. Joseph, head of the academy at Pumbeditha (d. 322 A.D.) by reference to the messianic predictions in Zechariah from a time long after Hezekiah.

[3] See above, pp. 324 f.

[4] What put them on this king in particular was presumably the miraculous destruction of Sennacherib's hosts beneath the walls of Jerusalem as narrated in 2 Kings 18, 13–19, 36.

In the hour of his death R. Johanan ben Zakkai bade his disciples, "Set a seat for Hezekiah king of Judah, who is coming." [1] One of the last of the Tannaim, Bar Ḳappara, in a homily at Sepphoris, took the closed *mem* in the middle of a word (לםרבה) in Isa. 9, 6 to signify the end of Hezekiah's messianic prospects: God proposed to make Hezekiah the Messiah and Sennacherib Gog and Magog, but the divine justice objected that that was unfair to David who had made so many hymns in praise of God, while Hezekiah for whom He had wrought so many miracles had not made even one. Further voices were raised on either side, and finally a heavenly voice (*bat ḳol*) was heard saying, It is my secret. The prophet exclaimed, Alas, alas! how long? and the same voice answered, 'The faithless deal faithlessly, with utter faithlessness do the faithless deal' (Isa. 24, 16).[2] A familiar appellation of the Messiah in later generations is Menahem (ben Hezekiah). Menahem (Comforter) is here symbolic, suggested by Lam. 1, 16, 'Far from me is a comforter (*menaḥem*),[3] one to restore my life,' and the phrase is in origin a symbol rather than a proper name. It was perhaps commended by another consideration; Menahem is equivalent to Ṣemaḥ, Scion (of David), the oldest designation of the coming king of the golden age,[4] the numerical value of each being 138.[5]

As we have seen, the "name of the Messiah" was in the mind of God before the creation of the world, but He had not revealed it. Guesses were free, but they are hardly meant even as serious guesses when the disciples of great teachers competed in puns on their masters' names — those of R. Shela (שילה) said that

[1] Berakot 28b.

[2] Sanhedrin 94a. See the interpretation which follows (4th century); "until there come robbers and robbers of the robbers" (one empire spoiling its predecessor).

[3] Lam. R. on 1, 16, near the end (ed. Wilna f. 18c). Cf. Lam. 1, 9.

[4] Above, pp. 324 f.

[5] Jer. Berakot 5a, above. Ḥanina bar Abahu, fourth century; Lam. R. l. s. c. In both places there follows in the name of the same fourth century Amora (Aibo) the story of how the 'Comforter' was born in Bethlehem on the night when Jerusalem was destroyed, and carried off by a storm wind.

it was Shiloh (Gen. 49, 10); those of R. Yannai that it was Yinnon (Psalm 72, 17); those of R. Ḥanina that it was Ḥanina (Jer. 16, 13).[1]

There is no trace in the Tannaite sources of any idea that the Messiah himself was an antemundane creation, or that he was regarded otherwise than as a man of human kind. Even if David was imagined to come again, that would be miraculous, but not more extraordinary than that Elijah should be taken up to heaven bodily, to be sent down to earth again before the great and terrible day of the Lord. In fact, as God had no mythical laws of nature to respect, there was no reason why he should always act according to men's observation of his ordinary ways. Nor did any mystery there might be about the person of the Messiah, or the mode and circumstance of his appearance, make a preternatural being of him. He might be, by God's singular favor, a wiser and better and greater king than was ever seen, but not a supernatural being. For demigods Jewish monotheism had no room. If the Messiah wrought miracles, that was no more than Moses had done, and Elijah, and many others. It was God who really did it, by what instruments he chose in ancient or modern times.[2]

In a sermon of Bar Ḳappara he allegorizes on the six measures of barley that Boaz gave to Ruth (Ruth 3, 15): Ruth was to have six descendants each of whom was to have six special "blessings" (gifts), beginning with David, whose six are recited in 1 Sam. 16, 18, and ending with the Messiah whose great qualities are enumerated in Isa. 11, 2, 'The Spirit of the Lord shall rest upon him, the spirit of wisdom and insight, the spirit of counsel and heroism, the spirit of knowledge and godliness.'[3] This seems to be the only reference to the passage in Tannaite sources.[4]

[1] Sanhedrin 98b. Schools of the third century; Shela in Babylonia, the other two in Palestine. [2] See Vol. I, pp. 276 ff.

[3] Literally, 'the fear of the Lord.' — Sanhedrin 93a–b and parallels in the Midrashim.

[4] In the sequel, Isa. 11, 3 is quoted by Raba in a story to show that Bar Kozibah did not come up to the test.

If it were asked under what conditions and in what circumstances the advent of the Son of David might be expected, two contradictory answers offered themselves, namely, When the people had made itself worthy of the great deliverance, or, When the decadence of religion and morals had reached its lowest point and made divine intervention necessary. The alternative is left in equipoise in the sentence, The Messiah son of David will come only in a generation that is wholly worthy or in one that is wholly guilty.[1]

The former is represented by the words of Levi elsewhere quoted: If Israel should keep only a single sabbath as it is prescribed, at once the Messiah would come.[2] A much older utterance to the same intent comes from R. Simeon ben Yoḥai: Should Israel keep two sabbaths according to rule (*halakah*), forthwith they would be delivered.[3] Of charity it is said, Great is charity, for it brings the deliverance nearer, as it is said, 'Thus saith the Lord, maintain ye justice and practise charity,[4] for my salvation is near to come and my loving kindness to be revealed' (Isa. 56, 1).[5]

Of more consequence than such sporadic dicta supported by subtleties of exegesis are the utterances which make the coming of the Messiah conditional on repentance, we might say, on a complete reformation. This is the burden of the prophets from first to last; it is written in some of the most pertinent and impressive chapters of the Law. The cumulative disasters of the century, the failure of one hope after another of the expected deliverance, put urgency into the efforts of the responsible leaders of Judaism to promote a revival of religion that should bring the people as a whole into that conformity with his will which was the only way to recover and secure God's favor. Great is re-

[1] Sanhedrin 98a; cf. Pesiḳta ed. Buber f. 51b. R. Johanan, for the former quoting Isa. 60, 21, for the latter Isa. 59, 16 and 48, 11.

[2] Jer. Ta'anit 64a, middle. Proof, Exod. 16, 25 combined with Isa. 30, 15.

[3] Shabbat 118b, middle. Isa. 56, 4 and 7. Cf. Sifrè Deut. § 41 (f. 79b): If ye keep the Law, expect Elijah (Mal. 3, 22 f.).

[4] *Ṣedaḳah*, almsgiving.

[5] Baba Batra 10a.

pentance, for it brings deliverance nearer, as it is said, 'There comes to Zion a deliverer, and to those who turn from transgression in Jacob' (Isa. 59, 20).[1]

R. Eliezer ben Hyrcanus maintained that if Israel did not repent they would never be delivered, quoting Isa. 30, 15, 'By repentance[2] and quietness ye shall be saved.' R. Joshua ben Hananiah replied, Really, if Israel stays as it is and does not repent, will it never be delivered? R. Eliezer replied, God will raise up over them a king as hard as Haman, and forthwith they will repent, and they will be delivered. 'It is a time of distress for Jacob, and out of it he shall be saved' (Jer. 30, 7).[3] Joshua thereupon quoted Isa. 52, 3, 'Ye were sold for nought and without silver shall ye be delivered.'[4] His position was, Whether they repent or do not repent, when the fixed time comes they will be delivered, as it is written, 'I, the Lord, in its time I will hasten it' (Isa. 60, 22). To similar effect a saying of R. Joshua ben Levi is cited: If ye are worthy I will hasten it; and if ye are not worthy, 'in its time.'[5]

In his plan of universal history God has set a definite time for the great deliverance, which not even the unrepented sin of Israel can postpone. For both opinions equally numerous and weighty proof-texts could be found. Later we find some holding the opinion that the time God intended has come and gone by, because the people was not fit. Thus Rab: All dates for the end have expired, and the matter now depends solely on repentance and good works.[6] It is sin that delays the inauguration of the golden age which by every reckoning should have begun long ago. On the six thousand year scheme,— two thousand 'empti-

[1] Yoma 86b, above; cf. Yalḳuṭ on Isa. l. c. (§ 498). R. Jose the Galilean (it brings deliverance to the world).

[2] Taking *shubah* in the sense of *teshubah*.

[3] The context should be noted.

[4] Jer. Ta'anit 63d, below; cf. Tanḥuma ed. Buber, Beḥuḳḳotai § 5 end. A slightly different version in Sanhedrin 97b–98a: Eliezer quotes Jer. 3, 22; Mal. 3, 7; Isa. 30, 15; Jer. 4, 1. R. Joshua finally cites Dan. 12, 7. This last silenced R. Eliezer. See Bacher, Tannaiten I, 144 f.

[5] Jer. Ta'anit l. c.

[6] Sanhedrin 97b.

ness' (תהו), two thousand Law (תורה), two thousand Messianic Age,—"By reason of our multiplied iniquities there have passed as many of them (years properly belonging to the Messianic Age) as have passed."[1]

Daniel had applied apocalyptic arithmetic to the date of the great revolution. Esdras found that Daniel had misunderstood his revelation, and revised the calculation so as to bring the fall of the Fourth Empire—now the Roman—within his own horizon; and this became a habit. It is probable that similar corrected computations were made in the time of the Bar Cocheba war. After the calamitous issue of the revolt had discredited its Messiah, mistrust of all attempts to fix a date for God and censure of those who tried it prevailed. Rabbi Nathan, who occupied a high station in the academy of Rabban Simeon ben Gamaliel and subsequently often appears in discussion with Rabbi, quotes Hab. 2, 3 as a verse which pierced to the profoundest depths: 'The vision is yet for the appointed time, and it hurries on to the end and does not deceive. If it delay, wait confidently for it, for it will surely come, and will not delay (indefinitely).'[2] The interpretations of earlier authorities ("our rabbis") are disapproved, who operated with the 'time, two times, and half a time' of Dan. 7, 25, and of R. Akiba, who relied on Hag. 2, 6, 'Yet one, a little it is, and I will convulse the heavens and the earth.'[3]

R. Samuel bar Naḥman in the name of his master Jonathan (ben Eleazar), a Palestinian teacher of the first half of the third century, pronounces an imprecation on the calculators: "Blast the bones of those who reckon out 'ends,' for when their computed 'end' comes and he (the Messiah) does not come, they say, Well then, he is not coming."[4]

[1] 'Abodah Zarah 9a; cf. Seder Eliahu Rabbah c. 2 (ed. Friedmann p. 6) and Friedmann's Introduction, p. 46.

[2] Sanhedrin 97b.

[3] The following context (vss. 7–9) must be considered as also in mind.—In what way Akiba extracted a prediction of time from the text is not plain. For different conjectures see Rashi in loc. and Meharsha.

[4] Sanhedrin l. c.

Jonathan ben Uzziel, the author of the Targum on the Prophets, is said to have contemplated doing a similar work for the Hagiographa, but was deterred by a mysterious voice (*bat ḳol*) saying, No more! This prohibition, it is explained, was because in the Hagiographa (Daniel) the fixed term for the Messiah was given.[1] An interpretative translation into the vernacular would put it into the power of laymen to speculate on the date of his coming as well as scholars, a thing of which they had a wholesome apprehension.

Renunciation of all attempts to compute the time is the meaning of Jose ben Ḥalafta, the great chronologist: "Whoever knows how many years Israel worshipped other gods, he knows when the Son of David will come." For this there are three proof-texts, Hos. 2, 15; Zech. 7, 13; Jer. 5, 19.[2] Another harmless term is set when it is said: The Son of David will not come until all the souls that are in the repository[3] are exhausted;[4] as it is written, ('I will not forever contend, nor will I eternally be wroth,) for the spirit would faint before me and the souls I have created' (Isa. 57, 16).[5]

Not all teachers were content to leave the question in complete abeyance. R. Ḥanina, in the first generation of the third century, reckoning, apparently, on the six thousand year scheme, said: When four hundred years have passed since the destruc-

1 Megillah 3a.

2 Lam. R. Proemium no. 21.

3 *Gūf.* The place in which souls not yet embodied are kept until it is time for them to be born. Cf. Lev. R. 15, 1 (opinion of the majority — Rabbanan) or, Until all the souls which it entered into God's intention to create are exhausted (same proof-text). Creationist hypothesis; whereas in the former the assumption is that all souls were created at the beginning.

4 'Abodah Zarah 5a; Niddah 13b; Yebamot 62a, 63b. In the last place, attributed by R. Huna to Rab Assi, in the other two it is ascribed to R. Jose. See Bacher, Pal. Amoräer, II, 172; Klausner, Die messianischen Vorstellungen des jüdischen Volkes, u. s. w., pp. 37 f.

5 The verb יעטוף is translated 'faint' in conformity to the context in Isaiah. It is possible that in the quotation the rabbis took it in the meaning 'be belated' (cf. Gen. 30, 42). For an interpretation in this sense see Rashi on Niddah 13b. Marriage with a little girl, who cannot conceive, 'retards the deliverance,' which will not come until every soul that God created has been implanted in an embryo.

tion of the temple, if a man offers you a piece of land worth a thousand dinars for one dinar, do not take it.[1] An otherwise unknown Tannaite tradition quoted in the same place has the same conclusion to a reckoning from the era of creation — "4231 years after the creation of the world." Ḥanina's date for the deliverance is a century or so in his own future, and the calculation from the creation closely coincides with it. The Messianic Age is still a long way off.[2]

Many prophecies dealt in signs of the impending crisis — signs among the nations, signs in nature, significant conditions among the Jews themselves. The critic looks in them for the marks of particular historical situations from the days of the Assyrians down, but to the Jewish interpreters they portended the great coming crisis, or at least were typical of it.

The Sibyllines and the apocalypses naturally abound in signs of the last times, which in accordance with their feigned origin, they habitually envelop in mystery and not infrequently in Delphic ambiguity.

The sole rivals to the Roman empire in the East were the Parthians. There were moments in the conflict of the two powers when the Roman armies suffered signal disasters at their hands; and it is not strange that Jewish hopes should sometimes have fastened upon them as the predestined instrument in God's plan for the destruction of Rome, as in a like situation Persia had destroyed the empire of Babylon and delivered the Jews. Jose ben Ḳisma, who in the time of Hadrian recognized the Roman rule as of God's ordaining,[3] and warned Ḥanina ben Teradion of the consequences of defying the edict against teaching, bade his disciples bury his coffin deep, for there is not a single palm tree in Babylonia to which a Persian horse will not be tied, and not

[1] 'Abodah Zarah 9b. When the deliverance comes all alienated lands will revert to the heirs of those to whom they were originally allotted.

[2] Cf. also the story of the roll found by a Jewish mercenary in "Roman" (Byzantine) service, in a Roman treasure-house. Sanhedrin 97b. Some editions of the Talmud have "Persian" instead of "Roman."

[3] See above, p. 114.

a single coffin in the land of Israel from which a Median horse will not be eating straw.[1] In the next generation R. Simeon ben Yoḥai, a disciple of Akiba, is reported to have said, When you see a Persian horse tied in the land of Israel then look for the feet of the Messiah.[2] These forecasts are as indefinite as another of Jose ben Ḳisma, that when the gate of the city (Caesarea Philippi or Tiberias?)[3] had fallen and been rebuilt twice, and a third time fallen,[4] before the rebuilding was again finished, the Son of David would come.[5]

Even such vague ventures are, however, unusual. Instead of conjectures when the Messiah is to come we find the formula: "The Son of David will not come until" this or that takes place; for example, until the good-for-nothing[6] kingdom has altogether ceased out of Israel, as it is said, 'He will cut off the good-for-nothing shoots[7] with pruning-hooks'[8] (Isa. 18, 5), and further on, 'In that time there shall be brought a present to the Lord of Hosts, a people,' etc. (vs. 9).[9] Or, until the arrogant cease out of Israel, as it is written, 'I will remove from the midst of thee those who exult in their eminence . . . and I will leave in the midst of thee a folk lowly and poor, and they will take refuge in the name of the Lord' (Zeph. 3, 11, 12).[10] Or, until all judges and other officials cease out of Israel (Isa. 1, 25 f.).[11] The author specifies things obnoxious to him as particular hindrances to the coming of the Messiah; the texts he cites in support are sometimes, as in the first saying quoted above, evidence of nothing but misplaced ingenuity.

[1] The stone coffins robbed from the tombs to use as feeding troughs. — Sanhedrin 98a–b. Persian and Median are the ancient historical names for the peoples of the Parthian empire.

[2] Lam. R. on 1, 13, with Mic. 5, 4 for biblical support. In Cant. R. on 8, 9, 'tied to tombs in the land of Israel.'

[3] See Bacher, Tannaiten, I, 398 f.

[4] Probably in a siege of the city.

[5] Sanhedrin 98a, end.

[6] *Zallah.*

[7] *Zalzallim.* The whole point lies in the play on the words.

[8] 'Pruning' is a frequent figure for the cutting off of nations; see e.g. Cant. R. on 2, 13 (Canaanites, Babylonians, etc.).

[9] Sanhedrin 98a.

[10] Ibid.

[11] Ibid.

Others aver that the Son of David will not come until informers multiply;[1] or until the whole empire goes over to heresy,[2] or until the Jews despair of ever being delivered—'None is left, confined or at large' (Deut. 32, 36),[3] as if, to speak reverently, Israel had no supporter or helper.[4]

The rabbis frequently dwell on the grave moral and religious declension which gives warning that the Messiah is at the door. Thus, R. Judah (ben Ila'i) said: "In the generation in which the Son of David comes, the meeting-house[5] will become a brothel; Galilee will be devasted and the Gaulan[6] laid waste; the Galileans[7] will go around from city to city and find no compassion; the learning of scholars will be a stench in men's nostrils, and those that fear sin will be despised; the countenance of the generation will be as impudent as a dog's, and truth not to be found" (Isa. 59, 15).[8]

R. Nehemiah, another of Akiba's disciples, said: "Before the days of the Messiah poverty will increase and high prices will prevail; the vine will give its fruit, but the wine will spoil. The whole empire will turn to heresy, and there will be no reprehension (of it)."[9] To adduce but one more illustration, R. Nehorai, in the same generation with the two scholars whose words are quoted above, said: "In the generation in which the Son of David comes youths will insult their elders, and elders will stand in the presence of youths. Daughter will rise up against her mother,

[1] As was no doubt the case in the days of Hadrian's edict.

[2] Reflecting the impression of the rapid spread of Christianity in the second century and the third (R. Isaac). Cf. R. Nehemiah, below.

[3] I.e. no one at all is left. A proverbial expression; cf. 2 Kings 14, 26; 1 Kings 14, 10.

[4] All these in Sanhedrin 97a.

[5] *Bet wa'd.* Place of learned assembly.

[6] The region east of the Sea of Galilee and the upper Jordan.

[7] So cod. Monac. The common text has אנשי הגבול, 'inhabitants of the borders.' Cf. Eccles. R. c. 1 § 6, R. Jacob נבולאי.

[8] Sanhedrin 97a. In Cant. R. on 2, 13, attributed to R. Simeon ben Yoḥai (with minor variations). Cf. also Pesiḳta ed. Buber f. 51b (R. Abin).

[9] Sanhedrin 97a. The translation follows the text in Cant. R. on 2, 13 as the more consistent and intelligible. Cf. also Soṭah 49b, top.

and daughter-in-law against her mother-in-law.[1] The countenance of the generation will be like a dog's for impudence; even a son will have no shame in the presence of his own father." [2]

A more particular description is given of the 'week' (seven years) in which the Son of David comes:[3] The first year fulfils this verse, 'I will make it rain on one city, and on another I will not make it rain' (Amos 4, 7). The second will be partial famine;[4] the third a great famine in which men, women, and little children will die, pious men and men of good works, and the Law will be forgotten by its students. In the fourth there will be enough food but not enough; in the fifth great abundance, they will eat and drink and rejoice, and the Law will come back to its students. In the sixth there will be thunderous sounds. In the seventh, wars; at the end of the seventh the Son of David comes.[5]

It is small wonder that a later Babylonian teacher, Rab Joseph, exclaimed, Ever so many such septennial periods have gone by, and he has not come! Abaye's answer to this was, "In the sixth thunders, in the seventh wars," — have these come to pass? and further, have these things occurred in just the order indicated? [6]

It was the universal belief that shortly before the appearance of the Messiah Elijah should return: 'Behold, I will send you Elijah the prophet before the coming of the great and terrible day of the Lord. And he will turn the heart of the fathers to the children and the heart of the children to their fathers, lest I come and smite the land with a ban' (Mal. 3, 23). There is no more

[1] Micah 7, 6. The Pesiḳta completes the quotation, 'a man's enemies are the men of his own household.' Matt. 10, 35 f.

[2] Sanhedrin 97a; cf. Pesiḳta ed. Buber 51b.

[3] Cf. Syr. Baruch. 27, 1–28, 2.

[4] Literally, 'arrows of famine' (Ezek. 5, 16).

[5] Sanhedrin 97a; cf. Cant. R. on 2, 13 (R. Johanan), with variants; Pesiḳta ed. Buber f. 51a–b. The 'thunderous sounds' (*kolot*) are perhaps suggested by Exod. 19, 16–19, proclaiming that God is at hand. Compare the 'sound of a horn growing louder and louder' vs. 16. Understood as the horn which announces the coming of the Son of David (Isa. 27, 13). Rashi on Sanhedrin 97b.

[6] In Cant. R. it is Abaye who makes the plaint here attributed to R. Joseph.

dramatic figure in all biblical story than Elijah, from the moment when he appears abruptly upon the scene announcing to Ahab in short, stunning words the coming years of drought and famine to the last act when he is rapt away into the heavens in a chariot of fire with horses of fire. The prophet was the incarnation of zeal for the Lord.[1] For the God of Israel, on Mount Carmel, against the intruder Baal, against all his priests and devotees, against his royal patrons, the king and queen. No god but Jehovah should be worshipped in Israel's land. For the Lord as the vindicator of the rights of the Israelite freeman, against Ahab and Jezebel in the crime of Naboth's vineyard. It was in the same zeal for the Lord that he was to come to earth again, precursor of the great and terrible day of the Lord, if by bringing the people to a better mind the impending ban might be averted. The impression his career and the mission assigned to him in Malachi made on later times may be read in Sirach in the paragraph allotted to him in the Praise of the Fathers.[2]

Elijah's historical mission was to bring Israel back to wholehearted allegiance to its own God and his righteous will, and the prophecy of his return spoke only of a work to be done in Israel. His part was the preparation of the people for the imminent crisis, which in the centuries we are dealing with was understood to be the appearance of the Messiah.

What, more precisely, he was to do is not made plain in Malachi, and various opinions are reported. Sirach interprets his mission, "to set to rights [3] the tribes of Jacob." Some thought that Elijah's business would be to settle questions of clean and unclean, about which the dissensions of the schools threatened to make the Law "two laws"; others that he would straighten out questions of ancestry — for which undoubtedly inspiration

[1] In this he is like Phineas, the typical zealot (Num. 25, 7–12; Psalm 106, 30 f.; Ecclus. 45, 23 f.), and comes finally to be identified with him, and thus to be a priest.

[2] Ecclus. 48, 1–12. Sirach does not connect the return of Elijah with the appearance of the Messiah, of whom, indeed, there is no mention in the book.

[3] להכין. Greek *καταστῆσαι*; cf. Isa. 49, 6, להקים, *στῆσαι*.

was necessary — in anticipation of the coming of the Messiah.[1] Was such and such a family of pure Israelite stock, and entitled to be registered as genuine Jews, or was it contaminated with alien blood?[2] Elijah would see that the former got their rights, and exclude the latter. Johanan ben Zakkai gave it out as a "Halakah of Moses from Sinai" (an immemorial tradition) that Elijah came to do neither, but to remove those who had been arbitrarily registered among the pure-blood Jews and restore such as had been arbitrarily struck out.[3] Other Tannaim held that he would restore but not remove; or remove but not restore. Others that he would compose differences in the schools;[4] or that Malachi's words meant to make peace in the world.[5]

None of the earlier sources makes it Elijah's especial mission to bring Israel to repentance. The Pirḳè de-R. Eliezer, however, quotes R. Judah: Unless Israel repents they will not be delivered; and Israel never repents except out of tribulations and oppression and exile and want of a living. Israel will not make the great repentance until Elijah comes (Mal. 3, 23).[6] The conception must be much older than this testimony; John the Baptist is a witness to it.

Nor does Elijah in any ancient source announce that the Messiah is shortly coming or is come. It was, however, expected that Elijah would restore to Israel three things that had been concealed with the ark before the destruction of the temple;

[1] Cf. Ḳiddushin 70b below (Ḥama bar Ḥanina): When God lets his Presence (*Shekinah*) rest (i.e. when He himself resides among them), he lets it rest only on pedigreed families in Israel (Jer. 31, 1).

[2] The question was of peculiar moment after the recent wars in which cities were sacked, and the country overrun by a licentious soldiery, many women enslaved, etc.

[3] Illustrations are given in the case of certain families in the region east of the Jordan.

[4] Various concrete questions in dispute or doubt are reserved "until Elijah comes," e.g. M. Sheḳalim 2, 5 end; Pesaḥim 13a, 20b.

[5] 'Eduyot 8, 7. On the whole subject see M. Friedmann, Seder Eliahu Rabba, Introduction, pp. 23–25.

[6] Pirḳè de-R. Eliezer c. 43, end; cf. c. 47, where 'repentance' (*teshubah*) is got out of a play on the words in 1 Kings 17, 1, Elijah was of the settlers (*toshebè*) of Gilead.

viz., the jar of manna, and the flask of water of lustration, and the flask of anointing oil; some added Aaron's rod with its almonds and blooms.[1] From Justin Martyr we learn that the Jews with whom he was acquainted believed that Elijah would anoint the Messiah and make him known to all.[2] To the anointing there is no reference in the Talmud or Midrashim; [3] but it was a current notion in the Middle Ages.

The Tannaim have, thus, little to tell about what Elijah will do when he comes at the end. In contrast to this is the abundance of tales of how he appeared in one guise or another to many of the rabbis of the time, and about his discourse with them.[4] In a later period such legends increased and multiplied. There is no reason to dwell upon these stories, nor upon the description of his coming and doings in later writings.[5]

To the connection of Elijah with the resurrection we shall return further on.

In many places in the prophetic books predictions of the golden age — however it may be conceived — follow abruptly upon denunciations of the direst calamities, and this juxtaposition gave ground for the belief that when evils of all kinds had reached their climax the deliverance would suddenly come. We have seen above in what dark colors the state of things in the generation in which the Son of David would come were depicted by some of the most influential teachers of the generation after the war under Hadrian. From an earlier date we have in the Gospel of Matthew (c. 24) a prophecy of the dreadful time that was to precede the coming of the Son of Man on the clouds

[1] Mekilta, Wayyassa' 5, on Exod. 16, 33 (ed. Friedmann f. 51b; ed. Weiss f. 59b–60a). See Horaiyot 12a, top (these and other things concealed by King Josiah), and Jer. Sheḳalim 49c. On the concealment and recovery of the sacred fire, 2 Macc. 1, 18–35; cf. 2, 1 ff.

[2] Dialogue with Trypho 8, 4; 49, 1.

[3] See, on the contrary, Sifra, Ṣau Pereḳ 18 (ed. Weiss f. 40b), and Rabad in loc. Ginzberg, Unbekannte jüdische Sekte, p. 348, n. 4.

[4] See L. Ginzberg, Legends of the Jews, IV, 202 ff. An exhaustive collection in M. Friedmann, Seder Eliahu Rabba, Introduction, pp. 27–44.

[5] E. g. Pesiḳta Rabbati ed. Friedmann, f. 161a; his appearance three days before that of the Messiah, etc.

of heaven, all which should come to pass within that generation. The first warnings of the approaching end would be wars among the nations, famines and earthquakes in various places. 'All these things are the beginning of pangs.'[1] It was evidently expected that these "pangs" would be understood of the travail in which the new age was to be born. The corresponding phrase in the rabbinical texts is "the travail of the Messiah,"[2] that is, not the sufferings of the Messiah himself, as it has sometimes been erroneously explained, but the throes of mother Zion which is in labor to bring forth the Messiah — without metaphor, the Jewish people.[3]

In the oldest contexts in which the phrase occurs (R. Eliezer, in the generation after the destruction of Jerusalem in 70 A.D.), it is one of three great punishments from which individuals will be saved by proper observance of the sabbath, namely, the travail of the Messiah, the days of Gog and Magog, and the great Judgment Day.[4] Similarly in a saying of Bar Ḳappara (early third century), the travail of the Messiah, the judgment of hell, and the war of Gog and Magog.[5] The biblical text alleged (by analogy of expressions) for the travail of the Messiah is Mal. 3, 23, 'Behold I send you Elijah the prophet before the coming of the great and terrible *day* of the Lord.' In the later and vaguer passages also it is deliverance from the travail of the Messiah that is in mind.

It appears that the phrase was originally applied, not to a period of general distress such as is described above,[6] but to a

1 ἀρχὴ ὠδίνων. Matt. 24, 8.

2 חבלו של משיח. Mekilta, Wayyassa' 5, on Exod. 16, 29 (ed. Friedmann 51a; ed. Weiss, f. 59a). R. Eliezer (ben Hyrcanus); cf. ibid. 4 near the end. See also Shabbat 118a; Pesaḥim 118a; Sanhedrin 98b. "חבלי המשיח," frequent in modern Christian books, is fictitious, like מלכות השמים. In Ketubot 111a, in an Aramaic context, the common editions have חבלי דמשיח, but the correct reading is חבליה דמשיח. The origin of the notion is Micah 5, 1 ff. (Sanhedrin l. c.); Yoma 10a.

3 The figure of a woman in travail is very common, especially in Jeremiah. The origin of the idea of the labor of which the Messiah is born is Mic. 5, 1–3; cf. the sequel, 5, 4–14, and 4, 9 ff. Cf. also Isa. 26, 17–19.

4 Mekilta l. s. c.

5 Shabbat 118a.

6 While in the Bible the plural is generally used as in Matt. 24, 8 (pangs, throes), in the rabbinical texts the word is invariably singular.

particular crisis of oppression (Micah 5, 2) which determines the fate of men, and in which some are saved while others perish.

That the sinners of Israel will be exterminated before the inauguration of the national golden age is expressly foretold in the prophets. The classical example is Amos 9, 10 f.: 'All the sinners of my people shall die by the sword, that say, The evil will not overtake nor confront us. In that day will I raise up the fallen hut of David,' [1] etc.

A similar expectation is found in rabbinical sources. R. Ḥiyya bar Abba [2] in an allegorical messianic exposition of Cant. 2, 13 ('The fig tree puts forth its green figs and the blossoming vines give their fragrance'), says: "Shortly before the days of the Messiah there will come a great pestilence, and the wicked will meet their end in it." [3] The fragrant blossoming vines are those who are left (the 'remnant,' Isa. 4, 3).[4] In the assimilation of the later (messianic) deliverance to the deliverance by Moses, the death of the wicked in this crisis is made to correspond with the death of all the wicked in the days of Egyptian darkness. Thus in Cant. R. on the same verse, the first clause is interpreted: These are the wicked of Israel who died in the three days of darkness, as it is said, 'There was dense darkness in all the land of Egypt three days; no man saw his brother.' [5] The fragrant blossoming vines are "the rest who repented and were delivered."[6]

That many of the Israelites died in Egypt on the eve of the exodus is a notion that is at least as old as the middle of the

[1] Take in the whole context, vss. 8–15. [2] About 200 A.D.

[3] The bad figs, according to Jer. 24, 2 f.

[4] The reference extends to the whole passage 4, 2–6.

[5] Exod. 10, 22 f. In Exod. R. 14, 3 it is explained that the darkness hid the death of the wicked Israelites from the Egyptians, and enabled the survivors to bury them unobserved.

[6] Cant. R. on 2, 13 (ed. Wilna f. 17b); Pesiḳta Rabbati c. 15 (ed. Friedmann f. 74a, 75a). See also Pesiḳta Rabbati c. 35 (ed. Friedmann f. 161a). Elijah, coming three days before the advent of the Messiah, proclaims salvation to Zion and her sons, but warns the wicked, who have broken out in loud rejoicing, that it is not for them.—Here "the wicked" are the nations of the world.

second century, and is ultimately derived from Ezekiel 20, 8. Among the explanations of the word *ḥamushshim* in Exod. 13, 18 (English version 'harnessed'), which seemed to be etymologically connected with the numeral *ḥamesh*, 'five,' some said that one in five of the Israelites in Egypt went out in the exodus; others said, one in fifty; still others, one in five hundred. R. Nehorai said, not even one in five hundred [1] (Ezek. 16, 7; Exod. 1, 7) went up; the greatest part of the Israelites died in Egypt in the three days of darkness ('they could not see one another'); they buried their dead, and gave thanks and were glad to God that their enemies did not see them and rejoice in their calamity.[2]

The coming of the Messiah is therefore a judgment of the generation to which he comes, and the announcement of its proximity by his precursor, Elijah, a call not to universal rejoicing but to heart-searching and repentance, as John the Baptist makes it in the Gospels, and Jesus after him. It may fairly be inferred from their words, 'Repent, for the reign of God is at hand,' that conceptions similar to those which we have found in the Midrash were current in their time. In this crisis the righteous or the repentant are to be saved, as they are to be saved from the days of Gog and Magog, and in the last judgment from the fate of the wicked in hell. It is a reasonable surmise that it is this crisis which is meant in the contexts where there is mention of the 'travail of the Messiah.'

The prophets abound in idealizing descriptions of the golden age to come, with its political, social, and economic blessings. The Jews drew on all this imagery in their pictures of the future, and embellished them with new traits discovered by ingenious midrash in other parts of the Scriptures. One of these is the inauguration banquet at which Behemoth and Leviathan furnish flesh and fish enough for everybody. The description of these fabulous terrestrial and marine monsters in Job 40–41 was spun out in the Haggadah not only into grotesque extravagances of

[1] Tanḥuma, Beshallaḥ § 1, not even one in five thousand (R. Nehorai).
[2] Mekilta, Beshallaḥ, Proem (ed. Friedmann f. 24a; ed. Weiss f. 29a).

monstrosity, but in an account of their creation on the fifth day,[1] of how they are to be slaughtered in preparation for the feast, and much more.[2]

Leviathan and Behemoth appear in Enoch 60, 7–10 (cf. vs. 24), but the angel declines to tell any more than that they are separated, one in the sea and the other on land. In 4 Esdras 6, 51 f., however, they are preserved from the fifth day of creation to be food for those whom God wills when he wills.[3] References to these creatures in the Tannaite sources are rare,[4] and there is in them no mention of the banquet.[5]

Johanan, a multifarious homilist of the third century, is the source of much that is told thenceforward about Leviathan and the feast upon his flesh, which he finds in Job 40, 30 ('The associates will feast upon him').[6] What is left of their portions they will put on sale in the markets of Jerusalem, etc.[7] Rab[8] also makes notable contributions to this mythology: God created a pair of Leviathans, but when he thought how much mischief might come of it, he castrated the male, and killed and pickled the female to preserve her flesh for the righteous in the time to come (Isa. 27, 1). He took care in a similar way that the pair of Behemoths should not multiply, but kept the female alive for the righteous in future time, instead of killing her.[9]

Behemoth and Leviathan represented land and sea; for the air an enormous bird called Ziz was discovered in Psalm 50, 11,

[1] The sea monsters (*tanninim*) of Gen. 1, 21 taken of Leviathan.

[2] For particulars see L. Ginzberg, Legends of the Jews, I, 27–29, with the Notes in Vol. V, 41–46.

[3] Similarly, Syr. Baruch 29, 1–4.

[4] Baba Batra 74b. R. Eliezer and R. Joshua were once on a voyage; Joshua saw by night a great light, which Eliezer thought might be the eyes of Leviathan (Job 41, 10). R. Meir saw an allusion to them in Job 12, 7 f.

[5] Antoninus' inquiry of Rabbi whether he should eat of Leviathan in the world to come (Jer. Megillah 72b) is a later legend.

[6] Ḥaberim, i.e. scholars (*talmidè ḥakamim*), or more generally, the righteous.

[7] Baba Batra 75a.

[8] Died in 247.

[9] Baba Batra 74b, middle. There is reflection in this difference: fish were commonly preserved in brine; the flesh of animals was not.

which also was as old as creation and should, like them, be served up to the righteous in the great banquet.[1]

A feast without something good to drink was unimaginable, and this is provided in the shape of wine preserved in the grapes since the six days of creation. (Isa. 64, 3.)[2]

Of the messianic banquet without such fantastic accessories there is repeated mention in the Gospels, and it was evidently part of the popular expectation.[3]

The fertility of the land of Israel is a theme on which numerous passages in the Scriptures expatiate; and that in the golden age to come nature would outdo herself was indubitable, even if there had been no express promises of it. In the Syriac Baruch,[4] in the immediate sequel of the Leviathan banquet, there follows a description of such marvellous productiveness. "The earth will yield her fruits ten thousand fold. On one vine will be a thousand clusters, each cluster of a thousand grapes, and each grape will yield a *kor* (about ninety gallons) of wine."[5]

Eulogies of the profuseness of nature in the land of Israel are found in rabbinical sources, especially in Sifrè on Deut. 32, 13 f.[6] In the future every grain of wheat will be as large as the two kidneys of a big bullock. As for wine, a man will not have to toil in gathering and treading the grapes; he will bring one grape in a cart and set it up in a corner, and will take as much as he wants and go, like one who drinks from a large jar. Another adds, there will not be a single grape that yields less than thirty jars of wine.

1 Ginzberg ll. cc. (p. 247, n. 2).

2 Sanhedrin 99a. R. Joshua ben Levi.

3 See Matt. 8, 11 f.; Luke 13, 29; 14, 15, and the following parable; 22, 16–18; Mark 14, 25; Matt. 26, 29.

4 Syr. Baruch 29, 5 ff.

5 Irenaeus (Haer. v. 33) quotes from Papias as a saying of Christ about his messianic kingdom an exaggerated parallel to this (*ten* thousand throughout, and two more multiplications-10 000 4), each grape yielding 25 *metretes* of wine — more than 200 gallons; and continues with wheat in similar lavishness of figures.

6 Sifrè Deut. § 317; cf. Midrash Tannaim, pp. 192–194. See also Ketubot 111b, later variations on the same theme.

Another bountiful source of such homiletic fertility was Psalm 72, 16. Rabban Gamaliel (II) [1] found in the first clause of this verse that in the future the land of Israel would produce rolls of bread and garments of fine wool.[2] Others learn from it that the wheat will shoot up like a palm tree. The obvious difficulty of harvesting such tall grain is foreseen in the next clause ('its fruit will rustle like Lebanon'): God will let a wind out of his treasury come and blow on it and set free the flour; a man will go out into the field and bring in a handful of it and from it supply himself and his household.[3]

In the prophets the return of the people of Israel to its own country from exile and dispersion is a conspicuous feature of the restoration of God's favor. 'For, lo, days are coming, saith the Lord, when I will turn the captivity of my people Israel and Judah . . . and I will return them to the land which I gave to their forefathers, and they shall possess it' (Jer. 30, 3). A little further on the theme is taken up again to introduce a foreglimpse of the golden age that follows the restoration (vss. 18–22).[4] Ezekiel has similar predictions.[5] The return is the motive with which Isa. 40 begins, and it is resumed and developed in the sequel with a wealth of poetic imagery.[6] The denunciations of calamity and captivity in the Law do not conclude without the assurance of restoration, if the misery of exile works in Israel a change of heart.[7]

The post-canonic writings bear witness to the vitality of this

[1] In the Yalkuṭ, R. Simeon ben Gamaliel.

[2] Shabbat 30b, end. Other wonders of the future in his sermons quoted there are that the trees will bear fruit every day (Ezek. 17, 8), and that a woman will bear a child daily (Jer. 31, 8). When an impertinent student quoted to him Eccles. 1, 9 — 'there is no new thing under the sun' — Gamaliel gave him an ocular demonstration that similar things happen in this present world; a hen lays an egg a day, the caper bush is always in fruit.

[3] Ketubot 111b.

[4] See also Jer. 23, 1–8; 29, 10–14; 32, 36–44; and especially c. 31.

[5] Ezek. 39, 25–29; 34, 11–16, etc.

[6] Isa. 40, 1–11; 43, 5–8; 49, 8–23; 52, 7–12; 60, 1–22. See also Isa. 11, 10–12, 15 f.; 27, 12 f.; Amos 9, 14 f.; Micah 4, 6 f.

[7] Deut. 30, 1–10; Lev. 26, 40–45; cf. also 1 Kings 8, 47–53.

hope in the wider dispersion of those centuries. It must suffice here to give references to some of the most memorable.[1] The older apocalypses have not much to say about the subject. Daniel is completely absorbed in the crisis in Judaea. In Enoch the return follows the destruction of the enemy in the last onslaught of the nations on Jerusalem (cc. 56–57);[2] in the vision of the whole history of the world (cc. 85–90) the assembly of the dispersed (90, 33–36) immediately precedes the birth of the white bull with great horns (the Messiah).[3]

The liberation of Israel from the dominion of the nations and the gathering of the dispersion to their own land has a place in the oldest prayers of the synagogue: "Sound the great horn[4] (as a signal) for our freedom; lift up the standard[5] for the assembling of our exiles," with the response, "Blessed art Thou, O Lord, who gatherest the dispersed of his people Israel."[6] The following petition is: "Restore our judges as at the first and our counsellors as at the beginning;[7] and reign over us, Thou alone. Blessed art Thou, O Lord, who lovest judgment." In succinct phrase the petition is included in the condensed prayer, Habinenu.

The exodus from Egypt had been the great miracle of history, a monument of God's almighty power and of his goodness to his people. But, as Jeremiah had foretold, it would be eclipsed by the greater miracle of their restoration from all the countries whither they had been dispersed. 'The days are coming, saith the Lord, when they shall no more say, As the Lord liveth, who

[1] Baruch 2, 30–35 (in prayer), and the jubilant hymn, 4, 36–5, 9; Ecclus. 33, 13–22; Tobit 13, 9–18; 2 Macc. 1, 27; 2, 18. Psalms of Solomon 8, 33 f.; 11; 17, 28–31 (following a messianic passage 21–26); and repeatedly in the Testaments of the Twelve Patriarchs.

[2] The Parthians and Medes, in the rôle of Gog and Magog.

[3] On the return of the ten tribes in 4 Esdras and the Syriac Baruch, see below.

[4] Isa. 27, 13; cf. Zech. 9, 14.

[5] Isa. 11, 12.

[6] The tenth of the Eighteen Prayers, in the Palestinian text (Dalman, Worte Jesu, p. 300). Slightly amplified in the Prayer Books. Cf. Megillah 17b–18a.

[7] Isa. 1, 26.

led up the children of Israel out of the land of Egypt, but, As the Lord liveth, who led up and brought the posterity of the children of Israel from the northern land, and from all the lands whither I drove them away; and they shall dwell on their own soil.'[1]

From Egypt they departed hurriedly, for they were thrust out and could not delay (Exod. 12, 39; Deut. 16, 3); but in the new exodus the prophet foretold, 'Ye shall not depart hurriedly, nor shall ye go in flight; for the Lord goeth before you and the God of Israel will bring up your rear' (Isa. 52, 12).[2]

In Isaiah the return of the exiles resembles a solemn procession; the way is made smooth for them, every obstacle removed (Isa. 40, 3-5). The clouds of the (divine) glory are a pavilion over their heads for shade by day (Isa. 4, 6), 'and the Lord's ransomed people will return and come to Zion with jubilant song, and everlasting joy will be upon their heads' (Isa. 35, 10).[3]

The idealizing expectation of the prophets was that the Jews who, when this turn of fortune came, were living in other countries would universally return to Judaea, and the representation of the Tannaim corresponds. Whether the descendants of the ten tribes who had been earlier deported by the Assyrians would also return to their own country, so that the golden age to come would see a reunited Israel, was a controverted question.

In 4 Esdras the peaceful multitude whom the Messiah calls to him (13, 12), after he has miraculously annihilated the host who gathered from every quarter to make war upon him,[4] are the ten tribes[5] who were carried away beyond the Euphrates by Shalmaneser king of Assyria (2 Kings 17, 1-6).[6] Thence they migrated to a far distant and inaccessible land[7] which had never

[1] Jer. 23, 7 f. Berakot 12b, end.
[2] Mekilta, Bo 7 (ed. Friedmann f. 7 b; ed. Weiss f. 9 b).
[3] Mekilta, Beshallah (Proem), ed. Friedmann f. 25a, top; ed. Weiss f. 29b-30a.
[4] 13, 2-11.
[5] Otherwise, 'nine and a half.'
[6] "In the days of king Josiah" is an early error for 'Hosea.'
[7] On the river 'Sanbation' beyond which the ten tribes were settled see Jewish Encyclopedia, X, 681-683.

been inhabited by men, that there they might keep laws which they had not kept in their home land. From this remote region God will bring them back in the latter days.[1]

Among the Tannaim of the second century there were conflicting opinions. Akiba interpreted Lev. 26, 38 ('And ye shall be lost [ואבדתם] among the heathen, and the land of your enemies shall devour you') of the ten tribes which were exiled to Media — they should perish there; others took the words 'be lost' in the light of the following verses to mean that they should be exiled thither.[2] In the Mishnah [3] R. Akiba maintains that the ten tribes will never return, arguing from Deut. 29, 27. ('The Lord . . . cast them into another land, as this day'): "As this day goes and does not return, so they go and do not return." R. Eliezer makes a contrary inference from the same words: "As the day is (first) dark and (then) light, so the ten tribes. As they were enveloped in darkness, so it will in future be light about them." A mediating solution is attributed to R. Simeon (ben Yoḥai), with another turn of the words 'as this day': "If their deeds are 'as (they are at) this day' (bad), they will not return; otherwise they will return."[4] In the corresponding Tosefta it is the participation of the ten tribes in the World to Come that is denied.[5]

The later opinion is more favorable to the ten tribes on both questions. Rabbi allowed them a share in the World to Come, and R. Johanan blames Akiba for lapsing from his usual charity in his harsh judgment, quoting against him Jer. 3, 12.[6]

[1] 4 Esdras 13, 38–47. Cf. Syriac Baruch 77, 17, 22, and the Epistle to the nine and a half tribes, 78, 1 ff. — On the ten tribes remaining in the East, see also Josephus, Antt. xi. 5, 2 §§ 131–133.

[2] Sifra, Beḥuḳḳotai Pereḳ 8, init. (ed. Weiss f. 112b). Cf. the commentary of Rabad.

[3] M. Sanhedrin 10, 3; Sanhedrin 110b.

[4] Sanhedrin 110b. On this subject and the variant attributions see Bacher, Tannaiten, I, 143, and Klausner, Messianische Vorstellungen u. s. w., pp. 77–79.

[5] Tos. Sanhedrin 13, 12: The ten tribes have no portion in the World to Come (Deut. 29, 27). Compare the preceding paragraphs of the Mishnah.

[6] Sanhedrin 110b.

In the apocalypses which lie between the fall of Jerusalem and the revolt under Hadrian, as has been shown above, the Messiah is to make an end of the Roman empire, sometimes himself putting to death the last emperor. After the war in which Bar Cocheba essayed this rôle and failed disastrously, all sane minds must have realized that such was not God's plan. The deliverance must be his work. When his time came, he would accomplish it in his way, and it was not for them to prescribe times for him or take his work into their own hands. This was, as we have seen, the attitude of the religious leaders in the century following the war.

A curious aberration, of which the first evidence comes from the latter part of this period, but which subsequently had a considerable development, was the discovery that besides the Judaean Messiah, Son of David, there was to come another, an Ephraimite Messiah ben Joseph.[1] The earliest mention of this Messiah is a report of a difference between a certain R. Dosa and the prevailing opinion of scholars on the question what the mourning in Zech. 12, 10 ('they will gaze on him whom they have run through,' etc.) is about. One — it is not clear which — said that it was for the Messiah ben Joseph who was killed, the other that it was for the 'evil impulse' which was slain.[2] The death of the Josephite Messiah is supposed also in a tradition introduced as Tannaite a little farther on in the same passage, where his fate alarms the Messiah son of David till God reassures him.[3] From the incidental way in which the Josephite Messiah and his death come in, it may be inferred that the notion was not unfamiliar; but it does not appear how commonly it was accepted among the authorities of the time.

[1] Of the tribe of Joseph.

[2] According to the words of R. Judah, in the time to come God will bring the 'evil impulse' (temptation personified) and slay it in the presence of the righteous and the wicked, etc. Both will mourn, but with different reasons. — The whole immediate context in Sukkah, it should be observed, is concerned with the 'evil impulse.'

[3] Sukkah 52a. The corresponding passage in Jer. Sukkah 55b has simply, 'the mourning for the Messiah.'

How it arose has been much discussed. Its main support, if not its origin, is Obadiah vs. 18: 'The house of Jacob will be fire and the house of Joseph flame, and the house of Esau stubble; and they will set them afire and consume them, and there will be nothing left of the house of Esau, for the Lord says so.' In this verse R. Samuel ben Naḥman, a homilist of the earlier part of the third century, found that Esau (Rome) would be delivered only into the hand of a descendant of Joseph.[1] From the second passage in Sukkah 52a it appears that the career of the Josephite Messiah and his death was imagined to precede the coming of the Messiah Son of David; but no other particulars are forthcoming.

The expectation of a golden age of the Jewish nation attached itself to the prophecies of liberation from foreign dominion, and restoration of independence under the rule of a wise and good king of the old line of kings of Judah, an age crowned with all the blessings of God. About the fate of other nations in that time there were diverse predictions: they should be subjugated, or destroyed, or converted. Whatever became of them they would no longer be an affliction or a menace or a temptation to God's people.

By the side of this political ideal of the promised golden age there was another conception of larger scope and more religious character, a time to come when all men would own and serve the one true God,[2] or in the prophet's words, 'the Lord shall be King over all the earth; in that day shall the Lord be One and His name one.'[3] For this supremacy of God the familiar Jewish phrase is Malkut Shamaim, "the kingdom of Heaven,"[4] by

[1] Baba Batra 123b. For the passages of the same intent in the Midrashim see Friedmann on Pesiḳta Rabbati f. 50a, note 54; Bacher, Pal. Amoräer, I, 525 n. 7.

[2] See Vol. I, pp. 226 ff.

[3] Zech. 14, 9; Obad. vs. 21, cf. vss. 17 ff.; Isa. 24, 23. This is the form of the expectation in Dan. 7.

[4] See Dalman, Worte Jesu, pp. 75 ff.; Strack-Billerbeck, Kommentar zum Neuen Testament aus Talmud und Midrasch, I, 172 ff.

which is to be understood not the realm over which God rules, but his *kingship*, his character of king.

God is *de jure* king over all the earth from creation on, but *de facto*, if one may say so, he is king only for those who in word and deed acknowledge his sovereignty. Israel alone of all the nations did this at Sinai,[1] and therefore he is in a peculiar sense the king of Israel, as he is the God of Israel. So in the individualizing of religion, a Jew renews his personal acknowledgment of God as his king every time he recites the Shema',[2] and he throws off his allegiance by ignoring God's law or acting in defiance of it.

The heathen, as nations and as individuals, reject the true God and his religion, they will not have the rightful king to reign over them. Thus it has been in all the past. But it will not always be so. The time will come when all mankind will bow to his rule, and do homage to him alone, and obey his law.[3] Then the reign of God will be universal; the end of all God's ways, the goal of human history, will be attained. Universal will be also the blessings of that age — all the good things men can think of. So it appears in the Sibylline Oracles iii, 767 ff.: "Then He will raise up a kingdom to all eternity over men, he who once gave a holy law to the godly,[4] to whom he promised to open all the earth, and the world, and the gates of the blessed, and all joys, and an immortal soul,[5] and eternal happiness."[6]

In this sense the consummation of the kingdom of Heaven may be best expressed for our understanding as the universality of the true religion, not alone professed by all men but realized in their lives in all their relations to God and to their fellow men.

[1] Exod. 24, 3 and 7.

[2] One who separates himself from heathenism, takes on him in fact the "yoke of the kingdom of Heaven." Sifra, Ḳedoshim, end (ed. Weiss f. 93 d).

[3] Zeph. 3, 9; Isa. 2, 2–4 (Mic. 4, 1–5); 42, 4–13; 49, 6 f.; 45, 3–6, 14–25; Zech. 8, 20–23, etc.

[4] To Israel.

[5] νοῦς, intellectual soul.

[6] The preceding (741 ff.) and following context should be taken with this. — Cf. also Assumption of Moses 10, 1: Et tunc parebit regnum illius in omni creatura illius; et tunc zabulus finem habebit, et tristitia cum eo abducetur, etc.

Such was the wider vision of some of the greatest of the prophets, and it became a firm article of Jewish faith. Prayer for the speedy coming of the time when it shall be a visible reality is one of the most constant elements in the liturgy. It is a reflection of this frequency when R. Johanan says: A prayer (*berakah*) in which there is no (mention of) "kingship" (*malkut*) is no prayer.[1] A special place is given to the "kingdom verses" (Malkuyot) in the additional service (Musaf) on New Years, introduced by the 'Alenu prayer, in the first part of which the Lord of the universe is praised and magnified as the God and king of Israel. The second is prayer for the speedy coming of the time when the kingdom of God shall be established in all the world, when all mankind shall call upon his name, and he shall make all the wicked of the earth turn their faces to him, taking on them the yoke of his kingship, and he be king over them forever, as it is written, The Lord shall reign for ever and ever.[2] In later times this prayer was introduced into the Daily Prayers, where it forms a fitting conclusion of the whole, with the addition of Zech. 14, 9.[3]

The universality of the true religion was naturally conceived as the universality of Judaism; the national religion becomes international, with Jerusalem as the seat of its cultus, to which the converted nations resort to worship the true God, bringing their offerings.[4] The Jews will be called 'priests of the Lord, ministers of our God';[5] but Isa. 66, 21, in the most natural interpretation, says, 'And also some of them (the Gentiles of

[1] I. e. in which God is not called king. Berakot 12a; Jer. Berakot 12d (attributed to Rab). See for this abstract sense Psalm 103, 19; 145, 11–13.

[2] Mic. 4, 7.

[3] This custom is unknown to the earlier writers on the liturgy, and to this day in the Sefardic rite only the first half is recited. It appears, however, in the Maḥzor Vitry, p. 75. In the common text some words have been omitted because obnoxious to Christians, who thought that they were meant for them. See Baer, 'Abodat Israel, p. 131 n.; Elbogen, Der jüdische Gottesdienst, pp. 80 f.; K. Kohler, Jewish Encyclopedia, I, 336–338.

[4] Isa. 56, 6–8; 60; 66, 18–21; Zech. 14, 16–21; see also Isa. 2, 2 f.

[5] Isa. 61, 5 f. (Exod. 19, 6).

vs. 20) will I take as priests (and) levites, saith the Lord' — an unparalleled utterance, but not beyond this prophet.[1]

There is no incompatibility between this conception of the future reign of God and the expectation of a king of Israel in the golden age, the so-called messianic hope, and such a ruler might well be supposed to have a part in the inauguration of the world-wide reign of God; but in their origin the two conceive the future from the different points of view of nationality and universality.[2]

It was natural that they should frequently be combined, all the more since the great obstacle to both was the heathen empire, as e. g. in the Sibylline Oracles iii, 46–50: "When Rome shall reign over Egypt . . . then will the most great kingdom of the immortal King be revealed [3] to men, and there will come a holy ruler to sway the sceptre over all the earth, to all the ages of swift-rushing time," with the sequel, the catastrophe of Rome.[4] In the Synoptic Gospels the kingdom of God is thought of not so much in its ultimate world-wide comprehension as with reference to the crisis which the advent of the kingdom will be for the Jews themselves,[5] and to what is required of those who aspire to a place in it.[6] It is closely associated with messianic ideas — both the Son of David and the Son of Man.[7] In attaching the messianic expectation to the person of Jesus of Nazareth and seeing in him the inaugurator of the kingdom of Heaven, the Gospels impressed on the latter phrase their own distinctive conceptions, and connected both with the World to Come.[8]

What Josephus calls the "fourth philosophy," whose founder was Judas the Galilean, on all other points in agreement with the Pharisees, had for its specific difference that its adherents held

[1] Cf. Mal. 1, 10–14. [2] See Part i, chapter 1.

[3] φανεῖται, cf. Luke 19, 11 ἀναφαίνεσθαι. The usual Jewish expression; e. g. Targ. Isa. 40, 9, איתגליאת מלכותא דאלהכון. See Dalman, Worte Jesu, p. 83.

[4] Quoted above, p. 330.

[5] Matt. 3, 2; 4, 17; 10, 7; 7, 21; 8, 11 f., etc.

[6] The Beatitudes; Parables of the Kingdom.

[7] Mark 10, 35 ff.; Matt. 16, 27, etc. [8] See below, p. 378.

God to be the only governor and ruler, and would give that title to no other.[1] The issue was first raised when, after the banishment of Archelaus (6 A.D.), Judaea, under a procurator, was attached to the province of Syria and made subject to Roman taxation; and it grew into a wildfire of popular fanaticism in the last years before the revolt under Nero, fomented by the abuse of his power by the procurator Gessius Florus.[2] The question put to Jesus by certain of the Pharisees and of the Herodians, Is it permissible to pay taxes to the emperor nor not? Shall we pay or not pay? was a trap;[3] but it shows that even in quiet times the radical party maintained its position in opinion, if not in practice.[4]

That the day should speedily come when God would be king over them, and He alone, was a common topic of prayer; the followers of Judas and their successors made His actual kingship a revolutionary principle.

In its original conception the national golden age inaugurated by the coming of the Messiah was of unmeasured duration. The newer eschatology with its general resurrection, last judgment, and final and endless Age to Come, did not supersede it; and, when the two were more clearly distinguished, could find place only beyond it. Consequently, as we have seen in 4 Esdras and the Revelation of John, the Messianic Age became an interim, which in Esdras is to last four hundred years,[5] in John, a thousand. In Sanhedrin 99a[6] various utterances about the duration of the Days of the Messiah are collected, with biblical texts from which they were extracted in the way of midrash, beginning with R. Eliezer (ben Hyrcanus) and R. Eleazar ben Azariah about the

1 Josephus, Antt. xviii. 1, 6. In xviii. 1, 1 § 4, Judas is described as a Gaulonite, from the city of Gamala.

2 Josephus, Antt. xviii, 1, 1; xx. 5, 2 § 102; Bell. Jud. ii. 8, 1; 17, 8 § 433; cf. Acts 5, 37.

3 Mark 12, 14 and parallels.

4 It may be conjectured that it had its principal strength among the Galileans.

5 So in the Latin version.

6 With the attributions in the Talmud there cf. Tanḥuma, 'Ekeb § 7, and Pesiḳta Rabbati ed. Friedmann f. 4a–b with the editor's notes.

beginning of the second century, the former of whom made them forty years,[1] the latter, seventy.[2] According to R. Dosa they would last four hundred years;[3] Rabbi said three generations,[4] or by another report three hundred and sixty-five years, corresponding to the days of the solar year,[5] and so on. The millennium is ascribed to R. Eliezer, son of Jose the Galilean, citing Psalm 90, 4 and Isa. 63, 4.[6] Others, especially later rabbis, would have the period much longer, Samuel, e.g., as much time as lay between the creation and his day (third century). There was no orthodoxy or consensus in such exegetical ingenuities. In one thing, however, all agreed: the Days of the Messiah are of limited duration.

[1] Psalm 95, 10; or Deut. 8, 2 f. and Psalm 90, 15. In the Tanḥuma attributed to Akiba.

[2] Isa. 23, 15.

[3] Gen. 15, 13 and Psalm 90, 15. In the Tanḥuma, Rabbi.

[4] Psalm 72, 5. Anonymous in Sifrè Deut. § 310 and elsewhere. Cf. also Mekilta de-R. Simeon ben Yoḥai ed. Hoffmann, p. 84 f.

[5] Isa. 63, 4.

[6] Pesiḳta Rabbati ed. Friedmann f. 4a. Tanḥuma, R. Eliezer. Other figures: 2000, 7000, 365000 years. Pesiḳta Rabbati f. 4b.

CHAPTER III

ESCHATOLOGY

We have seen how in Daniel the fulfilment of the national hope assumes an eschatological form with its forensic judgment and the resurrection of the righteous dead, and how in parts of the Book of Enoch the eschatological element has a larger development in a judgment of superhuman powers of evil; and, again, how in the apocalypses from the end of the first century a clearer division is made between the messianic golden age of Israel and its eschatological sequel, the general resurrection, the last judgment, and the new era of the world that is thus ushered in.

With the scheme of the later apocalypses rabbinical conceptions are in general accord. The beginning of the Messianic Age is a great crisis in the history of Israel and of the nations. As its close, the Last Things in the proper sense begin, the domain of eschatology, with the great assize in which living and dead appear before the judgment seat of God.

Jewish eschatology is the ultimate step in the individualizing of religion, as the messianic age is the culmination of the national conception. Every man is finally judged individually, and saved or damned by his own deeds. Therein lies its religious significance. Besides this it offered a solution of a tormenting problem, how to reconcile the facts of human experience, in which both the good and the bad often fare far otherwise than, as everybody sees, they deserve, with belief in divine providence; and above all how to harmonize these facts with the retributive justice of God which is so emphatically enunciated in the Scriptures. When once the sphere of retribution was extended beyond this brief life to an endless hereafter, theodicy need no longer harass faith.

From the historical development of the ideas we have under consideration it results that the periodization of the hereafter is not always consistent either in conception or in designation. To begin with the names. When the distinction is clearly made between the fulfilment of the national expectation and the new and final order of things beginning with the general resurrection and the last judgment, the proper name for the latter is the Coming World,[1] in contrast to the present order, This World.[2] The Days of the Messiah then intervene: This World, the Days of the Messiah, the World to Come.[3] Instead of the Coming World, we frequently find, in similar connections, the indefinite expression, 'the Future,' e.g. Tos. 'Arakin 2, 7[4]: This Time, the Days of the Messiah, the Future.[5]

In an earlier stage of the development, the national golden age, here called the Days of the Messiah, was the final period of history, and the names the World to Come or the Future were applied to it,[6] and this usage continued in later times. Where the great feast on the flesh of Leviathan and Behemoth, or allotments of land for cultivation, or the enormous fertility of the land of Israel, and the like, are assigned to the World to Come or to the Future, it is clearly the national golden age (Days of the Messiah) that is described, not that new order of things that is to endure after the general resurrection.[7]

There is in this sphere not merely an indefiniteness of terminology but an indistinctness of conception. In the sequel of the various conceits of the rabbis about the duration of the Messianic

[1] *'Olam ha-ba. 'Olam* (αἰών) is 'age, epoch.'

[2] *'Olam ha-zeh.*

[3] So, e.g., in Sifrè Deut. § 47 (ed. Friedmann f. 83a, above); Zebaḥim 118b, below (Rabbi).

[4] *'Atid la-bo*, 'What is to come.'

[5] Also in Pesiḳta Rabbati c. 21 (ed. Friedmann f. 99a) and the parallels cited in Friedmann's note there. — 'Arakin 13b reads, The World to Come.

[6] The earliest known occurrence of the phrase, the World to Come, is in Enoch 71, 15, He proclaims unto thee peace in the name of the world to come.

[7] See e.g. Baba Batra 74b, middle; ibid. 122a; Ketubot 111b (Sifrè Deut. § 317). Klausner, Messianische Vorstellungen u. s. w., pp. 17 f. Very many instances might be adduced from the Midrashim.

Age, a saying of R. Johanan is reported: All the prophets prophesied only about the Days of the Messiah; but of the World to Come, 'Eye hath not seen a God besides Thee who works for him who waits for Him' (Isa. 64, 4).[1] But most men were not content to renounce all imagination of the final state and leave it to future experience, and they pictured it in traits drawn from the predictive descriptions of the national golden age by the prophets and poets in the Scriptures. An opinion the opposite of Johanan's is attributed to Samuel: There is no difference between This World (the present time) and the Days of the Messiah except only our subjection to the dominion of the (heathen) empires.[2] This, if taken as a principle of interpretation, would leave all the prophecies of a different order of things to the eschatological hereafter. The diverse opinions of these two distinguished teachers of the third century is further evidence that there was not only no orthodoxy, but no attempt to secure uniformity in such matters.

The primary eschatological doctrine of Judaism is the resurrection, the revivification of the dead. The beginnings of this belief and the development of the conception from Daniel on have been exhibited in a former chapter. In the original apprehension this resurrection was to occur at the inauguration of the Messianic Age, and was for the righteous dead of Israel only, who were brought back to life to enjoy in their own land the blessings of that time. This belief was not displaced by the eschatological conception of a resurrection of righteous and wicked to judgment, but persisted beside it.

In the resurrection in the days of the Messiah the dead in Palestine would rise first; all the patriarchs desired, therefore, to be buried in it. It was the 'land of the living' (Psalm 116, 9). Only there, indeed, would the dead be brought to life again. Those who were buried outside the land would roll over and over

[1] Note the preceding clause, 'Whereof from of old men have not heard nor perceived by the ear.' Sanhedrin 99a, cf. Berakot 34b. Cf. 1 Cor. 2, 9.

[2] Sanhedrin 99a; Berakot 34b; Shabbat 63a, and elsewhere.

through underground tunnels made for them by God until they reached its borders; there alone would they receive souls (Ezek. 37, 14).[1] The opinion was even advanced that those who died outside the land would not rise,[2] and by another, contrariwise, that even a 'Canaanitish' (alien) slave girl in the land of Israel may confidently expect to be a daughter of the World to Come (sharing in the resurrection) [3] — a specimen of exegetical whimsicality, rather than an eccentricity of opinion.[4]

When the phrase "the revivification of the dead" is employed without other indication in the context, it is usually the general resurrection for the grand assize that is meant. The controversy over the question whether there is any such thing as a resurrection of the body comprehends both. The dissension between the Pharisees and the Sadducees on this point began in the stage of what may be called the immediate eschatology, represented in Daniel and parts of Enoch and in the Synoptic Gospels, before the discrimination of periods which is found in the apocalypses from the end of the first century (Revelation of John, 4 Esdras), and in the rabbis of the second century.

The question Paul puts into the mouth of a caviller, How are the dead raised? With what sort of a body do they come? (1 Cor. 15, 35), confronted the Jews also.[5] That they might be recognized, it seemed necessary to assume that they would rise with the defects and deformities they had in life, the lame, lame; the blind, blind.[6] After they thus appeared just as they had been, God would heal them of all their infirmities (Deut. 32,

[1] Jer. Kilaim 32c, above; Jer. Ketubot 35b, above. See Ketubot 111a; Tanḥuma ed. Buber, Wayyeḥi § 6, and the parallels cited in the editor's notes. The authors named include some Tannaim and several teachers of the fourth century. The subject is treated by them with a certain air of mystery. See also Targ. Cant. 8, 5.

[2] Ketubot 111a. R. Eleazar (ben Pedat).

[3] Ibid. R. Abahu.

[4] Isa. 42, 5, combined with Gen. 22, 5.

[5] Question and answer at length in Syr. Baruch cc. 49 f.

[6] Eccles. R. on 1, 4 ('A generation goes and a generation comes'): As a generation goes, so it comes. Ḥanina ben Ḥama. Cf. Tanḥuma ed. Buber, Wayyigash § 9.

39).[1] It was also believed that the dead would rise clothed as they had been in life, as the witch of Endor saw Samuel; [2] or in the garments in which they were buried.[3]

"Queen Cleopatra" is said to have questioned R. Meir: I know that the dead bodies will live again, for it is said, 'They will blossom out of the city like the grass of the earth' (Psalm 72, 16); but when they stand there, will they stand naked or in their clothes? He replied, *A fortiori* from wheat: as a grain of wheat which is buried naked comes forth clad in many garments, how much more the righteous who are buried in their garments! [4]

These are curious questions which are answered by contortions of exegesis. The fact of the resurrection itself is a dogma carrying an anathema: "The following are those who have no portion in the World to Come: Whosoever says that the revivification of the dead is not (proved) from the Torah; or the Torah is not from Heaven (God)," etc.[5] Against Gentile controversialists or scoffers other arguments might be employed, but with those who acknowledged the authority of the revelation in Scripture, like the Sadducees and other heretics (Minim) or the Samaritans,[6] the proof of the doctrine must be adduced from the Scripture itself. A great number and variety of such proof-texts are in fact alleged by a long succession of teachers from all parts of the Scripture, frequently, for complete demonstration, in threes, from the Law, the Prophets, and the Hagiographa, respectively.

[1] Tanḥuma l. s. c.; Gen. R. 95, 1. Even the wild animals would be cured (Isa. 65, 25) in the World to Come.

[2] Ibid.

[3] R. Nathan. Jer. Kilaim 32b, top; Tanḥuma ed. Buber, Emor § 4 (Job 38, 14).

[4] Sanhedrin 90b, below. The figure also in Ketubot 111b. — Mohammed let the dead rise for judgment naked as they were born, at which impropriety 'Ayesha protested.

[5] M. Sanhedrin 10, 1. The Babylonian Talmud (f. 90a, below) on these words comments: He denied the resurrection of the dead, accordingly he shall have no part in the resurrection of the dead; for God always requites measure for measure.

[6] In editions of the Baylonian Talmud the names of these classes of opponents are frequently interchanged in consequence of the activities of the censorship or in apprehension of them.

An illustration may be given from a discussion between Rabban Gamaliel (II) and the Sadducees: The Sadducees asked Rabban Gamaliel, Where is the evidence that the Holy One, blessed is He, brings the dead to life? He replied, In the Law and in the Prophets and in the Writings, but they did not accept his proof. In the Law, for it is written, 'And the Lord said to Moses, Thou wilt sleep with thy fathers, and wilt rise' (Deut. 31, 16). They objected, But it may mean rather, 'and this people will rise up [1] and go a-whoring (after the foreign gods of the land' etc.). — In the Prophets, for it is written, 'Thy dead shall live, my dead [2] bodies shall rise; awake and sing, ye that sleep in the dust, for a dew of lights is Thy dew, and the earth shall bring forth the shades' (Isa. 26, 19). The Sadducees answer, This may refer rather to the dead whom Ezekiel brought to life (Ezek. 37). — From the Writings, For it is written: 'Thy palate is like the best wine, that slips right down my love's throat, gently moving the lips of them that sleep' (in the tomb; Cant. 7, 10). — They rejoined, It may be only an ordinary movement of the lips (in sleep). (This agrees with R. Johanan in the name of R. Simeon ben Jehozedek: When a rule of Law (Halakah) is cited in this world in the name of a (dead) teacher, his lips move gently in the tomb [Cant. 7, 10]).[3] — Finally, Gamaliel quoted to them Deut. 11, 9: (The land which) 'the Lord sware to your fathers to give to them' — it is not said *to you*, but *to them*; from this the resurrection of the dead is proved.[4] Others say that he alleged Deut. 4, 4.[5]

Deuteronomy 11, 9 figures also in a controversy with the Samaritans, who denied that the resurrection of the dead was to

[1] This is the natural division of the clauses, as in the Massoretic text and the versions. The verse was nevertheless a favorite proof-text, cited by Joshua ben Hananiah (Sanhedrin 90b) and Simeon ben Yoḥai (ibid.).

[2] Probably the author wrote "thy."

[3] Yebamot 97a; Bekorot 31b (in the name of Simeon ben Yoḥai). The quotation from R. Johanan is probably not part of the Sadducees' reply.

[4] The patriarchs were dead before the occupation of the land; God's oath could only be fulfilled by raising them from the dead. — Cf. Matt. 22, 32.

[5] Sanhedrin 90b.

be found in the Law. R. Eliezer ben Jose charges them with mutilating their Scriptures by leaving out '*to them*,'[1] without gaining anything by it, for the resurrection is proved by Num. 15, 31, 'That person shall be utterly cut off; his guilt is in him.' 'Utterly cut off' in This World. 'His guilt is in him.' When? Is it not in the World to Come?[2]

An argument in which may be noted a certain resemblance to the answer of Jesus to the Sadducees in Matt. 22, 32 is used in Sanhedrin 90b: 'And thereof ye shall give the Lord's portion (Terumah) to Aaron the priest' (Num. 18, 28). Did Aaron live forever? Is it not true that he did not even enter the land of Israel, that they might give this portion? The words teach that he is to live in the future and the Israelities give him the portion.[3] In Exod. 15, 1 (E. V., Then Moses sang, etc.) the Hebrew has *yashir*, a future form; the particle *az* ('then') admits either. Some found in the future tense a proof of the resurrection: It is not said, Moses *sang* (*shar*), but, Moses *will sing*.[4] These specimens of proofs from the Scriptures may suffice to exemplify the method. Many other texts are alleged. R. Simai held that there was not a single weekly lesson (Parashah) which does not contain the resurrection of the dead, only that we lack the ability to bring it out. Simai follows this with an illustration of what can be done by sufficiently subtle exegesis. In Psalm 50, 4 ('He calls to the heavens above, and to the earth that he may judge his people') he finds the resurrection thus: 'He will call to the heaven above 'to bring the soul,' and to the earth 'to bring the body, and thereafter, 'to judge *with it*.'[5]

[1] The Samaritan-Hebrew and its Targum in our hands lack these words. In Sanhedrin 90b the editions read *Minim* or *Ṣaddukim*.

[2] Sanhedrin 90b. Others found the whole doctrine in the words, 'shall be utterly cut off' (*hikkaret tikkaret*), the repetition, on the hermeneutic principle of Akiba, signifying "cut off in this world and in the world to come." Other examples in 90b–92. Translations of many in Strack-Billerbeck, Kommentar zum Neuen Testament aus Talmud und Midrasch, I, 892–897.

[3] Sanhedrin 90b, above. Ascribed to Johanan.

[4] Mekilta, Shirah, init. (ed. Friedmann f. 34a; ed. Weiss f. 41a).

[5] Pronouncing '*immō* ('with it'; i. e. the one with the other), instead of '*ammō* ('his people'). Midrash Tannaim on Deut. 32, 2 (p. 185, below; cf.

The contention of soul and body is the subject of a parable given by Rabbi to Antoninus. Antoninus maintained that body and soul can both exculpate themselves in the judgment. The body says, it was the soul that sinned, for from the day it was separated from me, here I lie in the tomb, mute as a stone. The soul says, it was the body that sinned, for from the day I was separated from it, here am I flying in the air like a bird. Rabbi replied, I will give you a parable. What is the thing like? Like a king who had a delightful park, in which were fine rareripe figs. He put in it two keepers, one of them lame and one blind. The lame man said to the blind man, I see fine rareripe figs in the park. Let me mount on your back and we will get them to eat. So the lame man mounted on the blind man's back and they got them and ate them up. After a while the owner of the park came and asked, Where are the fine rareripe figs? The lame man said, Have I any legs to get about? The blind man said, Have I any eyes to see with? What did the king do? He made the lame man get on the back of the blind man and punished the pair of them together. So the Holy One, blessed is He, will bring the soul and install it in the body, and judge both together, as it is written, 'He will call to the heaven above and to the earth to judge with it.' He will call to the heaven above, that is the soul; and to the earth to judge with it, that is the body.[1]

The association of Elijah with the advent of the Messiah[2] gave him a part at the resurrection of the dead. In R. Phineas ben Jair's ascending scale of virtues,[3] the (indwelling of the) holy spirit conducts a man to the resurrection of the dead, "and the resurrection of the dead comes through the instrumentality of Elijah,"[4] or leads to Elijah.[5]

183). The text is clearer than in Sifrè Deut. § 306 (ed. Friedmann f. 132, end). See also Mekilta de-R. Simeon ben Yoḥai ed. Hoffmann, p. 59.

[1] Sanhedrin 91a–b. Cf. Mekilta, Shirah 2 (ed. Friedmann f. 36b; ed. Weiss f. 43b); Lev. R. 4, 5; Tanḥuma, Wayyiḳra § 6 (ed. Buber § 12).

[2] See above, pp. 357 f. [3] Above, p. 272. [4] [M.] Soṭah 9, end.

[5] Cant. R. on Cant. 1, 1 (c. 1 § 9); cf. Jer. Shabbat 3c, above; Jer. Sheḳalim 47c, below. See L. Ginzberg, Legends of the Jews, III, 234, and Notes (Vol. VI).

A curious notion was that in the reconstruction of the bodies of the dead the nucleus was one small bone which did not decay and could not be destroyed. "Hadrian" asks R. Joshua ben Hananiah, From what does God make a man blossom out in the Future Age? The rabbi replied, From the 'almond'[1] of the spinal column. The inquirer demanded proof, and experiment showed that this bone could not be dissolved in water, nor pulverized in a mill, nor burned in fire; they laid it on an anvil and went at it with a sledge-hammer; the anvil split, the hammer broke, but nothing was done to the bone.[2]

In the grand assize righteous and wicked stand before this judgment seat of God, soul and body, as they lived. Consequently where it is said that only the righteous Israelites are restored to life, it is the resurrection at the beginning of the messianic age that is meant, to participate in its blessings, not the general resurrection at its close, or the thought is not distinct.[3]

In some of the apocalypses the heathen as well as the Jews rise to appear in the last judgment. Especially dramatic is the scene in 4 Esdras 7, 37 f., where, with the abodes of happiness and repose and of fire and torment before their eyes, God bids them, "Behold and see whom you have denied, whom you have not served, whose commandments you have contemned."[4]

Rabbinical utterances on this point are less explicit. Two of the disciples of Johanan ben Zakkai, R. Eliezer ben Hyrcanus and R. Joshua ben Hananiah, maintained contradictory opinions about the ultimate fate of the Gentiles. The former, who thought very ill of them,[5] held: "No Gentiles have a portion in the World to Come, as it is said, 'The wicked shall return to Sheol, all the Gentiles, who forget God' (Psalm 9, 18). The first

[1] *Lūz*, the tip of the coccyx: so called from its shape.

[2] The text is Eccles. 12, 5, 'the almond (*shaḳed*) will blossom.' Lev. R. 18, near the beginning; Gen. R. 28, 3.

[3] On the notions of various classes of Jews about the resurrection and the future life see Maimonides Commentary on M. Sanhedrin 10, 1.

[4] Cf. Revelation of John 20, 11–15; Syr. Baruch 50, 2–51, 17.

[5] Giṭṭin 45b; Baba Batra 10b, middle.

clause, 'Those who *return* to Sheol' are the wicked of Israel; in the second, 'who forget God' includes all Gentiles."—R. Joshua replies that he had formerly held the same view of the fate of all Gentiles; but now takes the words of 'all the Gentiles who forget God,' implying that there are righteous men in the nations of the world who have a portion in the World to Come.[1] The "righteous Gentile" is often recognized with commendation; characteristic examples have been quoted in another connection.[2]

The opinion of R. Joshua prevailed. Thus Maimonides: The pious of the nations of the world (Gentiles) have a portion in the World to Come.[3]

In the preceding passage in the Tosefta a difference between Rabban Gamaliel and R. Joshua ben Hananiah is reported on the question whether the little children of the heathen will have a portion in the World to Come. Gamaliel excluded them, quoting Mal. 3, 19; while Joshua maintained, on the ground of Psalm 116, 6 and Dan. 4, 20, that they would come into the World to Come, and parried Gamaliel's rejoinder drawn from the last clause of Mal. 3, 19.[4] In the same connection an anonymous interpretation of Mal. 3, 19 is quoted — (the fire in the coming day of wrath 'will leave them neither root nor branch'): 'Root' is the soul; 'branch' is the body, and the children of the wicked of the Gentiles will neither be brought to life (in the resurrection) nor be punished.[5]

The predominant religious and moral interest of the rabbis in the Last Judgment was, however, not in the fate of the heathen,[6] but in the individual retribution which there awaits Israelites.

[1] Tos. Sanhedrin 13, 2; cf. Sanhedrin 105a. — This phrase is unambiguous. On the terminology see Bacher, Tannaiten, I, 140 f.

[2] Vol. I, pp. 278 f.

[3] Hilkot Teshubah 3, 5. Joseph Caro, Kesef Mishneh, *ad loc*. See also Maimonides Commentary on M. Sanhedrin 10, 2 (in the section immediately following the Thirteen Articles).

[4] Tos. Sanhedrin 13, 1; cf. Sanhedrin 110b (Akiba in place of Joshua).

[5] Tos. Sanhedrin 13, 2; cf. Sanhedrin 110b.

[6] In their imaginations of the messianic age, on the contrary, this is a prominent point.

We have already seen how the schools of Shammai and Hillel raised the question what was to become of the middle class (the *benonim*), who were neither good enough for the World to Come nor bad enough for hell, and differed about it.[1] As to the wicked, we read in the same source: The wicked of Israel in their bodies, and the wicked of the nations of the world in their bodies go down to hell and are punished in it for twelve months. After twelve months their souls become extinct, and their bodies are burned up, and hell casts them out, and they turn to ashes, and the wind scatters them and strews them beneath the soles of the feet of the righteous, 'for they shall be ashes under the soles of the feet of the righteous in the day which I make, saith the Lord of Hosts' (Mal. 3, 21).[2] But the heretics and the apostates and the informers and the epicureans and those who deny the revelation (Torah), and those who separate themselves from the ways of the community, and those who deny the resurrection of the dead, and all who sin and make the multitude sin, like Jeroboam and Ahab, and those who put the terror of them into the land of the living, and those who stretch out their hands against the temple[3]—on these hell will be locked, and they will be punished in it for all generations, as it is said, 'And they will go out and see the carcasses of the men who rebelled against Me, for their worm shall not die, nor their fire go out, and they will be an abhorrence to all men' (Isa. 66, 24). Hell will wear away but they will not wear away, as it is written 'And their form is to wear out (outlast) hell' (Psalm 49, 15).[4]

The orthodox corollary to the dogma of the resurrection is that every Israelite will ultimately be saved: "All Israelites have a portion in the World to Come."[5] Biblical proof is alleged: 'Thy

[1] Tos. Sanhedrin 13, 3; above, p. 318.
[2] Tos. Sanhedrin 13, 4.
[3] So *zebūl* is explained in the sequel (1 Kings 8, 13). These sinners are all Israelites.
[4] Tos. Sanhedrin 13, 5; Rosh ha-Shanah 17a.
[5] M. Sanhedrin 10, 1 (in the numeration of the Babylonian Talmud, 11, 1, f. 90 ff.). This is Zoroastrian and Mohammedan orthodoxy also.

people will all be righteous; forever shall they possess the land, the branch of My planting, the work of My hands, to be proud of' (Isa. 60, 21). This is immediately qualified by specific exceptions which emphasize the wide scope of the preceding assertion. "The following are those who have no portion in the World to Come: He who says that the resurrection of the dead is not proved from the Law, or that the Law is not from Heaven, and the epicurean." [1]

R. Akiba adds the man who reads out of the outside books,[2] and one who mutters (as an incantation) over illness, 'No disease that I inflicted on the Egyptians will I inflict on thee, for I am the Lord thy healer' (Exod. 15, 26). Abba Saul includes the man who pronounces the (ineffable) Name as it is spelled.[3] Over these particular comminations we need not here delay.[4]

The Mishnah continues: Three kings (Jeroboam, Ahab, Manasseh [5]) and four private persons (Balaam,[6] Doeg, Ahitophel, and Gehazi) have no portion in the World to Come. The generation of the Flood have no portion in the World to Come, and will not stand in the judgment (Gen. 6, 3); [7] the generation of the dispersion of nations have no portion in the World to Come (Gen. 11, 8); the men of Sodom (Psalm 1, 5); the spies (Num. 14, 37); the whole generation of the wilderness (ibid. vs. 35); Korah's rout (Num. 16, 33); the ten tribes [8] (Num. 29, 27), etc. These somewhat numerous restrictions of the general proposition at the head of the Mishnah are of the nature of midrash. The significant part of the dogma is in the first sentence, with the

[1] Perhaps one who denies divine providence and retribution in this life or another.

[2] Outside the accepted canon of the Scriptures.

[3] M. Sanhedrin 10, 1.

[4] The rabbis are very liberal with homiletical damnation.

[5] About Manasseh, R. Judah (ben Ila'i) dissented.

[6] Balaam was not an Israelite at all, and that he is thus singled out was in later times used as an argument that the Gentiles are not all in the same condemnation. Maimonides, Commentary on M. Sanhedrin 10, 2.

[7] Will not be brought to life.

[8] This is controverted. See above, p. 369.

exceptions immediately noted, the deniers of the resurrection, of revelation, and of providence or retribution. It is to be noted that they have incurred their fate by denying fundamental articles of orthodoxy — by misbelief, not by misconduct. The amplifications of what is to be regarded as the original anathema are of an essentially different character.

Any attempt to systematize the Jewish notions of the hereafter imposes upon them an order and consistency which does not exist in them. As has already been remarked, their religious significance lies in the definitive establishment of the doctrine of retribution after death, not in the variety of ways in which men imagined it. The variety of these imaginings is immensely increased in Judaism by the fact that not only were there widely different representations of the future of Israel and the nations in the Scriptures, which as prophetic revelations must all be equally true, but that the rabbis operated upon these and all other scriptures by hermeneutic methods which treated single verses, clauses, and even words, as independent oracles, without regard to the general or particular context, and combined them with other similarly isolated enunciations according to rules which were supposed to embody the logic of revelation, and not infrequently derived unsuspected meanings from the text by forcing a clause to submit to an unnatural division or a word to an arbitrary mispronunciation. Larger liberties in interpretation were taken because, properly speaking, the whole subject belonged to Haggadah; but the fundamental Mishnah, Sanhedrin 10, 3, shows how similar freedom might invade a law book.

In conformity with the purpose of the present work, we shall here confine ourselves to a summary of the more general and constant elements of the doctrine of retribution.

At death there is a separation of the souls of righteous Jews from those of the wicked. This takes place without the machinery of a judgment, such as we find in the Zoroastrian eschatology. The former go to a blessed abode, which is commonly thought to be in the heavens.

These abodes are treasuries, or store-chambers,[1] as we have seen in 4 Esdras [2] and the Syriac Baruch.[3] R. Eliezer son of Jose the Galilean says: As long as a man is alive, his soul is kept safe in the hand of his Creator (Job 12, 10); when he is dead, it is put into the treasury, as it is written, 'The soul of my lord will be bound up in the bundle of life' (1 Sam. 25, 29). From the application of this quotation, the "bundle of life" comes itself to be used for the safekeeping of the souls of the righteous dead. "He will keep thy soul in the hour of death, as he says, etc., 'bound up in the bundle of life.'" It is only the souls of the righteous that are thus kept, for the verse goes on to say, 'but the soul of thine enemies He will sling away in the hollow of the sling.' [4]

A catalogue of the seven heavens and what is in them, puts in the seventh and highest, 'Arabot, the souls of the righteous (dead) and the spirits and souls that are yet to be created (embodied), and the dew with which God is to vivify the dead.[5] There are also the Ofannim [6] and the Seraphim and the holy beasts [7] and the ministering angels, and the throne of glory. Above them all, but in the same heaven, is the King, the ever-living God, high and exalted.[8]

Another frequent name for the abode of blessed souls is the Garden of Eden,[9] with reflection of the meaning of Eden, 'de-

[1] Latin (4 Esdras) *promptuaria;* also *habitacula*, *habitationes*.

[2] E. g. 4, 35, 41; 7, 9, 121. See above, p. 339.

[3] *ausere*, 30, 2.

[4] Sifrè Num. § 139 (on 27, 16); ibid. § 40, on 6, 24, 'The Lord will bless thee and keep thee.' Cf. Shabbat 152b (the bodies of the righteous enter into peace, they rest in their bed. Isa. 57, 2); their souls are bound up in the bundle of life.

[5] Isa. 26, 19. See Vol. I, p. 368.

[6] Ezekiel's 'wheels' with eyes in the felloes (1, 15 ff.) become an order in the celestial hierarchy. Cf. Enoch 61, 10; 71, 7. Rosh ha-Shanah 24b.

[7] Ezek. 1, 5 ff.; Rev. John 4, 6 ff., etc.

[8] Ḥagigah 12b, with proof-texts for it all. See Vol. I, p. 408 f. The scheme of seven heavens is older and is found in a number of places.

[9] *Gan 'Eden;* Greek παράδεισος, Luke 23, 43; cf. 2 Cor. 12, 4; Rev. John 2, 7 ('the paradise of God'). See also Enoch 32, 3 ('paradise of righteousness'). To the celestial paradise (*pardes*) the four rabbis made their famous, but for three of them disastrous, visit. Ḥagigah 14b, seq.

light'; it is the celestial counterpart of the earthly paradise in which the first parents were put. R. Johanan ben Zakkai in conversation with his disciples on his deathbed said: Before me lie two ways, one leading to the Garden of Eden, and one to Gehenna, and I know not by which of them I am being conducted.[1]

Of this intermediate state — to use a modern term — the phrase the World to Come is sometimes used. A certain 'philosopher,' who was converted by the constancy of the martyrs, Ḥanina ben Teradion and his wife and daughter, and was sentenced to the same fate, said, You have told me good news; tomorrow my portion will be with them in the World to Come.[2]

The name Garden of Eden is often given also to the final state of the righteous,[3] and in many cases it is not evident whether the abode of disembodied souls or of the re-embodied — Paradise Regained — is meant. The ambiguity exists in the use of the World to Come, which, as we have seen, is sometimes the messianic age, sometimes the new order of things after the resurrection, and, as in the instance just cited, occasionally the state of the soul between death and the resurrection. It is probable that these stages of the future were not so sharply distinguished in thought as we should like to have them.

The miserable abode of the souls of the wicked between death and the resurrection is called Gehinnom; and the same name is given to the place of fiery torment to which at the last judgment they are sent down, soul and body, so that here, too, there is an ambiguity in terms.

When the time fixed in God's plan arrives, the bodies of the dead will be restored and rise from the tomb; the souls from the

[1] Berakot 28b. It is unnecessary to multiply examples. A list of occurrences is given by Kohut, Aruch Completum, II, 314.

[2] Sifrè Deut. § 307 (ed. Friedmann f. 133a, below). The parallel to the penitent robber in Luke 23, 43 to whom Jesus says, 'Today thou wilt be with me in Paradise,' is plain.

[3] This is meant when it is said that the Garden of Eden and Gehinnom were among the things created before the creation.

treasuries will rejoin their own bodies, and the whole man as he lived will answer to God for his character and conduct in the former life. Those who are condemned will go down to hell (Gehinnom), while the justified will live forever in blessedness. This is the second and final stage of retribution.

Jewish imagination did not indulge itself in inventing retaliatory modes of torment in hell, such as flourished in the Orphic and other Greek sects and in India. There was biblical warrant for the pit of fire, and there the Jews generally left it. It was less easy, as all eschatologies illustrate, to imagine the conditions, circumstances, and occupations of the righteous in the World to Come, and when the imagery is derived from biblical pictures of a golden age there is room for doubt how literally the authors took it. The ambiguity of the term, again, often leaves it uncertain what they are talking about. Rab, a Babylonian teacher of the third century, used to say: The World to Come is not like this world. In the World to Come there is no eating and drinking, no begetting of children, no bargaining, no jealousy and hatred, and no strife; but the righteous sit with their crowns on their heads enjoying the effulgence of the Presence (Shekinah), as it is said, 'They beheld God, and ate and drank' (Exod. 24, 11) [1] — they were satisfied with the radiance of God's presence; it was food and drink to them. With this modern scholars often compare the answer of Jesus to the question of the Sadducees, whose wife a woman should be in the resurrection who had passed from brother to brother in levirate marriage through the whole family: 'When they rise from the dead they neither marry nor are married, but are like angels in heaven.' [2]

To Rab's description of the World to Come no Tannaite parallel is found, and it does not appear to have been popular. It is echoed in Abot de-R. Nathan 1, 8, where the title of Psalm 92, 'A Hymn for the Sabbath Day,' is taken, "A day that is all

[1] Berakot 17a (Rab).

[2] Mark 12, 25; Matt. 22, 30; cf. Luke 20, 34–36, 'the children of this world marry and are married, but those who are found worthy to attain to that world and the resurrection of the dead,' etc.

sabbath, in which there is no eating and drinking, and no trading, but the righteous sit with their crowns on their heads, and are nourished by the effulgence of the Shekinah, as it is written, 'and they beheld God, and ate and drank' (Exod. 24, 10 f.) like the ministering angels."

In the (post-Talmudic) Kallah Rabbati[1] the saying of Rab is quoted anonymously as a Tannaite deliverance. In objection Psalm 72, 16 is quoted, 'There shall be a patch of grain in the land, on the top of the mountain,' with the application of this verse to the World to Come in Ketubot 111b,[2] and Jer. 31, 8, 'A woman shall conceive and bear a child at once': "In the future a woman will bear a child every day."[3] The two apparently conflicting presentations are reconciled by referring the former to the state before the resurrection of the dead (the intermediate state),[4] the latter to the days of the Messiah.

It is certain that most men would find little satisfaction in contemplating a passive eternity of sitting basking in the radiance of the Shekinah. The blessed hereafter was imagined by the Jews in much more concrete and picturesque fashion. Maimonides in his commentary on M. Sanhedrin 10, 1 classifies under four heads the crudely material notions of his contemporaries, and makes a fifth category — the largest — for those who confuse them all. The resurrection was a cardinal doctrine of religion, and as such is included in his Thirteen Articles of Faith. For his *philosophy* the "vivification of the dead" (*teḥīyat ha-mētīm*) means, not the restoration of the body, but the immortality of the disembodied soul, and to Aristotelian psychology immortality is an achievement, not an endowment.[5]

The common Christian imagination of the existence and occupation of the saints after the resurrection draws its picture of

[1] Perek 2, near the beginning.
[2] See above, p. 366.
[3] Shabbat 30b, below.
[4] Strack on Matt. 22, 30 (I, 890) regards this as the right understanding of Rab's utterance, and therefore as not a parallel to the words of Jesus.
[5] On this point Maimonides is not explicit.

that state after the Revelation of John, especially chapters 20–22, which itself is in the line of Jewish apocalyptic. The great mass of Christians have always taken these descriptions literally and their own hereafter physically, notwithstanding Paul's effort to dematerialize, or spiritualize, the resurrection.[1] The fundamental Christian creed declares unequivocally for the resurrection of the flesh.[2] The conflict with the Gnostics led to great emphasis on this article, as when Tertullian writes: Resurget igitur caro, et quidem omnis, et quidem ipsa, et quidem integra.[3] The Millenarians of all the centuries have looked for a bodily advent of Christ and a bodily reign of the saints with him on earth for a thousand years, and the whole programme of the Revelation of John, and have made innumerable calculations of the date of Christ's coming, just as Jews have done — both primarily based on Daniel.

The eschatology of Judaism has an unmistakable affinity to that of the Zoroastrian religion in the separation of the souls of righteous and wicked at death, and their happy or miserable lot between death and the resurrection, and in the doctrine of a general resurrection and the last judgment with its issues. The resemblances are so striking that many scholars are convinced that this whole system of ideas was appropriated by the Jews from the Zoroastrians,[4] as well as that Jewish angelology and demonology were developed under Babylonian and Persian influence.

Borrowings in religion, however, at least in the field of ideas,[5] are usually in the nature of the appropriation of things in the possession of another which the borrower recognizes in all good faith as belonging to himself, ideas which, when once they become

[1] 1 Cor. 15, 42–54; 2 Cor. 5, 1 ff.

[2] Apostles' Creed, *σαρκὸς ἀνάστασις*, *carnis resurrectio*.

[3] De resurrectione carnis c. 63. See c. 35, where he explains what he means by the body of man.

[4] The converse, that the Persians learned their eschatology from the Jews, though entertained by some scholars, is for various reasons improbable.

[5] The adoption of foreign rites and adaptation of myths are a different matter.

known to him, are seen to be the necessary implications or complements of his own.

In the present case the primitive conception of a revivification of the dead, as it emerges in Daniel or in Isa. 26, appears to be indigenous; there is nothing like it in Zoroastrianism. This notion may have prepared the way for a wider extension of the idea of resurrection; but the Persian scheme must have been most strongly commended by the fact that it seemed to be the logical culmination of conceptions of retribution which were deeply rooted in Judaism itself.

PREFACE TO THE NOTES

By "Judaism in the first centuries of the Christian Era, The Age of the Tannaim" I mean the religion which has acquired an historical right to the name "Judaism" in its own definition of it. In the Preface (Vol. I, p. vii) I defined the scope of the volumes as I proposed it to myself: "The aim of these volumes is to represent Judaism in the centuries in which it assumed definitive form as it presents itself in the tradition which it has always regarded as authentic." "The aim of the present work is to exhibit the religious conceptions and moral principles of Judaism, its modes of worship and observance, and its distinctive piety, in the form in which, by the end of the second century, they attained general acceptance and authority" (Vol. I, p. 125). "These primary sources come to us as they were compiled and set in order in the second century of the Christian Era, embodying the interpretation of the legislative parts of the Pentateuch and the definition and formulation of the Law, written and unwritten, in the schools, in the century and a half between the reorganization at Jamnia under Johanan ben Zakkai and his associates, after the fall of Jerusalem in the year 70, and the promulgation of the Mishnah of the Patriarch Judah" (Preface, Vol. I, p. vii).

The succession of the authoritative teachers who are called "Tannaim" may, for our purposes, be regarded as beginning with Shammai and Hillel and their schools in the time of Herod. In the historical Introduction I have endeavored to show how this type of Judaism gained the ascendency, while its exclusive supremacy was attained only after the fall of Jerusalem. "The older and younger contemporaries of Gamaliel II and their disciples, with their successors in the next generation, are the fundamental authorities of normative Judaism as we know it in the literature which it has always esteemed authentic" (Vol. I, p. 87, cf. 86).

The learned study of the Law is, however, much older, as is shown in the chapter on the Scribes (Vol. I, pp. 37–47), where the importance of Sirach (Ecclesiasticus, ca. 200 B.C.) as a landmark is recognized. The continuity of this development of Judaism with the Scriptures and its progress beyond them in some directions are evident. In numerous places I have endeavored to illustrate this in particulars by references to uncanonical writings from the two centuries preceding the Christian Era, emphasizing the appropriation and assimilation of the prophetic teaching (Vol. I, p. 113, cf. pp. 15 f.).

Until the supremacy of the type of Judaism represented by the Tannaim was achieved — before the fall of Jerusalem and the reorganization at Jamnia, Lydda, and in Galilee, — as I have recognized in various connections, Judaism was much less homgeneous than it appears in the Tannaite sources; parties, sects, schools, or looser groups differed and contended over points of major and minor importance. I have frequently directed attention to these diversities, but except for the controversies between the Sadducees and the Pharisees little or nothing is known about the parties by which these differences were cultivated. The recent discovery in the Cairo Genizah of parts of a Hebrew book proceeding from an organized schismatic sect in the region of Damascus leads to the surmise that the groups that sloughed off or were extruded may have been more numerous and more significant than we should have suspected.

Fortunately, for the task I have set myself the continuity and the progress of the main current of what is called rabbinical Judaism — I should prefer the name "normative Judaism" — with the Scriptures at one end and the Tannaite sources of the second century at the other is of greater importance than the diversity and dissent; and it is as evidence of continuity and progress that I have chiefly employed the writings of the preceding centuries from Sirach on.

I should perhaps have evaded some misunderstandings if I had said explicitly at the outset what I did *not* propose to do.

First, then, I did *not* propose to write on the history of the Jews in their wide dispersion and the multiplication of "Jews" by conversion, nor of the effects of contact with alien civilizations, religions, philosophical theologies, and superstitions, and the resulting varieties. What I have attempted to describe is the Judaism of Palestine in a limited period, which in its main features furnished the norms of worship, morals, charity, piety, and observance, for all subsequent times.

Second, I have *not* attempted a descriptive account of Judaism in New Testament times. Neither the Christian era nor the completion of the New Testament marks an epoch in the history of Judaism. The religion in which Jesus was brought up in Galilee, or Paul grew up at Tarsus and in which he pursued his studies "at the feet of Gamaliel" in Jerusalem, is the proper subject of investigations which would demand a different selection and critical evaluation of sources and an altogether different method.

The investigation of the religious environment of Jesus has acquired factitious importance in the modern turn of Christian theology and consequent direction of its apologetic. For this theology, revelation is not primarily the content of a body of inspired Scriptures comprised in the Old and the New Testaments, but the person of Jesus Christ, who was himself the supreme, if not the sole, revelation of the character of God, the Father in heaven, who is love. The "Kingdom of God" is the "regulative principle" of Christian theology; in it, as Jesus defined it, was revealed God's own purpose in the world, the final cause of creation, history, revelation, and redemption; and it is as a citizen of the Kingdom of Heaven that man is saved. The "essence" of Christianity is therefore to be sought in the religious and moral teaching of Jesus as the expression of his own religious life, or as might be said nowadays, his "religious experience."

The older apologetic found the essential peculiarity of Christianity in its doctrines of the divine nature of Christ and of redemption through his atoning death, appropriated by faith and communicated in the sacraments, which distinguished Christianity from Judaism and from all other religions that presented themselves as ways of salvation; the new apologetic seeks such a difference in the teaching of Jesus by word and example contrasted with the religion of the contemporary Scribes and Pharisees. As a system of professedly orthodox Protestant theology this may be called modern, but in so far as the "essence" is sought only in the teaching and example of Jesus it has precursors from the age of the Reformation down. It must suffice here to repeat that into this inquiry I have not transgressed.

Third, I have not meant to become involved in "Religionsgeschichtliche Probleme," the question when, where, and how the Jews got some of the notions which others seem to have entertained before them. In the period with which I have essayed to deal the most important of these notions had already been amalgamated, if not fully assimilated; the rabbis found them in their Scriptures and accepted them on the authority of revelation without any suspicion that they had any other origin. Some of these problems are very interesting and I have for years been much engaged with them; but the comparisons belong to the general history of religions, not specifically to Judaism. A general observation on the subject of borrowings in the sphere of ideas is expressed in Vol. II, pp. 394 f.

I have no intention of using the present supplementary sections for discussion of subjects which lie outside the scope of my work as defined above. Nor shall I fulfil in these Notes the desire or expectation that I give an "authority" for every statement. On the contrary, I have resisted the temptation to multiply references to the sources beyond the selection given in the foot-notes. For vast collections made for a wholly different purpose the reader may resort to Strack-Billerbeck, Kommentar zum Neuen Testament aus Talmud und Midrasch (4 volumes, 1922–1928); but he should be warned that the critical sifting of this miscellany devolves upon him who uses it for any particular purpose.

In the text of the volumes on Judaism I frequently had to pronounce a positive opinion on points on which I am well aware that the evidence is not of a nature to warrant confident assertion, or is susceptible of other interpretations. I think I have never delivered such an opinion without having weighed all the evidence or without acquaintance with the modern discussions; but as I have neither the right nor an inclination to conclude the argument with an *ipse dixit* I have taken occasion to present in the Notes at some length the views of scholars who entertain other opinions, for instance, on the Great Synagogue, or the membership and presidency of the Sanhedrin, or on the continuity of development in Judaism before and after the fall of Jerusalem, with the reasons adduced for them. On the other hand, I have made no attempt to give a bibliography of these controversies nor to enter into them, and it is not unlikely that some important contributions have been omitted.

For the rest, the Notes are supplementary to the text. Two classes of possible readers have been in mind, and I must crave the indulgence both of those to whom some of the notes seem superfluous and of those who find desired explanations lacking. Many notes not foreseen in Vol. I have been introduced, and some of those then contemplated will not be found in the present sections, generally because it seemed preferable consolidate the treatment of larger topics rather than to disperse it among many references.

Finally, I have availed myself of the opportunity to make numerous corrections. A second printing of the two volumes was necessary so soon after the first that there was time only to eliminate obvious typographical errors, and some even of such escaped notice. In the emendations in the Notes I have profited most by a detailed review by Professor Chaim Tschernowitz in two numbers of the periodical שבילי החנוך (1928), and by the extensive annotations of Professor Louis Ginzberg, kindly communicated to me in writing, some of which I have taken the liberty of inserting with his initials appended. To many other reviewers and correspondents I must content myself here in behalf of myself and my readers with a general acknowledgment of obligations.

Professor Louis Finkelstein of the Jewish Theological Seminary in New York has been so good as to verify in the library of the Seminary references to books and periodicals not accessible to me here; and, as in the previous volumes, my colleague, Professor H. A. Wolfson, has gone over the references to the Talmuds and Midrashim and called my attention to places where the statement in the text or the Note seemed to be inexact or not to be clear, for all of which I am most grateful.

The captions of the Notes are designed to make it possible to use for them the general indexes in Vol. II; to facilitate finding some of the longer detached notes I have subjoined here an indication of the pages on which they may be looked for.

NOTES

II, 7

That the Jewish teachers recognize the intrinsic difference between the distinctive observances of Judaism in the sphere of the cultus and the support of the ministry, or of domestic life, and universal moral laws, I have tried to make sufficiently plain here (II, 6–10) and in other places (II, 70–78). What I have maintained is that they also recognized that in a revealed religion which includes both kinds of duties or prohibitions the ground of obligation is the same for both, namely that thus and so is the revealed will of God. The gravity of the offense, in case of neglect or transgression, is dependent not on our natural notions, but upon revelation, which affixes the doom of extirpation (כרת) not solely to vile crimes such as incest but to eating flesh with a remainder of blood in it or the suet of certain animal kinds (p. 6). It belonged to the Jewish faith in God's wisdom and goodness to believe that in prohibiting the flesh of a "hare" (ארנבת) and in similar cases for which there was no reason apparent to men, God had reasons which were beyond human understanding, but that all such things were ordered for the good of his people. Philosophers, from Philo on (see Vol. I, 213 f.), endeavored to discern and explain the divine motive, but he would not admit that the discovery of the goodness and reasonableness of the laws (see, e.g., De specialibus legibus, iv. cc. 4 ff., ed. Mangey, II, 352 ff.) was the reason why Jews should observe them (Vol. II, p. 9). In the sphere of morals, so far as I can see, the Tannaim had no notion of a rationalistic ethics, still less of an intuitive ethics — "thus saith the Lord" was the beginning and end of their wisdom; 'He hath taught thee, O man, what is good; and what doth the Lord require of thee' (Micah 6, 8). Between this attitude and a rationalization like that in Maimonides' "Eight Chapters" lies Aristotle. Without ignoring that morality is integral in Judaism in a sense that cannot be affirmed, for example, of the religions of the Greeks, it may be said that attempts to define Judaism as essentially an "ethical religion," like similar definitions of the essence of Christianity (often in contrast not only to contemporary heathenism but to Judaism), are modernizations which belong to apologetics, not to history.

II, 10 ll. 13–18

Consequences, which when they were put in practice, shocked Paul greatly (see, e.g., his first epistle to the Corinthians, almost throughout).

II, 11 ll. 17–21

This restriction of the sacrificial cultus to one sanctuary had not always existed. Worship at the local "high places" was in its time general and entirely legitimate (e.g., 1 Sam. 9 f.). Deuteronomy 12 (cf. Lev. 17, 3–9) proposes to make an end of all this, and 2 Kings 22 f. narrates how Josiah put in force the provisions of the law in 622/621 B.C. (according to the generally accepted chronology). Doubts about the historical character of this account and about the age of the law itself have not been lacking. We know of a temple with a priesthood and sacrifices at Elephantine, a military colony garrisoned by Jews far up the Nile, which was destroyed by the Egyptians with the connivance of the local Persian governor in 410 B.C. and by the account of the Jews on the spot had existed there before the Persian conquest of Egypt in 525 B.C., and it may be suspected that there were such ἱερά in other places in Egypt before the Onias temple. The latter was erected, or at least reconstructed, under the lead of Palestinian refugees in the days of Antiochus Epiphanes, with a legitimate priesthood of the old Jerusalem line (Josephus, Antt. xii. 9, 7 § 387 f.; xiii. 3, 1–3; Bell. Jud. vii. 10, 2). See Valeton, "Jahwe-Tempels buiten Jerusalem" in Teyler's Theologisch Tijdschrift, 1910, pp. 33 ff.; S. Krauss, Synagogale Altertümer, pp. 72–92, and the literature there cited. — It is sufficient for our present purpose that rabbinical authorities agree in recognizing Jerusalem as the one place where public sacrifice can legitimately be offered.

II, 11 ll. 28–30

As the expansion of Islam made obsolete the annual attendance on the Feast at Mecca (*ḥajj*). Nowadays a man who has made such a visit once in his life adds to his name *hajji*, like a title of nobility. — Ceremonial uncleanness would not exclude from admission to the sacrificial rites and mingling with the throng of worshippers (Ḥagigah 4b), but distance might prevent a man from appearing in Jerusalem at all.

II, 12 ll. 1–4 and n. 1

See also Tos. Pesaḥim 4, 3: Once King Agrippa wanted to take a kind of census, and instructed the priests to save for him one testicle from each passover victim. There proved to be 600,000 pairs of testicles — twice the number of the Israelites who came out of Egypt (Exod. 12, 37) — and there was no passover company numbering less than ten persons; those who were on a far journey, or who were unclean were not included in the numeration. It is added that the "mountain of the house" would not hold them all, and that it was called the "Passover when men were crushed to death." But on this name see Levy III, 190. The resulting number of those present was 1,200,000. Cf. Pesaḥim 64b; Lam. R. on Lam. 1, 1, ed. Buber, f. 23a for the text and the editor's notes). For the name "Passover of the Crushed" a Baraita in Pesaḥim 64b gives another origin, referring it to an occasion in the time of Hillel when an old man was crushed to death by the crowds in the court of the Temple.

II, 12 ll. 16–24

On the prayers and readings in the Temple see M. Yoma 6, 1; Tos. Yom Kippurim, 4, 18; Jer. Yoma, vii. 1; Yoma 70a.[L. G.]

II, 12, end, 13 ll. 1 ff.

On the lay deputation (*ma'amad*) see Malter's note in his edition of Ta'anit (1928) on Ta'anit 15b (p. 105, n. 230), also pp. 198 f. (on M. Ta'anit 4, 1–4). — A private sacrifice was presented either by the offerer or by his representative (שליח).

I, 13 n. 5

Cf. Ta'anit 27b, where the purpose of these fasts is specified. Note also the reasons there given for not including Sunday. R. Johanan (third century) said מפני הנוצרים, etc.

II, 14 ll. 1–7

The blowing of the ram's horn and the waving of the palm branches were observed in the synagogues and at home before the destruction of the Temple, cf. M. Rosh ha-Shanah 4, 1; M. Sukkah 3, 12, but outside the Temple the ram's horn was not blown on the Sabbath, and, after the destruction of the Temple, the palm branches, which previously had been manipulated outside the Temple only on the first day of Tabernacles, were used on all the seven days. [L. G.]

II, 14 ll. 25 ff.

One may perhaps surmise that the idea had its starting point in the readings prescribed for the *ma'amadot* (the creation of heaven and earth, Gen. 1), rather than in the Haggadah about Abraham as is alleged in the Talmud. Or did the designation of Gen. 1 for the lessons rest on some such a connection? — In the days of the Amoraim named the temple-worship had long since ceased, but *ma'amadot* had an established place in the synagogue, which was long maintained. Baer, 'Abodat Israel p. 495 cites testimony of Rab Amram to the continuance of the custom in the voluntary practice of individuals, and gives reasons for its discontinuance as part of the synagogue service.

II, 15 n. 1

Reference should be made also to Menaḥot 110a, where the general principle is applied particularly to the various species of sacrifice. In the preceding context it may be noted that on the heavenly altar the great prince Michael offers sacrifice. It is perhaps such studious substitutes for material sacrifice that Rab has in mind.

II, 17 ll. 5–10.

This passage in Herodotus is quoted by Josephus, C. Apionem, i. c. 22 §§ 168–171; cf. Antt. xvii. 10, 3 §§ 260–262.

II, 18 ll. 22–27

R. Akiba would not admit any such delay.

II, 19 l. 15

The term *ger ṣedeḳ* is never applied to the manumitted slave, who is always described as עבד משחרר. . . . . The second baptism admitted him to full standing in the Jewish community, including the *connubium*, and imposed upon him the religious obligations, which as a slave he had been exempt from. [L. G.]

II, 19 ll. 19 ff.

See Note on Vol. I, p. 198, n. 3.

II, 22 ll. 19 f.

The inference from 2 Kings 4, that in old Israel people were accustomed to demit their ordinary occupations on the New Moon, and might use the opportunity to visit a "man of God" like Elisha, is one which I should not be inclined to press; our knowledge of what was customary in Israel in the ninth century is too small to warrant confidence.

II, 23 n. 2

Labor was not forbidden on the New Moon, but some made a voluntary or customary holiday of it; see also Megillah 22b. — In Jer. Pesaḥim 30d, top, reference is made to a woman's custom, to refrain, at least partially, from work on the New Moon; cf. Pirkè de-R. Eliezer, c. 45, where an historical origin is attributed to the custom. [L. G.] This is perpetuated and commended in the Codes: see Shulḥan 'Aruk, Oraḥ Ḥayyim § 417.

II, 24 n. 1

Unleavened bread at the Passover season could be the rule everywhere, as doubtless it had been before the destruction of the Temple (cf. Vol. II, p. 40). Other features of the festival rites were taken over, with adaptation, into the synagogue and the home; but the sabbatical observance was the main thing.

II, 26 ll. 3–8

In their wars with the Romans we find it the established rule that defensive operations were licit, but not *offensive*. Josephus, Bell. Jud. i. 7, 3 § 146 (Pompey); cf. ii. 16, 4 § 392 (Agrippa's speech); ii. 17, 10 § 456; iv. 2, 3 § 100. — The Jews represent that they are forbidden to take up arms, even in defense; but they are trying to deceive Titus. The Romans themselves had *feriae publicae* on which it was *nefas* "hostem lacessere bello." (Wissowa, Religion und Kultus der Römer; Festus p. 226). — In Titus's siege of Jerusalem the factions within the city were as little deterred by such scruples from breaking the Sabbath as from desecrating the Temple. — For the rabbinical rules of defensive and offensive military operations references may be made to Maimonides, Hilkot Shabbat 2, 23–25 and the passages of the Talmud there cited in the commentaries ('Erubin 45a; Shabbat 19a).

II, 28 ll. 4–11

This connection of the "thirty-nine" species of labor prohibited on the Sabbath with Deut. 25, 2 f., is very far-fetched, and should not have been asserted as if it were an authenticated fact — the combination seems, on the contrary, to be modern. — For other ways in which the number 39 was ciphered out, see Strack-Billerbeck, I, 617 (paragraph c).

II, 29 n. 2

According to Beṣah 12b, rubbing out the heads of grain in the hands is not threshing, and is therefore only rabbinically prohibited. [L. G.]

II, 31 n. 3

According to Joshua ben Levi "combinations of courts" were ordained only for the sake of peace (friendly relations in the neighborhood). Jer. 'Erubin 20d, below; and 24c, end; Tanḥuma ed. Buber, Noah 22. The rule has, however, been interpreted as a cautionary restrictive measure.

II, 35 n. 2

In the Morning Prayer on the Sabbath of Penitence to the same purport (ישמח משה,' in the fourth 'benediction'): "And thou didst not give it, O Lord our God, unto the Gentiles of the (other) lands, nor didst thou, O our King, make it a heritage of the worshippers of images, and in its resting place the uncircumcised do not abide; but to thy people Israel thou didst give it in love, to the seed of Jacob whom thou didst choose." (Singer, Prayer Book, p. 139; Baer, p. 219, and Baer's note with citations from Talmud and Midrash). Abrahams, Companion to the Daily Prayer Book, pp. cxlvi ff., calls particular attention to the resemblance to Jubilees as illustrating the antiquity of features of the liturgy which otherwise are known to us only from the Gaonic age or after it. Cf. also the Ḳiddush of the day, on the ẹve of the Sabbath (Singer, p. 124; Baer, p. 198).

II, 35 l. 31

The three meals are obligatory, even for a pauper who is dependent on alms. There seems to be no authority for making of the third a *light* repast; the codes treat them all alike, each of them presuming the regular provision of wine and the breaking of the two loaves (Maimonides, Hilkot Shabḅat 30, 9). The Shulḥan 'Aruk, however, contemplates the case of a man who has eaten to satiety at the previous meal; he may satisfy his obligation by eating a quantity no greater than an egg, and if he cannot do even that, he is not bound to force himself (Oraḥ Ḥayyim § 291, 1). A wise man will look out not to fill his belly at the forenoon meal, so as to have room for the third meal (ibid.).

II, 36 ll. 5–8

The statement about the sabbath lamp was corrected in the second printing to read as follows: "It was an ancient custom . . . on Friday afternoon before dark to light a lamp which was to be left burning through the evening of the holy day."

II, 36 ll. 15 ff.

This Kiddush belongs in the home, where the table has been spread for the family meal. In Tannaite times there were no congregational prayers in the afternoon, and the eve of the Sabbath was not an exception. The introduction of a Ḳiddush into the synagogue service on Friday afternoon, like this service itself, is later, and is thought to have begun in Babylonia. There is mention, however, of a Ḳiddush in the synagogue building, and over wine, in Mekilta Baḥodesh 7 (ed. Friedmann f. 69a–b; ed. Weiss f. 76b–77a; cf. Pesaḥim 106a), and on the other hand we hear from Samuel (Babylonia, 3d cent.), אין קדוש אלא במקום סעודה. The place of the Ḳiddush and Habdalah in the congregational prayer is a very tangled history, into which there is, fortunately no necessity to penetrate here. See I. Elbogen, "Eingang und Ausgang des Sabbats nach talmudischen Quellen," in Festschrift zu Israel Lewy's siebzigstem Geburtstag (1911), pp. 173–187; L. Ginzberg, REJ. LXVII (1914), pp. 133 f., 150. Ginzberg thinks that the Ḳiddush (קדושא רבא, Pesaḥim 106a, to which he would refer the passage in the Mekilta) originally had its place in the Sabbath morning service in the synagogue, the transposition to the eve of the Sabbath was later, since it presumes a Friday afternoon service.

The Ḳiddush in the home on the eve of the Sabbath is usually pronounced over the wine. It is permissible, however, to say it, omitting, of course, the blessing on the wine, over the two loaves of bread, if the householder likes it better than wine, or if he has no wine (Pesaḥim 106b; Maimonides, Hilkot Shabbat, 29, 9; Shulḥan 'Aruk, Oraḥ Ḥayyim § 271, 12).

II, 36 ll. 22 f.

This symbolism is a homiletic afterthought.

II, 36 n. 3

The form of blessing over the lights found in the prayer-books is mediaeval.

II, 36 n. 7

This note should be cancelled. — The כוס של ברכה is the cup following which the grace after meals (ברכת המזון) is said. On the Sabbath the grace after meals is expanded by the insertion of a prayer appropriate to the day, known from its initial word as רְצֵה (Singer, p. 281 f.; Baer, p. 557), which is in substance very old.

II, 37 ll. 11–14, n. 3

The text is not as clear as it should be: fasting on the Sabbath is never permissible (except when the Day of Atonement falls on a Sabbath); M. Ta'anit 3, 7 names certain emergencies in which an alarm may be sounded on the Sabbath (cf. Ta'anit 22b), but has nothing to say about fasting on that day.

II, 40

On the rules for Passover and Unleavened Bread a century or more before the Christian era, see Jubilees 49. The prescriptions closely follow the biblical laws and interpret them strictly (see especially 49, 20); nothing sectarian is discoverable in them.

II, 40 ll. 12–14

The obligation to partake of the *maṣṣot* on the eve of the fifteenth is treated as an independent requirement of the Law, binding everywhere and in all times. Maimonides, Hilkot Ḥamaṣ u-Maṣṣah, 6, 1; see also the discussion, Pesaḥim 120a. — "There can be no doubt that long before the destruction of the Temple, the Passover meal became a home ceremony entirely independent of the sacrifice. In the description of this ceremony in M. Pesaḥim 10, 1–7, though composed before 70 (cf. Hoffmann, Die erste Mischna, pp. 16–17), the sacrifice plays a very subordinate part." [L. G.]

II, 40 n. 4

As at the other pilgrim festivals, when all male Israelites were required to appear before the Lord at the sanctuary of his choice (Jerusalem), Exod. 23, 14, 17; Deut. 16, 16, the actual participation of women is not questioned. On the whole subject see M. Pesaḥim, 8, 1; cf. Pesaḥim 91a (discussion by disciples of R. Akiba).

II, 42 ll 1–21

The modern rule corresponds; see Shulḥan 'Aruk, Oraḥ Ḥayyim § 476, 1.

II, 42 ll. 21 f.

The cup of Elijah owes its origin to a misunderstood phrase. In Pesaḥim 117b (bottom) some authorities in the Middle Ages read, 'the fourth 'cup (רביעי) and others 'the third' (שלישי, see Tosafot *in loc.*). This question, like many others, Elijah would have to settle when he came. [L. G.] See below, Note on Vol. II, p. 359, n. 4.

II, 43 ll. 12 ff.

"The exact time of this procession is nowhere given. I am inclined to assume that it took place before Musaf, as is now the custom among Sephardim and has the authority of Sa'adia." (See Genizah Studies, II, n. 18). On p. 44, l. 1, for "the people" *read* "the priests." — "It is also very doubtful whether they marched with palm-branches; the text of the Mishnah rather favors the view given in Sukkot 43b that the weeping-willow was carried and not the palm-branches." [L. G.]

II, 45 ll. 7 ff.

See Feuchtwanger, "Die Wasseropfer und die damit verbundenen Zeremonien," Monatsschrift, LIV–LV.

II, 45 ll. 25 ff.

For a different interpretation ("Fackelhaus") which would explain the name of the illumination of the Temple, see Kohut, Aruch Completum, I, 85, where it is etymologically associated with the Syriac *shauba*, 'burning heat, *simmum* wind' (Bar Baḥlul, ed. Duval, 1939); it is employed to render the Greek καύσων (see Payne Smith, s.v., col. 4085 f.). That the word was ever used of a light or a torch, I find no evidence.

II, 49 ll. 5–10

The name *Simḥat Torah* is mediaeval; the earliest authority to mention it is Hai Gaon. Previously this day (23d of Tishri) was indicated merely as the second of Shemini 'Aṣeret. The one year cycle of Pentateuch lessons which ended and recommenced on this day is Babylonian, though it has become universal. Elbogen, Der jüdische Gottesdienst, pp. 167, 200.

II, 49 ll. 25–30

Josephus, Antt. xii. 7, 7 § 325; cf. c. Apionem, ii. 9 § 118. Apart from the reported difference between the Shammaites and the Hillelites (Shabbat 21b), there is not much about the Ḥanukkah lights in Palestinian sources, though Palestinian Amoraim are quoted in the Babylonian Talmud (Johanan, Joshua ben Levi, al.). The provision for putting them out of sight, or in a position where they might seem to be ordinary household lights, in case of danger, seems to point to countries under Sassanian (Zoroastrian) rule in the third century.

II, 56 n. 2

In M. Yoma 6, 8, the place is called בית חדודו (cf. Enoch, 10, 4, Dudael); in the editions of the Pal. Targum, בית חדורי. In the Mishnah of the Jer. Talmud (10, 9) בית חורון is not the *terminus ad quem*.

II, 59 l. 10

On the observance of the day, see Philo, De septenario c. 23, ed. Mangey, II, 296 f.; on the all-day supplications, § 196.

II, 61 ll. 18–21, and n. 4.

The quotation of Cant. 3, 11 in the Mishnah is the answer of the young man (*read* וכך הוא אומר, so Mishnah, ed. Lowe); see Malter, Ta'anit (1928), p. 203, n. 389. — The match-making of the day left its traces in the reading of the פרשת עריות at the afternoon service; Megillah 31a. [L. G.]

II, 62 ll. 5–10

In the liturgy note the prayer אתה זוכר in the Musaf service on New Years (Singer, p. 249 f.; Baer, pp. 400–402); cf. Elbogen, Der jüdische Gottesdienst, pp. 142, 143 f., 204. The age of this prayer prefatory to the Zikronot (see Vol. II, p. 64) is not known, but the ideas of God's all-comprehending knowledge and his perfect justice are both old and familiar; and his annual judgement on nations and individuals was long-established belief.

II, 63 l. 25

An error in this passage was corrected in the second printing: it should accordingly read: "it was transposed to a later hour, in the Musaf prayers," and in the sequel: "It retained this place in the liturgy, but what might be called an anticipatory horn-blowing was introduced when the congregation was seated after the close of the morning prayer and the reading of the law." See Rosh ha-Shanah 16a–b, where the question is raised why the ram's horn is blown when the congregation is seated and (again) when they are standing (in the Musaf prayers); see Maimonides, Hilkot Shofar, 3, 10–12; Elbogen, Der jüdische Gottesdienst, p. 140 f., 142.

II, 64 l. 4

On the significance of these three proper benedictions for New Years, cf. Rosh ha-Shanah 16a, bottom. — It may be noted that the verses selected in the Malkuyot refer to God's goodness to Israel, not to his discomfiture of the heathen.

II, 66 ll. 6 f.

That is, it was treated as a public fast in distinction from a fast of individuals.

II, 70 ll. 3-6

Vespasian converted this into an annual poll-tax on all Jews in whatever part of the empire, to be appropriated to the temple of Jupiter on the Capitoline in Rome, as previously they had paid it to the Temple in Jerusalem, Josephus, Bell. Jud. vii. 6, 6 § 218; Dio Cassius, lxv. 7, 2.

II, 70 n. 1

The portion of the sacrificing priests, defined in Lev. 7, 31-34. According to the Mishnah (M. Ḥullin, 10, 1; cf. Sifrè Deut. § 165) of an animal slaughtered for food (not a prescribed victim) the parts named in Deut. 18, 3 are customarily given to a priest (M. Ḥallah, 5, 9), both in the land of Israel and outside the land, and whether the Temple is standing or not. In the Talmud (Ḥullin 136a) the opinion of Rabbi Ila'i (contemporary of Ishmael and Akiba, early second century) was that these presents (מתנות), like the Terumah, were made only in the land of Israel, not outside of it.

II, 71 n. 1

On the character of some of the high priestly houses of this period see Pesaḥim 57a; Tos. Menaḥot 13, 18-22; cf. Tos. Sukkah 14, 6. In Jer. Yoma 38c the great number of high priests who served in the second temple is accounted for by their getting into office by murder (of their predecessors), "some say that they killed one another by sorcery" (בכשפים).

II, 71 n. 4

On the ratio of the Terumah to the whole, a difference of opinion between the Schools of Shammai and Hillel is reported in Tos. Terumot 5, 3, the former regarding 1/30 as liberal, the latter 1/40. The former is thought to have in view the well-to-do; the latter, the poor. [L. G.]

II, 71 n. 6

The burning of Ḥallah is prescribed in the Mishnah in certain regions in or adjacent to Palestine, where two Ḥallahs are required one of which is thrown into the fire; see M. Ḥallah 4, 5. See Büchler, Der galiläische 'Am ha-'Areṣ, pp. 255 ff. For modern rules see Shulḥan 'Aruk, Yoreh De'ah § 322 ff.

II, 71 n. 7

On the meaning and use of the phrase "Mosaic law from Sinai," see Vol. I, p. 256.

II, 72 n. 1

See Büchler, Der galiläische 'Am ha-'Areṣ, p. 16.

II, 72 n. 2

On the dire consequences of the neglect of tithing, see Abot 5, 8 f. M. Yadaim, 4, 3; the statement in Midrash Tehillim is not found in early sources. [L. G.]

II, 73 ll. 2–5

The Terumah Gedolah of agricultural products (Num. 18, 12 f.) and the tenth of the Levites' tithe (Terumat Ma'aser, Num. 18, 25–28) are the portion of the priests and their households (being in a state of ceremonial "cleanness"); Vol. II, p. 72 (Num. 18, 13–19), and are strictly prohibited to all others; while the remainder of the Levites' tithe is not sacred, and may be eaten by any one.

II, 74

On the so-called "dietary laws," and their educational importance, see Josephus, c. Apionem, ii. 17. On the meaning and wisdom of these laws, Philo, De special. legibus, iv. §§ 100 ff. (De concupiscentia, cc. 4 ff., ed. Mangey, II, 352 ff.). Allegorical interpretation, Ep. Aristeae, §§ 143 ff. (ed. Wendland). — On rules attributed to Pythagoras, Diogenes Laertius, viii. 19 ff., 33–35. — Abstinence from every kind of animal food was common in philosophical piety.

II, 74 ll. 25–75, l. 3

Such inspection (בדיקה) as is now practiced is of very late origin; it is not known in Talmudic times. (L. G.]

II, 75 l. 4

"Difficult" is hardly strong enough; for a strictly observant Jew it would have been impossible; particularly the cooking utensils used in a Gentile kitchen made anything prepared in them prohibited food.

II, 75 ll. 22 ff.

For a curious partial parallel in Unyoro (Central Africa) see Frazer, Taboo and the Perils of the Soul (Golden Bough, Vol. III, p. 272).

II, 75 n. 2

Cf. Esther (Greek), after 4, 17 (Esther says): *καὶ οὐκ ἐδόξασα συμπόσιον βασιλέως, οὐδὲ ἔπιον οἶνον σπονδῶν* [Perles].

II, 76 ll. 9 f.

Contact with *dead* animals is meant, and should have been said.

II, 76 ll. 13 ff.

See Büchler, Der galiläische 'Am ha-'Areṣ, p. 2 f., n., and pp. 157 ff.

II, 76 ll. 20f.

The purifications here meant are those which required an offering in the Temple. There were rites of purification in which the year 70 was no such crisis, and these may have been observed by scrupulous persons thereafter. For an example see Ḥagigah 25a, and on the question how long they thus continued see L. Ginzberg, Genizah Studies, p. 71.

II, 77 ll. 11–16

See Note on Vol. II, p. 7.

II, 81 ll. 20–22

See below on Vol. II, p. 83, n. 2.

II, 83 n. 2

Plato, Diogenes Laertius, iii. 90: *φρόνησις, δικαιοσύνη, ἀνδρεία, σοφρωσύνη*, with brief definitions of their several spheres.

II, 85 ll. 7–9

Numerous echoes and applications of this saying, or of the principles enounced in it, are collected by Kobryn *ad loc.* (f. 25a–27b). — The order, Truth, Justice, Peace, in which the three terms are sometimes found, seems to me to be a transposition, bringing the order into correspondence with Zech. 8, 16, quoted in the sequel.

II, 85 l. 24

בכל מאודך. In Berakot 61b the word is understood of material resources, *mammon*. A different interpretation is quoted from R. Akiba who finds in the word מדה, 'measure'; see Vol. II, p. 253 and n. 4.

II, 85 n. 1

Sifrè, l.c., is quoted in Ta'anit 2a, below.

II, 87 ll. 12 ff.

See King, "The Negative Golden Rule," Canadian Journal of Religious Thought (1928).

II, 95 n. 5

The term בעל חוב, 'creditor,' is used of God in his relation to man; Marmorstein, The Old Rabbinic Doctrine of God, p. 79, citing Shebu'ot 42b, top; Giṭṭin 51b (Rabbah). Other instances in which sin and its penalty are a debt to God are Jer. Shabbat, 15d, הניחו לנבאי שינבה חובו, and Jer. Ta'anit 66c, where God is מרי חובא. Büchler, Studies in Sin and Atonement (1928), p. 154, n. 2, p. 336, n. 1. On flogging in expiation of offenses against which the כרת is denounced, see Sifrè on Deut. 25, 3 (§ 286): כל חייבי כריתות שלקו נפטרו מיד כריתתן.

II, 96 n. 1

On פרס see Note on Vol. I, p. 35.

II, 98 ll. 6–9

See Vol. I, p. 367. Marmorstein, op. cit., pp. 105–107; though with his surmise that it means "the Father in Heaven" I do not agree.

II, 99

On the service of God out of love or fear, and the obedience of Job, see Büchler, Studies in Sin and Atonement (1928), pp. 122 ff.

II, 101

On the Ḳaddish, see Vol. I, p. 306, Notes **83**, **84**.

II, 102 ll. 4–12

Cf. Ecclus. 33 (36), 1–5.

II, 103 n. 2

In Sanhedrin 74a–b, the offense must be committed with publicity, which is defined as under the observation of at least ten Israelites; but it may be about so small a matter as changing the Jewish mode of lacing shoes for one customary among the heathen, in which the form of the knot had perhaps a magical or a superstitious significance. In the same passage a difference is made between ordinary occasions and a time of religious persecution when the government undertakes by edict to nullify the Jewish law. See Maimonides, Yesodè ha-Torah, 5, 1 ff.

II, 104 ll. 16f.

By an oversight to which Professor Perles has kindly called my attention, number 4 in the text is used twice, and the second of the two notes thus indicated was omitted altogether. The bit of Midrash on Psalm 123, 1 is preserved in the Yalkuṭ II § 548, end (on Amos 9, 6), from which Buber has restored it in his edition of Midrash Tehillim on the Psalm (f. 255a). The last clause in my quotation (l. 16) should read: Otherwise, *Thou wouldst* not be sitting in the heavens.

II, 105 ll. 7–14

The point of the story about Sarah is not the act of charity, but the demonstration that she had borne a child, thus hallowing the name of God. [L. G.].

II, 106 ll. 19 ff.

I. Halevy argues, against Graetz and others, that this conference was held before the fall of Bether (the last act of the war under Hadrian); see Doroth Harischonim, I e (Vol. II), pp. 371 f. For the purpose of the present work this question is not vital.

II, 113 ll. 15–19

Cf. what the Jewish deputation has to say before the Emperor Augustus against the succession of Archelaus, and their request that their country be annexed to Syria under the administration of governors of their own people in Josephus, Bell. Jud. ii. 6, 2; see also ii. 2, 3 § 22 (autonomy under the administration of a Roman governor).

II, 114 ll. 1 ff.

Cf. The Essene oath, Josephus, Bell. Jud. ii. 1, 7: At his initiation "he swears tremendous oaths, first, that he will reverence the Deity, then that he will deal justly with men, and injure no one, either of his own accord or under orders, will always hate the unjust and contend strenuously on the side of the just; that he will ever keep faith with all men, especially with those in power, for without God rule comes to no man," etc. See also Cant. R. (on Cant. 2, 7) and Ketubot 111a, top. — Biblical examples of honor paid to heathen governments and rulers, Mekilta Bo, 13 (ed. Friedmann, 13b–14a).

II, 115 n. 4

References may be added: Josephus Antt. xii. 10, 5 § 406 (for the Seleucid king); c. Apion. ii. 6 § 76 f. (for the Emperors and the Roman people).

II, 115 n. 6

See also the sequel, Bell. Jud. ii. 17, 3 f. (§§ 409–417).

II, 116 l. 8 and n. 1

The name "Vespasian" makes difficulty, for although Josephus (Bell. Jud. iv. 3, 2 § 130) brings Vespasian from Caesarea to Jamnia and Azotus, while Titus, after the fall of Gischala and the flight of John to Jerusalem, moved his headquarters to Caesarea, all this was before the investment of Jerusalem. The strife of factions, however, was already raging within the city as well as throughout the land.

II, 119 ff.

L. M. Epstein, The Jewish Marriage Contract. A study of the Status of Woman in Jewish Law. 1927. With a classified bibliography of the whole subject (pp. 301–304) and an index.

II, 119 ll. 19 f.

That eighteen is the proper age for a man to marry is to be found in Abot 5, 21, where the whole of life is laid off in a comprehensive scheme (Vol. I, p. 320). In foot-note 5 the reference to Ḳiddushin 29b has to do only with the words attributed to R. Ishmael. In the sequel other opinions about the best age for marriage are reported. See L. Ginzberg, Genizah Studies, I. 478. The actual ages most likely varied widely from any mean, with times and circumstances.

II, 120 n. 1

See Ginzberg, *l.s.c.* In Ḳiddushin 29b I have followed the interpretation of Rashi; the contrary explanation is given in the Tosafot.

II, 120 n. 7

One may compare the advice of Pittacus about such an alternative in the Anthology, vii. No. 89: τὴν κατὰ σαυτὸν ἔλα.

II, 121 n. 3

See also S. Krauss, "Die Ehe zwischen Onkel und Nichte," in Studies in Jewish Literature in honor of K. Kohler (1913), pp. 165–175.

II, 121 n. 6

See, however, Ḳiddushin 41a (repeated, 81b, below), in the name of Rab (or "as some say, R. Eleazar"): "A man is forbidden to give his daughter in marriage while she is a minor (*ḳeṭannah*), until she grows up and says, I want so and so." This rule is incorporated in the modern code (Shulḥan 'Aruk, Eben ha-'Ezer 37, 8; but see the Tosafot on Ḳiddushin 41a and commentators on Shulḥan 'Aruk l.c.).

II, 121 ll. 14 ff.

See A. Büchler, "Das jüdische Verlöbnis, u.s.w.," in Festschrift zu Israel Lewy's siebzigstem Geburtstag (1911), pp. 110 ff.

II, 122 ll. 1–3

The expressions used in these lines are exposed to misunderstanding. I did not mean to suggest a religious character in the Ḳiddushin; but the exclusive right of the husband in his wife, just as things and persons in which God has an exclusive right are said in the Bible to be *ḳadosh*, and as such not to be meddled with by others. An equivalent, and presumably older, term is קנה, 'acquire' (property rights). Professor Perles brings to my notice the fact that Rappoport associated the word Ḳiddushin with the Aramaic (and Syriac) קדשא 'ring,' (the man gave the woman a ring), but I should imagine that the ring was so-called because it was an amulet, and of an ancient Jewish ring ceremony in betrothal or wedding I know nothing. (See S. Krauss, Talmudische Archäeologie, II, 36 and p. 455, n. 298.)

II, 122 l. 5

Sexual relations of any kind with foreign female slaves are strictly prohibited; see M. Giṭṭin 4, 5. The kind of slavery of Jewish women contemplated in Exod. 21, 7–11 had gone out of use in the times of the Tannaim and Amoraim; the rabbis see in the union of a Jewish female servant and her master a regular marriage, not concubinage (Ḳiddushin 19b). [L. G.] — The statement in the text that "the rabbinical law corresponds" must be qualified accordingly.

II, 122 ll. 6–10

On polygamy see the article in the Jewish Encyclopedia, X, 120–122, especially for this period, p. 121 A. — "I know of only one case of polygamy among the Tannaim, Abba, the brother of Gamaliel II (Jewish Encyclopedia, I, 29)." [L. G.] — The nine wives of Herod — not all at once — by seven of whom he had offspring (Josephus, Bell. Jud. i. 28, 4 § 562), are to be regarded as privileges of uxorious royalty, not as examples of custom among his subjects.

II, 122 ll. 16 ff.

For the literature on divorce, see L. M. Epstein, The Jewish Marriage Contract, pp. 302 f.

II, 122 ll. 12–15

On the marriage contract (Ketubah) see Epstein, cited in the last note. That some form of marriage contract is older than Simeon ben Shaṭaḥ is demonstrable (Epstein, *op. cit.*, pp. 17–31); the precise nature of the changes introduced by Simeon ben Shaṭaḥ it is difficult to determine.

II, 123 ll. 6–9

Giṭṭin 90b. See Bacher, cited in n. 3, who surmises that the rabbis here named were the two sons of R. Ḥiyya (third century). It is possible that the two rabbis had in mind different cases.

Josephus' account of his own divorce from his second wife, who had borne him three children (Vita, c. 76 § 426), μὴ ἀρεσκόμενος αὐτῆς τοῖς ἤθεσιν ἀπεπεμψάμην, is indefinite enough.

II, 126 ll. 27 f.

The most significant advance beyond the biblical laws is to be seen in emancipation of the girl who has arrived at the age of puberty (בוגרת, גדולה) from the control of her father; she is thenceforth completely her own mistress. This is treated in Tannaite laws not as the kind of innovation that is nowadays called a "reform," but as an established principle. See, e.g., Mekilta on Exod. 21, 7 (ed. Friedmann, f. 74b; ed. Weiss, f. 84a).

II, 127 n. 4

The age was not the decisive factor, but the physical evidence of puberty. Since there were abnormal cases both of premature and of delayed development, the rule was that a girl remained under the authority of her father from twelve years to twelve years and six months.

II, 127 ll. 15–17

The earnings of a daughter belong to her father until she becomes *suae juris;* those of a boy in his minority are his own. [L. G.]

II, 128 n. 4

The obligation of fathers to teach their sons Torah and to begin talking Hebrew to them as soon as they began to speak, and that there is no similar duty to teach their daughters, see Sifrè Deut. § 146, on Deut. 11, 19.

II, 129 ll. 14–16

The rule that women are exempt from positive commandments for the observance of which a time is set (Sifrè Num. § 115, at the beginning, on Num. 15, 37 f.) was perhaps first formulated by R. Simeon (ben Yoḥai) who is named there. The Mishnah is frequently at variance with the general rule enounced by R. Simeon; e.g., M. Berakot, 3, 3, quoted in the text. [L. G.] — The commentators who feel obliged to harmonize these prescriptions with the general rule, are put to some straits.

II, 129 l. 17

The parenthesis (*at Tabernacles*) is accidentally misplaced: it should stand after "the palm-branches."

II, 129 n. 10

These rules affect all the relations of men with women.

II, 130 n. 5

See, however, Kiddushin 52b, at the bottom, and Tosafot, *ad loc.* (lemma, וכי).

II, 133 l. 19

This Dama ben Netina lived before the destruction of the Temple; see note 8, and add Tos. Parah 2, 1.

II, 135 ll. 7–10

In Sanhedrin 71a, R. Simeon (ben Yoḥai) is quoted as saying (in regard to some of the specifications of the rabbinical law defining Deut. 21, 20), "Such a case never arose and never will arise."

II, 135 ll. 20–22

The rules found in rabbinical sources about the Hebrew slave are purely theoretical. In 'Arakin 29a it is said that this form of servitude existed only as long as the year of Jubilee was observed, i.e., in the time of the first temple; this is probably an exegetical inference not an historical tradition, but we may safely infer that it had become obsolete long before the age of the Tannaim. See Vol. II, p. 138.

II, 136 ll. 1–4

On the "Canaanite" (alien) slave in Jewish law, see Maimonides, Hilkot 'Abadim, 5 ff. — The legal status of such a slave was better than in Roman law. See, in general, S. Krauss, Talmudische Archäologie, II, 91 ff.; Rubin, Das talmudische Recht, I, i, Die Sklaverei, 1920.

II, 136 n. 1

Whether the slave is real or personal property is in controversy between R. Meir and his colleagues. Baba Meṣi'a 100b. [L. G.]

II, 137 n. 1

The father is here supposed to be a *Gentile* or a Gentile freedman, not a Jew, to whom such relations were, according to most authorities, forbidden.

II, 138 l. 19

See Note on Vol. II, p. 135, ll. 20–22.

II, 142 ll. 13–20

Various kinds of adulteration are named in Eccles. R. 6, 1, along with fraudulent balances, etc.

II, 145 n. 5

The words of the usurer are euphemistically paraphrased in the Talmud. The meaning is "Moses was a *fool*, and his Torah is *not* true." [L. G.]

II, 149 n. 2

Note also the מלשינים in early forms of the Birkat ha-Minim (Shemoneh 'Esreh, 12).

II, 151 n. 1

On הגיון see L. Ginzberg, Unbekannte jüdische Sekte, pp. 70 f.

II, 152 n. 2

That is, a man should not insist on his rights to the utmost limit of the law, but have regard to the equity of the case and in fairness rather concede something to the other party. The Roman proverb *summum ius summa iniuria* (Cicero, De officiis, i. 10, 33) will occur to everyone.

II, 154 n. 4

Reference may also be made to Yoma 87a. For a form of confession, see Vol. I, p. 512 (N **225**).

II, 156 ff. (chap. vi)

See Bousset-Gressmann, Die Religion des Judentums, 3 ed. (1926), pp. 183 ff.

II, 157 ll. 21f.

In Seder 'Olam (c. 30, ed. Ratner f. 70b) the prophets prophesied till the time of Alexander of Macedon: "from that time on, incline thine ear and hear the words of the learned (*ḥakamim*), Prov. 22, 16 f."

II, 157 n. 5

See also Israel Abrahams, 'Am ha-'Areç, appended to Montefiore, The Synoptic Gospels (2 ed., 1927), II, 647–669.

II, 158 ll. 19–21

"In Tannaite times unclean food is *not* prohibited; men may partake of it if they are willing to take the consequence of becoming impure." [L. G.] See Maimonides, Hilkot Tum' at Okelin, 16, 7 ff.

II, 158 n. 1

The Babylonian Talmud does not lack reported answers to the question, Who is an *'am ha-'areṣ?*, and Babylonian scholars contribute their own (see, e.g., Berakot 29a).

II, 159 ll. 13 ff.

For the texts see Büchler, Der galiläische 'Am ha-'Areṣ, at the beginning; cf. I. Abrahams, 'Am ha-'Areç (above, Note on Vol. II, p. 157, n. 5).

II, 160 n. 1

Jesus son of Sirach was of the same way of thinking. See Bousset-Gressmann, Religion des Judentums, u.s.w., p. 164. In his case one might suspect something of upper-class feeling; but not in Hillel, who was himself a man of the people. For parallels to Hillel's saying, see Kobryn, Catena on Abot, f. 35b.

II, 162 n. 4

It is one of the most important differences between R. Ishmael and R. Akiba; see D. Hoffmann, Einleitung in die halachischen Midraschim, pp. 7–9. [L. G.]

II, 167 l. 5

On almsgiving in secret (בסתר) see Baba Batra 9b. R. Eliezer deduces from two texts that the man who gives alms in secret is greater than Moses.

II, 167 n. 5

Read העבט תעביטנו.

II, 168 n. 3

Hilkot Ṣedaḳah in R. Jacob ben Asher's Tur Yoreh De'ah (14th century) is in many respects superior to Maimonides' treatment of the subject. [L. G.] See also Schechter, Studies in Judaism, III.

II, 169 ll. 16–20

On the ups and downs of human life, cf. Philo, De somniis, i. 24 §§ 154–156, ed. Mangey I, 644 (symbolized by Jacob's ladder).

II, 171 ll. 15 f.

On the almsgiving of Gentiles different opinions are expressed. Johanan ben Zakkai is reported to have said, "as the sin-offering atones for Israel so almsgiving atones for the nations of the world" (Baba Batra, 10b, below; cf. his saying after the destruction of the Temple about the cessation of sacrificial atonement, Vol. I, p. 503; Vol. II, p. 172). The preceding context records the answers which the disciples of Johanan ben Zakkai made to a question he propounded to them, How do you interpret Prov. 14, 34 צדקה תרומם גוי וחסד לאומים חטאת? They took גוי to refer to Israel (quoting 2 Sam. 7, 23), and חטאת to mean 'sin': "Almsgiving exalts a nation (Israel), and the charity of the nations is sin," with various definitions of the nature of the sin — they do it to extend their dominion, to boast of it, to taunt Israel with, etc. After they had delivered these opinions one after another, R. Johanan gave his interpretation of the verse, in effect: Almsgiving exalts a Gentile (גוי), and the charity of the nations is a sin-offering (for them). All agree in taking חסד as synonymous with צדקה. The rendering of the English version, "but sin is a reproach to any people," said to have been anticipated by Symmachus (ὀνείδος δὲ λαοῖς ἁμαρτίαι — 'disgrace' as LXX in Lev. 20, 17, taking it as Aramaic equivalent of Hebrew חרפה). Cf. Pesiḳta ed. Buber, f. 12b (Abin bar Judah; see Bacher, Pal. Amoräer, III, 759).

II, 172–173

For a similar distinction attributed to Plato see Diogenes Laertius iii. § 95 f. (Εὐεργεσία . . . ἢ χρήμασιν ἢ σώμασιν, κ. τ. λ.)

II, 172 n. 7

On this interpretation of Psalm 89, 3, cf. L. Ginzberg, Legends of the Jews, VI, 145, n. 42. — The words are quoted in Sifra on Lev. 20, 17, apropos of Cain's wife (his sister).

II, 181 ll. 24–26

On the duty of giving evidence see also Tos. Shebu'ot, 3, 1 f.

II, 183 n. 1

Into the numerous and various cases in which excommunication could be pronounced — Maimonides, Hilkot Talmud Torah, 6, 14, enumerates twenty-four — and into the forms and degrees of excommunication there is no occasion to enter here; the important thing for us is that a court had power to excommunicate for contumacy of any kind.

II, 184 n. 4

Sifrè Num. § 161 and Tos. Sanhedrin 9, 4 refer to the witness *pleading* in behalf of the accused, not to *testifying*. [L. G.]

II, 187 l. 14

More exactly "eight rows back" (from the front, where God was); Akiba belonged to a later generation. See Vol. I, p. 256.

II, 188 ll. 18f.

On the order of these three things, see above, Note on Vol. II, p. 85.

II, 189 l. 7

That is, make up some *false* answer. Others understand תתבדה "be given the lie."

II, 189 n. 4

For הן as an affirmative particle see Mekilta on Exod. 19, 20 (ed. Friedmann, f. 66a; ed. Weiss, f. 73b); Ishmael and Akiba.

II, 189 n. 8

The equivalent biblical phrase is נבב לב (the heart as the seat of intelligence, the mind).

II, 191 l. 8

In the second Epistle of Clement, c. 12, this saying is attributed to Jesus. [L. G.] — See the prayer of Socrates at the end of Plato's Phaedrus: Ὦ φίλε Πάν τε καὶ ἄλλοι ὅσοι τῇδε θεοί, δοίητέ μοι καλῷ γενέσθαι τ'ἄνδοθεν. (The resemblance is rather verbal than real; the "ἔξωθεν" here are external circumstances) ἔξωθεν δ' ὅσα ἔχω, τοῖς ἐντὸς εἶναι μοι φίλια.

II, 193 ll. 15 ff.

On the bad Pharisees, see the advice of Alexander Jannaeus, when dying, to his wife (Soṭah 22b): Do not be afraid of the Pharisees, nor of those that are not Pharisees, but of the counterfeits (lit. "dyed") who resemble Pharisees (outwardly); whose deeds are like the deed of Zimri but claim a reward like Phineas" (Num. 25).

II, 194 ll. 20 ff.

On God's Truth see Marmorstein, The Old Rabbinic Doctrine of God, pp. 179–181.

II, 195 ll. 5 ff.

Cf. Josephus, Contra Apionem, ii. 22 § 190, ἀρχὴ καὶ μέσα καὶ τέλος οὗτος τῶν πάντων.

II, 196 n. 4

In the names of synagogues the singular is usual, Oheb Shalom, etc.

II, 202 ff.

See Marmorstein, The Old Rabbinic Doctrine of God, pp. 56–61, 109, 121 f., 136. — The earliest use of Abinu as an invocation in prayer is 1 Chron. 29, 10 (David): אבינו מעולם ועד עולם, 'our Father from eternity and to eternity' (forever and ever). [Perles.]

II, 204 l. 20

On these substitutes for the Name see N 113a (on Vol. I, p. 373).

II, 204 n. 4

Seder Eliahu Rabbah contains a good deal of older material.

II, 206 l. 13

The "sextons" (חזניא) probably in their frequent occupation as (elementary) teachers, assistants to the school-masters. See Bacher, Tannaiten, I², 105.

II, 210 n. 5

Bousset 3 ed. (Gressmann, 1926), p. 376.

II, 212 l. 22

See David de Sola Pool, The Old Jewish-Aramaic Prayer, The Kaddish, 1909, especially, pp. 10 ff. (Language and Date of the Kaddish). — Another view is that the "Kaddish contains some old phrases but is not an old prayer." [L. G.]

II, 216 ll. 17f.

Read (as in the second impression): "R. Eleazar (ben Pedat), contemporary of Johanan." — This R. Eleazar lived in the third century.

II, 217 ll. 19 f.

Vol. II, pp. 84 f. S. Krauss, Synagogale Altertümer, pp. 96 f.

II, 220 n. 2

Also Gen. R. 68, 8. On the way in which these origins were arrived at see S. Krauss, *op. cit.*, pp. 36–38.

II, 220 n. 4

Jer. Berakot 7b, above (R. Tanḥuma); cf. Gen. R. 68, 9. — The איברים ופדרים which were left burning on the altar all night furnish the desired correspondence with the sacrificial worship.

II, 220 ll. 16–19

See Vol. I, p. 292. The differences recorded in Tos. Rosh ha-Shanah 4 (2), 11, between the schools of Shammai and Hillel presume a fixed order in the daily prayer before the destruction of the Temple; cf. also Tos. Berakot 3, 11 (R. Eliezer). The point in dispute between R. Gamaliel and his colleagues was the obligation of the *individual* (מתפלל אדם) to conform in this point exactly to the form and order of the prayers in the synagogue. [L. G.]

II, 221 n. 3

The passages cited refer to the repetition of the Tefillah. [L. G.]

II, 223 n. 1

The general rule about sacrifices is M. Zebaḥim 1, 1; every sacrifice must be offered under its specific name; cf. M. Pesaḥim 5, 2; and, of course, with observance of the ritual particularly prescribed. The priest must therefore have definitely in mind the particular kind of sacrifice he is making.

II, 225 n. 4

If the "hour" is taken literally, it would be hard to see how such pious men found hours enough in the day for other occupations. The word is frequently less definite, "a while."

II, 234 n. 4

On the harmony between man's will and God's, see the more general counsel in Abot 2, 4: "Make His will as thy will," etc. Herford, Pirkè Aboth (1925) *ad loc.* quotes Abot de-R. Nathan (Schechter, second recension, p. 36a): "If thou hast done His will as thy will, thou hast not done His will as His will. If thou hast done His will against thine own will, thou hast done His will as His will," etc.

II, 239 n. 3

Cf. Abot 6, 5 (Knowledge of) Torah superior to priesthood or royalty; the forty-eight excellences by which it is acquired.

II, 240 n. 1

For Johanan *read* Jonathan. — חובה is a measurable obligation; in contrast to such an obligation מצוה is used of an action by the performance of which a man acquires merit, though it is not specifically commanded. The whole discussion in Menaḥot 99b is about Josh. 1, 8; all would agree that the study of Torah is one of the greatest, if not the greatest of מצוות in the sense defined above.

II, 240 n. 4

For a different application of the principle, great things or small, see the story of the two rabbis on the way to execution, in Mekilta on Exod. 22, 22 (ed. Friedmann, f. 95b; ed. Weiss, f. 101b).

II, 241 n. 2

Rosh ha-Shanah 35a very likely means that Rab Judah, instead of saying the prayers himself, attended the public service and listened to the recitation of the leader in prayer (שליח הצבור). On Tannaim who gave study the precedence over prayer see Shabbat 11a and Jer. Berakot 1, 5.

II, 242 n. 1

Others take the reference to be to the angels who preside over the heavenly bodies and the elements of nature; Jer. Rosh ha-Shanah 2, 5 (f. 58a, middle); cf. Peṣikta, f. 3a–b, where Michael and Gabriel are mentioned, both of whom are patrons and guardians of Israel. Abot de-R Nathan, ed. Schechter, p. 48 f.

II, 242 ll. 23 f.

The metaphor, 'fire-law' (אש דת, Deut. 33, 2), is developed in detail in Sifrè Deut. § 343 (ed. Friedmann, f. 143a–b; on the text see Friedmann's note 35). It is a deadly fire to those who abandon their studies: כל זמן שאדם עמל בהם חיים הם לו פירש מהם ממיתים אותו.

II, 248 ff.

With the chapter on Chastisement compare that on Expiatory Suffering (Vol. I, pp. 546 ff.). See also Marmorstein, The Old Rabbinic Doctrine of God, pp. 185–196.

II, 249 n. 3

The disease is noted as especially fatal among children, but not confined to them. It is probable that the ancients did not distinguish it from quinsy (acute suppurative tonsillitis).

II, 249 n. 10

On "measure for measure," see also Mekilta on Exod. 13, 21 (ed. Friedmann, f. 25a; ed. Weiss, f. 30a) and on 14, 4 (Friedmann, f. 26a; Weiss, f. 31a); cf. the anecdote of Hillel and the skull floating in the water, Abot 2, 6. Cf. L. Ginzberg, Legends of the Jews, V, 427, n. 172.

II, 252 n. 4

The Megillat Ta'anit was written by Hananiah ben Hezekiah and his associates, as a memorial of deliverances, שהיו מחבבין את הצרות; as Rashi explains it, the afflictions from which they had been delivered. The words of R. Simeon ben Gamaliel are taken in the same sense, the interventions of God to deliver his people in our time have been so frequent that we should not be able to record them. (L. G.] See Shabbat 13b.

II, 253–254

See Mekilta Mishpaṭim 9, end (ed. Friedmann, f. 85b; ed. Weiss, f. 91b) on Exod. 21, 27. See Vol. I, p. 547 with notes 1–3.

II, 257 ll. 18–22

On the penitence of Reuben (and Judah), Sifrè Deut. § 348 (on Deut. 33, 6 f.; cf. Gen. R. 84, 18; Pesiḳta ed. Buber, f. 159a–b (in connection with his return to the pit into which, at his instance, the brothers had put Joseph, Gen. 37, 29).

II, 258 n. 3

On the penitence of Adam see L. Ginzberg, Legends of the Jews, V, 114 f.

II, 258 n. 5

For a Christian parallel, see Hermas, Sim. 5. 3, 7 f. See also 2 Clement, 16, 4 (almsgiving as a mode of repentance is good; fasting superior to prayer; almsgiving to both).

II, 260 n. 4

See also Abot de-R. Nathan, c. 1 and the parallels cited by Schechter. [L. G.] Cf. Bacher, Tannaiten I^2, 383, also 380 n.

II, 261 n. 2

The services were held on these days because they were the market-days on which the country people came to town (Vol. I, p. 29, n. 2).

II, 262 ll. 14–16

On the date of the destruction of the Temple cf. Josephus, Bell. Jud. vi. 4, 5 § 250. — "Tenth of Lous" (Jer. 52, 12 f.).

II, 262 ll. 22–25

See Büchler, Priester und Cultus, u.s.w., p. 22.

II, 268 l. 8

Read Isa. 1, 15, and correct n. 4 accordingly.

II, 268 n. 4

Cf. Martial ix. 41 — a kind of murder ("istud quod digitis, Pontice, perdis, homo est"). Nocturnal pollution (Deut. 23, 11 f., Sifrè § 255 f.) has as its consequence serious uncleanness for the בעל קרי. He is forbidden to read in the Scriptures or to study any of the branches of the unwritten law (Tos. Berakot 2, 13; Berakot 22a. About the unwritten law certain exceptions are made, in which there is no unanimity). On the ordinance of Ezra see Note on Vol. I, p. 29, N 3. Inasmuch as the bath of purification could not be taken until toward evening, the disqualification lasted through the daylight hours of the day following the pollution.

II, 271 n. 1

Those who thus indulge in thoughts of sin are not admitted to the mansion (מחיצה) (of God) — the part of heaven where He abides.

II, 272 ll. 11–18

Cf. 2 Peter 1, 5–9.

II, 280 l. 25

There is a strong presumption that the language of the apocalypses written towards the close of the first century was the Hebrew of the times, "the language of scholars." Against the opinion formerly entertained that the original language of 4 Esdras was Greek, see Wellhausen, Skizzen und Vorarbeiten, VI, 234 ff., who operates, however, with Biblical Hebrew, e.g., p. 237, the frequency of the Infinitive Absolute with a finite verb, a use which has disappeared in the later Hebrew (Segal, Mishnaic Hebrew Grammar, p. 165). Perles contends for a Hebrew original for Enoch (Orientalistische Literaturzeitung, XVI (1913), 481 ff., 516).

II, 280 n. 2

With the esoteric books of the Essenes may be compared what is told of the Pythagoreans, Iamblichus, Vita Pyth. § 253.

II, 284 ll. 19 f.

The Georgian version is published by R. P. Blake in the Harvard Theological Review, XIX (1926), 299–375.

II, 287 n. 2

The burnings for kings furnished precedent for the burnings for Patriarchs (נשיאים) — the parallel is not without significance — not for private persons. Tos. Shabbat, 7 (8), 18; cf. Abodah Zarah 11a. The question what was burned is asked, and answered, "his bed and all the articles he had in daily use." But the following anecdote shows that others might contribute: "When Rabban Gamaliel the Elder [this appears to be an anachronism] died, the proselyte Onkelos burned for him more than seventy minas," i.e., things mounting up to that value — one may imagine costly gums and spices. The Talmud, l.c., guards itself against the suspicion of a heathenish custom.

II, 289 n. 4

On later Greek notions see Rohde, Psyche.

II, 289 n. 7

Virgil, Aeneid, vi, 425 (the *irremeabilis* unda, cf. ib. 436–439).

II, 290 n. 6

Read עמיו (his kinsfolk).

II, 291 ll. 9–11

Cf. Wisdom of Solomon, 5, 1. Grimm, in his commentary on 4, 20–5, 2 (p. 111), similarly finds in the verses, not the resurrection and last judgement (Böttcher, al.), but "eine *Dramatisierung* des Gedankens . . . , dass Gottlose wie Gerechte im Jenseits Bewusstseyn und Kenntniss von der durch Gottes Richterspruch erfolgten gänzlichen Umwandlung ihres beiderseitigen Schicksales haben," u.s.w.

II, 292 ll. 28 ff.

The speech put into the mouth of Eleazar, addressed to his followers at Masada (Josephus, Bell. Jud. vii. 8, 7 §§ 341 ff.), notwithstanding the appeal to the Scriptures (§ 343), is completely Greek in conception and expression.

II, 294 n. 4

Cf. ἐξετασμός, 4, 6.

II, 295 ll. 4–12.

See Vita Mosis, ii. 39 § 288 (ed. Mangey II, 189); Quod Deus immutabilis, c. 10 §§ 45–50 (Mangey I, 279 f.); De mundo opificio, c. 23 §§ 69–71 (Mangey, I, 15 f.).

II, 296 n. 3

For other references see L. Ginzberg, Legends of the Jews, V, 119.

II, 298 ll. 24–27

Cf. Dan. 11, 33.

II, 298 n. 5

On this commentary see Malter, Saadia Gaon (1921), p. 404.

II, 299 n. 1

With 2 Macc. 7, 9 (ἀναβίωσις) cf. Josephus, cited in Vol. II, p. 317 (ἀναβιοῦν).

II, 301 l. 26

In 45, 3 the judge is "the Elect One"; cf. 69, 27. See Vol. II, p. 333.

II, 302 l. 5

That the name Raphael may originally have been derived, not from רפא, 'heal,' but from רפאים, 'shades' (of the dead), so that he appears quite in character in 22, 3 ff., is conjectured by Ginzberg, Legends of the Jews, V, 71. He would accordingly take Tartarus away from Uriel and give it to Raphael, supposing that the translator mistakenly connected the words with the preceding clause instead of the following.

II, 302 l. 19

Why this category of sinners should be neither punished in the day of judgment nor raised up out of Hades is not manifest. Gunkel, Berliner philologische Wochenschrift, 1903, p. 203) would insert a negative before the second clause in the description, so that it would read, ἀλλ' οὐδ' ἁμαρτωλοὶ ἀσεβεῖς, they are not ὅσιοι, but also not godless sinners and accomplices of the wicked (heathen), and fittingly they do not share either the torments of the altogether bad or the resurrection of the righteous. This plausible emendation removes the main difficulty, but comparison of the Greek and Ethiopic shows that the text is otherwise not in order. — The rabbis had their opinions about the fate of the 'middling class'; see Vol. I, p. 495 f.; Vol. II, p. 318, and Note on the latter place.

II, 311 ll. 1–3

Cf. Exod. R. 44, 6.

II, 315 ll. 24 f.

The notion that the fallen angels are the authors of the corruption of mankind is almost entirely unknown to rabbinical sources. [L. G.]

II, 315 n. 4

Bousset, Religion des Judentums, 2 ed. p. 383, n. (3 ed. p. 333, n.) cites Clem. Hom. viii, 12 ff.

II, 316 ll. 24–26

Commonplaces about the universal and inevitable lot of man from the beginning, in the consolation of mourners, with prayer to God, the great comforter (בעל נחמות), closing with the benediction, "Blessed is He who comforts mourners," Ketubot 8b.

II, 317 ll. 10–13

When and where Ecclesiastes was written are questions which I have seen no reason to discuss. I do not find in Sirach any evidence of acquaintance with the book.

II, 317 ll. 20 ff.

Reference may be made also to Josephus, Bell. Jud. i. 23, 2 § 650, cf. § 653; iii. 8, 5 § 372; Contra Apionem, ii. c. 30 § 218.

II, 317 n. 3

With ἀναβιοῦν cf. 2 Macc. 7, 9 (ἀναβίωσις); Vol. II, p. 299, n. 1.

II, 318 l. 16 and n. 3

In Mekilta Mishpaṭim 14 (on Exod. 22, 5) מצפצפת is used of fire running along the surface of the ground, in distinction from a fire that jumps from point to point, and might perhaps be rendered 'scorching' or 'charring.' In Mekilta de-R. Simeon ben Yoḥai on the same verse (ed. Hoffmann, p. 141), though not in the same connection, מפספה occurs in a context where the meaning 'scorch' or 'singe' seems to be required. In M. Nazir 6, 3, a Nazirite who shaves or singes his hair (סיפסף), no matter how little, is accountable; see also Tos. Uḳaṣin 2, 16. אע״פ שסיפספן באור, "though one singe them with fire." Professor Ginzberg, to whom I owe this suggestion, with an etymological and critical discussion of the words in these and other passages, understands the opinion of the School of Shammai to be that these "betwixt and betweens" will go down to hell and *be singed* by its fires, and after this experience arise thence and be healed. It is evident that this figure for their fate is more appropriate than that which I dubiously employed in the text.

II, 319 n. 2

See Note on Vol. II, p. 321, n. 3.

II, 321 n. 2

See Origen on Matt. 15, 14.

II, 321 n. 3

In Beṣah 15b (cited on p. 319, n. 2) the contrast is between the fulfilment of a commandment (keeping the holiday festively, which belongs to חיי שעה) and the study of Torah (חיי עולם); see on the same page, below, on the division of time, etc. In Ta'anit 21a in the same phrase the current editions erroneously read חיי עולם הבא, the old editions simply חיי עולם. [L. G.]

II, 321 n. 4

Other examples, R. Eleazar ben Azariah, Gen. R. 93, 11; R. Ḥanina ben Teradion, 'Abodah Zarah 17b. Compare also the attitude of the author of 4 Esdras throughout. The relatively early date of these utterances may be observed.

II, 323 ff.

On the Messianic expectations of the Jews the most recent comprehensive monograph is that of Joseph Klausner, רעיון המשיחי בישראל מראשיתו ועד חתימת המשנה, 2 ed. Jerusalem, 1927, pp. 346 ff. — In three Parts: I. In the Age of the Prophets: II. In the Apocryphal and Pseudepigraphic Literature: III. In the Age of the Tannaim. The Third Part is a revision of Die messianischen Vorstellungen des jüdischen Volkes im Zeitalter der Tannaiten, Berlin, 1904.

In Strack-Billerbeck, Kommentar zum Neuen Testament aus Talmud und Midrasch, the subject is treated in long excursuses (nos. 29–33) on "Diese Welt, die Tage des Messias und die Zukünftige Welt; Vorzeichen und Berechnung der Tage des Messias; Scheol, Gehinnom und Gan 'Eden; Allgemeine oder teilweise Auferstehung der Toten?; Gerichtsgemälde aus der altjüdischen Literatur. Vol. IV (1928), pp. 799–1212. The index, s.v. Messias, should also be consulted.

See also Bousset, Religion des Judentums, 2 ed. (1926), pp. 213–301.

II, 326 n. 6

See Strack-Billerbeck, Excursus 28 (IV, 764–798), Der Prophet Elias nach seiner Entrückung aus dem Diesseits; Louis Ginzberg, Legends of the Jews, IV, 195–235, VI, 316–342.

II, 326 n. 7

Ekah Rabbati, ed. Buber, p. 45b.; Jer. Berakot 5a, above.

II, 327 ll. 15 ff.

See Torrey, The Second Isaiah (1928), pp. 5–19.

II, 329 ll. 10–12

In the Amoraic passages of the Talmud *ben David* is rarely used; more frequently in the Midrashim, where, however, *Messiaḥ ben David* is the common form. [L. G.]

II, 329, n. 3

See Vol. II, p. 347.

II, 329 ll. 20–22

In Lam. R. on Lam. 2, 2 a pun on this name is attributed to the Patriarch Judah: in Num. 24, 17, אל תקרי כוכב אלא כוזב read not "a star," but "a liar." In Buber's edition (1899), this piece of wit disappears; see the editor's note, f. 51a, n. 57.

II, 329 n. 2

On this constant usage see Jackson and Lake, The Beginnings of Christianity, I, 348, 353 f.

II, 333 n. 7

In the Talmud also there are several passages in which it is supposed that the Messiah will appear after the so-called "Messianic work" (the gathering of the dispersed and the punishment of sinners).— See L. Ginzberg, Unbekannte jüdische Sekte, p. 347, n. 2.

II, 333 ll. 21 ff.

Judgment by the Chosen One, Enoch 45, 3, cf. 36, 1 ff. (Vol. II, p. 301, and Note there).

II, 334 ll. 11 ff.

Reference should be made to Enoch 62, 7, the "Son of Man" hidden from the beginning. A Christian hand may be suspected in this passage, at least by way of expansion. — For literature on the "Son of Man" see Bousset, Religion des Judentums, 3 ed. (1926), p. 266.

II, 337 l. 18

The contrast between the peaceful prince and the militant Asmonaeans, John Hyrcanus and Alexander Jannaeus, may have been in the author's mind.

II, 337 ll. 26 f.
Cf. Enoch 62, 7 (Note on Vol. II, p. 334).

II, 341 l. 27
The book of life, see Vol. II, p. 297.

II, 342
Christians who took the Revelation of John literally held that there would be a millennium after the resurrection of the dead, when the kingdom of Christ was to be established in material form on this same earth (Eusebius, Hist. Eccles, iii. 39, 12 — Papias, not recognizing, as Eusebius says, that the Apostolic descriptions are to be understood mystically); Euseb. iii. 28, 1 ff. (Jerusalem his capital, Cerinthus); Justin Martyr, Dial. c. Tryphone, cc. 80–82 (for himself and many others of the same mind, c. 80, 2); the Montanists, *et al.*

II, 344 ll. 8–12
See Vol. II, p. 337, and Note above, p. 36.

II, 346 ll. 13 ff.
On the Messianic notions of the Tannaim see Joseph Klausner (titles above, p. 35.)

II, 347 ll. 20–23
See Note on Vol. II, p. 329.

II, 347 n. 2
Another Hillel was a brother of the Patriarch Judah (II), and it is thought by some that he is meant by Origen (on Psalm 1) when he speaks of Ιοῦλλος πατριάρχος. "He may have been prompted to this declaration (Sanh. 98b) by Origen's professed discovery in the Old Testament of Messianic passages referring to the founder of Christianity." — Jewish Encyclopedia VI, 401. — In the preceding context (Sanhedrin 99b, top) a מין (perhaps a Christian) asks R. Abbahu when the Messiah will come; and to such a question the answer of Hillel would be apposite. The identification with a contemporary of Origen is, however, very dubious.

II, 348 ll. 1 f.
A different explanation is preferred by Ginzberg: Hezekiah was the scholar on the throne, and R. Johanan ben Zakkai may have thought of Hezekiah as coming to meet him at his entrance on the

better life; cf. Baba Kamma 111b, where Raba hopes that when he dies R. Osha'ya may come to meet him because he has explained a tradition of that rabbi.

II, 348 n. 3
Ekah Rabbati, ed. Buber, f. 45a f.

II, 352
That Daniel misunderstood this revelation, see Megillah 12a, top (Raba). [L. G.]

II, 352 ll. 25–30
When the kingdom of the house of David will be re-established is one of the things that no man knows, Mekilta Wayassa 5 (on Exod. 16, 32), ed. Friedmann, 51a, below; ed. Weiss, 59b. [L. G.]

II, 353 ll. 1–5
One of the things which God adjured Israel not to reveal was "the end" (Levi). Ketubot 111a. Rashi understands this as an injunction laid particularly on the prophets; and probably this is what Levi had in mind.

II, 353 n. 3
See also Vol. I, p. 368; Vol. II, p. 390.

II, 354 n. 2
"Persian" (for Roman) is a favorite substitution of the censors, and is found here only in censored editions of the Talmud. [L. G.]

II, 355 ll. 5–9
On Jose ben Ḳisma's prognostications also Tanḥuma ed. Buber, Wayyishlaḥ 8 (f. 83b). Here the reference to Tiberias is explicit; they were staying in that city, and he said "this gate." Caesarea Philippi is suggested by the "sign" (אות) he gave his disciples — the waters in the grotto of Paneas should turn to blood.

II, 356 l. 8 ff.
On this and the following utterances see Klausner, רעיון המשיחי, pp. 284 ff. Klausner thinks that they had their origin in the experience of the generation which lived under the decrees of Hadrian after the Bar Kocheba war; the authors of these Baraitas are of the school of Akiba.

II, 356 l. 20

Nehorai is said to be equivalent in meaning to Meir ("he enlightened the eyes of scholars in Halakah") and is taken for the name of the well-known disciple of Akiba. 'Erubin 13b. See Vol. I, p. 95, n. 4 and Note *ad loc.* In 'Erubin *l.c.* the true reading is not נהוראי but מיישא or מיאשא; see Bacher, Tannaiten, II, 6, n. 1.

II, 356 n. 7

The patrial נבלאי may be from n. p. נבל Byblos, in Phoenicia for which Assyrian inscriptions have Guubli.

II, 357 n. 5

Later sources have רעש (or רעם), perhaps the rumbling sounds, precursors of an earthquake; and this may be the meaning in Sanhedrin, l.c. [L. G.]

II, 358 ll. 27–29

See Vol. I, p. 46, ll. 15 ff.

II, 358 n. 3

Cf. Mark 9, 12 ἀποκαθιστάνει πάντα.

II, 3_9 n. 3

See Büchler, Priester und Cultus, p. 20, n. 3.

II, 359 n. 4

For a complete collection of passages in which doubtful cases are reserved till the coming of Elijah see L. Ginzberg, Unbekannte jüdische Sekte, p. 304.

II, 362 n. 6

Also Pesiḳta ed. Buber, f. 50b.

II, 363 l. 2

Read *ḥamūshīm*.

II, 363 n. 2

Also Pesiḳta de-R. Simeon ben Yoḥai, ed. Hoffmann, p. 38, end.

II, 364 n. 5

The Messianic banquet is perhaps meant in a saying of Akiba, Abot 3, 16: והדין דין אמת והכל מתוקן לסעודה.

II, 365 n. 3

Cf. Enoch 62, 14 f.; see also Note on Vol. II, p. 364, n. 5 (Akiba).

II, 368 n. 7

The name of this land is *Arsareth* in the Latin version of 4 Esdras, 13, 45; cf. ארץ אחרת, Deut. 29, 27, quoted M. Sanhedrin 10, 3; Tos. Sanhedrin 13, 12. The Syriac version has Arzaph and the other Oriental versions otherwise. See Hilgenfeld, Messias Judaeorum (1869), p. 101, n. (v. Gutschmid, Zeitschrift für wissenschaftliche Theologie (1860), p. 76, compares Ἀρσαράτα, Ptolemy, v. 13, 11 (name of a city in Armenia Maior). See Violet, Die Apokalypsen des Esra und des Baruch in deutscher Gestalt (1924), p. 185, for other conjectures, among which "Ararat" may be particularly mentioned. See also Klausner, רעיון המשיחי, p. 305. — On "Sabbatical" rivers, see Josephus, Bell. Jud. vii. 5, 1 § 99 (in Phoenicia); Pliny, Nat. Hist. xxxi. 2, 18 (In Judaea rivos sabbatis omnibus siccatur), cf. R. Akiba in Sanhedrin 65b; but neither of these, of course, is the river beyond which the ten tribes were in exile.

II, 369 n. 1

Return of the Ten Tribes from beyond Sambation, Yalkuṭ II § 469 (on Isa. 49, 9) quoting Pesiḳta R. (ed. Friedmann, f. 146b–147).

II, 370 ll. 12 ff.

On the Ephraimite Messiah see Klausner רעיון המשיחי, pp. 313 ff. On the origin of the notion see also L. Ginzberg, Unbekannte jüdische Sekte, 337–340.

II, 373 n. 3

Cf. Vol. I, p. 434.

II, 378 n. 5

It should also be noted that in repetitions of the same saying in different sources the terms sometimes interchange, being equivalents in the mind of the scribes, as in the instance cited in note 5.

II, 379 ll. 28–31

The resurrection in Palestine, Midrash Tannaim on Deut. 12, 10 f. (ed. Hoffmann, p. 58). — "Some say forty days before other lands, some say forty years."

II, 380 n. 1

See also Pesiḳta Rabbati, ed. Friedmann, f. 147a (from beyond Sambation).

II, 381 l. 15

"From the Torah" is here a late addition not found in correct texts. [L. G.]

II, 381 n. 1

See also Pesaḥim 68a, end, where Deut. 32, 39, "I kill and I make alive; I have wounded, and I heal," furnishes an answer to those who say that the revivification of the dead is not in the Torah.

II, 383 l. 20

In Talmudic sources Parashah is never the "weekly lesson," but "section." [L. G.]

II, 384 n. 1

A Christian parallel is Athenagoras, De resurrectione, c. 18 f.

II, 386 ll. 2–6

Instead of "he had formerly held the same view," etc., the words of R. Joshua should be rendered: "If the verse had said,' 'The wicked shall return to Sheol, all the Gentiles,' and stopped there, I should have interpreted it as you do; but now since it says, 'who forget God,' there are righteous men among the nations who have a lot in the World to Come."

II, 386 ll. 9–11

The "nations of the world" with whom Maimonides was acquainted were Christians and Mohammedans.

II, 387 ll. 9 ff.

The translation reproduces the Tosefta. In the parallels, Seder 'Olam, c. 3 (ed. Ratner 9a) and Rosh ha-Shanah 17a, the clause "and those who stretch out their hands against the Temple," is not found. The Seder 'Olam has in place of it, "and those who deride the words of learned men" (*ḥakamim*); cf. 'Erubin 21b, where this class is promised a particularly offensive punishment. It may be suspected that the clause in the Tosefta had its origin in the desire of a haggadist to do something with the last words of Psalm 49, 15 (מִזְּבֻל לוֹ), as had been done with what went before it (וצורם לבלות שאול).

II, 388 l. 7

On the words "from the Law" see Note on Vol. II, p. 381, l. 15.

II, 388 l. 9

"Extraneous books" (חיצונים, cf. Baraita). Akiba's damnatory sentence is probably aimed at reading from such books in the synagogue. See Krochmal, Moreh Nebukè ha-Zeman (1851), p. 101 f. (הקורא בהם בצבור וגו׳).

II, 391 ll. 8–12

With this conversion one may compare the story in Eusebius Hist. Eccles. ii. 9, told of the martyrdom of the Apostle James.

II, 394 ll. 16–25

See E. Meyer, Ursprung und Anfänge des Christentums, II, 58–120; Bousset, Religion des Judentums, 3 ed. (1926). Das religionsgeschichtliche Problem, especially, pp. 501 ff.

II, 394 n. 4

See Pettazoni, Zarathustra, p. 106, n. 5.

INDEX

INDEX

SUBJECTS AND NAMES

In this index the title of a chapter is distinguished by full-faced limiting numerals (e. g. Chastisement, ii, **248–256**); an asterisk affixed to the page number indicates a principal reference (e. g. Alenu, prayer, i, 434*). Definitions of Hebrew terms in the index fit it to serve also as a glossary.

A

Aaron, peaceable, peacemaker, i, 392; ii, 196; gifts to Israel for his sake, i, 542; his death an expiation, i, 547.

Ab, Fast of the Ninth of Ab, ii, 65 ff., 262; festival of wood-offering on the 15th, i, 30; ii, 54, 61.

Abaddon, ii, 289 n.

Abahu, polemic against the deification of Christ, i, 165.

Abba Areka, *see* Rab.

Ability of man to keep God's commandments, i, 454 f.

Abinu, 'our Father,' in prayer, ii, 208; reason for plural form, ibid. *See* Father in Heaven.

Abinu Malkenu, 'Our Father, our King,' litany on the ten penitential days, ii, 210.

Ablutions, before prayer, ii, 222.

Abodah, Seder, on Day of Atonement, ii, 59.

'abōdah, 'worship' (the service of the altar), prayer is worship in the inner man, ii, 218; religious study is worship, ii, 246.

'abōdah, ha-, as an oath, i, 377.

'abōdah zarah, the first of the cardinal sins (*q. v.*). *See* Heathenism.

Abodat Israel, title of a prayer book, i, 177.

Abot, *see* Pirkê Abot.

Abot de-R. Nathan, i, 158.

Abraham, his good desert and favor with God, i, 538; the rock (πέτρα) God looked for to found the world on, ibid.; miraculous interventions in behalf of Israel for his sake, ibid.; love to God the motive of his obedience, i, 100, 194, 536; the great exemplar of faith, ii, 237; by it acquired both worlds, i, 538; ii, 237; ready to die for the hallowing of the Name, ii, 105 f.; his appeal for Sodom, i, 338 n.; a proselyte and maker of proselytes, i, 344 n.; versed in the written and the unwritten law, i, 275 f.

Abrahamic covenant (circumcision), ii, 18, 20.

Absolute, God, in Philo's religious philosophy, i, 361, 416; idea unknown in Palestinian Judaism, i, 421, 423 ff.

Abstinence, from flesh and wine, in mourning or as penance, ii, 257 f.; after the destruction of the temple, ii, 262 f.; self-imposed, disapproved, ii, 265. *See also* Fasting.

Abṭalion, one of the last Pair (with Shemaiah), i, 45, 77, 78; commonly identified with "Pollion" in Josephus, i, 313 n.

Acts of the Apostles, history of the disciples of Jesus in Jerusalem, i, 187.

Accusation, false, ii, 148 n.

Actions on contract, ii, 184 n.

Adam, 'man,' generic name, i, 445.

Adam, the first man, creation of, i, 452 f.; his huge size, ibid.; created androgynous, ibid.; God showed him all His works, and warned him not to spoil the world, i, 474 f.; freedom of choice, i, 453; his sin and its consequences, i, 474 f.; death entailed upon all his descendants,

Aristobulus (III), brother of Mariamne, i, 75, 76.
Aristotle, ethics and politics, ii, 112.
Artaxerxes, in the Books of Ezra and Nehemiah, i, 5–7, 23.
Ascriptions, in the Daily Prayer, i, 292, 295.
Asceticism, ii, 263 ff.
Aṣeret, Feast of Weeks, Pentecost, ii, 48 n.
asham talūy, trespass offering in doubtful cases, i, 498 f.
asham wadai, indubitable trespass offering, ibid.
asham ḥasīdīm, trespass offering of the pious, i, 499.
Ashamnu, litany of confession on the Day of Atonement, ii, 60, 214 n.
Asidaeans, ally themselves to the Maccabaean leaders, i, 59; sought to make peace with Alcimus, ibid.; derivation of the Pharisees from them, i, 61.
Asmonaeans, their achievements, ii, 113; loyalty of the Jews, i, 74; aggressive wars of expansion, i, 335 f.; feeling of the Pharisees toward them, ii, 113; toward the later rulers of the house, ii, 156, 328; prophecies of restoration seemed to be fulfilled in them, ii, 327.
Assembly, the Great, *see* Great Synagogue.
Associates (*ḥaberīm*), their pledge, ii, 159; dealings with the *'am ha-areṣ*, ibid.; ate their unconsecrated food in a state of ceremonial purity, ii, 76. *See also* Pharisees.
Athcism, dogmatic and practical, i, 360; as a crime in Roman law, definition, i, 350 n.
Atheist, in Jewish definition, i, 360 n.
Athenian law forbidding marriage of citizens with any but citizens, i, 20.
'atīd la-bō, the future age, ii, 398, *see also* World to Come.
Atonement, ritual, i, 497 ff.; sacrificial, ended with the ruin of the temple, i, 502; equivalent for it, i, 503; prophetic teaching, i, 503 f.; burnt offerings at Tabernacles an atonement for the seventy heathen nations, ii, 43 n. *See also* Expiation.
Atonement, Day of, *see* Day of Atonement.
Atonement, vicarious, by the sufferings and death of the righteous, i, 547 ff.
Attendance, Men of (*ma 'amad*), ii, 12 f., 14.
Attendant of the synagogue (*ḥazzan*), duties and functions, i, 289 f., 301, 303, 317.
Attention, in religious acts (*kawwanah*), ii, 223 f.
Attributes, of God, i, 373 ff., 380; moral attributes, i, 386 ff.; in Philo, i, 389 f.; Maimonides' philosophy excludes all attributes as anthropomorphisms, i, 437.
Augustine, nature and need of sacraments, ii, 4, 24; the consequences of Adam's fall, i, 479.
Autocracy of God, its significance, i, 432. *See also* Sovereignty.
Azazel, leader among the fallen angels, his doom in the final judgment, ii, 305.
Azazel, the scapegoat on the Day of Atonement sent to, ii, 56.

B

Baal worship, adopted from the Canaanites, i, 221; stigmatized by prophets as apostasy, adultery, ibid.
Baal of Tyre (Melkart), worship introduced by Ahab, i, 221.
Baalam, has no portion in the world to come, ii, 388.
Baba ben Buta, i, 499.
Babylonia, schools of the Law in, i, 77–79, 104; Shela, Rab, Mar Samuel, i, 105; relation to the Palestinian schools, i, 104, 107; Targums in, i, 102.
Bacchides, Syrian general, i, 59.
Bacher, W., Die Agada der Tannaiten; Die Agada der palästinensischen Amoräer, i, 215.
Backslider, repentance of, i, 521.
Bagohi, *see* Bagoses.

sume the name Sanhedrin, i, 85 n.; the Patriarch's, i, 96, 104.
Bet Din, the celestial, i, 408.
Bet ha-Midrash, place of more advanced biblical study, i, 312 ff.; name as old as Sirach, i, 312; frequently in proximity to the synagogue, i, 314; frequented on sabbath afternoons, i, 314; ii, 38; discourses in, i, 305 f., 314 f.
Bet ha-Sefer (-Sofer), elementary school, i, 316 f. *See* Schools.
bet shō'ebah, at the celebration of the Feast of Tabernacles in the temple, ii, 45 f., 47.
bet wa'ad, place of meetings of the learned, i, 311 f.
Bether, last stronghold of the Jews in the war under Hadrian, i, 90; fall of, commemorated on the Ninth of Ab, ii, 66, 262.
Bethlehem, the Messiah born there on the night on which Jerusalem was destroyed, rapt away by a storm wind, ii, 348 n.
Betrothal and marriage, ii, 121 f.
Bible, in historical and in religious apprehension, i, 318; *see also* Scripture, and Revelation.
Bible, canon, *see* Canon.
Bible, fixing of standard Hebrew text, i, 100; Greek translation of this text, i, 101; Aramaic, i, 102; Syriac, i, 103.
Bible reading in the synagogue, i, 296–302*; institution ascribed to Moses, supplemented by Ezra, i, 296; lessons from the Pentateuch, on festivals, holy days, and special sabbaths, i, 297 f.; ordinary sabbaths, i, 298 f.; the triennial cycle, i, 299 f.; annual cycle, ibid.; lessons from the Prophets, i, 300 f.; number of readers, i, 301 f.; accompanied by a vernacular translation, i, 302–305*; in Hellenistic synagogues, 322.
Bigamy, prohibited by the Damascus sect, i, 202; ii, 122 n.
Birkat Kohanim, last prayer in the Daily Prayer, i, 294.
Birkat ha-Minim, commination of heretics in the Daily Prayer, i, 292; variations in, i, 294.
Bishops of Jerusalem after Hadrian, Gentiles, i, 91.
Blasphemy, what legally constitutes, i, 427 f.
Blessing and curse, reality of, i, 414; God's, conditioned on obedience or disobedience, i, 453 f.
Blessings, at meals, ii, 36, 216 f.
Blind and lame, parable of soul and body, i, 486–488*; ii, 384*.
Blood, is the life, ii, 287; prohibition of eating blood, ii, 6, 74 f.; blood in rites of purification, ii, 55.
Body, physical organism of man not (as material) the source of evil, i, 485; contrary opinion of Greeks, ibid.; body not an irresponsible instrument of the mind in sin, i, 486 ff. *See* Soul and Body.
Boethus, disciple of Antigonus of Socho, i, 69 f.; name of a high priest of Herod's creation, i, 69 n.
Boethusians, akin to the Sadducees, i, 69 f.
Bonus, for a loan, form of usury, ii, 144.
Book of Life, ii, 62 f., 297, 341.
Books, record of each man's deeds, produced in judgment, i, 476; ii, 300, 341.
Booths, at Feast of Tabernacles, ii, 47 f.
Borrower, not to be turned away, ii, 143 n., 168 f.
Bousset, Wilhelm, on the Jewish thought of God as king, i, 431 f.; ii, 210 n.; on Lev. 24, 16, i, 427.
Box, G. H., on the Ezra Apocalypse, i, 8 n.
Brazen serpent, faith of Israel in their Father in heaven, ii, 206.
Breaking of bread, in the consecration of the Sabbath (*ḳiddūsh*), ii, 36 n.
Brevity in prayer, ii, 227.
Brother, honor due the eldest, ii, 131 n.
Bullocks of the lips (Hos. 14, 3), ii, 15, 218.
Bundle of life, the, ii, 390.

God's love, ibid.; rejoicing in chastisement, ii, 253 f.; leads to repentance, ii, 253 n.; brings remission of sins, ii, 253; atones for sin even better than sacrifice, ii, 253 f.; wipes out all a man's wickednesses, i, 547; brings a man to the world to come, ii, 254 f. *See also* Suffering.

Chastisements of love, i, 397; ii, 256.

Chastity, ii, 267–273.* *See also* Women, behavior with.

Cherubim, i, 404, 409.

Children, duty of parents to, ii, 127 f.; duty of children to parents, ii, 131–135; parental blessing on the Sabbath, ii, 37; children at synagogue service, i, 315; at the Passover celebration in the home, ii, 41 f.; suffer for the sins of their parents, i, 548; die because of them, ii, 249.

Choice, power of, *see* Freedom; initial choice determines subsequent particular choices, i, 455 f.; man led by God in the way he chooses to go, i, 456.

Chosen, the, ii, 303, 304, 309.

Chosen One, God's (Messiah, *q. v.*), usual designation in the Parables of Enoch, ii, 333; seated on His throne, ii, 304.

Christ, *see* Messiah.

Christian era, no epoch in the history of Judaism, i, 131.

Christian healing, *see* Jacob of Kefar Sekanya.

Christian writings, not sacred scripture, i, 87.

Christianity, rejection of the Law, ii, 10, 21, 93 f.; a new law, i, 236; Jewish controversies with Gentile Christians, i, 173; over the new law, i, 269 n.; the unity of the godhead, i, 364 f.; the deity of Christ, i, 165; before the coming of the Messiah the whole empire will go over to heresy (Christianity), ii, 356.

Chronicles, Book of, age, i, 27; authorship, i, 32.

Chronological order, not observed in the Bible, hermeneutical principle, i, 245.

Chronology, of the age of restoration, Persian and Greek periods (Seder 'Olam), i, 5–7; of the Book of Jubilees, i, 193 f.

Church, Christian, identified with the kingdom of Heaven, ii, 310 n.

Cicero, on man's place in the world, i, 449.

Circumcision, practised by many peoples, ii, 16 f.; fundamental observance of Judaism, i, 198; ii, 16; why not in the Decalogue, ii, 18; sign of the covenant, ii, 18; neglect of, threatened with extirpation, ii, 6, 18; obliterated by surgical operation, i, 49; father bound to have his son circumcised, ii, 127; grounds for postponement, ii, 19, 30; forbidden by Antiochus IV, ii, 19; made a capital crime by Hadrian, i, 351; ii, 20; permitted to Jews alone by Antoninus Pius, ii, 20.

Circumcision, of heathen slaves, i, 136; ii, 18 f.

Circumcision of converts (proselytes), i, 330 ff.; ii, 19; naturalization in Jewish people, i, 232; prohibited by Roman law, and by Christian emperors, i, 352; ii, 19 f.; effect on conversions, i, 108.

Circumlocution, reverential, in the Targums, i, 419–421. *See also* Memra, Shekinta (Shekinah), Yeḳara.

Circumstantial evidence, in criminal cases, not admitted, ii, 184.

Civil and criminal law, traditionin, i, 252.

Clean and unclean, religious sense, ii, 74 n.; among other peoples, ii, 76 f.; i, 21 n.; laws in the Priests' Code, i, 21 f.; decisions of Jose ben Jo'ezer, i, 46.

Collectors of tolls, publicans (*mōkesīn*), ii, 117; of communal charities (*gabba'īn*), ii, 174 ff.

Commandments, six given to Adam for all mankind, i, 274; renewed to Noah with an addition, ibid.; given to the patriarchs, i, 275; decalogue, i, 467; the 613 (248 + 365) commandments, ii, 28, 83; compendium of, ii, 83 f.; multiplied that Israel may acquire merit by obedience, ii, 92 f.; lightest and weightiest have the same sanction, ii, 5 f.; the light to be as scrupulously observed as the weighty, ii, 93; the weightiest of all is filial piety, ii, 5 f., 31; commandments to be kept for their own sake, ii, 96 f.; keeping them from inferior motives leads to doing it for their own sake, ii, 98; some held tenaciously, others laxly, ii, 20; commandments for which no rational or moral ground is apparent, i, 233 f. *See also* Law.

Commandments, the two great, ii, 85, 86; cf. 173 f.

Commensality with Gentiles, restriction of, i, 22; ii, 75; of Associates (*ḥaberīm*) and the common people, ii, 159.

Commination of heretics in the Daily Prayer, i, 292; variations of form, i, 294.

Compassion of God, with all in affliction, even by deserved inflictions, i, 393 f.; shown in corrective discipline, ii, 255; God has compassion like a father, comforts like a mother, i, 395; his almighty power linked with his compassion, i, 380. *See also* Mercy.

Compendium of the Law, ii, 83 ff.

Concentration of mind in prayer (*kawwanah*), ii, 223 f.

Confession of sin, by the penitent, i, 511–514*; formulas for private confession, i, 511, 512; public, on the Day of Atonement, i, 512; confession indispensable condition of divine forgiveness, i, 512 f., 513 f.; confession of a man under sentence of death, i, 547; confession on the Day of Atonement, high priest and people, ii, 57 f.; in the synagogue, ii, 59 f.; forms in the prayer-books, ibid.; multiplication of confessions and prayers for forgiveness (*selīḥōt*) in the liturgies, ii, 214.

Conflicting impulses, Paul, i, 485.

Conscience, approving or reproving, ii, 90; things left to (*masūr la-leb*), i, 148; ii, 92; have no norm or measure, ii, 82.

Conspiracy of witnesses, ii, 186

Continence, a moral ideal, ii, 270.

Contracts, actions on, ii, 184 n.; contracts of service, ii, 139.

Contributions to communal charities, compulsory, ii, 178; of Gentiles, voluntary, ibid. n.

Contrition for sin, an element in repentance, i, 510, 514.

Controversies between Jews and catholic Christians in the third century, i, 165.

Conventional lies, ii, 189.

Conversion of Gentiles, i, **323–353**; hindrances to, i, 325 f.; forcible conversion by the Asmonaeans (Idumaeans, people of northern Galilee, Ituraeans), i, 336; conversion from worldly motives, i, 336 f.; of foreign slaves, ii, 19; conversion to Judaism prohibited by Roman emperors, pagan and Christian, i, 352; ii, 20; penalties, ibid.; conversion in the messianic age, i, 346; in the last crisis, ii, 300, 304, 306.

Converts, *see* Proselytes, and God-fearing persons.

Converts, Christian, from proselytes and adherents of the synagogue, i, 92, 108.

Conviction, in courts, by a majority of the judges, ii, 186.

Cor malignum, in 4 Esdras, i, 486 f. *See also* Evil Impulse.

Cosmogony, esoteric (*ma'aseh berēshīt*), i, 383 f.

Councils, of rabbis, i, 81; at Lydda, i, 466 f.; ii, 30, 106; at Usha, i, 93, 94.

Council of Trent, i, 257; Vatican Council, ibid.

Courses of priests, ii, 13.

Courts of the temple, ii, 130.

Courts of justice, commandment to establish them given to Adam, i, 274; courts of three, twenty-three, seventy-one judges, ii, 183 f.; procedure, ii, 183 ff.

Cousins-german, marriage of, ii, 121.

Covenant, of God with the fathers, i, 537; the fundamental observances, circumcision and sabbath, ii, 16, 18, 20, 21.

Creation, i, 380–383*; by fiat, without toil and pains, i, 415; with no helper, i, 381; on a preconceived plan, i, 382; everything perfect, ibid.; *de nihilo?* i, 381 f.; worlds before this, i, 382; esoteric lore (*ma'aseh berēshīt*), i, 383 f.; limits of exposition and speculation, ibid.

Creed, obligation in divine law, i, 236 (Maimonides).

Criminal law, procedure in, ii, 183 ff.

Critical principles in the choice and use of sources, i, 125–132.

Cultus, peculiarities of Jewish, ii, 11 f.

Cup of blessing, ii, 36.

Curriculum of higher studies, i, 319.

Curse, reality of, ii, 134.

Cursing parents, biblical and rabbinical law, ii, 134.

Custom, local (*minhag*), in Passover observance, ii, 41; labor on the ninth of Ab, ii, 66 f.

Cyprus, insurrection of the Jews under Trajan, i, 107 f.

Cyrenaica, insurrection under Trajan, i, 107 f.

D

Dabar, in phrases, "word of the Lord," "word of God," and the like, i, 417; rendered in Targums by *pitgama* (*milla*) not *memra*, ibid.

Daily Prayer (Shemoneh 'Esreh, Eighteen Prayers, Tefillah), the Eighteen Prayers said to have been prescribed in their order by the Men of the Great Synagogue, i, 292; arranged under direction of Gamaliel I, ibid.; ii, 212; prayer for the extirpation of heretics added, i, 91, 292; content and order, i, 291–296*; ii, 219; antiquity of the standard prayers, i, 177 f. *See* Prayer.

Dama ben Netina, exemplary filial piety, ii, 133.

Damascus, seceding Jewish sect in the region of, i, 200; age of the migration thither, i, 204; strictness of their Halakah, ii, 27; relation to the Book of Jubilees and the Testaments of the XII Patriarchs, i, 203; polygamy condemned, ii, 122 n., 124 n.; and marriage with a niece, ii, 201 f. (cf. ii, 121); did not prohibit divorce, ii, 124 n.; sabbath observance, ii, 33; sabbath day's journey, ii, 32.

Dances, of maidens in the vineyards, on the 15th of Ab, ii, 54; on the Day of Atonement, ii, 61; challenge the young men to marry, ibid.

Danger to human life suspends the sabbath laws, ii, 30 f.; even the fast on the Day of Atonement, ii, 59.

Daniel, the visions of, ii, 281.

Daughters, upbringing and education of, ii, 128; rights of minor or unmarried daughters in their fathers' estate, ii, 126 n.

David, king in the golden age, ii, 325 ff.; Messiah, ii, 347.

Day of Atonement, a sabbath of eminent sanctity, ii, 58 f.; strict fast, ibid.; the day itself expiates, i, 500; rites in the Herodian temple, ii, 56 f.; disinfection of the sanctuary by blood and incense, ii, 55; general riddance of sins by the scapegoat, ii, 56; the high priest's confession of sins, ii, 57 f.; higher conception of the ritual, ii, 57 f.; repentance indispensable condition, i, 498; expiation, various cases, i, 498 f., 546; sins against a fellow man expiated only on condition of reparation and forgiveness, ii, 154; the sentence of the judgment at New Year's sealed on the Day of Atonement, i, 530, cf. 523; one of the great festivals of the year, ii, 55; joyous character, ii, 61; dances of maidens in the vineyards, ibid.; penitential character of the synagogue observance, i, 499; ii, 59.

Dead, abodes of the, ii, 287 ff.; tendance of the dead, ii, 288. *See also* Sheol *and* Souls.

Dead, the unburied (*mēt miṣwah*), i, 71.

Deadly sins, *see* Cardinal sins.

Death, primitive beliefs and customs, ii, 287 ff.; contagious uncleanness, ii, 76; Johanan ben Zakkai on the uncleanness of death and the prescribed purifications, ii, 7; death the common lot, ii, 316; is good, ii, 253 n.; nine hundred and three kinds of death, ii, 249; death brought into the world by the envy of the devil, i, 448, 478; Adam's sin brought death on all his descendants, i, 474 ff.; death an expiation, i, 546, 547; death personified, cast into the lake of fire, ii, 341; after the final judgment there will be no more death, ii, 342; the second death, ii, 341.

Debarim Rabbah, Midrash on Deuteronomy, i, 171.

Deceit, *see* Falsehood.

Debt, sin as, ii, 95.

Debts, septennial remission of, i, 80, 260; ii, 145.

Decadence, after destruction of the temple, ii, 206.

Decalogue, giving of, commemorated at the Feast of Weeks, ii, 48; restoration of the tables of the law (Exod. 34) on the Day of Atonement, ii, 61; once had a place in synagogue service, i, 291 n.

Deceit, the worst kind of theft, ii, 189.

Decorum, in prayer, ii, 222 f.

Decrees (*gezerōt*), widening the scope of prohibitive laws, i, 33, 46, 258 f.; authority for such additional restrictions, i, 33; eighteen adopted at one time by a vote, i, 81; not to be imposed if the majority cannot live up to them, ii, 263.

Dedication, Feast of, ii, 49.

Deeds of lovingkindness (*gemīlūt ḥasadīm*), ii, 92, 171 ff.; greater than almsgiving, ii, 171 f.; more than all sacrifices, ii, 172; God the great exemplar, ibid.

Delators, ii, 149 n.; have no share in the world to come, i, 525; punished in hell forever, ii, 387.

Deliverance, the great, the work of God, ii, 330 ff., 370; why so long delayed? ii, 231, 351; conditions, i, 520; ii, 231, 351; in the past and in the future, theme of Passover observance, ii, 42.

Demai, ii, 72 f., 158 f.

Demetrios Eukairos, called in by the rebels against Alexander Jannaeus, i, 63 f.

Demiurge, in Philo, i, 364.

Demons, ii, 259 f.; tempt and seduce to sin, ii, 316. *See also* Beliar, spirits of.

Destiny (Εἱμαρμένη), tenets of Jewish sects about, i, 457.

Deuteronomy, legal and prophetic character, i, 15; ii, 8; spirit of the cultus contrasted with the Priests' law book, ii, 34 f.

Δευτερώσεις (Mishnah), i, 186.

Development, idea of, at variance with the presumptions of revealed religion, i, 249, 358.

Devil, his envy brought death into the world, i, 448, 478; relation to the serpent in Genesis, i, 478 f.; chained and hurled into the abyss for a thousand years, ii, 340. *See also* Satan, Mastema, Beliar.

Devotion, spirit of, ii, 223, 226.

Dew, the reviving dew of the resurrection, i, 368; ii, 296 n., 390.

Diaspora, *see* Dispersion.

Didachè, Teaching of the Twelve Apostles, i, 188 f.

Didrachm (half-shekel) poll tax, ii, 70.

Dietary laws, i, 21; ii, 74 f.

Diphtheria, i, 149 n.; ii, 248.

Direction of the mind (*kawwanah*), in prayer and other religious acts, ii, 223 f.; study, ii, 240; and secular occupations, ibid.

Discourses, in the schoolhouse (*bet ha-midrash*), i, 305 f.

Dispersion of the Jews, i, 224 f.; future gathering and return of, ii, 300, 305, 366 ff. *See also* Ten Tribes.

Divine beings (*bene elōhīm*), angels, i, 402.

Divorce, biblical and rabbinical law, ii, 122 ff.*; conflicting interpretation of Deut. 24, 1–4, on grounds of divorce,

ibid.; barrenness a cause, ii, 125; woman could sue in courts for a divorce for cause, ibid.; formalities, ii, 122 f.; frequency of divorce, ii, 125 f.; disapproval of, ii, 123; Damascus sect did not forbid, i, 202 n.
Divorcement, bill of (*geṭ*), ii, 122.
Doeg, informer (I Sam. 22), ii, 149; has no portion in the world to come, ii, 388.
Domitian, collection of the *fiscus Judaicus*, i, 350.
Door of repentance, opened to Adam, i, 530; unlike the gates of prayer, is always open, i, 530.
Dowry, for orphan girls, a community charge, ii, 175.
Dual nature of man, akin to angels and to brutes, i, 451 f.; ii, 205; Greek conceptions, ii, 292, 311; Philo, i, 452; good and evil impulses, in rabbinical teaching, are not attributed to soul and body respectively, i, 485 f.
Dualism, i, 502; ii, 263 f.; heresy of 'two authorities,' or 'powers,' i, 364 ff.,* 502; refutation of arguments from the Bible, i, 366; Gentile Christianity, i, 364 f.; heretical expressions in prayers, i, 365. *See also* Monotheism.
Duty, conception of, in a revealed religion, i, 460; to be done "for its own sake," ii, 96–98; "for the sake of Heaven," ii, 98.

E

Eagle vision, 4 Esdras, ii, 343.
Ebal and Gerizim, *see* Gerizim.
Ecclesiastes (Kohelet), canonicity of, i, 86; inspiration, i, 238; controversy of the schools of Shammai and Hillel; decision at Jamnia, i, 242.
Ecclesiasticus (Wisdom of Jesus son of Sirach), *see* Sirach.
'*ed zōmem*, a witness who gives false testimony against a man with premeditation (Deut. 19, 16–19), ii, 148 n., 186.
Edom, sanguinary prophecies against, i, 399; applied to Rome, i, 400; Edom-Rome, ii, 115 n., 116 n. *See also* Esau.
Education, of sons, obligation of the father, ii, 127; of daughters, ii, 128; in the unwritten law disapproved, ibid.; elementary education, i, 316 ff.; higher, branches of learning, i, 319, 320; normal stages and ages, i, 320; religious education of the whole people, corollary of idea of revealed religion, i, 281–283.
Eighteen Prayers (Shemoneh 'Esreh), *see* Daily Prayer.
Egypt, Jews in, colony at Elephantine, i, 5; temple of Onias, i, 43 n., 230 n.; ii, 11 n.; Philo and his times, *see* Philo; rising of the Jews under Nero suppressed by Tiberius Alexander, i, 211; relation to the Palestinian authorities, i, 107, 214; decline of Hellenistic culture, i, 107 f.
Ejaculatory prayers, ii, 229 f.
Ekah Rabbati, Midrash on Lamentations, i, 167 f.
Elders, the early, i, 30.
Elders, the Twenty-four, in Revelation of John, ii, 307 n.
Eleazar, one of the leading scribes, Maccabaean martyr, i, 548 f.
Eleazar, R. (ben Shammua'), pupil of Akiba, ordained by R. Judah b. Baba, i, 106.
Eleazar ben 'Arak, disciple of Johanan ben Zakkai, Johanan's estimate of him, ii, 245 n.; in the line of esoteric tradition, i, 411 f., 413.
Eleazar ben Azariah, made head of the academy at Jamnia on the deposition of Gamaliel II (i, 86), ii, 220; visit to Rome, i, 106; anecdote about, i, 314 f.
Eleazar Ḥisma, visit to R. Joshua ben Hananiah, i, 315.
Eleazar (ben Pedat, Amora), anecdote of Johanan's visit to his sick bed, ii, 240.
Elect, the (in Enoch), ii, 301. *See* Chosen.
Election, of the Fathers, i, 536.
Election, of Israel, i, 398 f., 536; ii, 95; irrevocable, i, 542; of individuals, ibid.; ii, 303, 341.
Elementary schools, *see* Schools.

only, i, 364 n.; Pythagorean manner of life, i, 457; strict observance of the sabbath, ii, 32; relation to apocalyptic literature, ii, 280 f.; "Essene Baraita," ii, 273.

Essentials of the Law (*gūfe tōrah*), ii, 84, 103 n.

Esther, Book of, reading at Purim, i, 239; ii, 52 f.; objections to, i, 245; inspiration of the book, i, 238, 244 f.; decision in favor of its canonicity, i, 245; uncertainty in Christian lists, i, 246; to abide, like the Law, in the days of the Messiah, i, 245.

Eternal life, ii, 294 n., 297 f., 299 n., 308, 310, 319; "portion in the world to come," equivalent, ii, 95; what to do to attain it, ii, 321.

Eternal punishment, ii, 310, 341, 387.* *See also* Hell.

Ethical principles impressed on the Halakah, ii, 145, 146, 187 f. *See* Legislation, Tannaite.

Ethics, character of Jewish, ii, 79 f., 81 f.; political virtues, ii, 112.

Ethnarch, title of the Patriarch, I, 234.

Etrog, at Tabernacles, i, 63; ii, 43 f.

Euangelion (gospel), book of the Nazarenes, i, 244.

Eucharist, liturgical prayers in the Didachè, i, 189; reminiscent of the Ḳiddush, ibid.; blessing of the cup precedes the bread, ibid.

Eve, the first transgressor, i, 475, 478.

Evidence, in criminal cases, ii, 184 ff.; new, ii, 186. *See also* Testimony *and* Witnesses.

Evil Impulse (*yeṣer ha-ra'*), i, 479 ff.*; seven names, i, 493 n.; implanted by God, i, 481,* 490; ii, 94; the bad leaven in the dough, ii, 216; grain of evil seed sown in the heart of Adam, *cor malignum* in him and all his descendants, i, 477, 483; God regretted creating it, i, 480 f.; present in the infant from birth, i, 481; its seat not the body but the heart (mind and will), i, 485, 486; a kind of malevolent second personality, i, 482; a tempter within, i, 481 f.; progressive temptation, i, 469; specialized association with lust, ii, 267; evil impulse and sin, i, 482; a "strange god" within man, i, 469 f.; natural impulses not in themselves sinful, i, 482 f.; evil impulse personified, Satan, angel of death, i, 482 n., 492; can be defeated and subdued, i, 489; the most potent means the study of the Law, which God created as an antidote, i, 489–491*; by it the evil impulse can be shaped to good ends like iron in the fire, ibid.; man can come to love God with his evil impulse as well as with the good impulse, ibid.; the good impulse (*q. v.*) created by God to countervail the evil, i, 483; conflict of impulses, i, 484; the wicked are ruled by their evil impulse, the righteous by good impulse, i, 495, cf. 486 n.; if a man has yielded to evil impulse, the remedy is repentance, i, 490 f.; evil impulse will be extirpated (or slain) on the judgment day, i, 482, 493; ii, 370; has no dominion over angels, i, 406, 484; animals have neither evil nor good impulse such as men have, i, 483.

Evil-speaking of others, ii, 148 ff.*

'Evil tongue' (*lashōn ha-ra'*), calumny, on a level with the cardinal sins, i, 149 f.

Ewald, H., on the composition and age of the Pentateuch, i, 9 f.

Examination of witnesses, ii, 185.

Exclusiveness, of the relation between Jehovah and Israel, i, 219, 220, 221, 222, 225 f., 228.

Exclusiveness, Jewish, i, 19 ff. *See also* Intermarriage *and* Dietary laws.

Excommunication, ii, 183 n.

Execution of criminals, ii, 187 n.

Exegesis, atomistic character, i, 248. *See also* Hermeneutics.

Exiles, return of, ii, 367 f. *See also* Dispersion.

Exodus, only a small part of the Israelites in Egypt went out in the, ii, 362 f.

Exorcism, ii, 260.

Fat, abdominal (*ḥeleb*), prohibited food, ii, 75.
Fate (Heimarmenè), tenets of the Jewish sects about, i, 457. *See also* Freedom.
Father, obligations to his children, ii, 127 f.; fathers do not save their sons, etc., i, 544.
Father in heaven, God, i, 527; ii, 201–211; phrase new in our period, ii, 204; expresses an attitude of piety, ii, 211; use in prayer, ii, 208; in New Testament, ii, 204 f.
Fathers, the, name belongs by preëminence to Abraham, Isaac, and Jacob, i, 542; used of others, i, 468; election of, i, 536; God's peculiar love for the patriarchs, covenants, oath, i, 536–538; their good desert with God accrues to the benefit of their posterity, ibid., *see* Merit of the Fathers; were they without fault? i, 468, 513.
Fear of God, reverence, ii, 96; one of the primary elements of religion, i, 86; fear and love as motives, ii, 98 ff.*
Feast of Weeks (*shebū'ōt*), Pentecost, memorial significance, ii, 48.
Feelings of others, regard for, ii, 147 f., 152 f., 167.
Fence about the Law (*seyag la-tōrah*), cautionary rules, i, 259; biblical authority for, ibid.
Festivals, annual, ii, 23, 40–54*; memorial significance given to, ii, 47 f.; institution of, in Jubilees, i, 196, 275; concourse of pilgrims, ii, 12.
Fiat, creation by, i, 382, 415. *See also* Word of God.
Filial piety, ii, 92, 131–134*; honoring parents made equal with honoring God, ii, 131 f.; what it includes, ii, 132 f.; father and mother to be equally honored, ii, 131; anecdotes of exemplary piety, ii, 133; crimes against, in biblical and rabbinical law, ii, 134 f.
Firmaments, number, thickness, distances, i, 368, 530 f.
First fruits, of grain and fruits, the priest's due (*terūmah gedōlah*), ii, 71.
Fiscus Judaicus, i, 234, 350.
Flattery, a form of deceit, ii, 189 f.
Flavius Clemens, Flavia Domitilla, i, 349.
Flesh with milk, prohibition of, ii, 75.
Food, varieties of prohibited, i, 21; ii, 74 f.
Fool, moral implication, ii, 148 n.
Foreign religions in Israel, i, 221 f.; ii, 358.
Foreknowledge of God, i, 455.
Forgiveness of sins (God's), i, 117; a prerogative which he does not share nor depute, i, 535; the only remedy for sin as a breach of divine law, i, 117; motives of divine forgiveness, i, 535–545; repentance the sole but inexorable condition of sins against Himself, i, 500–502*; in the case of injuries against a fellow man, reparation and reconciliation required, i, 512, 514; ii, 153 ff.; forgiveness never refused to the genuine penitent, i, 520; ii, 58.
Forgiveness of sins, man's, of injuries done him by a fellow man, ii, 153 ff.; refusal a sin, ii, 154.
Formalism, in prayer, ii, 227.
Four cubits, the, ii, 32 n.
Fourth (Second) Esdras, ii, 283 ff. ,321 f.; chap. 7, 26–44, ii, 338 f.
Frauds in sale of wine, food, etc., ii, 142.
Freedom, man's, power of choice, ability, responsibility, i, 453 ff.*; in Sirach, Psalms of Solomon, 4 Esdras, i, 455; Philo, i, 458 f.; mediaeval philosophers, i, 454 n.; rabbinical teaching, i, 455 f.; freedom and divine providence, i, 454, 456.
Freedom and necessity, dissension of Jewish sects in Josephus, i, 456–458.
Friends, Society of, ii, 5.
Fritzsche und Grimm, commentary on the Apocrypha, i, 216.
Functional deities, i, 221 n.
Funeral feast, ii, 288.
Funeral procession, ii, 172.

G

gabbai ṣedaḳah, charity collector, ii, 174 f.
Gabriel, angel of revelation, i, 403.
Galilee, Judaizing of, i, 287; forcible conversion of Upper, i, 336; schools in Galilee after the war under Hadrian, i, 93.
Gamaliel II (of Jabneh), Patriarch, deposed for a time from the presidency of the academy, i, 86; ii, 220; with his colleagues and disciples the fundamental authorities of normative Judaism, i, 87; revision and regulation of the Daily Prayer, i, 103, 292; ii, 220; commination of heretics in the Daily Prayer, i, 91.
Games at Tyre, Jason sends an embassy to, i, 50.
Gan Eden, paradise, ii, 390 f.
ganaz, treasure up, put in safe-keeping, i, 247.
Garden of Delight, ii, 339.
Garden of Righteousness, ii, 303.
Gates of heaven, i, 530.
Gates of prayer and of repentance, i, 530.
gayyer, make a proselyte (*gēr*), i, 330; *nitgayyer*, become a proselyte, ibid.
Geburah, ha-, 'the Power' (the Almighty, God), i, 374, 472; ii, 335 n.
Gehinnom, Gehenna, ii, 391. *See* Hell.
gemīlūt ḥasadīm, deeds of lovingkindness, charity, ii, 85 n., 86 n., 92, 171 ff.; superior to almsgiving, ii, 85 n., 171 f.; God the great exemplar, i, 441; ii, 111, 172 f.; an atonement equal to the sacrificial atonement on the altar, i, 503.
Generation of the Flood, respite given them that they might repent, i, 492, 528.
Gentiles, laws given to Noah binding on all, i, 274 f., 453, 462; to be observed by the resident alien, i, 339; table companionship with Gentiles made difficult by regulation for slaughter of animals, ii, 75; dissension among disciples of Jesus on this point, ibid.
Gentiles, conversion of, i, **323–353**; ii, 320, *see also* Proselytes; in the last crisis, ii, 306 n., 315; opportunity for repentance given to, ii, 304; Gentiles in the general resurrection, ii, 385; their ultimate fate, ii, 385 f.; righteous Gentiles have a share in the world to come, i, 279; ii, 386.*
Genuflexions in prayer, ii, 222, 228.
George, G. F. L., on the composition and age of the Pentateuch, i, 10.
gēr, meaning and use of the word (resident: alien, convert to Judaism), i, 328 ff.; *gēr ben berīt*, i, 332 n., 339, 340 n.; *gēr ṣedeḳ*, i, 338; *gēr emet*, ibid. *See* Proselyte.
gēr tōshab, i, 339, 340.
gērīm gerūrīm, i, 337 f., 346.
Gerizim, temple on Mt., i, 23–26; dedicated by Antiochus IV to Zeus Xenios, i, 26, 52 n.; destroyed by John Hyrcanus, i, 26.
geṭ, certificate of divorce, ii, 122.
Ge'ullah, at Passover, ii, 42.
gezerōt, authoritative decrees widening the scope of prohibitive laws, i, 33, 46, 258 f.; biblical authority for such extension, i, 33; restrictions which the majority cannot live up to not to be imposed, ii, 263; eighteen adopted at a conference by a Shammaite majority, i, 81.
gillūy 'araiyōt, 'incest,' extended to all kinds of unchastity, i, 466 f.; ii, 267; a cardinal sin (*q. v.*), i, 466 f.
Girls, upbringing and education, ii, 128.
Gnostics, Jewish, i, 365.
God, i, **357–442**; ii, **201–211**; Jewish conceptions, summarized, i, 423; their undogmatic character, i, 357 ff.; God not transcendent, i, 361, 417, 421; supramundane but not extramundane, exalted but not remote, i, 368 f., 423 ff.; the Absolute in Philo, i, 416; the unity of God, *see* Monotheism; unity in Philo, i, 361; creator of the world, i, 227 f., 380 ff.; sustains in being all that

is, i, 384; everywhere present, all-knowing, all-powerful, i, 370 ff.; religious significance of these ideas, ibid.; justice and mercy the two primary 'norms' of his dealing with men, i, 386 ff.; character of his justice, i, 379 f., 387 f., *see also* Retribution; mercy the quality that best expresses his nature, i, 535; embraces all his creatures, i, 393, 535, *see also* Compassion; holiness of God, i, 386, 461; ii, 101 f., 109 f.; goodness, i, 390 ff.; deeds of loving-kindness, i, 441; ii, 110 f., 172 f.; an example for man's imitation, ibid.; truth, i, 395; ii, 194 f.; love, i, 396 ff.; peculiar love for Israel, i, 398; for the Fathers, i, 536 ff.; the Father in heaven, ii, 201 ff.; chastisement of his children, ii, 248 ff.; sovereignty of God, i, 401, 431 ff.; ii, 210, 372; history the unfolding of a plan of God, i, 384 f.; teleology, i, 375; providence and miracle, i, 384 f.; ii, 376 ff.; names of God, i, 387, 389, 424 ff.; ii, 134 n.; abode, the highest heaven, tabernacle, temple, i, 368 ff.; in the New Jerusalem, ii, 342; ministers and instrumentalities, i, 401 ff., 414 ff.

God-fearing persons (φοβούμενοι, σεβόμενοι, τὸν θεόν), i, 325 f., 340.

Gog and Magog, ii, 305 n., 333 n., 337 n., 344, 348, 367 n.

gōi ṣaddīḳ, a righteous Gentile, i, 279; ii, 386.

Golden Age, national, ii, 323 ff., 330; why so long delayed? ii, 231; calculations of the end, ibid. *See also* Messiah, Messianic Age.

Golden calf, Moses' intercession, i, 537.

Golden Rule, negative and positive forms; parallels, ii, 87 f.

Good Impulse (*yeṣer ṭōb*), i, 483 ff.; the righteous man is ruled by his good impulse, i, 495, cf. i, 486 n.

Good name, *see* Reputation, Honor.

Good works, of which man draws the interest in this world, while the capital is laid up in heaven, ii, 92; treasure in heaven, i, 544 f.; ii, 90 ff.; deeds of loving kindness, i, 514.

Goodness of God, the thirteen norms (Exod. 34, 6), i, 390, 395; to the unthankful and the evil, i, 394 f.; extends to man and beast, Jew and Gentile, righteous and wicked, i, 535.

Gospel (*euangelion*) not sacred scripture, i, 86 f., 243 f.

Gospels, witnesses to the teaching of the synagogue, i, 132, 183, 185, 288 f.; apologetic writings, i, 185; Greek gospels and Aramaic tradition, i, 184 f.

Gossip, peddling, ii, 148 f.

Government, general principle, ii, 117 f.; duty and limits of obedience to, ii, 113 ff.; Roman, good, because it protects its subjects and enforces justice, ii, 115.

Grace of God, i, 395; ii, 95, *see also* Goodness.

Grace after meals, ii, 217.

Graf, K. H., on the composition and age of the Pentateuch, i, 10 f.

Gratitude to God, for ill-fortune as well as for good, ii, 253.

Great Assembly, *see* Great Synagogue.

Great Synagogue, i, 31 ff.; institutions, i, 32 f.; motto, i, 33, 311; decision on the Book of Esther, i, 245; regulations about reading of Esther, ii, 52.

Greatest commandment, ii, 85.

Greek culture in Syria, i, 48 f.; Greek language in Palestine, i, 48, 322; in the home of Rabbi, ii, 128 n.

Greek translation of the Pentateuch (LXX), *see* Versions, Greek.

Grudge, not to be cherished, ii, 152, 154 f.

gūf, repository of unborn souls, ii, 353 n.

gūfe tōrah, essentials of the Law, ii, 84, 103 n.

Gymnasium in Jerusalem, i, 49.

H

Habdalah, at the close of Sabbath, ii, 37.

Ḥaberim, Associates, ii, 73, 206 n. *See also* Pharisees.

Habinenu, condensed prayer, ii, 212.

I

Ibn Ezra, on Dan. 12, 2, ii, 298.
Ideal (utopian) strain in biblical and rabbinical legislation; in teaching of Jesus, ii, 151 f.
Idleness, leads to sin, ii, 127 f.
Idolater, five names by which he is called in Scripture, i, 466 n.
Idolatry, antipathy of the religion of Israel to, i, 223; concomitant of polytheism, most heinous of sins, i, 362 f.; polemic against, i, 362 ff.; rejection of, is acknowledgment of the whole law, i, 325; began in the generation of Enosh, i, 473 n.; yielding to evil impulse is idolatry, i, 469 f. *See also* Heathenism.
Idols, sarcasm on, i, 227.
Idumaea, conquered and Judaized by John Hyrcanus, i, 336.
Illumination, in temple, at Tabernacles, ii, 46 f.; of houses, at Feast of Dedication, ii, 49 f.
Image of God in man, i, 446 ff.; fundamental principle of morals, ibid.; wherein it consists (Wisdom of Solomon, Philo), i, 448 f.; a likeness at third remove (Philo), i, 449 n.; not lost by Adam's sin, i, 479.
Imagination (devising) of man's heart is evil, i, 479 f. *See* Evil Impulse.
Imagination: the imagining of sin is sin, ii, 267, 271; if indulged is worse than actual transgression, ii, 271.
Imitation of God, i, 441; ii, 85, 109 ff.*, 172.
Immateriality, an abstraction, ii, 287 n.; Platonic, ii, 292 n.
Immortality, essential nature of deity, image of God in man, i, 448; Greek conceptions, ii, 311; Philo, 295; Maimonides, ii, 393; hope of immortality for the righteous only, ii, 293 f.
Imposition of hands, in sacrifice (*semīkah*), early subject of controversy, i, 46; in sacrifices of women, ii, 130.
Imprisonment, as form of punishment, ii, 187.
Incantations, over the sick, ii, 388.
Incense, in rites of purification (disinfection), ii, 55.
Incest (*gillūy ʿaraiyōt*), cardinal sin, i, 466 f.; includes all kinds of unchastity, ibid.; rabbinical enlargements of the list of prohibited degrees, ii, 120 f.; Damascus sect makes marriage with a niece incestuous, i, 201 f.
Individualizing of prophetic message to the people, i, 113 f.; retribution, i, 501; ii, 248 f., 292; repentance, i, 501 f., 509, 520 f.; salvation, i, 120 f. Cf. also i, 224 f.
Infidels, deniers of revelation, retribution, resurrection, etc., punished in hell forever, ii, 387 f.
Infidelity, fundamental, disbelief in God (*kōfer ba-ʿiḳkar* — the Root), i, 360, 467, 521, 522; ii, 149 f.
Informers (delators), ii, 149 n., 525; ii, 387.
Injuries to reputation or to honor, i, 394; ii, 141 f.; worse than to person or property, ii, 147 ff.*
Insincerity, ii, 191.
Inspection (*bedīkah*) of animals slaughtered for food, ii, 74 f.
Inspiration, of the authors of Scripture, i, 237 f.; ceased with the last prophets, i, 237, 243, 421; of Solomon, i, 238; Philo's theory, i, 239; verbal and literal, ibid., i, 88; associated with sacred joy, ii, 46.
Instrumental music, the levitical band at Tabernacles, ii, 46 f.
Insults, ii, 147 f., 149 n. *See* Injuries to honor.
Integrity (*ṣedeḳ*), ii, 191.
Intellect, the likeness of God in man, i, 448; the immortal element breathed into him by God (Philo), i, 452.
Intention (*kawwanah*), in religious acts, prayer, study, ii, 223 ff., 240, 245 f.
Intercession for others, in prayer, a duty, ii, 219; the intercession of Moses after the sin of the golden calf, i, 537, 550.
Intercession of angels, i, 438 f.

Jerome, account of the Nazarene sect, i, 186 f.

Jerusalem, restoration by Zerubbabel and Joshua, Ezra, Nehemiah, i, 4 ff.; repairs of the walls by the high priest Simeon, i, 34 f.; under Antiochus IV, i, 49, 51 f.; Judas Maccabaeus, i, 53 f.; taken by Pompey, i, 73; by Herod, i, 74; by Titus, i, 83; rebuilt by Hadrian as Aelia Capitolina, i, 89 f., 91, 93.

Jerusalem, sole legitimate seat of sacrificial worship, ii, 11; in the future to be the religious centre of the world, i, 230; the New Jerusalem, ii, 300, 332, 341 f., 343.

Jesus the Nazarene, disciples of, i, 90 ff., 183 ff.; pious and observant Jews, i, 90, 187; knowledge of the Scripture through the synagogue, i, 288; attitude to the law, i, 269 f.; ii, 9 f.; denunciation of the Scribes and Pharisees, i, 183; the merit of good works, ii, 90 f.; messianic beliefs, i, 90 f., 185 f.; ii, 309; the Son of David, ii, 309, 329; genealogies, ii, 329; the apocalyptic "Son of Man," i, 127 f., 186; ii, 309 f., 334 f., 335, 374. *See also* Nazarenes.

Jesus the Nazarene, illustrations of the teaching of Jesus: two great commandments, ii, 85 f.; civic and religious duties, ii, 118; non-resistance, ii, 151 f.; opprobrious words, i, 48; reproof and forgiveness, ii, 153; giving and lending, ii, 168; giving everything to the poor and acquiring treasure in heaven, ii, 90 f.; what to do to inherit eternal life, ii, 90 f., 321; adultery of the eyes, ii, 267; grounds of divorce, ii, 124 f.; response to another halakic question, ii, 250; proof of the resurrection of the dead, ii, 383, 392; charged with laxity in the observance of the Sabbath, ii, 29, 31; cures wrought by his disciples by the use of his name, i, 378; legality of his trial, ii, 187 n.; "Jesus the Nazarene," thrust away by Joshua ben Peraḥiah, i, 348.

Jesus, son of Sirach, *see* Sirach.

Jews, exceptional status and privileges in the Roman empire, i, 225, 233 f., 336, 350; not extended to proselytes, i, 233 f., 350.

Jews and Samaritans, i, 23 ff.

Job, motives for serving God, ii, 99 f.

Johanan, high priest in the Persian period, i, 23.

Johanan (John Hyrcanus, *q. v.*), regulations about Demai, ii, 72 n., 159.

Johanan ben Beroḳa, visit to R. Joshua (ben Hananiah), i, 315.

Johanan ben Nuri, anecdote about Akiba, ii, 153.

Johanan ha-Sandelar, at Nisibis, i, 106.

Johanan ben Torta, warning to Akiba about Bar Cocheba, i, 89; ii, 329 n.

Johanan ben Zakkai, disciple of Hillel, i, 84; leader of the Pharisees, i, 85; predicts the destruction of Jerusalem, ii, 116; escapes from the city, ibid.; establishes school at Jamnia and constitutes the High Court, i, 83 ff.; supremacy of Pharisaism and predominance of the school of Hillel, i, 85, 86, cf. 81; his work conservative, not reformatory, i, 131 f.; reputed fountainhead of the esoteric tradition, i, 411 f.

John Hyrcanus (Johanan), high priest and ruler, his wars of conquest, i, 56; forcible Judaizing of Idumaea, i, 336; breach with the Pharisees, i, 57 ff.; became a Sadducee, i, 58, 482; rebellion against him, i, 62; the last years of his reign, i, 63; heard a mysterious voice (*bat ḳōl*) announcing the victory of his sons, i, 422; charges against him (?) in Enoch 94–104, ii, 156.

John the Baptist, his message, ii, 309; in the rôle of Elijah, ii, 326.

John, Revelation of, *see* Revelation.

Jonathan, brother of Judas Maccabaeus, i, 55.

Jonathan (Jannai), high priest and king, *see* Alexander Jannaeus.

L

freedom and ability, i, 453 ff.; responsibility, i, 38, 445, 454 ff.; created with the evil impulse (*q. v.*), i, 480 f.; dual nature of man, i, 451 f.; in Philo, i, 452.

Manasseh, king of Judah, introduction of foreign religions, i, 221 f.; his repentance, i, 523 f., 530; the angels try to shut it out, ibid.; his prayer, *see* Prayer of Manasses; chastisement did for him what instruction did not, ii, 253; has no share in the world to come, i, 525; ii, 388; contrary opinion, i, 525.

Manslaughter, *see* Homicide.

Mariamne, Asmonaean princess, married to Herod, i, 75 f.

Marom, high heaven, abode of God, i, 430 n.

Marriage, a divine ordinance, ii, 119; prohibited degrees, ii, 120 f.; rabbinical extensions, ii, 121; marriage with a niece, ibid.; of cousins-german, ibid.; arranged by parents, ibid.; marriages made in heaven, i, 439 f.; ii, 234; early marriages favored, ii, 119 f.; marriage of students, ibid.; laws of the Damascus sect, i, 201 f.

Marriage contract (*ketūbah*), ii, 122 f., 127.

Martyrs, Maccabaean, their death a vicarious expiation, i, 548 f.; expect to be brought to life again, ibid.; under Trajan, ii, 107; under Hadrian, i, 106; Akiba, i, 93; ii, 106 n.; Hananiah ben Teradion, ii, 106 n., 174 n., 114.

Martyrs, Christian, appear in the first resurrection, ii, 341 f.

Martyrdom, hallows the Name, ii, 105 f.; not to be courted, ii, 107 f.

masseket, *massekta*, i, 152.

Masses, the ignorant and negligent, ii, 206; *see* People of the Land (*'amme ha-areṣ*).

Maṣṣot, unleavened cakes, ii, 40.

Mastema, Satan (in Jubilees), ii, 316 n.

Master, *see* Teacher.

Master and servant, ii, 138 ff.; slaves, ii, 135 ff.

Masturbation, ii, 268.

masūr la-leb, 'left to conscience,' obligations and duties for which no quantum can be fixed, ii, 82, 148 n.

Mathia ben Ḥeresh, head of a school in Rome, i, 106 f.

Measure for measure, ii, 249 n., 251 f., 253, 381 n.

Meat with milk, prohibition of combining, ii, 75.

Matthew, Gospel according to, i, 186.

Megillah (Roll of Esther), reading at Purim, ii, 52 f.; objections to it, i, 245.

Megillat Ta'anit, Fasting Scroll, i, 160; ii, 54, 68.

Megillot, the Five Rolls, reading at festivals, i, 241 n.

Megillot, Midrashim on, i, 171.

meḥussere amanah, men of scant faith, ii, 232 n.

Meir, disciple of Akiba, i, 94 f.; said to have been a proselyte, i, 95 n., 347; his Mishnah, ibid.; dialectic, i, 95; relations to Elisha ben Abuyah, i, 95 n., 395, 522.

Mekilta, Tannaite Midrash on Exodus, school of Ishmael, i, 135 ff.

Mekilta de-R. Simeon ben Yoḥai, from the school of Akiba, i, 138 ff.

Melchizedek, ii, 328.

Melkart, god of Tyre, i, 221; games at Tyre, i, 50.

Memra, in the Targums, i, 417 ff.; does not render "the word of the Lord" (God, etc.) in the Bible, i, 418; does not correspond to Logos in Philo, i, 416 ff.; not a personal being, i, 419; or "hypostasis," i, 437; Strack-Billerbeck on, i, 418 n.

memrī, 'myself,' ii, 327 n.

Men of the Great Assembly (Synagogue), i, 31 ff.; their motto, i, 33, 311; decision on the Book of Esther, i, 245, "restored the crown" (of the divine attributes), i, 380; ii, 229.

Menahem (ben Hezekiah), name of the Messiah, ii, 348.

350 ff.; calculations of the set time, and signs of its approach, ii, 352 ff.; shortly before it a great pestilence will sweep away the wicked of Israel, ii, 362 f.; fate of the heathen nations, ii, 371; return of the dispersion, ii, 366 ff., *see also* Ten Tribes; proselytes in that age, conflicting opinions, i, 346; the Law in the messianic age, i, 271 f.; marvellous fertility of Palestine, ii, 365 f.
Messianic banquet (Behemoth and Leviathan), ii, 364 ff.
Messianic expectations of hellenistic Jews, ii, 329 f.; of the Tannaim, ii, 346 ff.*; messianic expectation and the reign of God, ii, 374.
mēt miṣwah. The unburied dead, to perform the last offices for whom is a duty of the highest obligation, i, 71.
Meturgeman, interpreter in the synagogue, i, 174.
Meyer, Eduard, development of Kuenen's theory of the Priests' Code, i, 12 n.
Mezuzah, amulet on door-posts, ii, 129.
Michael, angelic champion of the Jews, i, 403; ii, 297.
Middle class (*bēnōnīm*), neither completely good nor completely bad, i, 485, 495 f.; ii, 62, 318 f., 387.
Middot, Dimensions, tract in the Mishnah on the plan of the Herodian temple, ascribed to Eliezer ben Jacob, i, 153.
middōt, 'norms,' attributes of God, i, 287; hermeneutic rules of Hillel, i, 77, 79 n.; of R. Ishmael, i, 88, 135.
Midrash, the higher exegesis of Scripture, i, 319; Midrash and Mishnah, branches of study, i, 150 f.; Tannaite, or Halakic, juristic exegesis of the Mosaic legislation, i, 89, 97, 132, 135 ff.; Midrash, Halakah, Haggadah, i, 319.
Midrash ha-Gadol, catena on the Pentateuch, i, 138 f., 144 f., 146.
Midrash Tannaim, on Deuteronomy, i, 146 f.
Midrash, homiletical (Haggadah), i, 133, 161 ff.; value of, i, 171.
miḳweh, 'hope,' 'font,' ii, 207 n.
Millenarians, Christian, ii, 394.
Mind, rational faculty, hellenistic conception, i, 485 f.
Minim, sectaries, heretics, sometimes particularly the Nazarenes, i, 85 f., 91; their books, i, 243 f.; dualists among them, i, 365, 366. See also *mīnūt*.
Minister of the synagogue (*ḥazzan*), duties and functions, i, 289 f., 301, 303, 317.
Ministers of God (angels, etc.), i, 401 ff.
Ministering angels, i, 410.
Minor girl, could be betrothed by her father, ii, 121 n.
mīnūt, heresy, sometimes Christianity, ii, 250 n., 356.
minyan, quorum of the synagogue for prayer, ten free adult males, i, 300; ii, 131.
Miracle, the idea of, i, 376; ii, 349; miracles no more wonderful than the ordinary operations of providence, i, 378 f.; the age of miracles not past, i, 376 f.; miracles in response to faith, ii, 205 f., 237; to prayer, i, 377 f.; ii, 235 f.; by the use of the secret Name, i, 426; wrought for Israel for the sake of Abraham, i, 538 f.; in the deliverance of martyrs, ii, 107 f.
Miracle-workers, i, 377 f.; ii, 206 n.
Miriam, i, 542; Miriam's well, ibid. (cf. Paul's allegory, i, 250); death of, expiatory, i, 547; leprosy, punishment for calumniating Moses, ii, 149.
Miscegenation of angels and women, i, 406. *See* Angels, fall of.
Mishnah, comprehensive term for the science of tradition, over against Miḳra, study of the Bible, i, 319; Mishnah and Midrash, i, 150 f., 319; especially, systematic compilations of rules of the traditional law, i, 132; in the school of Akiba's disciples, i, 94, 151; Meir, i, 94; the Large Mishnahs of Ḥiyya, Bar Ḳappara, Hosha'ya, i, 96, 156.
Mishnah, The, of the Patriarch Judah, i, 4, 94 f., 96; its authority, i, 105, 151;

N

magical formulas; miracles wrought by it, i, 426; in theosophy, ibid.; uttered in the temple only, i, 424 f.; exceptional ordinance, i, 427; pronunciation formerly taught to any one, later only to trustworthy men, i, 425; Samaritans uttered it in (judicial) oaths (Ιαβε), i, 427; names of 12, 42, 72, letters, i, 426 n.; the seven names that may not be erased, ii, 134 n.; no name or title of God to be employed lightly, even in prayer, i, 428 f.; IHVH designates God in his merciful and gracious character, in distinction from Elohim, i, 387, 389.

Name, The, *see* Name of God.

Name of the Messiah, premundane, i, 526; ii, 340, 344, 347 ff.

Narcissus story, ii, 264 f.

Nashim, Women, third division of the Mishnah, i, 152.

Nasi, *see* Patriarch.

Nathan the Babylonian, vice-president (Ab bet Dīn) under Simeon ben Gamaliel II, i, 104.

Nations, the seventy, i, 227, 278; the Law revealed to them and rejected, i, 453; the seventy bulls, burnt offerings, at Tabernacles an expiation for them, ii, 43 n.

Nations of the world, *see* Heathen Nations.

National character of the religion of Israel, i, 219 ff.; of Judaism, i, 233 f.; nationality and universality, i, **219–234**; reconciliation, i, 228.

Natural and supernatural, i, 376.

Nature, God's activity in, i, 375 f.; laws of nature divine ordinances, i, 376 n.

Nazarenes, disciples of Jesus the Nazarene, i, 90 ff., 183 ff. (*see* Jesus); their activity after the destruction of Jerusalem, i, 91, 243 f.; animosity of some of the leading rabbis of the time, ibid.; commination in the Daily Prayer, i, 91, 292; their books, i, 243 f.; separated from their countrymen by the war under Hadrian, i, 91, 172 f., 244; excluded from Aelia Capitolina (Jerusalem) with the rest of the Jews, i, 91; regarded by the church as heretics, i, 92; seats east of the Jordan, i, 91; in the region of Beroea (Aleppo), i, 91, 186 f. *See also* Kefar Sekanya.

Nearness of God, i, 368 f.; 440 ff.*

nebelah, flesh of animals not correctly slaughtered, i, 339; ii, 74.

Nebuchadnezzar, and the three Jewish youths in the fiery furnace, ii, 106.

Necessity, *see* Fate *and* Freedom.

Necromancy, ii, 290.

Needle, eye of, in a figure, i, 531.

ne'eman, 'trustworthy,' especially in matters of tithes, first fruits, etc., ii, 74, 159.

Nehardea, school at, i, 105.

Nehemiah, governor of the district of Judaea, i, 5; restoration of the walls of Jerusalem, i, 5 f.; some identified him with Zerubbabel, i, 31 n.; member of the Great Synagogue, i, 31, 32; second governorship, i, 5, 14 f.

Nehemiah, disciple of Akiba, anonymous element in the Tosefta ascribed to him, i, 155.

Neighbor, 'thou shalt love thy neighbor as thyself,' the most comprehensive rule of moral obligation, ii, 85 ff., 174; let thy neighbor's property be as dear to thee as thine own, i, 19; ii, 142, 151; thy neighbor's honor as thine own, i, 19; ii, 150, 151.

Ne'ilah, final service on the Day of Atonement, ii, 59; prayer at, ii, 211 n., 214.*

Nero, rebellion of the Jews under, i, 83; expectation of the reappearance of Nero, ii, 343.

Nerva, delations prohibited by, i, 351.

neshek, 'usury,' interest on loans, i, 340; ii, 142 f.

New creation, figure for the annulment of a sinner's past, i, 533.

New heaven, ii, 305; and new earth, ii, 341, 342.

New Jerusalem, ii, 300, 332; descends from heaven, habitation of God on earth, 341 f., 343.

P

Paedagogic principles, ii, 247.
Pairs (*zūgōt*), in the succession of tradition from Antigonus of Socho, ending with Shammai and Hillel, i, 45; names and times, i, 255 f.; president (*Nasi*) and vice-president (*Ab bet Dīn*) of the High Court, i, 45 n., 225 n.
Palestine, fabulous fertility in the messianic age, ii, 365 f.
Pantheism, i, 361.
Pappos, R., i, 379, 447.
Parables and proverbs cultivated by scholars, i, 309 f.; examples of parables, i, 487 f., 488, 490; ii, 384.
Paradise, the earthly, ii, 303, 339; celestial, abode of blessed souls, ii, 390 f.; antemundane creation, i, 526; visit of the four rabbis, i, 413; ii, 390 n.
Paraphrases, in Targums, for reverence, *see* Circumlocutions.
Parah (Red Heifer), i, 85; one of the four special sabbaths, i, 298.
Parashah, 'section,' of the Pentateuch for reading in the synagogue, i, 300; subdivisions of, i, 302.
Parents, honoring of, *see* Filial Piety.
Parthians, i, 74; ii, 343; their invasion a sign of the coming of the Messiah, ii, 350; Parthians and Medes, in the rôle of Gog and Magog, ii, 305, 367 n.
Particularism, i, 219 n.
Paschal meal, *see* Passover.
Passover, concurrence of the fourteenth of Nisan and a Sabbath, i, 78 f.; concourse of pilgrims at, ii, 12; rites and customs, domestic observance, ii, 40 ff.; proselytes to keep it just like native Israelites, i, 330 f.; Passover story (*Haggadah shel-Pesaḥ*), ii, 42 f.
Patriarch (*Nasi*), the title, i, 234; head of the Jewish nation after the fall of Jerusalem, i, 108 f.; regal authority, i, 234; his *apostoli;* taxes for his support, 109; Davidic lineage, through Hillel, i, 234; Gamaliel II, i, 86; Simeon ben Gamaliel (II.), i, 104; Judah, ibid.
Patriarchs, *see* Fathers.
Patriarchs, Testaments of the Twelve, *see* Testaments.
Paul, the dispensation of law as a whole at an end, ii, 10; no salvation by the works of the law, i, 282; ii, 93 f.; God cannot forgive without expiation, ii, 94 n.; accused of teaching Jews not to circumcise their sons nor observe the customs of their religion, ii, 21; the moral law and the indwelling spirit of Christ, ii, 10; the whole (moral) law in one sentence, ii, 85, 87; the conflict of impulses in man, i, 484, 485 f.; on Adam's sin and its consequences, i, 476, cf. 477, 478; attempt to dematerialize the resurrection, ii, 394; on subjection to authorities, ii, 113 f.; on marriage, ii, 120 n.; on the merit of the Fathers, i, 542.
Peace (*shalōm*), meaning, ii, 195; encomiums on, ii, 195 ff.; in heaven and on earth, ii, 242.
Peace-making, ii, 92, 196; Aaron an example, i, 392; Meir, ii, 196 f.
Peasants, untrustworthy in matters of religious taxation, ii, 72; work of the peasant and the scholar — the important thing the religious spirit in which it is done, ii, 240, 245 f.
Penance, self-imposed, i, 517; ii, 257 f.
Penitent thief, parallel to, ii, 391.
Penitential days, the ten, from New Year's to Day of Atonement, i, 530 n., 533; ii, 62 f.; litany on, ii, 210.
Penitential prayers, biblical examples, i, 501, 511; Jewish, ii, 59, 60, 214 n. *See also* 'Al Ḥeṭ *and* Ashamnu.
Pentateuch, composition and age, critical opinions, i, 9 ff.; Jewish belief, i, 7, 29; lessons in the synagogue, i, 297 ff.; divided into sections to be completed in a definite time; Palestinian cycle of three years (*sedarīm*), Babylonian, one year (*parashiyōt*), i, 299; normal number of readers, i, 301; Greek translation, letter of Aristeas, i, 322 n.; made for the use of the Jews, i,

the rational soul, i, 458 f.; the dual nature of man, i, 452; conception of sin, i, 484 n.; universality of sin, i, 468; on proselytes, i, 327 f.; acquaintance with Philo's ideas in the Midrash, i, 165.
Philo, Antiquitates Biblicae, ii, 285 n.
Phineas, covenant of the priesthood, i, 549; a perpetual atonement for the Israelites, ibid.; Elijah identified with Phineas, ii, 358 n.
Φοβούμενοι τὸν θεόν, God-fearing (religious) men, i, 325 n., 340.
Phylacteries (*tefillīn*), ii, 191.
Φῶτα, Feast of Lights, Ḥannukah, ii, 49 f.
Piacula, private and public, i, 499. *See* Atonement, Expiation, Scapegoat.
Pietism, ii, 5.
Piety, ii, **201–275**; in specific sense, subjective side of religion, ii, 3; its premises, ii, 201 f.; characteristics of Jewish, ii, 214; study an integral part of Jewish piety, ii, 239.
Pirḳè Abot, i, 152 n., 156 f.; taken up into synagogue service, i, 157; maxims and aphorisms of eminent teachers, i, 310 f.
pitgama, 'word,' in Targums, rendering of "word of God" in the Scriptures, i, 417; *see* Memra.
Place (*makōm*), metonymy for God, i, 373.
Plato, ethics and politics, ii, 112; influence on Philo's idea of God, i, 223 f.; of inspiration, i, 239.
Polemic, Jewish, against polytheism and idolatry, i, 323; sects and heresies: "two authorities," i, 364 ff.; the Nazarenes, i, 91, 243 f.; against Christianity, i, 165, 173, 269 n., 364 f.
Political conditions of the Jews under foreign rule, ii, 112; political virtues, ii, 112 f.
Poll-tax, the half-shekel, ii, 70.
Pollion and Sameas, leading Pharisees under Herod, i, 75; ii, 113.
Pollion, commonly identified with Abṭalion (*q. v.*), i, 313 n.
Polygamy, ii, 122; prohibited by the Damascus sect, i, 202; ii, 122 n.
Polytheism, in other ancient religions, i, 220 f.; its existence a problem for monotheism, proposed solutions, i, 226 ff.; idolatry its concomitant, i, 362 f. *See also* Heathenism *and* Monotheism.
Pompey, hears the rival claims of Aristobulus and Hyrcanus, i, 72 f.; ii, 113; takes Jerusalem and makes an end of Judaean independence, ibid.
Poor, the biblical solicitude for, laws for their relief, ii, 162 ff.; rabbinical interpretation and extension, ii, 165 ff.; organization of poor-relief, ii, 174 ff.; impostors, ii, 177; exhortation not to become a public charge, ibid.
Poor, the humble and pious, in contrast to the rich, ii, 156.
Poor-tithe, ii, 163 n.
Poseidonios, on the cities of Syria, i, 148.
Power, The (*ha-gebūrah*), metonymy for God, i, 374, 472; ii, 335 n.; the supernal (God), enfeebled by sin, increased by the righteous when they do His will, i, 472.
Praise of God, inordinate recital of in private prayer censured, ii, 229. *See also* Ascriptions.
Prayer, ii, **212–236**; biblical synonyms for prayer, ii, 217; common prayer (Shemoneh 'Esreh, Tefillah), *see also* Daily Prayer; revision and regulation under Gamaliel II, i, 103; institution of three daily hours of prayer attributed to Moses, or the patriarchs, ii, 219 f.; antiquity of the standard prayers, i, 177 f.; normal order, first, ascriptions, then petitions, closing with praise, ii, 219; may be said in any language, i, 295; recitation incumbent on women, ii, 129; prayer is worship ('*abōdah*) in the heart, ii, 15, 84 f., 217 f.; dearer to God than all good works and all sacrifices, ii, 218; place of common prayer in the religious life of Judaism, ii, 226; brevity in private prayer commended,

all inspired men were prophets, i, 237; forty-eight enumerated, besides seven prophetesses, ibid.; did not all leave their utterances in writing, i, 237 n.; neither added to the revelation given to Moses nor took anything from it, i, 239, 358; transmitters of tradition from Moses down, ibid.

Prophet, the False (Rev. of John), ii, 340.

Prosbul, i, 80, 259 f.

Proselytes (Conversion of Gentiles, i, **323–353**); in Greek Bible the usual rendering of Hebrew *gēr*, i, 328 f.; aliens who join themselves to the Jews, ii, 24; or "turn Jew," i, 329; their conversion as repentance, i, 529; Jews by naturalization, i, 231, 529; defined by Philo, i, 327 f.; "enter into the covenant" by circumcision, i, 332, 334, 340; keep Passover like native Jews, i, 330 f.; enjoy equal rights with born Jews, i, 327, 329, 330; subject to all the obligations of the Law, ibid.; legal status at the moment of reception, i, 334 f.; initiatory rites, circumcision, baptism, sacrifice, i, 331 f., 334; for a woman, baptism and sacrifice, i, 332; examination for admission, i, 333 f.; formalities of proselyte baptism, i, 333 f.; attitude of the religious leaders toward proselytes, i, 341 ff.; proselytes from worldly motives, i, 336 f.; righteous, or sincere, proselytes, who embrace Judaism for the sake of Heaven, i, 338, 340; "proselyte of the gate," i, 338, 340 f.; proselytes in mass (*gērīm gerūrīm*), i, 337, 338, 346; in the messianic age, i, 346; heathen kings and famous scholars, proselytes, i, 346 f.; proselytes are dear to God, i, 343 f.; treatment of, ii, 142, 148; numbers of proselytes, i, 348 f.

Προσευχαί, 'places of prayer,' synagogues, i, 307.

Prostrations, in prayer, ii, 222, 228.

Proverbs, Book of, inspiration of, i, 238; canonicity, i, 246.

Providence, particular and immediate ordering of God, i, 383 f.; its ordinary operations no less wonderful than miracles, i, 378 f.; providence determines man's fortunes but not his character, i, 456; denial of providence and retribution, i, 360.

Psalms, Davidic authorship, i, 242; from Maccabaean age, i, 27; in temple service, i, 241; in the synagogue, i, 296; Hallel psalms at festivals, ii, 42, 43; psalms appointed to be read at public fasts, ii, 68; influence of the Psalms on Jewish piety, ii, 226.

Psalms of Solomon, i, 180 ff.; ii, 113; messianic expectation, ii, 328; resurrection in them, ii, 308 f.

Publicans, collectors of octroi tolls, ii, 117.

Pugio Fidei, of Raimund Martini, i, 164, 474 n., 551.

pur'anūt, 'punishment,' ii, 252 n.

Purification, religious, unites the ideas of expiation and disinfection, ii, 55 f.; demanded by "uncleanness," i, 76; purification of the inner man, repentance (Philo), i, 532.

Purim, i, 244 f.; ii, 51 ff.; in an intercalary year, ii, 53 n.

Purim Epistle, ii, 51 f.

Purity of mind, ii, 267 ff.

Q

Quakers, ii, 5.

Quinsy (?), *see* Diphtheria.

R

Rab (R. Abba Arika), nephew of R. Ḥiyya, i, 104 f.; qualified ordination, return to Babylonia, i, 105; head of school at Sura, ibid.; his vexatious wife, ii, 126.

Rabbi, as title of an officially authorized teacher of the Law, i, 43 f.

Rabbi, by preëminence, Judah the Patriarch (*Nasi*), *q. v.*; Rabbi and Antoninus, *see* Antoninus.

to be presumed on, i, 508; ii, 522 f.; sins that make it difficult or impossible, i, 526; God tries in every way to bring men to repentance, i, 393, 527; punishment meant to lead to amendment, ii, 252; encourages them when they think their sin unforgivable, i, 527 f.; ii, 207; sin forgiven, the memory of it expunged, i, 532 f.; imputed to the penitent as if he had not sinned, ibid.; expiation remaining to be made, i, 514 f.; repentance, not sinlessness, mark the righteous man, i, 495; God seeks the repentance of the heathen, i, 528 f.; by turning from heathenism to the true religion, i, 327 f., 529; motives of repentance, fear and love, i, 514 f.; is the initiative on God's side or man's? i, 531; prayers for repentance, ibid.; a cure for evil impulse, i, 492; eulogies of repentance, i, 520, 530 f.; its preëminence, i, 533; brings (national) deliverance nearer, ii, 350 f.; necessary precedent of deliverance, ii, 351 f.; Elijah's mission, ii, 359; repentance in the New Testament, i, 518 f.

Repetition, in the Law, hermeneutic principle, ii, 162, 166 n., 167, 383 n.

Repository of righteous souls, between death and resurrection, ii, 302; in heaven, ii, 339, 390.

Representative piety, ii, 261 f.

Reproof, duty and difficulty, ii, 152 f.

Reputation, injury to, worse than monetary injury, ii, 148 ff.

Resh Galuta, i, 104, 109 n.

resha'im, wicked, ungodly, ii, 156 n.

Respect of persons (partiality), judgment without, ii, 182; *see* Equity.

Responsibility, of man for his misdeeds, cannot be shifted to God, i, 454 f.; God has given him knowledge of the law, i, 462; responsibility, distinction between legal and moral, ii, 141.

Restitution or reparation, in case of a wrong to a fellow man, condition of God's forgiveness, i, 512.

Resurrection (*teḥiyat ha-mētim*, revivification of the dead), in Isa. 26, 17–19, ii, 295 f.; Daniel, ii, 297 f.; 2 Maccabees, i, 207 f.; ii, 299; Enoch 85–90 (?), ii, 300; Enoch 92, 3–5; 102, 6–11, ii, 305; Enoch (Parables, 51, 1–5), ii, 304; Testaments of XII Patriarchs, ii, 307; Psalms of Solomon, ii, 308; Gospels, ii, 310 f.; 4 Esdras, ii, 338 f.; Revelation of John, ii, 341; genesis of the idea, ii, 311 ff.*; primary eschatological doctrine of Judaism, ii, 295, 379; tenet of the Pharisees, i, 68, 86, 172; ii, 317; Josephus on the Pharisaic doctrine, ii, 317; denied by Sadducees, Samaritans, and "heretics" (*mīnīm*), i, 68; ii, 381; a dogma, with an anathema, i, 172; ii, 381; biblical proofs alleged by rabbis, and other arguments, ii, 382 f.; in every Parashah of the Law, ii, 383; Jesus' argument, i, 250; nature of the resurrection — restoration of the body, reunion with the soul, i, 486 ff.; ii, 383 f., 391 f.; the indestructible nucleus of the body (*lūz*), ii, 385; the dew of resurrection, i, 168; ii, 296 n.; the dead rise with all their defects and deformities, and then are cured of them, ii, 380; rise clothed (analogy of wheat), ii, 381; who are restored to life? i, 297 f., 378; ii, 302 f., 306; return to a life on this earth, ii, 299, 302, 303, 304, 308, 314 f., 342; resurrection of Israelites at beginning of the messianic age, ii, 340, 379 f.; the dead in Palestine first, ii, 379 f.; the *first* resurrection, ii, 38, 342; general, to last judgment, at the end of the messianic age, ii, 381, 339, 341, 380; revivification of the dead in Maimonides' Articles of Faith; for his philosophy, ii, 393; Paul's attempt to dematerialize the resurrection, ii, 394; Christian doctrine, the resurrection of the flesh, ibid.

Retribution, national, prophetic doctrine, ii, 248, 291; individualized, i, 501; ii, 248 f., 292; in kind, ii, 251; measure for measure, ii, 249 n., 381 n.; in this

Sages (*ḥakamīm*), as a class of teachers, i, 310.
Saint (*ḳadōsh*), God calls no man saint till he is dead, i, 468.
Saintliness (*ḥasīdūt*), culmination of virtues, ii, 273, 384.
Saintly (*ḳadōsh*, 'holy'), epithet applied to one who keeps aloof from all unchastity, ii, 27.
Salvation, to have a portion in the world to come, ii, 94 f.; to inherit eternal life, ii, 321; the way, remission of sins procured through repentance, i, 500 ff.; origin of the Jewish idea of salvation, ii, 311 ff.*; its peculiar character, ii, 312, 313 f., 319; compared to the mysteries, ii, 320 f.; "are there few that be saved?" ii, 321 f.
sam ḥayyīm, 'elixir of life'; *sam mawet*, deadly poison, ii, 242.
Sameas (Samaios), leading Pharisee in the time of Herod, "disciple of Pollio," (? Shammai), i, 313.
Samaritans, the schism, i, 23 ff.; temple on Gerizim, i, 23 ff.; dedicated by Antiochus IV to Zeus Xenios, i, 26, 52 n.; destroyed by John Hyrcanus, i, 26; abortive rising (in 67) suppressed by Vespasian, i, 26 f.; Pentateuch, i, 25; archaic script, i, 25, 29; accepted the Pentateuch alone as Scripture, i, 27; accused of mutilating it, ii, 383; strict observance of the laws, i, 25; the sabbath, ii, 31; pronounced the name of God in oaths, i, 426 f. (Ιαβε); deny the resurrection, ii, 381 f.
Samuel the Little, formulated the prayer for the extirpation of heretics, i, 292; a mysterious voice (*bat ḳōl*) declares him worthy that the holy spirit should rest upon him, i, 422.
Samuel, Mar, head of the school at Nehardea, i, 105.
Sanballat, governor of Samaria, i, 23.
Sandalfon, tall angel, i, 415 n.
Sanhedrin (συνέδριον), name replacing the older γερουσία, senate, i, 26 f.; in Jerusalem, organization, i, 45 n., 82, 85; ii, 183; presidency, i, 255 n.; ii, 183; Sadducees and Pharisees in the Sanhedrin, i, 85, 260 f.; powers, under Herod, i, 82; the procurators, i, 82, 85; ii, 183; power to execute sentence of death, i, 82 n.; ii, 183, 187; came to an end with the fall of Jerusalem, the High Court (*Bet Dīn*) its successor, i, 85, 260 f.; ii, 183, 187 n.; the Patriarch as president, i, 261 f.
sar shel areṣ, 'esh, barad, gehinnom, yam, individual angels appointed over the earth, fire, hail, hell, the sea, i, 403 f.
Sarah, legend of, ii, 105.
Satan, 'adversary,' in Scripture, i, 406; accuses Israel every day in the year (364) except the Day of Atonement, i, 407; "evil impulse" identified with Satan, i, 478, 492; his fate in the Revelation of John, ii, 340 f. *See also* Mastema, Azazel, Beliar.
Satisfactio pro peccatis, in Catholic doctrine, i, 546.
Saul of Tarsus, i, 187. *See* Paul.
Scapegoat, rites of riddance, ii, 56; on the Day of Atonement, expiates for all sins, including insolent and rebellious transgressions, i, 464, 498; but only on condition of repentance, i, 499 f.
Schechter, S., Some Aspects of Rabbinic Theology, i, 470; Documents of Jewish Sectaries, i, 200.
Scholars and peasants respect each other's work, ii, 240.
Scholastic Hebrew, 'language of scholars,' i, 100.
Schools, i, **308–322**; school and synagogue, i, 308, 314; *see also* Bet ha-Midrash; antecedents and beginnings of schools of the Law, i, 46, 311 f.; elementary schools, i, 316 ff.; higher schools, i, 319 ff.; schools of the Law in Babylonia before Hillel, i, 104, 313 f., 321; Hananiah, i, 104; at Sura (Rab), i, 104 f.; at Nehardea (Mar Samuel), i, 105; in Syria, at Nisibis, i, 104, 105 f., 313; at Rome, i, 106 f.; in Greek-

speaking lands, i, 321; schools of the Law in the messianic age, i, 271 f.

Schools ('Houses') of Shammai and Hillel, controversial issues, i, 46, 77 ff., 80 f., 242; would it have been better for man if he had never been created? ii, 285 n.; were the heavens or earth created first? i, 381 n.; on legitimate grounds for divorce, i, 123 f.; on combination of domiciles, ii, 31 n.; on the permissibility of deceiving a toll-man, ii, 117; on conventional lies, ii, 189; more than three hundred school differences recorded in the Talmud, i, 80 f.: ultimate ascendancy of the school of Hillel, i, 81, 85, 86.

School-house (*Bet ha-Midrash*, *q. v.*), i, 312 ff.; elementary school (*Bet ha-Sefer*), i, 316 f.

School teachers, rank in the hierarchy of education, i, 317; supported by the community, i, 317 f.; synagogue attendants as teachers, ibid.; teachers as interpreters in the synagogue, i, 318.

Scion of David (*ṣemaḥ*), king in the golden age to come, ii, 213, 324 f., 348. *See* Messiah.

Scribe (*sōfer*), biblical scholar, the name, i, 4 n., 308 f.; education and attainments described by Sirach, i, 40 f., 309, 310; professional class, scholars and teachers, i, 42; part in development of jurisprudence, i, 42 f.; connection with the Pharisees, i, 43, 57, 286 f.; ii, 157; teachers in the synagogue, i, 286 f.; the name later restricted to older generations, i, 43 f.

Scribes, succeeded the prophets, i, 421; their enactments distinguished from biblical laws, i, 33; the authority of the words of the Scribes, i, 33 f., 262.

Scriptures, The, i, **235–250**; the name Scripture, Holy Scripture, i, 240; modes of citation, ibid.; the work of the Great Synagogue on the collection, i, 32, *see also* Canon; all sacred Scripture makes the hands unclean, i, 247 n.; God the *auctor primarius*, i, 358; all the books written by prophets (inspired men), i, 238; every syllable of divine verity and authority, i, 239 (*see also* Inspiration); reading in the synagogue, *see* Bible reading in the synagogue.

Seal, of God, is truth (*emet*), ii, 195.

Σεβόμενοι τὸν θεόν, God-fearing (religious) men, i, 325 n., 340.

Second Esdras, *see* Fourth Esdras.

Sects, the three Jewish, i, 57; their differences on the question of fate and freedom, i, 456 ff.; *see also* Pharisees, Sadducees, Essenes.

Sectarian Halakah, i, 198 f., 200 ff.

Sectaries of Damascus, *see* Damascus.

Sedarim, sections of the Pentateuch in the Palestinian (triennial) cycle, i, 299.

Seder Abodah, in synagogue service on Day of Atonement, ii, 59.

Seder 'Olam, chronological work, attributed to Jose ben Ḥalafta, i, 6, 158 f.

Seder (Siddur) Rab Amram, prayer book, i, 176.

ṣedaḳah, alms, almsgiving, ii, 170 f., 180; inferior to *gemīlūt ḥasadīm* (*q. v.*), ii, 85 n., 171 f.

ṣedeḳ, rectitude, integrity, ii, 180, 191.

Seleucids, kings of Syria and Babylonia, conquest of Palestine, i, 48; zealous Hellenizers, ibid.; *see* Antiochus IV, Epiphanes.

Seleucus IV, attempt on the treasures of the temple in Jerusalem, i, 51.

Self-determination of man, i, 453 ff., *see* Freedom.

Self-examination, under affliction, ii, 249 ff.

Self-love, natural and good, ii, 87.

seliḥōt, prayers for forgiveness, ii, 214.

Semi-proselytes, not proselytes in the Jewish sense at all, i, 326 f., 338, 340 f.

semīkah, imposition of hands on the head of the sacrificial victim, long-standing dissension over, i, 46; in women's sacrifice, ii, 130.

Separation, of Jews from heathen, i, 197; holiness is separateness, i, 61.

may be said in any language, i, 111; in reciting the first sentence man takes upon him the yoke of the kingdom of Heaven (acknowledges the sovereignty of God), i, 465; women exempt from the obligation, ii, 129.

Shemaiah, colleague of Abṭalion (*q. v.*), in the penultimate Pair, i, 45, 77, 78; their reputation as scholars and expositors, i, 313; Hillel an auditor in their school, i, 313; reports a halakic tradition from them, i, 78; in Josephus, Sameas (Samaios), i, 313 n.

shemīni 'aseret, eighth day of Tabernacles, ii, 43.

Shemoneh 'Esreh, The Eighteen Prayers, said to have been prescribed in their order by the Men of the Great Synagogue, i, 292; arranged under direction of Gamaliel II, ibid.; ii, 212. *See* Daily Prayer.

Shemot Rabbah, Midrash on Exodus, i, 167.

Sheol, the nether world, biblical representation, common abode of all the dead, ii, 289 ff.; separation of the souls (spirits) of the righteous and the wicked between death and the great judgment (Enoch), ii, 302; the souls of the righteous in a repository (in heaven), ii, 302, 303, 390; Sheol will give up what it has received, ii, 304. *See also* Hell (Gehinnom).

Shepherds, the seventy, angels who abused their power over Israel, ii, 300.

Sherira, Gaon of Pumbeditha, response (987 A.D.) to inquiries about writing down of the Mishnah, etc., i, 97 f., 154.

Shiloh, name of the Messiah, ii, 349.

Shir ha-Shirim, the Song of Songs, *see* Canticles.

Shir ha-Shirim, Midrash on, i, 171.

Signs, of the impending messianic crisis, ii, 354 f.

shōfar, ram's horn, sounded at New Year's, ii, 63 f.; at Tabernacles, ii, 44.

Shofarot, biblical verses in the New Year's liturgy, ii, 64.

Sifra (de-Be Rab), Tannaite Midrash on Leviticus, i, 140 ff.

Sifrè (de-Be Rab), Tannaite Midrash on Numbers and on Deuteronomy, i, 143 ff.

Sifrè Zuṭa, on Numbers, i, 144 f.

Simeon, his penance, ii, 257 f.

Simeon the Righteous, survivor of the Great Synagogue, i, 34; according to the Talmud went out to meet Alexander the Great, i, 34; probably contemporary of Sirach, subject of his eulogy (50, 1–24), i, 34 f., 310; repairs of temple and walls, i, 34, 48; his motto, the three foundations of the world, i, 35, 311; ii, 84, 172; the epithet, "the Righteous," i, 43.

Simeon ben 'Azzai, the most comprehensive principle of the Law, i, 446, 455 f.; ii, 85; why he never married, ii, 120; visit to paradise, i, 413.

Simeon of Mizpah, the anonymous element in, M. Yoma and M. Tamid attributed to him, i, 153.

Simeon ben Zoma, visit to paradise, i, 413.

Sin, nature and consequences, i, **460–473**; origin, i, 474–496; a religious, not primarily moral, conception, i, 461, 462, 463; definition of sin in a revealed religion, i, 460, 461 f.; in Judaism, disobedience to divine law, i, 461; ii, 89; consequence: God's forgiveness the only remedy, i, 117; New Testament teaching, ii, 89; the sin of the heathen, transgression of law, i, 276 ff., 278 f., 462; sin as debt, defaulted obligation, ii, 95; unwitting and defiant sins, i, 463 f.; sin as rebellion against God, i, 464 f.; extremity of sin, the deliberate rejection of the authority of God, i, 465 ff.; Philo's idea of sin, i, 484 n.; beings above and below man incapable of sin, i, 406, 483, 484; universality of sin, i, 467 ff., 476, 477 f.; Adam's sin and its consequences, i, 474 f., 476 ff.; the root of sin in man, *see* Evil Impulse; sin, a fault of the whole man, not of either soul or body alone, i,

lenistic Jews, i, 294 f.; Sadducees held that the soul perishes with the body, ii, 317; in the orthodox Judaism of our period all beliefs about souls are related to the doctrine of resurrection, ii, 295; the souls of all generations were created at the beginning of the world, and kept till the time of their birth in a repository (*gūf*), ii, 353 n.; a different (creationist) hypothesis, ibid.; in the highest heaven (*'arabōt*), i, 368; ii, 390; the souls of righteous and wicked, between death and the great judgment, occupy separate places in the west (Enoch), ii, 302; the souls of the righteous are in treasuries in the highest heaven, i, 368; ii, 389 f.; in the earthly life the soul pervades the whole body, i, 370 f.; is a transient guest in the body, i, 447.

Soul and Body, Greek conceptions, ii, 292 f.; the body, as material, evil, and source of evil appetites and passions, i, 485 f.; in Judaism, no divided responsibility, i, 486 ff.*; ii, 384*; the soul the more guilty, because it knows better, i, 488.

Sovereignty of God, ii, 371 ff.; religious interest in it, i, 401, 432 f.; teleology of religion, ibid.; sovereignty in history, ii, 210. *See also* Kingdom of Heaven.

Special sabbaths, the four, i, 297, 298.

Spirit, in ancient conception implied materiality, ii, 293.

Spirit of God, of the Lord, in the Bible, its operations, i, 421; medium of revelation, especially prophetic, i, 237; in Hellenistic writers, i, 371 f.

Spirit, holy, *see* Holy spirit.

Spirituality of God, i, 223 f.

Star out of Jacob (Num. 24, 7), applied by Akiba to the leader of the revolt under Hadrian, Bar Cocheba, i, 89; ii, 116, 329, 349 n.

Stars, the seven, bound and burning for 10,000 years (Enoch), ii, 301. *See* Heavenly bodies.

Stepfather and stepmother, honor of parents due to, ii, 131 n.

Strack, H., Einleitung in Talmud und Midrasch, i, 125.

Strack-Billerbeck, Kommentar zum Neuen Testament aus Talmud und Midrasch, i, 215 f.

Study of the Law (divine revelation), an integral part of Jewish piety, ii, 239; a means of grace, ii, 245; study is worship (*'abōdah*), ii, 15; demands attention and intention (*kawwanah*, *q. v.*), ii, 240; to be pursued "for its own sake," without self-regarding motive, ii, 96, 241 f.; out of love to God, ibid.; an elixir of life or a deadly poison, ii, 96 f., 242; irreligious study of religion, ii, 191; sin and penalty of neglecting study, ii, 247 n.; obligation not like a debt to be worked off, ii, 243; study of laws and fulfilling them in practice, priority of obligation, ii, 96 f., 246; study of ritual laws a surrogate for sacrifice, i, 505 f.; branches and sequence of study, ii, 240, 318, 319; study and secular occupations, ii, 127 f., 177, 244; study on Sabbath afternoons, ii, 38 f.; in the messianic age, 271 f.; in the world to come, i, 273.

Subjection to authorities, duty and limits, ii, 112–118.

Suffering, expiatory, i, **546–552**. *See also* Chastisement.

Suffering Messiah, i, 551 f.; ii, 370.

Sukkot, *see* Tabernacles.

Supplication for God's free grace (*teḥinnah*, *taḥnūnīm*), ii, 217.

Sura, in Babylonia, establishment of school by Rab, i, 105.

Surenhusius, edition of the Mishnah, i, 154.

Survivals, in observances, critical point of view, ii, 8, cf. i, 14.

Swine's flesh, unclean, ii, 74, 77.

Synagogue, i, **281–307**; its obscure beginnings, i, 283, 285 f.; attributed to Moses, i, 284; a public institution for worship and instruction in religion, i,

T

Y

Z

INDEX

Three additional indexes—Passages Cited, Talmud and Midrash, and Tannaim and Amoraim—are available in Volume II of the Harvard University Press edition of this work.